PROGRAMMING IN CLIPPER™

The Definitive Guide to the Clipper dBASE Compiler

The Second Edition

PROGRAMMING IN CLIPPER™

The Definitive Guide to the Clipper dBASE Compiler

The Second Edition

Stephen J. Straley

Addison-Wesley Publishing Company, Inc.
Reading, Massachusetts Menlo Park, California New York
Don Mills, Ontario Wokingham, England Amsterdam Bonn
Sydney Singapore Tokyo Madrid San Juan

DEDICATION

To my Mom, Aunt Pat, Sharon and Robert, and especially to Nicole – hang on to dreams and ideas, for one day they will become reality.

Many of the designations used by manufacturers and sellers to distinguish their products are claimed as trademarks. Where those designations appear in this book, and Addison-Wesley was aware of a trademark claim, the designations have been printed in initial caps or all caps.

dBASE II and *dBASE III* are registered trademarks of Ashton-Tate, Inc.
dBASE III Plus is a trademark of Ashton-Tate, Inc.
WordStar is a trademark of MicroPro International Corporation.
Lotus 1-2-3 is a trademark of Lotus Development Corporation.
SideKick is a trademark of Borland International, Inc.
Scrabble is a trademark of Selchow & Righter, Inc.
Plink86 is a trademark of Phoenix Software Associates, LTD.
Viewgen is a trademark of Software Tools Development Corporation.
HiLite is a trademark of Software Enhancement Technology.
Quickcode is a trademark of Fox & Geller, Inc.
Genifer is a trademark of Bytel Corporation.
Novell Netware is a trademark of Novell, Inc.
PC Net II is a trademark of AST Research, Inc.
3COM Ethernet is a trademark of 3Com Corporation.
Clipper and *Nantucket* are trademarks of Nantucket Corporation.
Steve Straley's Toolkit is a trademark of Stephen J. Straley & Associates.

Library of Congress Cataloging-in-Publication Data

Straley, Stephen J.
Programming in Clipper / Stephen J. Straley. -- 2nd ed.
p. cm.
Includes index.
ISBN 0-201-14583-9
1. Compilers (Computer programs) 2. Clipper (Computer program)
3. dBASE III (Computer program) 4. dBASE II (Computer program)
I. Title
QA76.76.C65S77 1988 88-19843
005.4'53--dc19 CIP

Copyright © 1987, 1988 by New York Communications Systems, Inc.

All rights reserved. No part of this book may be reproduced, stored in a retrieval system, or transmitted in any form or by any means, electronic, mechanical, photocopying, recording or otherwise, without the prior written permission of Addison-Wesley. Printed in the United States of America. Published simultaneously in Canada.

C D E F G H I J -HA- 89 *Third Printing, April 1989*

ABOUT THE AUTHOR: STEVE STRALEY

Stephen J. Straley, formerly the senior support engineer at Nantucket, Inc., was directly involved in the early development stages of Clipper. For over a year, he traveled across the country meeting with computer users, teaching and demonstrating the many aspects of the compiler. Currently, as President of Stephen J. Straley & Associates, he is owner of a software development and consulting firm in California and in New York, specializing in application development using Clipper and the C language.

ACKNOWLEDGMENTS

Brian Russell is a man with practical ideas for the "programming whiz-kid" in all of us. To give mere acknowledgment to a man who gave me the key for new insights and wonders is not just. Personally, I thank him for myself and for all of us who use his "child." As it matures, so do we!

Phil Kimble, Roger Clay, Steve Hilbourne, and Fred Ho are the backbone of this book; Cheryll Webber is the guardian of our sanity. The daily use and direction of this product is attributable to these individuals, who are the remaining force in the Technical Support Division of Nantucket, Inc. Never will there be a finer group of individuals dedicated to stretching the compiler to unimaginable parameters, finding answers to daily questions, solving problems with the product, and interfacing with the company and the market.

Due to space and time constraints, many people who should have been given credit in the first edition were not. They have been very important in my continuing development as a programmer, a businessman and as a person. So to my teachers David Dodson, Joseph King, Essor Maso, and William Lomax: many heart-filled "thanks". To John Ciardullo, David Karasek, Bob Cook, Ray Love, Dave Morgan, and Burt Durant: your support have been equally important and meaningful. Finally, to the thousands of users and supporters who have taken the time to suggest additional points and material: this book is for you.

SPECIAL OFFER

Source Code Disk for
PROGRAMMING IN CLIPPER

We have prepared a 5 1/4-inch disk to save you the time it takes to type in the examples and programs provided by Steve Straley. This disk will also save you the time it takes to find and correct the inevitable typing errors that keep programs from running properly.

The disk contains, in addition to the various examples and source code fragments, a complete *Code Generator*, a *Menu Generator*, and a sample *Call Tracking* application. Just compile them and use them to help you in your own program development. This disk is an invaluable tool for every Clipper programmer.

The Source Code Disk is only available from New York Communications Systems, Inc. To order, photocopy or clip out the coupon below.

New York Communications Systems, Inc.
P.O. Box 20024
New York, NY 10017-0001

YES! Please send me ____ copies of the Source Code Disk for
PROGRAMMING IN CLIPPER at only $19.95 each.
(New York residents add $1.65 sales tax.)

__Check enclosed __VISA __MasterCard __American Express
Account No. ______________________________
Exp. Date ________ Signature ______________________
Name ______________________________
Company ______________________________
Address ______________________________
City ____________________ State _____ Zip __________

(Please allow 4-6 weeks for delivery.)

B002

TABLE OF CONTENTS

PREFACE

My main objectives in writing this book were to remove some of the mystique surrounding compilers, to help change the thought patterns of first-time users of a compiler, and to provide helpful tips in programming. While this book assumes a basic familiarity with dBASE II or dBASE III, it is also useful for readers who have never used the dBASE interpreters. Personally, I hope to offer a new way of thinking to those programming in the dBASE III language. Please take note of that last phrase, "...the dBASE III language." With the advent of the Clipper compiler, dBASE III leaves the confines of database management and takes its first steps toward becoming a true high-level language for microcomputers.

Currently, there is some confusion in explaining the differences between dBASE III and Clipper. While advertising agencies are eager to label Clipper as a compiler, we must pay equal attention to dBASE III as an interpreter. One goal of this book is to bridge the gap between the two and to show how each relates to the real world and to the other. Sometimes, there will be cases where the application involved should be designed and executed under the environment of dBASE III. Also, there will be times where the code must execute under both systems. However, there will be more situations calling for the use of Clipper. The developer must identify which system is appropriate for each application. These chapters will enable you to make informed decisions.

Once you understand how a compiler is basically different from an interpreter, it will be clear how the coding in the respective environments will ultimately differ. The guidelines and examples we give for working in the two environments will be your tools for success. The examples should help change bad coding techniques to more structured, disciplined methods. No specialized university degrees are required, just effort and determination. Effort in training yourself to "do it better" and determination within yourself to find "the better way" will both pay off.

dBASE III allows many techniques that it should not allow if it is ever to be considered a structured language. Programming with dBASE III can be compared to programming with BASIC. A few years ago I heard that most BASIC and dBASE III programmers write "spaghetti code," a group of syntactically correct words and phrases jumbled together and thrown against the "wall of execution." If the jumbled code executes, the rule is "Don't touch it and walk away quietly." If it does not work and falls off the wall, programmers run over, twist the few pieces that fell off the wall, and throw them up again.

Structured programming emphasizes purpose and meaning; routines are not just thrown together haphazardly. The notion of modular coding is the key. Structured coding is like building a wall, with each brick carefully laid on top of another. The bricks on top rely on the brick below, yet each brick is small, clear, and well-defined in itself.

Clipper's power lies in its ability to understand the plate of spaghetti as well as the carefully constructed wall of bricks.

Look at Clipper as a foreign language. Suppose you had the chance to go to a foreign land and stay there on your own. One of the first requirements for survival would be learning the local language. There would be no better way to do this than to listen to the natives and practice speaking with them.

Reading textbooks without practical direction and examples is no different from trying to learn a foreign language in a classroom environment, where your survival is not dependent on understanding. For many individuals, understanding Clipper is vital to surviving in the world of microcomputers. This world is based on speed, portability, and money. Using Clipper is essential if one is to survive in the current market atmosphere.

No matter what your experience level is with dBASE or Clipper, this book provides ample coding examples to illustrate theories, rules, and principles. I hope that these programming samples provide additional insight that may ultimately reduce confusion and save you time and money. Granted, some of these sections may cover areas already understood, but reviewing them is never a waste of time. For others with little or no experience in application development or in using Clipper, the ground rules at the beginning of most chapters should be helpful. Following these are sample codes, illustrating the points being discussed. If after reviewing the section containing the sample coding, the concepts are not clear, stop. Reread the code first, then the theory, and then try to duplicate the situation yourself on your computer. Even if things do not work out initially, keep trying; persist and you will prevail. Eventually, you'll see the light and create bigger and better applications.

Use this book not only as a learning guide to Clipper, but as a reference text as well. A small function, procedure, or even a suggestion in tackling a problem may be initially overlooked. Keep referring to the chapters pertaining to your code. If something is finally found, time is ultimately saved in finishing your application. If time can be saved, money is earned. If money is earned, you have survived.

So now onto the world of Clipper, the first true dBASE III compiler. Prepare yourself for a language finally geared to the belief that anything is possible . . . for a computer. Happy Clipping!

HOW TO USE THIS BOOK

Some will view this text as a guide to the Clipper/dBASE III language. Others will look for specific commands and techniques unique to the compiler, while still others will search for the one or two pieces of additional insight that will solve their problems. Whatever your reasons are for using this book, read it all! No one section is more important than another.

The main theme I have tried to stress is better programming. The compiler allows the implementation of coding principles and techniques that were previously impossible or inconvenient. For the most part there are two types of users of the compiler: those converting old dBASE III applications to Clipper to increase their speed and those who have already converted and are now using the compiler to take advantage of its advanced features. In either case, clean coding and the expanded possibilities of structured programming are the main focuses of this book.

If you pick up this text simply to get additional background on one or two commands, you will miss its other advantages. There are many sections that can be looked at as a programming cookbook, but theories and techniques are implied recipes. They need to be reread, felt, simmered, and experienced in order to fully realize their thrust. This book should serve as a locksmith to the Clipper language. It can make the keys and can define the lock, but it actually takes a breathing soul to turn the keys inside of that lock in order to gain access. Expand your thinking to beyond the "now." Take the commands and concepts of "now" and apply them to future dreams and ideas. With some effort those ideas and dreams can become practical applications sitting on someone's desk in the future.

For the second edition, I have completely gone through and expanded every section. Particular interest should be given to the MEMO, ARRAY, DBEDIT, debugger, binary files, error handling, new windowing techniques, and new features never before thought possible with Clipper. I have also added a few personal tricks and tips throughout. Additionally, in the header of every programming sample there are three new lines of information that should be looked at carefully:

1. Compile Syntax
2. Release to Use
3. Linking Syntax

This edition is specifically oriented to the Summer '87 and later releases, while still documenting the differences with previous versions. This edition is dedicated to all readers of the previous edition. Through their comments and suggestions, this book is much more than the "definitive" guide. It has grown to answer more questions and solve more problems.

HOW TO USE CLIPPER

Frequently, the programming examples in the text should be compiled in order to see how they appear in final form. The following is the normal syntax for compiling:

```
C>clipper <filename> -m
The Clipper Compiler, Summer '87
Copyright (c) Nantucket Corp 1985-1987.  All Rights Reserved.
Microsoft C Runtime Library Routines,
Copyright (c) Microsoft Corp 1984-1987.  All Rights Reserved.

Compiling <filename>.PRG
Code Pass 1
Code Pass 2
Code size 1023, Symbols 496, Constants 1041

C>plink86
PLINK86plus ( Nantucket ) Version 2.24.
Copyright (C) 1987 by Phoenix Technologies Ltd.,
All Rights Reserved.
```

The following are three styles of linking:

1.

```
C>plink86
PLINK86plus ( Nantucket ) Version 2.24.
Copyright (C) 1987 by Phoenix Technologies Ltd.,
All Rights Reserved.

=>fi <filename>
=>lib \<path>\clipper
=>;

<FILENAME>.EXE (142 K)
```

2.

```
C>tlink <filename>,,,clipper/se:1024,,;

Microsoft (R) Overlay Linker  Version 3.60
Copyright (C) Microsoft Corp 1983-1987.  All rights reserved.
```

3.

```
C>turlink fi <filename>,,,clipper
Turbo Link  Version 1.0  Copyright (c) 1987 Borland International
```

NOTE: All subsequent examples of program code or screen output will use the typeface shown above.

If there is any variation in this syntax, the sequence of compiling and/or linking will be given.

So look at the commands, definitions, and theories for rules. The restrictions are only in your own capabilities!

CHAPTER ONE

Interfacing dBASE and Clipper

CLIPPER and dBASE II

dBASE II emerged when programmers were just beginning to introduce database management systems to microcomputers. Since those days, dBASE II has stabilized, while system capacities have increased and new standards have gradually evolved. Consequently, there are bound to be some differences between dBASE II and Clipper. These differences are not only in the command structure and syntax, but also in the mechanical constructs and theoretical approaches as well.

Most of the practical differences between Clipper and dBASE II parallel the differences between dBASE II and dBASE III. An immediate difference between dBASE II and Clipper is the expanded command and function base in Clipper. Another difference is in coding techniques. Because of Clipper's greater capabilities, code can be greatly condensed to accomplish the same task. Some of the more significant differences and the trouble areas to avoid are outlined in detail in this book.

BASIC FILE CONSTRUCT

In early days of Clipper, there was a difference between those dBASE II database files converted to dBASE III via dCONVERT and normal dBASE III and Clipper database files. If a dBASE II file has been converted via dCONVERT, a symptom of "Clippered" applications is that data in the database will be shifted by one character. For example, displayed fields will suddenly appear to contain a character from the previous field. Additionally, SEEKs and FINDs will no longer work. Because of the shift in the character position in a dBASE II dCONVERTED to dBASE III, the indexes built will be based on an incorrect record construct. This problem may still appear in some applications using a recent version of Clipper, so to get around this problem, do the following:

1. Create a duplicate structure of the database with a temporary name either in dBASE III or in Clipper's CREATE utility program.

2. Append the records from the old dCONVERTED database to the newly generated database. This may be accomplished either through the dBASE III interpreter or through a small compiled program.

3. Erase the old file and rename the newly appended file with the old file's name.

4. Reindex all pertinent index files.

Below are layouts of the basic file headers of a true dBASE III file, a Clipper database file, and, finally, a dBASE II-dCONVERTED-dBASE III database file. To examine these yourself, use the following procedure (be sure that DEBUG is either in the same directory as your .DBF files or in your DOS path):

```
C>debug <filename.dbf>
```

A hyphen will appear. Enter the letter "D" and a carriage return. The beginning of the header of the entered file will show across the screen. After a few lines, another hyphen will appear. To exit from DEBUG, just enter the letter "Q."

dBASE III database file:

```
C>debug dbase.dbf
-d
1D45:0100  03 56 03 16 00 00 00 00-42 00 0B 00 00 00 00 00 .V......B.......
1D45:0110  00 00 00 00 00 00 00 00-00 00 00 00 00 00 00 00 ................
1D45:0120  4F 4E 45 00 00 00 00 00-00 00 00 43 00 00 00 00 ONE........C....
1D45:0130  0A 00 00 00 00 00 00 00-00 00 00 00 00 00 00 00 ................
1D45:0140  0D 00 1A EA 00 00 00 00-2E 8F 06 56 77 2E 8F 06 ...j.......Vw...
1D45:0150  58 77 E8 21 F0 EA 00 00-00 00 2E 8F 06 68 77 2E Xwh!pj.......hw.
1D45:0160  8F 06 6A 77 E8 27 F0 EA-00 00 00 00 2E 8F 06 7A ..jwh'pj.......z
1D45:0170  77 2E 8F 06 7C 77 E8 2D-F0 EA 00 00 00 00 2E 8F w...|wh-pj......
-Q
```

CLIPPER database file:

```
C>debug clipper.dbf
-d
1D45:0100  03 56 03 16 00 00 00 00-42 00 0B 00 00 00 00 00 .V......B.......
1D45:0110  00 00 00 00 00 00 00 00-00 00 00 00 00 00 00 00 ................
1D45:0120  4F 4E 45 00 00 00 00 00-00 00 00 43 00 00 00 00 ONE........C....
1D45:0130  0A 00 00 00 00 00 00 00-00 00 00 00 00 00 00 00 ................
1D45:0140  0D 00 1A 01 00 00 02 00-00 00 41 63 6B 6E 6F 77 ..........Acknow
1D45:0150  6C 65 2E 00 28 00 00 00-01 00 02 00 0F 00 0D 01 le..(...........
1D45:0160  41 00 63 00 6B 00 6E 00-6F 00 77 00 6C 00 65 00 A.c.k.n.o.w.l.e.
1D45:0170  64 00 67 00 6D 00 65 00-6E 00 74 00 73 00 0D 00 d.g.m.e.n.t.s...
-q
```

dBASE II dCONVERTED dBASE III database file:

```
C>debug II.dbf
-d
1D45:0100  03 56 03 18 00 00 00 00-21 04 0B 00 00 00 00 00 .V......!.......
1D45:0110  00 00 00 00 00 00 00 00-00 00 00 00 00 00 00 00 ................
1D45:0120  4F 4E 45 00 00 00 00 00-00 00 00 43 00 00 00 00 ONE........C....
1D45:0130  0A 00 00 00 00 00 00 00-00 00 00 00 00 00 00 00 ................
1D45:0140  0D 00 00 00 00 00 00 00-00 00 00 00 00 00 00 00 ................
1D45:0150  00 00 00 00 00 00 00 00-00 00 00 00 00 00 00 00 ................
1D45:0160  0D 00 00 00 00 00 00 00-00 00 00 00 00 00 00 00 ................
1D45:0170  00 00 00 00 00 00 00 00-00 00 00 00 00 00 00 00 ................
-q
```

The first two headers are virtually identical. Note the first 4 bytes that contain the dBASE III database marker and the next 3 pertaining to the date of the last update. Also note that if either of the first two databases were to contain a memo field, the first byte would be an 83, not an 03.

Now compare either of these two headers with the header of the dCONVERTED database. Notice that the ninth and tenth bytes are different. These point to the beginning positions of the fields in the file. While both the dBASE III and Clipper headers contain a 42 00, the dCONVERTED file contains a 21 04. This small difference is magnified when indexing because the index process is then based on an incorrect database header.

MODIFY COMMAND

Clipper is external to any text editor. dBASE II has the ability to build and modify command files within itself. These ASCII files may be compiled by Clipper. However, there are occasional problems.

A major problem is that the wraparound symbol is acknowledged by the interpreter and not by the compiler. In MODIFY COMMAND <filename>, if a command line extends beyond the width of a screen, a CHR(141) is placed at the end of the line and the input is continued onto the next line. This extra character must be removed! Try using a true text editor for programming, such as EDIX, Pmate, or EX EDITOR. Notice the reference to text editor. There are some editors that leave high seventh-order bit markers, better known as high-byte markers. Avoid using word processors (such as WordStar in the document mode and SideKick's editor) that may have a tendency to leave formatting characters in the text itself.

BASIC COMMANDS

In Clipper there are additional commands and changes in basic syntax from dBASE II. Examples of this are the symbols for true and false that are changed from a simple **T** or **F** in dBASE II to a **.T.** or a **.F.** in Clipper. There are also many new functions in Clipper that under dBASE II would require many lines of extra coding but need only one or two command lines in Clipper (e.g., date conversions and string conversions). dCONVERT does not completely convert program files in dBASE II to program files that can be compiled. It may be extremely slow, but ultimately it may be to your advantage to completely recode a dBASE II application into code that will work efficiently in Clipper. Only you can decide if the time needed for such a project will ultimately pay off.

If you recode, you will obtain valuable experience in learning the proper syntax and structure for the compiler, as well as the practical experience of applying the additional commands and functions in Clipper and dBASE III. The experience will pay dividends in the future.

SEPARATE WORK AREAS

One significant difference between dBASE II and Clipper is in file handling. In dBASE II only two selectable areas are available; in Clipper there are 10. Clipper has greater capacity in the files: longer-length character fields, a memo field, more fields per database, and more records per database, to name just a few. Take some time to familiarize yourself with the new commands and look over the section comparing Clipper to dBASE III.

RELATIONS

The concept of "relations" was introduced in dBASE III. In dBASE II, for example, if information on a customer is separated into two files, the only way to print information from both files is to store the vital information to be printed in one file in memory variables. You then switch work areas or USE a new file, find the proper record, and then display all information, from both memory variables and fields. Or, you could have linked two files that were indexed on the same field and selected information from the primary or secondary file. However, this awkwardness can be avoided with Clipper and dBASE III by setting relations from one file into another. Relations are those "hooks" that can tie two or more databases together based on certain key fields. As the database pointer in the main or parent database moves, so do the pointers in its children. Information from all files can be displayed without the use of memory variables. Because of this connection, we say that the databases relate to one another based on certain key elements, fields.

MEMORY VARIABLES

Under dBASE II, only 64 memory variables can be used at any one time. It may seem impossible to use all 64 memory variables, yet it happens. As our applications and sophistication grew, so did the number of memory variables used. Eventually, all 64 variables were assigned and used. The two ways around this problem were to save some or all of those variables to a temporary memory file on disk and restore them later or to join a couple of variables together, especially string variables, and parse them out at the time needed. Indeed, there is a limit to the number of memory variables that is based on the amount of available memory on the machine running your application. With Clipper, the number of memory variables allowed may be as great as 2048. It is highly doubtful that an application will ever need more than 2048 variables. Additionally, since the Autumn '86 release, memory variables longer than 255 bytes may be saved to a .MEM file. While this is still supported with the Summer '87 release, greater string and array support has been implemented.

CLEAR GETS

This command, which normally is placed immediately after a READ command, completes the READ and clears all GETS, preparing the system for the next set of @...SAY/GET. Under the compiler, no CLEAR GETS command is necessary; the READ command will clear out all GETS before the next set.

Using CLEAR GETS can be useful, although it is not necessary after a READ command. The CLEAR GETS command can highlight variable input. Below is a piece of code using the CLEAR GETS and READ commands. Go through the program at least twice and notice how the CLEAR GETS command affects the screen.

```
*********************
* Name          Clearget.prg
* Date          March 22, 1986
* Notice        Copyright 1986, Stephen J. Straley
* Compile       Clipper Clearget
* Release       All versions
* Link          Plink86 fi clearget lib clipper;
* Note          This program shows how CLEAR GETS works.
*
*********************

STORE 0 TO a,b,c,d,e,f,g
DO WHILE .T.
   CLEAR
   SET DELIMITER OFF
   SET INTENSITY ON
   @ 3,10 SAY "Number of hours worked: " GET a PICT "##"
   @ 4,10 SAY "      Pay rate 1 hour: " GET b PICT "##.##"
   @ 5,10 SAY " Amount to be deducted: " GET c PICT "###.##"
   @ 6,10 SAY "           Federal tax: " GET d PICT "###.##"
   @ 7,10 SAY "             State tax: " GET e PICT "###.##"
   @ 8,10 SAY "             Local tax: " GET f PICT "###.##"
   @ 9,10 SAY "         Amount of pay: " GET g PICT "###.##"
   CLEAR GETS
   SET DELIMITER ON
   SET INTENSITY OFF
   @ 12,10 SAY "        How many hours worked? " GET a PICT "##"
   READ
   @ 13,10 SAY "What is the pay rate per hour? " GET b PICT "##.##"
   READ
   @ 14,10 SAY "How much extra to be deducted? " GET c PICT "###.##"
   READ
   @ 15,10 SAY "      What is the federal tax? " GET d PICT "###.##"
   READ
   @ 16,10 SAY "        What is the state tax? " GET e PICT "###.##"
   READ
   @ 17,10 SAY "        What is the local tax? " GET f PICT "###.##"
   READ
   g = a * b - c - d - e - f
```

```
   STORE .T. TO loop
   @ 20,10 SAY "      Do you want to continue? " GET loop
   READ
   IF .NOT. loop
      EXIT
   ENDIF
ENDDO
* End of File
```

Notice that there is no READ before the first CLEAR GETS. To distinguish between prompt and variable, the DELIMITERS and INTENSITY are set to highlight all GETS without a DELIMITER on them. Therefore, in this sample, the prompts are displayed in one fashion, while the GETS are displayed (highlighted) in another. If the GETS were not CLEARED before the first READ, the prompt would wait for input by the user on the first GET. Since the first seven GETS are only being used for display purposes and not for input, the CLEAR GETS command is used to clear out those seven GETS and wait only for input on the eighth GET. In dBASE III, CLEAR GETS is also allowed; not so in the compiler!

TO SEEK OR TO FIND

One of the biggest misjudgments by the developers of dBASE II was in the implementation of the FIND. It was never really planned that things to be "found" would first be stored in a variable. It was assumed that it was the contents of the variable and not the variable's name that were being searched for. To get the concept to work under dBASE II, a macro symbol was needed in front of the variable so its contents, not the variable name, were searched for with the FIND command. In dBASE III and in the compiler, the implementation of the SEEK command was added. In Clipper the SEEK command is preferred over the use of the FIND command. The SEEK command automatically looks at the value (or contents) of the memory variable and searches for that in the database. The FIND command is now reserved strictly for the interpreted and interactive environment.

A NAME BY ANY OTHER NAME...

File names under the compiler must follow the following conventions:

1. No hyphens are allowed in the root file name.

2. The file cannot begin with a character other than a letter.

3. Program file extensions can only be either .PRG, or .FMT. (If using CLiP files, which will be explained later, .FMT is ignored.)

SUMMING IT UP

Other than these overt differences, the biggest difference between Clipper and dBASE II is in theory. Applications programmed normally in dBASE II would look and act totally different when compiled under Clipper. The only way to get a better feel for this contrast is to look over some of the sample code, the discussions about some of the compiler's unique features, and the sample applications and then to practice what you have read!

CLIPPER and dBASE III/dBASE III Plus

No list of the differences between dBASE III and Clipper can really be complete. Even with the Summer '87 release, that list is constantly growing. Some variations are very subtle and will only surface when you are practicing the basics in the compiled environment. Other are blatant and obvious. And still, some difference are more in theory or practice. Keep in mind that while Clipper supports the syntax and basic structure of code of the dBASE III language, the environment is totally different.

What makes Clipper so powerful is that the compiler can take code running under the interpreter and make some logical, structured order of it, while allowing for a whole new branch of structured programming to flourish. This dual role allows for two totally different types of users: those individuals seeking to gain an improvement in performance and execution and those looking for power beyond the limits of the interpreter. And what a difference! In the Summer '87 release, what once seemed impossible now becomes possible. With this version, Clipper advances the language to even greater heights and possibilities. There will come a time for any developer to make a decision between the two environments. Clipper expands the realm of possibilities. The ideas and concepts of tomorrow may be programmed today. A good example of this is the left trim function (LTRIM()).

Prior to its implementation in Clipper (and later in dBASE III), there was a strong need for the left trim function (LTRIM()) in many applications. A user-defined function was the answer to the problem. There was no need to wait for the publishers to "get with it." Additionally, there were a few nice functions in dBASE III Plus, such as ABS(), MAX(), and MIN(), not supported in Clipper prior to the Autumn '86 version. In the Summer '87 release, those functions and even more were brought directly into the language. With just a few creative functions and procedures, most of those commands were simulated in Clipper. The point is that old versions of the compiler can be just as useful as new versions, and they do not restrict creativity.

A decision must be made whether to use Clipper or dBASE III. With the power of Clipper, the possibilities are endless. It is far less complicated to code for one environment than for both. dBASE III allows for many faults whereas Clipper does not. Clipper is more structured and restrictive than dBASE III. All of this is true only because of the differences in the fundamental natures of the products. One is an interpreter, and one is a compiler. In the following chapters, one goal is to help you decide between the two products. To be a good Clipper programmer you must work with Clipper. Never straddle the fence and work in both environments. To do so would restrict your potential and possibilities. dBASE III is meant for users wanting on-site query and on-the-fly report generating; Clipper is meant for programmers!

MEMORY VARIABLES

Clipper supports up to 2048 active memory variables, while dBASE III can only support 256. Also, internal to the Autumn '86 release of Clipper, string memory variables can have a length of 32,000 bytes as opposed to 255 bytes for dBASE III. The Summer '87 release expanded this capability to 64K bytes. The point to keep in mind here to maintain dual compatibility is that while Clipper has this internal capacity, these variables should not be saved directly to a memory file. Remember, dBASE III cannot handle variables that are longer than 255 bytes. In order for a string memory variable to be SAVEd to a memory file in Clipper and to be read by dBASE III, the string must be parsed out to separate memory variables, each with a length no greater than 255 bytes per string variable. When RESTORing from a memory file, remember to concatenate all of the previously parsed variables into one memory variable that is the sum of all of the string variables involved.

```
********************
* Name          Parse.prg
* Date          February 13, 1988
* Notice        Copyright 1988, Stephen J. Straley & Associates
* Compile       Clipper Parse
* Release       All versions
* Link          Plink86 fi parse lib clipper;
* Note          This sample program will save a screen to
*               a memory variable, then parse that variable into
*               a few memory variables, then SAVE those variables to
*               a MEMORY FILE, RESTORE that file, and eventually,
*               flash the screen back.  To be used with the Winter '85
*               version as well as earlier versions.
*
********************

STORE SPACE(4000) TO ascr
SAVE SCREEN TO ascr
FOR x = 1 TO 16
   temp = LTRIM(STR(x))
   ascr&temp = SUBSTR(ascr,(x-1)*250+1,250)
NEXT
RELEASE ascr
SAVE ALL LIKE ascr* TO Scrfile

NOTE > Now to restore from the file....
```

```
CLEAR
? "Now for the restoration...."
RESTORE FROM Scrfile
ascr = ""
FOR x = 1 TO 16
   temp = LTRIM(STR(x))
   ascr = ascr + ascr&temp
NEXT
WAIT
RESTORE SCREEN FROM ascr
@ 23,00 SAY ""          && To reposition the cursor to the bottom of the screen
* End of File
```

With the Autumn '86 version of Clipper, you can save the screen memory variable directly to a .MEM file without having to parse it into many 255-byte memory variables. One thing to keep in mind is that this .MEM file cannot be looked at by dBASE III. If you should try to RESTORE a .MEM file in dBASE that has in it a memory variable longer than 255 bytes, the following error message will be displayed by dBASE III:

```
. RESTORE FROM Memory
Memory Variable file is invalid.
                             ?
RESTORE FROM Memory
.
```

So for the sake of maintaining a sense of compatibility, you may opt to limit the size of your memory variables to 255 bytes with the newest version of Clipper. However, you may limit your potential by trying to be compatible in **both** environments.

FIELDS

Clipper allows 1024 fields per file while dBASE III allows only 256. This expansion must be carefully looked at for every application if maintaining compatibility is in any way a factor. Many times, databases can be consolidated by taking advantage of the extra capacity. However, an incompatibility with dBASE III might be the net result. If you decide to take this step, be consistent and code your procedures, program files, and user-defined functions for the compiler as well. It will serve no purpose to maintain compatible code between dBASE III and Clipper while the databases are incompatible.

Another feature of fields in Clipper is an extended capacity in the length of a character field. The compiler will support a character field length of over 32,000 bytes whereas dBASE III will only support 255 byte-long character fields. Again, look at the application closely to see if using this added feature will be an advantage or a nightmare. A quick example of an advantageous situation would be the following.

Let us say a compiled system would generate a series of variables to be saved from the application. In an accounting system, these values might be the last check number printed, the posting account number for the package, and other system-wide information. Saving these variables to a memory file would mean that the file could be accessed and modified from dBASE III. In order to avoid this, there is the other option of saving the variables to a temporary database. The problem with this approach is that dBASE III could have access to the information, thus allowing it to be modified at will when it should be left alone.

A solution to this problem would be to create a one-character field database that would have a length of 255 bytes. Now the trick is to parse all of the important information in one long character string and replace the character *field* with the character *string*. Since the developer would know the length of each piece of information, it could all be saved together as one. When executing the application, the program would have to take the database, look at the field, and separate out the important information into separate memory variables. The advantage to this solution is that the information would be saved according to changes dictated by the system. dBASE III cannot be used to modify any of the information because the expanded character field cannot be read by the interpreter.

So you see, incompatibility may or may not be a disadvantage. It all depends upon your specific need. Look over your situation carefully and choose wisely!

INDEX FILES

With versions prior to the Summer '87 release, any Clipper application using indexes to help order the data would have index files totally incompatible with dBASE III, and index files made under dBASE III are incompatible with Clipper. This remains true for the Summer '87 release only if special files needed to be added to the application are not linked in. If the special file is not included in the linking of the application (NDX.OBJ), the indexes will remain incompatible. The differences between the two index structures are two fold: in time and in size. The unique Clipper indexes are not only smaller than dBASE III indexes, but they are faster as well. Again, maintaining compatibility may not be a wise option for some applications.

There is no limit in Clipper to the number of index files you can have open on a file at one time. Under dBASE III, the limit is seven index files per database file. While Clipper has no limit, versions of DOS prior to 3.3 are still restricted to 20 files open at one time. The Summer '87 release has an additional DOS parameter to allow for more than 20 open files, provided your version of DOS can handle this and provided the CONFIG.SYS file on the machine running your application has been properly set. If you were to allow for the standard five files for the operating system and one for the application or program itself and one more for the database, that would leave 13 possible files that can be opened at one time. An example of this in action is shown below. Included is a structure for the database we are using in this example. Add data and note that the last index is updated with the rest.

For this example, we will use a database named MULTY.DBF:

```
Structure for database: C:MULTY.DBF     Number of data records:     0
Date of last update    : 07/03/86

Field  Field Name  Type       Width    Dec
    1  FIRST_NAME  Character     20
    2  LAST_NAME   Character     20
    3  INITIALS    Character      3
    4  SERIAL_NO   Numeric        8
    5  PURCHASED   Date           8
    6  COMPANY     Character     30
    7  CITY        Character     25
    8  STATE       Character      2
    9  PHONE       Character     10
```

```
********************
* Name           SAMPINDX.prg
* Date           March 5, 1988
* Notice         Copyright 1988, Stephen J. Straley & Associates
* Compile        Clipper Sampindx
* Release        Autumn '86 or Summer '87
* Link           Plink86 fi sampindx lib clipper;
* Note           This demonstrates how the indexes are updated
*                when there are more than seven index files
*                open at the same time.  The name of the database
*                is MULTY.DBF.
*
********************

@ 0,0 CLEAR
CREATE Template
USE Template
APPEND BLANK
REPLACE field_name with "FIRST_NAME", field_type WITH "C", field_len WITH 20
APPEND BLANK
REPLACE field_name WITH "LAST_NAME", field_type WITH "C", field_len WITH 20
APPEND BLANK
REPLACE field_name WITH "INITIALS", field_type WITH "C", field_len WITH 3
APPEND BLANK
REPLACE field_name WITH "SERIAL_NO", field_type WITH "N", field_len WITH 8
APPEND BLANK
REPLACE field_name WITH "PURCHASED", field_type WITH "N", field_len WITH 8
APPEND BLANK
REPLACE field_name WITH "COMPANY", field_type WITH "C", field_len WITH 30
APPEND BLANK
REPLACE field_name WITH "CITY", field_type WITH "C", field_len WITH 25
APPEND BLANK
REPLACE field_name WITH "STATE", field_type WITH "C", field_len WITH 2
APPEND BLANK
```

```
REPLACE field_name WITH "PHONE", field_type WITH "C", field_len WITH 10
USE
CREATE Multy FROM Template
USE Multy
ERASE Template.dbf
? "Test one"
INDEX ON initials TO Multy1
? "Test two"
INDEX ON serial_no TO Multy2
? "Test three"
INDEX ON purchased TO Multy3
? "Test four"
INDEX ON first_name TO Multy4
? "Test five"
INDEX ON company TO Multy5
? "Test six"
INDEX ON city TO Multy6
? "Test seven"
INDEX ON state TO Multy7
? "Test eight"
INDEX ON phone TO Multy8
? "Test nine"
INDEX ON last_name TO Multy9
? "Now opening them all"
USE Multy INDEX Multy1, Multy2, Multy3, Multy4, Multy5, Multy6, Multy7,
Multy8, Multy9
CLEAR
TEXT

     Try putting in at least three entries and pay strict attention to
     the last name.  Try putting the last names out of order, like a
     "T" record before a "J" record and before a "B" record.  This sample
     program would list the records in order of the last name, yet
     the last name index was the ninth open index file.

ENDTEXT
WAIT
CLEAR
DO WHILE .T.
   STORE "Y" TO cont
   CLEAR
   @ 5,5 SAY "Continue? " GET cont
   READ
   IF UPPER(cont) = "N"
      EXIT
   ENDIF
   CLEAR

   APPEND BLANK
   @  5, 5 SAY "Initials   " GET initials
   @  6, 5 SAY "Serial No  " GET serial_no
   @  7, 5 SAY "Purchased  " GET purchased
   @  8, 5 SAY "First Name " GET first_name
```

```
   @  9, 5 SAY "Company     " GET company
   @ 10, 5 SAY "City        " GET city
   @ 11, 5 SAY "State       " GET state
   @ 12, 5 SAY "Phone       " GET phone
   @ 13, 5 SAY "Last Name   " GET last_name
   READ
ENDDO
CLEAR
USE Multy INDEX Multy9
LIST last_name
* End of File
```

In addition to the differences with the extension defaults (.NDX for dBASE III index files and .NTX for Clipper index files), there are other differences as well.

There are two basic reasons why the default index file structure under Clipper is different from dBASE III's index file structure:

1. Under dBASE III, pages (see the explanation of pages below) may be lost during certain update operations (i.e., replacing key fields); in addition empty pages may take space without function.

2. Under dBASE III, pages are allocated and, upon change, the entire page is moved. Under the compiler, a page has an accompanying table, which is in essence a mini-index, and the table is updated accordingly.

Now, let's look at the implications of this.

The first problem to overcome is to make certain that updates to the key would not corrupt the index file, especially as the file size increased. Second, the dBASE III indexing in multiples of four with SET EXACT ON was looked at seriously and circumvented with a new algorithm. This last problem is known by all dBASE III users who have fallen into this trap. More important than these basic underlying reasons was the issue of speed and how to handle it. What came about was an improved algorithm, but before explaining how the new algorithm is used by the compiler, let us look at how indexes are viewed under the interpreter.

In dBASE III, the basic construct of an index is held in what is commonly referred to as a "page." This is no more than a 256-byte block of memory that the interpreter will look at one time to analyze. Now, let us say that we have two keys, the first being X in size, and a second larger one, Y in size. On the first pass, the key is updated and X is placed into a page. Since it is the first key, it is very simple to enter. When we come to the second pass, we see that Y is in front of X. A complete shift takes place while a temporary page is established for Y and a final page is established consisting of Y in front of X (note the diagram):

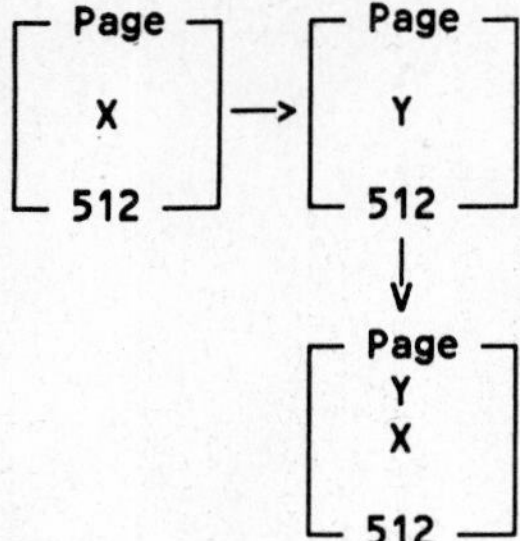

What transpires is the movement of the pages in memory and the creation of an extra page that is left dangling. The first level of pages serves no use, for all intents and purposes, since it is the second-level page that contains the actual index order. This constant shifting and managing of the pages of memory will have two effects:

1. Large index files with huge amounts of repetitively indexed data become astronomical in size.

2. Indexing is slow as the pages are adjusted. Memory is not used efficiently.

With the development of dBASE III Plus, the indexing scheme remained the same with one minor twist: the buffering techniques were changed to allow more memory (up to 640K of RAM) to be used by the indexing algorithm. Since indexing on machines with larger memories can now be accomplished entirely in RAM memory, the operation is relatively quick. Unfortunately, there is **no** increase in speed on those machines with less available memory!

Incidentally, very few applications do nothing but indexing; for example, screen formatting, printer output, and calculations are common parts of programs. So if the entire RAM is used for indexing, applications using other commands will slow down as buffers are flushed and the definitions of the commands are loaded into memory.

With the preceding information in mind, let us look at the algorithm the compiler employs.

Clipper also has pages. However, these pages are larger than those in dBASE III. A page of memory is 1024 bytes, or 1K. This will allow a larger amount to be viewed at one time, which is one way of being more efficient. Additionally, the page is broken up into two parts: a "front half " and a "back half." The front half is basically a mini-index routine. It is a series of pointers, or a table of pointers, indicating the order of the keys inside of the page itself. The back half of the page actually holds the key of the index.

Using the same example as above, on the first pass key X and the header of the index file are analyzed, and it is determined that there is nothing in the file. Key X is placed in the back half of the page and the pointer in the front half is also updated. Now the second key, Y, is analyzed and compared to the first key, X. The size is also examined to ensure that it is still under one full page (otherwise an entire new page would be created). It is then placed behind the key in the back half of the page. However, the pointer to it is placed in front of the pointer of key X. Since pointers are smaller than keys, this change can take place within the page of memory and will not create a secondary page to hold the change. The keys are generally left alone and only the pointers are updated, as described, so indexing is faster, and memory is used more efficiently. This is most noticeable when large database and index keys are being updated constantly. The following diagram shows what transpires during this operation:

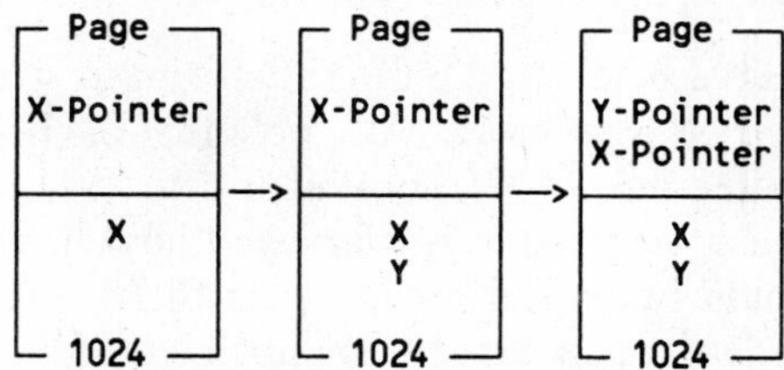

Note that the updating occurs entirely within a page of memory, indexing is rapid, and space is used efficiently. The trick occurs at the moment of indexing. The algorithm links all of the different tables together, pointing to the various keys inside of the pages. The pointer in the header is the address point of the first index in the b-tree operation.

Below is a listing of the two headers of similar index files, the first being in Clipper and the second in dBASE III. The important things to note are the completely different header structure and the contents of the header.

CLIPPER index file:

```
C>debug clipper.ntx
-d
1D45:0100  06 00 01 00 00 04 00 00-00 00 00 00 12 00 0A 00 ................
1D45:0110  00 00 32 00 19 00 6F 6E-65 00 00 00 00 00 00 00 ..2...one.......
1D45:0120  00 00 00 00 00 00 00 00-00 00 00 00 00 00 00 00 ................
1D45:0130  00 00 00 00 00 00 00 00-00 00 00 00 00 00 00 00 ................
1D45:0140  00 00 00 00 00 00 00 00-00 00 00 00 00 00 00 00 ................
1D45:0150  00 00 00 00 00 00 00 00-00 00 00 00 00 00 00 00 ................
1D45:0160  00 00 00 00 00 00 00 00-00 00 00 00 00 00 00 00 ................
1D45:0170  00 00 00 00 00 00 00 00-00 00 00 00 00 00 00 00 ................
-q
```

dBASE III index file:

```
C>debug dbase.ndx
-d
1D45:0100  01 00 00 00 02 00 00 00-00 00 00 00 0A 00 19 00 ................
1D45:0110  00 00 14 00 00 00 00 00-6F 6E 65 20 00 73 00 FF........one.s..
1D45:0120  FF FF 2E 00 28 00 00 00-01 00 02 00 04 00 0D 01 ....(...........
1D45:0130  42 00 69 00 6F 00 73 00-0D 00 05 00 B4 00 08 00 B.i.o.s....4...
1D45:0140  00 00 00 01 00 00 02 00-00 00 41 63 6B 6E 6F 77 ..........Acknow
1D45:0150  6C 65 2E 00 28 00 00 00-01 00 02 00 0F 00 0D 01 le..(...........
1D45:0160  41 00 63 00 6B 00 6E 00-6F 00 77 00 6C 00 65 00 A.c.k.n.o.w.l.e.
1D45:0170  64 00 67 00 6D 00 65 00-6E 00 74 00 73 00 0D 00 d.g.m.e.n.t.s...
-Q
```

Immediately obvious is the initial byte. In the dBASE III index structure, the initial byte is set to 01 while in Clipper it is set to 06. Also note that the beginning byte containing the key expression for the index file is located at byte 25 in dBASE III and at byte 23 in Clipper. If these headers were to be displayed further, you could see that the beginning of the file would begin further down in the file in Clipper than in dBASE III. This is due to the larger page size being implemented.

RELATIONS

Unlike the interpreter, which is limited to one relation per database file, Clipper will allow a series of relations to be established–up to eight "children" relating to a single "parent." Additive relations are allowed in the Summer '87 version, which means that a child database may become a parent database by ADDing a relation onto them. Thus former parent database will act like grandparents to the entire relation. Only one parent file may be established at a given time. Relations are vital for cross-referencing and report generating. Listed below is a fragment that shows how possible multichild relations can be established.

```
CLEAR
@ 5,0,23,79 BOX "*"
@ 7,5 SAY "One moment while all files are initialized"

file4 = "PRHIST"     && A History File
file3 = "PRCHECK"    && A Check File
file2 = "PREMPLOY"   && An Employee Master File
file1 = "PRTIME"     && A Timecard file

**********************************
* This section sets up all files *
**********************************

SELECT 4
USE &file4. INDEX Prhist_a
SELECT 3
USE &file3. INDEX Prchk_a.dat
ZAP
SELECT 2
```

```
USE &file2. INDEX Premp_a.dat
SELECT 1
USE &file1. INDEX Prtime_a.dat
SELECT 1
***************************************************************************
* This section adds the checks to be processed to the check file, based *
* completely on the number of timecards in the timecard file.           *
***************************************************************************
DO WHILE .NOT. EOF()
   @ 21, 5 SAY "Now adding employee number " + TRIM(employee) + ;
   " to the check file"
   temp_emp = employee
   SELECT 3
   APPEND BLANK
   REPLACE employee WITH temp_emp
   SELECT 1
   SKIP
ENDDO
******************************************************
* This section sets up final relation and then goes  *
* on to calculate federal, state, and local taxes.   *
******************************************************

@ 21, 5 SAY SPACE(73)
SELECT 3
GO TOP
SET RELATION TO employee INTO &file2., TO employee INTO &file1.

*********************************************
* Both files are indexed on employee, as is *
* the parent file.                          *
*********************************************

@  7, 5 SAY SPACE(73)

DO WHILE .NOT. EOF()

   ************************************************************
   * Calculate base pay                                       *
   *   AMT_REG_P is set to salary rate (if a salary employee) *
   *   else is set to the hourly rate X the number of         *
   *   straight hours worked                                  *
   ************************************************************
   IF &file2.->salaried
      REPLACE amt_reg_p WITH &file2.->pay_rate_s
   ELSE
      REPLACE amt_reg_p WITH &file1.->stra_time * &file2.->pay_rate_h
   ENDIF

   ****************************************************************************
   * Calculate Overtime pay, Total Gross Pay, and Exempted Pay                *
   *                                                                          *
   * Temp_pay is first the hourly rate X the rate for overtime X the          *
```

```
*     number of overtime hours worked.                                  *
* Temp_pay is then added to hourly rate X the rate for double time      *
*     X the number of double-time hours worked.                         *
* Temp_pay is finally added to the hourly rate X the rate for triple    *
*     time X the number of triple-time hours worked.                    *
*     AMT_OVR_P is then set to Temp_pay                                 *
*     AMT_VAC_P is set to the hourly pay rate X the rate for vacation time *
*     X the number of vacation hours worked                             *
*     AMT_SIC_P is set to the hourly pay rate X the hours of sick time  *
*     AMT_GRO_P is set to the regular pay + the overtime pay + vacation *
*     pay + the sick pay                                                *
*     Temp_pay is then set to the tips + the bonus + any misc. pay -    *
*     any gross pay deduction (master employee record)                  *
*     AMT_TGR_P is set to the gross pay(AMT_GRO_P) + temp_pay(all else) *
*     AMT_EXP_P is set to the amount of exempted pay                    *
*************************************************************************

   temp_pay = &file2.->pay_rate_h * prover * &file1.->half_time
   temp_pay = temp_pay + &file2.->pay_rate_h * prdouble * &file1.->doub_time
   temp_pay = temp_pay + &file2.->pay_rate_h * prtriple * &file1.->trip_time
   REPLACE amt_ovr_p WITH temp_pay, amt_vac_p WITH &file2.->pay_rate_h * prvaca *
&file1.->vaca_time
   REPLACE amt_sic_p WITH &file2.->pay_rate_h * &file1.->sick_time
   REPLACE amt_gro_p WITH amt_reg_p + amt_ovr_p + amt_vac_p + amt_sic_p
   temp_pay = &file1.->tips + &file1.->bonus + &file1.->misc_pay - &file>gross_pay
   REPLACE amt_tgr_p WITH amt_gro_p + temp_pay, amt_exp_p WITH &file1.->exem_pay
ENDDO
CLOSE DATABASES
```

In this sample fragment of code from a possible payroll section, everything is based on the contents of a check file. Based on related information in the employee master file and the employee's timecard file, the check will be cut. The concept is that relations are not only important for report generating (i.e., a database with the invoice header relating to a secondary database with the detail information or line item). Obtaining vital information for calculating purposes is just as important.

CUSTOMIZED HELP

An application in Clipper may be designed with a built-in help system. This feature can give dBASE III systems an extremely polished look and feel. If you take the view-point that manuals are never really read, the on-line help feature may be a viable method to save time in document preparation and to provide an accessible reference. For further information, please refer to Chapter 13, Clipper's Help Utility.

USER-DEFINED FUNCTIONS

Possibly the greatest feature of Clipper, the user-defined functions (UDFs) enable the programmer to create, develop, expand, and manipulate data in just about any situation. UDFs allow the experienced programmer to develop features that may not be available in Clipper and to have the ability to implement new features immediately, without update fees or problems.

PROCEDURES AND PROCEDURE FILES

If it is not a function, it is a procedure. Being a compiler, Clipper treats programming in two lights: functions and procedures. Any operation that performs a **task** is considered by the compiler to be a "procedure"; anything that **returns a value** is a "function." Keeping this in mind, program recursion is fully supported in Clipper. For further details, please refer to Chapter 8, Clipper Procedures.

NOTES FOR MEMOS AND STRINGS

Clipper has increased the functionality of memo fields and strings. Unlike the interpreter, a memo in Clipper may be edited on the entire screen or a portion of the screen. Indeed, under the compiler a memo can finally act like a paper memo: a note pad taking very little space on the screen, with a border as well. Under Clipper, strings may be treated and edited as memos as well.

MACRO SUBSTITUTION

An extensive effort was made to expand the use of macros in Clipper and their interface with the flow of any application. Some of the new advantages include the use of macros in a DO WHILE...ENDDO loop as well as the use of recursive macros. Clipper includes the standard uses for macros in the place of constants, variable names, literals, and most full expressions. However, one limitation of macros under Clipper is the prohibition of the use of a macro in a command line. Since the compiler needs to know the full command at the time of compilation, macros must be avoided and the command must be spelled out. Significant cases are commas inside of a macro being used in conjunction with the LIST command and full-screen addressing completely in a macro. Added to this basic understanding, the Summer '87 release permits macros used as expressions to be handled more efficiently with simple parentheses surrounding the macro expression. For further information on the differences, please refer to Chapter 11, Macros and Arrays.

ARRAYS AND MATRIXES

One of the most powerful tools of the Clipper language is its ability to handle arrays. This concept is totally new to the structure of the dBASE III language and is only available with the compiler. Equally useful is the ability to handle matrixes or multi-dimensional arrays and macro substitution in conjunction with arrays, simulating GATHER and SCATTER commands, and to save and restore arrays to and from the disk.

INTERFACING WITH OTHER LANGUAGES

Another added feature of the compiler is the ability to interface with and use routines and modules written in other languages, such as Assembler and C. With the introduction of the Summer '87 release, interfacing with Microsoft C is made easier.

CONTROL KEYS

The compiler contains an extended ability to SET specific keys, depending upon their ASCII value, and to DO specific tasks, programs, functions, or procedures. Not only is on-line help available, but with enhanced flexibility and control of the keyboard, entire applications can be organized and executed with minimal keystrokes.

MORE FUNCTIONS AND MORE COMMANDS

Appealing to the needs of many developers, the compiler adds several new and/or enhanced functions that both speed up applications and make coding techniques extremely simple. Under the compiled environment, what might have taken numerous lines of code will now take just one or two. Along with additional functions, including array functions and low-level functions, there are a few additional commands: CALL, COMMIT, BOX, SAVE SCREEN, FOR...NEXT, etc. All of these are designed with one intent: to expand the capabilities and capacity of the language.

SAVING SCREENS

Another added feature of the compiler is the capability of saving screens to memory variables, to temporary memory files, or even to databases. With the Summer '87 release, even portions of the screen may be saved to variables as well. Menu drawing, which became very fast under the compiler, now can be virtually instantaneous.

CLIPPER VARIABLE

Clipper also can distinguish between variable dBASE III code (code that may contain commands not supported by the compiler) and Clipper code. When the PUBLIC variable CLIPPER is declared, it is considered to be **true** under the compiler, while under the interpretive environment, it is considered **false**. Therefore, any code inside a logical test of the compiler (IF CLIPPER) will execute properly. Conversely, that same code would be ignored and the alternative code would be executed under the interpreter. This allows developers to code in parallel for both environments without maintaining two separately coded applications.

PARAMETER PASSING FROM DOS

Parameters can now be passed directly into an application from the operating system. With this flexibility, chaining a series of programs is within the realm of possibilities. The Autumn '86 and later versions of Clipper allow more than one parameter to be passed from DOS to a Clipper application. Remember that these parameters will be of *character* data type and so if numeric or date parameters are passed in from DOS, they must then be converted to the appropriate data type.

BASIC CODING TECHNIQUES

This is the most difficult feature of the compiler to explain and understand, but once you master it, many of the frustrations of working with an interpreter can be eliminated. Modular coding, expanded ideas, and program recursion are all features of the compiler. The main concept to grasp is that if it is possible, no matter how difficult, it is more feasible with the compiler than with the interpreter. Coding and programming with Clipper is an adventure into the world of possibilities!

DIFFERENCES

Along with the advantages of the compiler, the features **not** supported by the compiler should be understood. Most of these are not supported because by their nature they are better suited to an interpreter rather than a compiler. You will get a better understanding of this as we discuss the differences between a compiler and an interpreter. Suffice it to say that in many circumstances the interpreter takes care of a great many things for the programmer. Many times, these commands are really in control of the programmer and not vice versa. A compiler is very literal and precise; an interpreter does just that–it *interprets* meaning, and is placed between the developer and his code. Following is a list of those features not supported by Clipper. There are a few commands that have been simulated under the compiler's environment and are marked with an asterisk (*). They are discussed in Appendix F, Simulating dBASE III Commands.

```
ASSIST          HELP            BROWSE *        RETURN TO MASTER *
INSERT          SET             LIST STATUS     LIST STRUCTURE *
CREATE REPORT   CREATE LABEL    LIST MEMORY     DISPLAY STATUS
SET DEBUG       CHANGE          LIST FILES      DISPLAY STRUCTURE *
SET ECHO        SET HELP        DISPLAY FILES   DISPLAY MEMORY
SET MENU        SET STEP        MODIFY LABEL    MODIFY COMMAND
SET SAFETY      SET HEADING     MODIFY REPORT   MODIFY STRUCTURE *
SET TALK        EDIT *
```

In addition, there are many routines taken for granted in the interpreter that are not supported by the compiler. For example, one file might have a 1-byte *character field* that contains nothing but "Y" or "N." In comparison, a second database file might have a field with the same name as the character field, except its data type is *logical*. Let's set up a situation to copy from one file to the other. The code might look like this:

```
USE Two
APPEND FROM One
```

dBASE III's front end checks and handles the files as they are COPYing and APPENDing. The one character "Y" or "N" would be appended by dBASE III to the logical field (the same holds true for character fields that look like a date field). The interpreter will automatically handle the conversion to a date field. If we try to copy from one file to the other under the compiler, the following error message would be displayed on the screen:

```
proc:TEST line:2  Type conflict in REPLACE                    QUIT? (Q/A/I)
```

These situations, if overlooked during coding, will cause problems during execution. The best advice when converting a system from dBASE III to Clipper is to rethink the mechanics of the system. Take the flow of the application to the very bare essence and work from there. Yes, it once worked in dBASE III, but that is not the reason for running with the compiler. Get a feeling for the constraints of the compiler and see if your code fits!

CLIPPER AND dBASE III Plus

CHANGE IN HEADERS

When dBASE III Plus was released, there was an unexpected change in the structure of the header of database files. This obviously caused a great deal of consternation to Clipper users. However, the situation was resolved in the Winter '85 release and compatibility was restored. Below are headers of the dBASE III file and a dBASE III Plus file. The fourth byte was changed from a 16 to an 18. The result is a shift in the position of records being displayed, reported, and even indexed. The solution is either to use the Winter '85 or later release of the compiler or use dBASE III to create the databases. Once created, the system will function as planned.

dBASE III Header:

```
C>debug dbase.dbf
-d
1D45:0100 03 56 03 16 00 00 00 00-42 00 0B 00 00 00 00 00 .V......B.......
1D45:0110 00 00 00 00 00 00 00 00-00 00 00 00 00 00 00 00 ................
1D45:0120 4F 4E 45 00 00 00 00 00-00 00 00 43 00 00 00 00 ONE........C....
1D45:0130 0A 00 00 00 00 00 00 00-00 00 00 00 00 00 00 00 ................
1D45:0140 0D 00 1A EA 00 00 00 00-2E 8F 06 56 77 2E 8F 06 ...j.......Vw...
1D45:0150 58 77 E8 21 F0 EA 00 00-00 00 2E 8F 06 68 77 2E Xwh!pj.......hw.
1D45:0160 8F 06 6A 77 E8 27 F0 EA-00 00 00 00 2E 8F 06 7A ..jwh'pj.......z
1D45:0170 77 2E 8F 06 7C 77 E8 2D-F0 EA 00 00 00 00 2E 8F w...|wh-pj......
-q
```

dBASE III Plus Header:

```
C>debug plus.dbf
-d
1D45:0100 03 56 03 18 00 00 00 00-41 00 0B 00 00 00 00 00 .V......A.......
1D45:0110 00 00 00 00 00 00 00 00-00 00 00 00 00 00 00 00 ................
1D45:0120 54 48 52 45 45 00 00 00-00 00 00 43 00 00 00 00 THREE......C....
1D45:0130 0A 00 00 00 00 00 00 00-00 00 00 00 00 00 00 00 ................
1D45:0140 0D 1A 1A EA 00 00 00 00-2E 8F 06 56 77 2E 8F 06 ...j.......Vw...
1D45:0150 58 77 E8 21 F0 EA 00 00-00 00 2E 8F 06 68 77 2E Xwh!pj.......hw.
1D45:0160 8F 06 6A 77 E8 27 F0 EA-00 00 00 00 2E 8F 06 7A ..jwh'pj.......z
1D45:0170 77 2E 8F 06 7C 77 E8 2D-F0 EA 00 00 00 00 2E 8F w...|wh-pj.....
```

Notice the value of the ninth byte. In dBASE III, the value is 42, yet in dBASE III Plus, the value is dropped by one position to 41. This is the shift in the header previously described.

SINGLE-USER ENVIRONMENT

While most of the additional commands were brought on by the advent of dBASE III Plus, the main thrust of that program is to provide a multiuser environment. An entire section of this text is devoted to the discussion of Clipper and the world of multiuser programs. However, the main thrust of this book is using the compiler for single-user applications.

dBASE and CLIPPER COMMANDS

As with all vital products, enhancements are continuously introduced for dBASE III. An important feature of Clipper is its ability to stay compatible with these enhancements and to provide continued support for the dBASE III language, regardless of the number of commands and functions already built in. Below is a list of commands in dBASE III and Clipper and an indication of how Clipper supports the commands, using the following key: not at all (N), fully support (F), available in extended routines (E), or may be simulated (S). The dBASE III + column identifies those commands supported by dBASE III Plus. The next four columns are for the Autumn '86 release of Clipper and the last four are for the Summer '87 release.

		CLIPPER Autumn 1986 OPTIONS				CLIPPER Summer 1987 OPTIONS			
COMMAND	dBASE III+:	N:	F:	E:	S:	N:	F:	E:	S:
?	X	-	X			-	X		
??	X	-	X			-	X		
@BOX	-	-	X			-	X		
@CLEAR	X	-	X			-	X		
@GET	X	-	X			-	X		
@PROMPT	-	-	X			-	X		
@SAY	X	-	X			-	X		
@TO	X	-	X			-	X		
ACCEPT	X	-	X			-	X		
APPEND	X	X		X		-	X		X
APPEND BLANK	X	-	X			-		X	
APPEND FROM	X	-	X			-		X	
ASSIST	X	X				X			
AVERAGE	X	-	X			-	X		
BEGIN SEQUENCE...END		X				-	X		
BROWSE	X	X		X		X		X	
CALL		-	X			-	X		
CANCEL	X	-	X			-	X		
CHANGE	X	X				X			
CLEAR	X	-	X			-	X		
CLEAR ALL	X	-	X			-	X		
CLEAR FIELDS	X	X				X			
CLEAR GETS	X	-	X			-	X		
CLEAR MEMORY	X	-	X			-	X		
CLEAR TYPEAHEAD	X	-	X			-	X		
CLIPPER		-	X			-	X		
CLOSE ALL	X	X				-	X		
CLOSE ALTERNATE	X	-	X			-	X		
CLOSE DATABASE	X	-	X			-	X		
CLOSE FORMAT	X	-	X			-	X		
CLOSE INDEX	X	-	X			-	X		
COMMIT		X				-	X		
CONTINUE	X	-	X			-	X		
COPY	X	-	X			-	X		
COPY FILE	X	-	X			-	X		
COPY STRUCTURE	X	-	X			-	X		
COPY TO STRUCTURE EXTENDED	X	-	X			-	X		
COUNT	X	-	X			-	X		
CREATE		-	X			-	X		
CREATE FROM	X	-	X			-	X		
CREATE LABEL	X	-			X	-			X
CREATE QUERY	X	X				X			
CREATE REPORT	X	-			X	-			X
CREATE SCREEN	X	X				X			
CREATE VIEW	X	X				X			
CREATE VIEW FROM ENVIRONMENT	X	X				X			

		CLIPPER Autumn 1986 OPTIONS				CLIPPER Summer 1987 OPTIONS			
COMMAND	dBASE III+:	N:	F:	E:	S:	N:	F:	E:	S:
DECLARE		-	X			-	X		
DELETE	X	-	X			-	X		
DIR	X	-	X			-	X		
DISPLAY	X	-	X			-	X		
DISPLAY HISTORY	X	X				X			
DISPLAY MEMORY	X	X				X			
DISPLAY STATUS	X	X				X			
DISPLAY STRUCTURE	X	-			X	-			X
DO	X	-	X			-	X		
DO CASE	X	-	X			-	X		
DO WHILE	X	-	X			-	X		
EDIT	X	-			X	-			X
EJECT	X	-	X			-	X		
ERASE	X	-	X			-	X		
EXIT		-	X			-	X		
EXPORT	X	X				X			
EXTERNAL		-	X			-	X		
FIND	X	-	X			-	X		
FOR ... NEXT		-	X			-	X		
FUNCTION		-	X			-	X		
GO	X	-	X			-	X		
HELP	X	X				X			
IF	X	-	X			-	X		
IF...ELSEIF...ENDIF		X				-	X		
IMPORT	X	X				X			
INDEX ON	X	-	X			-	X		
INPUT	X	-	X			-	X		
INSERT	X	X				X			
JOIN	X	-	X			-	X		
KEYBOARD		-	X			-	X		
LABEL	X	-	X			-	X		
LIST	X	-	X			-	X		
LIST HISTORY	X	X				X			
LIST MEMORY	X	X				X			
LIST STATUS	X	X				X			
LIST STRUCTURE	X	-			X	-			X
LOAD	X	X				X			
LOCATE	X	-	X			-	X		
LOOP	X	-	X			-	X		
MENU TO		-	X			-	X		
MODIFY COMMAND	X	X				X			
MODIFY LABEL	X	X				X			
MODIFY QUERY	X	X				X			
MODIFY REPORT	X	X				X			
MODIFY SCREEN	X	X				X			
MODIFY STRUCTURE	X	-			X	-			X
MODIFY VIEW	X	X				X			
NOTE	X	-	X			-	X		
ON ERROR / ESCAPE / KEY	X	X				X			
PACK	X	-	X			-	X		

		CLIPPER Autumn 1986 OPTIONS				CLIPPER Summer 1987 OPTIONS			
COMMAND	dBASE III+:	N:	F:	E:	S:	N:	F:	E:	S:
PARAMETERS	X	-	X			-	X		
PRIVATE	X	-	X			-	X		
PROCEDURE	X	-	X			-	X		
PUBLIC	X	-	X			-	X		
QUIT	X	-	X			-	X		
READ	X	-	X			-	X		
RECALL	X	-	X			-	X		
REINDEX	X	-	X			-	X		
RELEASE	X	-	X			-	X		
RENAME	X	-	X			-	X		
REPLACE	X	-	X			-	X		
REPORT	X	-	X			-	X		
RESTORE	X	-	X			-	X		
RESTORE SCREEN		-	X			-	X		
RESUME	X	X				X			
RETRY	X	X				X			
RETURN	X	-	X			-	X		
RUN	X	-	X			-	X		
SAVE	X	-	X			-	X		
SAVE SCREEN		-	X			-	X		
SEEK	X	-	X			-	X		
SELECT	X	-	X			-	X		
SET ALTERNATE on/OFF	X	-	X			-	X		
SET ALTERNATE TO	X	-	X			-	X		
SET BELL ON/off	X	-	X			-	X		
SET CATALOG ON/off	X	X				X			
SET CATALOG TO	X	X				X			
SET CENTURY on/OFF	X	-	X			-	X		
SET COLOR ON/off	X	X				X			
SET COLOR TO	X	-	X			-	X		
SET CONFIRM on/OFF	X	-	X			-	X		
SET CONSOLE ON/off	X	-	X			-	X		
SET DATE	X	-	X			-	X		
SET DEBUG on/OFF	X	X				X			
SET DECIMALS TO	X	-	X			-	X		
SET DEFAULT TO	X	-	X			-	X		
SET DELETED on/OFF	X	-	X			-	X		
SET DELIMITERS on/OFF	X	-	X			-	X		
SET DELIMITERS TO	X	-	X			-	X		
SET DEVICE TO SCREEN	X	-	X			-	X		
SET DOHISTORY on/OFF	X	X				X			
SET ECHO on/OFF	X	X				-	X		
SET ESCAPE ON/off	X	-	X			-	X		
SET EXACT on/OFF	X	-	X			-	X		
SET EXCLUSIVE ON/off	X	-	X			-	X		
SET FIELDS ON/off	X	X				X			
SET FIELDS TO	X	X				X			
SET FILTER TO	X	-	X			-	X		
SET FIXED on/OFF	X	-	X			-	X		
SET FORMAT TO	X	-	X			-	X		

COMMAND	dBASE III+:	CLIPPER Autumn 1986 OPTIONS N:	F:	E:	S:	CLIPPER Summer 1987 OPTIONS N:	F:	E:	S:
SET FUNCTION TO	X	-	X			-	X		
SET HEADING ON/off	X	X				X			
SET HELP ON/off	X	X				X			
SET HISTORY TO	X	X				X			
SET INDEX TO	X	-	X			-	X		
SET INTENSITY ON/off	X	-	X			-	X		
SET KEY TO		-	X			-	X		
SET MARGIN TO	X	-	X			-	X		
SET MEMOWIDTH TO	X	X				X			
SET MENUS ON/off	X	X				X			
SET MESSAGE TO		-	X			-	X		
SET ORDER TO	X	-	X			-	X		
SET PATH TO	X	-	X			-	X		
SET PRINT TO	X	-	X			-	X		
SET PRINT on/OFF	X	-	X			-	X		
SET PRINTER TO	X	-	X			-	X		
SET PROCEDURE TO	X	-	X			-	X		
SET RELATION TO	X	-	X			-	X		
SET SAFETY ON/off	X	X				X			
SET SCOREBOARD ON/off		-	X			-	X		
SET SOFTSEEK on/OFF		X				-	X		
SET STATUS ON/off	X	X				X			
SET STEP on/OFF	X	X				X			
SET TALK ON/off	X	X				X			
SET TITLE ON/off	X	X				X			
SET TYPEAHEAD TO	X	X				-	X		
SET UNIQUE on/OFF	X	-	X			-	X		
SET VIEW TO	X	X				X			
SET WRAP on/OFF		X				-	X		
SKIP	X	-	X			-	X		
SORT	X	-	X			-	X		
STORE	X	-	X			-	X		
SUM	X	-	X			-	X		
SUSPEND	X	X				X			
TEXT	X	-	X			-	X		
TOTAL	X	-	X			-	X		
TYPE	X	-	X			-	X		
UNLOCK	X	-	X			-	X		
UPDATE	X	-	X			-	X		
USE	X	-	X			-	X		
USE...EXCLUSIVE	X	-	X			-	X		
WAIT	X	-	X			-	X		
ZAP	X	-	X			-	X		

FUNCTIONS	dBASE III+:	CLIPPER Autumn 1986 OPTIONS N:	F:	E:	S:	CLIPPER Summer 1987 OPTIONS N:	F:	E:	S:
$	X		X				X		
&	X		X				X		
&&	X		X				X		
ABS()	X		X				X		

		CLIPPER Autumn 1986 OPTIONS				CLIPPER Summer 1987 OPTIONS			
FUNCTIONS	dBASE III+:	N:	F:	E:	S:	N:	F:	E:	S:
ACHOICE()							X		
ACOPY()							X		
ADEL()			X				X		
ADIR()			X				X		
AFIELDS()							X		
AINS()			X				X		
ALIAS()	X		X				X		
ALLTRIM()					X		X		
ALTD()							X		
AMPM()					X		X		
ASC()	X		X				X		
ASCAN()			X				X		
ASORT()							X		
AT()	X		X				X		
BIN2I()							X		
BIN2L()							X		
BIN2W()							X		
BOF()	X		X				X		
CDOW()	X		X				X		
CHR()	X		X				X		
CMONTH()	X		X				X		
COL()	X		X				X		
CURDIR()							X		
DATE()	X		X				X		
DAY()	X		X				X		
DAYS()					X		X		
DBEDIT()							X		
DBF()	X				X		X		
DELETED()	X		X				X		
DISKSPACE()	X		X				X		
DOW()	X		X				X		
DBFILTER()							X		
DBRELATION()							X		
DBRSELECT()							X		
DESCEND()					X		X		
DOSERROR()							X		
DTOC()	X		X				X		
DTOS()			X				X		
ELAPTIME()					X		X		
EMPTY()			X				X		
EOF()	X		X				X		
ERROR()	X	X				X			
ERRORLEVEL()							X		
EXP()	X	X					X		
FCLOSE()							X		
FCOUNT()			X				X		
FCREATE()							X		
FERROR()							X		
FIELD()			X				X		
FIELDNAME()			X				X		

FUNCTIONS	dBASE III+:	CLIPPER Autumn 1986 OPTIONS N:	F:	E:	S:	CLIPPER Summer 1987 OPTIONS N:	F:	E:	S:
FILE()	X		X				X		
FKLABEL()	X				X		X		
FKMAX()	X				X		X		
FLOCK()	X		X				X		
FOPEN()							X		
FOUND()	X		X				X		
FREAD()							X		
FREADSTR()							X		
FSEEK()							X		
FWRITE()							X		
GETENV()	X	X				X			
GETE()			X						
HARDCR()			X				X		
HEADER()							X		
I2BIN()							X		
IIF()	X		X				X		
INDEXEXT()							X		
INDEXKEY()			X				X		
INDEXORD()							X		
INKEY()	X		X				X		
INT()	X		X				X		
ISAPLHA()	X				X		X		
ISCOLOR()	X				X		X		
ISLOWER()	X				X		X		
ISPRINTER()					X		X		
ISUPPER()	X				X		X		
L2BIN()							X		
LASTKEY()			X				X		
LASTREC()	X		X				X		
LEFT()	X		X				X		
LEN()	X		X				X		
LOCK()	X		X				X		
LOG()	X		X				X		
LOWER()	X		X				X		
LTRIM()	X		X				X		
LUPDATE()	X			X			X		
MAX()	X		X				X		
MEMOEDIT()			X				X		
MEMOLINE()							X		
MEMOREAD()			X				X		
MEMORY(0)			X				X		
MEMOTRAN()							X		
MEMOWRIT()			X				X		
MESSAGE()	X	X				X			
MIN()	X		X				X		
MLCOUNT()							X		
MLPOS()							X		
MOD()	X				X		X		
MONTH()	X		X				X		
NDX()	X				X	X			
NETERR()	X		X				X		

FUNCTIONS	dBASE III+:	CLIPPER Autumn 1986 OPTIONS N:	F:	E:	S:	CLIPPER Summer 1987 OPTIONS N:	F:	E:	S:
NETNAME()	X		X				X		
OS()	X				X		X		
PCOL()	X		X				X		
PCOUNT()			X				X		
PROCLINE()			X				X		
PROCNAME()			X				X		
PROW()	X		X				X		
RAT()							X		
READEXIT()							X		
READINSERT()							X		
READKEY()	X		X				X		
READVAR()			X				X		
RECCOUNT()	X		X				X		
RECNO()	X		X				X		
RECSIZE()	X				X		X		
REPLICATE()	X		X				X		
RESTSCREEN()							X		
RIGHT()	X		X				X		
RLOCK()	X		X				X		
ROUND()	X		X				X		
ROW()	X		X				X		
RTRIM()	X		X				X		
SAVESCREEN()							X		
SCROLL()							X		
SECS()					X		X		
SECONDS()			X				X		
SELECT()			X				X		
SETCANCEL()							X		
SETCOLOR()							X		
SETPRC()			X				X		
SOUNDEX()					X		X		
SPACE()	X		X				X		
SQRT()	X		X				X		
STR()	X		X				X		
STRTRAN()							X		
STRZERO()					X		X		
STUFF()	X				X		X		
SUBSTR()	X		X				X		
TIME()	X		X				X		
TONE()							X		
TRANSFORM()	X		X				X		
TRIM()	X		X				X		
TSTRING()					X		X		
TYPE()	X		X				X		
UPDATED()			X				X		
UPPER()	X		X				X		
USED()							X		
VAL()	X		X				X		
VERSION()	X				X		X		
WORD()	X		X				X		
YEAR()	X		X				X		

Most of these commands and functions were introduced in either dBASE II or in dBASE III. However, there are a few that are new in dBASE III Plus. As dBASE III Plus becomes more established in the market, more and more routines will be developed in Clipper to support it. Also, notice how many more functions have been added to the core base of the language, and also note how many functions and features are supported and enhanced with the Summer '87 version. The point to this is quite obvious: as the compiler matured, the language grew, the possibilities widened, and the end results were substantial.

RESERVED WORDS IN CLIPPER

Like most languages or compilers, Clipper has a list of reserved words. Using these words may produce strange results in your applications. Therefore, avoid using these words either for memory variables, function names, file names, or even procedure names. In addition, the double underscore character (__) is not allowed as the beginning character of a variable, function, or procedure name in conjunction with the Summer '87 release. Since this version was compiled with Microsoft C and Microsoft C automatically places an underscore in front of all symbols (variable, functions, procedures), what was a single underscore in earlier versions of Clipper now has become a double underscore symbol.

```
$START$     CXNDPB      FOPEN       MOVMEM      STPBLK CXNDPH
FORKL       STPCHR      ALLMEM      CXNDPL      FORKLP OPEN
STPCPY      ATOF        CXNM8       FORKV       STRCAT CXS55
FORKVP      POW         STRCMP      BDOS        CXS88 FREOPEN
POW2        STRCPY      BLDMEM      CXS_55      FREXP
STRCSPN     CXT5        RBRK        STRLEN      CLOSE
CXV05       GETENV      READ        STRNCAT     CREAT
CXV25       GETMEM      REMOVE      STRNCMP     CXA38
CXV52       GETML       RENAME      STRNCPY     CXA55
CXV53       RLSMEM      STRSPN      CXA_55      CXV54
HEADER*     RLSML       STSCMP      CXC33       CXV83
RST         SYSTEM      CXC55       CXVDF       IEXEC
CXC88       CXVFD       SBRK        UNLINK      CXC_55
CXV_45      LDEXP       SETMEM      CXD33       CXV_54
LOG         SIZMEM      WAIT        CXFNM4      ERRNO
LOG10       SORT        Winter85    CXFNM5      EXCEPT
LSBRK       STBCPY      WRITE       CXFXT4      EXIT
LSEEK       STCCPY      CXFXT5      EXP         STCI_K
XCEXIT      CXM33       MATHERR     STCIS       XCOVF
FABS        MKEXT       STCISN      CXM_55      FCLOSE
MKNAME      STCI_D      CXN5        FMOD        MODF
STCU_D
 * reserved word in Autumn '86 version
```

CLIPPER AND THE REST OF THE WORLD

With the entire computer industry constantly changing, it is extremely difficult to predict future developments. Who could have predicted such dramatic enhancements to Clipper from the Autumn '86 release to the Summer '87 release? Those in the industry appear to belong to one of two groups: the 20 percent group that is comfortable with new ideas and new technologies and the 80 percent group that waits to see what IBM does. The scenario has been and probably always will be the same. The problem is that the two groups are never completely in sync with each other. However, there are those rare instances when a product or a group of products seem to bridge the gap between the two. Clipper is one such product. While it establishes a new approach to database management practice on microcomputers, it is compatible with the current standards (dBASE III and IBM) yet at the same time looks toward the future by interfacing with Microsoft C and the UNIX operating system.

Some of the old conceptions of what a database manager should and should not be do not apply to Clipper. In the industry there are often simple solutions to many problems. But what about the future, other languages, other capabilities? After all, the entire world does not program in dBASE III alone.

To allow for this, any routine that is supported by Microsoft C, version 5.0, may be linked directly into the program with very little effort. Most of the C library is contained in the compiler's library; it becomes simply a question of addressing those routines. This also explains some of the capabilities of the compiler. In many instances it acts like dBASE III; in many more it acts like C. Second, the compiler can work with those Assembly routines that do many things including invoking direct interrupts, manipulating buffers and screen I/O, and locking records and files. Many developers who know the operating system or machine specific to their needs can program these tools to coexist with their applications. It is practical to have those routines interact with Clipper routines. Because of the advent of the CALL command (which dBASE III Plus enabled), these approaches are now possible.

Many programmers now use the C language. To have the flexibility to use such a language for many machine-level tasks while programming in Clipper makes for a very bright and profitable future!

WORD PROCESSING VERSUS TEXT EDITING

Many programs are written in dBASE III's pseudo (MODIFY COMMAND) text editor. With this editor, problems will occur with lines that are longer than one screen. dBASE III has a tendency to place a soft carriage return marker [CHR(141)] in the file, which will really confuse Clipper when compiling.

Regardless of the reason, almost all word processors and dBASE III's editor should **not** be used for programming in Clipper! Use programming-specific text editors such as Brief (and the add-on package dBRIEF), Pmate, EDIX, Norton's Editor, PC, XyWrite, and WordStar in the nondocument mode. Avoid using RAM resident editors such as Popcorn and SideKick.

CLIPPER VERSUS CLIPPER

The Summer '87 release is much more than just an update to the Clipper language. This release makes a firm statement to the entire industry: Clipper is a sophisticated development language that has all of the power of most major structured languages. There are many new and enhanced features to the Summer '87 release that allow programmers to give even more punch to their applications. Just because Clipper can access standard .DBF, .NTX, .LBL, and .FRM files does not mean that it is **just** a compiler to the dBASE language. I have outlined some of the new features and enhancements that any Clipper developer should seriously consider including in the next application.

COMPATIBLE DBASE III INDEXES

For those applications in which not only the file format must be compatible to the interpreter, but the index order as well, Clipper now can read and write both the default .NTX Clipper index format and the dBASE .NDX index file format. To have Clipper look at .NDX files, the NTX.OBJ file must be linked in with all other program modules for the application. Clipper will automatically know, if this object file is present in the .EXE file, to create, update, and access dBASE III standard index files. If this is the case, the file extension for the index files will be .NDX while the default file extension for Clipper indexes will continue to be .NTX. Be careful if you are overriding the default file extensions and the application tries to access an index file in the wrong format. For example, the index file is named PEOPLE.ORD. If the application to create this index file had the NDX.OBJ object module linked in, the index file would be compatible with dBASE III. However, if at some time in the future the same application was modified and the NDX.OBJ module was **not** linked in, a run-time error message would occur; it would be something like:

```
Proc T1 line 1, undefined identifier (in index key) COUNT
```

LARGER STRING SUPPORT

The Summer '87 version introduced a larger string capacity. In the previous version, a character string could be up to 32K in length. Now, Clipper support 64K strings for all operations and functions.

LOW-LEVEL FUNCTIONS

Probably one of the most welcomed enhancements, these functions round out the Clipper language so that they are more conventional, like other high-level languages. The low-level functions allow direct manipulation on any file, including specific byte manipulation on .FRM, .LBL, .DBF, and .NDX files. The key to remember with these functions is the new ability to open, read, write, and analyze information in any data format, including those files that do not fit the standard database file header.

MORE FILES

Using the Summer '87 version to compile applications that will run on machines with DOS version 3.3 or greater, the Clipper application may now access up to 255 files. This takes into consideration special settings for both the CONFIG.SYS file and the DOS environment.

RUN-TIME ERROR SYSTEM

All Clipper-compiled applications using the Summer '87 version may now have included a programmed error-handling system. This does not necessarily mean that the application can recover from errors encountered; rather, that the error can be programmed to be less cryptic and more user-friendly. In some cases, if the error can be recovered, the error system gives the end user of a Clipper compiled application the opportunity to recover and to continue with normal program flow. Again, this is not an automatic and guaranteed assumption; it must be provided for by the programmer.

EXTENDED EXPRESSIONS

This feature not only makes reading an application more legible, but it provides faster running as well. In many cases, a macro substitution may now be replaced with explicit parentheses around the expression. Clipper-compiled applications may now handle these embedded expressions far faster than the standard macro expansion techniques in previous versions of Clipper. This enhancement is included with all of the SET commands, provided the logical expression is still surrounded by parentheses. Alias expressions may be included now in field and database functions as well. Here is a list of commands to which the new expanded expression logic has been added:

```
APPEND FROM            SET DEFAULT TO
COPY FILE              SET DELETED
COPY TO                SET DELIMITERS
COPY STRUCTURE         SET ESCAPE
CREATE                 SET EXACT
DELETE                 SET EXCLUSIVE
DIR                    SET FIXED
ERASE                  SET INDEX TO
```

```
INDEX TO                SET INTENSITY
JOIN WITH               SET PATH TO
LABEL FROM              SET PRINT
RENAME                  SET PRINTER TO
REPORT FORM             SET RELATION TO
RESTORE FROM            SET SCOREBOARD
RUN                     SET SOFTSEEK
SAVE TO                 SET UNIQUE
SELECT                  SET WRAP
SET ALTERNATE           SKIP ALIAS
SET BELL                SORT TO
SET CENTURY             TEXT TO FILE
SET COLOR TO            TOTAL ON
SET CONFIRM             TYPE TO
SET CONSOLE             UPDATE ON
SET CURSOR              USE
```

NEW SCOPE ADDED

With the Summer '87 release, the REST scope for commands such as AVERAGE, SUM, TOTAL, COUNT, and even LABEL FORM have been added. This added scope feature allows the record pointer to move from the current position to either the EOF() or until the WHILE condition of the command (if specified) returns a logical false (.F.).

ARRAY SIZES

Array sizes have been doubled to handle up to 4096 elements. Additionally, the initial size of the array is now 14 bytes per element as opposed to previous versions of 22 bytes per element.

PARAMETER PASSING

One of the most sublime features of the Summer '87 release is the ability to pass parameters by reference instead of by value in user-defined functions. The default status of a parameter is by value unless the parameter is passed to the function with a processing @ sign.

NULL CHARACTERS

To support a move to graphic capabilities and enhanced printing features, a CHR(0) is now a legitimate character with a character length of 1. This does not change the value nor the length of a character string "".

OLD FUNCTIONS NOW PART OF THE LIBRARY

The functions listed below were included in many of the extended files in prior versions. These functions include:

ALLTRIM()	AMPM()	DAYS()	DBF()	ELAPTIME()
FKLABEL()	FKMAX()	ISALPHA()	ISLOWER()	ISUPPER()
LEFT()	LENNUM()	MOD()	OS()	READKEY()
RIGHT()	SECS()	SOUNDEX()	STRZERO()	STUFF()
TSTRING()	VERSION()			

All in all, the Summer '87 version of Clipper provides more than just increased speed: it provides more power for the programmer!

CHAPTER TWO

Compiling

EXAMINING CLIPPER AS A COMPILER

To help us understand compilers, let's start with some definitions:

Compiler: A programming routine that enables a computer to convert a program expressed in pseudo-code language into machine language or another pseudo-code language for later translation.

Compilation: The end results of a compile.

Pseudo-code: A program requiring a conversion of code for use by the computer. This code is independent of the hardware; it is also called "symbolic code."

Now for a more practical interpretation of the definitions:

A compiler is no different from any other program. In many instances, many commonly known programs were created using a compiler, programs such as dBASE III, WordStar, or Lotus 1-2-3. Each of these can also be called a "programming routine." Clipper is indeed a programming routine, but what does it do? According to the definition, a compiler allows the computer to "convert a program expressed in pseudo-code into machine language." For example, dBASE III programs are written in a form of pseudo-code. They are text files that need to be translated to a language the computer can understand before they can be run. A compiler takes the files containing pseudo-code and translates those instructions into machine language. There are several theories on compilers. Here is a brief overview relevant to the Clipper compiler.

Clipper is a "two-pass" compiler. The first pass generates "tokens," and the second generates "code." A token is a logical symbol generated by the compiler for a logical group or entity. It consists of one or more lines of code (e.g., a STORE command, a FOR...NEXT command, etc.). These symbols can be more easily understood by Clipper than can a line of code.

Think of the first pass as a scan for code that can be interpreted all at one time. A STORE command is simple and can be symbolically represented with one token. Similarly, a simple counting FOR...NEXT loop, consisting of four or five lines, may be represented by a single token. Compilers, in theory, act like people. There is only so much information we can process at one time. In our thought process we break things down automatically into logical chunks of information that we know we can process at one time. This does not mean that we have processed the information, just that we have broken it down to be processed. To us these breaks may be represented by sentences, paragraphs, or even pages, but to the compiler, the breaks are represented by a symbol or a token.

The second pass is the code-generating pass. On this pass the compiler will actually make a secondary file containing machine language code representing the pseudo-code it was fed. The compiler then refers to the tokens generated by the first pass and begins to break up the code logically for the second pass. If there is a token that is not understood, an error occurs. What happens then is that the second pass is out of sync with the first pass (or the tokens). This out-of-sync condition is known as a "phase error." This is like threading a motion picture projector with film that has torn holes on one side. One side of the film might slip. Eventually the two sides will not be parallel. If enough tension is placed on the film itself, a rip will occur. That rip is comparable to a phase error. We will discuss solutions to this in later sections of this book.

As we said, dBASE III programs are a form of pseudo-code. The compiler translates words or commands into a code that the computer can understand directly (machine language). How is that any different from dBASE III? The difference between Clipper and dBASE III is that dBASE III does this with an *interpreter.*

Interpreter: A program that translates a stored program expressed in pseudo-code into machine language and performs the operations as they are translated.

dBASE III translates programs into a language the computer can understand and **performs the operations as they are translated**. This is a clear case in which more is **not** better. With an interpreter, code is read, translated, and executed one line at a time, resulting in a direct one-to-one relationship for every line of code. A compiler, on the other hand, prepares code to be executed later. It translates the code for the machine.

Think of a human interpreter and what happens in a typical scenario. The interpreter listens to what is being said, translates it into a different language, then conveys the same thoughts in the second language. This is a slow and cumbersome process. Consider how much faster the communication process would be if, instead of needing an interpreter, you were able to speak directly in another language.

Let us set up an example of code and see how the differences between compiling and interpreting are magnified. Consider the following fragment:

```
STORE 1 TO looping
DO WHILE looping <= 500
   @ 10,10 SAY looping
   STORE looping + 1 TO looping
ENDDO
```

The compiler would take these six lines of code and make an equivalent set of machine language instructions. These instructions would tell the computer to display a variable 500 times, incrementing it by 1 each time at a certain position on the screen. However, the interpreter works differently. On the first pass the interpreter reads every line and acts accordingly. Finally, when it finishes the first pass and gets to the

ENDDO command, it loops back to the beginning of the DO WHILE... command, rereads it, evaluates the expression, and then proceeds. From here, the interpreter would then read the next two lines **again**, translate and perform them, and then continue. Have any of these lines been changed? No! So why is there a need to REREAD them? There is no reason. What were six lines of simple code have suddenly grown to 2002 lines of code. (We get 2002 lines this way: The basic format of the loop consists of four lines. Multiply this by 499, the number of repetitions after the initial pass, and the result is 1996. Add the first six lines of code to 1996 and we have 2002.)

The compiler is more efficient. The translation of pseudo-code to machine code is the same as with interpreting. However, compiling a program is only half the process necessary to make a program file in dBASE III run without the aid of an interpreter. The next step is called *linking.*

The compiler takes the words in a dBASE III application and makes a secondary file with an .OBJ extension (better known as an *object file*) that consists of the now converted machine language words. Think of a dictionary for a moment. Every dictionary entry has basically two parts: the first is the listing of the word and the second is the corresponding definition of that word. The object file is no more than the listing of the word, the first part of the dictionary with the spellings, the pronunciations, and the etymologies. These words do not "do" anything; they are just ordered and translated into a common language that the computer can understand.

The other half of our dictionary entry, the half containing what the words mean, must be added to the words in order to get them to perform properly. The definitions for all of the dBASE III words are grouped together in what is called a *library file* (a file with a .LIB extension). In order to function properly, these words need to be tied together, or "linked" with their appropriate definitions that are located in the Clipper library file. This is the purpose of a linker; it is further discussed in Chapter 3. Remember that while a compiler condenses code to a level understood by the computer, this is only half of the necessary operation. The compilation must be linked to the proper definitions found in a library file. A linker and a library file are vital.

COMPILING WITH CLIPPER

There are certain things we need to cover specifically regarding the Clipper compiler. The Clipper compiler is a true compiler. However, it reflects certain aspects that are unique to the dBASE III language and certain rules about compiling with Clipper may not be applicable to other compilers. First, think like a compiler. The error checking routines prominent in an interpreter are not present, so the control of the process is the responsibility of the developer or programmer. The code is going to be translated to its literal value at the time of compilation. The compiler will not look at values of variables and understand those values to mean "bring in this definition from the library when I link." It does not work like that. A good example of this would be the following:

```
STORE "@ 2,3 SAY 'Hello there.'" TO prompt
&prompt
```

That line will work with the interpreter but **not** with the compiler. The compiler does not interpret the meaning of the variable PROMPT when it is translating your code. All that the compiler will do is set up an address point labeled "prompt" to hold a certain value at the time of execution. The compiler library knows to move a certain value into that address because you specifically told it to with the STORE command. However, on the second line there is no command, just a macro. The compiler translates this line of code to expand the macro at the time of execution. It does not know that an @ SAY...GET... command will be executed, so it does not pull that routine from the library into your executable file. Your application will not run as it did before because of the differences between the interpreter (which allows for these programming maneuvers) and the compiler (which does not).

Let's look at another example, one in which we wish to branch off from a main menu to go to submenus with the branching choice made by the user. Many times program names are generic root names with numbers attached to them in order to have them correspond to the options chosen by the users. Here is some sample code:

```
@ 20,15 SAY "Enter Choice: " GET option PICT "9"
READ
DO Submenu&option
```

This is a perfectly legitimate command in both dBASE III and Clipper, but when compiling these three lines of code, we must think like a compiler and not rely on the interpreter. This will probably compile and link properly, but when you execute those lines of code, you will receive an error message. Why? Again, the macro is not interpreted when it is being compiled. Therefore it does not tell the compiler to go out to the disk drive and look for and compile all of the possible options obtained from the macro. In other words, the compiler will not assume you want to have programs SUBMENU1, SUBMENU2, SUBMENU3, and SUBMENU4 compiled. You must think ahead and compile those programs yourself (using CLiP files, which we will discuss in the next sections) and link them into your main file with the Clipper library. There are certain guidelines we must follow in order to have our applications compile, link, and execute properly.

Another consideration in using the Clipper compiler is the use of names for program files and procedures. The same routine for field verification and validity is used for files as for fields. That's why file and procedure names cannot contain hyphens or start with numbers. Fields cannot have them and neither can files! Make file names describe the operation with clear labels. The same is true for procedures and functions. If a symbol for separation is required or desired, use the underscore and avoid the hyphen. Finally, if numbers are also needed, put them closer to the end of the routine's name. Whatever technique you use, **be consistent**.

CLIPPER SWITCHES

Let's take a look at the switches available with the compiler to see what they do and how they are activated. Try not to mix object files that were compiled with a particular switch with other object files that were not. Also be very careful never to mix object files compiled with different compiler versions. People tend to forget to recompile all of their files when updating from one Clipper version to the next. The result is that they forget some object files and don't realize the mistake until the program hangs or, when linking the application together, the _PLANKTO error message appears.

Summer '87 Switches:

- -l No line numbers
- -m Compile only one module
- -o Redirect object file output
- -p Pause to allow change of disk
- -q Suppress line numbers for displaying
- -s Check for proper syntax only
- -v Assume all memory variable to be M->

Autumn '86 Switches:

When using switches make sure that you use lowercase rather than uppercase letters. If you use uppercase letters, the compiler will tell you there was an illegal switch call, ignore it, and compile as though no switch had been called. Furthermore, use the switches **after** the name of the program being compiled or **after** the name of the CLiP file being compiled. Also, if more than one switch is desired, separate each switch with an additional space and hyphen like this:

```
C>Clipper Myfile -m -l
```

or (for CLiP files)

```
C>Clipper @Myfile -m -q
```

The first switch is the **-l** option or the line number switch. Using this switch will strip the reference bits for line numbers associated with your source code. This will lower the size of the object file by 3 bytes per source line.

Next, the **-m** option tells Clipper to only compile the source file specified, regardless of any called ancillary files.

Applying the **-o** switch will instruct the Clipper compiler to redirect the to-be-generated object file (.OBJ) to the directory or path specified after the switch.

The **-p** switch tells the compiler to pause and to allow for a change of disk.

The fifth switch, the **-q** switch, basically suppresses the display of line numbers while Clipper is compiling the source file.

Using the **-s** switch tells the compiler to go through the file(s) mentioned and check for syntax problems. All illegal syntax is flagged just as though you were trying to compile without the switch. The only difference is that the compiler **will not** generate object code. This saves time because the second pass through your application is totally avoided.

Finally, the **-v** option instructs Clipper to assume that all variables are M-> in nature. This means that variables of the same name as fields will take initial precedence over fields.

For releases prior to the Autumn '86 version, the **-n** option switch stands for the enhanced native code option. Using this feature, Clipper will compile true native code, optimizing your application. The net results will slightly increase the size of the object files as well as increase the final execution speed of the application. For most applications, this option is not necessary. This option is somewhat beneficial when developing test programs and small utility programs.

ERROR MESSAGES

Errors can and will occur, especially with large applications. It can be frustrating to sit in front of a screen and jot down every error spotted by the compiler. Depending on the nature of the error, in most cases the type of error or problem must be noted as well as the line number and module in which the error occurred. These notes would then be referenced when fixing the program errors. Magnify this routine a hundredfold for large applications. Taking notes manually is not efficient. Let the computer do the work for you! Port the errors out to an alternate file using the DOS switch, the greater than sign (>). Using this switch in conjunction with the Clipper compiler will redirect all error messages to a disk file with the name you give it. An example of this would be as follows:

```
C>Clipper Myfile > Errors.lst
```

The compiler is called up, the source code read in, and if any compiler errors are found, they are redirected to a file called ERRORS.LST. This file can then be printed or viewed on the screen. With some text editors that provide split screen editing, the trouble spots can be on the screen at the same time as the source code. Use whatever tools are available to you, including your operating system, in order to save time and energy!

COMMON PROBLEMS

Below are listed some common problems that occur when trying to compile either a small program or a large application using Clipper. Each problem is defined and followed by a brief explanation and the way to solve the problem, if any exists. Use these solutions when you are trying to compile your own programs.

Command Syntax in Macros

UNlike dBASE III, any statement that would be considered part of the syntactical structure of the command will not work in a macro under Clipper. A good example is the following:

```
STORE "@ 5,10 SAY 'Hello Federal...'" TO command
&command
```

The compiler does not evaluate the macro at the time of compilation. A compiler error would point to the macro and would look like the following:

```
^ ASSIGNMENT error
```

Instead, place the "@ 5,10 SAY" literally in the file for the compiler to see and to compile. So now the command lines read:

```
STORE "Hello world..." TO command
@ 5,10 SAY command
```

Another error with macros is trying to put commas in the macro, especially if a field listed is being generated. An example is:

```
STORE "field_one, field_two, field_three" TO listing
LIST &listing
```

Under Clipper, these lines would indeed compile and link with no apparent problems. When you try to run it, however, you would only get the listing of "field_one"–the other fields would be lost. Again, since the macro is not being evaluated (interpreted) at the time of the compilation, it does not know whether to allow for one field or two fields, let alone three fields. Since the commas are viewed as part of the command syntax of the command line, problems will arise with this sort of statement. Solutions for this problem are either to replace the commas with plus signs or store the name of each field to be listed in its own separate variable or macro. For the latter option, if there are three fields to be listed, there must be three separate macros. The command would look like this:

```
STORE "field_one" TO list_one
STORE "field_two" TO list_two
STORE "field_three" TO list_three
```

```
LIST &list_one., &list_two., &list_three
```

Using the Nantucket Batch File to Compile

With early versions of Clipper, a batch file was provided with the compiler and quite often people use this batch file to get their .PRG files turned into .EXE files. Often, a problem arises with its use. When the batch file is called with the file name of the application along with the .PRG extension, problems occur such as in the following:

```
C>CL keys.prg
The Clipper Compiler, Winter '85
Copyright (c) 1985, 1986 Nantucket Inc., All Rights Reserved.

Compiling KEYS.PRG
Code size:177        Symbols:80        Constants:224

C>Plink86 fi keys.prg
PSA Linkage Editor (Nantucket Clipper) Version 1.46.c
Copyright (C) 1984 by Phoenix Software Associates Ltd.

Warning 7:    Unknown record type 2A in File KEYS.PRG

Fatal error 41
Premature end of file at offset 5422 in File KEYS.PRG

C>
```

Does it look familiar? Even the words "fatal error" sound so dreadful and final. Nevertheless, all is not lost. The problem here is not with the compiler but with the way the batch file works with the linker. Notice that Clipper compiled the program with no errors and produced a code size message that means that an object file was indeed generated.

Take a look at the line where the linker is being called. Notice that the file name is passed to the linker exactly as it was passed to the batch file, including the .PRG extension. That is the problem. Clipper will always assume you are initially trying to compile a .PRG file; it does not need to be passed that extension by the batch file and it will ignore it. However, the linker assumes it is getting a file with a .OBJ extension (which is what Clipper will produce after a successful compilation). The problem is that the batch file is passing the .PRG extension to the linker and the linker is trying to link your ordinary text file with the library of machine language routines. You can see why this is indeed a fatal error.

To get rid of this problem, just remove the .PRG extension when using the batch file to compile and to link your applications.

External Programs Needed but NOT Compiled

Consider the following piece of code:

```
STORE "0" TO choice
@ 10,10 SAY "<1> Enter Transaction"
@ 11,10 SAY "<2> Edit Transaction"
@ 12,10 SAY "<3> Scan Transaction"
@ 13,10 SAY "<4> Delete Transaction"
@ 14,10 SAY "What is Choice? " GET choice PICT "9" VALID(choice $"1234")
READ
DO Trans&choice
```

Here is an example of a macro not being evaluated during the compiling process. Clipper will not know from the last command line to go out to the disk and compile TRANS1.PRG, TRANS2.PRG, TRANS3.PRG, and TRANS4.PRG with your application. You will have to compile those four programs separately and link them to your main files; otherwise, you will assuredly get an error message when you run the program.

Another problem occurs when using on-line help with a program file called HELP.PRG. Since this file is called by striking the F1 key and not by a direct DO command, Clipper will not know to compile it with your application. Program files containing nothing but user-defined functions also fall into the category of being needed and being referenced but not compiled and, worse yet, not linked.

The only way to avoid these situations is to plan ahead! If HELP.PRG is referenced, if a function in a user-defined function file is called, or if a macro can call a program or procedure file at any time, those files **must** be compiled and linked with your application.

Phase Errors

This is the most difficult error to explain. Clipper makes two passes through a file. The first pass translates commands into tokens. The second pass uses those tokens to generate appropriate machine code. A phase error occurs when the tokens generated on the first pass are not understood by the code generated on the second pass. This can be quite confusing because many things may cause this problem ranging from bad memory chips to high-bit graphic characters in a program file. In either case check for the following conditions:

1. Remove any RAM-resident programs when compiling.
2. Check your computer's expansion boards.
3. Avoid using word processors that may leave high-bit characters in the file, specifically those used for word wrap and hyphen marking.

Symbol Redefinition Error

This problem occurs when a procedure file has the same name as a procedure within that file. Simply change the name of either the procedure file or the name of the procedure within that file and the error should go away.

Unbalanced Conditions

Many times the compiler will yield an error message "Unbalanced DO WHILE" or "Unbalanced ENDDO" when in fact all DO WHILEs and ENDDOs match up. Whenever this condition occurs, check not only for all DO WHILEs, but all IFs, DO CASEs, and corresponding ENDDOs, ENDIFs, and ENDCASESs. All must match and must follow standard operating procedures. Because dBASE III is an interpreter and only holds roughly 1K worth of source code information, it is quite possible to have an unbalanced condition in dBASE III that still works. Clipper, however, will pick up on this and report it.

Mixing Clipper Switches

While this error occurs during the linking of your application (and is described in detail in Chapter 3), the problem is listed here because of the cause. If the enhanced native code option is chosen for some modules and not for others and these are linked together, a major catastrophe occurs. Choose a standard code option for your compilations and stick to it. A suggested approach is compiling all programs without any switch until they are completely developed and tested. Then recompile using the switches you want.

Using a Word Processor

As I said earlier, word processors can cause problems. Don't confuse a word processor with a text editor; there is a big difference. A text editor just edits text. With a word processor, text files are normally formatted for output to the printer, including wraparounds, soft carriage returns, boldfacing routines, etc. Codes inserted for these functions are not understood by the compiler. Even dBASE III's MODIFY COMMAND automatically wraps a word around from one side of the screen to the next. Take a look at a dBASE III procedure file by using DOS to TYPE it to the console; look at the odd graphic characters throughout. DBASE III knows to ignore these characters because it wrote them, but Clipper does not ignore them. Make sure that there are no high-bit characters embedded in your code.

Sometimes symptomatic error messages appear on the last line of the code, even on a simple READ. Adding a line of code, even a remark line, only moves the error message one line further down. Other times, phase errors occur. All of these errors may indicate a high-bit character inside the text file. WordStar in document mode and Borland's SideKick are notorious for causing these situations.

The best way to avoid this condition is to use a text editor rather than a word processor for your coding.

Too Many Constants, Too Many Symbols, Fatal at 0– Too Many procs

This problem occurs when too much code is compiled at one time. There is a process in the compiling referred to as *parsing*. Parsing involves making a reference pointer for commands, statements, variables, and their respective names–in fact, just about everything that is referenced by the compiler. From the parsing process, the tokens are generated into logical segments to be handled at one time. However, the parser has a size limitation. It is like a Scrabble board, with each parse a tile to be placed on the board. Every new and unique parse requires the placement of a new tile. Eventually, there comes a point when the board is filled with little tiles, and yet there is more code to be parsed. That's when you get this error message. From that point on, nothing is compiled properly.

The solution is to learn how to use CLiP files to break your application into a number of separate compiles. Generally, the program files can be placed in two or more separate CLiP files. These then create separate compiled (object) files. Consider the process carefully. Each time the compiler is called upon initially, it generates three tables: one for the code, one for the symbols, and one for the constants. Each unique symbol, code, and constant marker in your files generates a unique code to be placed in the appropriate table.

Eventually, one or more of the tables gets filled. Sometimes, changing code alleviates the problem. This solution works only in cases in which the compilation is extremely close to completion. The most likely table to fill up first is the constant table followed by the symbol table. The problem is knowing how many more codes will be placed in the table. There is no way to determine that ahead of time. Therefore, the simplest solution is to break up the programs into separate compiles and join them together through the linking step. To accomplish this task, we employ what are termed CLiP files.

CLiP FILES

The following diagram shows the flow of operation of an application:

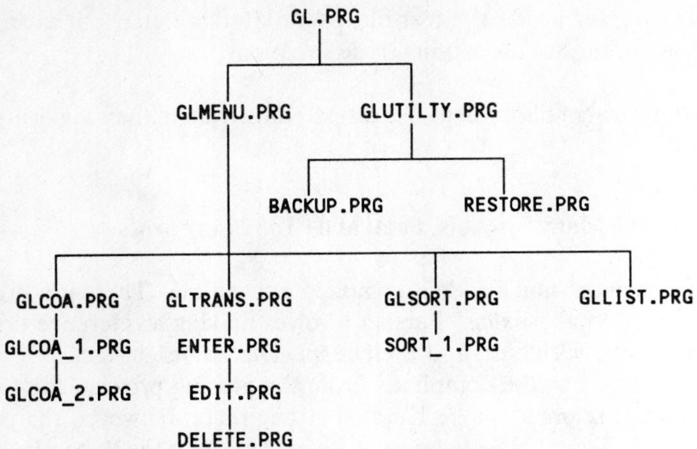

In this structure, GL.PRG calls both GLMENU.PRG and GLUTILTY.PRG, which in turn call their respective subroutines. Now let's say that you tried to compile this. Clipper would go down the list of program names that it recognizes, pull them into one object file, and try to compile it all. If there is too much to compile at one time, an error message referring to "Too Many <Constants> <Symbols>" would appear. If you want to use overlays, separate object files would need to be generated for the code to be properly structured for the linker.

To compile the files individually or in preselected groups, we create CLiP files, which are ordinary text files with .CLP extensions. The CLiP file contains the names of the programs (without the .PRG extensions) to be compiled exclusively. It doesn't matter if a program calls another program (subroutine) or procedure. Only those programs listed in the CLiP file will be compiled. Referring to the example above, let's make three unique CLiP files.

First, create a text file called GL.CLP, which contains the following list of programs without extensions:

```
GL
GLMENU
GLUTILTY
BACKUP
RESTORE
```

Close the file and create another text file called GLCOA.CLP. Inside of this file will be the names of the following programs:

```
GLCOA
GLCOA_1
GLCOA_2
GLTRANS
ENTER
EDIT
DELETE
```

Finally, close that file and create yet another file called FINAL.CLP. Inside this text file will be the following file names:

```
GLSORT
GLSORT_1
GLLIST
```

Keep in mind that all files listed in a CLiP file must have a .PRG extension; format files and procedure files with an extension other than .PRG must be renamed before you compile the CLiP file.

Compile each CLiP file by using the following command line syntax:

```
C>CLIPPER @GL
C>CLIPPER @GLCOA
C>CLIPPER @FINAL
```

The result will be three separate object (.OBJ) files with the names of the associated CLiP files. Note that the major difference on the command line between a massive compile (looking at GL.PRG and compiling its subroutines) and the CLiP file is the additional character (the @ sign). This special character tells the compiler that there is a CLiP file with the following name and to compile each listed program file collectively, yet exclusive to the list, no matter what else is called by a listed program. After the compilation of these CLiP files, there would be three new files created on the disk:

```
GL.OBJ
GLCOA.OBJ
FINAL.OBJ
```

Notice that it does not matter what is being compiled inside the CLiP file. The name of the CLiP file can be anything as long as the extension is .CLP. The compiler takes the name of the CLiP file and uses that as the name of the object file. In this example, the last CLiP file is called FINAL.CLP for a good reason. Sometimes we compile code that has problems in it, and these problems may not surface until we try to run our application. It can be frustrating to change one or two lines of code in GLLIST.PRG, for example. Once we have made the necessary changes, we have to recompile and relink our application. By using CLiP files properly, we can isolate code that is clean from that which we are still trying to finish.

In this example, all we have to do once we change the desired lines of code in GLLIST.PRG is to recompile the FINAL.CLP file by itself and then link it with the remaining two files previously compiled. This method is very helpful in saving time and energy when trying to get an application up and running. The final step is to link all the object files with the library. To do this, you need to either build a LiNK file or use Plink86 interactively. The LiNK file is just a text file with a .LNK extension in which you put the commands for Plink86. An example follows:

```
GL.LNK

     FI GL
     FI GLCOA
     FI FINAL
     LIB CLIPPER
```

To activate the linker with this link file you would type in the following:

```
     C>PLINK86 @GL
```

The default name of the executable file will be the name of the first object file seen by the linker. In the above example, it would be GL.EXE. Further information on the linker is available in Chapter 3.

After the linker connects the three object files with the Clipper library, the executable file is created. The .PRG file that normally begins the application **must be** the first file in the list of files in the first linked CLiP (now converted to object) file.

The following program demonstrates one way of automating the writing of CLiP files. Study this code and, if you choose, type it in and compile it. You will find that you use it often in your development work. In addition, this program demonstrates how to use contextual help, user-defined functions, and program flow and development. Much of the explanatory help repeats what has been covered above; if you choose, you need not include it in your program.

```
********************
* Name          Compile.prg
* Date          August 1, 1986 / Revised: March 5, 1988
* Notice        Copyright 1986-8, Stephen J. Straley & Associates
* Compile       Clipper Compile -m
* Release       Summer '87 release
* Link          Tlink Compile,,,extend + clipper
* Note          This program will check the directory for files, write
*               CLiP files, and then write a batch file for the compile.
*               An extensive HELP module is included to demonstrate the
*               compiler in process and the advantages of CLiP files.
********************

SET SCOREBOARD OFF
 scrframe = CHR(201) + CHR(205) + CHR(187) + CHR(186) + CHR(188) + ;
            CHR(205) + CHR(200) + CHR(186) + CHR(32)
 scrbar    = CHR(204) + REPLICATE(CHR(205),78) + CHR(185)
 scrlin    = CHR(186)
 STORE SPACE(4000) TO scr_page1, scr_page2

 DO Scrinit
 DO Input_it
 CLOSE DATABASES
 DO Port_it1
```

```
 CLOSE DATABASES
 DO Port_it2
 CLOSE DATABASES
 DO Port_it3
 CLOSE DATABASES
 DO Choice
 DO Exiting

********************

 PROCEDURE Scrinit

    ***********************************************************************
    * This Procedure will initialize the screen with the main menu message. *
    * Save it to an array for future display, and then display a brief     *
    * opening message.                                                      *
    ***********************************************************************
    CLEAR SCREEN
    @ 0,0,20,79 BOX SUBSTR(scrframe,1,8)
    @ 4,0 SAY scrbar
    FOR x = 1 TO 3
       @ x,1 SAY REPLICATE(CHR(219),78)
    NEXT
    @ 1,5 SAY " COMPILE "
    @ 1,RIGHT_JUST(" Version 2.00 ", 75) SAY " Version 2.00 "
    @ 3,CENTER(" The Clipper Utility Program - Main Menu ") SAY " The Clipper Util-
ity Program - Main Menu "

    SAVE SCREEN TO scr_page1
    * Summer 87 acceptable: CALL __scrsave WITH scr_page1
    * Prior versions: CALL _scrsave WITH scr_page1

    @ 10,5 SAY "The following program was designed to make CLiP files out of all"
    @ 12,5 SAY "program, format, and procedure files available to the program on
the"
    @ 14,5 SAY "registered directory/drive.  If you are unsure what CLiP files are
or"
    @ 16,5 SAY "their purpose, please strike FUNCTION KEY 1 (F1) for a descrip-
tion."
    STORE "Y" TO continue
    @ 18,25 SAY "Would you like to continue? " GET continue PICT "!" VALID(continue
$"YN")
    READ
    IF continue = "N"
       @ 23,0 SAY ""
       QUIT
    ENDIF

********************

PROCEDURE Input_it

    ***********************************************************************
```

```
    * This routine will take a directory of all .PRG, .PRC, and .FMT files *
    * in the current directory.                                            *
    ************************************************************************

    @ 0,0 CLEAR   && Summer 87 acceptable: CLEAR SCREEN

    @ 4,0,20,79 BOX SUBSTR(scrframe,1,8)
    SAVE SCREEN TO scr_page2
    @ 10,10 SAY ""
    ?? "Reading Disk Information"
    @ 11,10 SAY ""
    IF !FILE("*.PRG")    && This is the same as .NOT. FILE
       ?? "There are no Program Files Available on drive"
    ELSE
       RUN DIR *.PRG > CAPTURE.TXT
    ENDIF
    @ 12,10 SAY ""
    IF !FILE("*.PRC")
       ?? "There are no Procedure Files Available on drive"
    ELSE
       ?? "Procedure FIles Present.  Make a note to Rename them *.PRG"
       RUN DIR *.PRC >>CAPTURE.TXT
    ENDIF
    @ 13,10 SAY ""
    IF !FILE("*.FMT")
       ?? "There are no Format Files Available on drive"
    ELSE
       ?? "Format FIles Present.  Make a note to Rename them *.PRG"
       RUN DIR *.FMT >>CAPTURE.TXT
    ENDIF

********************

PROCEDURE Port_it1

    ****************************************************************
    * This procedure will take the captured file and port it into a *
    * raw database.                                                 *
    ****************************************************************

    CREATE Template   && This creates a database file on the fly!
    USE Template
    APPEND BLANK
    REPLACE field_name WITH "TEMP", field_type WITH "C", field_len WITH 80
    USE
    CREATE Port1 FROM Template
    ERASE Template
    USE Port1
    APPEND FROM Capture.txt SDF
    USE

********************
```

```
 PROCEDURE Port_it2

    ***********************************************************
    * This procedure takes the ported database in PORT1.DBF,   *
    * sorts it into a secondary database by root file name and *
    * extension, and notes if it is going to be a major file   *
    * (a file at the head of a CLiP file).                     *
    ***********************************************************

    CREATE Template
    USE Template
    APPEND BLANK
    REPLACE field_name WITH "ROOT", field_type WITH "C", field_len WITH 8
    APPEND BLANK
    REPLACE field_name WITH "EXT", field_type WITH "C", field_len WITH 3
    APPEND BLANK
    REPLACE field_name WITH "MAJOR", field_type WITH "L", field_len WITH 1
    USE
    CREATE Port2 FROM Template
    ERASE Template

********************

PROCEDURE Port_it3

    ****************************************************
    * This will port between the two files created by *
    * Procedures Port_it1 and Port_it2.                *
    ****************************************************

    SELECT 2
    USE Port2
    SELECT 1
    USE Port1
    DO WHILE !EOF()
       IF SUBSTR(temp,1,1) # " "
          SELECT 2
          APPEND BLANK
          REPLACE root  WITH SUBSTR(A->temp,1,8), ext WITH SUBSTR(A->temp,10,3)
          REPLACE major WITH .F.
          SELECT 1
       ENDIF
       SKIP
    ENDDO

********************

PROCEDURE Choice

    ***********************************************************************
    * This procedure branches off into two directions, depending upon the *
    * response of the user.  If a "Y" is entered. then every .PRG, .PRC,  *
    * and/or .FMT file is set up to be compiled individually.  Otherwise, *
```

```
    * the program will branch off to prompt the user to enter which      *
    * files to compile together.                                          *
    ***********************************************************************

    RESTORE SCREEN FROM scr_page1
    * Summer 87 acceptable: CALL __scrrest WITH scr_page1
    * Prior versions: CALL _scrrest WITH scr_page1

    STORE "Y" TO input
    @ 10,15 SAY "Would you like to compile every file separately? " GET input PICT
"!" VALID(input $"YN")
    READ
    IF input = "Y"
       DO Separate
    ELSE
       DO Indiv
    ENDIF

********************

PROCEDURE Indiv

    *********************************************************************
    * This is the procedure that allows for a selective compiling list. *
    *********************************************************************

    SELECT 1
    USE Port2
    COPY STRUCTURE TO Port4
    screen_no = 0
    SET MESSAGE TO 22 CENTER   && The CENTER options intro. in Summer 87
    DO WHILE screen_no >= 0
       RESTORE SCREEN FROM scr_page1
       position  = RECNO()
       down      = 6
       over      = 5
       option    = 1
       count     = 1
       ending    = LASTREC()
       IF EOF()
          DO Exiting
       ENDIF
       DO WHILE count <= 30
          DO CASE
          CASE ext = "PRG"
             info = "This is a Program File"
          CASE ext = "PRC"
             info = "This is a Procedure File"
          OTHERWISE
             info = "This is a Format File"
          ENDCASE
          IF DELETED()
             info = info + " --- FILE ALREADY SELECTED/USED"
```

```
        ENDIF
        info = SPACE(5) + info
        @ down, over PROMPT root MESSAGE info

        * Without the CENTER option, "PROMPT root MESSAGE CENTRING(info)"

        over = over + 15
        IF over > 70
           down = down + 2
           over = 5
        ENDIF
        count = count + 1
        SKIP
        IF EOF()
           EXIT
        ENDIF
     ENDDO
     @ down, over PROMPT "Write File" MESSAGE "Selected Files will be now writ-
ten"
     over = over + 15
     IF over > 70
        down = down + 2
        over = 5
     ENDIF
     IF !EOF()
        @ down, over PROMPT "Next Screen" && MESSAGE SPACE(78)
     ENDIF

     SET KEY -1 TO Review
     SET KEY 24 TO Downprmt
     SET KEY  5 TO Upprmt

     MENU TO option

     SET KEY -1 TO
     SET KEY 24 TO
     SET KEY  5 TO

     DO CASE
     CASE option = 0
        screen_no = screen_no - 1
        IF screen_no >= 0
           GO position
           SKIP - 30
        ENDIF
     CASE option = 32
        screen_no = screen_no + 1
        count = 1
        RESTORE SCREEN FROM scr_page1
     CASE option = count
        DO Writfile
        screen_no = 0
     OTHERWISE
```

```
         GO (screen_no * 30 + option)
         IF DELETED()
            RECALL
         ELSE
            DELETE
         ENDIF
         GO position
         count = 1
      ENDCASE
   ENDDO

********************

PROCEDURE Writfile

   ****************************************************
   * This Procedure starts to write the chosen files *
   * out to disk in the form of the CLiP file.        *
   ****************************************************

   SET FILTER TO DELETED()
   GO TOP
   rec_count = 0
   DO WHILE !EOF()
      rec_count = rec_count + 1
      SKIP
   ENDDO
   IF rec_count > 32 .OR. rec_count = 0
      IF rec_count > 32
         a_mess = ALLTRIM(STR(rec_count)) + " is too many files in " + ;
                  "a CLiP file. Unselect " + ALLTRIM(STR(32 - rec_count)) + ;
                  " files. "
      ELSE
         a_mess = "An empty file cannot be written.  Any Key to Continue."
      ENDIF
      @ 22,0 SAY CENTRING(a_mess)
      INKEY(0)
      SET FILTER TO
      GO TOP
      RETURN
   ENDIF
   COPY TO Port3
   STORE .F. TO Abort_it
   DO Outfile
   IF Abort_it
      RETURN
   ENDIF
   USE Port2
   PACK
   GO TOP

********************
```

```
PROCEDURE Outfile

    ****************************************************************
    * In this procedure, the user is given the choice of which     *
    * of the selected files will head the list, after which the    *
    * CLiP file will be named.                                     *
    ****************************************************************

    option = 0
    down_out = 6
    over_out = 5
    USE Port3
    RESTORE SCREEN FROM scr_page1
    @ 3,1 SAY REPLICATE(CHR(219),78)
    @ 3,26 SAY "CLiP File Selection Menu"
    DO WHILE !EOF()
       visual = TRIM(root) + "." + ext
       @ down_out, over_out PROMPT visual
       over_out = over_out + 15
       IF over_out > 70
          down_out = down_out + 2
          over_out = 5
       ENDIF
       SKIP
    ENDDO
    MENU TO option
    IF option = 0
       STORE .T. TO Abort_it
       RETURN
    ENDIF
    GO option
    REPLACE major WITH .T.
    DO Finalout

********************

PROCEDURE Finalout

    ****************************************************
    * This is the routine that actually writes the CLiP *
    * file in the order assigned by Outfile.            *
    ****************************************************

    LOCATE FOR major = .T.
    outfile = TRIM(root) + ".CLP"
    SET ALTERNATE TO &outfile
    @ 11,20,14,60 BOX scrframe
    @ 12,21 SAY SUBSTR(CENTRING("Now creating " + outfile),21,38)
    @ 13,21 SAY SUBSTR(CENTRING(" Listing " + TRIM(root) + "." + ext),21,38)
    SET CONSOLE OFF
    SET ALTERNATE ON
    ? TRIM(root)
    SET ALTERNATE OFF
```

```
    SET CONSOLE OFF
    GO TOP
    DO WHILE .NOT. EOF()
       IF !major
          @ 13,21 SAY SUBSTR(CENTRING(" Listing " + TRIM(root) + "." + ext),21,38)
          SET CONSOLE OFF
          SET ALTERNATE ON
          ? TRIM(root)
          SET ALTERNATE OFF
          SET CONSOLE OFF
       ENDIF
       IF ext = "PRC" .OR. ext = "FMT"
          ths_is_in = TRIM(root) + "." + ext
          ths_is_out = TRIM(root) + ".PRG"
          RENAME &ths_is_in. TO &ths_is_out
       ENDIF
       SKIP
    ENDDO
    GO option
    SELECT 2
    USE Port4
    APPEND BLANK
    REPLACE root WITH A->root, ext WITH A->ext, major WITH A->major
    SELECT 1
    ZAP

********************

PROCEDURE Separate

    ****************************************
    * This routine will separate all files *
    * into individual CLiP files.          *
    ****************************************

    USE Port2
    REPLACE ALL major WITH .T.
    @ 12,01 SAY SUBSTR(CENTRING("Manipulating Data FIle for Output"),1,78)
    COPY TO Port4
    GO TOP
    SET CONSOLE OFF
    DO WHILE .NOT. EOF()
       outfile = TRIM(root) + ".CLP"
       a_mess = "Now working with " + TRIM(root) + "." + ext
       @ 12,01 SAY SUBSTR(CENTRING(a_mess),1,78)
       SET ALTERNATE TO &outfile
       SET ALTERNATE ON
       ? root
       SET ALTERNATE OFF
       CLOSE ALTERNATE
       SKIP
       @ 12,20 SAY SPACE(40)
    ENDDO
```

```
    SET CONSOLE ON

********************

 PROCEDURE Exiting

    ************************************************************
    * This routine gives the option to write a batch file that *
    * automatically compiles the selected CLiP files.          *
    ************************************************************

    CLOSE DATABASES
    RESTORE SCREEN FROM scr_page1
    STORE "Y" TO input, ynput
    @ 10,15 SAY "Would you like a BATCH file to compile your CLiP files? " GET in-
put PICT "!" VALID(input $"YN")
    READ
    @ 10,15 SAY SPACE(60)
    IF input = "Y"
       @ 10,15 SAY "Would you like to PAUSE between every compile? " GET input PICT
"!" VALID(ynput $"YN")
       READ
       @ 10,15 SAY SPACE(60)
       batch = SPACE(8)
       @ 10,15 SAY "Enter desired name of batch file: " GET batch PICT "!!!!!!!!"
       READ
       batch = IF(LEN(TRIM(batch)) = 0, "CLIPCOMP.BAT", TRIM(batch) + ".BAT")
       USE Port4
       GO TOP
       @ 10,01 SAY SUBSTR(CENTRING("Now Writing " + batch + " to drive"),1,78)
       SET ALTERNATE TO &batch
       SET CONSOLE OFF
       DO WHILE !EOF()
          a_mess = "Now Writing for Clipper @" + TRIM(root)
          @ 12,1 SAY SUBSTR(CENTRING(a_mess),1,78)
          SET ALTERNATE ON
          ? "CLS"
          ? "CLIPPER @" + TRIM(root)
          IF input = "Y"
             ? "PAUSE"
          ENDIF
          SET ALTERNATE OFF
          SKIP
       ENDDO
       CLOSE ALTERNATE
       @ 10,1 SAY SPACE(78)
       @ 12,1 SAY SPACE(78)
       a_mess = "Run Batch File, "
    ELSE
       a_mess = "Compile CLiP Files, "
    ENDIF
    a_mess = a_mess + "then run 'LINKIT' to determine Link Structure"
    @ 11,1 SAY SUBSTR(CENTRING(a_mess),1,78)
```

```
    @ 13,1 SAY SUBSTR(CENTRING("Thank you for running COMPILE.  A product of NOS
Development"),1,78)
    ERASE Capture.txt
    ERASE Template.dbf
    ERASE Port1.dbf
    ERASE Port2.dbf
    IF FILE("Port3.dbf")
       ERASE Port3.dbf
    ENDIF
    @ 23,00 SAY ""
    QUIT

*********************

PROCEDURE Review

    **************************************************************
    * This procedure will display all selected files for group *
    * CLiP files.  This routine is called by striking          *
    * the F2 key.  Because it was called by the SET KEY TO     *
    * command, the parameters listed below are never used yet  *
    * are necessary for the procedure to function properly.    *
    **************************************************************

    PARAMETER p, l, v

    SAVE SCREEN
    RESTORE SCREEN FROM scr_page2
    down_rev = 6
    over_rev = 5
    SET FILTER TO DELETED()
    GO TOP
    DO WHILE !EOF()
       @ down_rev, over_rev SAY root
       over_rev = over_rev + 15
       IF over_rev > 70
          down_rev = down_rev + 2
          over_rev = 5
       ENDIF
       SKIP
    ENDDO
    a_mess = "All Files Listed.  Any Key to Return to Main Menu"
    @ 22,00 SAY CENTRING(a_mess)
    qw = INKEY(0)
    SET FILTER TO
    GO position
    RESTORE SCREEN

******************

FUNCTION Right_just

   PARAMETERS right_st, right_col
```

```
   * This is part of the Steve Straley Toolkit.
   * Copyright (c) 1988 Stephen Straley & Associates

   IF PCOUNT() = 1
      right_col = 79
   ENDIF
   RETURN(IF(LEN(right_st) > right_col, right_st, right_col - LEN(right_st)))

********************

FUNCTION Center

   PARAMETERS centa, centb

   * This is part of the Steve Straley Toolkit.
   * Copyright (c) 1988 Stephen Straley & Associates

   IF PCOUNT() = 1
      centb = 40
   ENDIF

   RETURN(centb - (LEN(centa)/2))

********************

FUNCTION Centring

   PARAMETERS a1

   the_len = LEN(a1)
   half_space = INT(40 - the_len / 2)
   tot_len = 79 - the_len - half_space
   RETURN(SPACE(half_space) + a1 + SPACE(tot_len))

********************

 PROCEDURE Counting

    *************************************************
    * This procedure will just simulate a compiling *
    * process.  It is used in the HELP routine.     *
    *************************************************

    PARAMETER end_count

    posit = ROW()+1
    FOR qw = 1 TO end_count
      @ posit,00 SAY "Line " + LTRIM(STR(qw))
    NEXT
```

```
*********************

 PROCEDURE Downprmt

   *****************************************************
   * This procedure simulates going down five prompts. *
   *****************************************************

   PARAMETER p, l, v

   KEYBOARD REPLICATE(CHR(4),5)

*********************

 PROCEDURE Upprmt

   **************************************************
   * This procedure simulates going up five prompts *
   **************************************************

   PARAMETER p, l, v

   KEYBOARD REPLICATE(CHR(19),5)

* End of File
```

Summary

The fundamental point of this chapter is that there are very big differences between an interpreter and a compiler. As developers, we can use those differences to our advantage, while as managers we can go after the similarities for functionality. The differences, both big and small, must be understood.

It is normal to question why an application that worked under the interpreter fails to compile, but the answer isn't always simple. For example, consider a program that has 85 consecutive IF statements but one ENDIF is missing, or a DO program inside an IF statement where the terminating ENDIF is located in a program being called. Because the interpreter can handle only so much source code at one time, it is possible that both cases would function with apparent ease under the interpreter; however, this would not be the case under the compiler. Is the compiler wrong for not allowing faulty coding? Is the interpreter wrong? The main point is that there is a difference, and you must code accordingly.

MEMORY REQUIREMENTS AND CLIPPER

Memory Boundaries

Clipper automatically requires an additional 64K of memory above the given load size of the program in order to execute. (The load size is provided by Plink86 after a successful link.) This additional memory is needed to handle some of the basic commands as well as most of the conditional statements and macro substitutions. However, to take advantage of larger systems, the compiler will attempt to take hold of more memory, provided the additional memory is not being used by another program or by the system. The amount of extra memory that Clipper takes is directly proportional to the amount available above the minimum 64K the compiler demands. Developers who do not allow for this may plan a system or an overlay scheme around the 64K requirement. This can become a special problem for those applications that are programmed to run another program. If the Clipper program is loaded in first and additional memory is free, the application will try to take more than just the 64K minimum. Then when it comes time to run a word processor, for example, an "insufficient memory" message will appear, even when all calculations show that there should be enough memory for both programs.

Consider the following program fragment:

```
CLEAR
RUN C:COMMAND
WAIT
```

Once the program cleared the screen and reloaded DOS, we ran CHKDSK to check the amount of available memory. Here are the results:

Test.exe = 128,076 bytes + 71,536 Req. = 199,612 bytes minimum required

Memory	Machine I	Machine II	Machine III
Before:	480,672	544,464	358,800
During:	233,872	297,600	123,136
Taken:	246,800	246,864	234,664

Notice that machine III has almost 200K less available to run a program than does machine II. Interestingly, the same program used **more memory on machine II than on machine III**. The program automatically used a proportional amount of the extra memory. Also notice that the amount taken on all three machines is not even close to the minimum amount required by the program. On the larger machine an additional 47K was taken by the application.

This is just a small example of a situation that may cause large troubles. Be careful when designing, coding, and linking the application. The minimum amounts quoted are just that, minimums, and should not be used as the absolute figures when calculating a memory management scheme. Following is an additional diagram of the internal memory mechanisms for a computer with 256K of RAM available:

```
64K for DOS
---
128K for Clipper.lib
---
64K for memory variables
        buffers
        memory management
```

In this configuration, only 16K is allotted for index buffering and only 500 memory variables (roughly) will be allowed. However, on a machine with more RAM available, the following memory schematic would pertain:

```
64K for DOS
---
128K+ for Clipper.lib
---
128K for memory variables
         buffers
         memory management
---
64K for miscellaneous memory
        values (e.g., screens)
```

In this scheme, the larger allocation for memory variables, buffers, and basic memory management means a faster indexing routine and over 2000 memory variables. Also, the additional 64K for miscellaneous memory variables allows faster execution and performance.

Clipper and Memory – Summer '87

A few words on the memory management in the Autumn '86 release of Clipper are in order. There are four items to be aware of when developing an application with this release of Clipper:

1. The number of memory variables
2. The number of buffers used for INDEXing
3. The need to run other programs within a Clipper application
4. The amount of free memory pool to be used for data manipulation

Unless specifically directed otherwise, Clipper will automatically allocate values to each of these four areas. However, if you wish to control the environment under which Clipper will operate, you must use a DOS SET command.

If no SET command is issued, Clipper will allocate all available memory in the following order:

1. The size of the executable (.EXE) program is loaded into memory.

2. 24K bytes are set aside for "free memory pool." This area is used for data manipulation.

3. 20 percent of the remaining available memory will be used for allocating memory variables.

4. After memory variables have been allocated, 33 percent of the remaining memory will be set aside for the RUN command and for index buffers. This value will always be at least 16K bytes.

5. The rest of the available memory will be added to the free memory pool. This value will be added to the previously established 24K bytes. If you have an expanded memory system, a Clipper application will automatically make use of the extra memory. However, keep in mind that a Clipper application will allocate up to 1 megabyte for buffers, depending on the amount of that memory that is actually available. Also, if there is any expanded memory available, the Clipper application will automatically require a minimum of 16K bytes from the expanded memory system.

Modifying the Memory of Summer '87 Applications

As stated before, the memory configuration can be altered to better fit each application's requirements and needs. To do so, you must issue a SET command at DOS, either directly or through a batch file, preferably AUTOEXEC.BAT. The command syntax would be as follows:

```
SET CLIPPER= [vXXX;] [rXXX;] [eXXXX;] [xXXX;] [fXXX] ; [sX;]
```

Make sure that you do not place an extra space between the word "CLIPPER" and the equal sign. If you do, this command will be ignored by your applications. Here are the explanations for each of the parameters:

1. **The v parameter.**

   This parameter is used to restrict the amount of memory that will be allocated for a memory variable table to XXX kilobytes. If it is not specified, a Clipper application will automatically allocate 20 percent of the available memory, up to a maximum of 44 K.

   Since Clipper will allow up to 2048 memory variables and each memory variable will take up 14 bytes for a position in the memory table, the maximum usage would be roughly 29K. For the Autumn '86 release, this would be roughly 44K because each memory variable used would take up 22 bytes.

   However, programs converted from dBASE III applications won't use more than 256 variables. Here is how to figure out how much space should be allocated for the memory table:

   256 memory variables * 14 bytes = 3584 bytes / 1024 = 3.5 kilobytes

   To implement this, use the following SET command:

   ```
   SET CLIPPER= v006;
   ```

   By doing this, you would have freed roughly 25K bytes from the allocated memory.

   If you set the v parameter to more than 28K bytes (or v028), your application will allocate the memory accordingly, but Clipper will not recognize it and the memory would be wasted.

2. **The r parameter.**

   This parameter is used to allocate space for both the RUN command and for indexing buffers. If you try to RUN a program that allocates for itself as much available memory as possible, the space used for the indexing buffers will be given up to the external program.

   Once the external program returns control to the Clipper application, the space will be reassigned to the indexing buffers.

   If more memory is requested by the r parameter than the amount of available memory left in the free pool, the following error message will appear:

   ```
   Not enough memory
   ```

   If you are using the Autumn '86 release, the same error will yield this message:

   ```
   proc:<startup> line:  System error not enough memory    QUIT? (Q/A/I)
   ```

The maximum number allowed for this parameter is equal to the free pool of memory less the number entered for the v parameter. If expanded memory is available, the r parameter will be used only for the RUN command while the space required by the indexing buffers will be moved to the expanded memory area. Of course, this is dependent on the e parameter.

3. **The e Parameter.**

   This parameter is used to specify the maximum amount of expanded memory the application will use. If no parameter is issued, the application will allocate all available expanded memory up to a maximum of 1 megabyte.

   If the expanded memory is present and available, the application will use this memory space for indexing buffers.

   The minimum number allowed for this parameter is 16K bytes. The command would look like this:

```
SET CLIPPER= e016;
```

4. **The x Parameter.**

   This parameter is used to exclude a specified amount of memory from being allocated and is primarily used to test various environments under which an application might run; you can restrict the application from taking advantage of all the available memory present at the time the application is executed.

   For instance, to make a 640K system look like a 512K machine, the value in the x parameter would be 128.

   No matter how much memory is blocked from your application allocation process, the RUN command can still use this area of memory.

5. **The f Parameter.**

   This parameter is used to specify the maximum number of files the Clipper application may open at any one time. Keep in mind that this parameter is to be used on the machine running the compiled application. It is not necessary for the machine actually compiling the application unless that machine will be used for testing. If no parameter is used, the default number of files allowed to be opened for an application will be set to 8.

   This parameter is also used in conjunction with the FILES parameter located in the CONFIG.SYS file. For example, if the maximum number of files set by the CONFIG.SYS file is 15, no matter what the f parameter is set at, only 15 files will be allowed open. Conversely, if the f parameter is set to 12, only 12 files will be set no matter what value the FILES parameter in the CONFIG.SYS file is set for.

Additionally, for those machines running DOS 3.3 or higher, the maximum number of files that are allowed open is 255. Both the DOS CLIPPER switch and the CONFIG.SYS file may reflect these new maximums.

6. **The s Parameter.**

   This parameter was added for those machines where snow may still appear on the screen while running a Clipper compiled application. To remove the screen flickering, set the value of the s parameter to 1. The default value is 0. Setting the parameter to a value of 1 will cause the application screen writes to be a bit slower than normal.

All of these parameters can be evaluated from within a program by using the GETE() function. By checking for the word "CLIPPER" in your environmental table, you can see if there is enough memory to actually RUN a command, thus preserving the integrity of the system. If you are manipulating large memory variable strings, you can test to see the amount of available memory and restrict the size of the memory variables accordingly.

The first four parameters are present in both the Autumn '86 and Summer '87 releases: the last two are only included in the Summer '87 version.

CHAPTER THREE

Linking

PLINK86

BASIC COMMANDS

Below are listed some of the commands available in Plink86. Along with each command is a brief description of its purpose. For further details on how these commands can be used in linking your application, please refer to the section on Overlay Management.

FILE / FI

The FILE command tells the linker that what follows is the name of the object file to be linked. When this command is used, the file extension (.OBJ) is assumed. FI is an abbreviation for the FILE command.

OUTPUT

The OUTPUT command labels the file created by the linker at the end of linking. The output file will have an .EXE extension. If no label is given, the root name of the executable file will be the name of the first object file in the link list. The .EXE extension will still be assigned.

LIB

The LIB command identifies which run-time libraries need to be linked with the given object modules. The version of Plink86 provided with the compiler automatically assumes that the library to be linked will be CLIPPER.LIB. If there are other files to be linked, such as OVERLAY.LIB for the creation of overlays, they need to be specified.

MAP

The MAP command is used to obtain reports that detail the memory map location of the program symbols, codes, and constant tables, as well as all library routines intrinsic to Clipper and/or Plink86. The basic format for the MAP command is:

MAP = <filename> flag1,... , flagn.

Map Flags:

G - This flag will produce a file of all global public symbols. They are listed in alphabetical order with their assigned addresses.

S - This flag will produce a file that contains a map of all the sections in input order. The report contains the following headings:

Maddr - memory address where section will be loaded.
Msize - memory space used by the section.
Daddr - address where section is stored within disk file.
Dsize - disk space used by the section.
Lev - the level number of this section. A zero indicates a section that is not overlayed that will reside in the main memory module.
Ov# - Overlay number of this section. A zero indicates the main or "root" section. A non-zero indicates a section loaded by the overlay loader.
Fth - Overlay number of the "father" section within the overlay structure. A zero indicates an overlay that has no ancestors.
Pload - Pre-Load flag. A "Yes" indicates that the overlay will be loaded by the loader before execution of the actual program because of its level of zero.

A - This flag will print all reports. If no flag is given, this report is the default report.

M - This flag will print a report on the modules. Each module and its segments are listed in input order. Listed under each segment are its symbols and addresses. Common blocks and absolute symbols are listed separately in front of the report.

E - This flag will print a report of the error messages and warning messages thatare normally displayed to the screen. Messages generated by the VERBOSE command are not part of this report.

WIDTH

This statement will change the page width of the memory map reports. The default value is 80.

HEIGHT

This statement will change the number of lines per page for the memory map reports. The default value is 65 lines.

NWIDTH

This statement changes the width of symbol names and other identifiers printed in the map. The default is nine characters.

VERBOSE

This command will display the current operation of the linker while it is in session. The last line on the screen is used for the display. Do not use this command if redirecting the output to file or printer.

BEGINAREA

This command is used to initiate the beginning of an area for an overlay. BEGIN can be used as an abbreviation for this command.

ENDAREA

This command is used to conclude an area for an overlay. END can be used as an abbreviation for this command.

SECTION

This command separates the following object module files to be contained in an internal overlay.

SECTION INTO

This command separates the following object module files to be contained in an external overlay file. This file will have an .OVL extension.

OVERLAY

This command specifies the names of the segment classes that can remain in the overlay structure.

DEBUG

This command will display to the screen the name of the overlay section that is currently being executed.

WARNING ERRORS

If any of the following error messages appear, the linking process will finish, but there is no guarantee that your application will run.

Error Number:	Cause:
1	There are several causes for this error condition. One is that the address being referenced is lower in memory than the segment register addressing it. In theory it is like a variable that has not been initialized at a higher level or made PUBLIC being called by a lower program. This is not a common error message. Also see ERROR 10, below.

2 Under the operating system, the designated stack location of the application is kept in the header of the executable file. This is then used to set the SS and SP registers when the program is called and executed. The linker looks for a stack segment marked as either SS or SP by the compiler or assembler. If it is found, the eventual address is placed in the header. If it is not found, zeroes are placed in the header at that location, and the program will not function correctly. This can be avoided if the SS and SP registers are set by the application itself. Even then the application could halt if such an interruption occurs before it has had a chance to establish a valid stack. In normal compiling of Clipper or dBASE code, this error should not appear.

3 A *group* is a collection of segments that must reside within 64K of memory space. Sixteen-bit addresses can then be used to access objects within the group. A part of the group cannot be accessed if the group is too large; the group size must then be reduced. Even if the segment is less than 64K, verify with the memory map that segments have not been separated by intervening segments from another group. If this error message occurs, and the segment is close to 64K, reduce the segment even further, to around 40K, to make certain it will link.

This is similar to large .OBJ modules. Sometimes, when there is too much compiling, the code, symbol, and constant tables may exceed their 32K limit. If this should occur, the amount compiled at one time must be reduced. The same theory holds true for linking.

Also, this situation often occurs when attempting to link assembly language modules with high-level language modules. The class and segment names used in assembly language code should match those used in the high-level language code.

4 The module name given in the MODULE command was not found in any of the linked files.

5 The 8086 processor uses a dual addressing scheme, making the offset portion of a long address relative to the physical segment selected by the paragraph. Though the offset can be determined at linkage, the paragraph address, being an absolute address point in memory, must be adjusted according to where the operating system loads the application into memory. The linker outputs a long address relative to the start of the program and continues linking.

6 Relevant only for CP/M-86.

7 The given module contains a record type unfamiliar to the linker. The entire record will be skipped. Included with this will be FATAL ERROR

41, which means that the linker is looking for a file that follows standard relocatable object module format and one of the files given to the linker does not follow this rule. This is a common error when developers try to use batch files that not only call the compiler but call the linker as well. If this is the case, check to see if file extensions are being used. Predictably, the .PRG extension is given with the file name, which Clipper does not mind. However, that file extension will be passed to the linker. Instead of linking in the newly compiled .OBJ file, the batch file is telling the linker to use the .PRG file. Make sure that no file extensions are used with batch files unless absolutely necessary. Let the compiler and the linker assume their default values.

8 Each record in an object file will contain a check field at the end for validation purposes. This message indicates that the checksum value was bad; linking will continue, however. If object files are patched, the checksum must be changed to reflect the possible change in the file size.

9 Plink86 reached the end of the record and found that the number of bytes processed is different from the specified size. Each record in an object file is preceded by the record size. This is the source of the discrepancy.

10 A reference to the named modules was made to the given target object and assumed that the segment register to be used for the access will point to the given frame object.

The target cannot be accessed as desired if a 16-bit address is being used and the target is more than 64K bytes away from a frame (or an 8-bit address with a distance greater than 256 bytes). The address actually used will be wrapped around to fit into the required offset size. If there is a group larger than 64K, make it smaller for proper access.

11 There may be only one definition for each public global symbol in the program being linked. Another definition was found for the named symbol, either in another module or created by the DEFINE command. The linker will ignore the duplicate definition, retain the first one, and continue linking. However, to insure that the application's integrity is maintained, the duplication should be found and removed.

This is a frequent error if either of the following things should happen:

a. You compile a user-defined function library and some of the same functions are defined and compiled at the end of another program module. When these two files are linked and a reference is made to one of those user-defined functions, the linker sees two symbols for the same call.

b. Sometimes, developers use the same set of procedure names in different procedure files. For example, a procedure named ADDTHEM may be defined in procedure file POLICY and defined again in procedure file CODES. Each version of ADDTHEM would be slightly different depending on which SET PROCEDURE TO file is being used. Since the compiler makes no distinction between program files and procedures, one of the ADDTHEM procedures will have to be changed and all subsequent and relative calls similarly changed to fit the new name.

12 The named public segment was assigned to more than one group. One module placed the segment in one group, while another module placed the same segment in another group. System integrity will be in question if this occurs.

13 The name segment was first defined as a public segment and then later redefined as a common block, or the other way around. All definitions of the segment should be changed to be the same type.

14 A duplicate stack segment was defined within the named module. The linker will use the last stack definition made to specify the stack in the executable file's header. If this stack segment is empty or too small, the application will, in all probability, halt during execution.

Verify that all stack segment definitions use the same name and class name, for they will be combined into one segment having the same size.

FATAL ERRORS

Many errors are the result of a series of previously reported errors, usually in the compiling process. These errors are sometimes ignored and compiling continues. If a batch file is used, the error does not stop all processing until the process invokes the linker. Below is a listing of the possible error messages and, where applicable, the probable cause.

Error Number: **Cause:**

1 @ files are nested too deeply for the linker The linker will only accept three @ files at any given time. If there are any loops, each loop will count as a legitimate pass.

2 There was a disk error while attempting to read the designated @ file. Try to rebuild the file.

3 The file name entered after the @ was not found on the specified drive or directory.

5 The expression given has too many characters for input. The maximum number of characters allowed in an expression is 64.

6 There was an invalid digit in a number. Valid digits depend on the radix being used (the default for addresses is hex and for everything else, it is decimal).

10 An invalid file name was given.

11 The linker was expecting a statement. A key word that begins a command statement should be present. With some versions of the compiler, the batch file (CL.BAT) that was provided with the compiler was missing the letters "FI." Here is what it looked like:

```
clipper %1
plink86 %1
```

It should have been:

```
clipper %1
plink86 FI %1
```

14 The linker was expecting an identifier. A section, segment, module, or symbol name must be entered.

15 Expecting "="

16 A value was expected. At this point a 16-bit quantity must be given.

17 No files were given to link. The FI statement must be used and at least one file must be linked.

18 The ")" was expected at the end of a CLASS statement. If a list of segment names is used, the names must be enclosed in parentheses.

WORK FILE ERRORS

Error Number: **Cause:**

30 The given work file cannot be created, probably because of lack of space in the disk directory.

31 There was an I/O error while writing the work file.

32 There was an I/O error while reading the work file.

33 There was an I/O error while attempting to reposition the work file (doing an *lseek*, for example).

34 Too many object modules (symbols, segments, groups) are defined. Basically, the program being created is too large for the linker to handle as specified.

INPUT OBJECT FILE ERRORS

Error Number: Cause:

41 A premature end of the input file was found. This error occurs when compiling and linking with the help of a batch file, normally CL.BAT. If an extension is given with the batch file, the compiler accepts both the main name and the file (.PRG) extension. However, the file name and extension of .PRG were passed to the linker, which will try to link the .PRG file instead of the .OBJ file to the library. Just remove the file extension when using the batch file. The compiler will assume .PRG extensions, and the linker will assume .OBJ extensions.

42 There was a fatal read error in object file input.

43 Plink86 could not locate the named object file. When an object file cannot be located, the linker will ask for the name prefix such as a drive or path name. If using batch files, the linker will just abort the operation and not prompt the user for the correct response.

OUTPUT FILE ERRORS

Error Number: Cause:

45 The linker cannot create the output file on the disk. Check to see if the disk directory is full or if the disk is write protected.

46 The output file type given is not valid. If this option is used, the output file must be either an .EXE or .CMD type.

47 A fatal disk write error has occurred. Either this is because the disk is full or write protected or there is some type of hardware error.

48 A fatal disk read error has occurred while being output to file. Probably caused by an unrecoverable hardware error, or the disk is full or write protected.

49 The output file cannot be closed. Check to see if the disk is write protected or if a hardware error has occurred.

50 The memory map cannot be created because the disk directory is full or the disk is write protected.

MISCELLANEOUS ERRORS

Error Number: **Cause:**

51 Undefined symbols are present. The linker will list the symbols that are undefined, meaning that there was no reference to a library routine containing the definition. The name of the object file in which the symbol was initially compiled will be given with the symbol name. Only the name of the object file will be listed. If several program files are compiled collectively to make up one object file, the reason for the error could be in any one of those files.

For example, let's say we misspell the function SPACE() as SAPCE() in a program module named OVER.PRG. OVER.PRG was called in and compiled by UNDER.PRG and both are in an object file labeled UNDER.OBJ. Clipper will make a symbol for SAPCE(), assuming that it will be a user-defined function and will be defined later. Therefore, the compiler will not report an error. Since it is only a misspelling, there will not be a user-defined function so labeled and no matching symbol will be present either in another object file or in the library. Here is what linking would look like:

```
C>plink86 fi under lib \dbase\clipper
PSA Linkage Editor (Nantucket Clipper) Version 1.46.c
    Copyright (C) 1984 by Phoenix Software Associates Ltd.


    Can't find file CLIPPER.LIB.
    Enter new file name prefix (drive:  or path name/)
    or . to quit =>\dbase\

    Can't find file CLIPPER.LIB.
    Enter new file name prefix (drive:  or path name/)
    or . to quit =>\dbase\

    The following 1 symbols are undefined:
```

```
Symbol SAPCE was accessed from Module UNDER File UNDER

Fatal error 51
Undefined symbols exist
```

Note: Just correct the spelling, recompile, and relink.

52 The linker is informing the user that the specified symbol is self-defined. Generally this error occurs when the DEFINE command was used to define a symbol relative to another symbol, which was in turn used to define another symbol. Finally, the chain of references goes back to the original symbol, completing the circle. In actuality, no symbol ever gets defined.

54 There is not enough available memory to execute the linker. The minimum amount of memory required to run Plink86 is 256K of RAM.

57 There is a problem with the OVERLAY.LIB file.

58 The stack segment is too large for the linker to handle. The largest segment can be no greater than 64K bytes. Remember that the stack segments that are defined in each module are concatenated by Plink86 similarly to the way public segments are concatenated.

INTEL FORMAT OBJECT FILE ERRORS

These errors are caused by problems with the format of the input structure of the object files given to the linker. Normally this implies that the input file is trying to use a feature that the linker will not support. Clipper is not subject to this error. However, since object files compiled outside Clipper can be linked in, it may apply to those.

Error Number: **Cause:**

61 An LTL segment appeared in an Intel module. Unfortunately Plink86 does not support these for input.

62 A REGINT (register initialize) record specified a register to be initialized in a way unsupported by the executable file format. The linker will only support CS:IP (the program starting address point) and SS:SP (the stack pointer). These may be preinitialized with a REGINT record.

63 A LIDATA subrecord has a repeat count of zero that is strictly disallowed by the standards of the INTEL format.

64 An Intel format object library file was used that has an illegally built library index. A possible solution would be to rebuild the library.

65 Plink86 does not support an absolute starting address in the given module. The linker will only support a starting address that is given relative to some segment.

66 The given module uses a group element type that is not supported by Plink86. At present, the linker will only support segments that are included in groups (group component descriptor code = FFH).

70 An invalid location was specified for a fixup. The LOC field must be greater than 4 for all segments relative for a fixup.

71 An invalid location was specified for a fixup. The LOC field must be greater than 1 for all segments relative to the fixup.

73 A frame specification type is unsupported by Plink86. Normally, this frame type is either 6 or 7.

PROGRAM STRUCTURE ERRORS

Error Number: Cause:

80 Overlays are nested too deeply. Check the structure of the overlays being generated and remove a level.

81 There are too many ENDAREA statements. There are more ENDAREA statements than the number of BEGINAREA statements that have not yet been closed.

82 An unbalanced situation exists between BEGINAREA and ENDAREA. Treat these two statements like a DO WHILE...ENDDO loop or a FOR...NEXT loop.

83 The program being linked will not fit into a 1-megabyte address space.

DOS AND MSLINK LINKERS

COMMANDS AND SYNTAX

Review your DOS manual concerning the LINK program provided with your operating system. If you use the MicroSoft Linker, refer to that manual for the specific commands and syntax.

The default allotted segment size with Microsoft Linker version 3.05 has decreased, but it can be increased by command. In order to link any Clipper application with this linker, use the following format:

```
mslink %1 ,,,\path\/se:1024,,;
```

The %1 is used for a batch file, passing the name of the program to be compiled and linked. The \path\ tells the linker where CLIPPER.LIB is located, and the remaining characters are needed to increase the segment size. In this example, the segments have been set to the maximum size, 1024 bytes.

OVERLAY MANAGEMENT WITH PLINK86

OVERLAY BASICS

An overlay is simply a section of the application that is organized so that it will use the same memory area as another section of the application. No special programming commands are necessary to establish an overlay; this is accomplished by the linker. The theory is that since portions of large applications will share the same memory area, the overall memory requirements on a system will be lessened. The disadvantage in using overlays is the immediate increase of execution time because of an increase of I/O needed to load each overlay from the disk drive.

Try to link your application as is, without the use of overlays. Even if the application is larger than 640K, get a benchmark from which to start. Avoid using overlays if you can; they slow down an application and are difficult to manage. If you do decide to use overlays, establish a series of test programs to compile and to link or follow the examples in the *call tracking* application located in Appendix I.

There are no simple rules for utilizing overlays. Two points must first be made:

1. Overlay management is never the total solution.
2. Make sure when planning for the implementation of overlays that you consider the computer system on which the application will run.

Overlay Management Is Never the Total Solution

There is more to overlay management that just adding a few extra statements to the linker. Three factors affect overlay management:

a. The way we code
b. The way we compile
c. The way we link

Obviously, linking has a direct effect on the memory scheme of the application. The compiling and coding are equally important but are more difficult to plan and handle. The linking and compiling are handled after the application has been coded and at least one attempt has been made at creating an overlay. After one attempt, a good developer can adjust the overlay via the coding, compiling, or even linking techniques. All three methods are elaborated upon later in this chapter.

Plan the Application for the Computer on Which it Will Run

Some applications may never run because of the restrictions of a machine's memory, the capacity of the disk, the restriction of the operating system, the execution speed, or a combination of all four. Quite often, and usually after a few attempts with overlays, a decision must be made whether or not to use overlays. Sometimes, the amount of time necessary to create the ideal overlay scheme is not cost effective.

MEMORY REQUIREMENTS

Every application has a specific memory requirement. That requirement fluctuates from system to system and from application to application. Below are 10 factors that determine the amount of RAM required by any one specific application on any one machine. Once this base is established, each of these factors may be manipulated to decrease the amount of memory required.

1. The size of any required program file that will remain in the main load module (i.e., code, symbol, and constant size)

2. The code size (from the compiler) of the object files that may reside in an overlay

3. The symbol size (from the compiler) of the object files that may reside in overlays

4. The constant size (from the compiler) of the object files that may reside in an overlay

5. The size of any outside programs that may be executed

6. The size of any "called" routine that will be linked in with the application

7. The size of any RAM resident program or RAM drive

8. The required amount of memory needed for macros and memory variables

9. The required memory for the basic Clipper library

10. The size of the operating system

The following is a brief discussion of each of the 10 memory size issues:

1. The Size of the Object File in the Main Load Module:

   This pertains to the specific size of the constant, symbol, and code tables for those modules that must reside in the main load module. An example of these types of modules would be the HELP program, the main calling program, a user-defined function library, or even a special chaining program. Any module that needs to be accessed by an overlay module should reside in the main load module.

2. The Code Size of the Object File for Overlays:

   After every compilation, the compiler will generate three numbers, the first of which pertains to the size of the code table generated by the compiler. The compiler takes source code and generates intermediate code that represents the commands being issued. For example, for a simple STORE command, a series of push, move, and pop instructions would be generated.

3. The Symbol Size of the Object File for Overlays:

   The second number reported after compilation is the size of the symbol table. A symbol is a reference to a greater part. The compiler will generate a symbol for procedure or function names, memory variables, macros, etc., that refers to the item. This reference is either linked to its definition or is expanded to its true value.

4. The Constant Size of the Object File for Overlays:

   The last number reported is the size of the constant table. A constant is a quote or a value (for example). The prompt messages in an @SAY, @GET, or @PROMPT are all constants, while the STORE 0 TO x command would generate some room in the constant table for the zero.

5. The Size of Any Outside Executed Programs:

   In some cases, a CHKDSK command is needed or perhaps the MODE command has to be used to change printer direction. In these cases, DOS is reloaded, and the size is figured into the memory size one more time. Additionally, any program that is called upon to execute via the RUN command must be calculated. The main program remains in memory while the secondary application is loaded into memory on top of the original. The main program is still in control even though the secondary application is executing. Upon completion of processing, the second application will turn control of the system back to the original program. However, the secondary program or application will not load if there is not enough room for **both** programs to fit in memory. Keep in mind that compiled applications initially try to grab as much memory as possible proportional to the amount available. Because of this, it is **very** difficult to design applications that will RUN another large application (such as a word processor).

6. The Size of any Called Programs:

   In some applications, special programs may be written in C or in Assembler to be linked in with Clipper applications. These routines increase the size of the application.

7. The Size of RAM Resident Programs:

   Some utility programs can reside in the background until called upon, at which time they execute as prescribed. They take space away from the amount of RAM available to the application. Some of these programs are not clean in the way they interface with the operating system. This means that errors may occur even if there is enough available RAM memory for both the compiled application and the background program. It is not advisable to run Clipper programs concurrently with active RAM resident programs.

8. The Size of the Macro Library and Memory Variables:

   Along with the basic memory size as quoted by Plink86, an additional 64K minimum is needed for memory variables and macro substitutions. If the system has more than 64K available, the application will take as much memory as possible, proportional to the amount available. For more information on this see Chapter 16, Programming Structure and Application Layout.

9. The Size of the Clipper Library:

   Every application, even the simplest one-line program, will yield a high-load module. This is because the Clipper library is loaded into the executable file. For example, in a program with only a one-line CLEAR command, the object file size is 532 bytes, yet the executable size is 128,524 bytes. The entire library is not linked into the file; some commands, if used, will link in more code. For example, if in place of our CLEAR command a REPORT FORM <filename> is used, the object file would be 567 bytes with an executable file of 140,668 bytes. The basic library file size is roughly 128K and cannot be decreased.

10. The Size of DOS:

    This is the simplest factor to calculate, but remember that each version of DOS is different. Verify the version of DOS on the computer for which the application is being designed, not the machine on which the application is being developed, compiled, and linked. The way to determine the RAM size required by your version of DOS is to run the DOS program CHKDSK when no other programs or devices are loaded.

```
C>chkdsk

  10592256 bytes total disk space
    258048 bytes in 6 hidden files
    147456 bytes in 32 directories
   9576448 bytes in 530 user files
     12288 bytes in bad sectors
    598016 bytes available on disk

    524288 bytes total memory
    480672 bytes free
```

In this example, the amount of available memory on the machine is 512K. However, after DOS has been loaded into the system, the amount available to run programs is 470K. On this particular machine, DOS required almost 43K.

THE WAY WE CODE

Too often, this is the most overlooked factor in attempting to minimize RAM overhead and maximize overlay efficiency. Developers can get caught up in their own coding techniques, which may be the very root of many problems in creating the perfect overlay structure.

With Plink86, we are allowed to have the constants of an overlay move with the overlay rather than reside in the main load module. If we can tailor our coding to have more constants than symbols, our main load module will be smaller while our overlays grow. However, this may not be really necessary. Main load modules and overlay modules can also be reduced in size if we simply make better use of memory variables, reusing stale ones, or recoding a specific section of code. The way we code plays a subtle yet significant role in our memory management scheme. Below are just a few samples relating to this topic.

Command Differences

Let's code a simple loop to count from 1 to 500. First we will use a DO WHILE loop; then we will do the same thing with a FOR command.

Sample 1.

```
STORE 1 TO x
DO WHILE x <= 500
   STORE x + 1 TO x
ENDDO
```

Sample 2.

```
FOR x = 1 TO 500
NEXT
```

	Sample 1	**Sample 2**
Code Size:	59	66
Symbol Size:	48	48
Constant Size:	64	48

Notice that even though there are fewer lines of code in sample 2, the code size is 7 bytes larger. On the other hand, the constant size for sample 1 is 16 bytes larger than sample 2, yielding a total of 9 more bytes than the first sample. Multiplying these figures over entire applications, the numbers become significant. This type of information is also critical when choosing an overlay structure. Since constants move in and out with their corresponding overlay sections, it may be beneficial to have a larger constant size that resides only in the overlay. On the other hand, if multiple sections and overlays are nested, the corresponding code sizes and constant sizes will move with one another. Therefore, the overall smaller code or constant size in sample 2 may be more usable.

Literals or Macros?

Sometimes commands and their respective conditions may be stated in more than one fashion. For example, conditional clauses can reside in a macro rather than being entered as a literal. The following two samples establish a simple SET FILTER command, the first using a literal structure and the second a macro substitution.

Sample 1.

```
USE Test
SET FILTER TO SUBSTR(name,1,3)="STE" .AND.;
   LEN(TRIM(SUBSTR(phone,10,4)))<>0
```

Sample 2.

```
USE Test
STORE "SUBSTR(name,1,3)="STE" .AND. ;
   LEN(TRIM(SUBSTR(phone,10,4)))<>0" TO test
SET FILTER TO &test
```

	Sample 1:	**Sample 2:**
Code Size:	62	45
Symbol Size:	80	64
Constant Size:	144	128

In the first sample, the literal command is larger on all sections, which suggests that the second method of coding is more efficient than the first, especially when developing with the intent of using overlays. However, because of the nature of the command and the fact that the macro will be expanded for every record in TEST.DBF, the second example may slow down execution speed drastically. If a large database is to be used and execution time is a major concern, code the routine as a literal. If the size ofthe application is of supreme concern and if the file in use is relatively small, the macro is more appropriate.

Just Bad Code

Bad code not only affects the readability and flow of the application but the memory scheme as well. Below are two samples of a testing situation inside HELP, each checking for the name of the program and for the memory variable involved. The first sample uses nested IF commands while the second uses a more structured DO CASE flow.

Sample 1.

```
IF p = "ONE"
   IF v = "TEST"
   ELSE
      IF v = "NEW"
      ELSE
         IF v = "THIS"
         ELSE
         ENDIF
      ENDIF
   ENDIF
ELSE
   IF p = "TWO"
      IF v = "A"
      ELSE
         IF v = "B"
         ELSE
            IF v = "C"
            ELSE
            ENDIF
         ENDIF
      ENDIF
   ELSE
      IF v = "X"
      ELSE
         IF v = "Y"
         ELSE
            IF v = "Z"
            ELSE
            ENDIF
         ENDIF
      ENDIF
   ENDIF
ENDIF
```

Sample 2.

```
DO CASE
CASE p = "ONE"
   DO CASE
   CASE v = "TEST"
   CASE v = "NEW"
   CASE v = "THIS"
```

```
    OTHERWISE
    ENDCASE
 CASE p = "TWO"
    DO CASE
    CASE v = "A"
    CASE v = "B"
    CASE v = "C"
    OTHERWISE
    ENDCASE
 OTHERWISE
    DO CASE
    CASE v = "X"
    CASE v = "Y"
    CASE v = "Z"
    OTHERWISE
    ENDCASE
 ENDCASE
```

	Sample 1	Sample 2
Code Size:	317	302
Symbol Size:	64	64
Constant Size:	208	208

Obviously, the code in the first sample is larger by 15 bytes. This might seem insignificant in this test environment. However, in a real HELP procedure or over an entire application, this difference will magnify and may present a problem.

Simply having the computer wait for a keystroke from the operator to signal it to continue can be a challenge to code. As with all functions, this routine returns a value, and that value can either be stored to a memory variable, displayed on the screen, or hidden in some fashion. Depending how we code even the simplest wait routine, our application space and speed can increase or decrease. Here are a few more samples:

Sample 1.

```
CLEAR
@ 10,10 SAY "Any Key to continue..."
temp = INKEY(0)
```

Sample 2.

```
CLEAR
@ 10,10 SAY "Any Key to continue..."
SET CONSOLE OFF
?? INKEY(0)
SET CONSOLE ON
```

Sample 3.

```
CLEAR
@ 10,10 SAY "Any Key to continue..."
IF INKEY(0) <> 0
ENDIF
```

	Sample 1:	Sample 2:	Sample 3:
Code Size:	42	51	51
Symbol Size:	48	32	32
Constant Size:	96	96	96

The major difference to note is that in sample 1 a temporary memory variable is used in conjunction with the INKEY() function. In the other samples the INKEY() function is either being displayed or tested. With the temporary variable the code size is less than the other two. However, the symbol size is greater, while the constants remain the same. Symbols are important to the main load module of an application, while the code size is important to the overlay modules. If less symbol size is important, sample 3 is preferred to sample 2 because it has fewer command lines.

THE WAY WE COMPILE

The way we compile our applications also plays a very important role in the final memory scheme. First consider the following samples of code:

Sample 1.

```
********************
* Name      CODESIZE.prg
* Date      August 29, 1986
* Author    Stephen Straley
* Notes     This is the first tested file in the compiling example.
*
********************

CLEAR
@ 10,10 SAY "Do you want to continue (Y/N) ? "
IF VERIFY()
   @ 12,10 SAY "O.k.  I continued...."
ELSE
   @ 12,10 SAY "Program Terminated"
ENDIF

********************
* Name      FUNC.prg
* Date      April 29, 1986
* Author    Stephen Straley
* Notes     This is the function library that goes
*           with TEST.prg to illustrate how to compile.
*
********************
```

```
FUNCTION Verify

   SET CONSOLE OFF
   WAIT TO intemp
   SET CONSOLE ON
   IF UPPER(intemp) = "Y"
      ?? " Yes"
      RETURN(.T.)
   ENDIF
   ?? "  No"
   RETURN(.F.)
```

Each file was compiled separately, yielding the following code, symbol, and constant sizes.

	CODESIZE.PRG:	FUNC.PRG:	COMBINED:
Code Size:	96	97	193
Symbol Size:	48	64	112
Constant Size:	167	112	279

When these two object files are linked together, the final executable file size is 129,036 bytes.

Now we'll try compiling the two files together with the aid of a CLiP (.CLP) file. The file (called TEST.CLP) will look like this:

```
Test
Func
```

And the compiling command would be: CLIPPER @Test

The resulting code, symbol, and constant sizes are:

Sample 2:

	TEST.PRG / FUNC.PRG
Code Size:	193
Symbol Size:	80
Constant Size:	272

When this file is linked with the library, the final executable file size is 128,988 bytes.

The only major difference in this test situation is that the symbol size decreased by 32 bytes; however, the size of the executable file decreased by 48 bytes. Obviously, the linker has less overhead to add in order to handle the fewer symbols in the second test.

Let's try one more example, one in which we code the user-defined function directly in with the test program. The file would look like this:

Sample 3.

```
*********************
* Name      TESTSIZE.prg
* Date      August 29, 1986
* Author    Stephen Straley
* Notes     This file includes the user-defined function.
*
********************

CLEAR
@ 10,10 SAY "Do you want to continue (Y/N) ? "
IF VERIFY()
   @ 12,10 SAY "O.k.  I continued...."
ELSE
   @ 12,10 SAY "Program Terminated"
ENDIF

FUNCTION Verify

   SET CONSOLE OFF
   WAIT TO intemp
   SET CONSOLE ON
   IF UPPER(intemp) = "Y"
      ?? " Yes"
      RETURN(.T.)
   ENDIF
   ?? "  No"
   RETURN(.F.)
```

In this test example, the code, symbol, and constant sizes are:

	TEST.PRG
Code Size:	181
Symbol Size:	64
Constant Size:	247

This results in a final executable file size of 128,924 bytes.

On all three sections--code, symbols, and constants--the size decreased and the final decrease in the executable file size was proportional.

In the second example, the compiler established a separate code and constant table for each file in the CLiP file, while the symbol size is reduced. Again, symbols always remain in the main load module with references to global memory variables, macros, and functions or procedures. In sample 3, when the two programs and functions were combined into one file, all factors reduced in size. The compiler will handle most of the management of code, symbol, and constants if the information is present.

The point of this can best be seen in major applications, not in test programs. Most applications require similar items: a help file, a procedure library, a function library, and so on. Since there is no real limit to the number of procedures in a procedure file (since program files are in essence procedures, and since user defined functions can reside within a procedure file), it is obvious that we can combine specific files into one large file. This file can be compiled once, saving on all fronts: code size, symbol size, and constant size.

Compiling plays a direct role in determining file sizes. And only because of certain system criteria are we restricted from compiling with complete freedom.

THE WAY WE LINK

The most important factor in memory requirements is the way we link our applications with each other and with outside routines, outside libraries, the overlay library, and the Clipper library. Overlays help overcome large memory requirements of an application. In other words, overlays would be unnecessary if every microcomputer had a minimum of 640K of memory and every application required far less. But since this is not the situation, the creation, understanding, and use of overlays is crucial.

An overlay is a partitioned section of memory used to swap different sections of the application in and out according to need. This allows available memory to be used more efficiently. Specific procedures or program files can share the same section of memory, thus reducing the overall demand on RAM. Up to this point, we have stressed that many factors play a major role in how we can link and what the results will be when we do link.

In discussing both coding and compiling, we made several references to the code, symbol, and constant sizes. These three values play an important role in what we can do with overlays. With the linker we also control where these tables reside with the main load module and even within the overlays themselves. The next section looks carefully at the relationships of memory requirements, overlay and main load module sizes, and code, symbol, and constant sizes.

The next few sections center on the application source code called "MENU GENERATOR." There is one more example of small differences in coding and compiling. Using the MENU GENERATOR as the example, note the following figures:

```
Compiled in one Program File:                                  143,400 bytes

Compiled in one CLiP File:                                     144,204 bytes

Compiled in separate CLiP Files and LINKed by one LiNK file:   148,256 bytes
```

SOME COMMON RULES

1. Important files should remain in the main load module.

   Quite often this rule is ignored, and subsequent run-time errors, especially the EXEC SEQUENCE ERROR, will occur. Be very careful that any function or procedure library, help utility, screen driver, or any other object file pertinent to the operation of the application is linked to the main object file. This constitutes the main load module. A pertinent file is a file that may be called upon by any program, in or out of an overlay, regardless of its section. Clearly, a HELP file would fall into this classification, for the user should be allowed to call upon it at **any** point in the application without causing a major disturbance to the overlay scheme and memory manager.

2. Never have sections call other sections within the same overlay.

   If a section manages to call another section of code within the same overlay, an EXEC SEQUENCE ERROR will occur and the system will automatically stop running. Overlay files can call other overlay files but not sections within the same overlay. In mapping the execution of your applications, be careful to follow sibling branches and verify that they do not call the same level of sibling at any time.

3. Never calculate an overlay based upon the directory size of the object file.

   Use the three table sizes generated after each compilation: the code, symbol, and constant sizes. With every overlay, Plink86 adds additional bytes to the load module in order to handle the overlay scheme. For the first overlay used, add an additional 20 bytes; for every subsequent overlay add 16 bytes.

4. Never assume that the application will fit in 256K with the use of overlays.

   In some cases it just cannot be accomplished. Every overlay generates additional overhead with the linker and in many cases a <u>Catch 22</u> scenario develops. In this situation we use overlays to reduce overhead but because of the increase of linkage overhead needed to handle those overlays, the system will still not execute under a certain memory requirement.

5. The LOAD size is not the EXE size.

   At the end of a successful linkage, Plink86 will generate a number for the basic load module size. It does not mean that this is the memory requirement for that application. All that number includes are the sizes of the library(s) and object file(s) used. Therefore, the basic memory overhead to handle macros and memory variables has not been included, nor has the size of the operating system. As a general rule, add an additional 100K to this generated number to arrive at the approximate memory requirement for that application.

CODE, CONSTANT, AND SYMBOL TABLES

Code, constant, and *symbol* table sizes are generated at the completion of every successful compilation. Each number plays a significant role in the size of our main load module and has equal importance in the overlay size. More than the size of the largest section in an overlay determines its overall size. Each number refers to a specific function of your code.

The code section is that table that equates the specific steps or commands as written in the dBASE III language and converts them to tokens or symbols representing those actions. Of course, these tokens are linked to the library with regard to their specific machine-level action. The smallest code section size will be 12 bytes. Both the main load module and overlay modules have a certain area set aside for the code section or table.

The constant table is that table of the specific data that never changes. Examples of constant tables are the string of a SAY, a PROMPT, and a specific value assigned to a variable. These constants are a part of the overlay file, yet they may move in and out of memory with the overlay itself. The smallest constant section table size is 32 bytes. Depending on how it is linked, either the main load module or the overlay module has a designated area established for this table.

The symbol table refers to functions, program names, memory variables, and macro substitutions. This table is often ignored in calculating the memory requirement of an application. The smallest symbol table size generated by the compiler will be 32 bytes. The symbol table always remains in the main load module, regardless of the size and number of overlays.

Depending on many factors, the linker loads extra overhead in with the application to handle the designated overlay scheme as well as the compiling scheme. For example, more overhead is needed to link many object files together than is required for just a couple of object files. Remember that a user-defined function generates a symbol to the compile. If many .PRG files are separated, preventing one massive object file, each object file has an identical symbol every time the UDF is used. At link time the linker consolidates these identical symbols the best it can. This process takes up extra overhead. The solution is to compile larger amounts at one time, such as all .PRG files that make use of unique symbols. This allows the compiler to generate a more efficient symbol table. The table below illustrates this:

.PRG:	A:	B:	C:	D:	E:
Symbol:	UNIQUE()	"hello"	DO A	READ	UNIQUE()
	TRIM()	x =	"bye"	DO A	LTRIM()
	DATE()	SET KEY TO	STR()	SET FORMAT TO	DATE()
	x =	TRANSFORM()	CHR()	SET ALTERNATE ON	?
	"hello"	STR()	DAY()	??	QUIT
	x =	SET KEY TO	"bye"		DATE()
	x =				

If each .PRG file were compiled separately, the code, symbol, and constant tables would look something like this:

.PRG:	A:	B:	C:	D:	E:
Symbol:	UNIQUE()	"hello"	DO A	READ	UNIQUE()
	DATE()	x =	"bye"	DO A	LTRIM()
	"hello"	SET KEY TO	STR()	SET FORMAT TO	DATE()
	TRIM()	TRANSFORM()	CHR()	SET ALTERNATE ON	?
	x =	STR()	DAY()	??	QUIT

Regardless of the number of symbols stuffed in the table, the minimum sizes of the table are set in advance. Each is unique. The minimum size of the code table is 12 bytes, the symbol table size is 32 bytes, and the constant table size is 32 bytes. Below is a screen dump of a compile on an empty .PRG file named TEST.PRG:

```
C:\>clipper test
The Clipper Compiler, Winter '85
Copyright (c) 1985, 1986 Nantucket Inc., All Rights Reserved.

Compiling TEST.PRG
Code size:12     Symbols:32     Constants:32
```

The way to get around the extra overhead used by the linker would be to combine each of those table markers into one, combining like markers and reordering them within one unique table. If you were to compile all of these different .PRG files into one massive program file allowing the compiler to make one pass, the resulting .OBJ table would look something like this:

A:

```
UNIQUE()
TRIM()
DATE()
x =
"hello"
SET KEY TO
TRANSFORM()
STR()
DO A
"bye"
```

```
CHR()
DAY()
READ
SET FORMAT TO
?
??
LTRIM()
SET UNIQUE ON
QUIT
```

It is clear that this table is more consolidated and there would be less work for the linker. Allowing the compiler to cross-reference and establish some sort of prelink order to the tables also saves some overhead.

The linker adds extra overhead to move more symbols out of overlay files and down to the main load module. This amount fluctuates and cannot be specifically calculated. Just be aware of it and allow for it. Unfortunately, there is nothing you can do to prevent this extra overhead from being added. Not all situations require one massive compile. Sometimes, more frequently in larger applications, the amount of space used by the linker for the overlays and reshuffling is far less than that used by one huge load module from one massive compile and link.

Here are a few key figures (all are approximations) to use when designing an overlay scheme:

The basic Clipper library (without REPORT/LABEL commands)	126,200
Additional bytes to support REPORT/LABEL commands	12,000
Size of DOS (varies)	36,000
Partitioned area for memory variables	64,000
TOTAL..	238,200

A series of linking techniques is shown in the next section, each with a small diagram of its internal workings and a brief description of the technique. The examples refer to the MENU GENERATOR application. The 11 program files of MENU GENERATOR were compiled separately using CLiP files. Below is a list of the object files and their code, symbol, and constant sizes. All figures shown below refer to the number of bytes per table, not kilobytes. These numbers will be referred to in all subsequent overlaying techniques we discuss.

Object File	Code Size	Symbol Size	Constant Size
Genmen.obj	1968	608	3600
Startoff.obj	747	80	496
Begin.obj	328	320	192
Promptng.obj	736	576	320

Menuentr.obj	1108	432	752
Menudraw.obj	726	528	272
Move_cur.obj	655	336	224
Drawbox.obj	385	128	208
Movetitl.obj	380	176	106
Moveesc.obj	380	176	106
Finished.obj	1071	544	1024

In the next two sections, each linking will show the LiNK file used, any memory map that may be pertinent, the file sizes, a diagram of how the memory scheme is laid out, and a summary of the theory involved.

INTERNAL OVERLAYS

In this series of overlays and linking options it is assumed that the entire file, including overlays, fits on a 360K floppy disk. Therefore, with internal overlays the only hurdles to overcome are those pertaining to memory. External overlays will be covered in the next section.

Sample 1:

This LiNK file will link all 11 object modules together to make one executable file with no overlays. This link file was the one used to quote a file size of 148,256K.

```
     Command at DOS:   Plink86 @One

   Name of LiNK file:  One.lnk

   Contents of file:   FI Genmen
                       FI Startoff
                       FI Begin
                       FI Promptng
                       FI Menuentr
                       FI Menudraw
                       FI Move_cur
                       FI Drawbox
                       FI Movetitl
                       FI Moveesc
                       FI Finished
                       LIB \DBASE\Clipper

          Load Size:   139,264

     Directory Size:   148,352
```

Here the library file is located in the subdirectory labeled DBASE. Notice that the load module that starts the entire application is located at the top of the link list. Without the OUTPUT command, Plink86 takes the name of this object file as the name of the application. It is generally advisable when using CLiP files and compiling exclusively (compiling a specific set of program files, regardless of the number of program files that the file may call) that the root name of the CLiP file be that of the first program file in the CLiP list. It then follows that the application root name is the first listed name in the link list.

GENMEN.EXE via One.lnk:

```
   Total Symbols    3904
 Total Constants    7300
      Total Code    8484
 Clipper Library  119576
```

Sample 2:

The following is a LiNK file that has the main program in the main load module and every other program in one overlay in multiple sections. The additional overhead listed in the overlay file is used to handle the multiple sections within that overlay. The size of the overlay, including basic overhead, is based on the largest code section within the overlay and the largest constant section within the same overlay.

```
    Command at DOS:     Plink86 @Two

 Name of LiNK file:     Two.lnk

  Contents of file:     FI Genmen
                        LIB \DBASE\CLIPPER
                        BEGIN
                          SECTION FI Startoff
                          SECTION FI Begin
                          SECTION FI Promptng
                          SECTION FI Menuentr
                          SECTION FI Menudraw
                          SECTION FI Move_cur
                          SECTION FI Drawbox
                          SECTION FI Movetitl
                          SECTION FI Moveesc
                          SECTION FI Finished
                        END

         Load Size:     137,216

    Directory Size:     151,408
```

It is impossible to have programs call other programs in different SECTIONs within the same overlay area. Therefore, this link would eventually yield an EXEC SEQUENCE ERROR and abort the program. However, for the purpose of this demonstration the following is a sample of how the overlay would be viewed, if it were possible to execute.

GENMEN.EXE via Two.lnk:

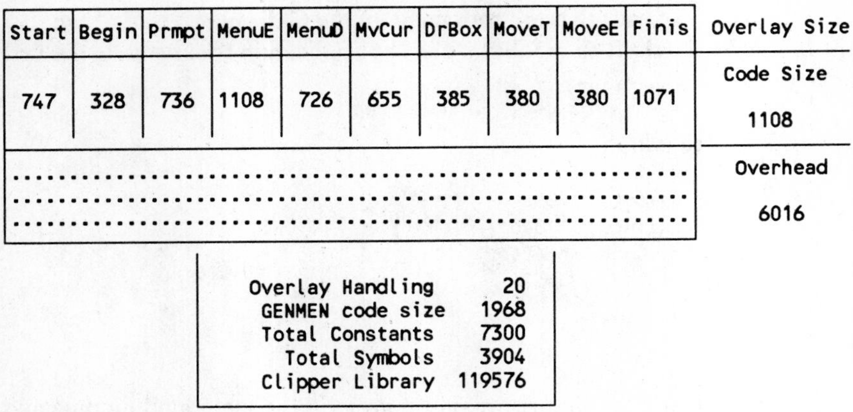

Start	Begin	Prmpt	MenuE	MenuD	MvCur	DrBox	MoveT	MoveE	Finis	Overlay Size
747	328	736	1108	726	655	385	380	380	1071	Code Size 1108
....										Overhead 6016

Overlay Handling	20
GENMEN code size	1968
Total Constants	7300
Total Symbols	3904
Clipper Library	119576

Sample 3:

This sample is basically the same as sample 2 except that the overlay does not have any SECTIONs within it. Thus, the amount of overhead used by the linker is less. Also, the overlay sizes for each type (code and constants) are combined for each (excluding the figure for GENMEN that are calculated in the main load module).

```
     Command at DOS:     Plink86 @Three

  Name of LiNK file:     Three.lnk

   Contents of file:     FI Genmen
                         LIB \DBASE\CLIPPER
                         BEGIN
                           FI Startoff
                           FI Begin
                           FI Promptng
                           FI Menuentr
                           FI Menudraw
                           FI Move_cur
                           FI Drawbox
                           FI Movetitl
                           FI Moveesc
                           FI Finished
                         END

          Load Size:     142,336

     Directory Size:     151,120
```

In this sample the SECTION command has been removed and all of the remaining object files are put together in one overlay. All of the symbols are in the main load module, yet the code and constant sizes are combined. Because there is no SECTION command, any program in any module may call and DO any other program in any other module.

GENMEN.EXE via Three.lnk:

Remaining Code Sizes 3700		Startoff Begin Promptng Menuentr Menudraw Move_cur Drawbox Movetitl Moveesc Finished
(3052)		Overhead
Overlay Handling	20	
GENMEN Constant Size	3600	
Total Constants	7300	
Total Symbols	3904	
Clipper Library	119576	

Sample 4:

This sample is the same as the previous one except for the additional command, OVERLAY PROG, $CONSTANTS (this is for summer '87; the command for Autumn '86 is OVERLAY NIL, $CONSTANTS). This command moves the constant data up from the main load module to the overlay module. Since there is only one overlay, the effect is the same except that the .EXE file is a little smaller. The linker will now require less symbolic information to handle the file.

```
     Command at DOS:     Plink86 @Four

  Name of LiNK file:     Four.lnk

   Contents of file:     FI Genmen
                         LIB \DBASE\CLIPPER
                         OVERLAY PROG, $CONSTANTS
                         BEGIN
                           FI Startoff
                           FI Begin
                           FI Promptng
                           FI Menuentr
                           FI Menudraw
                           FI Move_cur
                           FI Drawbox
                           FI Movetitl
```

```
        FI Moveesc
        FI Finished
      END

Load Size:        142,336

Directory Size:   151,072
```

GENMEN.EXE via Four.lnk:

Remaining Constant Sizes 6516	Startoff Begin Promptng Menuentr Menudraw Move_cur Drawbox Movetitl Moveesc Finished
Remaining Code Sizes 3700	
(3052)	Overhead
Overlay Handling 20 GENMEN Constant Size 3600 GENMEN Code Size 1968 Total Symbols 3904 Clipper Library 119576	

USING MULTIPLE SECTIONS

This section of the discussion on linking introduces the subject of multiple sections and overlaying the file. Because of the recursive program calling, it is difficult to make an overlay file with many sections in it and not have problems. Therefore, in order to save on space and strive for multiple sections, more than one overlay must be established. Using a diagrammed map of the system is a handy way to show the proper way of setting up the linkage.

Sample 1:

Consider the following link file:

```
FI Genmen
MAP = Ten a
LIB \Dbase\Clipper
BEGIN
   SECTION FI Moveesc
   SECTION FI Movetitl
   SECTION FI Finished
END
```

```
BEGIN
   SECTION FI Menudraw, Promptng
   SECTION FI Move_cur
   SECTION FI Drawbox
END
BEGIN
   SECTION FI Menuentr
   SECTION FI Startoff
END
BEGIN
   SECTION FI Begin
END
```

Following is the memory map that the linker provides:

```
Groups:

    Name         Address  Size  DSalloc
    DGROUP        1EFF0   3130

Segments:

    Section :  Maddr=0, Msize=1B3B0, Daddr=1C00, Lev=0, Ovly#=0

        Name          Addr    Size   Name          Addr    Size
        GENMEN.NIL       0     15F   CENTER.NI      160      3A
        SHORT.NIL      1A0      27   VERIFY.NI      1D0      6B
        PROCHEAD.      240      39   HELP.NIL       280     4A4
        DOITAGAIN      730      2E   CHAINA.NI      760      24
        CHAINB.NI      790      29   $START.NI      7C0      DF
        $INTERFAC      89F     6F4   $INTERFAC      F93      8B
        $DRIVERS.     101E     54F   EXEC.C.NI     156D    136B
        _PROG.NIL     28D8     1CA   NDEBUG.C.     2AA2       B
        SYMSYS.C.     2AAD     523   CTERM.C.N     2FD0     915
        STACK.C.N     38E5    12B1   DB.C.NIL      4B96    4B00
        OPS.C.NIL     9696    261E   STERM.C.N     BCB4    377E
        SET.C.NIL     F432     BCB   CSUPPORT.     FFFD    1861
        MACRO.C.N    1185E     36A   $HACKJOB.    11BC8     271
        _PROG.NIL    11E39      5D   _PROG.NIL    11E96     2DD
        _PROG.NIL    12173       0   _PROG.NIL    12173       0
        _PROG.NIL    12173       0   _PROG.NIL    12173     120
        INDEX.C.N    12293    27E9   RPAR.C.NI    14A7C    1D4B
        _PROG.NIL    167C7      6A   _PROG.NIL    16831     5DB
        _PROG.NIL    16E0C      15   NATION.C.    16E21     19C
        _PROG.NIL    16FBD      41   _PROG.NIL    16FFE      1D
        _PROG.NIL    1701B      6A   _PROG.NIL    17085      38
        _PROG.NIL    170BD      2E   _PROG.NIL    170EB      25
        _PROG.NIL    17110       0   _PROG.NIL    17110       0
        _PROG.NIL    17110     A59   _PROG.NIL    17B69      1B
        _PROG.NIL    17B84     12F   _PROG.NIL    17CB3      41
        _PROG.NIL    17CF4      2D   _PROG.NIL    17D21      1E
        _PROG.NIL    17D3F     456   _PROG.NIL    18195      9A
        _PROG.NIL    1822F      1D   _PROG.NIL    1824C      33
```

```
    _PROG.NIL  1827F     2D  _PROG.NIL  182AC     A8
    _PROG.NIL  18354      C  _PROG.NIL  18360      C
    _PROG.NIL  1836C     C4  _PROG.NIL  18430    41A
    _PROG.NIL  1884A    178  _PROG.NIL  189C2     92
    _PROG.NIL  18A54     4C  _PROG.NIL  18AA0     3C
    _PROG.NIL  18ADC     15  _PROG.NIL  18AF1    423
    _PROG.NIL  18F14    106  _PROG.NIL  1901A     A0
    _PROG.NIL  190BA     43  _PROG.NIL  190FD     AF
    _PROG.NIL  191AC     15  _PROG.NIL  191C1      0
    _PROG.NIL  191C1      E  _PROG.NIL  191CF     84
    _PROG.NIL  19253    164  _PROG.NIL  193B7     5B
    _PROG.NIL  19412    11F  _PROG.NIL  19531     F9
    _PROG.NIL  1962A     50  _PROG.NIL  1967A     24
    _PROG.NIL  1969E     20  _PROG.NIL  196BE     32
    _PROG.NIL  196F0    1A4  _PROG.NIL  19894      0
    _PROG.NIL  19894     21  _PROG.NIL  198B5     3E
    _PROG.NIL  198F3     58  _PROG.NIL  1994B    2CD
    _PROG.NIL  19C18     34  _PROG.NIL  19C4C    2AE
    _PROG.NIL  19EFA    241  _PROG.NIL  1A13B     A8
    _PROG.NIL  1A1E3    17F  _PROG.NIL  1A362      0
    _PROG.NIL  1A362      B  _PROG.NIL  1A36D     12
    _PROG.NIL  1A37F     1B  _PROG.NIL  1A39A     7B
    _PROG.NIL  1A415     9C  _PROG.NIL  1A4B1     34
    _PROG.NIL  1A4E5     EB  _PROG.NIL  1A5D0     2B
    _PROG.NIL  1A5FB     28  _PROG.NIL  1A623     6B
    _PROG.NIL  1A68E    125  _PROG.NIL  1A7B3     7C
    _PROG.NIL  1A82F     EA  $OVTB$.OV  1A920    128
    OVDATA.OV  1AB00    1EC  OVCODE.OV  1ACF0    6B6

Section : Maddr=1B3B0, Msize=170, Daddr=1CFD0, Lev=1, Ovly#=1
    MOVEESC.N  1B3B0    161

Section : Maddr=1B3B0, Msize=170, Daddr=1D150, Lev=1, Ovly#=2
    MOVETITL.  1B3B0    161

Section : Maddr=1B3B0, Msize=420, Daddr=1D2E0, Lev=1, Ovly#=3
    FINISHED.  1B3B0    207  FINISHED_  1B5C0    208

Section : Maddr=1B7D0, Msize=550, Daddr=1D720, Lev=1, Ovly#=4
    MENUDRAW.  1B7D0    2A5  PROMPTNG.  1BA80    29C

Section : Maddr=1B7D0, Msize=260, Daddr=1DC80, Lev=1, Ovly#=5
    MOVE_CUR.  1B7D0    25F

Section : Maddr=1B7D0, Msize=160, Daddr=1DEF0, Lev=1, Ovly#=6
    DRAWBOX.N  1B7D0    15A

Section : Maddr=1BD20, Msize=3C0, Daddr=1E060, Lev=1, Ovly#=7
    MENUENTR.  1BD20    3BD

Section : Maddr=1BD20, Msize=2C0, Daddr=1E430, Lev=1, Ovly#=8
    STARTOFF.  1BD20    2BB
```

```
Section : Maddr=1C0E0, Msize=140, Daddr=1E700, Lev=1, Ovly#=9
    BEGIN.NIL   1C0E0    136

Section : Maddr=1C220, Msize=5F00, Daddr=1F0F0, Lev=0, Ovly#=10, Pre-Loaded

        $EXPR.$EX   1C220      0  $EXPR.$EX   1C220      0
        $EXPR.$EX   1C220      0  $EXPR.$EX   1C220     27
        $EXPR.$EX   1C250     13  $EXPR.$EX   1C270     26
        $EXPR.$EX   1C2A0      0  $EXPR.$EX   1C2A0      0
        $EXPR.$EX   1C2A0     39  $EXPR.$EX   1C2E0      0
        $EXPR.$EX   1C2E0      0  $MDATA.$M   1C2E0     B0
        $SYMSTART   1C390      0  $SYMBOLS.   1C390    260
        $SYMBOLS.   1C5F0     B0  $SYMBOLS.   1C6A0     B0
        $SYMBOLS.   1C750    220  $SYMBOLS.   1C970    210
        $SYMBOLS.   1CB80    240  $SYMBOLS.   1CDC0    150
        $SYMBOLS.   1CF10     80  $SYMBOLS.   1CF90    1B0
        $SYMBOLS.   1D140     50  $SYMBOLS.   1D190    140
        $SYMEND.$   1D2D0      2  $CONSTANT   1D2E0    E30
        $CONSTANT   1E110     A0  $CONSTANT   1E1B0     A0
        $CONSTANT   1E250    400  $CONSTANT   1E650    110
        $CONSTANT   1E760    140  $CONSTANT   1E8A0     E0
        $CONSTANT   1E980     D0  $CONSTANT   1EA50    2F0
        $CONSTANT   1ED40    1F0  $CONSTANT   1EF30     C0
        DATA.DATA   1EFF0   2D70  $LIB_TABL   21D60    33C
        STACK.DAT   220A0     80
```

The basic load module from this is 139,424 bytes. Look at the "Section : Maddr =" points in the map for each individual overlay. For the first overlay, the beginning address point is at 1B3B0 and the ending address point is 1B7CF. The difference between the two is 41F hex or 1055 bytes. This is close to the number for the largest code module (FINISHED), which was 1071 (the code size for that object file). Obviously, this overlay must allow for the largest section's code value. The remaining two object files, MOVEESC and MOVETITL, are both smaller than FINISHED, so theoverlay will accommodate the relative code, constant, and symbol size of FINISHED.OBJ.

In the next overlay area the ending address point minus the beginning address point yields a total overlay area of 1359 bytes. Look at the sections involved. There are four object files comprising three sections. The total of the code values generated by the compiler from the two object files in the first section is 1426 bytes. This figure is larger than the code size of MOVE_CUR.OBJ (655) and DRAWBOX.OBJ (385). Therefore, this overlay is the size of the largest section, which is the combination of MENUDRAW and PROMPTING.

These overlays sit on top of one another. The basic picture for this linkage would be something like this:

```
+--------------------------------------+
| Overlay BEGIN                        |        319 bytes
+--------------------------------------+
| Overlay MENUENTR                     |        959 bytes
|         STARTOFF                     |
+--------------------------------------+
| Overlay MENUDRAW + PROMPTING         |
|         Move_cur                     |       1426 bytes
|         Drawbox                      |
+--------------------------------------+
| Overlay MOVEESC                      |
|         MOVETITL                     |       1071 bytes
|         FINISHED                     |
+--------------------------------------+
| Symbols/Expressions/Constants        |
|                                      |
| Clipper.lib                          |    ≈ 135,000 bytes
|                                      |
| Code: GENMEN                         |
+--------------------------------------+
```

We can reduce some of the main load size by moving the $CONSTANTS out of the preload section and into the overlay in which each $CONSTANT belongs. For instance, according to the table chart, the symbol size for GENMEN.OBJ is 608. In the previous memory map the first $CONSTANT symbol has a value of hex E30. When converted to decimal, it equals 3632. This is close to the compiled figure of 3600. The next $CONSTANT size has a value of A0. This equates to 160, which is roughly the constant size of either MOVETITL.OBJ or MOVEESC.OBJ. In our link list the second object file linked into the system in the first overlay area is MOVEESC.OBJ. There is a definite pattern to these numbers and where they reside in the memory map.

In order to move the corresponding $CONSTANT symbols to their respective places, an additional linking command needs to be issued **before** the first overlay area.

OVERLAY PROG, $CONSTANT

The following example shows how this command would look in the link list:

```
FI Genmen
MAP = Ten2 a
LIB \Dbase\Clipper
OVERLAY PROG, $CONSTANTS
BEGIN
   SECTION FI Moveesc
   SECTION FI Movetitl
   SECTION FI Finished
END
BEGIN
   SECTION FI Menudraw, Promptng
   SECTION FI Move_cur
   SECTION FI Drawbox
```

```
END
BEGIN
   SECTION FI Menuentr
   SECTION FI Startoff
END
BEGIN
   SECTION FI Begin
END
```

The corresponding memory map looks like this:

```
Groups:

   Name         Address  Size  DSalloc
   DGROUP        1EAE0   3130

Segments:

   Section :  Maddr=0, Msize=1C1B0, Daddr=1C00, Lev=0, Ovly#=0

      Name           Addr    Size   Name          Addr    Size
      GENMEN.NIL        0     15F   CENTER.NI      160      3A
      SHORT.NIL       1A0      27   VERIFY.NI      1D0      6B
      PROCHEAD.       240      39   HELP.NIL       280     4A4
      DOITAGAIN       730      2E   CHAINA.NI      760      24
      CHAINB.NI       790      29   $START.NI      7C0      DF
      $INTERFAC       89F     6F4   $INTERFAC      F93      8B
      $DRIVERS.      101E     54F   EXEC.C.NI     156D    136B
      _PROG.NIL      28D8     1CA   NDEBUG.C.     2AA2       B
      SYMSYS.C.      2AAD     523   CTERM.C.N     2FD0     915
      STACK.C.N      38E5    12B1   DB.C.NIL      4B96    4B00
      OPS.C.NIL      9696    261E   STERM.C.N     BCB4    377E
      SET.C.NIL      F432     BCB   CSUPPORT.     FFFD    1861
      MACRO.C.N     1185E     36A   $HACKJOB.    11BC8     271
      _PROG.NIL     11E39      5D   _PROG.NIL    11E96     2DD
      _PROG.NIL     12173       0   _PROG.NIL    12173       0
      _PROG.NIL     12173       0   _PROG.NIL    12173     120
      INDEX.C.N     12293    27E9   RPAR.C.NI    14A7C    1D4B
      _PROG.NIL     167C7      6A   _PROG.NIL    16831     5DB
      _PROG.NIL     16E0C      15   NATION.C.    16E21     19C
      _PROG.NIL     16FBD      41   _PROG.NIL    16FFE      1D
      _PROG.NIL     1701B      6A   _PROG.NIL    17085      38
      _PROG.NIL     170BD      2E   _PROG.NIL    170EB      25
      _PROG.NIL     17110       0   _PROG.NIL    17110       0
      _PROG.NIL     17110     A59   _PROG.NIL    17B69      1B
      _PROG.NIL     17B84     12F   _PROG.NIL    17CB3      41
      _PROG.NIL     17CF4      2D   _PROG.NIL    17D21      1E
      _PROG.NIL     17D3F     456   _PROG.NIL    18195      9A
      _PROG.NIL     1822F      1D   _PROG.NIL    1824C      33
      _PROG.NIL     1827F      2D   _PROG.NIL    182AC      A8
      _PROG.NIL     18354       C   _PROG.NIL    18360       C
      _PROG.NIL     1836C      C4   _PROG.NIL    18430     41A
      _PROG.NIL     1884A     178   _PROG.NIL    189C2      92
```

```
  _PROG.NIL  18A54     4C   _PROG.NIL  18AA0     3C
  _PROG.NIL  18ADC     15   _PROG.NIL  18AF1    423
  _PROG.NIL  18F14    106   _PROG.NIL  1901A     A0
  _PROG.NIL  190BA     43   _PROG.NIL  190FD     AF
  _PROG.NIL  191AC     15   _PROG.NIL  191C1      0
  _PROG.NIL  191C1      E   _PROG.NIL  191CF     84
  _PROG.NIL  19253    164   _PROG.NIL  193B7     5B
  _PROG.NIL  19412    11F   _PROG.NIL  19531     F9
  _PROG.NIL  1962A     50   _PROG.NIL  1967A     24
  _PROG.NIL  1969E     20   _PROG.NIL  196BE     32
  _PROG.NIL  196F0    1A4   _PROG.NIL  19894      0
  _PROG.NIL  19894     21   _PROG.NIL  198B5     3E
  _PROG.NIL  198F3     58   _PROG.NIL  1994B    2CD
  _PROG.NIL  19C18     34   _PROG.NIL  19C4C    2AE
  _PROG.NIL  19EFA    241   _PROG.NIL  1A13B     A8
  _PROG.NIL  1A1E3    17F   _PROG.NIL  1A362      0
  _PROG.NIL  1A362      B   _PROG.NIL  1A36D     12
  _PROG.NIL  1A37F     1B   _PROG.NIL  1A39A     7B
  _PROG.NIL  1A415     9C   _PROG.NIL  1A4B1     34
  _PROG.NIL  1A4E5     EB   _PROG.NIL  1A5D0     2B
  _PROG.NIL  1A5FB     28   _PROG.NIL  1A623     6B
  _PROG.NIL  1A68E    125   _PROG.NIL  1A7B3     7C
  _PROG.NIL  1A82F     EA   $CONSTANT  1A920    E30
  $OVTB$.OV  1B750    128   OVDATA.OV  1B900    1EC
  OVCODE.OV  1BAF0    6B6

Section : Maddr=1C1B0, Msize=210, Daddr=1DDD0, Lev=1, Ovly#=1
    MOVEESC.N  1C1B0    161   $CONSTANT  1C320     A0

Section : Maddr=1C1B0, Msize=210, Daddr=1DFF0, Lev=1, Ovly#=2
    MOVETITL.  1C1B0    161   $CONSTANT  1C320     A0

Section : Maddr=1C1B0, Msize=820, Daddr=1E220, Lev=1, Ovly#=3
    FINISHED.  1C1B0    207   FINISHED_  1C3C0    208
    $CONSTANT  1C5D0    400

Section : Maddr=1C9D0, Msize=7A0, Daddr=1EA60, Lev=1, Ovly#=4
    MENUDRAW.  1C9D0    2A5   PROMPTNG.  1CC80    29C
    $CONSTANT  1CF20    110   $CONSTANT  1D030    140

Section : Maddr=1C9D0, Msize=340, Daddr=1F210, Lev=1, Ovly#=5
    MOVE_CUR.  1C9D0    25F   $CONSTANT  1CC30     E0

Section : Maddr=1C9D0, Msize=230, Daddr=1F560, Lev=1, Ovly#=6
    DRAWBOX.N  1C9D0    15A   $CONSTANT  1CB30     D0

Section : Maddr=1D170, Msize=6B0, Daddr=1F7A0, Lev=1, Ovly#=7
    MENUENTR.  1D170    3BD   $CONSTANT  1D530    2F0

Section : Maddr=1D170, Msize=4B0, Daddr=1FE60, Lev=1, Ovly#=8
    STARTOFF.  1D170    2BB   $CONSTANT  1D430    1F0

Section : Maddr=1D820, Msize=200, Daddr=20320, Lev=1, Ovly#=9
    BEGIN.NIL  1D820    136   $CONSTANT  1D960     C0
```

```
Section : Maddr=1DA20, Msize=41F0, Daddr=20DD0, Lev=0, Ovly#=10, Pre-Loaded

        $EXPR.$EX   1DA20     0   $EXPR.$EX   1DA20     0
        $EXPR.$EX   1DA20     0   $EXPR.$EX   1DA20    27
        $EXPR.$EX   1DA50    13   $EXPR.$EX   1DA70    26
        $EXPR.$EX   1DAA0     0   $EXPR.$EX   1DAA0     0
        $EXPR.$EX   1DAA0    39   $EXPR.$EX   1DAE0     0
        $EXPR.$EX   1DAE0     0   $MDATA.$M   1DAE0    B0
        $SYMSTART   1DB90     0   $SYMBOLS.   1DB90   260
        $SYMBOLS.   1DDF0    B0   $SYMBOLS.   1DEA0    B0
        $SYMBOLS.   1DF50   220   $SYMBOLS.   1E170   210
        $SYMBOLS.   1E380   240   $SYMBOLS.   1E5C0   150
        $SYMBOLS.   1E710    80   $SYMBOLS.   1E790   1B0
        $SYMBOLS.   1E940    50   $SYMBOLS.   1E990   140
        $SYMEND.$   1EAD0     2   DATA.DATA   1EAE0  2D70
        $LIB_TABL   21850   33C   STACK.DAT   21B90    80
```

All of the $CONSTANTs have been moved. The first went to the section of the map before the first overlay (that $CONSTANT is for GENMEN.OBJ). Each section in the overlay has the corresponding $CONSTANT size. The last address for the file is now 21B90 hex, or 138,128 bytes. This is a decrease in file size of 1296 bytes. Where the extra bytes went is easy to explain. By moving the $CONSTANT tables in with the overlay, the overlay increases by the size of the largest $CONSTANT map. The overlay, parsed by many sections, now has two basic parts: a part of memory to house the largest code module, and a part to house the largest constant module. Looking at the first overlay, the largest $CONSTANT table is FINISHED.OBJ. Therefore, the remaining two object files' constants size can fit inside the first one. With this approach the overlay module grows by about 1024 bytes, but the overall application saves about 212 bytes. A diagram of the memory scheme shows the following:

Overlay BEGIN	Code: 310 Constants: 192	511 bytes
Overlay MENUENTR STARTOFF	Code: 909 Constants: 752	1711 bytes
Overlay MENUDRAW+PROMPTNG Move_cur Drawbox	Code: 1345 Constants: 592	1951 bytes
Overlay MOVEESC MOVETITL FINISHED	Code: 1039 Constants: 1024	2079 bytes
Symbols/Expressions Clipper.lib Constants + Code of GENMEN		131,876 bytes

The topmost overlay size is (1DA20 - 1) - 1D820 hex, which is 1FF or 511 decimal. This is obviously bigger than the code size for BEGIN.OBJ. It is the combination of the code size and the constant size for BEGIN.OBJ, which is 520. Always allow for a small variance in the calculations. In the second overlay the largest code section is from MENUENTR.OBJ, as is the largest constant section. Using the same method for calculating the overlay size, we find that the overlay is roughly 1711 bytes, while the combined code and constant size for MENUENTR.OBJ is 1860. This is well within the range of tolerance. The total of all of the constant sizes from the files that are saved within the other constants' tables is:

FILE	BYTES
Startoff.obj	496
Drawbox.obj	208
Move_cur.obj	224
Movetitl.obj	106
Moveesc.obj	106
TOTAL................	1,140

This is very close to the difference between the first and second links.

Going back to the first example, look at the basic code sizes of the sections, remembering that the overlay size is based on the size of the largest code table in a section. If only some SECTION commands were issued, the overlay size would be based on the code size of the object file outside of the SECTION within the same overlay, plus the size of the largest SECTION's code size. However, in this example, look at the code size of the first overlay. Note that FINISHED.OBJ is the largest and the other two SECTIONs (MOVEESC.OBJ and MOVEESC.OBJ) can move in and out of the space set aside for FINISHED.OBJ.

Suppose we move FINISHED.OBJ down with MENUENTR.OBJ and STARTOFF.OBJ. First, the first overlay would decrease in size relative to the largest section code size. Since both remaining files (MOVEESC.OBJ and MOVETITL.OBJ) are the same in code size, their overlay would not establish room for either of their respective sizes. Looking at the overlay that now contains FINISHED.OBJ, we see that the size of MENUENTR.OBJ and FINISHED.OBJ are approximately equal in size. Therefore, in theory, the overlay should not be much bigger than it already is. Make sure that the object file being moved (FINISHED.OBJ) is not called by any of the other object files in other sections of the new overlay. Since in this case neither procedure MENUENTR nor procedure STARTOFF makes any calls to FINISHED, we can place FINISHED.OBJ in a separate section in this overlay. Looking at the link file we would see:

```
FI Genmen
MAP = Ten a
LIB \DBASE\Clipper
```

```
BEGIN
   SECTION FI Moveesc
   SECTION FI Movetitl
END
BEGIN
   SECTION FI Menudraw, Promptng
   SECTION FI Move_cur
   SECTION FI Drawbox
END
BEGIN
   SECTION FI Menuentr
   SECTION FI Startoff
   SECTION FI Finished
END
BEGIN
   SECTION FI Begin
END
```

Here is the map generated by this link:

```
Groups:

   Name         Address  Size  DSalloc
   DGROUP        1EDA0   3130

Segments:

   Section :  Maddr=0, Msize=1B3B0, Daddr=1C00, Lev=0, Ovly#=0

      Name          Addr   Size   Name          Addr   Size
      GENMEN.NIL       0    15F   CENTER.NI      160     3A
      SHORT.NIL      1A0     27   VERIFY.NI      1D0     6B
      PROCHEAD.      240     39   HELP.NIL       280    4A4
      DOITAGAIN      730     2E   CHAINA.NI      760     24
      CHAINB.NI      790     29   $START.NI      7C0     DF
      $INTERFAC      89F    6F4   $INTERFAC      F93     8B
      $DRIVERS.     101E    54F   EXEC.C.NI     156D   136B
      _PROG.NIL     28D8    1CA   NDEBUG.C.     2AA2      B
      SYMSYS.C.     2AAD    523   CTERM.C.N     2FD0    915
      STACK.C.N     38E5   12B1   DB.C.NIL      4B96   4B00
      OPS.C.NIL     9696   261E   STERM.C.N     BCB4   377E
      SET.C.NIL     F432    BCB   CSUPPORT.     FFFD   1861
      MACRO.C.N    1185E    36A   $HACKJOB.    11BC8    271
      _PROG.NIL    11E39     5D   _PROG.NIL    11E96    2DD
      _PROG.NIL    12173      0   _PROG.NIL    12173      0
      _PROG.NIL    12173      0   _PROG.NIL    12173    120
      INDEX.C.N    12293   27E9   RPAR.C.NI    14A7C   1D4B
      _PROG.NIL    167C7     6A   _PROG.NIL    16831    5DB
      _PROG.NIL    16E0C     15   NATION.C.    16E21    19C
      _PROG.NIL    16FBD     41   _PROG.NIL    16FFE     1D
      _PROG.NIL    1701B     6A   _PROG.NIL    17085     38
      _PROG.NIL    170BD     2E   _PROG.NIL    170EB     25
      _PROG.NIL    17110      0   _PROG.NIL    17110      0
```

```
    _PROG.NIL  17110    A59  _PROG.NIL  17B69     1B
    _PROG.NIL  17B84    12F  _PROG.NIL  17CB3     41
    _PROG.NIL  17CF4     2D  _PROG.NIL  17D21     1E
    _PROG.NIL  17D3F    456  _PROG.NIL  18195     9A
    _PROG.NIL  1822F     1D  _PROG.NIL  1824C     33
    _PROG.NIL  1827F     2D  _PROG.NIL  182AC     A8
    _PROG.NIL  18354      C  _PROG.NIL  18360      C
    _PROG.NIL  1836C     C4  _PROG.NIL  18430    41A
    _PROG.NIL  1884A    178  _PROG.NIL  189C2     92
    _PROG.NIL  18A54     4C  _PROG.NIL  18AA0     3C
    _PROG.NIL  18ADC     15  _PROG.NIL  18AF1    423
    _PROG.NIL  18F14    106  _PROG.NIL  1901A     A0
    _PROG.NIL  190BA     43  _PROG.NIL  190FD     AF
    _PROG.NIL  191AC     15  _PROG.NIL  191C1      0
    _PROG.NIL  191C1      E  _PROG.NIL  191CF     84
    _PROG.NIL  19253    164  _PROG.NIL  193B7     5B
    _PROG.NIL  19412    11F  _PROG.NIL  19531     F9
    _PROG.NIL  1962A     50  _PROG.NIL  1967A     24
    _PROG.NIL  1969E     20  _PROG.NIL  196BE     32
    _PROG.NIL  196F0    1A4  _PROG.NIL  19894      0
    _PROG.NIL  19894     21  _PROG.NIL  198B5     3E
    _PROG.NIL  198F3     58  _PROG.NIL  1994B    2CD
    _PROG.NIL  19C18     34  _PROG.NIL  19C4C    2AE
    _PROG.NIL  19EFA    241  _PROG.NIL  1A13B     A8
    _PROG.NIL  1A1E3    17F  _PROG.NIL  1A362      0
    _PROG.NIL  1A362      B  _PROG.NIL  1A36D     12
    _PROG.NIL  1A37F     1B  _PROG.NIL  1A39A     7B
    _PROG.NIL  1A415     9C  _PROG.NIL  1A4B1     34
    _PROG.NIL  1A4E5     EB  _PROG.NIL  1A5D0     2B
    _PROG.NIL  1A5FB     28  _PROG.NIL  1A623     6B
    _PROG.NIL  1A68E    125  _PROG.NIL  1A7B3     7C
    _PROG.NIL  1A82F     EA  $OVTB$.OV  1A920    128
    OVDATA.OV  1AB00    1EC  OVCODE.OV  1ACF0    6B6

Section :  Maddr=1B3B0, Msize=170, Daddr=1CFD0, Lev=1, Ovly#=1
    MOVEESC.N  1B3B0    161

Section :  Maddr=1B3B0, Msize=170, Daddr=1D150, Lev=1, Ovly#=2
    MOVETITL.  1B3B0    161

Section :  Maddr=1B520, Msize=550, Daddr=1D2E0, Lev=1, Ovly#=3
    MENUDRAW.  1B520    2A5  PROMPTNG.  1B7D0    29C

Section :  Maddr=1B520, Msize=260, Daddr=1D840, Lev=1, Ovly#=4
    MOVE_CUR.  1B520    25F

Section :  Maddr=1B520, Msize=160, Daddr=1DAB0, Lev=1, Ovly#=5
    DRAWBOX.N  1B520    15A

Section :  Maddr=1BA70, Msize=3C0, Daddr=1DC20, Lev=1, Ovly#=6
    MENUENTR.  1BA70    3BD

Section :  Maddr=1BA70, Msize=2C0, Daddr=1DFF0, Lev=1, Ovly#=7
    STARTOFF.  1BA70    2BB
```

```
Section :  Maddr=1BA70, Msize=420, Daddr=1E2D0, Lev=1, Ovly#=8
   FINISHED.  1BA70    207   FINISHED_   1BC80    208

Section :  Maddr=1BE90, Msize=140, Daddr=1E700, Lev=1, Ovly#=9
   BEGIN.NIL  1BE90    136

Section :  Maddr=1BFD0, Msize=5F00, Daddr=1F0F0, Lev=0, Ovly#=10, Pre-Loaded

   $EXPR.$EX  1BFD0      0   $EXPR.$EX   1BFD0      0
   $EXPR.$EX  1BFD0      0   $EXPR.$EX   1BFD0     13
   $EXPR.$EX  1BFF0     26   $EXPR.$EX   1C020      0
   $EXPR.$EX  1C020      0   $EXPR.$EX   1C020     39
   $EXPR.$EX  1C060      0   $EXPR.$EX   1C060     27
   $EXPR.$EX  1C090      0   $MDATA.$M   1C090     B0
   $SYMSTART  1C140      0   $SYMBOLS.   1C140    260
   $SYMBOLS.  1C3A0     B0   $SYMBOLS.   1C450     B0
   $SYMBOLS.  1C500    210   $SYMBOLS.   1C710    240
   $SYMBOLS.  1C950    150   $SYMBOLS.   1CAA0     80
   $SYMBOLS.  1CB20    1B0   $SYMBOLS.   1CCD0     50
   $SYMBOLS.  1CD20    220   $SYMBOLS.   1CF40    140
   $SYMEND.$  1D080      2   $CONSTANT   1D090    E30
   $CONSTANT  1DEC0     A0   $CONSTANT   1DF60     A0
   $CONSTANT  1E000    110   $CONSTANT   1E110    140
   $CONSTANT  1E250     E0   $CONSTANT   1E330     D0
   $CONSTANT  1E400    2F0   $CONSTANT   1E6F0    1F0
   $CONSTANT  1E8E0    400   $CONSTANT   1ECE0     C0
   DATA.DATA  1EDA0   2D70   $LIB_TABL   21B10    33C
   STACK.DAT  21E50     80
```

The diagram for this file is as follows:

Overlay BEGIN	319 bytes
Overlay MENUENTR STARTOFF FINISHED	1055 bytes
Overlay MENUDRAW + PROMPTING Move_cur Drawbox	1426 bytes
Overlay MOVEESC MOVETITL	367 bytes
Symbols/Expressions/Constants Clipper.lib Code: GENMEN	≈ 135,000 bytes

The difference between the two linked files is 592 bytes (take the last address points in each memory map, 220A0 and 21E50, and subtract the second from the first). The difference between the code size of FINISHED.OBJ and MOVEESC.OBJ (or

MOVETITL.OBJ) is roughly 691 bytes. The overlay now containing FINISHED.OBJ increased by 96 bytes. Subtract the 96 bytes gained from the 691 bytes saved and the net result is a total saving of 596 bytes. This shows that the space is being better utilized in this linking scheme than in the first.

If possible, keep similar sizes together in as many sections as necessary. However, remember that the linker will add bytes for each additional section and for each overlay. In many cases, when the code is broken down to many separate overlays or sections, the number of bytes added by the linker offsets the number of bytes saved by an elaborate linking scheme. Fortunately, this is not the case here. Above all, make sure that the sections in an overlay do not call any other section within the same overlay.

To finish this example, here is the LiNK file and memory map of the previous example with the additional command OVERLAY PROG, $CONSTANTS. The use of this command allows the constant tables to be out of the preload section and in their respective overlays. Since constants pertain only to the code used in the overlay, it is beneficial to do this. After looking at the command syntax, note the preceding memory map and the one following, especially the overlays and the preload section.

```
FI Genmen
MAP = Ten6 a
LIB \DBASE\Clipper
OVERLAY PROG, $CONSTANTS
BEGIN
   SECTION FI Moveesc
   SECTION FI Movetitl
END
BEGIN
   SECTION FI Menudraw, Promptng
   SECTION FI Move_cur
   SECTION FI Drawbox
END
BEGIN
   SECTION FI Menuentr
   SECTION FI Startoff
   SECTION FI Finished
END
BEGIN
   SECTION FI Begin
END
```

Once again, here is the memory map:

```
Groups:

  Name      Address  Size  DSalloc
  DGROUP     1E640   3130

Segments:
```

```
Section :  Maddr=0, Msize=1C1B0, Daddr=1C00, Lev=0, Ovly#=0

    Name          Addr    Size    Name          Addr    Size
    GENMEN.NIL       0     15F    CENTER.NI      160      3A
    SHORT.NIL      1A0      27    VERIFY.NI      1D0      6B
    PROCHEAD.      240      39    HELP.NIL       280     4A4
    DOITAGAIN      730      2E    CHAINA.NI      760      24
    CHAINB.NI      790      29    $START.NI      7C0      DF
    $INTERFAC      89F     6F4    $INTERFAC      F93      8B
    $DRIVERS.     101E     54F    EXEC.C.NI     156D    136B
    _PROG.NIL     28D8     1CA    NDEBUG.C.     2AA2       B
    SYMSYS.C.     2AAD     523    CTERM.C.N     2FD0     915
    STACK.C.N     38E5    12B1    DB.C.NIL      4B96    4B00
    OPS.C.NIL     9696    261E    STERM.C.N     BCB4    377E
    SET.C.NIL     F432     BCB    CSUPPORT.     FFFD    1861
    MACRO.C.N    1185E     36A    $HACKJOB.    11BC8     271
    _PROG.NIL    11E39      5D    _PROG.NIL    11E96     2DD
    _PROG.NIL    12173       0    _PROG.NIL    12173       0
    _PROG.NIL    12173       0    _PROG.NIL    12173     120
    INDEX.C.N    12293    27E9    RPAR.C.NI    14A7C    1D4B
    _PROG.NIL    167C7      6A    _PROG.NIL    16831     5DB
    _PROG.NIL    16E0C      15    NATION.C.    16E21     19C
    _PROG.NIL    16FBD      41    _PROG.NIL    16FFE      1D
    _PROG.NIL    1701B      6A    _PROG.NIL    17085      38
    _PROG.NIL    170BD      2E    _PROG.NIL    170EB      25
    _PROG.NIL    17110       0    _PROG.NIL    17110       0
    _PROG.NIL    17110     A59    _PROG.NIL    17B69      1B
    _PROG.NIL    17B84     12F    _PROG.NIL    17CB3      41
    _PROG.NIL    17CF4      2D    _PROG.NIL    17D21      1E
    _PROG.NIL    17D3F     456    _PROG.NIL    18195      9A
    _PROG.NIL    1822F      1D    _PROG.NIL    1824C      33
    _PROG.NIL    1827F      2D    _PROG.NIL    182AC      A8
    _PROG.NIL    18354       C    _PROG.NIL    18360       C
    _PROG.NIL    1836C      C4    _PROG.NIL    18430     41A
    _PROG.NIL    1884A     178    _PROG.NIL    189C2      92
    _PROG.NIL    18A54      4C    _PROG.NIL    18AA0      3C
    _PROG.NIL    18ADC      15    _PROG.NIL    18AF1     423
    _PROG.NIL    18F14     106    _PROG.NIL    1901A      A0
    _PROG.NIL    190BA      43    _PROG.NIL    190FD      AF
    _PROG.NIL    191AC      15    _PROG.NIL    191C1       0
    _PROG.NIL    191C1       E    _PROG.NIL    191CF      84
    _PROG.NIL    19253     164    _PROG.NIL    193B7      5B
    _PROG.NIL    19412     11F    _PROG.NIL    19531      F9
    _PROG.NIL    1962A      50    _PROG.NIL    1967A      24
    _PROG.NIL    1969E      20    _PROG.NIL    196BE      32
    _PROG.NIL    196F0     1A4    _PROG.NIL    19894       0
    _PROG.NIL    19894      21    _PROG.NIL    198B5      3E
    _PROG.NIL    198F3      58    _PROG.NIL    1994B     2CD
    _PROG.NIL    19C18      34    _PROG.NIL    19C4C     2AE
    _PROG.NIL    19EFA     241    _PROG.NIL    1A13B      A8
    _PROG.NIL    1A1E3     17F    _PROG.NIL    1A362       0
    _PROG.NIL    1A362       B    _PROG.NIL    1A36D      12
    _PROG.NIL    1A37F      1B    _PROG.NIL    1A39A      7B
```

```
    _PROG.NIL  1A415    9C  _PROG.NIL  1A4B1    34
    _PROG.NIL  1A4E5    EB  _PROG.NIL  1A5D0    2B
    _PROG.NIL  1A5FB    28  _PROG.NIL  1A623    6B
    _PROG.NIL  1A68E   125  _PROG.NIL  1A7B3    7C
    _PROG.NIL  1A82F    EA  $CONSTANT  1A920   E30
    $OVTB$.OV  1B750   128  OVDATA.OV  1B900   1EC
    OVCODE.OV  1BAF0   6B6

Section :  Maddr=1C1B0, Msize=210, Daddr=1DDD0, Lev=1, Ovly#=1
    MOVEESC.N  1C1B0   161  $CONSTANT  1C320    A0

Section :  Maddr=1C1B0, Msize=210, Daddr=1DFF0, Lev=1, Ovly#=2
    MOVETITL.  1C1B0   161  $CONSTANT  1C320    A0

Section :  Maddr=1C3C0, Msize=7A0, Daddr=1E220, Lev=1, Ovly#=3
    MENUDRAW.  1C3C0   2A5  PROMPTNG.  1C670   29C
    $CONSTANT  1C910   110  $CONSTANT  1CA20   140

Section :  Maddr=1C3C0, Msize=340, Daddr=1E9D0, Lev=1, Ovly#=4
    MOVE_CUR.  1C3C0   25F  $CONSTANT  1C620    E0

Section :  Maddr=1C3C0, Msize=230, Daddr=1ED20, Lev=1, Ovly#=5
    DRAWBOX.N  1C3C0   15A  $CONSTANT  1C520    D0

Section :  Maddr=1CB60, Msize=6B0, Daddr=1EF60, Lev=1, Ovly#=6
    MENUENTR.  1CB60   3BD  $CONSTANT  1CF20   2F0

Section :  Maddr=1CB60, Msize=4B0, Daddr=1F620, Lev=1, Ovly#=7
    STARTOFF.  1CB60   2BB  $CONSTANT  1CE20   1F0

Section :  Maddr=1CB60, Msize=820, Daddr=1FAF0, Lev=1, Ovly#=8
    FINISHED.  1CB60   207  FINISHED_  1CD70   208
    $CONSTANT  1CF80   400

Section :  Maddr=1D380, Msize=200, Daddr=20320, Lev=1, Ovly#=9
    BEGIN.NIL  1D380   136  $CONSTANT  1D4C0    C0

Section :  Maddr=1D580, Msize=41F0, Daddr=20DD0, Lev=0, Ovly#=10, Pre-Loaded

    $EXPR.$EX  1D580     0  $EXPR.$EX  1D580     0
    $EXPR.$EX  1D580     0  $EXPR.$EX  1D580    13
    $EXPR.$EX  1D5A0    26  $EXPR.$EX  1D5D0     0
    $EXPR.$EX  1D5D0     0  $EXPR.$EX  1D5D0    39
    $EXPR.$EX  1D610     0  $EXPR.$EX  1D610    27
    $EXPR.$EX  1D640     0  $MDATA.$M  1D640    B0
    $SYMSTART  1D6F0     0  $SYMBOLS.  1D6F0   260
    $SYMBOLS.  1D950    B0  $SYMBOLS.  1DA00    B0
    $SYMBOLS.  1DAB0   210  $SYMBOLS.  1DCC0   240
    $SYMBOLS.  1DF00   150  $SYMBOLS.  1E050    80
    $SYMBOLS.  1E0D0   1B0  $SYMBOLS.  1E280    50
    $SYMBOLS.  1E2D0   220  $SYMBOLS.  1E4F0   140
    $SYMEND.$  1E630     2  DATA.DATA  1E640  2D70
    $LIB_TABL  213B0   33C  STACK.DAT  216F0    80
```

The basic load size is 216F0 hex, or 136,994 bytes, or 134K when Plink86 is finished linking.

The remaining modules in the preload section of the file ($SYMBOLS and $EXPR) cannot be added to the OVERLAY PROG command, or the program would no longer function. One of the reasons $SYMBOLS cannot be moved is that once a program starts up, if there is a symbol that connects it to another symbol (e.g., DO Proca) and that connecting symbol has no reference point in the preload but is now in the overlay, the program stops running. This is similar to giving someone an outdated roadmap when important landmarks have been moved. The programs stop running because they get lost, and you are forced to start again. Other than $CONSTANTS, nothing should be moved out of the preloaded section of the file into the overlays.

NESTING OVERLAYS

There are two reasons for nesting overlays. First, with multiple overlay areas, extra memory is sometimes wasted because each overlay sits on top of the previous overlay area. Second, space is often wasted inside an overlay because it has smaller sections. A nested overlay may be able to reside in that empty area, thus filling up space set aside for other assigned sections and overlays.

The problem with nesting overlays lies in the SECTION command. Suppose we look at the same layout of files that we had in the previous example. The use of the SECTION command allows object files to be moved in and out of the same overlay area. If a file in a nested overlay branches off a SECTIONed file in a lower-level overlay and a call is made to a lower-level SECTIONed file, major problems will occur. The following examples will show the problems involved, the advantages of nesting overlays, and the ultimate solution. First, look at the following two LiNK files and note the advantages each has over nonnested overlay files, as well as over one another.

Example 1:

```
FI Genmen
MAP = Ten7 a
LIB \DBASE\Clipper
BEGIN
   SECTION FI Menuentr
   SECTION FI Finished
   SECTION FI Startoff
   BEGIN
      SECTION FI Menudraw, Promptng
      SECTION FI Move_cur
      SECTION FI Drawbox
      BEGIN
         SECTION FI Moveesc
         SECTION FI Movetitl
         BEGIN
```

```
            SECTION FI Begin
         END
      END
   END
END
```

The following is the memory map:

```
Groups:

    Name        Address  Size  DSalloc
    DGROUP       1E990   3130

Segments:

    Section :  Maddr=0, Msize=1B3B0, Daddr=1C00, Lev=0, Ovly#=0

        Name          Addr    Size  Name          Addr   Size
        GENMEN.NIL       0     15F  CENTER.NI      160     3A
        SHORT.NIL      1A0      27  VERIFY.NI      1D0     6B
        PROCHEAD.      240      39  HELP.NIL       280    4A4
        DOITAGAIN      730      2E  CHAINA.NI      760     24
        CHAINB.NI      790      29  $START.NI      7C0     DF
        $INTERFAC      89F     6F4  $INTERFAC      F93     8B
        $DRIVERS.     101E     54F  EXEC.C.NI     156D   136B
        _PROG.NIL     28D8     1CA  NDEBUG.C.     2AA2      B
        SYMSYS.C.     2AAD     523  CTERM.C.N     2FD0    915
        STACK.C.N     38E5    12B1  DB.C.NIL      4B96   4B00
        OPS.C.NIL     9696    261E  STERM.C.N     BCB4   377E
        SET.C.NIL     F432     BCB  CSUPPORT.     FFFD   1861
        MACRO.C.N    1185E     36A  $HACKJOB.    11BC8    271
        _PROG.NIL    11E39      5D  _PROG.NIL    11E96    2DD
        _PROG.NIL    12173       0  _PROG.NIL    12173      0
        _PROG.NIL    12173       0  _PROG.NIL    12173    120
        INDEX.C.N    12293    27E9  RPAR.C.NI    14A7C   1D4B
        _PROG.NIL    167C7      6A  _PROG.NIL    16831    5DB
        _PROG.NIL    16E0C      15  NATION.C.    16E21    19C
        _PROG.NIL    16FBD      41  _PROG.NIL    16FFE     1D
        _PROG.NIL    1701B      6A  _PROG.NIL    17085     38
        _PROG.NIL    170BD      2E  _PROG.NIL    170EB     25
        _PROG.NIL    17110       0  _PROG.NIL    17110      0
        _PROG.NIL    17110     A59  _PROG.NIL    17B69     1B
        _PROG.NIL    17B84     12F  _PROG.NIL    17CB3     41
        _PROG.NIL    17CF4      2D  _PROG.NIL    17D21     1E
        _PROG.NIL    17D3F     456  _PROG.NIL    18195     9A
        _PROG.NIL    1822F      1D  _PROG.NIL    1824C     33
        _PROG.NIL    1827F      2D  _PROG.NIL    182AC     A8
        _PROG.NIL    18354       C  _PROG.NIL    18360      C
        _PROG.NIL    1836C      C4  _PROG.NIL    18430    41A
        _PROG.NIL    1884A     178  _PROG.NIL    189C2     92
        _PROG.NIL    18A54      4C  _PROG.NIL    18AA0     3C
        _PROG.NIL    18ADC      15  _PROG.NIL    18AF1    423
        _PROG.NIL    18F14     106  _PROG.NIL    1901A     A0
```

```
      _PROG.NIL   190BA      43   _PROG.NIL   190FD      AF
      _PROG.NIL   191AC      15   _PROG.NIL   191C1       0
      _PROG.NIL   191C1       E   _PROG.NIL   191CF      84
      _PROG.NIL   19253     164   _PROG.NIL   193B7      5B
      _PROG.NIL   19412     11F   _PROG.NIL   19531      F9
      _PROG.NIL   1962A      50   _PROG.NIL   1967A      24
      _PROG.NIL   1969E      20   _PROG.NIL   196BE      32
      _PROG.NIL   196F0     1A4   _PROG.NIL   19894       0
      _PROG.NIL   19894      21   _PROG.NIL   198B5      3E
      _PROG.NIL   198F3      58   _PROG.NIL   1994B     2CD
      _PROG.NIL   19C18      34   _PROG.NIL   19C4C     2AE
      _PROG.NIL   19EFA     241   _PROG.NIL   1A13B      A8
      _PROG.NIL   1A1E3     17F   _PROG.NIL   1A362       0
      _PROG.NIL   1A362       B   _PROG.NIL   1A36D      12
      _PROG.NIL   1A37F      1B   _PROG.NIL   1A39A      7B
      _PROG.NIL   1A415      9C   _PROG.NIL   1A4B1      34
      _PROG.NIL   1A4E5      EB   _PROG.NIL   1A5D0      2B
      _PROG.NIL   1A5FB      28   _PROG.NIL   1A623      6B
      _PROG.NIL   1A68E     125   _PROG.NIL   1A7B3      7C
      _PROG.NIL   1A82F      EA   $OVTB$.OV   1A920     128
      OVDATA.OV   1AB00     1EC   OVCODE.OV   1ACF0     6B6

Section :  Maddr=1B3B0, Msize=3C0, Daddr=1CFD0, Lev=1, Ovly#=1
    MENUENTR.  1B3B0    3BD

Section :  Maddr=1B3B0, Msize=420, Daddr=1D3B0, Lev=1, Ovly#=2
    FINISHED.  1B3B0    207   FINISHED_  1B5C0    208

Section :  Maddr=1B3B0, Msize=2C0, Daddr=1D7E0, Lev=1, Ovly#=3
    STARTOFF.  1B3B0    2BB

Section :  Maddr=1B670, Msize=550, Daddr=1DAC0, Lev=2, Ovly#=4
    MENUDRAW.  1B670    2A5   PROMPTNG.  1B920    29C

Section :  Maddr=1B670, Msize=260, Daddr=1E020, Lev=2, Ovly#=5
    MOVE_CUR.  1B670    25F

Section :  Maddr=1B670, Msize=160, Daddr=1E290, Lev=2, Ovly#=6
    DRAWBOX.N  1B670    15A

Section :  Maddr=1B7D0, Msize=170, Daddr=1E400, Lev=3, Ovly#=7
    MOVEESC.N  1B7D0    161

Section :  Maddr=1B7D0, Msize=170, Daddr=1E580, Lev=3, Ovly#=8
    MOVETITL.  1B7D0    161

Section :  Maddr=1B940, Msize=140, Daddr=1E700, Lev=4, Ovly#=9
    BEGIN.NIL  1B940    136

Section :  Maddr=1BBC0, Msize=5F00, Daddr=1F0F0, Lev=0, Ovly#=10, Pre-Loaded

    $EXPR.$EX  1BBC0      0   $EXPR.$EX  1BBC0     39
    $EXPR.$EX  1BC00     27   $EXPR.$EX  1BC30      0
```

```
$EXPR.$EX   1BC30     13   $EXPR.$EX   1BC50     26
$EXPR.$EX   1BC80      0   $EXPR.$EX   1BC80      0
$EXPR.$EX   1BC80      0   $EXPR.$EX   1BC80      0
$EXPR.$EX   1BC80      0   $MDATA.$M   1BC80     B0
$SYMSTART   1BD30      0   $SYMBOLS.   1BD30    260
$SYMBOLS.   1BF90    1B0   $SYMBOLS.   1C140    220
$SYMBOLS.   1C360     50   $SYMBOLS.   1C3B0    210
$SYMBOLS.   1C5C0    240   $SYMBOLS.   1C800    150
$SYMBOLS.   1C950     80   $SYMBOLS.   1C9D0     B0
$SYMBOLS.   1CA80     B0   $SYMBOLS.   1CB30    140
$SYMEND.$   1CC70      2   $CONSTANT   1CC80    E30
$CONSTANT   1DAB0    2F0   $CONSTANT   1DDA0    400
$CONSTANT   1E1A0    1F0   $CONSTANT   1E390    110
$CONSTANT   1E4A0    140   $CONSTANT   1E5E0     E0
$CONSTANT   1E6C0     D0   $CONSTANT   1E790     A0
$CONSTANT   1E830     A0   $CONSTANT   1E8D0     C0
DATA.DATA   1E990   2D70   $LIB_TABL   21700    33C
STACK.DAT   21A40     80
```

This example's basic load size is 21A40 or 137,792 bytes. The basic rule to follow is that the code size of a nested overlay is added to the basic code size of the file or section from which the nested overlay branched. Using this LiNK file, the code size of BEGIN.OBJ is added to that of MOVETITL.OBJ. To determine the size of the overlay area in which MOVETITL.OBJ resides, compare the two sections. When MOVETITL.OBJ is called, BEGIN.OBJ is included and the two of them are bigger than MOVEESC.OBJ. Some loading time is also saved. Whenever BEGIN.OBJ is in operation, MOVETITL.OBJ is ready to be executed in memory. If BEGIN did in fact call upon MOVETITL, the computer would not have to load another module or take any extra time to execute.

To get a better understanding of how nested overlay areas work and the amount of space taken by the main overlay, let's review a memory diagram of the overlay scheme.

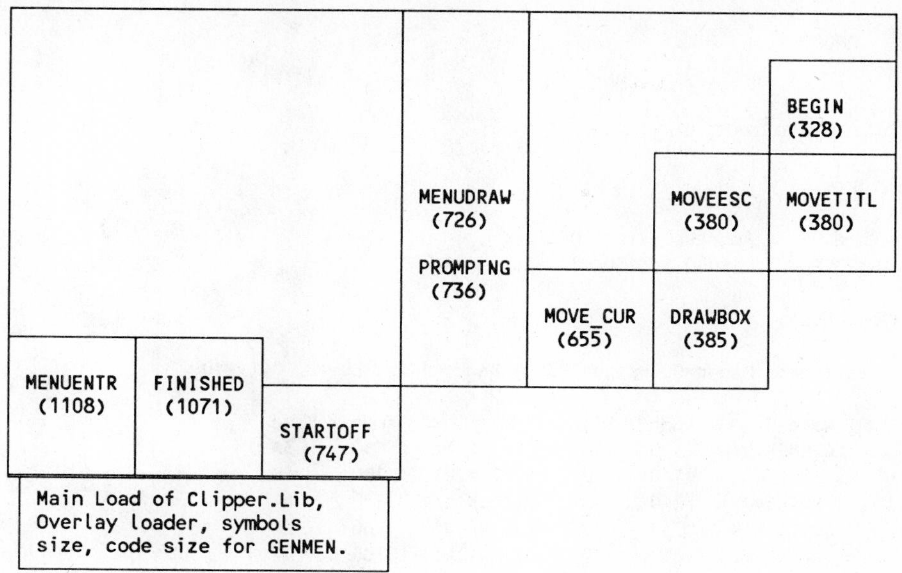

The size of the overlay is determined by the size of STARTOFF, MENUDRAW, and PROMPTNG: approximately 2209 bytes. If we turn to the memory map, the relative address points for the overlay area are approximately 2063 bytes. This difference is attributable to the linker's ability to condense and consolidate the various tables. Notice that regardless of the size of any other overlay or sectioned area, the entire overlay is based upon the size of STARTOFF, MENUDRAW, and PROMPTNG. It is evident that there is wasted space. It is possible to move the order of object files in the LiNK file to increase the SECTION sizes, even those SECTIONS with branch-off overlays. To get a better understanding of this, study the following LiNK and map files, comparing them with the previous ones.

```
FI Genmen
MAP = Ten8 a
LIB \DBASE\Clipper
BEGIN
   SECTION FI Startoff
   SECTION FI Finished
   SECTION FI Menuentr
   BEGIN
      SECTION FI Drawbox
      SECTION FI Move_cur
      SECTION FI Menudraw, Promptng
      BEGIN
         SECTION FI Moveesc
         SECTION FI Movetitl
         BEGIN
            SECTION FI Begin
         END
```

```
      END
   END
END
```

And this is the memory map:

```
Groups:

 Name        Address  Size  DSalloc
 DGROUP       1ED40   3130

Segments:

 Section :  Maddr=0, Msize=1B3B0, Daddr=1C00, Lev=0, Ovly#=0

     Name          Addr    Size   Name          Addr   Size
     GENMEN.NIL       0     15F   CENTER.NI      160     3A
     SHORT.NIL      1A0      27   VERIFY.NI      1D0     6B
     PROCHEAD.      240      39   HELP.NIL       280    4A4
     DOITAGAIN      730      2E   CHAINA.NI      760     24
     CHAINB.NI      790      29   $START.NI      7C0     DF
     $INTERFAC      89F     6F4   $INTERFAC      F93     8B
     $DRIVERS.     101E     54F   EXEC.C.NI     156D   136B
     _PROG.NIL     28D8     1CA   NDEBUG.C.     2AA2      B
     SYMSYS.C.     2AAD     523   CTERM.C.N     2FD0    915
     STACK.C.N     38E5    12B1   DB.C.NIL      4B96   4B00
     OPS.C.NIL     9696    261E   STERM.C.N     BCB4   377E
     SET.C.NIL     F432     BCB   CSUPPORT.     FFFD   1861
     MACRO.C.N    1185E     36A   $HACKJOB.    11BC8    271
     _PROG.NIL    11E39      5D   _PROG.NIL    11E96    2DD
     _PROG.NIL    12173       0   _PROG.NIL    12173      0
     _PROG.NIL    12173       0   _PROG.NIL    12173    120
     INDEX.C.N    12293    27E9   RPAR.C.NI    14A7C   1D4B
     _PROG.NIL    167C7      6A   _PROG.NIL    16831    5DB
     _PROG.NIL    16E0C      15   NATION.C.    16E21    19C
     _PROG.NIL    16FBD      41   _PROG.NIL    16FFE     1D
     _PROG.NIL    1701B      6A   _PROG.NIL    17085     38
     _PROG.NIL    170BD      2E   _PROG.NIL    170EB     25
     _PROG.NIL    17110       0   _PROG.NIL    17110      0
     _PROG.NIL    17110     A59   _PROG.NIL    17B69     1B
     _PROG.NIL    17B84     12F   _PROG.NIL    17CB3     41
     _PROG.NIL    17CF4      2D   _PROG.NIL    17D21     1E
     _PROG.NIL    17D3F     456   _PROG.NIL    18195     9A
     _PROG.NIL    1822F      1D   _PROG.NIL    1824C     33
     _PROG.NIL    1827F      2D   _PROG.NIL    182AC     A8
     _PROG.NIL    18354       C   _PROG.NIL    18360      C
     _PROG.NIL    1836C      C4   _PROG.NIL    18430    41A
     _PROG.NIL    1884A     178   _PROG.NIL    189C2     92
     _PROG.NIL    18A54      4C   _PROG.NIL    18AA0     3C
     _PROG.NIL    18ADC      15   _PROG.NIL    18AF1    423
     _PROG.NIL    18F14     106   _PROG.NIL    1901A     A0
     _PROG.NIL    190BA      43   _PROG.NIL    190FD     AF
     _PROG.NIL    191AC      15   _PROG.NIL    191C1      0
```

```
   _PROG.NIL  191C1      E   _PROG.NIL  191CF      84
   _PROG.NIL  19253    164   _PROG.NIL  193B7      5B
   _PROG.NIL  19412    11F   _PROG.NIL  19531      F9
   _PROG.NIL  1962A     50   _PROG.NIL  1967A      24
   _PROG.NIL  1969E     20   _PROG.NIL  196BE      32
   _PROG.NIL  196F0    1A4   _PROG.NIL  19894       0
   _PROG.NIL  19894     21   _PROG.NIL  198B5      3E
   _PROG.NIL  198F3     58   _PROG.NIL  1994B     2CD
   _PROG.NIL  19C18     34   _PROG.NIL  19C4C     2AE
   _PROG.NIL  19EFA    241   _PROG.NIL  1A13B      A8
   _PROG.NIL  1A1E3    17F   _PROG.NIL  1A362       0
   _PROG.NIL  1A362      B   _PROG.NIL  1A36D      12
   _PROG.NIL  1A37F     1B   _PROG.NIL  1A39A      7B
   _PROG.NIL  1A415     9C   _PROG.NIL  1A4B1      34
   _PROG.NIL  1A4E5     EB   _PROG.NIL  1A5D0      2B
   _PROG.NIL  1A5FB     28   _PROG.NIL  1A623      6B
   _PROG.NIL  1A68E    125   _PROG.NIL  1A7B3      7C
   _PROG.NIL  1A82F     EA   $OVTB$.OV  1A920     128
   OVDATA.OV  1AB00    1EC   OVCODE.OV  1ACF0     6B6

Section :  Maddr=1B3B0, Msize=2C0, Daddr=1CFD0, Lev=1, Ovly#=1
    STARTOFF.  1B3B0    2BB

Section :  Maddr=1B3B0, Msize=420, Daddr=1D2B0, Lev=1, Ovly#=2
    FINISHED.  1B3B0    207   FINISHED_  1B5C0    208

Section :  Maddr=1B3B0, Msize=3C0, Daddr=1D6E0, Lev=1, Ovly#=3
    MENUENTR.  1B3B0    3BD

Section :  Maddr=1B770, Msize=160, Daddr=1DAB0, Lev=2, Ovly#=4
    DRAWBOX.N  1B770    15A

Section :  Maddr=1B770, Msize=260, Daddr=1DC20, Lev=2, Ovly#=5
    MOVE_CUR.  1B770    25F

Section :  Maddr=1B770, Msize=550, Daddr=1DEA0, Lev=2, Ovly#=6
    MENUDRAW.  1B770    2A5   PROMPTNG.  1BA20    29C

Section :  Maddr=1BCC0, Msize=170, Daddr=1E400, Lev=3, Ovly#=7
    MOVEESC.N  1BCC0    161

Section :  Maddr=1BCC0, Msize=170, Daddr=1E580, Lev=3, Ovly#=8
    MOVETITL.  1BCC0    161

Section :  Maddr=1BE30, Msize=140, Daddr=1E700, Lev=4, Ovly#=9
    BEGIN.NIL  1BE30    136

Section :  Maddr=1BF70, Msize=5F00, Daddr=1F0F0, Lev=0, Ovly#=10, Pre-Loaded

    $EXPR.$EX  1BF70      0   $EXPR.$EX  1BF70       0
    $EXPR.$EX  1BF70     27   $EXPR.$EX  1BFA0      39
    $EXPR.$EX  1BFE0      0   $EXPR.$EX  1BFE0       0
    $EXPR.$EX  1BFE0     13   $EXPR.$EX  1C000      26
```

```
$EXPR.$EX   1C030     0   $EXPR.$EX   1C030     0
$EXPR.$EX   1C030     0   $MDATA.$M   1C030    B0
$SYMSTART   1C0E0     0   $SYMBOLS.   1C0E0   260
$SYMBOLS.   1C340    50   $SYMBOLS.   1C390   220
$SYMBOLS.   1C5B0   1B0   $SYMBOLS.   1C760    80
$SYMBOLS.   1C7E0   150   $SYMBOLS.   1C930   210
$SYMBOLS.   1CB40   240   $SYMBOLS.   1CD80    B0
$SYMBOLS.   1CE30    B0   $SYMBOLS.   1CEE0   140
$SYMEND.$   1D020     2   $CONSTANT   1D030   E30
$CONSTANT   1DE60   1F0   $CONSTANT   1E050   400
$CONSTANT   1E450   2F0   $CONSTANT   1E740    D0
$CONSTANT   1E810    E0   $CONSTANT   1E8F0   110
$CONSTANT   1EA00   140   $CONSTANT   1EB40    A0
$CONSTANT   1EBE0    A0   $CONSTANT   1EC80    C0
DATA.DATA   1ED40  2D70   $LIB_TABL   21AB0   33C
STACK.DAT   21DF0    80
```

Based on the ending address points, the link file is approximately 944 bytes larger. Looking at the link file and the resulting diagram, it is easy to see where the increase took place.

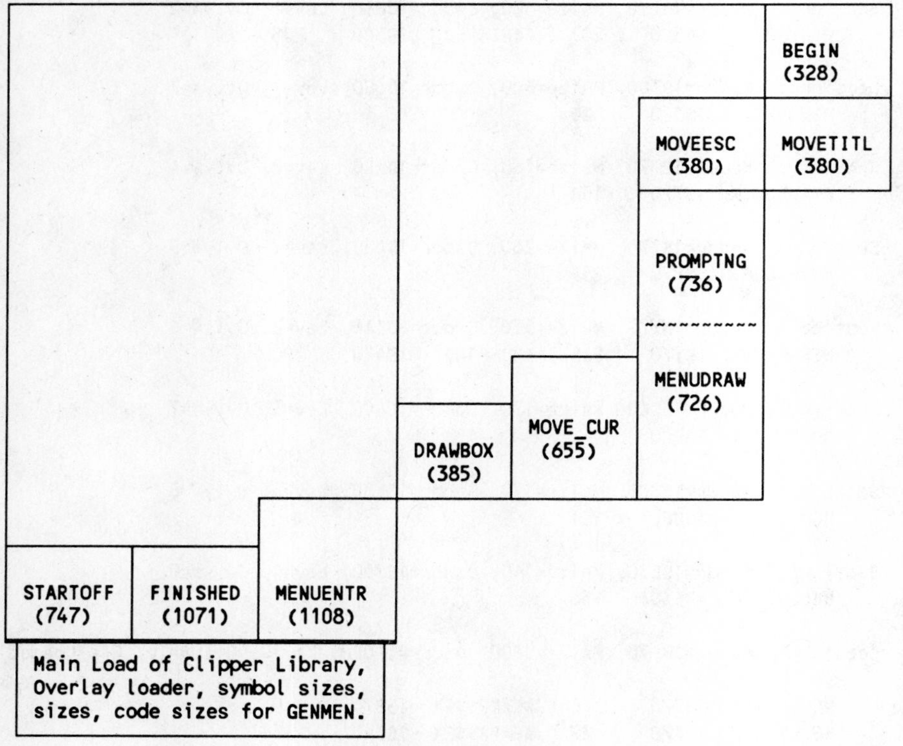

The overlay size is based upon the combined sizes of five files: MENUENTR, MENUDRAW, PROMPTNG, MOVETITL, and BEGIN. The combined code size is 3278 bytes. The increase in size, using this LiNK file instead of the previous LiNK file, is roughly 1069 bytes. Compared with the figure generated by the linker, this makes sense. Notice that just a few files were changed in order, not in content. The result was a general increase in the size of the overlay file. Even though this link is still just 135K, it can be made smaller. Of course, both LiNK files can be decreased in size with the addition of the OVERLAY PROG, $CONSTANTS command.

There is one problem with this linking method. If this program is run as linked, an EXEC SEQUENCE ERROR will occur. As stated before, files in one SECTION within the same overlay cannot call files from other SECTIONs. The LiNK file and the map diagram relating to the flow of operation indicate that immediately after GENMEN starts, BEGIN is called. Once BEGIN is called and loaded, STARTOFF, DRAWBOX, and MOVETITL are also loaded. After BEGIN executes, the flow branches either to STARTOFF or to MENUENTR. If the files are not present, STARTOFF is called. This is no problem because STARTOFF is loaded in with BEGIN. However, if the database files are present and STARTOFF is skipped, MENUENTR is called. This presents a major problem. Even though BEGIN is calling MENUENTR, BEGIN resides with STARTOFF. This means that in essence STARTOFF is calling MENUENTR, leading to the EXEC SEQUENCE ERROR.

Nesting overlays depends on the method of compiling or program calling used, especially if the SECTION command is used in conjunction with them. Be careful! Many problems can occur other than an EXEC SEQUENCE ERROR. For example, memory variables can get lost, resulting in UNDEFINED VARIABLES or TYPE CONFLICT errors. The program can just stop executing and the cursor will hang in the upper left corner of the screen.

One point should be made clear. Nesting overlays is only advantageous when (1) there is a clear route to and from programs, (2) recursive program calling is not utilized, and (3) the SECTION command is used at the highest level in the program. If several files have been compiled, labeled A through F, and files A, B, and C all require file D, a possible LiNK option would be:

```
BEGIN
   FILE D
   BEGIN
      SECTION FILE A
      SECTION FILE B
      SECTION FILE C
   END
   SECTION FILE E
   SECTION FILE F
END
```

The constraints for this linkage are as follows:

1. Files A, B, and C cannot call one another, nor can they call on Files E and F.

2. Files A, B, and C all require File D to be loaded in order to execute properly.

3. The size of the overlay is determined by one of the following:

   a. D + E
   b. D + F
   c. D + the largest section in the nested overlay (A, B, or C). Notice that file D is included in all calculations. You may choose to SECTION file D, which would alter the calculations as follows;

      i. E
      ii. F
      iii. D + the largest section in the nested overlay (A, B, or C)

4. All files are called from the main load file that is not shown in the LiNK file.

Nesting overlays can be quite useful because there is extra code added to the executable file that handles each and every overlay. The amount added is less for nested overlays than for multiple overlays. Unnested overlays sit on top of one another, while nested overlays reside in one large overlay. The same module should not be placed into two different overlays. By nesting overlays, you can "factor out" duplicate routines without having to place them in the main load module.

EXTERNAL OVERLAYS

As with internal overlays, external overlays are used in order to save space, both in memory and on disk. The only advantage external overlays have over internal overlays is that all relative code (or constant) information is placed on the disk and removed from the .EXE file. This does not mean that the amount of RAM memory decreases, just the actual file size. The main program still needs to partition the proper memory area to hold the overlay as it comes in and out of RAM.

The disadvantage of external overlays is protection. For example, an overlay file may be copied improperly to the disk drive or may be accidentally erased. Both examples are impossible with internal overlays because all overlays reside within the executable file. The overlays may not actually be loaded from the disk drive, as would be expected with external overlays. At least with internal overlays, a file will always be intact.

The only time it is imperative to use external overlays is when disk file size is paramount. Since with internal overlays, the code resides within the executable file, the .EXE file may grow to an astronomical size. The executable file may even become larger than 360K. In order to transfer the file from one machine to another, in such a case, the external overlay scheme is vital. Here are some examples to show how external overlays actually work.

First, let's review briefly the LiNK files to be used for the comparison.

```
Internal Overlay:                     External Overlay:

FI Genmen                              FI Genmen
MAP = Two a                           MAP = Two a
LIB \DBASE\Clipper                    LIB \DBASE\Clipper
BEGIN                                 BEGIN
  SECTION FI Startoff                    SECTION INTO Cmenover FI Startoff
  SECTION FI Begin                       SECTION INTO Cmenover FI Begin
  SECTION FI Promptng                    SECTION INTO Cmenover FI Promptng
  SECTION FI Menuentr                    SECTION INTO Cmenover FI Menuentr
  SECTION FI Menudraw                    SECTION INTO Cmenover FI Menudraw
  SECTION FI Move_cur                    SECTION INTO Cmenover FI Move_cur
  SECTION FI Drawbox                     SECTION INTO Cmenover FI Drawbox
  SECTION FI Movetitl                    SECTION INTO Cmenover FI Movetitl
  SECTION FI Moveesc                     SECTION INTO Cmenover FI Moveesc
  SECTION FI Finished                    SECTION INTO Cmenover FI Finished
END                                   END
```

Each "INTO <filename>" clause places the code tables for the object files in the external overlay. The filename "Cmenover" entered may be up to eight characters long and will have a file extension, .OVL, which denotes that the file is an overlay file. The following is a directory stamp of the overlay generated by the linker.

```
C>dir *.ovl

 Volume in drive C has no label
 Directory of  C:\FW\WORK

CMENOVER OVL      6272   5-12-86   3:58p
        1 File(s)  12718080 bytes free
```

The total of the code table sizes of the object modules involved with the overlay file is a relative code size of 6516 bytes. Allowing for the linker to condense the code tables and for organizing the object files, this compares nicely with a directory file size for the overlay of 6272 bytes. As will be shown, the overlay file size increases if the constant tables are also moved into the overlay. Following are the memory maps:

Internal Overlay:

```
Groups:

 Name        Address  Size  DSalloc
 DGROUP       1E5A0   3130
```

```
Segments:

 Section :  Maddr=0, Msize=1B3B0, Daddr=1C00, Lev=0, Ovly#=0

     Name          Addr    Size   Name         Addr    Size
     GENMEN.NIL       0     15F   CENTER.NI     160      3A
     SHORT.NIL      1A0      27   VERIFY.NI     1D0      6B
     PROCHEAD.      240      39   HELP.NIL      280     4A4
     DOITAGAIN      730      2E   CHAINA.NI     760      24
     CHAINB.NI      790      29   $START.NI     7C0      DF
     $INTERFAC      89F     6F4   $INTERFAC     F93      8B
     $DRIVERS.     101E     54F   EXEC.C.NI    156D    136B
     _PROG.NIL     28D8      1CA  NDEBUG.C.    2AA2       B
     SYMSYS.C.     2AAD     523   CTERM.C.N    2FD0     915
     STACK.C.N     38E5    12B1   DB.C.NIL     4B96    4B00
     OPS.C.NIL     9696    261E   STERM.C.N    BCB4    377E
     SET.C.NIL     F432     BCB   CSUPPORT.    FFFD    1861
     MACRO.C.N    1185E     36A   $HACKJOB.   11BC8     271
     _PROG.NIL    11E39      5D   _PROG.NIL   11E96     2DD
     _PROG.NIL    12173       0   _PROG.NIL   12173       0
     _PROG.NIL    12173       0   _PROG.NIL   12173     120
     INDEX.C.N    12293    27E9   RPAR.C.NI   14A7C    1D4B
     _PROG.NIL    167C7      6A   _PROG.NIL   16831     5DB
     _PROG.NIL    16E0C      15   NATION.C.   16E21     19C
     _PROG.NIL    16FBD      41   _PROG.NIL   16FFE      1D
     _PROG.NIL    1701B      6A   _PROG.NIL   17085      38
     _PROG.NIL    170BD      2E   _PROG.NIL   170EB      25
     _PROG.NIL    17110       0   _PROG.NIL   17110       0
     _PROG.NIL    17110     A59   _PROG.NIL   17B69      1B
     _PROG.NIL    17B84     12F   _PROG.NIL   17CB3      41
     _PROG.NIL    17CF4      2D   _PROG.NIL   17D21      1E
     _PROG.NIL    17D3F     456   _PROG.NIL   18195      9A
     _PROG.NIL    1822F      1D   _PROG.NIL   1824C      33
     _PROG.NIL    1827F      2D   _PROG.NIL   182AC      A8
     _PROG.NIL    18354       C   _PROG.NIL   18360       C
     _PROG.NIL    1836C      C4   _PROG.NIL   18430     41A
     _PROG.NIL    1884A     178   _PROG.NIL   189C2      92
     _PROG.NIL    18A54      4C   _PROG.NIL   18AA0      3C
     _PROG.NIL    18ADC      15   _PROG.NIL   18AF1     423
     _PROG.NIL    18F14     106   _PROG.NIL   1901A      A0
     _PROG.NIL    190BA      43   _PROG.NIL   190FD      AF
     _PROG.NIL    191AC      15   _PROG.NIL   191C1       0
     _PROG.NIL    191C1       E   _PROG.NIL   191CF      84
     _PROG.NIL    19253     164   _PROG.NIL   193B7      5B
     _PROG.NIL    19412     11F   _PROG.NIL   19531      F9
     _PROG.NIL    1962A      50   _PROG.NIL   1967A      24
     _PROG.NIL    1969E      20   _PROG.NIL   196BE      32
     _PROG.NIL    196F0     1A4   _PROG.NIL   19894       0
     _PROG.NIL    19894      21   _PROG.NIL   198B5      3E
     _PROG.NIL    198F3      58   _PROG.NIL   1994B     2CD
     _PROG.NIL    19C18      34   _PROG.NIL   19C4C     2AE
     _PROG.NIL    19EFA     241   _PROG.NIL   1A13B      A8
     _PROG.NIL    1A1E3     17F   _PROG.NIL   1A362       0
```

```
    _PROG.NIL  1A362     B   _PROG.NIL  1A36D     12
    _PROG.NIL  1A37F    1B   _PROG.NIL  1A39A     7B
    _PROG.NIL  1A415    9C   _PROG.NIL  1A4B1     34
    _PROG.NIL  1A4E5    EB   _PROG.NIL  1A5D0     2B
    _PROG.NIL  1A5FB    28   _PROG.NIL  1A623     6B
    _PROG.NIL  1A68E   125   _PROG.NIL  1A7B3     7C
    _PROG.NIL  1A82F    EA   $OVTB$.OV  1A920    138
    OVDATA.OV  1AB00   1EC   OVCODE.OV  1ACF0    6B6

Section :  Maddr=1B3B0, Msize=2C0, Daddr=1CFD0, Lev=1, Ovly#=1
    STARTOFF.  1B3B0   2BB

Section :  Maddr=1B3B0, Msize=140, Daddr=1D2A0, Lev=1, Ovly#=2
    BEGIN.NIL  1B3B0   136

Section :  Maddr=1B3B0, Msize=2A0, Daddr=1D3F0, Lev=1, Ovly#=3
    PROMPTNG.  1B3B0   29C

Section :  Maddr=1B3B0, Msize=3C0, Daddr=1D6A0, Lev=1, Ovly#=4
    MENUENTR.  1B3B0   3BD

Section :  Maddr=1B3B0, Msize=2B0, Daddr=1DA70, Lev=1, Ovly#=5
    MENUDRAW.  1B3B0   2A5

Section :  Maddr=1B3B0, Msize=260, Daddr=1DD30, Lev=1, Ovly#=6
    MOVE_CUR.  1B3B0   25F

Section :  Maddr=1B3B0, Msize=160, Daddr=1DFA0, Lev=1, Ovly#=7
    DRAWBOX.N  1B3B0   15A

Section :  Maddr=1B3B0, Msize=170, Daddr=1E110, Lev=1, Ovly#=8
    MOVETITL.  1B3B0   161

Section :  Maddr=1B3B0, Msize=170, Daddr=1E290, Lev=1, Ovly#=9
    MOVEESC.N  1B3B0   161

Section :  Maddr=1B3B0, Msize=420, Daddr=1E420, Lev=1, Ovly#=10
    FINISHED.  1B3B0   207   FINISHED_  1B5C0    208

Section :  Maddr=1B7D0, Msize=5F00, Daddr=1F0F0, Lev=0, Ovly#=11, Pre-Loaded

    $EXPR.$EX  1B7D0     0   $EXPR.$EX  1B7D0      0
    $EXPR.$EX  1B7D0     0   $EXPR.$EX  1B7D0     26
    $EXPR.$EX  1B800    39   $EXPR.$EX  1B840     13
    $EXPR.$EX  1B860     0   $EXPR.$EX  1B860      0
    $EXPR.$EX  1B860     0   $EXPR.$EX  1B860      0
    $EXPR.$EX  1B860    27   $MDATA.$M  1B890     B0
    $SYMSTART  1B940     0   $SYMBOLS.  1B940    260
    $SYMBOLS.  1BBA0    50   $SYMBOLS.  1BBF0    140
    $SYMBOLS.  1BD30   240   $SYMBOLS.  1BF70    1B0
    $SYMBOLS.  1C120   210   $SYMBOLS.  1C330    150
    $SYMBOLS.  1C480    80   $SYMBOLS.  1C500     B0
    $SYMBOLS.  1C5B0    B0   $SYMBOLS.  1C660    220
```

```
$SYMEND.$   1C880      2   $CONSTANT   1C890    E30
$CONSTANT   1D6C0    1F0   $CONSTANT   1D8B0     C0
$CONSTANT   1D970    140   $CONSTANT   1DAB0    2F0
$CONSTANT   1DDA0    110   $CONSTANT   1DEB0     E0
$CONSTANT   1DF90     D0   $CONSTANT   1E060     A0
$CONSTANT   1E100     A0   $CONSTANT   1E1A0    400
DATA.DATA   1E5A0   2D70   $LIB_TABL   21310    33C
STACK.DAT   21650     80
```

External Overlay:

```
Groups:

 Name        Address  Size  DSalloc
 DGROUP       1E5A0   3130

Segments:

 Section :  Maddr=0, Msize=1B3B0, Daddr=1C00, Lev=0, Ovly#=0

    Name          Addr    Size   Name          Addr    Size
    GENMEN.NIL       0     15F   CENTER.NI      160      3A
    SHORT.NIL      1A0      27   VERIFY.NI      1D0      6B
    PROCHEAD.      240      39   HELP.NIL       280     4A4
    DOITAGAIN      730      2E   CHAINA.NI      760      24
    CHAINB.NI      790      29   $START.NI      7C0      DF
    $INTERFAC      89F     6F4   $INTERFAC      F93      8B
    $DRIVERS.     101E     54F   EXEC.C.NI     156D    136B
    _PROG.NIL     28D8     1CA   NDEBUG.C.     2AA2       B
    SYMSYS.C.     2AAD     523   CTERM.C.N     2FD0     915
    STACK.C.N     38E5    12B1   DB.C.NIL      4B96    4B00
    OPS.C.NIL     9696    261E   STERM.C.N     BCB4    377E
    SET.C.NIL     F432     BCB   CSUPPORT.     FFFD    1861
    MACRO.C.N    1185E     36A   $HACKJOB.    11BC8     271
    _PROG.NIL    11E39      5D   _PROG.NIL    11E96     2DD
    _PROG.NIL    12173       0   _PROG.NIL    12173       0
    _PROG.NIL    12173       0   _PROG.NIL    12173     120
    INDEX.C.N    12293    27E9   RPAR.C.NI    14A7C    1D4B
    _PROG.NIL    167C7      6A   _PROG.NIL    16831     5DB
    _PROG.NIL    16E0C      15   NATION.C.    16E21     19C
    _PROG.NIL    16FBD      41   _PROG.NIL    16FFE      1D
    _PROG.NIL    1701B      6A   _PROG.NIL    17085      38
    _PROG.NIL    170BD      2E   _PROG.NIL    170EB      25
    _PROG.NIL    17110       0   _PROG.NIL    17110       0
    _PROG.NIL    17110     A59   _PROG.NIL    17B69      1B
    _PROG.NIL    17B84     12F   _PROG.NIL    17CB3      41
    _PROG.NIL    17CF4      2D   _PROG.NIL    17D21      1E
    _PROG.NIL    17D3F     456   _PROG.NIL    18195      9A
    _PROG.NIL    1822F      1D   _PROG.NIL    1824C      33
    _PROG.NIL    1827F      2D   _PROG.NIL    182AC      A8
    _PROG.NIL    18354       C   _PROG.NIL    18360       C
    _PROG.NIL    1836C      C4   _PROG.NIL    18430     41A
    _PROG.NIL    1884A     178   _PROG.NIL    189C2      92
```

```
    _PROG.NIL  18A54      4C  _PROG.NIL  18AA0      3C
    _PROG.NIL  18ADC      15  _PROG.NIL  18AF1     423
    _PROG.NIL  18F14     106  _PROG.NIL  1901A      A0
    _PROG.NIL  190BA      43  _PROG.NIL  190FD      AF
    _PROG.NIL  191AC      15  _PROG.NIL  191C1       0
    _PROG.NIL  191C1       E  _PROG.NIL  191CF      84
    _PROG.NIL  19253     164  _PROG.NIL  193B7      5B
    _PROG.NIL  19412     11F  _PROG.NIL  19531      F9
    _PROG.NIL  1962A      50  _PROG.NIL  1967A      24
    _PROG.NIL  1969E      20  _PROG.NIL  196BE      32
    _PROG.NIL  196F0     1A4  _PROG.NIL  19894       0
    _PROG.NIL  19894      21  _PROG.NIL  198B5      3E
    _PROG.NIL  198F3      58  _PROG.NIL  1994B     2CD
    _PROG.NIL  19C18      34  _PROG.NIL  19C4C     2AE
    _PROG.NIL  19EFA     241  _PROG.NIL  1A13B      A8
    _PROG.NIL  1A1E3     17F  _PROG.NIL  1A362       0
    _PROG.NIL  1A362       B  _PROG.NIL  1A36D      12
    _PROG.NIL  1A37F      1B  _PROG.NIL  1A39A      7B
    _PROG.NIL  1A415      9C  _PROG.NIL  1A4B1      34
    _PROG.NIL  1A4E5      EB  _PROG.NIL  1A5D0      2B
    _PROG.NIL  1A5FB      28  _PROG.NIL  1A623      6B
    _PROG.NIL  1A68E     125  _PROG.NIL  1A7B3      7C
    _PROG.NIL  1A82F      EA  $OVTB$.OV  1A920     140
    OVDATA.OV  1AB00     1EC  OVCODE.OV  1ACF0     6B6

Section :  Maddr=1B3B0, Msize=2C0, Daddr=10, Lev=1, Ovly#=1
    STARTOFF.  1B3B0     2BB

Section :  Maddr=1B3B0, Msize=140, Daddr=2E0, Lev=1, Ovly#=2
    BEGIN.NIL  1B3B0     136

Section :  Maddr=1B3B0, Msize=2A0, Daddr=430, Lev=1, Ovly#=3
    PROMPTNG.  1B3B0     29C

Section :  Maddr=1B3B0, Msize=3C0, Daddr=6E0, Lev=1, Ovly#=4
    MENUENTR.  1B3B0     3BD

Section :  Maddr=1B3B0, Msize=2B0, Daddr=AB0, Lev=1, Ovly#=5
    MENUDRAW.  1B3B0     2A5

Section :  Maddr=1B3B0, Msize=260, Daddr=D70, Lev=1, Ovly#=6
    MOVE_CUR.  1B3B0     25F

Section :  Maddr=1B3B0, Msize=160, Daddr=FE0, Lev=1, Ovly#=7
    DRAWBOX.N  1B3B0     15A

Section :  Maddr=1B3B0, Msize=170, Daddr=1150, Lev=1, Ovly#=8
    MOVETITL.  1B3B0     161

Section :  Maddr=1B3B0, Msize=170, Daddr=12D0, Lev=1, Ovly#=9
    MOVEESC.N  1B3B0     161

Section :  Maddr=1B3B0, Msize=420, Daddr=1460, Lev=1, Ovly#=10
    FINISHED.  1B3B0     207  FINISHED_  1B5C0     208
```

```
Section :  Maddr=1B7D0, Msize=5F00, Daddr=1D870, Lev=0, Ovly#=11, Pre-Loaded

    $EXPR.$EX   1B7D0      0   $EXPR.$EX   1B7D0      0
    $EXPR.$EX   1B7D0      0   $EXPR.$EX   1B7D0     26
    $EXPR.$EX   1B800     39   $EXPR.$EX   1B840     13
    $EXPR.$EX   1B860      0   $EXPR.$EX   1B860      0
    $EXPR.$EX   1B860      0   $EXPR.$EX   1B860      0
    $EXPR.$EX   1B860     27   $MDATA.$M   1B890     B0
    $SYMSTART   1B940      0   $SYMBOLS.   1B940    260
    $SYMBOLS.   1BBA0     50   $SYMBOLS.   1BBF0    140
    $SYMBOLS.   1BD30    240   $SYMBOLS.   1BF70    1B0
    $SYMBOLS.   1C120    210   $SYMBOLS.   1C330    150
    $SYMBOLS.   1C480     80   $SYMBOLS.   1C500     B0
    $SYMBOLS.   1C5B0     B0   $SYMBOLS.   1C660    220
    $SYMEND.$   1C880      2   $CONSTANT   1C890    E30
    $CONSTANT   1D6C0    1F0   $CONSTANT   1D8B0     C0
    $CONSTANT   1D970    140   $CONSTANT   1DAB0    2F0
    $CONSTANT   1DDA0    110   $CONSTANT   1DEB0     E0
    $CONSTANT   1DF90     D0   $CONSTANT   1E060     A0
    $CONSTANT   1E100     A0   $CONSTANT   1E1A0    400
    DATA.DATA   1E5A0   2D70   $LIB_TABL   21310    33C
    STACK.DAT   21650     80
```

Notice that the load module for the first LiNK file is exactly the same as that of the second LiNK file. Also the address points in memory where the external overlay is brought into the main program are the same as in the internal overlay. Clearly, the only advantage to external overlays is the disk space used.

The best approach is to develop the application to run on a hard-disk system. Even if external overlays are used, they can be loaded onto the hard disk and executed. The real use for external overlays is when you need to distribute an application that is larger than 360 kilobytes. Develop the proper overlay technique and link accordingly. Note the respective file sizes and then add a small chaining routine to the main program that will prompt the user for the appropriate disk and check for the necessary overlay file. If you use this technique, don't let the internal mechanisms of the linker display its message:

```
PLINK86 Overlay Loader - Can't find file CMENOVER.OVL.
Enter file name prefix (X: or path name/) or '.' to quit=>
```

This is not very user-friendly! The best way to avoid this is to add a FILE() function that looks for the existence of the overlay file itself. If it appears, have the application continue by chaining to that overlay. If it does not appear, simply add some code that prompts the user to either exit the program or to insert a new disk. Keep in mind that even functions can be called in an external overlay. If any of these functions are called, the existence of the overlay file must be checked prior to the actual function call. Following is the overlay file size for the same LiNK file. Notice the sizes of the files moved into the external overlay.

```
C>dir *.ovl

 Volume in drive C has no label
 Directory of  C:\PROJECT\PROGRAMS\TEST

CMENOVER OVL     10080   5-13-86   8:31a
        1 File(s)    290816 bytes free
```

Subtracting the size of the old overlay file from this new figure shows an increase in size of 3808 bytes. The constant sizes, not including the constant size for GENMEN.OBJ, are 3700 bytes. The extra file size exists because code was added by the linker to handle the constants separately from the code tables. The overlay file increased in size because the constant tables were moved out of the main load module and into the overlay file. The executable file decreased by 3856 bytes.

With Plink86, version 1.46.c., if external overlays are used, even though you may have a path set to a subdirectory containing the OVERLAY.LIB, the linker will not find it. If the linker cannot find the OVERLAY.LIB file on the currently logged directory, Plink86 will generate the following message:

```
Can't find file OVERLAY.LIB.
Enter new file name prefix (drive:  or path name/)
or . to quit =>
```

Just type in the subdirectory name containing the OVERLAY.LIB file. You may have to do this once or twice. To completely avoid the problem simply copy the OVERLAY.LIB file into the same subdirectory in which you are currently working.

A CHAINING PROGRAM

There are two types of chaining programs: one allows a program in an overlay section to go to another program in the same overlay, while the second checks for an overlay file on the disk drive and prompts the user accordingly.

Chaining to other overlay files depends entirely on each application and on programming techniques. In many cases memory variables are saved to a memory file containing the drive designators for both program and data drives. In this case only the name of the overlay would vary from program to program. This program should be written as a procedure and should reside in the main load module.

Chaining to other sections, though not directly possible and not recommended, is a bit more tricky. It is not as simple as adding an extra command line. Procedural considerations must be foreseen, and memory variables dependent on both procedures (the one chaining to the other) must be PUBLIC to both. A possible example would be the following:

```
*********************

PROCEDURE Chainto

   PARAMETERS goto_prog, ret_prog

   DO &goto_prog
   DO &ret_prog
```

Remember that when returning to the original calling program, the chain goes back to the beginning of the procedure or program file that originally called the CHAINTO procedure. The reason for this is that the control of the original calling program is washed out of memory as the second section in the overlay comes into memory. Without the returning program parameter, the RETURN does not know where to go and an EXEC SEQUENCE ERROR or similar memory-related error occurs. Programs using a chaining program must be coded accordingly. Conditional testing for flags set and reset by the chaining program jumps the execution of a program file or procedure from the beginning to some other point within the application.

Finally, if it is necessary to use a chaining program, make sure that the procedure for the chain resides in the main load module. Otherwise, an EXEC SEQUENCE ERROR may occur (which is the reason why you program for the chaining in the first place).

USING THE MAP

A memory map showing all of the entry points of an application is available through a command in Plink86 or is automatically available in Microsoft's 3.05 LINK program. These entry points are either the dBASE programs, the internal Clipper routines, or the Lattice C routines. The areas used for data, constants, etc., are shown. Below is an example of a memory map from the application called CREATE.PRG that is located in the **application** section of this text. It was linked with Microsoft's LINK, version 3.05.

```
       Start  Stop   Length Name                     Class

     ┌─ 00000H 000A6H 000A7H CREATE
 P   │  000B0H 00147H 00098H FIRST
 r   │  00150H 0043AH 002EBH SECOND
 o   │  00440H 00A86H 00647H THIRD
 c   │  00A90H 00D74H 002E5H FOURTH
 e   │  00D80H 0172EH 009AFH FIFTH
 d   │  01730H 018ACH 0017DH SIXTH
 u   │  018B0H 0198BH 000DCH SEVENTH
 r   │  01990H 01AA7H 00118H EIGHT
 e   │  01AB0H 01F55H 004A6H NINE
 s   │  01F60H 022D1H 00372H TEN
     │  022E0H 022EEH 0000FH CREATE1
 a   │  022F0H 026DBH 003ECH ELEVEN
 n   │  026E0H 02773H 00094H TWELVE
 d   │  02780H 02CD5H 00556H THIRTEEN
     │  02CE0H 02FEDH 0030EH FOURTEEN
```

Functions

```
02FF0H 03185H 00196H FIFTEEN
03190H 032DCH 0014DH SIXTEEN
032E0H 033BDH 000DEH SEVENTEEN
033C0H 0348DH 000CEH EIGHTEEN
03490H 035EFH 00160H NINETEEN
035F0H 03766H 00177H TWENTY
03770H 03825H 000B6H TWENTY1
03830H 03868H 00039H PROCHEAD
03870H 038A8H 00039H FUNCHEAD
```

Clipper Routines

```
038B0H 0391AH 0006BH VERIFY
03920H 039FEH 000DFH $START
039FFH 040F2H 006F4H $INTERFACE
040F3H 0417DH 0008BH $INTERFACE
0417EH 054E8H 0136BH EXEC.C
054E9H 05A37H 0054FH $DRIVERS
05A38H 05CA8H 00271H $HACKJOB
05CA9H 07509H 01861H CSUPPORT.C
0750AH 087BAH 012B1H STACK.C
087BBH 0ADD8H 0261EH OPS.C
0ADD9H 0F8D8H 04B00H DB.C
0F8D9H 0FDFBH 00523H SYMSYS.C
0FDFCH 11B46H 01D4BH RPAR.C
11B47H 12711H 00BCBH SET.C
12712H 1271CH 0000BH NDEBUG.C
1271DH 14F05H 027E9H INDEX.C
14F06H 1526FH 0036AH MACRO.C
15270H 15B84H 00915H CTERM.C
15B85H 19302H 0377EH STERM.C
```

Lattice C Routines

```
19303H 1949EH 0019CH NATION.C
1949FH 194B3H 00015H _PROG
194B4H 1967DH 001CAH _PROG
1967EH 196BEH 00041H _PROG
196BFH 19728H 0006AH _PROG
19729H 19785H 0005DH _PROG
19786H 19A62H 002DDH _PROG
19A63H 19A63H 00000H _PROG
19A63H 19A63H 00000H _PROG
19A63H 19A63H 00000H _PROG
19A63H 19B82H 00120H _PROG
19B83H 1A15DH 005DBH _PROG
1A15EH 1A18AH 0002DH _PROG
1A18BH 1A5A4H 0041AH _PROG
1A5A5H 1A5B0H 0000CH _PROG
1A5B1H 1A5F1H 00041H _PROG
1A5F2H 1AA47H 00456H _PROG
1AA48H 1AA65H 0001EH _PROG
1AA66H 1AA98H 00033H _PROG
1AA99H 1ABC7H 0012FH _PROG
1ABC8H 1ABD3H 0000CH _PROG
1ABD4H 1AC97H 000C4H _PROG
1AC98H 1ACB2H 0001BH _PROG
1ACB3H 1AE2AH 00178H _PROG
1AE2BH 1AEBCH 00092H _PROG
1AEBDH 1AF08H 0004CH _PROG
1AF09H 1AFB7H 000AFH _PROG
1AFB8H 1AFE4H 0002DH _PROG
1AFE5H 1B08CH 000A8H _PROG
1B08DH 1B0A9H 0001DH _PROG
1B0AAH 1BB02H 00A59H _PROG
1BB03H 1BB9CH 0009AH _PROG
1BB9DH 1BBB9H 0001DH _PROG
1BBBAH 1BCBFH 00106H _PROG
1BCC0H 1BCFBH 0003CH _PROG
```

```
    1BCFCH 1BD65H 0006AH _PROG
    1BD66H 1BD9DH 00038H _PROG
    1BD9EH 1BDCBH 0002EH _PROG
    1BDCCH 1BDF0H 00025H _PROG
    1BDF1H 1BDF1H 00000H _PROG
    1BDF1H 1BDF1H 00000H _PROG
    1BDF1H 1BE90H 000A0H _PROG
    1BE91H 1BEA5H 00015H _PROG
    1BEA6H 1C2C8H 00423H _PROG
    1C2C9H 1C30BH 00043H _PROG
    1C30CH 1C33DH 00032H _PROG
    1C33EH 1C4E1H 001A4H _PROG
    1C4E2H 1C645H 00164H _PROG
    1C646H 1C6A0H 0005BH _PROG
    1C6A1H 1C7BFH 0011FH _PROG
    1C7C0H 1C8B8H 000F9H _PROG
    1C8B9H 1C908H 00050H _PROG
    1C909H 1C92CH 00024H _PROG
    1C92DH 1C94CH 00020H _PROG
    1C94DH 1C96DH 00021H _PROG
    1C96EH 1C9ABH 0003EH _PROG
    1C9ACH 1CA03H 00058H _PROG
    1CA04H 1CCD0H 002CDH _PROG
    1CCD1H 1CD04H 00034H _PROG
    1CD05H 1CFB2H 002AEH _PROG
    1CFB3H 1D1F3H 00241H _PROG
    1D1F4H 1D1FEH 0000BH _PROG
    1D1FFH 1D1FFH 00000H _PROG
    1D1FFH 1D20CH 0000EH _PROG
    1D20DH 1D290H 00084H _PROG
    1D291H 1D291H 00000H _PROG
    1D291H 1D338H 000A8H _PROG
    1D339H 1D4B7H 0017FH _PROG
    1D4B8H 1D4CCH 00015H _PROG
    1D4CDH 1D4CDH 00000H _PROG
    1D4CDH 1D568H 0009CH _PROG
    1D569H 1D583H 0001BH _PROG
    1D584H 1D5FEH 0007BH _PROG
    1D5FFH 1D632H 00034H _PROG
    1D633H 1D71DH 000EBH _PROG
    1D71EH 1D748H 0002BH _PROG
    1D749H 1D770H 00028H _PROG
    1D771H 1D7DBH 0006BH _PROG
    1D7DCH 1D7EDH 00012H _PROG
    1D7EEH 1D912H 00125H _PROG
    1D913H 1D98EH 0007CH _PROG
    1D98FH 1DA78H 000EAH _PROG
    1DA80H 1DA98H 00019H $EXPR          $EXPR
M   1DAA0H 1DAA0H 00000H $EXPR          $EXPR
e   1DAA0H 1DABFH 00020H $MDATA         $MDATA
m   1DAC0H 1DAC0H 00000H $SYMSTART      $SYMSTART
o   1DAC0H 1DD5FH 002A0H $SYMBOLS       $SYMBOLS
r   1DD60H 1DF4FH 001F0H $SYMBOLS       $SYMBOLS
y   1DF50H 1DF51H 00002H $SYMEND        $SYMEND
    1DF60H 2343FH 054E0H $CONSTANTS     $CONSTANTS
S   23440H 2669FH 03260H $CONSTANTS     $CONSTANTS
e   266A0H 29413H 02D74H DATA           DATA
g   29420H 2975BH 0033CH $LIB_TABLE     DATA
.   29760H 297DFH 00080H STACK          DATA

     Origin   Group
    266A:0   DGROUP
```

To determine the precise load module size, take the last map figure (297DF) and subtract the stack figure (80). To this number, add 1000 for the allotted internal stack in Clipper and convert the hex number to decimal. The result is the basic load module.

297DF - 80 + 1000 = 2A75F hex = 173,919 bytes

Here is the memory map for the same file (which is generated by Plink86):

```
Groups:

 Name          Address  Size  DSalloc
 DGROUP         266A0   3130

Segments:

 Section :  Maddr=0, Msize=297D0, Daddr=2400, Lev=0, Ovly#=0

     Name          Addr    Size   Name          Addr    Size
     CREATE.NI        0      A7   FIRST.NIL       B0      98
     SECOND.NI      150     2EB   THIRD.NIL      440     647
     FOURTH.NI      A90     2E5   FIFTH.NIL      D80     9AF
     SIXTH.NIL     1730     17D   SEVENTH.N     18B0      DC
     EIGHT.NIL     1990     118   NINE.NIL      1AB0     4A6
     TEN.NIL       1F60     372   CREATE1.N     22E0       F
     ELEVEN.NI     22F0     3EC   TWELVE.NI     26E0      94
     THIRTEEN.     2780     556   FOURTEEN.     2CE0     30E
     FIFTEEN.N     2FF0     196   SIXTEEN.N     3190     14D
     SEVENTEEN     32E0      DE   EIGHTEEN.     33C0      CE
     NINETEEN.     3490     160   TWENTY.NI     35F0     177
     TWENTY1.N     3770      B6   PROCHEAD.     3830      39
     FUNCHEAD.     3870      39   VERIFY.NI     38B0      6B
     $START.NI     3920      DF   $INTERFAC     39FF     6F4
     $INTERFAC     40F3      8B   EXEC.C.NI     417E    136B
     _PROG.NIL     54E9     1CA   NDEBUG.C.     56B3       B
     $DRIVERS.     56BE     54F   SYMSYS.C.     5C0D     523
     CTERM.C.N     6130     915   STACK.C.N     6A45    12B1
     DB.C.NIL      7CF6    4B00   OPS.C.NIL     C7F6    261E
     STERM.C.N     EE14    377E   SET.C.NIL    12592     BCB
     CSUPPORT.    1315D    1861   MACRO.C.N    149BE     36A
     $HACKJOB.    14D28     271   _PROG.NIL    14F99      5D
     _PROG.NIL    14FF6     2DD   _PROG.NIL    152D3       0
     _PROG.NIL    152D3       0   _PROG.NIL    152D3       0
     _PROG.NIL    152D3     120   INDEX.C.N    153F3    27E9
     RPAR.C.NI    17BDC    1D4B   _PROG.NIL    19927      6A
     _PROG.NIL    19991     5DB   _PROG.NIL    19F6C      15
     NATION.C.    19F81     19C   _PROG.NIL    1A11D      41
     _PROG.NIL    1A15E      1D   _PROG.NIL    1A17B      6A
     _PROG.NIL    1A1E5      38   _PROG.NIL    1A21D      2E
     _PROG.NIL    1A24B      25   _PROG.NIL    1A270       0
     _PROG.NIL    1A270       0   _PROG.NIL    1A270     A59
     _PROG.NIL    1ACC9      1B   _PROG.NIL    1ACE4     12F
     _PROG.NIL    1AE13      41   _PROG.NIL    1AE54      2D
```

```
_PROG.NIL   1AE81     1E   _PROG.NIL   1AE9F    456
_PROG.NIL   1B2F5     9A   _PROG.NIL   1B38F     1D
_PROG.NIL   1B3AC     33   _PROG.NIL   1B3DF     2D
_PROG.NIL   1B40C     A8   _PROG.NIL   1B4B4      C
_PROG.NIL   1B4C0      C   _PROG.NIL   1B4CC     C4
_PROG.NIL   1B590    41A   _PROG.NIL   1B9AA    178
_PROG.NIL   1BB22     92   _PROG.NIL   1BBB4     4C
_PROG.NIL   1BC00     3C   _PROG.NIL   1BC3C     15
_PROG.NIL   1BC51    423   _PROG.NIL   1C074    106
_PROG.NIL   1C17A     A0   _PROG.NIL   1C21A     43
_PROG.NIL   1C25D     AF   _PROG.NIL   1C30C     15
_PROG.NIL   1C321      0   _PROG.NIL   1C321      E
_PROG.NIL   1C32F     84   _PROG.NIL   1C3B3    164
_PROG.NIL   1C517     5B   _PROG.NIL   1C572    11F
_PROG.NIL   1C691     F9   _PROG.NIL   1C78A     50
_PROG.NIL   1C7DA     24   _PROG.NIL   1C7FE     20
_PROG.NIL   1C81E     32   _PROG.NIL   1C850    1A4
_PROG.NIL   1C9F4      0   _PROG.NIL   1C9F4     21
_PROG.NIL   1CA15     3E   _PROG.NIL   1CA53     58
_PROG.NIL   1CAAB    2CD   _PROG.NIL   1CD78     34
_PROG.NIL   1CDAC    2AE   _PROG.NIL   1D05A    241
_PROG.NIL   1D29B     A8   _PROG.NIL   1D343    17F
_PROG.NIL   1D4C2      0   _PROG.NIL   1D4C2      B
_PROG.NIL   1D4CD     12   _PROG.NIL   1D4DF     1B
_PROG.NIL   1D4FA     7B   _PROG.NIL   1D575     9C
_PROG.NIL   1D611     34   _PROG.NIL   1D645     EB
_PROG.NIL   1D730     2B   _PROG.NIL   1D75B     28
_PROG.NIL   1D783     6B   _PROG.NIL   1D7EE    125
_PROG.NIL   1D913     7C   _PROG.NIL   1D98F     EA
$EXPR.$EX   1DA80     19   $EXPR.$EX   1DAA0      0
$MDATA.$M   1DAA0     20   $SYMSTART   1DAC0      0
$SYMBOLS.   1DAC0    2A0   $SYMBOLS.   1DD60    1F0
$SYMEND.$   1DF50      2   $CONSTANT   1DF60   54E0
$CONSTANT   23440   3260   DATA.DATA   266A0   2D70
$LIB_TABL   29410    33C   STACK.DAT   29750     80
```

As with the previous map, take the last address point (29750) and subtract the 80 hex from it for the stack brought in by the linker. Then add 1000 hex for Clipper's stack, and convert this figure to decimal for the basic load module linking with Plink86.

29750 - 80 + 1000 = 2A6D0 hex = 173,776 bytes

QUIT_TO VERSUS CHAINING BIG PROGRAMS

When developing an application, don't forget that the environment of the compiler is different from that of the interpreter. The syntax and structure look the same as dBASE III, but Clipper is still a more powerful language. Think of Clipper as a set of the dBASE III language. Programs that once chained from one program file to another, to word processors, or to other applications, may not do so under the compiled environment. Your program files are now totally memory resident. This takes up more memory than the same files did in the interpreter's environment.

Some recoding and rethinking may be necessary to make the program function as before. Below are just a few examples of how to accomplish this.

THE QUIT_TO BATCH FILE

One way to get programs to chain together is through the aid of a batch file. Below is one such example:

```
* Procedure: QTO.PRG
* Author ..: Barry Grant
* Date ....: 05-29-85, modified 06-26-85 by Ray Love
* Notes ...: Based on a routine by Tom Rettig from the "Advanced
*            Programmer's Guide", copyright (c) 1985 Luis Castro,
*            Jay Hansen, and Tom Rettig, Published by Ashton-Tate.
*
* This program allows programs to call one another by starting
* execution with a batch file, then modifying that batch file to
* call the next program.  This is done by passing the name of the
* next program to the procedure QUIT_TO.   For example,
*
*    DO Quit_to WITH Next
*
* where the contents of next is the program to execute.  The called
* routines can return by using the same procedure.  To exit the
* batch file, pass "GOTO END" to QUIT_TO.
*
* -IMPORTANT-
* The length of the memory variable passed to QUIT_TO must always
* be eight characters.  The file pointer used by DOS must find the
* instruction GOTO START at the same location in the batch file
* every time.
*
* Any memory variables that need to be passed may be SAVEd to a
* .MEM file.
*
* This example uses the names START.BAT for the batch file and
* MAIN.EXE for the initial program to execute.  The file START.BAT
* contains the following:
*
*    ECHO OFF
*    MAIN
*    GOTO START
*    :START
*    GOTO END
*    GOTO START
*    :END
*    ECHO ON
```

```
PROCEDURE QUIT_TO

PARAMETERS program

   SET ALTERNATE TO START.BAT
   SET ALTERNATE ON
   SET CONSOLE OFF
   ? "ECHO OFF"
   ? "MAIN"
   ? "GOTO START"
   ? ":START"
   ? program
   ? "GOTO START"
   ? ":END"
   ? "ECHO ON"
   SET ALTERNATE TO
   SET CONSOLE ON
   QUIT

* The following three programs demonstrate the use of QUIT_TO.
* Compile separately, create START.BAT, and enter "START" at the
* DOS prompt.

* MAIN.prg
* Notes ...: Main menu of a procedure to call other programs.

   SET PROCEDURE TO QTO
   DO WHILE .T.
      CLEAR
      @ 10,30 SAY "M A I N   M E N U"
      @ 12,30 PROMPT " 1.   Program 1 "
      @ 13,30 PROMPT " 2.   Program 2 "
      @ 14,30 PROMPT " 3.     QUIT    "
      MENU TO choice
      DO CASE
      CASE choice = 1
         * Add spaces to make next string 8 character long...
         next = "TEST_1  "
      CASE choice = 2
         next = "TEST_2  "
      OTHERWISE
         next = "GOTO END"
      ENDCASE
      DO QUIT_TO WITH next
   ENDDO
   * EOF MAIN.PRG

   * TEST_1.prg

   SET PROCEDURE TO QTO
   CLEAR
   WAIT "This is TEST_1.PRG   Press any key to return to MAIN."
   next = "MAIN    "
```

```
DO QUIT_TO WITH next
* EOF TEST_1.prg

* TEST_2.prg
SET PROCEDURE TO QTO
CLEAR
WAIT "This is TEST_2.prg   Press any key to return to MAIN."
next = "MAIN    "
DO QUIT_TO WITH next
* EOF TEST_2.prg
```

COMING BACK TO THE MAIN PROGRAM

A major concern in chaining two or more large applications together is the inability to leave one program to run another and then to return to the correct position in the original application. If the RUN command is invoked, the line immediately following it will be executed once control is regained by the original program. However, with large applications this is not that easy. The original program will remain in memory while the RUN command will try to load the second application (or program) on top of the first one. In most environments, the second program will not be able to be loaded into memory either because of file size, restricted memory size, or both. This is a common problem in applications that call up an external word processor.

The major problem with a batch file fix is the inability to get back to the exit point of the original application without being forced to go through the entire menu scheme as if starting up the program for the first time. The following example demonstrates a solution to this problem with the batch file fix and some minor recoding.

```
********************
* Name          CHAINIT.prg
* Date          September 21, 1986
* Notice        Copyright 1986, Stephen J. Straley
* Note          This example shows how, with minor coding, a program
*               can exit to another program and reenter the application
*               close to the exit point.
*
********************

   ****************************************************************
   * This section of code is needed in order to check the disk      *
   * to see if the system or environment file is out there.  If it  *
   * is, chain to that procedure; otherwise, go directly to the     *
   * Main Menu.                                                     *
   ****************************************************************
   CLEAR
   IF FILE("ALLMEM.MEM")
      RESTORE FROM Allmem
      ERASE Allmem.mem
      DO &goproc
```

```
ENDIF
DO Aamen1

*********************

PROCEDURE Aamen1

DO WHILE .T.
   CLEAR
   scrframe = CHR(201) + CHR(205) + CHR(187) + CHR(186) + ;
              CHR(188) + CHR(205) + CHR(200) + CHR(186) + CHR(32)
   STORE 0 TO option
   @ 6, 12, 16, 55 BOX scrframe
   @ 5, 29 SAY "Main Menu"
   @ 8, 14 PROMPT " Account Charts "
   @ 10, 14 PROMPT " Transactions "
   @ 12, 14 PROMPT " Postings "
   @ 14, 14 PROMPT " Reports "
   @ 8, 38 PROMPT " Listings "
   @ 10, 38 PROMPT " Other Systems "
   @ 12, 38 PROMPT " Utilities "
   @ 14, 38 PROMPT " End of Period "
   @ 17, 27 SAY "ESC to RETURN"
   MENU TO option
   DO CASE
   CASE option = 1
      DO Aamen11
   CASE option = 2
      **************************
      * Do subprocedure here. *
      **************************
   CASE option = 3
      **************************
      * Do subprocedure here. *
      **************************
   CASE option = 4
      **************************
      * Do subprocedure here. *
      **************************
   CASE option = 5
      **************************
      * Do subprocedure here. *
      **************************
   CASE option = 6
      **************************
      * Do subprocedure here. *
      **************************
   CASE option = 7
      **************************
      * Do subprocedure here. *
      **************************
   CASE option = 8
      DO Aamen18
```

```
    CASE option = 0
       @ 19, 15 SAY "All Files Closed, Returning to Operating System"
       QUIT
    ENDCASE

 ENDDO

 *********************

 PROCEDURE Aamen18

 DO WHILE .T.
    STORE 0 TO option1
    @ 15, 40, 22, 65 BOX scrframe
    @ 17, 46 PROMPT " Month End "
    @ 18, 46 PROMPT " Quarter End "
    @ 19, 46 PROMPT " Year End "
    @ 21, 47 SAY "ESC to RETURN"
    MENU TO option1
    DO CASE
    CASE option1 = 1
       **************************
       * Do subprocedure here. *
       **************************
    CASE option1 = 2
       **************************
       * Do subprocedure here. *
       **************************
    CASE option1 = 3
       **************************
       * Do subprocedure here. *
       **************************
    CASE option1 = 0
       EXIT
    ENDCASE

 ENDDO

 *********************

 PROCEDURE Aamen11

 DO WHILE .T.
    STORE 0 TO option2
    @ 8, 32, 20, 54 BOX scrframe
    @ 8, 39 SAY "Sub-Menu"
    @ 10, 33 PROMPT " 1> Enter Accounts "
    @ 13, 33 PROMPT " 2> Edit Accounts "
    @ 16, 33 PROMPT " 3> Scan Accounts "
    @ 19, 33 PROMPT " 4> Delete Accounts "
    @ 21, 37 SAY "ESC to RETURN"
    MENU TO option2
    DO CASE
```

```
      CASE option2 = 1
         ***************************
         * Do subprocedure here. *
         ***************************
      CASE option2 = 2
         ***************************
         * Do subprocedure here. *
         ***************************
      CASE option2 = 3
         ***************************
         * Do subprocedure here. *
         ***************************
      CASE option2 = 4
         DO Aamen114
      CASE option2 = 0
         EXIT
      ENDCASE

   ENDDO

   ********************

   PROCEDURE Aamen114

   DO WHILE .T.
      STORE 0 TO option3
      @ 17, 13, 21, 33 BOX scrframe
      @ 18, 18 PROMPT " Quit File "
      @ 19, 18 PROMPT " Go to Top "
      @ 21, 17 SAY "ESC to RETURN"
      MENU TO option3
      DO CASE
      CASE option3 = 1
         goproc = PROCNAME()
         SAVE TO Allmem
         QUIT
      CASE option3 = 2
         DO Aamen1
      CASE option3 = 0
         EXIT
      ENDCASE

   ENDDO
* End of CHAINIT
```

This example has five major considerations:

1. The number of variables stored to one MEMory file is still limited to 254 variables. If more variables exist, additional files will have to be created to properly save the environment.

2. It doesn't get to the exact point of departure. However, with additional coding, this too may be simulated.

3. Files must be reopened, relations reestablished, and record pointers properly positioned when returning to the main application.

4. Screen variables (those variables that contain the screen mapping) may be saved to the memory file. However, proper parsing must take place.

5. The routine must be able to exit to the top-level routine and not be expected to pop to the procedure immediately preceding the routine.

CHAINING THE PROGRAMS...WITH A FLAIR!

There is yet another way to circumvent the chaining problem. Many developers don't want to start their application via the batch file approach. They want the chaining to be managed entirely from within their programs. The problem is that there is no command in Clipper or in dBASE III that is equivalent to dBASE II's QUIT TO command.

If a CANCEL or a QUIT command is given, memory is released, but everything is turned over to the operating system. To chain from the operating system, a batch file would have been generated prior to running the application, which is, as we stated, not the intent. On the other hand, if a RUN command is issued, the application remains in memory and there may be insufficient memory space as the other program is loaded.

The solution to the problem is not simple and not clean. It may cause problems and user-interfacing difficulty. The solution consists of a batch file approach and the technique of saving the environment to a MEMory file. If the AUTOEXEC.BAT is saved to a temporary file and then changed with the proper chaining calls followed by a cold boot, the first application could chain to the second program, clear out memory space for it, and save the environmental conditions for reentry.

Keep in mind that if this is done there will be considerable lag time as the computer goes through the booting process and chains to the second application. If the second application is anything other than a program with the capabilities of writing batch files, the AUTOEXEC.BAT file must have the name of the original calling program in it as well. Also, upon reentry of the original program, the old AUTOEXEC.BAT file must be restored. When the program has completed processing, one more cold boot must be activated in order to reset the system to its original condition.

Below is an example of just that process:

```
********************
* Name          AMENU.prg
* Date          August 21, 1986
* Notice        Copyright 1986, Stephen J. Straley
* Note          This is the first application.  Try this under a 256K
*               environment space.
*
********************

   CLEAR
   STORE .F. TO reboot
   IF FILE("ALLMEM.MEM")
      RESTORE FROM Allmem
      ERASE Allmem.mem
      RUN CD\
      RUN DEL Autoexec.bat
      RUN REN Autoexec.tem Autoexec.bat
      RUN CD\FW\WORK\TEST     && The name of the sub-directory for program
      DO &goproc
      STORE .T. TO reboot
   ENDIF
   DO Aamen1

   ********************

   PROCEDURE Aamen1

   DO WHILE .T.
      CLEAR
      scrframe = CHR(201) + CHR(205) + CHR(187) + CHR(186) + ;
                 CHR(188) + CHR(205) + CHR(200) + CHR(186) + CHR(32)
      STORE 0 TO option
      @ 6, 12, 16, 55 BOX scrframe
      @ 5, 29 SAY "Main Menu"
      @ 8, 14 PROMPT " Account Charts "
      @ 10, 14 PROMPT " Transactions "
      @ 12, 14 PROMPT " Postings "
      @ 14, 14 PROMPT " Reports "
      @ 8, 38 PROMPT " Listings "
      @ 10, 38 PROMPT " Other Systems "
      @ 12, 38 PROMPT " Utilities "
      @ 14, 38 PROMPT " End of Period "
      @ 17, 27 SAY "ESC to RETURN"
      MENU TO option
      DO CASE
      CASE option = 1
         DO Aamen11
      CASE option = 2
         *************************
         * Do subprocedure here. *
         *************************
      CASE option = 3
```

```
      **************************
      * Do subprocedure here. *
      **************************
   CASE option = 4
      **************************
      * Do subprocedure here. *
      **************************
   CASE option = 5
      **************************
      * Do subprocedure here. *
      **************************
   CASE option = 6
      **************************
      * Do subprocedure here. *
      **************************
   CASE option = 7
      **************************
      * Do subprocedure here. *
      **************************
   CASE option = 8
      DO Aamen18
   CASE option = 0
      @ 19, 15 SAY "All Files Closed, Returning to Operating System"
      IF reboot
         RUN Coldboot
      ELSE
         QUIT
      ENDIF
   ENDCASE

ENDDO

********************

PROCEDURE Aamen18

DO WHILE .T.
   STORE 0 TO option1
   @ 15, 40, 22, 65 BOX scrframe
   @ 16, 12 SAY ""
   @ 17, 46 PROMPT " Month End "
   @ 18, 46 PROMPT " Quarter End "
   @ 19, 46 PROMPT " Year End "
   @ 21, 47 SAY "ESC to RETURN"
   MENU TO option1
   DO CASE
   CASE option1 = 1
      **************************
      * Do subprocedure here. *
      **************************
   CASE option1 = 2
      **************************
      * Do subprocedure here. *
      **************************
```

```
   CASE option1 = 3
      ***************************
      * Do subprocedure here. *
      ***************************
   CASE option1 = 0
      EXIT
   ENDCASE

ENDDO

********************

PROCEDURE Aamen11

DO WHILE .T.
   STORE 0 TO option2
   @ 8, 32, 20, 54 BOX scrframe
   @ 8, 39 SAY "Sub-Menu"
   @ 10, 33 PROMPT " 1> Enter Accounts "
   @ 13, 33 PROMPT " 2> Edit Accounts "
   @ 16, 33 PROMPT " 3> Scan Accounts "
   @ 19, 33 PROMPT " 4> Delete Accounts "
   @ 21, 37 SAY "ESC to RETURN"
   MENU TO option2
   DO CASE
   CASE option2 = 1
      ***************************
      * Do subprocedure here. *
      ***************************
   CASE option2 = 2
      ***************************
      * Do subprocedure here. *
      ***************************
   CASE option2 = 3
      ***************************
      * Do subprocedure here. *
      ***************************
   CASE option2 = 4
      DO Aamen114
   CASE option2 = 0
      EXIT
   ENDCASE

ENDDO

********************

PROCEDURE Aamen114

DO WHILE .T.
   STORE 0 TO option3
   @ 17, 13, 21, 33 BOX scrframe
   @ 18, 10 SAY ""
```

```
      @ 18, 18 PROMPT " Quit File "
      @ 19, 18 PROMPT " Go to Top "
      @ 21, 17 SAY "ESC to RETURN"
      MENU TO option3
      DO CASE
      CASE option3 = 1
         goproc = PROCNAME()
         SAVE TO Allmem
         CLEAR ALL
         RUN CD\
         RUN REN AUTOEXEC.BAT AUTOEXEC.TEM
         SET CONSOLE OFF
         TEXT TO FILE Autoexec.bat
   cd\fw\work\test
   BMENU
   AMENU
         ENDTEXT
         RUN Coldboot
      CASE option3 = 2
         DO Aamen1
      CASE option3 = 0
         EXIT
      ENDCASE

   ENDDO
* End of AMENU.prg
```

And now for the second program...

```
*********************
* Name          BMENU.prg
* Date          September 21, 1986
* Notice        Copyright 1986, Stephen J. Straley
* Note          This is just a simple subprogram that checks the
*               amount of memory available.
*
*********************

   CLEAR
   ? "I am in BBMENU..."
   RUN chkdsk
   WAIT
* End of BMENU
```

This technique works because there is a program called COLDBOOT residing on the main directory. For a listing of the COLDBOOT program, please refer to the section in Chapter 11, Extent Files with C and Assembly.

CHAPTER FOUR

Commands

This chapter includes explanations of all the Clipper commands. If you are converting code from dBASE III to Clipper solely for the sake of increasing speed, take particular note of the different ways the two environments use the same commands. However, if you are converting an application with the intent of marketing it (which means protecting the source code as well), take note of the additional commands, for they can greatly enhance your product.

The listing for each command includes the command *name*, proper *syntax*, *description*, *command type*, *library required* (Autumn '86 and Summer '87 applicable), any *variances*, and one or more *samples*. If a command is labeled "standard," it works like the standard dBASE III command. If the command is somewhat different or enhanced under Clipper, the command is labeled "enhanced." The standard version of Clipper is the Winter '85 release. If the command is unique to the Summer '87 or Autumn '86 versions of Clipper, the command will begin with "Summer '87: Clipper Enhanced" or "Autumn 86: Clipper Enhanced." However, if only a clause or a small variance is unique in the Summer '87 or Autumn '86 versions, that clause or variance will follow the words "Summer '87" or "Autumn 86." It will be understood that if a command was implemented for the Autumn '86 version, it will still be in effect for all following versions, unless specified.

The following notation is used in describing the commands:

<expC>: A character expression, normally a string
<expL>: A logical expression, either .T. or .F.
<expD>: A date expression
<expN>: A numeric expression (a number or a formula)

@

Syntax: @ <row,column> [SAY <exp> [PICTURE <clause>]]
[GET <exp> [PICTURE <clause>]
[RANGE <exp,exp]
[VALID <exp>]]
[CLEAR]

Description: Used to display information to the screen or to the printer at specific locations. The CLEAR clause will clear the portion of the screen beginning at the <row,column> position, continuing across from that column marker, and panning down from that row marker.

Command: Standard

Library Called: Clipper.lib

Variance: The implementation of the VALID option is new. With the VALID option, the program can test for immediate input validation. The @ command is not completed until the expression in the VALID option is true. Escape is possible if ESCAPE is SET ON and the key is entered.

An added capability with the compiler is the ability to have a user-defined function work on the PICTURE clause. This capability is not possible with other interpreters.

Below is a list of accepted PICTURE functions and their meanings

@A Allows only alphabetic character into a GET command.

@B All numbers will be left-justified within the PICTURE area.

@C All positive numbers will be displayed with a CR after them.

@D Dates will be displayed in the SET DATE format.

@E Dates will be displayed in British format; numbers will be displaced in European format.

@R Nontemplate characters will be inserted.

@X All negative numbers will be shown with a DB after them.

@(Negative numbers will be enclosed in parentheses with leading spaces.

@Z Displays zero as blanks.

@! All alphabetic characters will be converted to uppercase

@) For negative numbers (credit balances), the leading spaces are not displayed within the parentheses.

@K Allows a suggestion value to be seen within the GET area, but it will be cleared if any key, including the Enter key, is struck.

@S<expN> Will allow horizontal scrolling of the field or variable <expN> characters wide.

Below is a list of allowed template symbols:

A Only alphabetic characters will be displayed.

N Only alphabetic and numeric characters will be displayed.

X Any character will be displayed.

9 Only digits, including signs, will be displayed for any data type.

Only digits, signs, and spaces will be displayed for any data type.

L Only "T" or "F" will be displayed for logical data types.

Y Only "Y" or "N" will be displayed for logical data types.

! Alphabetic character are converted to uppercase.

$ Dollar sign will be displayed in place of leading spaces for numeric data types.

* Asterisk will be displayed in place of leading space for numeric data types.

. Position of decimal point.

, Position of comma.

Sample:

```
CLEAR
STORE "A" TO input
@ 10,10 SAY "I only want you to enter in any of the"
@ 11,10 SAY "  first three letters of the alphabet."
@ 15,10 SAY "Enter character " GET input PICT "@K !";
        VALID( input$"ABC" )
@ 20,10 SAY "Very good..."
WAIT
@ 10,10 CLEAR
```

@...TO

Syntax: @<row,column> [CLEAR] TO <row2, column2> [DOUBLE]

Description: Used to draw a single or double line box or to clear an area of the screen. The [CLEAR] clause and the [DOUBLE] clause cannot both exist with this command.

Command: Standard

Library Called: Clipper.lib

Autumn 86: This command was implemented in the Autumn '86 version.

![<expC>]

Syntax: ![<expC>]

Description: Introduced in Clipper - Winter '85. This operator is equivalent to the .NOT. operator. It offers additional compatibility with other languages some developers may be acquainted with.

Command: Clipper enhanced

Library Called: Clipper.lib

Variance: This operator may not be used in place of the < > sign in versions prior to Autumn '86. For that operation, as well as the other mathematical operators, maintain the standard conventions.

The ! operator must not have a blank space between it and <expC> or else it will be interpreted as a RUN command.

Sample:

```
IF !EOF()        && In Place of IF .NOT. EOF()
```

The following would **not** be legal in versions prior to Autumn '86:

```
IF test !="Sample"  && in place of IF test <> "Sample"
```

! (See RUN)

?

Syntax: ? <expression list>

Description: This operator displays and evaluates the value of an expression. The single question mark will issue a carriage return and line feed **before** the expression is displayed or evaluated. A question mark without an expression list will generate a blank line.

Command: Standard

Library Called: Clipper.lib

Samples:

```
? RECNO()    && Will display the current record number
? last_name && Will print out the contents of the
            && last_name field.
? DATE() = DATE()  && Will display a .T. for this true
                   && expression.
```

??

Syntax: ?? <expression list>

Description: This operator displays and evaluates the value of an expression. The double question mark will **not** issue a carriage return and line feed before the expression is displayed or evaluated. All that will be displayed or evaluated will be the expression either on the screen, to the printer, or to an alternate file.

Command: Standard

Library Called: Clipper.lib

Samples:

```
?? RECNO()    && Will display the current record number
?? last_name && Will print out the contents of the
             && last_name field.
?? DATE() = DATE()  && Will display a .T. for this true
                    && expression.
```

==

Syntax: <expression> = = <expression>

Description: Similar to SET EXACT ON; however, this operator will look for a perfect match: it must have the same characters, length, and value on both sides of the equation. SET EXACT ON evaluates characters, not value.

Command: Clipper enhanced

Library Called: Clipper.lib

Variance: Below is a list of examples showing the use of the = = operator with SET EXACT ON and with SET EXACT OFF and what each would yield. If there should ever be a case in which two variables do not match but are equal (e.g., X = 0 and Y = 0, but X < > Y) or there is a case in which -0 = 0, use the double equal sign.

Sample:

```
SET EXACT ON      "Test this" = "Test this "       && True

"Test this " = "Test this"        && True
SET EXACT OFF     "Test this" = "Test this "        && False
"Test this " = "Test this"        && True
SET EXACT ON      "Test this" == "Test this "       && False
"Test this " == "Test this"       && False
SET EXACT OFF     "Test this" == "Test this "       && False
"Test this " == "Test this"       && False
```

ACCEPT

Syntax: ACCEPT [<prompt message>] TO <memvar>

Description: Prompts the user for specific input. All data input by the user is treated as character type. Therefore, if numeric input is desired in conjunction with this command, the VALue() of the string must be converted. The prompting message will appear to the left-most side of the screen; the cursor immediately follows the string, waiting for input.

The memory variable does not have to be initialized prior to the issuance of this command. If the memory variable does exist, that value will be replaced by the new input.

If the Enter key is hit without any value for the memory variable, the memory variable will then be set to a NULL value with LEN() of 0.

A maximum of 255 characters can be entered into the variable with the ACCEPT command.

Command: Standard

Library Called: Clipper.lib

Sample:

```
********************
* Name          ACCEPT.prg
* Date          August 3, 1986
* Notice        Copyright 1986-1988, Stephen J. Straley
* Compile       Clipper Accept
* Release       All versions
* Link          Plink86 fi accept lib clipper
* Note          Demonstrates the ACCEPT command.
**********************
```

```
test = 4
FOR x = 1 TO 2
   CLEAR
   ACCEPT "What is the variable: " TO test
   ? test
   ? LEN(test)
   WAIT
NEXT
* End of File
```

APPEND BLANK

Syntax: APPEND BLANK

Description: This command places a blank record at the end of the file and positions the record pointer or counter to that blank record. All character fields are filled with spaces, numeric fields have a value of zero (0), logical fields are set to a value of .F. (false), and date fields are set to a value of " / / ." From this point, data entry may be performed with a series of @... SAY... GET on the fields that were just opened.

Command: Standard

Library Called: Clipper.lib

Autumn '86: Attempts to APPEND and lock a new record whenever SET EXCLUSIVE is OFF. If another user has locked the file on which the APPEND BLANK is to be performed, the NETERR() function will return a .T.

Sample:

```
********************
* Name        APPEND.prg
* Date        August 3, 1986
* Notice      Copyright 1986-1988, Stephen J. Straley
* Compile     Clipper Append
* Release     All versions
* Link        Plink86 fi append lib clipper;
* Note        This program will demonstrate the use of the
*             APPEND BLANK command.  There are a few other
*             commands mixed in, but study the main thrust
*             of this program.
*
********************

CREATE Temp
USE Temp
APPEND BLANK
```

```
REPLACE field_name WITH "CHARACT", field_len WITH 15, field_type
WITH "C"
APPEND BLANK
REPLACE field_name WITH "NUMERIC", field_len WITH 10, field_type
WITH "N"
APPEND BLANK
REPLACE field_name WITH "DATE", field_len WITH 8, field_type WITH
"D"
APPEND BLANK
REPLACE field_name WITH "logic", field_len WITH 1, field_type WITH
"L"
USE
CREATE Append FROM Temp
ERASE Temp
USE Append
CLEAR
APPEND BLANK
? "Positioned on record: "
?? RECNO()
?
? "Character field is set to: "
?? charact
? LEN(charact)
? "Numeric field is set to: "
?? numeric
? "Date field is set to: "
?? date
? "Logical field is set to: "
?? logic
WAIT
CLEAR
@ 10,10 SAY "Input the character field: " GET charact
@ 12,10 SAY "  Input the numeric field: " GET numeric
@ 14,10 SAY "     Input the date field: " GET date
@ 16,10 SAY "  Input the logical field: " GET logic
READ
USE
ERASE Append
* End of File
```

APPEND FROM

Syntax: APPEND [scope][FIELDS <field list>] FROM <file name> [FOR <condition>][WHILE <condition>][SDF/Delimited [WITH BLANK/<delimiter>]]

Description: Allows records to be added to the currently selected and open database from one database.

Command: Standard

Library Called: Clipper.lib

Variance: The APPEND FROM command in Clipper supports a field list. This list is an optional argument. The word "FIELDS" must be present if this option is used. If used, when the data from the FROM database is brought in, only fields listed in the <fields list> are appended. Also, the data types **must** be the same for the fields listed in the list in both the source and target files. If the widths vary, Clipper will truncate the source data if the target field is smaller and will pad the source data if the target field is larger. The scope of the appended records may also be specified.

Sample:
```
APPEND Record 10 FIELDS name, city, state FROM Alter
```

AVERAGE

Syntax: AVERAGE [<scope>] <field list> TO <memvar list> [FOR <condition>][WHILE <condition>]

Description: Enables an average of specified fields to be calculated based on a specific condition in the currently selected and open database.

Command: Standard

Library Called: Clipper.lib

Variance: Both arguments (the <field list> and the <memvar list>) are mandatory. Only the Summer '87 version will recognize the REST scope clause.

Sample:
```
AVERAGE myage, yourage, ourage TO a_age, b_age, c_age;
FOR myage > 20
```

BEGIN SEQUENCE

Syntax: BEGIN SEQUENCE <statements>... [BREAK] <statements>... END

Description: The BEGIN SEQUENCE command allows you to define program control for error trapping and conditional breaking within the flow of a program. The BREAK statement will turn over program execution to the statement immediately following the matching END statement.

The BEGIN SEQUENCE command may be nested up to 16 times. Any more than 16 BEGIN SEQUENCE commands without releasing the command with a BREAK command will cause problems with the Clipper internal stack and may cause the computer to lock up.

Command: Clipper enhanced - Summer '87

Library Called: Clipper.lib

Sample: Please see the Breakout.prg in Chapter 7 for a complete description and sample of the BEGIN SEQUENCE command.

BOX

Syntax: @ <top,left,bottom,right> BOX <string>

Description: The BOX command is used mainly for drawing boxes quickly and efficiently, especially in the implementation of frames for screen designs. The string parameter of the BOX command either must be a string of nine characters or a null string. If the null string is passed to the BOX command, the area specified by the four coordinates is cleared. Otherwise, the string being passed represents the characters designated for: (1) the top left corner, (2) the line across the top, (3) the top right corner, (4) the line down the right side, (5) the bottom right corner, (6) the line across the bottom, (7) the bottom left corner, (8) the line up the left side, and (9) the character to fill the space framed by the box.

Command: Clipper enhanced

Library Called: Clipper.lib

Variance: With the Summer '87 release, the ability to allow a single character to represent the border characters and the fill character has been removed.

Sample:

```
********************
* Name        BOXES.prg
* Date        August 4, 1986
* Notice      Copyright 1986, Stephen J. Straley
* Compile     Clipper Boxes
* Release     All versions
* Link        Plink86 fi boxes lib clipper;
* Note        This program will draw many boxes using the
*             BOX command.
*********************
```

```
frame = CHR(201) + CHR(205) + CHR(187) + CHR(186) + ;
        CHR(188) + CHR(205) + CHR(200) + CHR(186) + ;
        CHR(32)
STORE  1 TO top
STORE  0 TO left
STORE 22 TO bottom
STORE 79 TO right
FOR x = 1 TO 10
   @ top, left, bottom, right BOX frame
   STORE top + 1 TO top
   STORE left + 3 TO left
   STORE bottom - 1 TO bottom
   STORE right - 3 TO right
NEXT
@ 11,35 SAY "FINISHED!"
@ 23,00 SAY ""
* End of File
```

CALL

Syntax: CALL <process> [WITH <parameter list>]

Description: This command gives you access to separately compiled and/or assembled routines. These routines must be linked in at the same time as the other object files produced by Clipper. All CALLed programs must conform to the following rules:

1. They must follow C language calling and parameter passing conventions.
2. They must be in the "Intel 8086 relocatable object file format" with the .OBJ file extension.
3. They must be available to the linker.
4. The library of the compiler of the calling program must be available to the Clipper linker. Remember that additional runtime support will be necessary for any language other than assembly language.
5. Up to seven parameters may be passed to the CALLed routine.
6. The FAR process is necessary for CALLed programs.
7. All data references consist of 4-byte pointers of the form SEGMENT:OFFSET. They are on top of the stack in the order passed. All data types are passed by reference.
8. CALLed programs must preserve the BP, SS, and DS registers.
9. Character strings are passed by reference and are null terminated.
10. Data item lengths must be preserved.
11. Numeric variables are passed as 8-byte floating point representation. They maintain a 53-bit characteristic and an 11-bit exponent biased by 1023.

Command: Clipper enhanced

Autumn '86: [WITH WORD(<expN>)] has been added. This will convert numeric parameters from type double to type int, reducing the overhead of the CALLed routine. If the value of the numeric expression expressed in the WORD function does not exceed plus or minus 32K, there is no need to pass a larger parameter.

Summer '87: Microsoft C 5.0 places leading underscores on function names. In order to access these functions, use the form: CALL _<function>. As with the Autumn '86 version, in order to convert numeric parameters from type double to type int, use the [WITH WORD(<expN>] clause. Now, the CALL command allows a parameter list to consist of up to seven parameters. As with dBASE III Plus, the DX:BX and ES:BX registers point to the first parameter in the list. Required commands with the LOAD module are:

```
PUBLIC <proc>
```

and

```
mov ds,dx
```

Characters data types are passed by reference. The length of the data string must be preserved. Since data items reside consecutively in memory, if the data types are not preserved and if they are lengthened, other data may be written over.

Numeric data types are passed as an 8-byte floating point. It consists of a 53-bit character and an 11-bit exponent biased by 1023. If the value is greater than ±<F128M><145>32,767, it cannot be passed using the WORD clause.

Sample: See Chapter 11, Extend Files with C and Assembly.

CANCEL

Syntax: CANCEL

Description: Just as effective as the QUIT command, this command stops the execution of a procedure or command file and the program and returns to the operating system.

Command: Standard

Library Called: Clipper.lib

Sample:

```
*********************
* Name          CANCEL.prg
* Date          August 4, 1986
* Notice        Copyright 1986, Stephen J. Straley
* Compile       Clipper Cancel
* Release       All versions
* Link          Plink86 fi cancel lib clipper;
* Note          This will show the CANCEL command stopping
*               the execution of the program within a
*               subroutine from the main program.
**********************

CLEAR
DO WHILE .T.
   to_quit = .F.
   ? "Currently in the main section of the program..."
   DO Subroute
ENDDO

PROCEDURE Subroute

   @ ROW()+1, 5 SAY "Do you want to Cancel? " GET to_quit
   READ
   IF to_quit
      CANCEL
   ENDIF
* End of File
```

CLEAR

Syntax: CLEAR

Description: This command clears the screen and positions the cursor at ROW = 0, COL = 0 or at the upper left-most corner of the screen.

Command: Standard

Library Called: Clipper.lib

Variance: This command **cannot** be used in your HELP.PRG file, in procedures called via the SET KEY TO command, or in functions called via the VALID clause. If used, it will clear all GET/READs from the calling program. To get around this problem, issue an @ 0,0 CLEAR command to clear the screen or, for the Summer '87 release, use the CLEAR SCREEN command.

CLEAR ALL

Syntax: CLEAR ALL

Description: This command clears all memory variables from the system, closes all open databases and associated indexes and memo fields (if applicable), and releases any SET RELATION TO command and filter conditions. It SELECTs work area 1.

Command: Standard

Library Called: Clipper.lib

CLEAR GETS

Syntax: CLEAR GETS

Description: Used in conjunction with associated @ SAY/GET commands, a CLEAR GETS command releases all GET statements prior to this command.

Command: Standard

Library Called: Clipper.lib

Variance: In Clipper, the addition of the "S" on GETS is required for the compiler to function properly.

Notes: This command is used to help display a memory variable pertinent to the system in reverse video if the normal attributes of the screen are maintained.

Sample:

```
********************
* Name          ANOTHGET.prg
* Date          August 4, 1986
* Notice        Copyright 1986, Stephen J. Straley
* Compiler      Clipper Anothget
* Release       All versions
* Link          Plink fi anothget lib clipper;
* Note          This program demonstrates how CLEAR GETS can
*               be used as a display command on GETs rather
*               than as an input command.
*********************

STORE 0 TO testvar1
STORE "This is a test" TO testvar2
```

```
CLEAR
@ 01,10 SAY "There is this way..."
@ 04,10 SAY " The first variable: "
@ ROW(),COL()+1 SAY testvar1
@ 05,10 SAY "The second variable: "
@ ROW(),COL()+1 SAY testvar2
@ 10,10 SAY "Now there is this way..."
@ 14,10 SAY " The first variable: " GET testvar1
@ 15,10 SAY "The second variable: " GET testvar2
CLEAR GETS
@ 23,00 SAY ""
* End of File
```

CLEAR MEMORY

Syntax: CLEAR MEMORY

Description: This command releases and clears all memory variables from the system.

Command: Standard

Library Called: Clipper.lib

CLEAR SCREEN

Syntax: CLEAR SCREEN

Description: The CLEAR SCREEN command clears the entire screen without clearing any pending GETs.

Command: Clipper enhanced - Summer '87 release

Library Called: Clipper.lib

Note: This command may now replace the @ 0,0 CLEAR command in order to clear the screen and preserve the active GETs. It is extremely useful in conjunction with procedures called via the SET KEY TO command or functions called via the VALID clause.

CLEAR TYPEAHEAD

Syntax: CLEAR TYPEAHEAD

Description: The CLEAR TYPEAHEAD command clears the keyboard buffer.

Command: Clipper enhanced - Summer '87 release

Library Called: Clipper.lib

Note: This command replaces the Winter '85 CALL _cclr and the Autumn '86 KEYBOARD.

For the Summer '87 release, CALL __cclr is accepted.

CLOSE

Syntax: CLOSE <file type>

Description: The CLOSE ALTERNATE command closes an open alternate file.

The CLOSE DATABASES command closes all open databases and all associated indexes.

The CLOSE ALL command is a Summer '87 enhancement; it closes all types of files including alternate files, databases, and index files. It will also release all active files, formats, and relations.

The CLOSE ALTERNATE command closes the current open alternate file.

The CLOSE INDEX command closes all open index files that are currently in use.

The CLOSE FORMAT/PROCEDURE command closes all open FORMAT/PROCEDURE files. Keep in mind that format files are treated no differently from any other program or procedure file. In a compiled application, there is no real distinction between a program file and open format and procedure files.

Command: Standard

Library Called: Clipper.lib

Variance: The Summer '87 version now allows the CLOSE ALL command.

COMMIT

Syntax: COMMIT

Description: The COMMIT command performs a solid-disk write for all work areas. Before the disk write is performed, all buffers are flushed to DOS.

Command: Clipper enhanced - Summer '87 release

Library Called: Clipper.lib

Note: This command will only work with versions of DOS 3.3 or higher.

Sample:

```
DO Addgets
READ
IF LASTKEY() < > 27
   DO Rep_vals  && Array / memory variables are REPLACED
into the database.
  COMMIT
ENDIF
```

CONTINUE

Syntax: CONTINUE

Description: This command resumes a search initiated by a LOCATE FOR command, continuing to search for records that meet the search criteria. If a CONTINUE is successful in its search, the record pointer is placed on that record; otherwise, the EOF() marker is set to .T. (true) and the record pointer is placed on the last record.

Command: Standard

Library Called: Clipper.lib

COPY FILE

Syntax: COPY FILE <source file> TO <destination file>

Description: The COPY FILE command makes an exact copy of <source file> with the name <destination file>. Both file names **must** have the file extension included as well as the drive and directory designator if it is any different from that of the default drive and directory.

The COPY FILE command will not work on a currently open file.

Command: Standard

Library Called: Clipper.lib

Variance: If used as noted with the Autumn '86 release, a DOS message (1 file(s) copied) will appear on the screen immediately following the completion of this command. This is because Clipper uses DOS for the copying and DOS messages appear as well. To avoid this, send the output of the messages to a NUL device in the following way:

```
COPY FILE <source file> TO <destination file>>NUL
```

The >NUL must appear immediately after the name of the destination file, without any blank spaces.

Below are a few samples both with the additional clause and without.

Sample:

```
COPY FILE Mainfile.dbf TO Temp.dbf
COPY FILE Mainfile.dbt TO Temp.dbt>NUL
USE Mainfile
COPY FILE C:\DBASE\Myprog.prg TO A:\Myprog.bak>NUL
```

COPY STRUCTURE

Syntax: COPY STRUCTURE TO <filename> [FIELDS <field list>]

Description: The COPY STRUCTURE command only copies the structure of the currently active database to <filename>.

Command: Standard

Library Called: Clipper.lib

Variance: The <field list> cannot be in a macro substitution. The fields must be either in separate variables or coded as literals in the program or procedure file. As with all other similar commands, the <filename> must include the drive and directory designator if the file being generated is not to be on the default drive and directory. If no file extension is given, the file is assumed to carry a .DBF extension.

If the FIELDS <field list> option is not included, the entire structure of the active database will be copied to the TO <filename>.

Sample:

```
USE Mainfile
COPY STRUCTURE TO Temp
USE Temp
```

COPY TO <filename>

Syntax: COPY TO <filename> [<scope>] [FIELDS <field list>] [FOR <condition>] [WHILE <condition>] [SDF/DELIMITED WITH BLANK/<delimiter>]

Description: The COPY TO <filename> command copies the currently selected database to another database or to an alternate text file. The copied file can consist of selected fields within the selected database and/or can be copied with a specific condition. The FOR and WHILE clauses may be used together. If the SDF/DELIMITED clause is used, the copied file will be an ASCII text file.

Command: Standard

Library Called: Clipper.lib

Variance: With the Summer '87 the DELIMITED WITH BLANK, DIF, SYLK, and WKS are not supported.

Sample:

```
USE Hist

COPY TO Nufi FIELDS last_name, total_hours;
    FOR total_hours > 40
```

COPY TO STRUCTURE EXTENDED

Syntax: COPY TO <filename> STRUCTURE EXTENDED

Description: The COPY TO STRUCTURE EXTENDED command creates a new database consisting of only four fields: field_name, field_type, field_len, and field_dec. Fields of the open database become records in the structure extended database.

Command: Standard

Library Called: Clipper.lib

Notes: If used, this command can allow databases to be modified structurally within an application, especially if used in conjunction with the CREATE FROM command.

Sample:

```
********************
* Name          COPYSTRU.prg
* Date          August 3, 1986
* Notice        Copyright 1986, Stephen J. Straley
* Compile       Clipper Copystru
* Release       All versions
* Link          Plink86 fi Copystru lib clipper;
* Note          This will take the database MULTY.DBF and
*               convert the fields to records in
*               CONVERTD.DBF.
*********************

USE Multy
COPY TO Convertd STRUCTURE EXTENDED
CLEAR
USE Convertd
LIST field_name, field_type, field_len, field_dec
```

COUNT

Syntax: COUNT [<scope>][FOR <condition>][WHILE <condition>] TO <memvar>

Description: This command counts how many records in the currently active and open database file meet a specific condition, and it stores that figure to a memory variable.

Command: Standard

Library Called: Clipper.lib

Variance: The COUNT command must store the final figure of its operation to a memory variable. Additionally, the FOR and WHILE conditional clauses may coexist.

Sample:

```
USE Phonbook
COUNT FOR state = "CA" .AND. TRIM(city) = "San Diego";
TO how_many
CLEAR
@ 10,10 SAY "I know "
?? LTRIM(STR(how_many))
?? " People in San Diego, California"
```

CREATE

Syntax: CREATE <database file name>

Description: This command allows an application to create the necessary databases without a preexisting template and empty database or an available template and empty structure extended database.

Command: Clipper enhanced

Notes: Using the CREATE command results in a new file consisting of four fields: field_name, field_type, field_len, and field_dec. In essence, a STRUCTURE EXTENDED file will be created from scratch, without the previous existence of a database. Since Clipper can handle fields greater than 255 bytes and a character field defined with a length greater than 999 (i.e., for screens), the field_len field must be replaced with INT(length % 256) and the field_dec field must be replaced with the INT(length / 256). Records may then be added and, from this, new databases established.

Sample:

```
********************
* Name          PRINIT.prg
* Date          August 4, 1986
* Notice        Copyright 1986, Stephen J. Straley
* Compile       Clippper Prinit
* Release       All versions
* Link          Plink86 fi prinit lib clipper;
* Note          This will create the history file for a
*               payroll program.
*********************

STORE "C:" TO scrdata
IF !FILE(scrdata + "Prhist.dat")
   CREATE Template
   USE Template
   APPEND BLANK
   REPLACE field_name WITH "EMPLOYEE", field_type WITH "C",;
           field_len WITH 15
   APPEND BLANK
   REPLACE field_name WITH "PERIOD", field_type WITH "N",;
           field_len WITH 1
   APPEND BLANK
   REPLACE field_name WITH "HOURS", field_type WITH "N",;
           field_len WITH 8, field_dec WITH 4
   APPEND BLANK
   REPLACE field_name WITH "MARRIED", field_type WITH "L",;
           field_len WITH 1
   APPEND BLANK
   REPLACE field_name WITH "SCREEN", field_type WITH "C",;
```

```
            field_len WITH INT(4000 % 256), field_dec WITH INT(4000
/ 256)
   GO TOP
   CLEAR
   LIST field_name, field_type, field_len, field_dec
   USE
   file = scrdata + "PRHIST.DAT"
   CREATE &file. FROM Template
   ?
   ? "File created..."
   ERASE Template
   ?
   ? "Template erased..."
ENDIF
* End of File
```

CREATE FROM

Syntax: CREATE <newfile> FROM <structure extended file>

Description: The CREATE FROM command forms a new database file based on the contents of a structure extended file.

Command: Standard

Library Called: Clipper.lib

Variance: Issue a CLOSE DATABASES or a USE command immediately following this command if the newly created file is to be opened. With the CREATE FROM command, records in a structure extended database file are converted to be the actual structure for the file specified by the <newfile> parameter. To initially CREATE the structure extended file, refer to the CREATE command or the COPY STRUCTURE EXTENDED command.

This command can create any standard database with more than 128 fields and a character field length greater than 255 bytes.

Sample: See PRINIT.prg in the CREATE command

DECLARE

Syntax: DECLARE <memvar> [<expN>] [, <array list>]

Description: This command establishes a PRIVATE array named <memvar> of <expN> items. The items may be of any type and may be mixed.

Keep in mind that arrays are always private if initialized with this command. Public arrays may be initialized with the PUBLIC command only with the Summer '87 release. The brackets ([]) around <expN> must be included when working with arrays.

A few other things to keep in mind when using arrays are:

1. The LEN() function will return the number of items in the array if the array name is the only parameter used; otherwise it will return the LEN of the element addressed.

2. The TYPE() function will always return an "A" indicating an array type if the array name without element numbers is passed to the function.

3. Establishing a memory variable with the same name as an array will destroy the array and release the contents of the array; an array cannot be saved to an external file (SAVE TO <memfile>).

4. Arrays cannot be passed as a parameter with the CALL command.

5. Arrays may be used with macros but with limited usage (see samples below).

6. Arrays may be passed to procedures with the following regulations:

   a. DO <procedure> WITH (<memvar>[<expN>])
   passing element to procedure by value.

   b. DO <procedure> WITH (memvar)
   passing the entire array by reference by just passing the name of the array to the procedure.

7. The memory space required by an array is considered to be dynamic (it grows as items are added, much like a MEMO FILE) and follows the following formula:

   a. The array itself is 22 bytes times the number of elements to be stored in it.

   b. If an element to be added to the array is longer in width than 22 bytes, an address is added in place of the element that refers to the actual position in memory where that element resides.

Command: Clipper enhanced

Library Called: Summer '87 - Clipper.lib
Autumn '86 - Dbu.lib

Variance: With the Summer '87 release, the maximum number of array elements is 4096. In the Autumn '86 release, the maximum was set to 2048.

Sample:

```
********************
* Name          SAMPARRY.prg
* Date          August 4, 1986
* Notice        Copyright 1986, Stephen J. Straley
* Compile       Clipper Samparry
* Release       Autumn '86 or greater
* Link          Summer '87: Plink86 fi Samparry lib clipper;
*                 Autumn '86: Plink86 fi Samparry lib dbu lib clip-
per;
* Note          This program will initialize the months and
*               the days of the week to two memory
*               variables and pass them to procedures.
*********************

DECLARE month_a[12], day_a[7], date_a[50], numb_a[25],
hodge_a[100]

******************************************
* The following initializes the arrays. *
******************************************

FOR x = 1 TO 50
   DO CASE
   CASE x <= 7
      day_a[x]   = CDOW(DATE() + (1 *x))
      month_a[x] = CMONTH(DATE() + (30 * x))
      numb_a[x]  = x * 324
      date_a[x]  = DATE() + x * 84
   CASE x > 7 .AND. x <= 12
      month_a[x] = CMONTH(DATE() + (30 * x))
      numb_a[x]  = x * 324
      date_a[x]  = DATE() + x * 84
   CASE x > 12 .AND. x <= 25
      numb_a[x]  = x * 324
      date_a[x]  = DATE() + x * 84
   CASE x > 25
      date_a[x]  = DATE() + x * 84
   ENDCASE
NEXT
CLEAR
```

```
*****************************************************
* This section displays the values of the arrays. *
*****************************************************

@ 01,05 SAY "Days of the week are ... "
FOR x = 1 TO 7
   ? day_a[x]
   hodge_a[x] = day_a[x]
NEXT
WAIT
CLEAR

@ 01,05 SAY "Months of the year are ... "
FOR x = 1 TO 12
   ? month_a[x]
   hodge_a[x + 7] = month_a[x]
NEXT
WAIT
CLEAR

STORE 1 TO temp_col
STORE 3 TO temp_row

@ 01,05 SAY "A random set of 25 numbers are ... "
FOR x = 1 TO 25
   @ temp_row, temp_col SAY numb_a[x]
   DO Chngescr
   hodge_a[x + 19] = numb_a[x]
NEXT
WAIT
CLEAR

STORE 1 TO temp_col
STORE 3 TO temp_row

@ 01,05 SAY "A random of 50 dates are ... "
FOR x = 1 TO 50
   @ temp_row, temp_col say date_a[x]
   DO Chngescr
   hodge_a[x + 44] = date_a[x]
NEXT
WAIT
CLEAR

STORE 1 TO temp_col
STORE 3 TO temp_row

@ 01,05 SAY "The total is ... "
FOR x = 1 TO 100
   @ temp_row, temp_col SAY hodge_a[x]
   DO Chngescr
NEXT
WAIT
CLEAR
```

```
****************************************************
* This displays information using the LEN() and   *
* TYPE () functions.                               *
****************************************************

@ 10,15 SAY "The following will show the depth "
?? "of each array ... "
@ 12,10 SAY "The number of elements in the Month Array   "
?? LEN(month_a)
@ 13,10 SAY "The number of elements in the Day Array     "
?? LEN(day_a)
@ 14,10 SAY "The number of elements in the Number Array  "
?? LEN(numb_a)
@ 15,10 SAY "The number of elements in the Date Array    "
?? LEN(date_a)
@ 16,10 SAY "The number of elements in Hodge Podge Array "
?? LEN(hodge_a)
@ 20,10 SAY "The type of the arrays are ...              "
?? TYPE("month_a")
WAIT
CLEAR
STORE "" TO in_temp

************************************************************
* This section passes the array to a procedure by value. *
************************************************************

DO Passarry WITH month_a[3]
@ 14,10 SAY "Month_a[3] is out of the procedure and equal to: "
@ 14,60 SAY month_a[3]
WAIT

************************************************************
* This section passes the array by value yet shows how to *
* reassign the value back to the array.                    *
************************************************************

DO Passarry WITH month_a[3]
month_a[3] = in_temp
@ 14,10 SAY "Month_a[3] is out of the procedure and equal to: "
@ 14,60 SAY month_a[3]
WAIT

************************************************************
* This section passes the entire array to a procedure by  *
* reference.                                               *
************************************************************

DO Anotarry WITH numb_a
CLEAR

STORE 3 TO temp_row
STORE 1 TO temp_col
```

```
@ 01,05 SAY "The numbers are now set to ... "
FOR x = 1 TO 25
   @ temp_row, temp_col SAY numb_a[x]
   DO Chngescr
NEXT

********************

PROCEDURE Passarry

   PARAMETERS in_val

   CLEAR
   @ 04,23 SAY "The value of the passed array is ... "
   @ 04,60 SAY in_val
   @ 06,23 SAY "Let us change the value ... " GET in_val
   READ
   @ 08,23 SAY "The new value is ... "
   @ 08,60 SAY in_val
   @ 10,20 SAY ""
   in_temp = in_val
   WAIT

********************

PROCEDURE Anotarry

   PARAMETERS b

   CLEAR
   temp_col = 1
   temp_row = 3
   @ 01,05 say "You may edit this Number Array ... "
   FOR x = 1 TO 25
      @ temp_row, temp_col GET b[x]
      DO Chngescr
   NEXT
   READ

********************

PROCEDURE Chngescr

   temp_col = temp_col + 15
   IF temp_col > 65
      temp_col = 1
      temp_row = temp_row + 1
   ENDIF
* End of File
```

DELETE

Syntax: DELETE [<scope>][FOR <condition>][WHILE <condition>]

Description: The DELETE command marks a record(s) in the currently open and active database for future deletion. Without any conditional clause accompanying the DELETE command, only the current record is marked for deletion. Both a FOR condition and a WHILE condition may exist simultaneously; however, the FOR condition will take precedence.

Records are noted as DELETEd with an asterisk located in the first position on the screen, printer, or file (used in conjunction with the DISPLAY and LIST commands).

Command: Standard

Library Called: Clipper.lib

Variance: The REST scope is permitted with the Summer '87 release. With all versions of Clipper, the FOR and WHILE conditions are allowed together with this command.

Sample:

```
GO 5
DELETE   && this command will mark record 5 for deletion.

GO TOP
DELETE ALL FOR state = "CA" WHILE SUBSTR(phone,1,2) = "(2"
*
* All records in the state of CA and with a phone number
* starting with a "(2" will be marked for deletion.
*
```

DIR

Syntax: DIR [<drive>][<path>][<skeleton>]

Description: The DIR command displays the file names, number of records, size of the file in bytes, and date of last update for all databases on the designated drive or path. Not only database information but general file information as well may be displayed.

If no <skeleton> is passed, a search for .DBF files will be made. Other files may be displayed by using DOS wild cards in the <skeleton> as in the DOS DIR command.

Command: Standard

Library Called: Clipper.lib

Sample:

```
DIR *.*
DIR *.NTX
DIR *.PRG
DIR A:\ONE\*.*
```

DISPLAY

Syntax: DISPLAY [OFF][scope] FIELDS <field list> [FOR <condition>] [WHILE <condition>] [TO PRINT] [TO FILE <file>]

Description: This command allows the contents of fields to be displayed.

Command: Standard

Library Called: Clipper.lib

Variance: To display any field, the FIELDS clause is mandatory with the Autumn '86 release; the field names are not displayed as a header and there is no automatic pausing after each 20 lines.

Autumn 86/ Summer 87: [TO PRINT/TO FILE <filename>] is an additional clause for the DISPLAY command.

Sample:

```
DISPLAY FIELDS name, city, state FOR state = "CA"
```

DO

Syntax: DO <file name> [WITH <parameter(s)>]

Description: The DO command begins execution of a program file or procedure.

Command: Standard

Library Called: Clipper.lib

Variance: Since the application is compiled, just the name of the file is required to begin execution of that program or procedure. At the conclusion of the program or procedure, control is returned to the calling program. In the case of the top-level program, control will be returned to DOS. There is, in theory, no restriction to the number of consecutive DOs; therefore, Clipper supports recursive programming. However, an unlimited number of recursive DOs will cause your application to fail because of the finite size of the internal stack.

Any number of parameters up to 128 may be passed to a program file or to a procedure by reference or by value. If a parameter is passed by reference, the parameter is passed without parentheses and the called routine can change the value of the parameter that may be accessed by higher-level routines. If a parameter is passed by value, it is contained within parentheses and only the value of the parameter is passed to the program or procedure; even if that value is changed, the original value of the variable is retained in the calling program.

Sample: 1. This sample demonstrates recursive programming.

```
*********************
* Name          RECURSE.prg
* Date          August 4, 1986
* Notice        Copyright 1986, Stephen J. Straley
* Compile       Clipper Recurse
* Release       All versions
* Link          Plink86 fi recurse lib clipper;
* Note          This program will demonstrate recursive
*               program calling.
**********************

CLEAR
x = 1
DO Sub1 WITH (x)

*********************

PROCEDURE Sub1

   PARAMETERS y

   ?? y
   ?? SPACE(5)
   IF y > 10
      CANCEL
   ENDIF
   y = y + 1
   DO Sub1 WITH (y)
* End of File
```

2. This sample demonstrates the two methods of passing parameters.

```
*********************
* Name          PASSING.prg
* Date          August 4, 1986
* Notice        Copyright 1986, Stephen J. Straley
* Compile       Clipper Passing
* Release       All versions
* Link          Plink86 fi passing lib clipper;
* Note          This program will demonstrate passing
*               variables to a subroutine.
**********************
STORE 0 TO x, y
CLEAR
DO Readj WITH x, (Y)          && pass x by reference
? x                           && pass  Y by value
? y

*********************

PROCEDURE Readj

   PARAMETERS a, y

   a = a + 5
   y = y + 15
   ? a
   ? y
   WAIT
* End of File
```

DO CASE

Syntax:

DO CASE
CASE <condition>
   <commands>
CASE <condition>
   <commands>
CASE <condition>
   <commands>
OTHERWISE
   <commands>
ENDCASE

Description: The DO CASE command allows for structured programming control that selects a specific set of commands to perform based upon the evaluation of <condition>. The DO CASE commands should be used if more than two sets of actions are to be taken. Otherwise, an IF...ELSE...THEN command would be appropriate.

The OTHERWISE statement allows the program to take an alternate path of action when all CASE statements evaluate false.

The ENDCASE statement terminates the DO CASE structure.

DO CASEs may be nested.

Command: Standard

Library Called: Clipper.lib

Variance: The Summer '87 version of Clipper allows the word END to terminate a DO CASE command.

Sample:

```
DO CASE
 CASE option = 1
    DO Enter
 CASE option = 2
    DO CASE
    CASE subopt = 1
       DO Brnchoff
    CASE subopt = 2
       DO Whichway
    OTHERWISE
       DO Thisway
    ENDCASE
CASE option = 3
   DO Edit
CASE option = 4
   DO Append
OTHERWISE
   DO Scan
ENDCASE
```

DO WHILE

Syntax:

```
DO WHILE <condition>
         <commands>
ENDDO
```

Description: The DO WHILE command allows command statements within the DO WHILE and associated ENDDO statement to be repeated so long as the condition specified by the DO WHILE command remains true.

The ENDDO statement must terminate the structure of the DO WHILE command; this does not terminate the flow of operation of the DO WHILE command. If the condition prescribed by the DO WHILE command evaluates true (.T.), the subsequent commands will be executed; otherwise, those commands within the structure of the DO WHILE command will be skipped and the command following the associated ENDDO statement will be executed.

Macro substitution is permissible within the confines of the DO WHILE command.

DO WHILEs may be nested.

Command: Standard

Library Called: Clipper.lib

Variance: With the Summer '87 release, the EXIT command will unconditionally break from the loop and execute the command immediately following the ENDDO or END. Additionally with this release, the END command will terminate the DO WHILE command.

Sample:

```
STORE 0 TO looping
DO WHILE looping <> 501
   ?? looping
   ?? SPACE(10)
   looping = looping + 1
ENDDO
?
? "All finished..."

CLEAR
DO WHILE .T.
   ? DATE()
   input = "Y"
   @ ROW()+1,0 SAY "Do you want to go on? " GET input;
               PICT "!" VALID(input$"YN")
   READ
   IF input = "N"
      EXIT
   ENDIF
ENDDO
```

EJECT

Syntax: EJECT

Description: The EJECT command issues a form feed command to the printer. If the printer is not properly hooked up to the computer, an error will **not** be generated and the command will be ignored.

Command: Standard

Library Called: Clipper.lib

ERASE

Syntax: ERASE <file name>

Description: The ERASE command removes a file from the disk directory. The use of wild card characters (*) as parameters is permitted with this command.

Command: Standard

Library Called: Clipper.lib

Sample:

```
ERASE Temp.dbf
ERASE Temp.*
ERASE *.ntx
```

EXIT

Syntax: EXIT

Description: The EXIT command stops the execution of commands within a DO WHILE...ENDDO loop and FOR...NEXT loop and transfers execution to the command statement immediately following the appropriate ENDDO or NEXT command.

Command: Clipper enhanced

Library Called: Clipper.lib

Sample:

```
CLEAR
DO WHILE .T.
   ? DATE()
   input = "Y"
   @ ROW()+1,0 SAY "Do you want to go on? " GET input;
               PICT "!" VALID(input$"YN")
   READ
   IF input = "N"
      EXIT
   ENDIF
ENDDO
?
? "All finished..."
```

EXTERNAL

Syntax: EXTERNAL <procedure list>

Description: This command is used to declare a symbol during compiling for later use by the Plink86 linker (or any other linker used such as LINK and TLINK). This allows procedures to be placed in overlays and still be called with a macro.

Command: Clipper enhanced

Library Called: Clipper.lib

Note: For any procedure (including those called via the SET KEY TO command) or user-defined functions called within a macro or placed in an overlay area, the EXTERNAL command must be used.

Sample:

```
EXTERNAL Program1, Program2, Program3
which_one = "2"
* Program2 would be in an overlay
DO Program&which_one
```

FIND

Syntax: FIND <expC>/<expN>

Description: The FIND command searches the active, indexed database for the first record with a matching key as specified by the character expression or numeric expression.

Command: Standard

Library Called: Clipper.lib

Variance: A search for criteria stored in a variable specified by the user at run-time should use the SEEK command. Use the FIND command for literal FINDs, such as FIND "CA."

When searching for a match based on the contents of a memory variable, the FIND command may only be used in conjunction with the MACRO (&) function. If leading blanks are present, quotations must surround the macro substitution.

When searching for a match based on a numeric key, Clipper stores leading zeros to the key. In order to FIND a value, padding the argument with enough leading zeros to match the index key is required.

The FIND command will rewind the record pointer and start the search from the top of the indexed database file.

If no match occurs, EOF() is set to .T. and FOUND() is set to .F.

With the Summer '87 version and using the SET SOFTSEEK command, the record pointer is positioned to the record with the first key value greater than the search argument. The FOUND() function returns .F.; however, EOF() also returns false, provided there are values greater than the specified search argument.

Sample:

```
USE Phonbook Index Namebook
FIND "Jones"
? "The record was " + IF(FOUND(), "found!", "not found...")
```

FOR...NEXT

Syntax: FOR <memvar> = <expN> TO <expN> [STEP <expN>]
<commands>
[EXIT]...<commands>
NEXT

Description: This command allows looping for a range of values, where the value of <memvar> may increment or decrement by the amount of the STEP expression at each loop.

While the memory variable and expressions are mandatory, the STEP operator is optional and may increment or decrement <memvar>. If the STEP clause is not used, a STEP of +1 is assumed.

The EXIT command will unconditionally terminate the control of program execution from within the FOR...NEXT loop and execute the statement immediately following the NEXT command.

Command: Clipper enhanced

Library Called: Clipper.lib

Sample:

```
*****************************************************
* This routine will initialize 20 memory variables.
*****************************************************
```

```
FOR x = 1 TO 20
   STORE LTRIM(STR(x)) TO value
   STORE 0.00 TO temp&value
NEXT
```

FUNCTION

Syntax: FUNCTION <name>
<commands>
RETURN(<value>)

Description: This command initializes user-defined functions. As with procedures, functions may or may not have parameters passed to them.

Command: Clipper enhanced

Library Called: Clipper.lib

Variance: In the Summer '87 version, parameters passed to a user-defined function may be by value or by reference. Array names are passed by reference. Any variable passed with a preceded @ (at sign) will be passed by reference.

Sample: Refer to Chapter 12, Designing User-Defined Functions (UDFs).

GO / GOTO

Syntax: GO/GOTO <exp>/TOP/BOTTOM

Description: The GO/GOTO command places the record pointer in the currently selected area at the specified record or location in the database.

Command: Standard

Library Called: Clipper.lib

Variance: GOTO RECORD <exp> is not supported. The record pointer may be placed at a specific record by including that record number in the GO/GOTO command, or the record pointer may be placed at the logical TOP or logical BOTTOM of the file.

With an index file open, the logic of the TOP and BOTTOM options are dictated by the order prescribed by the index file in use. Only the first index file in a series will affect the logical order of the active database. Specifying the record number affects the database directly, ignoring the index file.

Sample:

```
USE Temp
GO 1
? "I am at record "
?? RECNO()

USE Temp INDEX Temp
GO TOP
*
* This position will be in logical order based on the
* order of the index file.  It may be different from
* the actual order in the database.
? "I am at record "
?? RECNO()
```

IF

Syntax:

IF <condition>
<commands>
[ELSE]
<commands>
[ELSEIF]
<commands>
ENDIF

Description: The IF command allows a branching depending on <condition> in a structured programming environment.

Command: Standard

Library Called: Clipper.lib

Variance: With the Summer '87 version, the ELSEIF clause has been added. This addition allows testing for multiple conditions within the same IF...END command.

Notes: Nested IF commands are permissible within the same procedure, function, or program file. All IF commands must terminate with a corresponding local ENDIF.

Under the compiler, all IF and corresponding ENDIFs are counted. There may be an extreme situation where an ENDIF is missing and the procedure is able to run under the interpreter, but the compiler will flag this as an error.

Sample:

```
CLEAR
STORE SPACE(8) TO indate
@ 10,10 SAY "Enter Date: " GET indate PICT "99/99/99"
READ
indate = CTOD(indate)
IF DATE() = indate
   @ 15,10 SAY "Hey, you picked today's date."
ELSEIF DATE() < indate
   @ 15,10 SAY "The date you picked is out of range."
ELSE
   @ 15,10 SAY "Sorry, the date you chose is not today."
ENDIF
```

INDEX ON

Syntax: INDEX ON <key expression> TO <file name>

Description: The INDEX command creates a file; contained in the head of that file is the key structure specified by <key expression>. This key structure is associated with the database that was open at the time the INDEX command was invoked. The main purpose is to build a series of keys that will instruct the compiler to put some order to the database, either alphabetically, chronologically, numerically, or any combination thereof. The index is no more than a file pointer to the record numbers in the database, in the order set by the key.

Command: Standard

Library Called: Clipper.lib

Variance: Clipper builds the key based on a blank record. If a TRIM() is performed, a null results. Therefore, if a TRIM() is necessary, allowance must be made for the largest possible data that might be in the key field. However, this is only half of the problem since the compiler performs implicit SEEKs on nonprimary indexes. This means that Clipper, when executing, could alter the index keys, especially where REPLACE or READ is involved. To solve this, explicit control must be forced onto the compiler. To accomplish this, the key expression must include the padding of the calculated length of the key expression. As a result, the key expression will always equal the maximum value that key can ever hold.

With the Summer '87 version, if the NDX.OBJ file is linked with the application, the index file created with the INDEX ON command will be dBASE compatible. Otherwise, Clipper standard indexes will be generated.

With the Summer '87 release, indexes may be generated in descending order with the use of the DESCEND() function. Otherwise, the default order will be in ascending order.

A user-defined function is permitted within the key of the index; however, if used with the .NDX object file, the index file will no longer be dBASE compatible.

The following code would accomplish this:

```
SUBSTR(<expC> + SPACE(<number>), 1, <number>)
```

This string <expC> is padded with blank spaces for length <number>, and a SUBSTR of this is taken, beginning at position 1 of string <expC> to <number>. Example:

```
INDEX ON SUBSTR(TRIM(last_name) + ", " +;
TRIM(first_name) + " " + middle +;
SPACE(LEN(last_name + ", ") + ;
LEN(first_name + " ") +;
LEN(middle)), 1, LEN(last_name) + ;
2 + LEN(first_name) + 1 + LEN(middle))
```

Unless otherwise instructed, Clipper will assume an index file extension of .NTX.

An index key may be a field, an expression, a function, or any combination thereof.

Logical and memo fields **cannot** be part of a key expression.

Keys must be built on similar types: in joining numeric, date, and character fields to an index, the appropriate function must be used in order to convert them all to one type.

Sample:

```
USE Phonbook
INDEX ON DTOC(date_ent) + STR(age) + last_name TO Phon1

* This would build an index in date order, followed by
* the order of the string representation of the age
* field, then followed by the order of the last_name
* field.
```

INPUT

Syntax: INPUT [<expC>] TO <memvar>

Description: The INPUT command accepts user-entered data from the keyboard. The INPUT can be of any data type and is completed by striking the Enter key.

Command: Standard

Library Called: Clipper.lib

Notes: The <expC> is the prompt for the INPUT command. This is an optional clause. If a memory variable is used in place of the character string, the content of the memory variable is used as the prompt.

If a character string is INPUT, the variable must be preinitialized. Otherwise, an undefined variable message will appear at run-time.

Mathematical expressions are legal.

Variance: If nothing is entered, the old value of the variable is retained, whereas in dBASE III the INPUT message is repeated until a valid response is entered.

Sample:

```
DO WHILE .T.
   CLEAR
   INPUT "[Enter in something ]" TO value
   ?
   ? value
   ? TYPE("value")
   ?
   ?
   WAIT
ENDDO
```

JOIN

Syntax: JOIN WITH <alias> TO <new filename> FOR <condition> [FIELDS <field list>]

Description: The JOIN command creates a new database based on two open databases by merging specified records and fields to that new file.

Command: Standard

Library Called: Clipper.lib

Notes: If not specified, the <new filename> will assume the default drive, directory and .DBF extension. If there are common fields in both open databases, the desired field is specified with the use of the Alias->field syntax. To specify a field in the currently open and selected database, only the name of the field without an Alias-> clause is required. If no FIELDS clause is specified, the field assignment will begin with the active database. The fields from the second file are then added until the 1024-field limit has been reached.

Duplicate field names will not appear in the created database file.

The record pointer is set at the top of the file in the current area. Each record in the secondary file is then evaluated for the FOR <condition>. If the FOR <condition> is **true**, the record is added to the new file. When all of the records in the second file are looked at, the record pointer in the current area is advanced one record and the process is repeated. This continues for all of the records in the currently active database.

Sample:

```
*********************
* Name          JOINIT.prg
* Date          August 4, 1986
* Notice        Copyright 1986, Stephen J. Straley
* Compile       Clipper Joinit
* Release       All versions
* Link          Plink86 fi joinit lib clipper;
* Note          This is a small procedure that will create
*               three databases: two for entry and one to
*               be joined.  The case established is purely
*               hypothetical and was created to show how
*               the command works.
*
*********************

CREATE Temp
APPEND BLANK
REPLACE field_name WITH "EMPLOYEE", field_type WITH "C", ;
        field_len WITH 10
APPEND BLANK
REPLACE field_name WITH "AGE", field_type WITH "N", ;
        field_len WITH 3
APPEND BLANK
REPLACE field_name WITH "HOURLY", field_type WITH "L", ;
        field_len WITH 1
USE
CREATE Master FROM Temp
CREATE Temp
```

```
APPEND BLANK
REPLACE field_name WITH "PERSON", field_type WITH "C", ;
        field_len WITH 10
APPEND BLANK
REPLACE field_name WITH "WAGE", field_type WITH "N", ;
        field_len WITH 8, field_dec WITH 2
APPEND BLANK
REPLACE field_name WITH "DATE_IN", field_type WITH "D", ;
        field_len WITH 8
USE
CREATE Second FROM Temp
CLOSE DATABASE
SELECT 2
USE Second
SELECT 1
USE Master
DO WHILE .T.
   STORE SPACE(10) TO in_name
   CLEAR
   @ 05,05 SAY "Enter Name of Person:  " GET in_name
   READ
   IF LEN(TRIM(in_name)) = 0
      EXIT
   ENDIF
   APPEND BLANK
   REPLACE employee WITH in_name
   @ 07,05 SAY "      Enter age: " GET age
   @ 09,05 SAY "Hourly Employee: " GET hourly
   READ
ENDDO
CLEAR
SELECT 2
DO WHILE .T.
   STORE SPACE(10) TO in_name
   CLEAR
   @ 03,25 SAY "Enter either a different name from before or"
   @ 04,25 SAY "    the same ... for testing, mix it up!"
   @ 07,05 SAY "  Enter name: " GET in_name
   READ
   IF LEN(TRIM(in_name)) = 0
      EXIT
   ENDIF
   APPEND BLANK
   REPLACE person WITH in_name
   @ 09,05 SAY "Enter wage: " GET wage
   @ 11,05 SAY "Enter date: " GET date_in
   READ
ENDDO
CLEAR
@ 01,05 SAY "Here is the first database: "
SELECT 1
FOR x = 1 to 3
   ? FIELDNAME(x)
```

```
NEXT
?
? "There are " + LTRIM(STR(LASTREC())) + ;
  " records in the database."
WAIT
CLEAR
@ 01,05 SAY "Here is the second database: "
SELECT 2
FOR x = 1 TO 3
   ? FIELDNAME(x)
NEXT
?
? "There are " + LTRIM(STR(LASTREC())) + ;
  " records in the database."
WAIT
CLEAR
@ 01,05 SAY "Now Joining to make Third.dbf"
SELECT 1
JOIN WITH Second TO Third FOR A->employee <> B->person ;
    FIELDS A->employee, B->wage, A->age, B->date_in
USE Third
FOR x = 1 TO 4
   ? FIELDNAME(x)
NEXT
?
? "There are " + LTRIM(STR(LASTREC())) + ;
  " records in the database."
WAIT
GO TOP
LIST fields employee, wage, age, date_in
* End of File
```

KEYBOARD

Syntax: KEYBOARD <expC>

Description: This command stuffs the Clipper input buffer with <expC>. It may be used to simulate "RETURN TO MASTER" (use the BEGIN SEQUENCE command as well in the Summer '87 release) by stuffing several characters, stringing them together, simulating key strokes that would emulate leaving lower levels to return to higher ones.

Command: Standard

Library Called: Clipper.lib

Sample:

```
FOR x = 1 TO 2
   STORE SPACE(35) TO input
   CLEAR
```

```
   @ 1, 5 SAY "Press the Esc key for keyboard stuff..."
   IF INKEY(0) = 27
      KEYBOARD "Hi there, this is a test..."
   ENDIF
   @ 10,10 GET input
   READ
NEXT
```

LABEL

Syntax: LABEL FORM <file name> [<scope>] [FOR <condition>] [WHILE <condition>] [SAMPLE] [TO PRINT] [TO FILE <file name>]

Description: The LABEL command allows labels to be printed based on the format outlined in a .LBL file on the disk.

Command: Standard

Library Called: Clipper.lib

Variance: Contents of a LABEL field **must** be a valid expression. Clipper will ignore anything following a comma in a label.

The Summer '87 release supports the REST scope option. Additionally, all versions of Clipper support both the FOR condition and the WHILE condition.

Sample:

```
* In Clipper
TRIM(last_name) + " " + first_name

* In dBASE III
last_name, first_name
```

Notes:

1. Drive designators must be included if files reside anywhere other than the default drive, and file extensions must be included if the extension is anything **other** than .LBL.
2. Both the FOR and WHILE conditions may be used in the LABEL command. If no conditions are specified, all records are selected.
3. The SAMPLE option is used to print test labels.
4. The TO FILE option is used to send the labels to a standard ASCII text file.

LIST

Syntax: LIST [OFF] [scope] <field list> [FOR <condition>] [WHILE <condition>] [TO PRINT] [TO FILE <filename>]

Description: The LIST command displays the contents of a database.

Command: Standard

Library Called: Clipper.lib

Variance: The TO PRINT and the TO FILE options have been added to the syntax of the command.

Notes: The OFF option turns off the display of record numbers.

Both the FOR condition and the WHILE condition may be present in the command line; the FOR condition will take precedence over the WHILE condition.

Sample:

```
USE Employees
LIST OFF last_name, first_name FOR state = "CA";
         WHILE age <= 50 TO FILE Output
*
*  A list of records with just the last name and first name
*  will be printed to an alternate file with the name of
*  OUTPUT.TXT.  Only those records with fields (state =
*  "CA") and (age <= 50) will be printed.
```

LOCATE

Syntax: LOCATE [<scope>] [FOR <condition>] [WHILE <condition>]

Description: The LOCATE command searches the open and selected database for the first record that meets the condition specified.

Command: Standard

Library Called: Clipper.lib

Notes: LOCATE does not require an INDEX file to be in USE.

The LOCATE command rewinds the record pointer to the top of the file and searches sequentially, unless otherwise specified by a scope or a WHILE condition.

If a NEXT scope is used, the limit of the search will be bound by the specified number in the NEXT clause.

If no match is made, EOF() is set to .T. and FOUND() is set .F.

If a match is made, the record pointer remains on the record number that satisfied the condition specified.

To search further, without moving back to the top of the file, the CONTINUE command is invoked.

Sample:

```
USE Phonbook
LOCATE FOR state = "CA" .AND. prefix = "(714)"
? phone_num
WAIT
CONTINUE
? EOF()
```

LOOP

Syntax: LOOP

Description: The LOOP command immediately jumps to the beginning of the current DO WHILE... ENDDO loop. Any command or series of commands following the LOOP command are ignored.

Command: Standard

Library Called: Clipper.lib

Notes: Good structured program techniques dictate avoidance of this command; however, there are cases where nothing but a LOOP command can be used. Be very careful in planning program flow and use false (DO WHILE .NOT. ...ENDDO) conditions to avoid a LOOP command, if possible, rather than true (DO WHILE...ENDDO) conditions. Also use the EXIT command to escape from the DO WHILE. Below is an example that shows two options.

Sample:

```
********************
* Name        LOOPING.prg
* Date        August 5, 1986
* Notice      Copyright 1986, Stephen J. Straley
* Compile     Clipper Looping
* Release     All versions
* Link        Plink86 fi looping lib clipper;
* Note        Sample 1 demonstrates the use of the LOOP
*             command and Sample 2 show a way to avoid it.
********************
```

```
* Sample 1.
*
STORE .T. TO looping
DO WHILE looping
   CLEAR
   @ 10,10 SAY "<First Pass> Would you like the time? (Y/N) "
   SET CONSOLE OFF
   WAIT TO temp
   SET CONSOLE ON
   IF UPPER(temp) = "N"
      STORE .F. TO looping
      LOOP
   ENDIF
   @ 12,10 SAY "The time is ... "
   ?? TIME()
   ?
   ?
   WAIT
ENDDO
*
* Sample 2. ... the second way...
*
DO WHILE .T.
   CLEAR
   @ 10,10 SAY "<Second Pass> Would you like the time? (Y/N) "
   SET CONSOLE OFF
   WAIT TO temp
   SET CONSOLE ON
   IF !UPPER(temp) = "N"
      @ 12,10 SAY "The time is ... "
      ?? TIME()
      ?
      ?
      WAIT
   ELSE
      EXIT
   ENDIF
ENDDO
* End of File
```

MENU TO

Syntax: MENU TO <memvar>

Description: The MENU TO command allows the creation of menu prompts and options with greater ease and efficiency.

This command is to be used in conjunction with the PROMPT commands. Think of the MENU TO command as you do a READ on a GET command. It is vital to initialize the <memvar>.

MENU TO <memvar> highlights the first PROMPT command and will allow the cursor to move from PROMPT command to PROMPT command. MENU TO also places in the <memvar> the numeric value of the PROMPT command selected. The values are determined by the order of the PROMPT commands.

There can be a maximum of 32 PROMPT commands per MENU TO command.

User-defined HELP can be activated from within a series of PROMPT/MENU TO commands. The parameter passed to the HELP.PRG as the input variable (input_var) is the <memvar> created by the MENU TO command.

Command: Clipper enhanced

Library Called: Clipper.lib

Note: Active Keys for MENU TO command:

Up arrow	-> Previous PROMPT
Down arrow	-> Next PROMPT
Home	-> First PROMPT
End	-> Last PROMPT
Left arrow	-> Previous PROMPT
Right arrow	-> Previous PROMPT
PgUp	-> Select PROMPT; return #
PgDn	-> Select PROMPT; return #
Return	-> Select PROMPT; return #
Esc	-> Abort MENU TO; return 0
First character	-> Select first PROMPT with same initial character; return #

Sample: See PROMPT ... MESSAGE Command

NOTE / * / &&

Syntax: NOTE/* <text>
<command line> && <text>

Description: The NOTE/*/&& commands allow text to be entered into the program or procedure code that can be used to describe the action being taken by the procedure or command.

This command should be used extensively for the sake of properly commenting the intent of a procedure or program file. However, do not bog down your application with redundant comments or unnecessary notations.

Comments cannot be continued onto a new line with a semicolon.

The asterisk and the NOTE syntax must begin the command line. The double ampersand notations (&&) can occur anywhere on the command line **other** than at the beginning.

Command: Standard

Library Called: Clipper.lib

Variance: Clipper strips all comment lines out of the code or text file so they do not appear in the object file. However, 3 bytes are reserved for properly noting the line number of the command line(s) that contained the notation or comment.

Because comment lines do not slow down the process of a compiled application, they should be used more rather than less, which is the tendency under dBASE III.

Blank lines are also omitted when compiling and only take up 3 bytes of space to trace the line numbers; therefore, a good practice to follow would be to use blank lines to help the readability of a program, procedure, or function.

Note: Use the following as a guide for different ways to comment a program.

* <Formatting and General Notation> Used for headings, procedure and function separations, for distinct differences in program flow from one section to another.

NOTE <Section Notation, Less General Notation> To generally note the purpose of the following or preceding section of code, yet maintain the basic flow of the entire program, procedure, or function.

&& <Line Notation, Specific Commenting> To comment directly on a line, generally stating the purpose or intent of a specific command on that line.

Sample:

```
*********************
* Name          NOTES.prg
* Date          August 5, 1986
* Notice        Copyright 1986, Stephen J. Straley
* Compile       Clipper Notes
* Release       All versions
* Link          Plink86 fi Notes lib clipper;
* Note          This will show the different ways to
*               comment a program.  Notice that the
*               asterisk (*) is generally used for the
*               header of a program, procedure, or
*               function, while the NOTE command is
*               directly in the flow of the program, and
*               the double macro symbol (&&) is in the
*               command line itself.
*********************

STORE 1 TO counter

NOTE > Initialize a counter to 1 and use the counter to <
NOTE > go until it reaches 500 <

CLEAR
DO WHILE counter <= 500

   @ 10,15 SAY "The current count is: " GET counter PICT "###"
   CLEAR GETS
   STORE counter + 1 TO counter   && Increment the value
   *                                 of counter
ENDDO
* End of File
```

PACK

Syntax: PACK

Description: The PACK command removes from the currently open and selected database those records that were previously marked for deletion.

Command: Standard

Library Called: Clipper.lib

Notes: With the use of the PACK command, all open indexes are automatically REINDEXed.

PARAMETERS

Syntax: PARAMETERS <parameter list>

Description: The PARAMETERS command assigns local variables with the names given. The values in those variables will be either referenced or valued as determined by the calling program.

Command: Standard

Library Called: Clipper.lib

Variance: If a PARAMETER is established for a variable and none is passed to it, the variable is set to a null value. A passed PARAMETER may be any legitimate expression including formulas, character strings, etc.

Autumn 86: More than one parameter may be passed to a program directly from DOS. However, if an intended numeric parameter is passed from the DOS command line, the application will see it as a character data type and it must be converted to a numeric data type with the VAL() function.

Sample: Refer to PARAM.prg in the section on parameters in Chapter 8, Clipper Procedures.

PRIVATE

Syntax: PRIVATE <memvar list> / <array name>

Definition: The PRIVATE command allows memory variables to be hidden from either higher-level variables, previously PUBLIC declared variables, or other variables within the same function or procedure.

Command: Standard

Library Called: Clipper.lib

Variance: With the Summer '87 release, arrays may be declared with the DECLARE or the PRIVATE command. Arrays declared via the DECLARE statement will be private in nature.

PROMPT ... MESSAGE

Syntax: @ <row>,<col> PROMPT <expC> [MESSAGE <expC>]

Description: The PROMPT...MESSAGE command places menu selections on the screen, highlights menu choices, and allows the cursor to be moved via the cursor pad or direct input.

Command: Clipper enhanced

Library Called: Clipper.lib

Notes: 32 PROMPTs per MENU command are allowed. If the MESSAGE clause is used, the SET MESSAGE TO command must be used if a row position other than 0 is desired.

The order of the PROMPT is important because it is the order that is evaluated once a menu item is chosen.

The **Enter** key will return the value of the current highlighted bar. The **PgUp** key will immediately move the highlighted bar to the first PROMPT; the **PgDn** key will immediately move the highlighted bar to the last PROMPT. Striking the Esc key will cause a value of 0 to be passed to the variable in the MENU TO command.

The HELP.PRG and all subsequently established SET KEY TO commands work in conjunction with the MENU TO command. The input variable passed to the procedure will be the variable in the MENU TO command.

A user-defined function may be used to center the MESSAGE string.

Each <expC> in the PROMPT command should have unique beginning characters. In addition to having the cursor keys move to the appropriate choices, striking the first letter in <expC> will complete the MENU TO command and move the highlight to the appropriate PROMPT area. Preceding spaces and tabs are ignored as the first character in <expC>.

Sample:

```
********************
* Name          SET_MESS.prg
* Date          August 5, 1986
* Notice        Copyright 1986, Stephen J. Straley
* Compile       Clipper Set_mess
* Release       All versions
```

```
* Link          Plink86 fi set_mess lib clipper;
* Note          This procedure will simulate a possible
*               menu using the SET MESSAGE TO command at
*               line 24.  CENTERING is a user-defined function
*               that centers the message.

*               With the Summer '87 release, the CENTRING()
*               function is not necessary because of the SET
*               MESSAGE <expN> CENTER option.
*
********************

STORE 1 TO menu_choic
SET MESSAGE TO 24
DO WHILE menu_choic <> 0
   CLEAR
   @  1,25 PROMPT "1> Enter Account Information" ;
           MESSAGE CENTRING("This is for general accounts")
   @  3,25 PROMPT "2> Enter Special Information" ;
           MESSAGE CENTRING("This is for the Special Accounts")
   @  5,25 PROMPT "3> Enter Transactions" ;
           MESSAGE "This will be for all accounts"
   @  7,25 PROMPT "4> Balance Normal Accounts"
   @  9,25 PROMPT "5> Balance Special Accounts" ;
           MESSAGE CENTRING("This Requires a PASSWORD")
   @ 11,25 PROMPT "6> Special Utility Submenu"
   @ 13,25 PROMPT "7> End of Period Processing"
   @ 15,25 PROMPT "0> EXIT TO OPERATING SYSTEM"
   @ 18,00 SAY;
     CENTRING("Please choose an option by moving the cursor")
   @ 19,00 SAY;
     CENTRING("or striking the appropriate number")
   MENU TO menu_choic
   IF menu_choic = 8
      QUIT
   ENDIF
   @ 22,10 SAY "Five Seconds will elapse or Any Key to Continue."
   IF INKEY(5) = 32
   ENDIF
ENDDO

FUNCTION Centring

   PARAMETERS string

   STORE (80 - LEN(string)) / 2 TO temp
   IF 2 * temp + LEN(string) < 80
      RETURN(SPACE(temp) + string + SPACE(temp) + " ")
   ENDIF
   RETURN(SPACE(temp) + string + SPACE(temp))
* End of File
```

PROCEDURE

Syntax: PROCEDURE <procedure name>

Description: A PROCEDURE is a group of commands that perform a specific task.

Command: Standard

Library Called: Clipper.lib

Variance: With all versions of Clipper, a RETURN statement is not necessary to terminate the program control of a PROCEDURE. Clipper automatically assumes a RETURN to occur prior to the next encountered FUNCTION or PROCEDURE statement.

Notes: The names of procedures may be up to 10 characters long and follow the same format as do fields. Procedure files still follow the 8-character format.

Variance: Procedure files **must** have a unique name; it cannot be the same as the name of a procedure.

A procedure **may** be included at the bottom of a program file.

Sample:

```
*********************a
* Name          ATTHEBOT.prg
* Date          August 5, 1986
* Notice        Copyright 1986, Stephen J. Straley
* Compile       Clipper Atthebot
* Release       All versions
* Link          Plink86 fi atthebot lib clipper;
* Note          This small routine will show that a
*               procedure may reside at the end of the
*               program that calls it.  This
*               technique will keep unusual routines
*               with the "mother" program.
*
*********************

DO WHILE .T.
   STORE 0 to temprow, tempcol
   CLEAR
   @ 10,12 SAY "What row do you want?    " GET temprow ;
           RANGE 0,21
   READ
   @ 12,12 SAY "What column do you want? " GET tempcol ;
           RANGE 0,65
   READ
```

```
   IF temprow = 0 .AND. tempcol = 0
      EXIT
   ENDIF
   DO Theverybot WITH temprow, tempcol
   @ 22,00 SAY ""
   WAIT
ENDDO

*********************

PROCEDURE Theverybot

   PARAMETERS at_this, at_that

   CLEAR
   FOR x = 1 TO 500
      @ at_this, at_that SAY x
   NEXT
* End of File
```

PUBLIC

Syntax: PUBLIC <memvar list> [, Clipper]

Description: The PUBLIC command declares memory variables to be PUBLIC in nature and available to all procedure and functions within an application.

Command: Clipper enhanced

Library Called: Clipper.lib.

Variance: The PUBLIC Clipper command is used to allow one set of source code to work both in Clipper and in dBASE III without modification.

With the Summer '87 release, arrays may be declared PUBLIC in nature. For more examples on this variation, please see Chapter 12, Macros & Arrays.

Notes: At the beginning of any application or program, declare one variable as PUBLIC and call that variable "Clipper." However, **do not** assign this variable a value. Under dBASE III, variables without value automatically assume a .F. value. This is true as well with all variables under Clipper except the one variable titled "Clipper," which assumes the value of .T.

Therefore, code that will only work with the compiler and code that is specific to dBASE III can be isolated by an IF statement.

Sample:

```
*********************
* Name          CLIPVAR.prg
* Date          August 6, 1986
* Notice        Copyright 1986, Stephen J. Straley
* Compile       Clipper Clipvar
* Release       All versions
* Link          Plink86 fi Clipvar lib clipper;
* Note          To demonstrate the use of the CLIPPER
*               variable in a "real" situation.
*
*********************

CLEAR
PUBLIC Clipper

IF Clipper
   @ 5,10,20,70 BOX REPLICATE(CHR(177), 9)
ELSE
   STORE  5 TO temprow
   STORE 10 TO tempcol
   DO WHILE temprow <= 20
      DO WHILE tempcol <= 70
         @ temprow, tempcol SAY CHR(177)
         STORE tempcol + 1 TO tempcol
      ENDDO
      STORE 10 TO tempcol
      STORE temprow + 1 TO temprow
   ENDDO
ENDIF
* End of File
```

QUIT

Syntax: QUIT

Description: The QUIT command closes all open files, clears all memory variables, and returns control to the operating system.

Command: Standard

Library Called: Clipper.lib

Notes: All compiled programs should have at least one safe method or flow in which the QUIT command is executed. This will insure that once the application is through executing, all database files and index files are closed safely.

Sample:

```
   CLEAR
@ 10,10 SAY "Do you want to continue? "
SET CONSOLE OFF
WAIT TO temp
SET CONSOLE ON
IF UPPER(temp) <> "Y"
   QUIT
ENDIF
DO Go_on
```

READ

Syntax: READ [SAVE]

Description: The READ command activates all current @...GETs invoked since the last CLEAR, CLEAR ALL, CLEAR GETS, or READ.

Command: Standard

Library Called: Clipper.lib

Variance: Prior to the Summer '87 release, the [SAVE] option is not supported.

Notes: This command is used in full screen entry and editing modes. Since dBASE interactive commands for editing are not supported by the compiler, the use of APPEND BLANK and @...GET, READ is the manner by which data is entered and edited.

Sample:

```
STORE SPACE(10) TO name
CLEAR
@ 10,10 SAY "Enter the name: " GET name
READ
STORE 1 TO a,b,c,
@ 14,10 SAY "Enter a number: " GET a
@ 15,10 SAY "   and again..: " GET b
@ 16,10 SAY " and one more.: " GET c
READ
```

RECALL

Syntax: RECALL <scope> [[FOR <condition>] [WHILE <condition>]

Description: The RECALL command unmarks those records marked for deletion and reactivates them in the current and open database.

Command: Standard

Library Called: Clipper.lib

Variance: Both the FOR <condition> clause and the WHILE <condition> clause can be in use at the same time. The FOR <condition> will take precedence over the WHILE clause.

Notes: Unless specified by the <scope> clause or the FOR/WHILE <condition> clauses, the RECALL command will only affect the current record.

Once records have been marked for deletion and the PACK or the ZAP command has been issued, the RECALL command will have no effect on the database.

A general RECALL command will have no effect on the database if that database is under the restraints of the SET DELETED ON command. Under this condition, all records for RECALL must be specified.

Sample:

```
USE Phonbook
GO 5
RECALL
USE Temp
RECALL ALL FOR state = "CA"
```

REINDEX

Syntax: REINDEX

Description: The REINDEX command rebuilds all of the active index files in the currently open and selected area.

Command: Standard

Library Called: Clipper.lib

Notes: In effect this command is an easier way to update an index file based on the current information in the database once the index files have been created. It would be equivalent to the INDEX ON <expC> TO <filename> command.

In an network environment, the REINDEX command requires an EXCLUSE USE command to be set on the current database file.

Sample:

```
USE Phonbook INDEX Phon1
REINDEX

NOTE \ another way to do the same is the following \
USE Phonbook
SET INDEX TO Phon1
REINDEX
```

RELEASE

Syntax: RELEASE <memory variable>
RELEASE <memory variable list>
RELEASE [ALL [LIKE/EXCEPT <skeleton>]]

Description: The RELEASE command deletes from memory a memory variable(s) and reallocates memory space for future use.

Command: Standard

Library Called: Clipper.lib

Notes: If the <skeleton> clause is used, a question mark (?) and an asterisk (*) are treated just as they are in DOS: a ? will mask a single character; an * will mask one or more characters. Since Clipper has an expanded capacity to handle memory variables, you may not find it necessary to invoke this command.

Sample:

```
STORE "Hi There" TO prompt
STORE 1 TO position
STORE "Returning to Operating System" TO depart
RELEASE ALL LIKE p*
* The only memory variable left will be "depart"
RELEASE ALL
* No more memory variables are present
```

RENAME

Syntax: RENAME <filename.1> TO <filename.2>

Description: The RENAME command changes the name of the first <filename> to that of the second <filename>.

Command: Standard

Library Called: Clipper.lib

Notes: Both <filename>s must include the file extension. Included with the <filename> must be the drive and directory designator if either is other than the default drive and directory.

The new <filename> cannot be that of an existing file on the same designated drive and directory.

Open files cannot be RENAMEd.

This command can be used in conjunction with the FILE() function in order to simulate file locking.

A memo file must be RENAMED as well if the associated database file has been renamed.

Sample:

```
IF FILE(Mainfile.dbf)
   RENAME Mainfile.dbf TO Temp.dbf
   USE Temp
ELSE
   CLEAR
   @ 10,25 SAY "That file is already in use."
   @ 12,25 SAY "    Any Key to Continue."
   tkey = INKEY(0)
ENDIF
```

REPLACE

Syntax: REPLACE [<scope>] <field> WITH <exp> [, <field> WITH <exp> ...] [FOR <condition>] [WHILE <condition>]

Description: The REPLACE command changes the contents of specified fields in the active database.

Command: Standard

Library Called: Clipper.lib

Variance: A FOR clause and a WHILE clause may exist simultaneously with the FOR option taking precedence over the WHILE option.

Autumn '86: Values may be REPLACED into another area so long as an open database is active in that area. To do so, the ALIAS name must precede the field in the field list.

In order to call that area, use the ALIAS of that area:

```
SELECT 2
USE History
SELECT 1
USE Timecard
REPLACE History->prev_quart WITH Timecard->reg_hours * 40
```

Summer '87: The REST clause is supported in the <scope> condition.

Notes: Unless otherwise specified by the scope, the FOR clause, or the WHILE clause, only the current record is affected by the REPLACE command.

The field and the expression must be of the same data type.

Each REPLACE on a key field with the indexed file open will update the index.

Sample:

```
    USE Phonbook INDEX Namebook
REPLACE first_name WITH "Nomad"

*******************************************************
* Now replace all state fields in the proper index    *
* file with "CA" for the phone number prefix = (213). *
*******************************************************

USE Phonbook INDEX Statbook
REPLACE ALL state WITH "CA" FOR prefix = "(213)"
```

REPORT FORM

Syntax: REPORT FORM <file name> [<scope>] [FOR <condition>] [WHILE <condition>] [TO PRINT] [TO FILE <file name>] [PLAIN] [HEADING <expC>][NOEJECT]

Description: The REPORT FROM command allows forms to be printed based on the format outlined in a .FRM file on the disk.

Command: Standard

Library Called: Clipper.lib

Variance: If an attempt is made to run a REPORT FORM with a division on a field or variable where the divisor is zero or is left blank, a run-time error will occur stating such. A user-defined function can be written and implemented to overcome this problem. See the UDF **DIVIDE0()** in Chapter 14, Designing User-Defined Functions (UDFs).

Notes: The default extension for the FORM file is .FRM, while the default extension for the TO file for output is .TXT.

Both the FOR <condition> and WHILE <condition> may be used, with the FOR option taking precedence over the WHILE option.

The PLAIN option causes the report to print without page numbers or a system date. The HEADING option with a character expression defines an extra heading that is printed on the page line of each page. The NOEJECT option in conjunction with the TO PRINT option will suppress the initial form feed.

RESTORE FROM

Syntax: RESTORE FROM <filename> [ADDITIVE]

Description: The RESTORE FROM command retrieves from disk a memory variable file and activates all memory variables stored in that file.

Command: Standard

Library Called: Clipper.lib

Variance: There is virtually no limit on the allocated space for active memory variables since many machines cannot handle the expanded capacity of the compiler.

Autumn 86: This version allows memory variables longer in length than 255 bytes to be RESTORED from a .MEM file. Thus, full screens previously saved with the SAVE SCREEN or the CALL command can be saved completely to a memory file without being parsed into 255-character substrings.

Notes: Unless otherwise specified, the <filename> will be assumed to have a .MEM file extension.

If the RESTORE FROM command is used without the ADDITIVE clause, all currently active memory variables are deleted and only those memory variables in the memory file will be present.

In order to maintain all current memory variables, the ADDITIVE clause must be included with the RESTORE FROM command. If there are any memory variables with the same name as a memory variable in the RESTOREd memory file, the memory variable in the system is overwritten by the variable from the file.

Sample:

```
STORE 1 TO x
? x
SAVE TO Temp
STORE 5 TO x
? x
RESTORE FROM Temp
? x
```

RESTORE SCREEN

Syntax: RESTORE SCREEN

Description: The RESTORE SCREEN command brings back a screen that was previously saved in memory.

Command: Clipper enhanced

Library Called: Clipper.lib

Notes: This command was included to help design applications with a more polished look to them. It is especially handy when used in conjunction with a HELP.PRG file: the original screen can be saved in memory while the help screen is displayed to the user.

Using this command is a one-shot situation. Once the screen is RESTOREd, it cannot be RESTOREd again without being SAVEd again. Screens that have been saved to memory variables by using the CALL command can be restored repeatedly by using those variables in conjunction with the CALL command to the Clipper library.

Review the SAVE SCREEN command for further information.

Addition: Using the CALL variation can be **extremely** hazardous to anything else that is residing in memory whenever this command is CALLed. For a complete description of the complications using these CALL routines, see SAVE SCREEN, below, and DRAWMEN1.prg in the section on Windowing for Menus and Submenus in Chapter 16.

Autumn '86: The sample listed below is just as effective as [FROM <memvar>], which was added with this version.

Sample:

```
CALL _scrsave WITH screen[1] && available in all releases
* This sample shows how to RESTORE a screen directly from a
* memory variable.

tempscr = screen[1]
RESTORE SCREEN FROM tempscr
* Again, this syntax is only available in the Autumn '86
* release.
```

Summer '87: The CALL _scrsave and CALL _scrrest is no longer supported. To use a similar command construct, and because of Microsoft C, use CALL __scrsave and CALL __scrrest instead.

RETURN

Syntax: RETURN

Description: The RETURN command restores control to the program or procedure which originally called the current program or procedure. If there is no program file or procedure to return control to, control is returned to DOS.

Command: Standard

Library Called: Clipper.lib

Variance: RETURN TO MASTER is not supported; however, with a combination of KEYBOARD and RETURN commands, this command may be simulated.

Sample:

```
*********************
* Name          RETURNTO.prg
* Date          August 5, 1986
* Notice        Copyright 1986, Stephen J. Straley
* Compile       Clipper Returnto
* Release       All versions
* Link          Plink86 fi returnto lib clipper;
* Note          To show the use of RETURN and the simulation of
*               a RETURN TO MASTER.
*
*********************

DO WHILE .T.
   CLEAR
   STORE "2" TO option
   @ 0,0 SAY "Top Level"
   @ 5,10 SAY "Exit to the system .......   1"
   @ 6,10 SAY "Go down next level .......   2"
```

```
   @ 8,10 SAY "Enter option ............   " GET option ;
        PICT "X" VALID(option$"12")
   READ
   IF option = "2"
      DO Down1
   ELSE
      EXIT
   ENDIF
ENDDO

*********************

PROCEDURE Down1

   DO WHILE .T.
      CLEAR
      STORE "2" TO option
      @ 0,0 SAY "Level One"
      @ 5,10 SAY "Return to Top Level ......   1"
      @ 6,10 SAY "Go down next level .......   2"
      @ 8,10 SAY "Enter option ............    " GET option ;
           PICT "X" VALID(option$"12")
      READ
      IF option = "2"
         DO Down2
      ELSE
         RETURN
      ENDIF
   ENDDO

*********************

PROCEDURE Down2

   CLEAR
   STORE "2" TO option
   @ 0,0 SAY "Level Two"
   @ 5,10 SAY "Return to Master ..........   1"
   @ 6,10 SAY "Return to Previous Level ...  2"
   @ 8,10 SAY "Enter option ..............   " GET option ;
        PICT "X" VALID(option$"12")
   READ
   IF option = "1"
      KEYBOARD "1"
   ENDIF
   RETURN
* End of File
```

RUN / (!)

Syntax: RUN <filename>
! <filename>

Description: The RUN / ! command executes a program from a currently running Clipper application.

Command: Standard

Library Called: Clipper.lib

Notes: When the RUN command has completed execution of the given file, control is returned to the application on the command line immediately following the RUN command.

In order for the RUN command to execute, the total of the amount of memory of the initial application, the amount of memory loaded by COMMAND.COM, and the amount of memory for the program to be RUN must be at least 100K less than the allotted memory of the machine.

COMMAND.COM must be available on the drive and directory path of the initial application performing the actual RUN.

Sample:

```
DO WHILE .T.
   STORE "Today's Date is " + CDOW(date()) + ;
         ", " + CMON(date()) TO prompt
   STORE prompt + " " + STR(DAY(date()),2) + ;
         ", " + STR(YEAR(date()),4) TO prompt
   @ 14,40-LEN(prompt)/2 SAY prompt
   @ 18,25 SAY "Is this the Correct Date?  "
   SET CONSOLE OFF
   WAIT TO temp
   SET CONSOLE ON
   IF UPPER(temp) = "Y"
      mdate = date()
      @ 18,0 SAY SPACE(80)
      @ 18,29 SAY "Enter Date:  " GET mdate
      READ
      mdate = DTOC(mdate)
      RUN DATE &mdate
   ELSE
      EXIT
   ENDIF
ENDDO
```

SAVE SCREEN

Syntax: SAVE SCREEN [TO <memvar>]

Description: This command SAVEs a screen in memory.

Command: Clipper enhanced

Library Called: Clipper.lib

Notes: This command was included to help design applications with a more polished look to them. It is especially handy when used in conjunction with a HELP.PRG file: the original screen can be saved in memory while the help screen is displayed to the user. For restoring the screen, review the RESTORE SCREEN command.

Remember to allow an additional 4K of RAM to be used by the application for the screen you want to keep in memory (2000 characters possible on the screen plus 1 attribute byte for each character).

Using this command is a one-shot situation. That is, one cannot save screens to databases or even to memory variables with this command. To do so, you must SAVE SCREEN TO <memvar> with the following consideration:

1. The amount of space needed for every screen saved will be 4000 bytes.

2. Screens cannot be saved directly to arrays or databases. Temporary variables must be established and the arrays or databases must be replaced by the values of the variables.

Addition: With versions prior to the Summer '87 release, using the CALL _scrsave variation can be **extremely** hazardous to anything else that is residing in memory when this command is CALLed. For example, let us say that a database is open with three index files and a screen is saved. On the surface this is simple. However, for the sake of this example, let us say that you do not allot enough space for the temporary variable (tempscr) and you CALL the library subroutine to save the screen to that variable. The result might be corrupted index files, database header problems, or even an application that once worked, working no longer. **Be very careful!** I can't stress this point enough. Remember, you are dealing with RAM when using this feature and many other "things" reside in RAM as well: databases, indexes, memory variables, macros, DOS, and even your application!

Autumn '86: [TO <memvar>] has been added with this version. It is now the same as the CALL command as shown below.

Sample 1.

```
STORE SPACE(4000) TO tempscr
CALL _scrsave WITH tempscr      && This is available in all
STORE tempscr TO screen[1]      && releases
```

Sample 2.

```
STORE SPACE(4000) TO tempscr     && This form is available in
SAVE SCREEN TO tempscr           && the Autumn '86 release.
STORE tempscr TO screen[1]
```

SAVE TO

Syntax: SAVE TO <filename> [ALL LIKE/EXCEPT <skeleton>]

Description: The SAVE TO command stores all or part of the current set of memory variables to a designated file.

Command: Standard

Library Called: Clipper.lib

Autumn '86: Memory variables of character type and longer than 255 bytes may be saved to a memory file without any program parsing.

Notes: If the <filename> does not include the drive and directory designator, the default drive and directors designator is assumed.

Unless otherwise specified, the file extension for all memory files is .MEM.

With the use of the <skeleton> clause, a question mark (?) represents a single character, while an asterisk (*) represents one or more characters.

If the ALL LIKE/EXCEPT clause is not used, all current memory variables are saved to the designated file.

Sample:

```
STORE "!" TO this
STORE "@" TO that
STORE "#" TO what
SAVE ALL LIKE th* TO Memfile
NOTE This memory file will contain only this and that.
```

SEEK

Syntax: SEEK <expression>

Description: The SEEK command searches for the first record in a database file with a key of an open index file that matches <expression>.

Command: Standard

Library Called: Clipper.lib

Variance: Should be used instead of the dBASE command: FIND &expression.

Summer '87: Using this command with the SET SOFTSEEK ON command means that if the SEEK command does not find a matching key, the record pointer is placed on the record with the first key value greater than the search argument. FOUND() will return .F.; EOF() will also return false.

Notes: The SEEK command always "rewinds" the database pointer and starts the search from the top of the file.

Macro substitution is not required when the expression being searched for is contained in a memory variable.

If the search is unsuccessful, FOUND() is set to .F. and EOF() is set to .T.

If a file is indexed on more than one field, the expression must refer to the first field only.

Sample:

```
STORE SPACE(10) TO search_name
CLEAR
@ 10,10 SAY "Enter Name to search for: " GET search_name
READ
USE Phonbook Index Namebook
SEEK search_name
@ 12,10 SAY IF(FOUND(), "Yes I found it", "Nope, not here")
```

SELECT

Syntax: SELECT <expN>
SELECT <expC>

Description: The SELECT command moves Clipper's internal primary focus and allows changes in the selected work area.

Command: Standard

Library Called: Clipper.lib

Autumn '86: SELECT 0 will now select the first unused area.

Summer '87: 254 work areas are supported. Each work area now allows a maximum number of 15 index files.

Notes: Without any command, the initial SELECTed area is 1.

The range of valid work areas is 1 through 10 (or A through J). If the alias name is used to SELECT the area, it will take precedence over the letter representation.

Record pointers are not connected between work areas unless a SET RELATION TO command has been previously used.

Information from another previously SELECTED area may be obtained provided the letter of the work area precedes the name of the field in question, using the syntax A->field_name.

Alias->field_name is supported; however, the specific work area should be used in place of the file or alias name whenever referring to another selected area or database.

Sample:

```
SELECT 1
USE Temp
SELECT 2
USE Mainfile
IF A->name = name
   ?? "The name in the TEMP is the name in MAINFILE"
ELSE
   ?? "The name in the TEMP is NOT the name in MAINFILE"
ENDIF
```

SET ALTERNATE TO

Syntax: SET ALTERNATE TO [<filename>]

Description: The SET ALTERNATE TO command creates a text file for the SET ALTERNATE ON command to port to.

Default: No file set

Command: Standard

Library Called: Clipper.lib

Notes: The file name must include a drive and directory designator if it is other than the default drive and directory.

If no file extension is specified, .TXT will be used.

Not using the <filename> clause will close the ALTERNATE file. You may also issue a CLOSE ALTERNATE command.

Until the alternate file is closed, there is a risk of losing information that is to be added to the file because of an improper flush of the buffers.

SET ALTERNATE

Syntax: SET ALTERNATE ON/OFF

Description: The SET ALTERNATE ON/OFF command actually tells the computer that the information that follows is to be appended to the alternate file, provided the information is not being displayed using the @...SAY/GET commands.

Default: OFF

Command: Standard

Library Called: Clipper.lib

Notes: The SET ALTERNATE ON command will redirect all non-full-screen entries and displays to the named file.

The file created by the SET ALTERNATE commands is an ASCII text file.

Summer '87: A logical switch is accepted along with the ON or OFF clauses.

Sample:

```
SET ALTERNATE TO Text
? "Hi there"
SET ALTERNATE ON
? "I said 'Hi there...'"              && This goes to Text.txt
CLEAR
@ 10,10 SAY "This should print out here..." && This doesn't
WAIT
SET ALTERNATE OFF
CLOSE ALTERNATE
```

SET BELL

Syntax: SET BELL ON/OFF

Definition: The SET BELL command toggles the bell to sound whenever the last character position in a GET is entered or if an invalid data type is entered into a GET.

Default: OFF

Command: Standard

Library: Clipper.lib

Summer '87: A logical switch is accepted along with the ON or OFF clauses.

SET CENTURY

Syntax: SET CENTURY ON/OFF

Description: The SET CENTURY ON/OFF command allows the input and the display of dates within the century prefix. It will be in standard MM/DD/YYYY format. The Autumn '86 version supports all dates in the range of 01/01/0100 through 12/31/2999.

Default: OFF

Command: Clipper enhanced - Autumn '86

Library Called: Clipper.lib

Summer '87: A logical switch is accepted along with the ON or OFF clauses.

SET COLOR TO

Syntax: SET COLOR TO [<standard> [,<enhanced> [,<border>] [,<background>] [,<unselected>]]]]]

Description: This command changes the colors displayed on the screen.

Default: "W/N, N/W,,,N/W"

Command: Clipper enhanced - Summer '87

Library Called: Clipper.lib

Autumn '86: [,<unselected>] is a new clause that is to follow the optional [<border>] clause. This allows the current and selected GET to be displayed in a different color than all other unselected GETs.

Summer '87: [,<background>] followed by [,<unselected>] now follows the optional [<border>] clause. This allows the background color to be different and allows the current and selected GET to be displayed in a different color than all other unselected GETs.

Variance: The <standard> is used by all output created by commands such as @ SAY and ?. The <enhanced> section of this command affects the GET portion of the command.

Macros are supported with this command; unlike other cases, these macros can contain commas and slashes (which normally are considered part of the syntactical structure of the command). Options such as the "+" and the "*" are also supported with letters rather than numbers and will only affect the foreground of the screen.

Keep in mind that if numbers are used to represent the desired colors rather than letters, the number to the left of the slash is written to the **high-order 4 bits** of the color attribute byte, while the number to the right of the slash is written to the **low-order 4 bits** of the color attribute byte. In other words, to get the best results, make sure you use numbers less than 8 with the SET COLOR TO command in conjunction with the "standard" color set.

High-intensity (+) and blinking (*) attributes are allowed to the foreground color.

The SET COLOR TO command does not support the use of numbers when used in conjunction with ANSI.OBJ.

To reset the screen to the original default values, use SET COLOR TO without parameters.

Guide:

Color	Number	Letter
Black	0	N
Blue	1	B
Green	2	G
Cyan	3	BG
Red	4	R
Magenta	5	RB
Brown	6	GR
White	7	W
Underline		U - Monochrome Only
Inverse		I
Blank		X
Gray	8	N+
Yellow	9	GR+

Sample:

```
*********************
* Name          COLOR.prg
* Date          August 5, 1986
* Notice        Copyright 1986, Stephen J. Straley
* Compile       Clipper Color
* Release       All versions
* Link          Plink86 fi color lib clipper;
* Note          This sample program shows the
*               SET COLOR TO command in operation.
*
*********************

STORE SPACE(30) TO input
CLEAR
DO WHILE .T.
   @ 10,10 SAY "Leave Blank to QUIT"
   @ 12,10 SAY "Set Color to what? " GET input
   READ
   IF EMPTY(input)
      EXIT
   ENDIF
   SET COLOR TO &input
ENDDO

CLEAR
SET COLOR TO
SET COLOR TO 7/7, 0/0
STORE SPACE(10) TO password
@ 10,22 SAY "And now to set the screen to hide input"
@ 11,22 SAY "    for the sake of a password!"
@ 14,22 SAY "Enter Password => " GET password
READ
@ 16,22 SAY "The password was &password."
SET COLOR TO
* End of File
```

SET CONFIRM

Syntax: SET CONFIRM ON/OFF

Description: With the SET CONFIRM ON command, the Enter key is required to end each and every GET.

Otherwise, once a GET is filled with the proper number of designated characters (either by the attributes of the variable or by the PICTURE clause), the cursor automatically advances to the next GET. If the READ is completed, the flow of the program will continue.

Default: OFF

Command: Standard

Library Called: Clipper.lib

Summer '87: A logical switch is accepted along with the ON or OFF clauses.

Sample:

```
STORE SPACE(15) TO test1, test2
SET CONFIRM ON
@ 2,10 SAY "Enter 20 characters to test1: " GET test1
@ 3,10 SAY "                         test2: " GET test2
READ
SET CONFIRM OFF
@ 2,10 SAY "Enter 20 characters to test1: " GET test1
@ 3,10 SAY "                         test2: " GET test2
READ
```

SET CONSOLE

Syntax: SET CONSOLE ON/OFF

Description: The SET CONSOLE command turns the screen either off or on for screen display other than @...SAY commands.

Default: ON

Command: Standard

Library Called: Clipper.lib

Summer '87: A logical switch is accepted along with the ON or OFF clauses.

Notes: The SET CONSOLE command will not affect output to a printer.

This command is normally used to shut off the screen so that those commands that route some type of a message back to the screen can be handled by other programming techniques and commands.

Sample:

```
@ 10,10 SAY "Press Any Key to Continue or Q to Quit..."
SET CONSOLE OFF
WAIT TO temp
SET CONSOLE ON
IF UPPER(temp) = "Q"
   RETURN
ENDIF
```

SET CURSOR

Syntax: SET CURSOR ON/OFF

Description: The SET CURSOR command toggles the cursor on and off.

Default: ON

Command: Clipper enhanced - Summer '87

Library Called: Clipper.lib

Summer '87: A logical switch is accepted along with the ON or OFF clauses.

SET DATE

Syntax: SET DATE AMERICAN/ANSI/BRITISH/FRENCH/GERMAN/ ITALIAN

Definition: The SET DATE command sets the date type format for function arguments and returned values and for display purposes.

Default: AMERICAN

Command: Clipper enhanced

Library Called: Clipper.lib

SET DECIMALS TO

Syntax: SET DECIMALS TO <expN>

Description: The SET DECIMALS TO command establishes the number of decimal places that Clipper will display in mathematical calculations, functions, memory variables, and fields.

Default: 2

Command: Standard

Library Called: Clipper.lib

Variance: In some functions, dBASE III will assume the decimal place by the number of places in the passed parameter. In Clipper, all results are bound by the SET DECIMALS TO command.

The SET DECIMAL TO command will only apply to calculations involved with division, the SQRT(), LOG(), and EXP() functions.

Sample:

```
? LOG(1)
SET DECIMALS TO 4
? LOG(1)
```

SET DEFAULT TO

Syntax: SET DEFAULT TO <disk drive>/<path>

Description: The SET DEFAULT TO command changes the drive and directory used for reading and writing of database, index, memory, and alternate files.

Default: <current logged drive>

Command: Standard

Library Called: Clipper.lib

Notes: Because of the compiled environment, the SET DEFAULT TO command does not pertain to format files, procedure files, and other program files in the manner that it would under the interpreter. This is because the compiler will compile the format and procedure files in with the main program files and they will be included in the final executable program.

Sample:
```
SET DEFAULT TO B
USE Phonbook
```

SET DELETED

Syntax: SET DELETED ON/OFF

Description: The SET DELETED command is, in essence, a filter placed on the database to mask out those records marked for deletion. A SET DELETED ON command is just as effective as a SET FILTER TO .NOT. DELETED().

Default: OFF

Command: Standard

Library Called: Clipper.lib

Summer '87: A logical switch is accepted along with the ON or OFF clauses.

Notes: Whether SET DELETED ON or OFF is used in conjunction with the INDEX and REINDEX command, all records are included.

If the SET DELETED command is ON, RECALL ALL does not recall any records.

Sample:
```
USE Temp
DISPLAY ALL
SET DELETED ON
DISPLAY ALL
```

SET DELIMITERS

Syntax: SET DELIMITERS ON/OFF

Description: The SET DELIMITERS ON command allows specific characters to delimit field area input. See SET DELIMITERS TO.

Default: OFF

Command: Standard

Library Called: Clipper.lib

Summer '87: A logical switch is accepted along with the ON or OFF clauses.

Notes: If left OFF, the fields are delimited by reverse video or highlighting.

SET DELIMITERS TO

Syntax: SET DELIMITERS TO [<expC>][DEFAULT]

Description: The SET DELIMITERS TO command changes the characters that delimit the area before and after field or variable input.

Default: ::

Command: Standard

Library Called: Clipper.lib

Notes: The character string expressed in <expC> may be either one or two characters. If only one character is used, that character is used both before and after field or variable input areas. If two characters are entered, the first character represents the character before the field, and the second character is used after the field.

If the DEFAULT clause is used in place of <expC>, the characters are reset to ::.

No matter what the DELIMITERS are SET TO, if the SET DELIMITERS OFF command is in effect, no delimiters are used. SET DELIMITERS ON must be used before SET DELIMITERS TO.

Sample:

```
SET DELIMITERS ON
SET DELIMITERS TO "[]"
STORE 0 TO value
CLEAR
@ 10,10 SAY "Get value: " GET value
READ
```

SET DEVICE TO

Syntax: SET DEVICE TO <PRINT/SCREEN>

Description: The SET DEVICE TO command determines where the @...SAY command will be displayed (either the screen or the printer).

Default: SCREEN

Command: Standard

Library Called: Clipper.lib

Notes: If the SET DEVICE TO PRINT is used in conjunction with a series of @...GET commands, the values for the GETS will all be ignored. If a position command requires that the printer either back up on the paper in column position or in row position, a page eject is issued.

This command is not to be confused with the SET PRINT ON command. This command is only connected with @...SAY commands.

Sample:

```
CLEAR
@ 10,10 SAY "Hi there..."
SET DEVICE TO PRINT
@ 10,10 SAY "I am over here now..."
EJECT
SET DEVICE TO SCREEN
@ 12,10 SAY "I am now here..."
```

SET ESCAPE

Syntax: SET ESCAPE ON/OFF

Description: The SET ESCAPE ON command allows an Alt-C to terminate the execution of the program and ignores VALID. If the SET ESCAPE OFF command is issued, Alt-C will **not** terminate an operation and no escape from a READ (VALID) is possible.
Also controls the Esc key.

Default: ON

Command: Clipper enhanced

Library Called: Clipper.lib

Summer '87: A logical switch is accepted along with the ON or OFF clauses.

Notes: This command may be used to offer alternate escape routes from an application.

Though it **is** an option, allowing a user to use Alt-C inside an application is **extremely** dangerous to the integrity of the open and active databases and indexes.

If SET ESCAPE is off and an Alt-C is entered, Clipper issues the (Q/A/I) error message for those applications compiled with the Autumn '86 release or prior ones. Otherwise, in Summer '87 the Q/A/I is replaced with several new messages, including "Paused?" and "Retry?"

SET EXACT

Syntax: SET EXACT ON/OFF

Description: The SET EXACT command determines how much of a comparison will be performed between two character expressions.

Default: OFF

Command: Standard

Library Called: Clipper.lib

Summer '87: A logical switch is accepted along with the ON or OFF clauses.

Variance: Index files with key fields **not** in multiples of 4 bytes may now be found with the SET EXACT command ON. In some applications, where the key wasn't precisely in a multiple of 4 bytes, items under the interpreter were rarely found with a SEEK or a FIND.

Notes: The SET EXACT OFF command makes a character by character comparison and allows for a match to be made if the short string is to the right of the equal sign. For example:

```
? "Monday" = "Monday Night Bowling"     .F.
? "Monday Night Bowling" = "Monday"     .T.
```

With SET EXACT ON, both sides of the equation are evaluated and must be equal. Therefore, the second test would now yield a .F. to the screen.

The SET EXACT ON command is equivalent to the = = operator for string evaluations. For most numeric evaluations, the = = operator is preferred.

SET EXCLUSIVE

Syntax: SET EXCLUSIVE ON/OFF

Description: The SET EXCLUSIVE ON/OFF command determines the way in which the database and related memo and index files are opened.

ON means nonshared file access; OFF means shared files.

Default: ON

Command: Clipper enhanced - Autumn '86

Summer '87: A logical switch is accepted along with the ON or OFF clauses.

SET FILTER TO

Syntax: SET FILTER TO [<expression>]

Description: The SET FILTER TO command masks a database so that only those records that meet the condition prescribed by the <expression> will be shown.

Default: No filter set

Command: Standard

Library Called: Clipper.lib

Notes: Using the SET FILTER TO command without an expression will turn off the filter on the active database and allow all records to be accessed.

If the SET FILTER TO command is used, a GO TOP command should follow immediately. GO TOP will reposition the record pointer to the top of the newly FILTERed database.

The SET FILTER TO command will only apply to the currently open and active database. A separate and unique FILTER may be set for each open area.

Sample: Consider the following database:

```
File: Main.dbf
Record #        Name        Age
   1          Stephen        26
   2          Ray            36
   3          Cheryl         34
   4          Barry          45
   5          David          27
   6          Steve          29
   7          Stan           88
   8          Marilyn        36
   9          Rita           19
  10          Terri          22
```

Now issue the following commands:

```
SET FILTER TO SUBSTR(name,1,2) = "St" .OR. age = 22
GO TOP
```

The database, if displayed, would now look like this:

```
File: Main.dbf
Record #        Name        Age
   1          Stephen        26
   6          Steve          29
   7          Stan           88
  10          Terri          22
```

SET FIXED

Syntax: SET FIXED ON/OFF

Description: The SET FIXED command activates a system-wide fixed placement on the number of decimal places shown for all numeric output.

Default: OFF

Command: Standard

Library Called: Clipper.lib

Notes: The number of decimal places that are FIXED is determined by the default or set value of the SET DECIMAL TO command.

When SET DECIMALS OFF is used, the following rules apply to the number of decimal places displayed:

Addition/Subtraction	Same as the operand with the greatest number of decimal digits.
Multiplication	Sum of the operand decimal digits
Division	SET DECIMAL TO
Exponentiation	SET DECIMAL TO
LOG()	SET DECIMAL TO
EXP()	SET DECIMAL TO
SQRT()	SET DECIMAL TO
VAL()	Same as operand

SET FORMAT TO

Syntax: SET FORMAT TO <file name>

Description: The SET FORMAT TO command selects a custom format that has been previously stored in a format (.FMT) file.

Default: No file

Command: Standard

Library Called: Clipper.lib

Variance: Files with a .FMT extension will not be recognized if CLiP files are used to compile an application. Files with a .FMT extension must be renamed to .PRG files in order to be pulled in by the compiler.

The SET FORMAT TO command does not automatically CLEAR the screen upon entry of the format file.

Sample:
```
SET FORMAT TO Editscr
```

SET FUNCTION

Syntax: SET FUNCTION <expN> TO <expC>

Description: The SET FUNCTION TO command allows each function key to be reprogrammed to represent a character expression.

Default: No keys set

Command: Standard

Library Called: Clipper.lib

Variance: Unlike dBASE III, the character expression is not limited to 30 characters. Additionally, function keys cannot be set to commands but can call procedures, functions, and programs. <expC> can also contain control characters, such as Ctrl-C.

Notes: The <expN> represents the numeric value for the function key as depicted by the INKEY() function. Function key 1 is set to HELP if it is available; function keys 2 through 10 are accessed by pressing the appropriate key; function keys 11 through 20 are accessed by pressing Shift plus the key; function keys 21 through 30 are combined with Control; and function keys 31 through 40 are combined with the Alt key. Also see the SET KEY command.

Any SET KEY TO definition will take precedence over a SET FUNCTION assignment.

Sample:

```
DO WHILE .T.
   CLEAR
   @ 0,10 SAY "Strike a Key..."
   qw = INKEY(0)
   IF qw = 28
      LOOP
   ELSE
      IF qw = 32
         EXIT
      ENDIF
   ENDIF
   @ 4,9,21,71 BOX REPLICATE(CHR(219), 9)
   STORE "" TO test
   SET FUNCTION qw TO MEMOEDIT(test,5,10,20,70,.T.)
ENDDO

DO WHILE .T.
   CLEAR
   STORE SPACE(500) TO test
   @ 10,0 GET test
   READ
   IF LEN(TRIM(test)) = 0
      EXIT
   ENDIF
   WAIT
ENDDO
```

SET INDEX

Syntax: SET INDEX TO [< file list >]

Description: This command opens an index file to the active and open database. If more than one file is listed in < file list >, the order of the database will be determined by the first index file in the < file list >. All file operations will be based on the first index file; however, all index files in the < file list > will be updated if the database is updated.

Default: None

Command: Standard

Library Called: Clipper.lib

Variance: While macros are supported with the SET INDEX TO command, the rule remains that syntax verbs are unsupported in macros. In other words, the use of commas in a macro in conjunction with the SET INDEX TO command is **not** supported. Each file being listed must be in a separate macro; it is suggested that the macro be "dot terminated" before the use of a comma.

Sample:

```
STORE "C:" TO drive
STORE "Time_a.dat" TO file1
USE Time
SET INDEX TO &drive.&file1., &drive.Time_b.dat
```

see also: SET ORDER TO

SET INTENSITY

Syntax: SET INTENSITY ON/OFF

Description: The SET INTENSITY command sets the field input color to either highlighted (inverse video) or normal color.

Default: ON

Command: Standard

Library Called: Clipper.lib

Summer '87: A logical switch is accepted along with the ON or OFF clauses.

Notes: Rather than using the SET DELIMITER TO command and establishing a set of delimiters, the video attributes may be used instead. For most data entry procedures, this is more effective.

Sample:

```
STORE SPACE(10) TO sample
CLEAR
@ 10,10 SAY "Enter with Intensity:      " GET sample
READ
SET INTENSITY OFF
@ 12,10 SAY "Enter without Intensity:   " GET sample
READ
```

SET KEY TO

Syntax: SET KEY <expN> TO [<proc>]

Description: This command is used where <expN> is equal to the value given by INKEY() for any keyboard key and <proc> is a procedure. Through Winter '85, extended codes had not been converted. As a result, compatibility with dBASE III was maintained.

Default: No Key SET except F1 to HELP.PRG, if HELP.PRG is present.

Command: Clipper enhanced

Notes: The <proc> is the name of the procedure or program that will be called whenever the designated key is entered and the program control is in a "wait" state. These states are defined by the following commands:

ACCEPT
INPUT
MENU TO
READ
WAIT

Special program control may be used in conjunction with the SET KEY command. For example, additional GETS may be added to the current and active READ by setting a key to a procedure with a few additional GETS. Once in the READ, if the specially assigned KEY is pressed, the additional GETS are added to the stack and thus made available to the current READ. All cursor control and movement will work between previously displayed GETs and those added with the SET KEY TO command.

Regardless of use, three parameters are passed to the procedure. Therefore, any procedure that may be called by the use of the SET KEY TO command **must** have the PARAMETER command with the calling program name (p), the line number of the READ or

MENU TO command (l), and the input variable name of either the GET or the MENU TO command (v).

Sample:

```
*********************
* Name          SET_KEY.prg
* Date          August 6, 1986
* Notice        Copyright 1986, Stephen J. Straley
* Compile       Clipper Set_key
* Release       Autumn '86 and later
* Link          Plink86 fi set_key lib clipper;
* Note          This shows the use of the SET KEY command.
*
*********************

SET KEY 28 TO One_cnt
SET KEY -1 TO Two_cnt
SET KEY -2 TO Three_cnt
SET KEY -3 TO Four_cnt
SET KEY -4 TO Five_cnt
SET KEY -5 TO Six_cnt
DO WHILE .T.
   CLEAR
   TEXT
       F1 will count to 600 by one
       F2 will count to 600 by two
       F3 will count to 600 by three
       F4 will count to 600 by four
       F5 will count to 600 by five
       F6 will count to 600 by six

       Enter 'QUIT' to exit program

   ENDTEXT
   STORE "    " TO temp_var
   @ 20,20 SAY "Strike a key or type QUIT to exit -> " GET ;
        temp_var
   READ
   IF UPPER(TRIM(temp_var)) = "QUIT"
      QUIT
   ENDIF
ENDDO

*********************

PROCEDURE One_cnt

   PARAMETERS p, l, v

   CLEAR
   FOR x = 1 TO 600
      @ 12,25 SAY "Total count: "
      ?? x
   NEXT
   WAIT
```

```
*********************

PROCEDURE Two_cnt

   PARAMETERS p, l, v

   CLEAR
   FOR x = 1 TO 600 STEP 2
      @ 12,25 SAY "Total count: "
      ?? x
   NEXT
   WAIT

*********************

PROCEDURE Three_cnt

   PARAMETERS p, l, v

   CLEAR
   FOR x = 1 TO 600 STEP 3
      @ 12,25 SAY "Total count: "
      ?? x
   NEXT
   WAIT

*********************

PROCEDURE Four_cnt

   PARAMETERS p, l, v

   CLEAR
   FOR x = 1 TO 600 STEP 4
      @ 12,25 SAY "Total count: "
      ?? x
   NEXT
   WAIT

*********************

PROCEDURE Five_cnt

   PARAMETERS p, l, v

   CLEAR
   FOR x = 1 TO 600 STEP 5
      @ 12,25 SAY "Total count: "
      ?? x
   NEXT
   WAIT
```

```
*********************

PROCEDURE Six_cnt

   PARAMETERS p, l, v

   CLEAR
   FOR x = 1 TO 600 STEP 6
      @ 12,25 SAY "Total count: "
      ?? x
   NEXT
   WAIT
* End of File
```

SET MARGIN TO

Syntax: SET MARGIN TO <expN>

Description: The SET MARGIN TO command adjusts the left-hand margin for all printed output according to the value expressed in the <expN>.

Default: 0

Command: Standard

Library Called: Clipper.lib.

Notes: Once a SET MARGIN TO is set and after printing has occurred, the margin must be reestablished at 0 in order for all video display to appear in the proper positions.

Sample:

```
SET DEVICE TO PRINT
@ 10,10 SAY "The margin is set to 0"
SET MARGIN TO 5
@ 15,10 SAY "Now it is set to 5"
SET DEVICE TO SCREEN
@ 15,10 SAY "It is off position..."
SET MARGIN TO 0
@ 15,10 SAY "It is now on position."
```

SET MESSAGE TO

Syntax: SET MESSAGE TO <expN> [CENTER]

Description: This command is designed to work with the MENU TO and PROMPT commands. With the SET MESSAGE TO command, choose a line number between 1 and 24 inclusive where a special prompt message will appear every time the cursor is placed on a PROMPT option. By using the SET MESSAGE TO line number option, every prompt to the screen may have an additional message giving more information to the user regarding that menu choice.

Default: 24

Command: Clipper enhanced

Library Called: Clipper.lib

Summer '87: With the Summer '87 release, the [CENTER] optional clause was added. Using this optional clause means that the message will be automatically centered on the specified row.

Notes: Keep in mind that the SET MESSAGE TO <expN> does not set the message that will be displayed; that happens in the PROMPT command. All the SET MESSAGE TO <expN> command will do is establish the line number on which the additional message will appear whenever the MESSAGE clause is used with the PROMPT command.

Sample: Refer to the PROMPT ... MESSAGE command.

SET ORDER TO

Syntax: SET ORDER TO [<expN>]

Description: The SET ORDER TO command selects a new active index from the index list. If <expN> is 0, the current index list order will be maintained.

Default: 1

Command: Clipper enhanced - Autumn '86

Library Called: Clipper.lib

Notes: The number expressed for the SET ORDER TO command may be from 0 to 15.

SET PATH TO

Syntax: SET PATH TO <expC>

Description: This command will change the system PATH.

Default: None set

Command: Standard

Library Called: Clipper.lib

Variance: Using this command in conjunction with a continuation marker (a semicolon) is not supported. The entire path must be entered on one line.

Sample:

```
SET PATH TO C:\EDP, C:\EDP\STATION1,C:\EDP\STATION2
```

SET PRINT

Syntax: SET PRINT ON/OFF

Description: The SET PRINT command directs all output that is not controlled by the @...SAY command to the printer and the console.

Default: OFF

Command: Standard

Library Called: Clipper.lib

Summer '87: A logical switch is accepted along with the ON or OFF clauses.

Notes: In order to prevent output from being displayed on the screen when it should go exclusively to the printer, the SET CONSOLE OFF command may have to be invoked as well, especially when using ? and ?? to display information.

Sample:

```
? "This is a test"
SET PRINT ON
? "This is another test with both..."
SET CONSOLE OFF
? "This is only printing on the printer..."
```

SET PRINTER TO

Syntax: SET PRINTER TO [<device>/<filename>]

Description: If you are redirecting the full screen output to a file, the SET DEVICE TO PRINT command is also required. This command is extremely useful when used in conjunction with the SET KEY TO command in order to trap screen messages and program location.

Default: OFF

Command: Clipper enhanced - Autumn '86

Library Called: Clipper.lib

Note: If a device name is applicable, trailing colons are not supported. Using the <device> option will send all printed output to the network or to the local device.

Sample:

```
SET DEVICE TO PRINT
SET PRINTER TO Screen.txt
a = 1
@ 5,10 SAY "This is a test, so enter a value -> " GET a
READ
SET PRINTER TO                  && This closes the printer file.
SET PRINTER TO LPT1
@ 10,10 SAY "This is now going to line printer 1"
SET PRINTER TO
SET DEVICE TO SCREEN
```

SET PROCEDURE TO

Syntax: SET PROCEDURE TO <filename>

Description: The SET PROCEDURE TO command allows a series of procedures that are contained in a .PRG file to be pulled into the application and used accordingly.

Default: None set

Command: Standard

Library Called: Clipper.lib

Variance: There is no maximum number of procedures allowed in a PROCEDURE file.

The PROCEDURE file does not constitute an open file during run-time.

The PROCEDURE <filename> must not have the same name as any name of a procedure.

Further detailed information regarding procedures and their functions under Clipper is in Chapter 10, Clipper Procedures.

Sample:

```
SET PROCEDURE TO Proclist
DO Proclis1
```

SET RELATION TO

Syntax: SET RELATION [ADDITIVE] TO <keyexp>/RECNO()/ /<expN> INTO <alias> [,TO <key exp>/RECNO()/<expN> INTO <alias> ...]

Description: The SET RELATION TO command links two or more database files according to a key expression that is common to all files.

Command: Standard

Library Called: Clipper.lib

Variance: Up to eight child RELATIONs are supported from one mother file. Cyclical relations are not supported.

Summer '87: The ADDITIVE clause allows relations to be added to the current set of relations previously defined in the current work area.

Notes: The SET RELATION command will link the currently selected database file to an open file in another area.

The second and subsequent files are identified by their aliases.

With the key expression option, the key must be contained in the selected database, and the linked file(s) must be indexed on the key expression. Whenever the active file is repositioned, the linked file is searched for the first record matching the key expression from the active file.

With the RECNO() option, the files may be linked by record numbers.

If a matching record cannot be found in the linked file, the linked file is positioned to the end of the file and a blank record is appended.

Sample:

```
CLEAR
@ 5,0,23,79 BOX "*"
@ 7,5 SAY "One moment while all files are initialized"

file4 = "PRHIST"     && A History File
file3 = "PRCHECK"    && A Check File
file2 = "PREMPLOY"   && An Employee Master File
file1 = "PRTIME"     && A Timecard File

*************************************************************
* This section sets up all files and subsequent relations. *
*************************************************************

SELECT 4
USE &file4. INDEX Prhist_a
SELECT 3
USE &file3. INDEX Prchk_a.dat
ZAP
SELECT 2
USE &file2. INDEX Premp_a.dat
SELECT 1
USE &file1. INDEX Prtime_a.dat
SELECT 1

*****************************************************************
* This section adds checks to be processed to the check file   *
* based on the number of timecards in the timecard file.       *
*****************************************************************
DO WHILE .NOT. EOF()
  @ 21, 5 SAY "Now adding employee number " + TRIM(employee) + ;
  " to the check file"
  temp_emp = employee
  SELECT 3
  APPEND BLANK
  REPLACE employee WITH temp_emp
  SELECT 1
  SKIP
ENDDO
*******************************************************
* This section sets up final relation and then goes  *
* on to calculate federal, state, and local taxes.   *
*******************************************************
@ 21, 5 SAY SPACE(73)
SELECT 3
GO TOP
SET RELATION TO employee INTO &file2., TO employee INTO &file1.
*******************************************************
* Both files are indexed on employee, and the parent *
* file has a similar field as well.                  *
*******************************************************
```

```
@ 7, 5 SAY SPACE(73)

DO WHILE .NOT. EOF()

*****************************************************************
* Calculate base pay                                            *
*   AMT_REG_P is set to salary rate (if a salary employee)      *
*             else is set to the hourly rate X the number of    *
*             straight hours worked                             *
*****************************************************************
  IF &file2.->salaried
    REPLACE amt_reg_p WITH &file2.->pay_rate_s
  ELSE
     REPLACE amt_reg_p WITH &file1.->stra_time * &file2.-
>pay_rate_h
  ENDIF

****************************************************************
* Calculate Overtime pay, Total Gross Pay, and Exempted Pay.  *
*                                                              *
* Temp_pay is first the hourly rate X the rate for overtime X *
*     the number of overtime hours worked.                     *
* Temp_pay is then added to hourly rate X the rate for         *
*     double time X the number of double-time hours worked.    *
* Temp_pay is finally added to the hourly rate X the rate for *
*     triple time X the number of triple-time hours worked.    *
* AMT_OVR_P is then set to Temp_pay.                           *
* AMT_VAC_P is set to the hourly pay rate X the rate for       *
*     vacation time X the number of vacation hours worked.     *
* AMT_SIC_P is set to the hourly pay rate X the hours of       *
*     sick time.                                               *
* AMT_GRO_P is set to the regular pay + the overtime pay +     *
*     vacation pay + the sick pay.                             *
* Temp_pay is then set to the tips + the bonus + any misc.     *
*     pay--any gross pay deduction (master employee record)    *
* AMT_TGR_P is set to the gross pay(AMT_GRO_P) +               *
*     temp_pay(all else)                                       *
* AMT_EXP_P is set to the amount of exempted pay               *
****************************************************************

  temp_pay = &file2.->pay_rate_h * prover * &file1.->half_time
  temp_pay = temp_pay + &file2.->pay_rate_h * prdouble * &file1.-
>doub_time
  temp_pay = temp_pay + &file2.->pay_rate_h * prtriple * &file1.-
>trip_time
  REPLACE amt_ovr_p WITH temp_pay, amt_vac_p WITH &file2.-
>pay_rate_h * prvaca * &file1.->vaca_time
  REPLACE amt_sic_p WITH &file2.->pay_rate_h * &file1.->sick_time
  REPLACE amt_gro_p WITH amt_reg_p + amt_ovr_p + amt_vac_p +
amt_sic_p
  temp_pay = &file1.->tips + &file1.->bonus + &file1.->misc_pay -
&file1.->gross_pay
  REPLACE amt_tgr_p WITH amt_gro_p + temp_pay, amt_exp_p WITH
```

```
&file1.->exem_pay
ENDDO
CLOSE databases
```

SET SCOREBOARD

Syntax: SET SCOREBOARD ON/OFF

Definition: The SET SCOREBOARD command will toggle the display area in the upper right corner of the screen for the READ command and the MEMOEDIT() function.

Default: ON

Command: Clipper enhanced

Library Called: Clipper.lib

Summer '87: A logical switch is accepted along with the ON or OFF clauses.

SET SOFTSEEK

Syntax: SET SOFTSEEK ON/OFF

Description: The SET SOFTSEEK command toggles for a "relative" seeking condition to exist.

If the SET SOFTSEEK command is ON, if a SEEK or FIND command is issued, and if no match is found, the record pointer will be set to the next record in the index with a higher key value than the expression in the SEEK or FIND command. The FOUND() function will return .F. as well as the EOF() function.

Default: OFF

Command: Clipper enhanced - Summer '87

Library Called: Clipper.lib

Summer '87: A logical switch is accepted along with the ON or OFF clauses.

Note: This is a Summer '87 command enhancement.

SET TYPEAHEAD

Syntax: SET TYPEAHEAD <expN>

Description: The SET TYPEAHEAD command sets the size of the keyboard buffer.

Command: Clipper enhanced - Summer '87

Library Called: Clipper.lib

Note: The maximum number of characters allowed in the keyboard buffer is 32,768.

SET UNIQUE

Syntax: SET UNIQUE ON/OFF

Description: The SET UNIQUE command determines whether all records with the same value on a key expression will be included in the index file.

An index created with SET UNIQUE ON will create an index based solely on each unique value within the database. Only the first record with duplicate keys will be included in the new index file.

Default: OFF

Command: Standard

Library Called: Clipper.lib

Summer '87: A logical switch is accepted along with the ON or OFF clauses.

Variance: Under dBASE III, the index file based on SET UNIQUE ON will be smaller than the original file; under Clipper, the second index file based on the unique field will be the same size as the original index file because of the manner in which Clipper handles indexing.

SET WRAP

Syntax: SET WRAP ON/OFF

Description: The SET WRAP command toggles MENU wrapping.

Default: OFF

Command: Clipper enhanced - Summer '87

Library Called: Clipper.lib

Summer '87: A logical switch is accepted along with the ON or OFF clauses.

SKIP

Syntax: SKIP [expN] [ALIAS <expN>/<expC>]

Description: The SKIP command moves the record pointer in either the active database or in any other open database.

Command: Clipper enhanced

Variance: The ALIAS clause allows the pointer in another preopened area, not currently selected, to be moved without having to go directly to the selected area and move the pointer. The pointer will be repositioned in that file by using either the ALIAS number <expN> or the ALIAS name <expC>.

SKIP 0 allows the buffer of the current database to be flushed. This does not cause a disk write. To accomplish that, the COMMIT command is necessary.

Sample:

```
SKIP ALIAS 2
* The old way to do the same would have been
* SELECT 2
* SKIP
* SELECT 1

SKIP 5 ALIAS Employee
* The old way to do the same would have been
* SELECT Employee
* SKIP 5
* SELECT 1
```

SORT

Syntax: SORT <scope> TO [<newfile>] ON <field> [/A][/C][/D][,<field2>][/A][/C][/D] [FOR <condition>] [WHILE <condition>]

Description: The SORT command copies the currently selected database to <newfile> with the records in alphabetical, chronological, or numerical order as specified by the ON <field> clause.

Command: Standard

Library Called: Clipper.lib

Variance: In the Autumn '86 version only, the /D option will not work on date fields.

Summer '87: In Summer '87 release, the SORT command now performs as much of the operation as possible in memory, spooling out the information to a temporary file (Clipsort.tmp). This operation requires three file handles.

Notes: The <newfile> will have a .DBF extension unless otherwise specified.

A file cannot be SORTed to itself or any other open file.

The switches mean the following:

/A = ASCENDING order
/D = DESCENDING order
/C = Ignore CASE

Combining switches is valid: /AC or /CD, etc....

To SORT on multiple fields, the most important key must be specified first. Separate field names with commas. This cannot be used in macro substitution.

SORTing is not allowed on memo fields or logical fields.

SORT does not work with substring functions or complex expressions.

Sample:

```
USE Phonbook
SORT ON state, city, prefix /C TO Newbook
```

STORE

Syntax: STORE <expression> TO <memory variable>/<memory variable list>

Description: The STORE command initializes a memory variable(s) to a specific value. An acceptable alternate syntax would be:

```
<memory variable> = <expression>
```

Command: Standard

Library Called: Clipper.lib

Notes: With the alternative syntax, only one variable can be initialized to an expression at one time. The primary syntax structure should be used if a series of variables needs to be initialized to one value.

If a memory variable has the same name as an active field name, the field name will take precedence over the memory variable unless the memory variable is explicitly specified as M-> <memory variable>.

Sample:

```
STORE 0 TO memvar1, memvar2, memvar3, memvar4

memvar1 = 0
memvar2 = 0
memvar3 = 0
memvar4 = 0
STORE 5 TO M->last_name  && where there is also an active
*                           field named last_name.
```

SUM

Syntax: SUM <scope> <field list> TO <memvar list> [FOR <condition>] [WHILE <condition>]

Description: The SUM command sums to a <memvar> the values of fields in a database, depending upon the condition set.

Command: Standard

Library Called: Clipper.lib

Variance: With this command, the memory variable or the memory variable list is mandatory, and the lists on each side of the TO section maintain a one-to-one relationship.

Sample:

```
USE Example
SUM amount_owe, past_due TO owe_amount, due_amount ;
    FOR state = "CA" WHILE .NOT. priority
```

TEXT

Syntax: TEXT [TO PRINT/TO FILE <filename>]
<commands>
ENDTEXT

Description: The TEXT command prints large quantities of information without using the @...SAY command.

Command: Standard

Library Called: Clipper.lib.

Variance: The [TO PRINT/TO FILE] clauses allow the TEXT/ENDTEXT to print to the printer or to an alternate file. This feature is useful for uniform report writing; with one routine you can send TEXT/ENDTEXT to screen, to printer, or to a file for output or format at a later time.

TOTAL ON

Syntax: TOTAL ON <key field> [<scope>] [FIELDS <field list>] TO <newfile> [FOR <condition>] [WHILE <condition>]

Description: The TOTAL command is used to sum numeric fields in the currently selected database file and send the results to a second database file. The numeric fields in the second database will contain the total for all records that have the same key value as the fields in the original database.

Command: Standard

Library Called: Clipper.lib

Variance: In the Autumn '86 release, the FIELDS clause must be included in the TOTAL ON command.

In the Summer '87 release, there are two separate modes for the TOTAL command. If the FIELDS clause is used, the TOTAL command will sum the specified numeric fields to the target database, grouped by the specified key expression. If the FIELDS clause is **not** used, the TOTAL command will only copy those records with unique fields to the target database.

Notes: The currently selected database file must be either INDEXed or SORTed on the key to be TOTALed.

The second database name must have a drive designator if the file is to be written to a drive or directory other than the default drive or directory. Unless specified, a .DBF extension will be given the <newfile>.

The structure of the secondary database is identical to that of the selected database. Memo fields are not copied to the new file.

All records are TOTALed to the <newfile> unless specified by the scope or by a FOR <condition> or a WHILE <condition> or by both.

All records with the same value in the specified key field will be condensed to a single record in the secondary database.

Sample:

```
USE Phonbook INDEX Statbook
TOTAL ON state TO A:Summary FIELDS owe, paid FOR owe > 0

* This will produce a secondary database called A:SUMMARY.DBF
* that will have in it two fields: the amount owed and the
* amount paid.  This database will have a record for each state
* that will be a total of the monies owed and paid.
```

TYPE

Syntax: TYPE <file name> [TO PRINT]/[TO FILE <filename>]

Description: The TYPE command types out the contents of an ASCII file.

Command: Standard

Library Called: Clipper.lib

Variance: The DOS redirectional option is not supported. In order to get output to a printer, use the TO PRINT option and use the TO FILE option rather than setting an alternate file.

Sample:

```
* The following is legal under Clipper: *
*
TYPE Results.txt TO PRINT              && goes to the printer
TYPE Results.txt                       && goes to the screen
TYPE Results.txt TO FILE Outfile.txt   && goes to a file

* The following is not legal under Clipper: *
*
TYPE Results.txt >PRN
TYPE Results.txt >Outfile.txt
```

UNLOCK

Syntax: UNLOCK [ALL]

Description: The UNLOCK command releases the file or record lock in the selected work area. If the [ALL] clause is used, all current locks in all work areas will be removed.

Command: Clipper enhanced - Autumn '86

Library Called: Clipper.lib

UPDATE ON

Syntax: UPDATE ON <key field> FROM <Alias> REPLACE <field> WITH <exp> [,<field2> WITH <exp> ...] [RANDOM]

Description: The UPDATE command uses data from an existing file and changes data records accordingly in the currently selected database. The alterations are made by matching records in the two database files on a single key field.

Command: Standard

Library Called: Clipper.lib

Variance: The RANDOM clause must be used; this saves Clipper from having to open an index file for the FROM database.

Notes: The file being UPDATEd must be the currently selected database and must be either SORTed or INDEXed on the key field; the FROM (<Alias>) file must be in one of the unselected work areas and it may be in any order.

The key field must have the same name in both files.

If the REPLACE expression involves a field in the secondary file, the field listed in the FROM statement must be identified as ALIAS-> character field.

Sample:

```
SELECT 2
USE Statbook
SELECT 1
USE Phonbook INDEX Namebook
UPDATE ON state FROM Statbook REPLACE B->paid WITH ;
        B->paid + paid
```

USE

Syntax: USE [<file name>][INDEX <index file list>]
[ALIAS <expC>]

Description: The USE command opens an existing database in the selected work area.

Command: Standard

Library Called: Clipper.lib.

Autumn '86: EXCLUSIVE [ALIAS <alias name>] will set the specified file to be USED EXCLUSIVEly by the user, thus locking it from USE by all other users.

Notes: If the database file contains an associated memo file, that file is opened automatically.

Depending on the number of previously open files, there is no limit to the number of index files to be opened at one time.

Without any parameter, the USE command will close the active database, associated memo file, and all open index files. The USE command will also flush all buffers associated with that file.

Unless otherwise specified, a file extension of .DBF will be assumed. If the file extension is .DBF, it is recommended that no file extension be used either as a literal or in a macro substitution.

If no ALIAS clause is used, the alias for the selected work area or file will be the root name of the file itself.

Issuance of the USE command without any associated INDEX files will place the record pointer at the top of the file. If the INDEX clause is used, the record pointer is positioned at the first logical record based on the first index file listed in the INDEX file list.

Sample:

```
USE Temp

* The record pointer is positioned at 1.
* The ALIAS is set to TEMP.

USE

* Closes the active database Temp and flushes the
* buffers accordingly.

USE Temp INDEX Temp1.dat, Temp2, Temp3 ALIAS Test

* The file TEMP.DBF is opened and any associated memo
* file will be opened as well.
*
* The record pointer will be positioned at the first
* logical record in the database as dictated by the
* file TEMP1.DAT.  The remaining index files are
* assumed to have an extension of .NTX.
*
* The ALIAS of the file is set to TEST.
```

WAIT

Syntax: WAIT [<expC>][TO <memvar>]

Description: The WAIT command pauses all processing and execution until any key is pressed.

Command: Standard

Library Called: Clipper.lib

Notes: <expC> is any string to be used as a prompt message. If none is used, the default prompt of "Press any key to continue..." will be used.

If the TO clause is added, the value of the key pressed is stored to <memvar>. This is character type and does not need to be initialized prior to the issuance of this command.

Sample:

```
WAIT "Press any key to continue or Q to quit..." TO input
IF UPPER(input) = "Q"
   RETURN
ENDIF
```

ZAP

Syntax: ZAP

Description: The ZAP command removes all records from the active database.

Command: Standard

Library Called: Clipper.lib

Notes: If the ZAP command is issued, **all** records within the database, whether marked for deletion or not, will be completely removed. All open indexes will be reinitialized as well.

Sample:

```
USE Temp INDEX Temp1.dat, Temp2, Temp3
ZAP
```

CHAPTER FIVE

Functions

This chapter describes all Clipper functions. The format used is identical to that used in the previous chapter describing Clipper commands. Each function summary includes *syntax*, *description*, *function type*, *variances*, and one or more *code samples*. All functions also are identified as either enhanced by Clipper, following the dBASE III standard, or simulated by programming. [Some of the simulated functions, e.g., VERSION(), do not seem to have any meaningful purpose; nevertheless, they are included here as a reference.]

Releases Since Autumn '86:

Functions may now be issued without an associated command. In other words, if the function really performs an operation [e.g., INKEY(0) and SETPRC(5,10)], it may be issued on a command line by itself.

```
Example:   ? "Press Any Key to Continue..."
           INKEY(0)
           RETURN
```

Additionally, I have included **all** of the functions available in the Summer '87 release. Some functions previously found in the extended files of the Autumn '86 release are now incorporated into the Summer release. For these functions, the "source" will be either "Summer '87 - Extend.lib" or "Autumn '86 - " and the name of the extended file. Notes within the description of the functions provide linking information.

The following notation is used in describing the function:

<expC>: a character expression, normally a string
<expL>: a logical expression, either .T. or .F.
<expD>: a date expression
<expN>: a numeric expression (a single number, a complete numeric expression, or a formula)

$ - SUBSTRING COMPARISON

Syntax: <<expC1>> $ <<expC2>>

Desciption: This function returns a logical true (.T.) if the character or string in <<expC1>> is found in <<expC2>>

Function: Standard

Source: Clipper.lib

Sample: ?? "A"$"ABCDEF" .AND. "NY"$"CANYNJCT"

& - MACRO SUBSTITUTION

Syntax: &< character string >

Description: This function allows the value of a memory variable to be evaluated and, where necessary, acted upon.

Function: Standard

Source: Clipper.lib

Variance: *Macro* substitutions in Clipper must conform to the requirements of a compiler. Keep in mind that the macros in your application do not have any values during the time of compiling. They are marked for future reference and a place for them is reserved in memory, but they are not looked at and interpreted. Therefore, commands and the syntax of commands cannot be included in the macro. The compiler must see each command and compile it accordingly for linking with the library. Also, you must not use a Macro in conjunction with a function [e.g., @ 2,3 SAY &FIELDNAME(2)].

However, macros can be used in DO WHILE loops and the parameters of commands may be within the macro, as long as no part of the syntactical structure of the command is included (i.e., you cannot use a macro with a LIST command and have the listed fields separated with commas).

As with dBASE, a period (.) immediately following a macro will preclude the possibility of an extra space being added.

One last thing concerning macro substitution: while Clipper is still restricted to a line length of 255 characters, Clipper is also restricted to no more than 15 iterations or parses per macro. Anything more than that will yield a macro expansion error. To avoid this, break up the number of logical parses to a macro and add an additional macro for anything greater than 15 parses.

Sample:

```
file4   = "PRTIME"
file2   = "PREMPLOY"
file1   = "PRCHECK"
scrdata = "C:"
SELECT 4
USE &scrdata.&file4..dat INDEX &scrdata.Prtime_a.dat
SELECT 2
USE &scrdata.&file2..dat INDEX &scrdata.Premp_a.dat
SELECT 1
```

```
USE &scrdata.&file1..dat INDEX &scrdata.Prchk_a.dat
SET RELATION TO employee INTO &file4., ;
        TO employee INTO &file2.
```

ABS()

Syntax: ABS(<expN>)

Pass: <numeric expression>

Return: <numeric expression>

Description: The ABS() function yields the absolute value of a numeric expression.

Function: Standard

Source: Clipper.lib

Sample:

```
? ABS(-5)    && This will yield a 5
```

ACHOICE()

Syntax: ACHOICE(<expN1>, <expN2>, <expN3>, <expN4>, <array1> [, <array2>, [, <expC1> [, <expN4> [, <expN6]]]])

Pass: <top>, <left>, <bottom>, <right coordinates>, <array name> [, <array name> [, <function name> [, <numeric value> [, <numeric value]]]]

Return: <numeric expression>

Description: This function displays a list-box window with top, left, bottom, right row and column coordinates of <expN1 - 4>.

The first array contains the to-be displayed menu choices. If used, the second array contains a parallel array of logical values, each for the menu choices in <array1>. Those menu choices set to a logical false will tell ACHOICE() that the option is **not** available. The default for all menu options will be logical true.

If used, this character expression contains the name of a user-defined function that will be executed whenever a key is pressed. The function name is named **without** parentheses and without any arguments.

If used, this value will contain the initial choice element. The default value will be the first element in <array1>.

If used, this value will contain the initial relative window row for the first choice in the window. The default position is 0.

Function: Clipper Enhanced - Summer '87

Source: Summer '87 - Extend.lib

Notes:

Active Keys	Default
Up Arrow	Up one element
Down Arrow	Down one element
PgUp	Up the number of elements defined for the menu window to the same relative row position
PgDn	Down the number of elements defined for the menu window to the same relative row position
Ctrl-PgDn	First Element
Ctrl-PgUp	Last Element

Active Keys	Without User Function
Home	First element
End	Last element
Return	Select element, return position
Esc	Abort function, return 0
Left Arrow	Abort function, return 0
Right Arrow	Abort function, return 0
First Character	Next element with same first letter

Passed Mode	(for UDF Only)
0	Idle
1	Cursor past top of list
2	Cursor past end of list
3	Keystroke exception
4	No item selectable

Returned Mode	(for UDF Only)
0	Abort selection, return 0
1	Make selection, return cursor element
2	Continue ACHOICE() function
3	Go to next element whose first character matches the last key pressed

For a complete description of the various modes for user-defined functions, please refer to Chapter 14.

Sample:

```
********************
* Name      Clipmand.prg
* Author    Stephen J. Straley
* Notice    Copyright (c) 1988 Stephen J. Straley & Associates
* Date      March 15, 1988
* Compile   Clipper Clipmand -m
* Release   Summer '87
* Link      Tlink Clipmand,,,extend + clipper
* Note      This demonstrates the ACHOICE() and ADIR() functions
with some
*           help for BEGIN SEQUENCE and the MEMOEDIT() function.
*
********************

PUBLIC setpos, startat, scrat, fulldisp, direct

SET SCOREBOARD OFF

setpos = 0
startat = 1
scrat = 0
fulldisp = .F.
diskstr = FILLOUT("*.*", 12)
direct = "\" + CURDIR()

DO Fillars WITH ALLTRIM(diskstr)

CLEAR SCREEN
WAIT ACHOICE(2,2, 16, 40, files, good)
CLEAR SCREEN
WAIT ACHOICE(2, 2, 16, 40, files)

SET COLOR TO W+/BR
CLEAR SCREEN
@ 0,0 SAY "Clipper Commander!"
@ 0,68 SAY "Version 1.0"
IF ISCOLOR()
   SET COLOR TO W+/B, B/W, I, I, GR/B
   @ 1,0 CLEAR
ENDIF

fullscreen = SAVESCREEN(2,0,18,79)

DO WHILE .T.
   BEGIN SEQUENCE
      RESTSCREEN(2,0,18,79, fullscreen)
      @ 1,1 SAY "Currently in " + FILLOUT(direct, 78)
      IF !fulldisp
         @ 2,1 TO 18,41 DOUBLE
         ACHOICE(3, 2, 17, 40, dispit, "", "AFUNC", startat,
scrat)
      ELSE
         @ 2,1 TO 18,79 DOUBLE
```

```
            ACHOICE(3, 2, 17, 78, fulld, "", "AFUNC", startat, scrat)
         ENDIF
         EXIT
      END
   ENDDO
   RESTSCREEN(2,0,18,79, fullscreen)
   @ 1,0 CLEAR
   @ 1,0 SAY "Operation Completed..."
   CANCEL

   ********************

   FUNCTION Afunc

      PARAMETERS amode, apos, ascr

      * The mode of the achoice()
      * The array element number currently on
      * The screen element number

      whatkey = LASTKEY()
      IF whatkey = 27
         RETURN(1)
      ENDIF

      @ 24,00 SAY amode
      @ 24,15 SAY apos
      @ 24,30 SAY ascr
      @ 24,45 SAY whatkey

      IF amode = 2 && The end of the list
         KEYBOARD CHR(31)
         RETURN(2)
      ELSEIF amode = 1
         KEYBOARD CHR(30)
         RETURN(2)
      ELSEIF amode = 3
         DO CASE
            CASE whatkey = 6
               KEYBOARD CHR(30)
               RETURN(2)
            CASE whatkey = 1
               KEYBOARD CHR(31)
               RETURN(2)
            CASE whatkey = 13 .AND. fattr[apos] = "D"
               IF apos == 1
                  @ 23,00 SAY "GO to DOS Shell? "
                  IF VERIFY()
                     SAVE SCREEN
                     CLEAR SCREEN
                     SET CURSOR ON
                     RUN \Command
                     RESTORE SCREEN
```

```
                  SET CURSOR OFF
               ENDIF
               @ 23,00 CLEAR
               RETURN(2)
            ELSE
               temp = ALLTRIM(files[apos])
               RUN CHDIR &temp
               direct = "\" + CURDIR()
               DO Fillars WITH diskstr
               BREAK
            ENDIF

         CASE whatkey = 102 .OR. whatkey = 70
            SET CURSOR ON
            @ 20,10 SAY "Enter the disk criteria ë" GET diskstr
PICT "@KXXXXXXXXXXXX"
            READ
            DO Fillars WITH ALLTRIM(diskstr)
            SET CURSOR OFF
            @ 20,10 SAY SPACE(60)
            BREAK
         CASE whatkey = 118 .OR. whatkey = 86
            IF !(".COM" $ files[apos] .OR. ".EXE" $ files[apos])
               IF fsize[apos] < 34000
                  SET CURSOR ON
                  saveit = ""
                  SAVE SCREEN TO saveit
                  @ 13,0 CLEAR
                  @ 14,0 SAY "Press ESC to Return..."
                  @ 15,1 SAY "Ö" + REPLICATE("—", 78)
                  @ 16,0 SAY "°"
                  @ 17,0 SAY " °"
                  @ 18,0 SAY " °"
                  @ 19,0 SAY "°"
                  @ 20,0 SAY "°"
                  @ 21,0 SAY " °"
                  @ 22,0 SAY " °"
                  @ 23,0 SAY " °"
                  @ 24,0 SAY "°"
                  MEMOEDIT(MEMOREAD(files[apos]), 16, 2, 23, 79,
.T., "RESTRICT", 150)
                  RESTORE SCREEN FROM saveit
                  RELEASE saveit
                  SET CURSOR OFF
               ENDIF
            ENDIF
            RETURN(2)


         CASE whatkey = 68 .OR. whatkey = 100
            fulldisp = !fulldisp
            startat = 1
            scrat = 0
```

```
            BREAK

         CASE whatkey = 117 .OR. whatkey = 85
            IF fattr[apos] $ "RA"
               tagged[apos] = .F.
               DO Storeit WITH apos
               startat = apos
               scrat = ascr
               *
               * By setting "scrat" to ascr, the highlighted
               * element will be in the same relative screen
               * position.  Otherwise, the first element displayed
               * will be the selected item
               *
               KEYBOARD CHR(24)
               BREAK
            ELSE
               RETURN(2)
            ENDIF

         CASE whatkey = 116 .OR. whatkey = 84
            IF fattr[apos] $ "RA"
               tagged[apos] = .T.
               DO Storeit WITH apos

               startat = apos
               scrat = ascr
               KEYBOARD CHR(24)
               BREAK
            ELSE
               RETURN(2)
            ENDIF

         CASE whatkey = 7
            @ 3+ascr, IF(!fulldisp,20,58) SAY " <= Delete This? "
            IF VERIFY()
               thefile = ALLTRIM(files[apos])
               NOTE ERASE &thefile.
               ADEL(files, apos)
               ADEL(dispit, apos)
               ADEL(fulld, apos)
               setpos = apos
               BREAK
            ELSE
               RETURN(2)
            ENDIF
         OTHERWISE
            RETURN(2)
      ENDCASE
   ELSE
      RETURN(2)
   ENDIF
```

```
* Note: The next two functions VERIFY() and FILLOUT() are
* part of the Steve Straley Toolkit.
* Copyright (c) 1988 by Stephen J. Straley & Associates
* All rights reserved.
*
*********************

FUNCTION Verify

   PARAMETERS comp, extra_key

   DO CASE
      CASE PCOUNT() = 0
         comp = "YyNn"
         extra_key = .F.
      CASE PCOUNT() = 1
         extra_key = .F.
   ENDCASE

   IF TYPE("scrpause") = "U"
      scrpause = 100
   ENDIF
   DO WHILE .T.
      the_var = ""
      inside = INKEY(0)
      DO CASE
      CASE inside = 4
         the_var = "Y"
      CASE inside = 19
         the_var = "N"
      OTHERWISE
         the_var = CHR(inside)
      ENDCASE
      IF the_var$comp
         EXIT
      ENDIF
   ENDDO
   IF the_var$SUBSTR(comp,1,2)
      ?? "Yes"
      IF extra_key
         INKEY(0)
      ELSE
         FOR qaz = 1 TO scrpause
         NEXT
      ENDIF
      RETURN(.T.)
   ELSE
      ?? "No "
      IF extra_key
         INKEY(0)
      ELSE
         FOR qaz = 1 TO scrpause
         NEXT
```

```
      ENDIF
      RETURN(.F.)
   ENDIF

********************

FUNCTION Fillout

   PARAMETERS fill_a, fill_b

   * fill_a = the string to be filled out
   * fill_b = the length to fill out the string to

   IF PCOUNT() = 1
      fill_b = 80
   ELSE
      IF TYPE("fill_b") = "C"
         fill_b = VAL(b)
      ENDIF
      fill_b = IIF(fill_b <= 1, 80, fill_b)
   ENDIF

   IF fill_b <= LEN(fill_a)
      RETURN(fill_a)
   ENDIF
   RETURN(fill_a + SPACE(fill_b - LEN(fill_a)))

********************

FUNCTION Restrict

   PARAMETERS the_mode, the_line, the_col

   rest_key = LASTKEY()

   IF rest_key = 27
      RETURN(0)
   ELSEIF rest_key = 24
      RETURN(32)
   ELSEIF rest_key = 5
      RETURN(32)
   ELSEIF rest_key = 6
      RETURN(32)
   ELSEIF rest_key = 118 .OR. rest_key = 86
      RETURN(0)
   ELSEIF rest_key > 31 .AND. rest_key < 500
      KEYBOARD CHR(27)
      RETURN(101)
   ENDIF
   RETURN(0)

********************
```

```
PROCEDURE Fillars

   PARAMETERS fillstr

   PUBLIC files[1], good[1], tagged[1], dispit[1]
   PUBLIC fsize[1], fdate[1], ftime[1], fulld[1]
   PUBLIC fattr[1]

   redl = ADIR(fillstr, files, fsize, fdate, ftime, fattr)

   oldcolor = SETCOLOR()
   IF redl > 1.8 * MEMORY(0)
      SET COLOR TO W+*/R
      @ 19,2 SAY " Partial Directory! "
      redl = (MEMORY(0) * 1.8)
   ELSE
      @ 19,2 SAY "                    "
   ENDIF
   SET COLOR TO &oldcolor.

   * This next section is totally ridiculous!

   * PUBLIC files[ADIR(fillstr)], good[ADIR(fillstr)], tag-
ged[ADIR(fillstr)], dispit[ADIR(fillstr)]
   * PUBLIC fsize[ADIR(fillstr)], fdate[ADIR(fillstr)],
ftime[ADIR(fillstr)], fulld[ADIR(fillstr)]
   * PUBLIC fattr[ADIR(fillstr)]

   PUBLIC files[redl], good[redl], tagged[redl], dispit[redl]
   PUBLIC fsize[redl], fdate[redl], ftime[redl], fulld[redl]
   PUBLIC fattr[redl]

   ADIR(fillstr, files, fsize, fdate, ftime, fattr)

   AFILL(tagged, .F.)

   FOR x = 1 TO LEN(good)
      DO Storeit WITH x
   NEXT

********************

PROCEDURE Storeit

   PARAMETERS setval


   IF fattr[setval] = "D"
      addto = "<DIR>"
   ELSEIF fattr[setval] = "S"
      addto = "<SYS>"
   ELSEIF fattr[setval] = "H"
      addto = "<HID>"
```

```
    ELSE
       addto = "      "
    ENDIF
    IF "." == ALLTRIM(files[setval])
       files[setval] = SUBSTR(CURDIR(), RAT("\", CURDIR()) + 1)
    ENDIF
    good[setval] =  !EMPTY( AT( ".PRG", files[setval]) )
    dispit[setval] = IF(tagged[setval], CHR(16), " ") + " " + FIL-
LOUT(files[setval], 13) + addto
    fulld[setval] = IF(tagged[setval], CHR(16), " ") + " " + FIL-
LOUT(files[setval], 13)
    fulld[setval] = fulld[setval] + addto + " ¤ " + TRANS-
FORM(fsize[setval], "99,999,999") + " ¤ " + DTOC(fdate[setval]) +
" ¤ " + ftime[setval]
```

ACOPY()

Syntax: ACOPY(<expC1>, <expC2> [, <expN1> [, <expN2> [,<expN3>]]])

Pass: <array name>, <array name> [, <numeric expression> [,<numeric expression> [, <numeric expression>]]]

Return: Nothing

Description: This function copies array elements from <expC1> to <expC2>.

<expN1> is the starting element position in <expC1>.

<expN2> is the number of elements to copy from <expC1> to <expC2>.

<expN3> is the starting element position in <expC2> to begin the ACOPY() function.

Function: Clipper Enhanced - Summer '87

Source: Extend.lib

ADEL()

Syntax: ADEL(<expC>, <expN>)

Pass: <character expression>,<numeric expression>

Return: Nothing

Description: This function deletes an element in an array named <expC> at the <expN> position. All array elements lower in the array list from the given numeric expression will move up one position in the array. In other words, the old sixth array element will now become the fifth element. However, the length of the array will remain unchanged, with an undefined element at the end of the array list.

Function: Clipper enhanced - Autumn '86

Source: Autumn '86 - Dbu.lib
Summer '87 - Extend.lib

Sample:

```
********************
* Name        ADELTEST.prg
* Date        December 1, 1986
* Notice      Copyright 1986, Stephen J. Straley
* Compile     Clipper Adeltest
* Release     Autumn '86 or later
* Link        Autumn '86: Plink86 fi adeltest lib dbu lib clipper;
*             Summer '87: Plink86 fi adeltest lib extend lib
*             clipper;
* Note        This sample program demonstrates how the ADEL()
*             function will delete an element from an array list.
*
*             In order for this function to work, the Autumn '86
*             version must be used and the DBU.LIB file must be
*             linked in with the CLIPPER.LIB.  For the Summer '87
*             version, link in the EXTEND.LIB
********************

   CLEAR
   DECLARE counter[10]
   FOR x = 1 TO 10
      counter[x] = x
   NEXT
   @ 1,5 SAY "Here is a list of numbers..."
   ?
   FOR x = 1 TO 10
      ? counter[x]
   NEXT
   ?
   WAIT "Press any key to DELETE the 5th element in array list"
   CLEAR
   ADEL(counter, 5)
   @ 1,5 SAY "Here is the new list..."
   ?
   ? "The number of elements in the array is "
   ?? LEN(counter)
   ?
```

```
   FOR x = 1 TO 10
      ? counter[x]
   NEXT
   ?
   ?
   TEXT
   Notice that the length of the array remained at 10 while there
   are only 9 elements showing on the screen.  Also notice that
   the fifth element was removed from the array and that all lower
   elements moved up one position within the array.
   ENDTEXT
* End of File
```

ADIR()

Syntax: ADIR(<expC1> [,<expC2> [, <expC3> [, <expC4> [,<expC5> [, <expC6>]]]]])

Pass: <character expression> [, <array name> [, <array name> [,<array name> [, <array name> [, <array name>]]]]]

Return: <numeric expression>

Description: This function returns the number of files that match a pattern specified by the first <expC> on the currently logged disk and directory. The pattern specified may be *.ext or even *.*.

The <expC2> is used for the name of a previously declared array. If this is used, the names of all files matching the pattern of the <expC1> will be inserted into this array.

The <expC3> is used for the name of a previously declared array. If used, the file sizes for each corresponding file will be inserted.

The <expC4> is used for the name of a previously declared array. If used, the file dates for each corresponding file will be inserted.

The <expC5> is used for the name of a previously declared array. If used, the directory file times for each corresponding file will be inserted.

The <expC6> is used for the name of a previously declared array. If used, the directory file attribute bytes for each corresponding file will be inserted.

If the last array is used, the values inserted are as follows:

A	Archive file
D	Directory
H	Hidden file
R	Read only file
S	System file

Function: Clipper enhanced - Autumn '86

Source: Autumn '86 - Dbu.lib
Summer '87 - Extend.lib

Variance: With the Autumn '86 release, only the directory skeleton and one array are allowed as parameters.

Note: With the Summer '87 release and subsequent manual, it is suggested to use this function to DECLARE the arrays to their proper sizes, then to use this function to fill those arrays with the information based on the directory skeleton. It should be noted that ADIR() will yield **different** results in different circumstances, so using it to DECLARE the initial array size may not be accurate. Therefore, if ADIR() is to be used with all array parameters, make sure that ADIR() is not initialized with just the directory skeleton. For example, if all five arrays are passed to a directory skeleton of *.*, ADIR() will yield a value that is 2 greater than if only four arrays are passed. For an example, please see the ACHOICE() description and the following sample program.

Sample:

```
*********************
* Name      ADIRTEST.prg
* Date      December 1, 1986
* Notice    Copyright 1986, Stephen J. Straley
* Compile   Clipper Adirtest
* Release   Autumn '86 or later
* Link      Autumn '86: Plink86 fi adirtest lib dbu lib clipper;
*           Summer '87: Plink86 fi adirtest lib extend lib clipper;
* Note      This sample program first demonstrates how the ADIR()
*           function will yield the number of matching elements
*           on the current logged disk and directory.  It then
*           shows how to load those matching file names into an
*           array, which eventually gets displayed back to the
*           screen.
*
*           In order for this function to work, the Autumn '86
*           version must be used and the DBU.LIB file
*           must be linked in with the CLIPPER.LIB.
*********************

   CLEAR
```

```
    DECLARE dir_files[ADIR("*.*")]

    ADIR("*.*", dir_files)

    @ 2, 10 SAY "The number of file(s) on this disk\directory is "
    ?? LEN(dir_files)
    ?
    WAIT "Press any key to get a listing of those files...."
    ?
    FOR x = 1 TO LEN(dir_files)
       ? dir_files[x]
    NEXT
    ?
    ? "End of Listing"
 * End of File
```

Note: If using the ADIR() function to declare the array size to fit the directory skeleton or using it to later fill the array with those values, the anticipated results may vary if the fifth array parameter is passed.

So if the <expC6> is used, the system, hidden, and directory files will be included in the specified directory skeleton.

If using the ADIR() function to find out the correct number of directory elements that match the criteria in <expC1>, DECLARE all arrays to dummy values, then find out the number of correct elements to reDECLARE the arrays to, then after reDECLARING the array, use ADIR() to properly fill them.

For a precise example of this, please refer to the program CLIPMAND.PRG and the use of the ADIR() function.

AFIELDS()

Syntax: AFIELDS(<expC1> [, <expC2> [,<expC3> [,<expC4>]]])

Pass: <array expression>, [, <array expression> [, <array expression> [, <array expression>]]]

Return: <expN>

Description: This function will fill a series of arrays with the field names, field-types, field lengths and field decimals for the currently selected and open database. Each array parallels the different file descriptors. The first array will be filled with the names of the fields in the open and selected database. All other arrays are optional and will be filled with the corresponding data.

The function will return a zero is no parameters are specified or if no database is available. Otherwise, the number of fields or the length of the shortest array argument, whichever is less, will be returned.

Function: Clipper enhanced - Summer '87

Source: Summer '87 - Extend.lib

Sample:

```
USE People
DECLARE names[FCOUNT()], types[FCOUNT()],;
   length[FCOUNT()], deci[FCOUNT()]
IF !EMPTY (AFIELDS (names, types, length, deci))
   ACHOICE(5,10,20,35,names)
ELSE
   WAIT "Error in storing information"
ENDIF
```

AFILL()

Syntax: AFILL(<expC1>, <exp> [,<expN1> [,<expN2>]])

Pass: <character expression>, <expression> [, <numeric expression> [, <numeric expression>]]

Return: Nothing

Description: <expC> is the name of an array into which <exp> is filled. The first optional parameter is the beginning element for the fill operation (the default is 1). The second optional parameter is the count parameter (the default is the length of the array).

All elements from <expN1> to <expN2> will be filled with the same fill value <exp>.

The fill character <exp> may be of any valid data type (other than memo).

Function: Clipper enhanced - Autumn '86

Source: Autumn '86 - Dbu.lib
Summer '87 - Extend.lib

Sample:

```
********************
* Name         AFILLTEST.prg
* Date         December 1, 1986
* Notice       Copyright 1986, Stephen J. Straley
* Compile      Clipper Afilltest
* Release      Autumn '86 or later
* Link         Autumn '86: Plink86 fi afilltest lib dbu lib clipper;
*              Summer '87: Plink86 fi afilltest lib extend lib
*              clipper;
* Note         This sample program demonstrates how the AFILL()
*              function will fill an array with a given <exp>,
*              starting at the first <expN> position and continuing
*              for <expN> positions.
*
*              In this demonstration, a portion of an array list
*              is put through the AINS() function and then is filled
*              with the AFILL() function
*
*              In order for this function to work, the Autumn '86
*              version must be used and the DBU.LIB file
*              must be linked in with the CLIPPER.LIB.
*
********************

   CLEAR
   DECLARE counter[20]
   FOR x = 1 TO 20
      counter[x] = DATE() + x
   NEXT
   @ 1,5 SAY "Here is a list of dates..."
   ?
   FOR x = 1 TO 20
      ? counter[x]
   NEXT
   ?
   WAIT "Press any key to FILL the array list"
   CLEAR
   FOR x = 5 TO 14
   AINS(counter, x)
   NEXT

   AFILL(counter, "ZZZZZZZZZ", 5, 10)

   @ 1,5 SAY "Here is the new list..."
   ?
   ? "The number of elements in the array is "
   ?? LEN(counter)
   ?
   FOR x = 1 TO 20
      ? counter[x]
   NEXT
   ?
   WAIT
```

```
    ?
    TEXT
    Note that the array length remained at 20 and that the elements
    at the fifh through fourteenth positions were shifted down.
    After that, note that the string of Zs was placed into the
    new, empty positions by using the AFILL() function.
    ENDTEXT
* End of File
```

AINS()

Syntax: AINS(<expC>, <expN>)

Pass: <character expression>,<numeric expression>

Return: Nothing

Description: This function inserts a blank space in the array named <expC> at the <expN>th position.

The new position opened by this function becomes an undefined element.

All array elements starting with the <expN>th position will be shifted down one position in the array list and the last item in the array will be removed completely. In other words, the old fifth array element will now become the sixth element.

The length of the array will stay at its DECLAREd value.

Function: Clipper Enhanced - Autumn '86

Source: Autumn '86 - Dbu.lib
Summer '87 - Extend.lib

Sample:

```
********************
* Name      AINSTEST.prg
* Date      December 1, 1986
* Notice    Copyright 1986, Stephen J. Straley
* Compile   Clipper Ainstest
* Release   Autumn '86 or later
* Link      Autumn '86: Plink86 fi ainstest lib dbu lib clipper;
*           Summer '87: Plink86 fi ainstest lib extend lib
*           clipper;
* Note      This sample program first demonstrates how the AINS()
*           function will insert a space within the array at the
*           <expN>th position.
*
*           In order for this function to work, the Autumn '86
*           version must be used and the DBU.LIB file
*           must be linked in with the CLIPPER.LIB.
*
*           For the Summer '87 version, the EXTEND.LIB library
*           must be used.
********************

   CLEAR
   DECLARE counter[10]
   FOR x = 1 TO 10
      counter[x] = x
   NEXT
   @ 1,5 SAY "Here is a list of numbers..."
   ?
   FOR x = 1 TO 10
      ? counter[x]
   NEXT
   ?
   WAIT "Press any key to INSERT the 5th element in array list"
   CLEAR

   AINS(counter, 5)

   @ 1,5 SAY "Here is the new list..."
   ?
   ? "The number of elements in the array is "
   ?? LEN(counter)
   ?
   FOR x = 1 TO 10
      ? counter[x]
   NEXT
   ?
   ?
   TEXT
   Notice that the length of the array remained at 10 though there
   are only 9 elements showing on the screen.  Also notice that
   the 5th element is now blank and needs to have a value assigned
```

```
    to it.  Further, notice that all lower elements in the array
    were moved down one position, including the old fifth element,
    and that the last element in the array is removed from
    the list.

    ENDTEXT
* End of File
```

ALIAS()

Syntax: ALIAS(<expN>)

Pass: <numeric expression>

Return: <character expression>

Description: This function yields the alias name of the work area specified by <expN>. If no parameter is passed, the alias name of the current work area is returned. If no database is in use, a null string is returned.

Function: Clipper enhanced - Autumn '86

Source: Autumn '86 - Clipper.lib
Summer '87 - Clipper.lib

Sample:

```
USE History
? ALIAS()       && Displays the word 'History'
? ALIAS(2)      && Displays a null string
```

ALLTRIM()

Syntax: ALLTRIM(<expC>)

Pass: <character expression>

Return: <character expression>

Description: This function returns <expC> with leading and trailing blanks removed.

Function: Cliper enhanced - Summer '87

Source: Autumn '86 - Extenddb.obj
Summer '87 - Extend.lib

Note: With the Summer '87 release, this function was placed directly into the Clipper language. For the Autumn '86 release, the EXTENDDB.PRG file must be compiled first and then linked in with all other object files.

With the Summer '87 release, the maximum string capacity for this function is set to 64K in length.

ALTD()

Syntax: ALTD([<expN>])

Pass: [<numeric expression>]

Return: Nothing

Description: The ALTD() function executes the DEBUG.OBJ file or enables or disables the use of it.

If no parameters are passed, the debugger is considered invoked and will display on top of the last screen displayed in the application.

If <expN1> is set to 0, the debugger is considered disabled.

If <expN> is set to 1, the debugger is considered invoked.

If <expN> is set to 3, the debugger is invoked and the "Variables:View Parameters" screen is displayed rather than the standard DEBUG.OBJ main menu.

Function: Clipper enhanced - Summer '87

Source: Summer '87 - Extend.lib

Note: This function allows the DEBUG.OBJ file to be linked in with any application, and direct program control dictates its use or not.

AMPM()

Syntax: AMPM(<expC>)

Pass: <character expression>

Return: <character expression>

Description: The passed <expC> must be in the form of a time string. The AMPM function yields an 11-byte character string based on the time string and will be in the 12-hour a.m. and p.m. format.

Function: Clipper simulated - Autumn '86.
Clipper enhanced - Summer '87

Source: Extenddb.prg - Autumn '86
Extend.lib - Summer '87

Autumn '86: In order to use this function, the EXTENDDB.PRG file must be compiled and linked in with your application and must appear in your link list with all other .OBJ files.

ASC()

Syntax: ASC(<expC>)

Pass: < character expression >

Return: < numeric expression >

Description: The ASC() function returns the ASCII number for the left-most character of any character expression.

Function: Standard

Source: Clipper.lib

Sample:

```
CLEAR
@ 10,10 SAY ASC("This function")  && Will yield a 84
STORE "N" TO test
@ 12,10 SAY ASC(test)             && Will yield a 78
```

ASCII TABLE

Char.	Number	Char.	Number	Char.	Number	Char.	Number
NUL	0	SPACE	32	@	64	`	96
^A	1	!	33	A	65	a	97
^B	2	"	34	B	66	b	98
^C	3	#	35	C	67	c	99
^D	4	$	36	D	68	d	100
^E	5	%	37	E	69	e	101
^F	6	&	38	F	70	f	102
^G	7	'	39	G	71	g	103

<table>
<tr><td>^H</td><td>8</td><td>(</td><td>40</td><td>H</td><td>72</td><td>h</td><td>104</td></tr>
<tr><td>^I</td><td>9</td><td>)</td><td>41</td><td>I</td><td>73</td><td>i</td><td>105</td></tr>
<tr><td>^J</td><td>10</td><td>*</td><td>42</td><td>J</td><td>74</td><td>j</td><td>106</td></tr>
<tr><td>^K</td><td>11</td><td>+</td><td>43</td><td>K</td><td>75</td><td>k</td><td>107</td></tr>
<tr><td>^L</td><td>12</td><td>,</td><td>44</td><td>L</td><td>76</td><td>l</td><td>108</td></tr>
<tr><td>^M</td><td>13</td><td>-</td><td>45</td><td>M</td><td>77</td><td>m</td><td>109</td></tr>
<tr><td>^N</td><td>14</td><td>.</td><td>46</td><td>N</td><td>78</td><td>n</td><td>110</td></tr>
<tr><td>^O</td><td>15</td><td>/</td><td>47</td><td>O</td><td>79</td><td>o</td><td>111</td></tr>
<tr><td>^P</td><td>16</td><td>0</td><td>48</td><td>P</td><td>80</td><td>p</td><td>112</td></tr>
<tr><td>^Q</td><td>17</td><td>1</td><td>49</td><td>Q</td><td>81</td><td>q</td><td>113</td></tr>
<tr><td>^R</td><td>18</td><td>2</td><td>50</td><td>R</td><td>82</td><td>r</td><td>114</td></tr>
<tr><td>^S</td><td>19</td><td>3</td><td>51</td><td>S</td><td>83</td><td>s</td><td>115</td></tr>
<tr><td>^T</td><td>20</td><td>4</td><td>52</td><td>T</td><td>84</td><td>t</td><td>116</td></tr>
<tr><td>^U</td><td>21</td><td>5</td><td>53</td><td>U</td><td>85</td><td>u</td><td>117</td></tr>
<tr><td>^V</td><td>22</td><td>6</td><td>54</td><td>V</td><td>86</td><td>v</td><td>118</td></tr>
<tr><td>^W</td><td>23</td><td>7</td><td>55</td><td>W</td><td>87</td><td>w</td><td>119</td></tr>
<tr><td>^X</td><td>24</td><td>8</td><td>56</td><td>X</td><td>88</td><td>x</td><td>120</td></tr>
<tr><td>^Y</td><td>25</td><td>9</td><td>57</td><td>Y</td><td>89</td><td>y</td><td>121</td></tr>
<tr><td>^Z</td><td>26</td><td>:</td><td>58</td><td>Z</td><td>90</td><td>z</td><td>122</td></tr>
<tr><td>ESC</td><td>27</td><td>;</td><td>59</td><td>[</td><td>91</td><td>{</td><td>123</td></tr>
<tr><td>FS</td><td>28</td><td><</td><td>60</td><td>\</td><td>92</td><td>|</td><td>124</td></tr>
<tr><td>GS</td><td>29</td><td>=</td><td>61</td><td>]</td><td>93</td><td>}</td><td>125</td></tr>
<tr><td>RS</td><td>30</td><td>></td><td>62</td><td>^</td><td>94</td><td>~</td><td>126</td></tr>
<tr><td>US</td><td>31</td><td>?</td><td>63</td><td>_</td><td>95</td><td>DEL</td><td>127</td></tr>
</table>

ASCAN()

Syntax: ASCAN(<expC>, <exp> [,<expN1> [,<expN2>]])

Pass: <character expression>, <expression>
[, <numeric expression> [, <numeric expression>]]

Return: <numeric expression>

Description: This function scans the contents of an array named <expC> for <exp>. The returned value is the position in the array in which it was found. If <exp> is not found, 0 is returned.

The two optional <numeric expression> values are the beginning element number to start the search and the count value. The beginning default is 1 and the count default value is the length of the array.

SET EXACT ON/OFF does have an effect on the matching ability of this function.

Function: Clipper enhanced - Autumn '86

Source: Autumn 86 - Dbu.lib
Summer 87 - Extend.lib

Sample:

```
*********************
* Name         ASCANTST.prg
* Date         December 1, 1986
* Notice       Copyright 1986, Stephen J. Straley
* Compile      Clipper Ascantst
* Release      Autumn '86 or later
* Link         Autumn '86: Plink86 fi ascantst lib dbu lib clipper;
*              Summer '87: Plink86 fi ascantst lib extend lib
*              clipper;
* Note         This sample program demonstrates how the
*              ASCAN() function scans through an array and
*              SEEKs a specific value.
*
*              In order for this function to work, the Autumn '86
*              version must be used and the DBU.LIB file
*              must be linked in with the CLIPPER.LIB.
*
*              For the Summer '87 version, link in EXTEND.LIB.
*
*********************

   CLEAR
   DECLARE name[10]
   AFILL(name, SPACE(20))
   FOR x = 1 TO 10
      wording = LTRIM(STR(x))
      @ 2, 4 SAY "Enter in number &wording. name => " GET name[x]
      READ
      @ 2, 4 SAY SPACE(70)
   NEXT
   DO WHILE .T.
      CLEAR
      search = SPACE(20)
      @ 4, 5 SAY "What name should I find? " GET search
      @ 6, 5 SAY "Leave Blank to QUIT"
      READ
      IF EMPTY(search)
         EXIT
      ENDIF
      IF ASCAN(name, search) = 0
         @ 10, 10 SAY TRIM(search) + " was not found in the list"
      ELSE
         @ 10, 10 SAY TRIM(search) + " was found in position "
         ?? ASCAN(name, search)
      ENDIF
      ?
      WAIT "Press any key to try another name...."
   ENDDO
   ?
* End of File
```

ASORT()

Syntax: ASORT(<expC>, [, <expN1> [, <expN2>]])

Pass: <character expression> [, <numeric expression> [, <numeric expression>]]

Return: Nothing

Description: The ASORT() function sorts the contents of an array expressed as <expC> in ascending order.

The sort will default to begin with the first element in the array unless specified by <expN1>.

The sort will default to sort all elements in the array. The number of elements to sort may be changed by <expN2>. <expN2> **cannot** be greater than the LEN() of the array <expC>.

Function: Clipper enhanced - Summer '87

Source: Summer '87 - Extend.lib

Note: Only elements with the same data type may be sorted using this function. If there are mixed data types a run-time error will occur.

Sample:

```
********************
* Name      Sortit.prg
* Author    Stephen J. Straley
* Notice    Copyright (c) 1988 Stephen J. Straley & Associates
* Date      March 15, 1988
* Compile   Clipper Sortit -m
* Release   Summer '87
* Link      Plink86 fi sortit lib extend lib clipper
* Note      This program shows how to sort an array of elements
*           using the ASORT function.   The ACOPY function will
*           be used as well.
*
********************

PUBLIC files[ADIR("*.*")], test[ADIR("*.*")]

ADIR("*.*", files)
ACOPY(files, test)

CLEAR SCREEN
FOR x = 1 TO LEN(files)
  ? files[x]
NEXT
```

```
WAIT

ASORT(files)

CLEAR SCREEN
FOR x = 1 TO LEN(files)
  ? files[x]
NEXT

start = test[LEN(test)/2]

?
?
? "The next array will be sorted starting with this element."
WAIT start

ASORT(test, ASCAN(test, start))
CLEAR SCREEN
FOR x = 1 TO LEN(test)
   ? test[x]
NEXT
WAIT

* End of File.
```

AT()

Syntax: AT(<expC>,<expC>)

Pass: <character expression>, <character expression>

Return: <numeric expression>

Description: The AT() function searches the second string expression for the starting position of the characters in the first string expression. If the substring (i.e., the first character expression) is not contained within the second expression, the substring function AT() returns a zero (0).

Function: Standard

Source: Autumn '86 - Clipper.lib
Summer '87 - Clipper.lib

Note: With the Summer '87 release, the maximum string capacity for this function is 64K in length.

Sample:

```
STORE "Bert" TO search
```

```
STORE "Bill Jim  SteveRogerRay  Bert David" TO string
STORE AT(search,string) TO which_one
?  "B in 'BERT' is the "
?? which_one                       && This will display a 26
?? "th character in the string."
```

BIN2I()

Syntax: BIN2I(<expC>)

Pass: <character expression>

Return: <numeric expression>

Description: This function converts a character string <expC> that is formatted as a 16-bit signed integer to a numeric value.

Function: Clipper enhanced - Summer '87

Source: Extend.lib

Note: If more than two characters are specified, the remaining bytes are ignored.

Sample: Please see Chapter 13, Low-Level File Logic.

BIN2L()

Syntax: BIN2L(<expC>)

Pass: <character expression>

Return: <numeric expression>

Description: This function converts a character string <expC> formatted as a 32-bit signed long integer to a numeric value.

Function: Clipper enhanced - Summer '87

Source: Extend.lib

Note: If more than four characters are specified, the remaining bytes are ignored.

Sample: Please see Chapter 13, Low-Level File Logic

BIN2W()

Syntax: BIN2W(<expC>)

Pass: <character expression>

Return: <numeric expression>

Description: This function converts a character string <expC> that formatted as a 16-bit unsigned integer to a numeric value.

Function: Clipper enhanced - Summer '87

Source: Extend.lib

Note: This function allows numeric data to be read in its native form.

Sample: Please see Chapter 13, Low-Level File Logic.

BOF()

Syntax: BOF()

Pass: Nothing

Return: <logical expression>

Description: The BOF() function determines if the beginning of file marker has been reached. If it has, the function will yield a logical true (.T.); otherwise, a logical false (.F.) will be returned.

Function: Standard

Source: Clipper.lib

Sample:

```
USE file     & Any standard .DBF file
GO TOP
? "Have we reached the beginning of file marker?  "
?? IF(BOF(), "Yes", "No")
SKIP - 1
? "Now are we there?   "
?? IF(BOF(), "Yes", "No")
```

CDOW()

Syntax: CDOW(<expD>)

Pass: <date expression>

Return: <character expression>

Description: This function returns a character string of the day of the week (Monday, Tuesday, etc.) from a date expression passed to the function.

Function: Standard

Source: Clipper.lib

Sample:

```
STORE DATE() TO indate
STORE indate + 4 TO indate
CLEAR
@ 10,10 SAY "What do you have planned for this " + ;
CDOW(indate)
```

CHR()

Syntax: CHR(<expN>)

Pass: <expression number>

Return: <character expression>

Description: The CHR() function returns the ASCII character code for <expN>. The number **must** be an integer within the range of 0 to 255, inclusive. These ASCII codes send their true value to whatever device is set. The CHR() function can be used for special printing codes as well as normal and graphics character codes.

Function: Standard

Source: Clipper.lib

Note: With the Summer '87 release, CHR(0) will now have a length of 1 and will be treated as any other character. However, a null byte symbolized as ("") will continue to have a length of 0.

Sample:

```
* This routine will set an Epson MS/RX/FX series printer
* to condensed print mode.

SET CONSOLE OFF
SET PRINT ON
?? CHR(15)
SET PRINT OFF
SET CONSOLE ON
```

CMONTH()

Syntax: CMONTH(<expD>)

Pass: <date expression>

Return: <character expression>

Description: This function returns a character string of the month (January, February, etc.) from a date expression passed to the function.

Function: Standard

Source: Clipper.lib

Sample:

```
CLEAR
STORE CTOD("05/23/86") TO temp_date
@ 10,10 SAY "This is the merry month of " + CMONTH(temp_date)
```

COL()

Syntax: COL()

Pass: Nothing

Return: <numeric expression>

Description: The COL() function returns the current cursor column position. The COL() value may be tested for or passed to a memory variable.

Function: Standard

Source: Clipper.lib

Sample:

```
sample = COL()
? REPLICATE("-",sample)
```

```
DO WHILE COL() < 65
   ?? values + "  "
ENDDO

CLEAR
@ 01,COL() + 10 SAY "This starts in position 10 on the screen."
```

CTOD()

Syntax: CTOD(<expC>)

Pass: <character expression>

Return: <date expression>

Description: This function converts a date that has been entered as a character expression to a date expression. The character expression will be in the form of MM/DD/YY. The default will be in the American date format.

Function: Standard

Source: Clipper.lib

Note: A SPACE(8), a "", or a " / / " signifies a null date value for this function.

Sample:

```
STORE "03/23/64" TO indate
STORE CTOD(indate) TO outdate
? "The date 10 days from now will be: "
?? outdate + 10
```

CURDIR()

Syntax: CURDIR([<expC>])

Pass: [<character expression>]

Return: <character expression>

Description: This function returns the current DOS directory path of a specified drive. If <expC> is not specified, the current logged drive is assumed.

Function: Clipper enhanced - Summer '87

Source: Extend.lib

Note: If the returned character expression is a null string (""), one of two conditions may have occurred: either an error has taken place, or the root directory is the current drive.

DATE()

Syntax: DATE()

Pass: Nothing

Return: < date expression >

Description: The DATE() function returns the current system date.

Function: Standard

Source: Clipper.lib

Notes: To change the system date, RUN the DOS DATE command.

Sample:

```
? "The system is set to: "
?? DATE()
newdate = DTOC(DATE() - 1)
RUN date &newdate.
? "The system is now set to: "
?? DATE()
```

DAY()

Syntax: DAY(< expD >)

Pass: < date expression >

Return: < numeric expression >

Description: The DAY() function returns the numeric value of the day of the month from a date expression passed to the function.

Function: Standard

Source: Clipper.lib

Sample:

```
?? "This is the "
?? DAY(DATE())
?? " of the month"

CLEAR
FOR x = 1 TO DAY(DATE())
   ?? x
   ?? " "
NEXT
```

DAYS()

Syntax: DAYS(<expN>)

Pass: <numeric expression>

Return: <numeric expression>

Description: This function converts <expN> seconds to the equivalent number of days. 86,399 seconds represents one day, 0 seconds being midnight.

If you maintained a log of elapsed time using the SECONDS() function, DAYS() could calculate the number of elapsed days.

Function: Clipper simulated - Autumn '86.
Clipper enhanced - Summer '87

Source: Extenddb.prg - Autumn '86
Extend.lib - Summer '87

Autumn '86: In order to use this function, the EXTENDDB.PRG file must be compiled and linked in with your application and must appear in your link list with all other .OBJ files.

DBEDIT()

Syntax: DBEDIT([expN1> [, <expN2> [, <expN3> [, <expN4>]]]] [,<expC1> [, <expC2> [, <expC3> [, <expC4> [, <expC5> [, <expC6> [, <expC7>]]]]]]])

Pass: [<numeric expression> [, <numeric expression> [, <numeric expression> [, <numeric expression>]]]] [, <character expression> [, character expression> [, <character expression> [, character expression> [, <character expression> [, <character expression> [, <character expression>]]]]]]]

Return: <logical expression>

Description: The DBEDIT() function displays and edits records from one or more work areas. The displayed area is in a window area with top, left, bottom, and right coordinates listed in <expN1>, <expN2>, <expN3>, and <expN4>, respectively.

<expC1> is the name of the array containing the field names for the selected database. If not used, the default is all fields.

<expC2> is the name of a user-defined function that will execute when a key is pressed. Only the root name of the function, without parentheses, is allowed.

<expC3> is the name of an array containing characters to be used as PICTURE strings for formatting the columns. A specific <expC> may be globally used for all columns instead of the name of the array containing those possible formats.

<expC4> is the name of an array containing the headings for the columns to be displayed.

<expC5> is the name of an array containing the characters used to draw lines separating the headings and the field area displayed. A specific <expC> may be used instead of an array name that will globally affect the displayed area.

<expC6> is the name of an array containing the characters used to draw lines separating the displayed columns. A specific <expC> may be used instead of an array that will globally effect the displayed area.

<expC7> is the name of an array of characters used to display the column footings. Footings may be forced onto more than one line so long as an embedded semicolon is used. Specific footers may be globally used if an <expC> is used instead of an array.

DBEDIT() Modes

0 Idle, any cursor movement keys have been handled and no keys are pending
1 Attempt to cursor past BOF()
2 Attempt to cursor past EOF()
3 Database file is empty
4 Any keystroke exception

DBEDIT() Returned values from UDF

0 Quit DBEDIT()
1 Continue DBEDIT()
2 Force data to be reread (replace the screen) and continue DBEDIT()

Function: Clipper enhanced - Summer '87

Source: Autumn '86 - Dbu.lib
Summer '87 - Extend.lib

Variance: The Autumn '86 version of this function is not as extensive or as comprehensive as the Summer '87 version. For more information, please refer to Chapter 6.

Note: For more information and tips on how to use this function in the Summer '87 release, please refer to Chapter 6.

DBF()

Syntax: DBF()

Pass: Nothing

Return: < character expression >

Description: This function returns the alias name of the currently selected and active database. Thus, in Clipper, it does not differ from the ALIAS function.

Difference: In dBASE III, this function will actually yield the name of the database even if the alias name is different. In the Clipper simulated function, only the alias name will be returned.

Function: Clipper simulated - Autumn '86
Clipper enhanced - Summer '87

Source: Extenddb.prg - Autumn '86
Extend.lib - Summer '87

Autumn '86: In order to use this function, the EXTENDDB.PRG file must be compiled and linked in with your application and must appear in your link list with all other .OBJ files.

Sample:

```
USE Hist
? DBF()     && Yields 'Hist'
USE Hist ALIAS History
? DBF()     && Yields 'History'
```

DBFILTER()

Syntax: DBFILTER()

Pass: Nothing

Return: < character expression >

Description: The DBFILTER() returns the expression of the current SET FILTER TO the condition present in the currently selected work area.

If no filter condition is present, a null string will be returned.

Function: Clipper enhanced - Summer '87

Source: Summer '87 - Clipper.lib

DBRELATION()

Syntax: DBRELATION(< expN >)

Pass: < numeric expression >

Return: < character expression >

Description: The DBRELATION() function returns the expression used by the SET RELATION TO command that exists in the work area specified by < expN >.

If there is no relation set in that work area, a null string will be returned.

Function: Clipper enhanced - Summer '87

Source: Summer '87 - Clipper.lib

DBSELECT()

Syntax: DBSELECT(<expN>)

Pass: <numeric expression>

Return: <numeric expression>

Description: The DBSELECT() function returns the work area number that is tied via the SET RELATION TO command to the work area expressed as <expN>.

Function: Clipper enhanced - Summer '87

Source: Summer '87 - Clipper.lib

DELETED()

Syntax: DELETED()

Pass: Nothing

Return: <logical expression>

Description: The DELETED() function returns a logical true (.T.) if the current record has been marked for deletion. Otherwise, this function will return a logical false (.F.).

Function: Standard

Source: Clipper.lib

Sample:

```
[[[ LINE DELETED HERE ]]]
GO 5
? DELETED()
DELETE
? DELETED()
GO TOP
DO WHILE .NOT. EOF()
   IF DELETED()
```

```
        ? RECNO()
      ENDIF
      SKIP
    ENDIF
```

DESCEND()

Syntax: DESCEND(<exp>)

Pass: <expression>

Return: <expression>

Description: The DESCEND() function creates the same data type as is passed to the function. It is intended to be used to create indexes in descending order.

In order to SEEK or FIND an expression in an INDEX created with the DESCEND() function, the SEEK or FIND expression must also be with the DESCEND() function.

Function: Clipper enhanced - Summer '87

Source: Summer '87 - Extend.lib

DISKSPACE()

Syntax: DISKSPACE([<expN>])

Pass: <numeric expression>

Return: <numeric expression>

Description: This function yields the number of bytes available on the specified disk drive. The disk drive is designated by the <expN>, where 1 is for A:, 2 for B:, 3 for C:, etc. If no <expN> is passed to the function, the space available on the currently logged drive will be returned.

Function: Clipper enhanced - Summer '87
Clipper extended - Autumn '86

Source: Autumn '86 - Extendc.obj
Summer '87 - Extend.lib

Autumn '86: In order to use this function, the EXTENDC.OBJ file must be linked in with your application and must appear in your link list after CLIPPER.LIB.

Sample:

```
IF DISKSPACE(1) < RECSIZE() * LASTREC()
?? "There is not enough room for this file on drive A:"
ENDIF
```

DOSERROR()

Syntax: DOSERROR()

Pass: Nothing

Return: < numeric expression >

Description: The DOSERROR() function returns the number of the last DOS error number encountered.

Function: Clipper enhanced - Summer '87

Source: Summer '87 - Clipper.lib

Note: For a complete listing of DOS error messages, see Appendix C.

DOW()

Syntax: DOW(< expD >)

Pass: < date expression >

Return: < numeric expression >

Description: The DOW() function returns the number representing the day of the week for the date expression passed to it.

1 = Sunday
2 = Monday
3 = Tuesday
4 = Wednesday
5 = Thursday
6 = Friday
7 = Saturday

Function: Standard

Source: Clipper.lib

Sample:

```
STORE DATE() TO indate
? DOW(indate)
```

DTOC()

Syntax: DTOC(<expd>)

Pass: <date expression>

Return: <character expression>

Description: The DTOC() function converts any date expression (field or variable) to a character expression.

Function: Standard

Source: Clipper.lib

Sample:

```
STORE DTOC(DATE()) TO indate
CLEAR
@ 10,10 SAY "Enter in the correct date: " ;
GET indate PICT "99/99/99"
READ
```

DTOS()

Syntax: DTOS(<expD>)

Pass: <date expression>

Return: <character expression>

Description: This function returns a string in year, month, day order.

Function: Clipper enhanced

Source: Clipper.lib

Notes: This function is extremely useful for indexing on dates and character expressions.

Sample:

```
STORE SUBSTR(DTOS(DATE()),1,4) TO in_year
STORE SUBSTR(DTOS(DATE()),5,2) TO in_month
STORE SUBSTR(DTOS(DATE()),7,2) TO in_day
? in_year
? in_month
? in_day
```

ELAPTIME()

Syntax: ELAPTIME(<expC>, <expC>)

Pass: <character expression>, <character expression>

Return: <character expression>

Description: This function returns a string that will show the difference between the starting time, the first <expC>, and the ending time, the second <expC>. If the starting time is greater than the ending time, the function will assume that the day changed once.

Function: Clipper simulated - Autumn '86.
Clipper enhanced - Summer '87

Source: Extenddb.prg - Autumn '86
Extend.lib - Summer '87

Autumn '86: In order to use this function, the EXTENDDB.PRG file must be compiled and linked in with your application and must appear in your link list with all other .OBJ files.

Sample: ? "The time difference was " + ELAPTIME(oldtime, TIME())

EMPTY()

Syntax: EMPTY(<exp>)

Pass: <expression>

Return: <logical expression>

Description: This function is used to test variables for an EMPTY condition.

Function: Clipper enhanced

Source: Clipper.lib

Notes: The following is a list of conditions for various types of variables that would yield a .T. if evaluated.

```
Character variable:   EMPTY() = .T.
                      IF variable = "" .OR.
                         variable = "       "

Numeric variable:     EMPTY()= .T.
                      IF variable = 0

Date variable:        EMPTY() = .T.
                      IF variable = CTOD("  /  /  ")

Logical variable:     EMPTY() = .T.
                      IF variable = .F.
```

Sample: Please see the section, "Creating Batch, Databases, and Indexes with in Application" in Chapter 16.

EOF()

Syntax: EOF()

Pass: Nothing

Return: <logical expression>

Description: The EOF() function determines if the end of file marker has been reached. If it has, the function will yield a logical true (.T.); otherwise, a logical false (.F.) will be returned.

Function: Standard

Source: Clipper.lib

Sample:

```
USE file     & Any standard .DBF file
GO BOTTOM
? "Have we reached the end of file marker?  "
?? IF(EOF(), "Yes", "No")
SKIP + 1
? "Now are we there?   "
?? IF(EOF(), "Yes", "No")
```

ERRORLEVEL()

Syntax: ERRORLEVEL([<expN>])

Pass: [<numeric expression>]

Return: <numeric expression>

Description: The ERRORLEVEL() function returns the current DOS error level. If a <expN> contains a value, that value will be used to set the DOS error level. This value can be between 0 and 255, inclusive.

Function: Clipper enhanced - Summer '87

Source: Summer '87 - Clipper.lib

Note: For a complete listing of the DOS error levels, please see Appendix C.

Sample:

```
IF !EMPTY(ERRORLEVEL())
    ? "An error occurred.  Now setting the DOS error level back."
    ERRORLEVEL(0)
ENDIF
```

EXP()

Syntax: EXP(<expN>)

Pass: <numeric expression>

Return: <numeric expression>

Description: The EXP() function returns the exponential of any given real number.

Function: Standard

Source: Clipper.lib

Variance: For a more accurate exponential of any number, the SET DECIMAL TO command must be invoked to carry the results out to the desired number of places. Remember that the default is 2.

In dBASE III, all that is needed to carry out the results is to pass a number to the EXP() function with x number of places representing the number of carried places.

Run the following example under dBASE III and Clipper and note the difference.

Sample:

```
CLEAR
? EXP(1)
? EXP(1.000)
? EXP(1.000000)
SET DECIMAL TO 8
? EXP(1)
? EXP(1.000)
? EXP(1.000000)
```

FCLOSE()

Syntax: FCLOSE(<expN>)

Pass: <numeric expression>

Return: <logical expression>

Description: The FCLOSE() function closes an open file with a DOS handle of <expN>, writing the associated DOS buffer to disk. The <expN> is determined via the FOPEN() or FCREATE() function.

Function: Clipper enhanced - Summer '87

Source: Summer '87 - Extend.lib

Sample: Please refer to the Chapter 13, Low-Level File Logic.

FCOUNT()

Syntax: FCOUNT()

Pass: Nothing

Return: <numeric expression>

Description: The FCOUNT() function returns the number of fields in the current and active database.

Function: Clipper enhanced - Autumn '86

Source: Clipper.lib

Sample:

```
USE History
FOR x = 1 TO FCOUNT()
? FIELDNAME(x)
NEXT
```

FCREATE()

Syntax: FCREATE(<expC> [, <expN>])

Pass: <character expression> [, <numeric expression>]

Return: <numeric expression>

Description: The FCREATE() function creates a new file with the name expressed as <expC>. <expN> is defaulted to 0 and contains the DOS attribute of the new file <expC>.

The returned value will be the DOS file handle that is associated with the new file. This number will be between 0 and 65,535, inclusive. If an error occurs, this value will be -1.

If the file <expC> already exists, the existing file will be truncated to a file length of 0 bytes.

Function: Clipper enhanced - Summer '87

Source: Summer '87 - Extend.lib

Notes: The DOS file attribute values are as follows:

0	Normal	Read/write
1	Read only	Attempting to open for output returns an error
2	Hidden	Excluded from normal DIR searches
4	System	Excluded from normal DIR searches

The value returned by this function (the file handle) should be stored to a memory variable for later use with the other low-level file functions.

The FCREATE function does not adhere to the default values set by the SET DEFAULT TO or SET PATH TO commands. If the directory path is necessary, it must be explicitly stated in <expC>.

Sample: Please see Chapter 13, Low-Level File Logic.

FERROR()

Syntax: FERROR()

Pass: Nothing

Return: < numeric expression >

Description: The FERROR() returns the DOS error from the last file operation. A 0 is returned if there is no error condition present.

Function: Clipper enhanced - Summer '87

Source: Summer '87 - Extend.lib

Sample: Please see Chapter 13, Low-Level File Logic.

FKLABEL()

Syntax: FKLABEL(< expN >)

Pass: < numeric expression >

Return: < character expression >

Description: This function returns the name assigned to the function key specified by < expN >. If < expN > is less than 0 or greater than 40, a "[]" will be returned.

Function: Clipper simulated - Autumn '86
Clipper enhanced - Summer '87

Source: Extenddb.prg - Autumn '86
Extend.lib - Summer '87

Autumn '86: In order to use this function, the EXTENDDB.PRG file must be compiled and linked in with your application and must appear in your link list with all other .OBJ files.

FKMAX()

Syntax: FKMAX()

Pass: Nothing

Return: <numeric expression>

Description: This simulated function will always return 40, which is the number of function keys available for the IBM PC/XT/AT.

Function: Clipper simulated - Autumn '86
Clipper enhanced - Summer '87

Source: Extenddb.prg - Autumn '86
Extend.lib - Summer '87

Autumn '86: In order to use this function, the EXTENDDB.PRG file must be compiled and linked in with your application and must appear in your link list with all other .OBJ files.

FIELDNAME()

Syntax: FIELDNAME(<expN>)

Pass: <numeric expression>

Return: <character expression>

Description: The FIELDNAME() function yields the name of the <expN>th field within the currently active database. A null string is returned if <expN> is greater than the number of the last field present.

Function: Clipper enhanced

Source: Clipper.lib

Note: In the Summer '87 release, the FIELD() function is acceptable as well as the FIELDNAME() function.

Sample:

```
* List names of the first six fields of the open
* database to the screen.
USE test
FOR x = 1 TO 6
```

```
    option = FIELDNAME(x)
    ? option
NEXT
```

FILE()

Syntax: FILE(<expC>)

Pass: <character expression>

Return: <logical expression>

Description: The FILE() function returns a logical true (.T.) if the given file name exists on the default or specified drive and directory.

Function: Standard

Source: Clipper.lib

Note: In the Summer '87 release, wild cards are accepted as part of the <expC>.

Sample:

```
STORE "C:" TO drive
? FILE(drive + "Employ.dbf")
? FILE("C:Employ.dbf")
STORE "A:Employee.dbf" TO file
? FILE(file)
```

FLOCK()

Syntax: FLOCK()

Pass: Nothing

Return: <logical expression>

Description: This function returns a logical true (.T.) if a file lock is attempted and is successful. This function will also unlock all record locks placed by the same station.

Function: Clipper enhanced

Source: Clipper.lib

Notes: This function was installed into the language with the Autumn '86 release.

FOPEN()

Syntax: FOPEN(<expC> [, <expN>])

Pass: <character expression> [, <numeric expression>]

Return: <numeric expression>

Description: The FOPEN() function opens the name of the file expressed as <expC>. The <expN> represents how the file will be opened. The default value is 0. The DOS file open modes are as follows:

0 Read only
1 Write only
2 Read/write

The returned value is the DOS file handle for the file <expC>. If there is an error in opening the file, a -1 will be returned. File handles may be in the range of 0 to 65,535, inclusive.

Function: Clipper enhanced - Summer '87

Source: Summer '87 - Extend.lib

Notes: The FOPEN() function does not adhere to the values set by the SET DEFAULT TO or the SET PATH TO commands. In order to access a directory path, it must be specified in the <expC> explicitly.

Sample: Please see Chapter 13, Low-Level File Logic.

FOUND()

Syntax: FOUND()

Pass: Nothing

Return: <logical expression>

Description: The FOUND function is used to test if the previous SEEK, LOCATE, CONTINUE, or FIND was successful.

Function: Clipper enhanced

Source: Clipper.lib

Notes: Takes the place of setting logical variables if conditions were true and removes lines of code that otherwise would have to test for EOF() conditions.

Sample:

```
STORE "Los Angeles" TO temp_city
SEEK temp_city
IF FOUND()
  DO Edit_rec
ELSE
   @ 10,10 SAY "That city does not exist.  Please enter"
   @ 11,10 SAY "in database.  Any Key to Continue..."
   SET CONSOLE OFF
   WAIT
   SET CONSOLE ON
ENDIF
```

FREAD()

Syntax: FREAD(<expN1>, @<expC>, <expN2>)

Pass: <numeric expression>, @<character expression>, <numeric expression>

Return: <numeric expression>

Description: The FREAD() function reads characters from a file expressed as <expN1> into a character memory variable expressed as <expC>.

The <expN1> is the file handle obtained from either the FOPEN or FCREATE functions.

The <expC> is passed by reference and must be predefined before this function is called. It also must be at least the same length as <expN2>.

The <expN2> is the number of bytes to read starting at the current DOS file pointer position. If the FREAD() is successful, the length of <expN2> will be the returned value.

The returned value is the number of bytes successfully read from the file. If a 0 is returned, the EOF file pointer has been reached in <expN1>.

Function: Clipper enhanced - Summer '87

Source: Summer '87 - Extend.lib

Sample: Please see Chapter 13, Low-Level File Logic.

FREADSTR()

Syntax: FREADSTR(<expN1>, <expN2>)

Pass: <numeric expression>, <numeric expression>

Return: <character expression>

Description: The FREADSTR() function is like the FREAD() function except this function returns the number of bytes read from the file handle <expN1>.

<expN1> is the file handle for the file to be read that is obtained from either the FOPEN() for FCREATE() functions.

<expN2> is the number of bytes to read from the file represented by <expN1>.

The returned value will be the characters read until a EOF file condition is encountered, at which time a null byte will be returned.

Function: Clipper enhanced - Summer '87

Source: Summer '87 - Extend.lib

Sample: Please see Chapter 13, Low-Level File Logic.

FSEEK()

Syntax: FSEEK(<expN1>, <expN2 [, <expN3>])

Pass: <numeric expression>, <numeric expression> [, <numeric expression>]

Return: <numeric expression>

Description: The FSEEK() function sets the file pointer in the file depicted by the file handle <expN1> and moves the file pointer by <expN2>

bytes from the file position <expN3>. The returned value is the relative position of the file pointer to the BOF marker.

<expN1> is the file handle for the file that the pointer is to move in. This number is obtained via the FOPEN() or FCREATE() functions.

<expN2> is the number of bytes to move the file pointer from the position provided by <expN3>. If there is no value for <expN3>, <expN2> may set the file pointer using the same table for <expN3>.

<expN3> set the method for moving the file pointer in <expN1>. These values are:

0 Beginning of file
1 Current pointer position
2 End of file

Function: Clipper enhanced - Summer '87

Source: Summer '87 - Extend.lib

Sample: Please see Chapter 13, Low-Level File Logic.

FWRITE()

Syntax: FWRITE(<expN1>, <expC1> [, <expN2>])

Pass: <numeric expression> <character expression [, <numeric expression>]

Return: <numeric expression>

Description: The FWRITE() function writes the contents of <expC> to the file handle <expN1>. If used, <expN2> is the number of bytes in <expC1> to write.

The returned value is the number of bytes successfully written to the DOS file. If the returned value is 0, an error has occurred. A successful write is depicted by the number returned by FWRITE(), which is equal to the LEN() of <expC1>.

<expC1> is the variable containing the contents to be written to the file.

<expN2> is the number of bytes to write out to the file. The disk write begins with the current file position. If this variable is not used, the entire contents of <expC1> is written to the file.

Function: Clipper enhanced - Summer '87

Source: Summer '87 - Extend.lib

Sample: Please see Chapter 13, Low-Level File Logic.

GETE()

Syntax: GETE(<expC>)

Pass: <character expression>

Return: <character expression>

Description: The GETE() function yields a string that is the value of the environmental variable <expC>, stored at the DOS level with the SET command.

Function: Clipper enhanced - Summer '87

Source: Autumn '86 - Extendc.obj
Summer '87 - Extend.lib

Autumn '86: In order to use this function, the EXTENDC.OBJ file must be linked in with your application and must appear in your link list after CLIPPER.LIB.

Summer '87: This function is now included as part of the library.

Note: With the Autumn '86 release, the allowed variable size for Clipper programs can be checked with this function by issuing GETE("CLIPPER"). If a null string is returned and there is not enough room to run the application, a SET CLIPPER=vXXX may be issued at the DOS level.

vXXX represents the allowed variable table size. XXX is the number of kilobytes to be allowed. If none is issued, 20 percent of available memory will be allocated for the application, up to 44K bytes. Each unique variable in an application will take up 22 bytes; therefore, in applications with only 256 memory variables, the value for XXX may be set to 006. If this is the case, 38K bytes will be saved for the application.

Sample: Please see the section entitled "Batch, Databases, and Indexes within an Application" in Chapter 16.

HARDCR()

Syntax: HARDCR(<expC>)

Pass: <character expression>

Return: <character expression>

Description: This function replaces all soft carriage returns [CHR(141)] found in the character expression with hard carriage returns [CHR(13)].

This function only will work for a CHR(141) + CHR(10) combination. If a CHR(141) exists by itself, it will be not replaced by a CHR(13).

Function: Clipper enhanced

Source: Autumn '86 - Memo.lib
Summer '87 - Extend.lib

Sample:

```
? HARDCR(memostr)
```

HEADER()

Syntax: HEADER()

Pass: Nothing

Return: <numeric expression>

Description: The HEADER() function returns the number of bytes in the header of the currently active and selected database file.

Function: Clipper extended - Summer '87

Source: Autumn '86 - Extendc.obj
Summer '87 - Extend.lib

Autumn '86: In order to use this function, the EXTENDC.OBJ file must be linked in with your application and must appear in your link list after CLIPPER.LIB.

Summer '87: This function is now included as part of the library.

Notes: If used in conjunction with the RECCOUNT(), RECSIZE(), and DISKSPACE() functions, this function may be useful for backup and restoration routines.

I2BIN()

Syntax: I2BIN(<expN>)

Pass: <numeric expression>

Return: <character expression>

Description: This function takes a numeric integer <expN> and converts it to a character string formatted as a 16-bit unsigned integer.

Function: Clipper enhanced - Summer '87

Source: Extend.lib

Sample: Please see Chapter 13, Low-Level File Logic.

IF()

Syntax: IF(<exp1>,<exp2>,<exp3>)

Pass: <condition>,<expression>,<expression>

Return: <expression>

Description: This function is similar to dBASE III's imperative IIF function. This function returns <exp2> if <exp1> is true, or it returns <exp3> if <exp1> is false.

Function: Standard

Notes: All three expressions are required and all three are evaluated. In other words, the IF() function **may not** be used in conjunction with a divide overflow situation. IF() may be used to prevent a value being divided by zero; i.e., IF(y=0,0,x/y).

Sample:

```
STORE .T. TO dep_ded_fl  && dependent deduction flag
@ 10,15 SAY "Deduct Dependents "
?? IF(dep_ded_fl, "Before", "After")
?? "Calculating Taxes"
```

INDEXEXT()

Syntax: INDEXEXT()

Pass: Nothing

Return: <character expression>

Description: The INDEXEXT() function returns a string telling that indexes will be used or created: Clipper .NTX or dBASE .NDX files.

The returned value will either be .NTX for Clipper indexes or .NDX for dBASE-compatible indexes.

Function: Clipper enhanced - Summer '87

Source: Summer '87 - Clipper.lib

INDEXKEY()

Syntax: INDEXKEY(<expN>)

Pass: <numeric expression>

Return: <character expression>

Description: This function returns the key expression of an active index file where <expN> is the placement in the index list of that index file. If <expN> is 0 (zero), the key of the current controlling index is returned. A null string is returned if <expN> is greater than the number of indexes in use.

Function: Clipper enhanced

Source: Clipper.lib

Sample:

```
********************
* Name       INDEXKEY.prg
* Date       December 1, 1986
* Notice     Copyright 1986, Stephen J. Straley
* Compile    Clipper Indexkey
* Release    Autumn '86 or later
* Link       Plink86 fi indexkey lib clipper;
* Note       This sample program demonstrates how the
*            INDEXKEY() function yields the index key
*            expression for the selected index file.
********************

   USE Client
   INDEX ON name TO client1
   INDEX ON phone TO client2
   INDEX ON location TO client3
   INDEX ON build_code TO client4
   INDEX ON acct_num TO client5

   USE Client INDEX Client1, Client2, Client3, Client4, Client5
   CLEAR
   FOR x = 1 TO 5
      ? "The index expression is: "
      ?? INDEXKEY(x)
   NEXT

   DO WHILE .T.
      store 1 to which
      @ 10,10 SAY "Which index order? " GET which RANGE 0,5
      @ 12,10 SAY "Enter 0 to Exit (or ESC key)"
      READ
      IF EMPTY(which) .OR. LASTKEY() = 27
         EXIT
      ENDIF
      SET ORDER TO which
      @ 14,10 SAY "That key expression is set to: "
      ?? INDEXKEY(0)
      ?
      WAIT "Press any key to try again..."
      @ 10,00 CLEAR
   ENDDO
* End of File
```

INDEXORD()

Syntax: INDEXORD()

Pass: Nothing

Return: < numeric expression >

Description: The INDEXORD() function returns the numeric position of the controlling index currently in use.

A returned value of 0 indicates no active index is present.

Function: Clipper enhanced - Summer '87

Source: Summer '87 - Clipper.lib

INKEY()

Syntax: INKEY()

Pass: Nothing

Return: < numeric expression >

Description: The INKEY() function allows direct input from the keyboard at specific times during an operation.

Function: Standard

Source: Clipper.lib

Notes: May be used for testing the cursor and function keys.

Sample:

```
STORE 0 TO value
CLEAR
DO WHILE value = 0
   @ 10,10 SAY "Strike any key... "
   value = INKEY()
   IF value <> 0
      @ 15,10 SAY value
      STORE 0 TO value
   ENDIF
ENDDO
```

INKEY(0)

Syntax: INKEY(0)

Pass: <0>

Return: < numeric expression >

Description: This version of INKEY() is more like a WAIT command ; it returns the ASCII value of the key struck.

Function: Clipper enhanced

Source: Clipper.lib

Notes: The function remains in effect until a key is struck. Keep in mind that with this variation the INKEY() function does not need to be placed inside a loop in order to trap the keyboard input.

Sample:

```
CLEAR
STORE 0 TO value
DO WHILE .T.
   @ 10,10 SAY "Strike any key... "
   value = INKEY(0)
   @ 15,10 SAY value
ENDDO
```

INKEY(number)

Syntax: INKEY(<expN>)

Pass: <numeric expression>

Return: <numeric expression>

Description: With this variation, the function waits for <expN> seconds or any keyboard input, whichever comes first, before continuing.

Function: Clipper enhanced

Source: Clipper.lib

Notes: This can be very useful for painting help screens and allotting a specific time to wait for a specific key to continue.

Sample:

```
CLEAR
DO WHILE .T.
   @ 10,10 SAY "Here is the first screen ... "
   @ 12,10 SAY "This will wait for 10 seconds or until"
   @ 13,10 SAY "the ESCAPE key is struck..."
   IF INKEY(10) = 27
      @ 15,10 SAY "That routine has completed."
      WAIT
      CLEAR
```

```
        ENDIF
    ENDDO
```

Inkey Values: Here are some of the INKEY() values of keys not necessarily expressed in the ASCII table.

Key Pressed	Inkey Value	Key Pressed	Inkey Value	Key Pressed	Inkey Value
F1	28	Ctrl F1	- 20	Home	1
F2	- 1	Ctrl F2	- 21	Up Arrow	5
F3	- 2	Ctrl F3	- 22	Down Arrow	24
F4	- 3	Ctrl F4	- 23	Left Arrow	19
F5	- 4	Ctrl F5	- 24	Ctrl Home	29
F6	- 5	Ctrl F6	- 25	Ctrl Left Arrow	26
F7	- 6	Ctrl F7	- 26	Ctrl Right Arrow	2
F8	- 7	Ctrl F8	- 27	PrtSc	42
F9	- 8	Ctrl F9	- 28	Esc	27
F10	- 9	Ctrl F10	- 29	Ins	22
Shift F1	- 10	Alt F1	- 30	Space Bar	32
Shift F2	- 11	Alt F2	- 31	Tab	9
Shift F3	- 12	Alt F3	- 32	Del	7
Shift F4	- 13	Alt F4	- 33	Ctrl *	16
Shift F5	- 14	Alt F5	- 34	Back Tab	271
Shift F6	- 15	Alt F6	- 35	Ctrl Page Down	30
Shift F7	- 16	Alt F7	- 36	Ctrl Page Up	31
Shift F8	- 17	Alt F8	- 37	Ctrl Scroll	3
Shift F9	- 18	Alt F9	- 38	-	45
Shift F10	- 19	Alt F10	- 39	+	43
End	6	Alt Right Arrow	6	Right Arrow	4
Ctrl End	23	Alt Page Down	3	Page Down	3
Enter	13	Alt Down Arrow	2	Page Up	18
Backspace	8	Alt End	1		
Alt 1	376	Alt Q	272	Alt D	0
Alt 2	377	Alt W	273	Alt F	289
Alt 3	378	Alt E	274	Alt G	290
Alt 4	380	Alt R	275	Alt H	291
Alt 5	381	Alt T	276	Alt J	292
Alt 6	382	Alt Y	277	Alt K	293
Alt 7	383	Alt U	278	Alt L	294
Alt 8	384	Alt I	279	Alt Z	300
Alt 9	385	Alt O	280	Alt X	301
Alt 0	385	Alt P	281	Alt V	303
Alt -	386	Alt A	286	Alt B	304
Alt =	387	Alt S	287	Alt N	305
				Alt M	306

INT()

Syntax: INT(<expN>)

Pass: <numeric expression>

Return: <numeric expression>

Description: The INT() function converts a numeric expression to an integer. All decimal digits are truncated.

Function: Standard

Source: Clipper.lib

ISALPHA()

Syntax: ISALPHA(<expC>)

Pass: <character expression>

Return: <logical expression>

Description: This function returns a logical true (.T.) if the first character in <expC> is alphabetic.

Function: Clipper enhanced - Summer '87

Source: Autumn '86 - Extenddb.prg
Summer '87 - Extend.lib

Autumn '86: In order to use this function, the EXTENDDB.PRG file must be compiled and linked in with your application and must appear in your link list with all other .OBJ files.

Summer '87: With the Summer '87 release, this function was incorporated directly into the EXTEND.LIB file.

Sample:

```
? ISALPHA("Yes")     && This would yield a .T.
? ISALPHA("212")     && This would yield a .F.
```

ISCOLOR()

Syntax: ISCOLOR(<expC>)

Pass: Nothing

Return: <logical expression>

Description: This function returns a logical true (.T.) if a color graphics card has been installed in the computer.

Function: Clipper enhanced - Autumn '86

Source: Clipper.lib

Sample:

```
IF ISCOLOR()
   SET COLOR TO R/B
ELSE
   SET COLOR TO U
ENDIF
```

ISLOWER()

Syntax: ISLOWER(<expC>)

Pass: <character expression>

Return: <logical expression>

Description: This function returns a logical true (.T.) if the first character in <expC> is a lowercase alphabetic character.

Function: Clipper enhanced - Summer '87

Source: Autumn '86 - Extenddb.prg
Summer '87 - Extend.lib

Autumn '86: In order to use this function, the EXTENDDB.PRG file must be compiled and linked in with your application and must appear in your link list with all other .OBJ files.

Summer '87: With the Summer '87 release, this function was incorporated directly into the EXTEND.LIB file.

Sample:

```
? ISLOWER("Yes")    && Yields a .F.
? ISLOWER("212")    && Yields a .F.
? ISLOWER("no")     && Yields a .T.
```

ISPRINTER()

Syntax: ISPRINTER()

Pass: Nothing

Return: < logical expression >

Description: This function yields a logical true (.T.) if a parallel printer is on-line and ready. Otherwise a logical false (.F.) is returned. This function will not work with a serial printer.

Function: Clipper extended - Summer '87

Source: Autumn '86 - Extenda.obj
Summer '87 - Extend.lib

Autumn '86: In order to use this function, the EXTENDA.OBJ file must be linked in with your application and must appear in your link list after CLIPPER.LIB.

Summer '87: With the Summer '87 release, this function was incorporated directly into the EXTEND.LIB file.

Sample:

```
IF !ISPRINTER()
   ? "Your Printer is not ready.  Any Key to Continue..."
   IF INKEY(0) = 0
   ENDIF
ENDIF
```

ISUPPER()

Syntax: ISUPPER(< expC >)

Pass: < character expression >

Return: < logical expression >

Description: This function returns a logical true (.T.) if the first character in < expC > is an uppercase alphabetic character.

Function: Clipper enhanced - Summer '87

Source: Autumn '86 - Extenddb.prg
Summer '87 - Extend.lib

Autumn '86: In order to use this function, the EXTENDDB.PRG file must be compiled and linked in with your application and must appear in your link list with all other .OBJ files.

Summer '87: With the Summer '87 release, this function was incorporated directly into the EXTEND.LIB file.

Sample:

```
? ISUPPER("Yes")    && Yields a .T.
? ISUPPER("212")    && Yields a .F.
? ISUPPER("no")     && Yields a .F.
```

L2BIN()

Syntax: L2BIN(<expN>)

Pass: <numeric expression>

Return: <character expression>

Description: This function takes a numeric integer <expN> and converts it to a character string formatted as a 32-bit signed integer.

Function: Clipper enhanced - Summer '87

Source: Extend.lib

Sample: Please see Chapter 13, Low-Level File Logic.

LASTKEY()

Syntax: LASTKEY()

Pass: Nothing

Return: <numeric expression>

Description: The LASTKEY() function returns a number representing the ASCII value of the last key pressed.

Function: Clipper enhanced

Source: Clipper.lib

Notes: This includes all control keys and is helpful when used to determine how a READ was completed. Values of keys not in the ASCII table are listed in the INKEY() section above.

Sample:

```
USE File
FOR x = 1 TO 32
APPEND BLANK
NEXT
GO TOP
down = 1
DO WHILE .NOT. EOF()
    @ 5,1 SAY "Prompt Message " + LTRIM(STR(down)) + ;
          "-> " GET prompt PICT "XXXXXXXXXXXXXXXXXXXXXXXXXXXXXX"
    READ
    **************************************************
    * If the PgUp key is pressed, the previous
    * record is brought back and reentered.
    *
    **************************************************
   IF LASTKEY() = 18
      IF .NOT. BOF()
         down = down - 1
         SKIP - 1
      ENDIF
      LOOP
   ENDIF
   IF EMPTY(prompt) = 0 .OR. LASTKEY() = 27
      EXIT
   ENDIF
ENDDO
```

LASTREC()

Syntax: LASTREC()

Pass: Nothing

Return: <numeric expression>

Description: The LASTREC() function returns the number of records present in the active database.

Function: Clipper enhanced

Source: Clipper.lib

Notes: May be used in place of GO BOTTOM and STORing the RECNO() of the database to a temporary memory variable.

It is not dependent on an INDEX file being opened.

Sample:

```
USE Test
? "The number of records on file is "
?? LASTREC()
GO BOTTOM
STORE RECNO() TO testing
IF testing = LASTREC()
   ? "It is equal to the last record number"
ELSE
   ? "It is NOT equal"
ENDIF
```

LEFT()

Syntax: LEFT(<expC>, <expN>)

Pass: <character expression>, <numeric expression>

Return: <character expression>

Description: This function returns the left-most <expN> characters of <expC>.

Function: Clipper enhanced - Summer '87

Source: Autumn '86 - Extenddb.prg
Summer '87 - Extend.lib

Autumn '86: In order to use this function, the EXTENDDB.PRG file must be compiled and linked in with your application and must appear in your link list with all other .OBJ files.

Summer '87: With the Summer '87 release, this function was incorporated directly into the EXTEND.LIB file.

Note: With the Summer '87 release, the maximum string capacity for this function is set to 64K in length.

Sample:

```
? LEFT("This is a test", 4)    && This would yield 'This'
```

LEN()

Syntax: LEN(<expC>)

Pass: <character expression>

Return: <numeric expression>

Description: The LEN() function returns the length of the string passed to it. If <expC> is the name of an array, it returns the array length.

Function: Standard

Source: Clipper.lib

Note: With the Summer '87 release, the maximum string capacity for this function is set to 64K in length.

Sample:

```
STORE SPACE(20) TO name
CLEAR
@ 10,10 SAY "Enter a name: " GET name
READ
@ 12,10 SAY "You entered in "
?? LEN(name)
?? " characters..."
```

LENNUM()

Syntax: LENNUM(<expN>)

Pass: <numeric expression>

Return: <numeric expression>

Description: This function will yield the length of the given <expN>. It is useful in determining relative column positions for numeric values.

Function: Clipper simulated - Autumn '86
Clipper enhanced - Summer '87

Source: Extenddb.prg - Autumn '86
Extend.lib - Summer '87

Autumn '86: In order to use this function, the EXTENDDB.PRG file must be compiled and linked in with your application and must appear in your link list with all other .OBJ files.

LUPDATE()

Syntax: LUPDATE()

Pass: Nothing

Return: < date expression >

Description: This function returns the date DOS entered when the selected and active database was last written to disk.

Function: Clipper enhanced - Summer '87

Source: Autumn '86 - Extendc.obj
Summer '87 - Extend.lib

Autumn '86: In order to use this function, the EXTENDC.OBJ file must be linked in with your application and must appear in your link list after CLIPPER.LIB.

Summer '87: With the Summer '87 release, this function was incorporated directly into the EXTEND.LIB file.

Sample:

```
USE Hist
IF LUPDATE() < DATE() - 3
    ? "It's time to backup your data"
ENDIF
```

LOG()

Syntax: LOG(< expN >)

Pass: < numeric expression >

Return: < numeric expression >

Description: The LOG() function returns the natural logarithm of the number passed to it.

Function: Standard

Source: Clipper.lib

Sample:

```
CLEAR
? LOG(2.72)
? LOG(EXP(1))
SET DECIMALS TO 8
? LOG(2.72)
? LOG(EXP(1))
? 1 = LOG(EXP(1))
```

LOWER()

Syntax: LOWER(<expC>)

Pass: <character expression>

Return: <character expression>

Description: The LOWER() function converts any character to its lowercase representation.

Function: Standard

Source: Clipper.lib

Sample:

```
STORE "Clipper is 20 times FASTER than ....." TO show
CLEAR
? LOWER(show)
```

LTRIM()

Syntax: LTRIM(<expC>)

Pass: <character expression>

Return: <character expression>

Description: The LTRIM() function trims leading blanks from a character string.

Function: Standard

Source: Clipper.lib

Notes: This function is useful for formatting output in conjunction with numeric values and specific screen and printer formats.

With the Summer '87 release, the maximum string capacity for this function is set to 64K in length.

Sample:

```
@ 10,10 SAY 1
@ 11,10 SAY STR(1)
@ 12,10 SAY LTRIM(STR(1))
? LEN(STR(1))
? LEN(LTRIM(STR(1)))
```

MAX()

Syntax: MAX(<exp1>, <exp2>)

Pass: <expression>, <expression>

Return: <expression>

Description: The MAX() function returns the larger of the two passed expressions. If <exp1> and <exp2> are of numeric data type, the returned value will be of numeric data type. If the two parameters are of date data type, the returned value will be of date data type.

Function: Clipper enhanced - Summer '87

Source: Autumn '87 - Extenddb.prg
Summer '87 - Clipper.lib

MEMOEDIT()

Syntax: MEMOEDIT(<expC1>, <expN1>, <expN2>, <expN3>, <expN4>, [, <expL> [, <expC2> [, <expN5> [, <expN6> [,<expN7> [, <expN8> [, <expN9> [, <expN10>]]]]]]]])

Pass: <memo field> / <character expression>, <numeric expression>, <numeric expression>,<numeric expression>,<numeric expression> [, <logical expression> [, <character expression> [,<numeric expression> [, <numeric expression> [, <numeric expression> [, <numeric expression> [, <numeric expression> [,<numeric expression>]]]]]]]]

Return: <character expression>

Description: The MEMOEDIT() function expands the ability to edit a memo field or a character string. MEMOEDIT() is a function with its own built-in word processer. Additionally, the MEMOEDIT() function allows specific windowing areas to be partitioned for the edit.

The first parameter is the name of the memo field or the character string. The second, third, fourth, and fifth parameters provide the top, left, bottom, right coordinates of the window in which the edit will take place. The last parameter is an update flag. If the memo is to be edited, the flag should be set to **true**; otherwise, to merely display the memo, the flag should be set to **false.**

The following remarks all apply to the **Summer '87 release:**
<expC2> is the name of a Clipper user-defined function that executes whenever a key is pressed. Only the root name of the function is allowed to be passed, without either parameter arguments or parentheses.

<expN5> is the line length for the MEMOEDIT() function. If <expN5> is greater than the (<expN4> - <expN2> - 1), the window area will scroll horizontally until the maximum line length is reached.

<expN6> is the tabs size. The default value is 4.

<expN7> is the initial line for the MEMOEDIT() function to place the cursor

<expN8> is the initial row for the MEMOEDIT() function to place the cursor.

<expN9> is the initial row to place the cursor relative to the current window position. The default value is 0.

<expN10> is the initial column to place the cursor relative to the current window position. The default value is 0.

The Summer '87 MEMOEDIT() modes are as follows:

Modes	Description
0	Idle
1	Reconfigurable or unknown keystroke; <expC1> remains unaltered.
2	Reconfigurable or unknown keystroke; <expC1> is altered.
3	Startup condition.

The Summer '87 user-defined function returns values as follows:

Value	Action
0	Perform the default action.
1 - 31	Perform the action that corresponds to a key value (e.g., 7 = Ctrl-G; 22 = Ctrl-V = the insert key).
32	Ignore the current key pressed.
33	Process the current key and toggle the insert control key.
34	Toggle the word-wrap ability.
35	Toggle the scrolling ability.
	For situations resolving key value collisions:
100	Next word (2 = CTRL-B: REFORM).
101	Bottom right of the window area (23 = CTRL-W / SAVE and EXIT).

Function: Clipper enhanced

Source: Autumn '86 - Memo.lib
Summer '87 - Extend.lib

Autumn '86: If you are using this function with the Autumn '86 release, you must link in the MEMO.LIB with your application in your library list after listing CLIPPER.LIB first.

Notes: MEMOEDIT() is a function and follows all standard conventions as such; therefore, it has a value and will need to be used accordingly.

With this release, only the first five parameters are permitted. Their remaining parameters were included with the Summer '87 release.

For detailed information regarding memo fields and the MEMOEDIT() function, please refer to Chapter 8, Memo Fields.

Sample:

```
REPLACE memo_fld WITH MEMOEDIT(memo_fld, 5, 20, 10, 60, .T.)
```

or

```
IF "" = MEMOEDIT(memo_field, 5, 20, 10, 60, .F.)
ENDIF
```

Commands within Memoedit():

```
Cursor Movement:
        Up one line........................... ^E/Up Arrow
        Down one line........................ ^C/Down Arrow
```

```
        Left one character ................. ^S/Left Arrow
        Right one character................ ^D/Right Arrow
        Left one word....................... ^A/^Left Arrow
        Right one word.................... ^F/^Right Arrow
        Beginning of current line .................. HOME
        End of current line ......................... END
        Beginning of memo/string.................... ^HOME
        End of memo/string ......................... ^END
        Window Up .................................. PgUp
        Window Down ................................ PgDn
        Beginning of current window ............... ^PgUp
        End of current window ..................... ^PgDn

Editing Keys:
        Finish editing ............................... ^W
        Abort editing/keep old memo ................. Esc
        Delete current line .......................... ^Y
        Delete word right ............................ ^T
        Reformat memo/string in window ............... ^B
```

Addition: The MEMOEDIT() function will also scroll within a specific windowed area, especially on one line. For example, if you want to edit a field that is larger than a screen, try the following:

```
CLEAR
SET FUNCTION 10 TO CHR(23)
STORE "" TO test
@ 5,0 SAY "Enter:"
STORE MEMOEDIT(test,5,15,5,80,.T.) TO test
WAIT
CLEAR
test
```

With this, keep two things in mind:

1. The arrow keys will work like PgUp and PgDn keys.

2. HARDCR() or a user-defined function to strip out soft carriage returns [CHR(141)] is necessary if the output is ever to be displayed **other than** by using the MEMOEDIT() function.

Sample: For more information, please see Chapter 8 for an explanation of the complete MEMOEDIT() function.

MEMOLINE()

Syntax: MEMOLINE(<expC1>, <expN1>, <expN2>)

Pass: <character expression>, <numeric expression>, <numeric expression>

Return: <character expression>

Description: The MEMOLINE() function extracts a formatted line from <expC1> based on the number of characters to a line expressed as <expN1> and the line expressed as <expN3>.

If <expN2> is greater than the number of lines in <expC1>, MEMOLINE() will return a null byte.

Function: Clipper enhanced - Summer '87

Source: Summer '87 - Extend.lib

MEMOREAD()

Syntax: MEMOREAD(<filename>)

Pass: <character expression>

Return: <character expression>

Description: This function retrieves the contents of <filename> from the disk.

Function: Clipper enhanced

Source: Autumn '86 - Memo.lib
Summer '87 - Extend.lib

Autumn '86: When using this function, you must link in the MEMO.LIB library file with the rest of your application and it must follow the CLIPPER.LIB in the link list.

Sample:

```
REPORT FORM Payhist TO FILE Outhist.txt
? MEMOREAD("Outhist.txt")
```

MEMORY(0)

Syntax: MEMORY(0)

Pass: 0

Return: < numeric expression >

Description: This function returns the amount of free memory in kilobytes.

Function: Clipper enhanced

Source: Clipper.lib

Sample:

```
IF MEMORY(0) < 60
  CLEAR
  ? "In order to run this application, you must have more
  ? "available memory.  Please check to see if there are any"
  ? "RAM resident programs that can be removed."
  QUIT
ELSE
  DO Mainmenu
ENDIF
```

MEMOTRAN()

Syntax: MEMOTRAN(expC > [,hard-fix][, soft-fix])

Pass: < character expression > [, < character expression >] [, < character expression >]

Return: < character expression >

Description: This function returns < expC > with the hard carriage returns and/or the soft carriage returns replaced with a special value.

Hard carriage returns with line feed characters [CHR(13) + CHR(10)] will be replaced with a semicolon unless a different character is specified by the [hard-fix] option.

Soft carriage returns with line feed characters [CHR(141) + CHR(10)] will be replaced with a space unless a different character is specified by the [soft-fix] option.

To strip all formatting characters from a memo field or from a character string returned by the MEMOEDIT() function, a MEMOTRAN(string, " ", " ") may be used.

Function: Clipper enhanced

Source: Autumn '86 - Memo.lib
Summer '87 - Extend.lib

Autumn '86: When using this function, you must link in the MEMO.LIB library file with the rest of your application and it must follow the CLIPPER.LIB in the link list.

Sample:

```
newstring = MEMOTRAN(oldstr, CHR(252), CHR(251))
```

MEMOWRIT()

Syntax: MEMOWRIT(<filename>, <expC>)

Pass: <filename>, <character expression>

Return: <logical expression>

Description: This function writes <expC> to disk as <filename>. If no drive designator is given with <filename>, the currently logged in drive and directory will be assumed.

If the write operation to the disk is successful, the function returns a logical true (.T.) value; otherwise, a false (.F.) will be returned.

Function: Clipper enhanced

Source: Autumn '86 - Memo.lib
Summer '87 - Extend.lib

Autumn '86: When using this function, you must link in the MEMO.LIB library file with the rest of your application and it must follow the CLIPPER.LIB in the link list.

Sample:

```
IF MEMOWRIT("C:Outfile.txt", newstring)
   WAIT "File has been written.  Any Key to continue."
ELSE
  WAIT "Write error.  Process aborted.  Any key to continue."
ENDIF
```

MIN()

Syntax: MIN(<exp1>, <exp2>

Pass: <expression>, <expression>

Return: <expression>

Description: The MIN() function returns the smaller of two expressions <exp1> and <exp2>.

If <exp1> and <exp2> are of numeric data types, the returned value will be of numeric data type. If <exp1> and <exp2> are of date data types, the returned value will be date data type,

Function: Clipper enhanced

Source: Autumn '86 - Extenddb.prg
Summer '87 - Clipper.lib

MLCOUNT()

Syntax: MLCOUNT(<expC>, <expN>)

Pass: <character expression>, <numeric expression>

Return: <numeric expression>

Description: The MLCOUNT() function returns the number of CHR(141) characters within <expC> based on a character length per line of <expN>.

Function: Clipper enhanced

Source: Autumn '86 - Memo.lib
Summer '87 - Extend.lib

MLPOS()

Syntax: MLPOS(<expC>, <expN1>, <expN2>)

Pass: <character expression>, <numeric expression>, <numeric expression>

Return: <numeric expression>

Description: This function determines the position of a specified line number <expN2> in a string or memo field expressed as <expC> with <expN1> characters per line.

Function: Clipper enhanced - Summer '87

Source: Extend.lib

Note: If <expN2> is greater than the number of lines in <expC>, the function returns the LEN(expC>).

MOD()

Syntax: MOD(<expN>, <expN>)

Pass: <numeric expression>, <numeric expression>

Return: <numeric expression>

Description: This function returns the remainder of the first <expN> divided by the second <expN>.

Differences: Below is a list of numeric values passed to this function that yield a different value in Clipper than in dBASE III.

```
Extended Clipper:           dBASE function:

 3 %  0 ::=  0.00           MOD( 3, 0) ::=  3
 3 % -2 ::=  1.00           MOD( 3,-2) ::= -1
-3 %  2 ::= -1.00           MOD(-3, 2) ::=  1
-3 %  0 ::=  0.00           MOD(-3, 0) ::= -3
-1 %  3 ::= -1.00           MOD(-1, 3) ::=  2
-2 %  3 ::= -2.00           MOD(-2, 3) ::=  1
 2 % -3 ::=  2.00           MOD( 2,-3) ::= -1
 1 % -3 ::=  1.00           MOD( 1,-3) ::= -2
```

Function: Clipper simulated - Autumn '86
Clipper enhanced - Summer '87

Source: Extenddb.prg - Autumn '86
Extend.lib - Summer '87

Autumn '86: In order to use this function, the EXTENDDB.PRG file must be compiled and linked in with your application and must appear in your link list with all other .OBJ files.

Summer '87: In the Summer release, the MOD() function may be expressed as:

< numeric expression > % < numeric expression >

MONTH()

Syntax: MONTH(<expD>)

Pass: < date expression >

Return: < numeric expression >

Description: The MONTH() function returns a number that represents the month of the given date expression.

Function: Standard

Source: Clipper.lib

Sample:

```
CLEAR
? DATE()
? MONTH(DATE())
? 28 + MONTH(DATE())
```

NDX()

Syntax: NDX(<expN>)

Pass: < numeric expression >

Return: < character expression >

Description: This function returns the root file name expressed as a character expression (regardless of the .NDX or .NTX file extension) for the <expN>th selected index.

Difference: In dBASE III, this function will actually return the name of the index file located in the <expN>th position in the index list.

Function: Clipper simulated

Source: Autumn '86 - Extenddb.prg

Autumn '86: In order to use this function, the EXTENDDB.PRG file must be compiled and linked in with your application and must appear in your link list with all other .OBJ files.

NETERR()

Syntax: NETERR()

Pass: Nothing

Return: < logical expression >

Description: This function returns a logical true (.T.) if a USE, an APPEND BLANK, or a USE...EXCLUSIVE command is issued and fails in a network environment.

Function: Clipper enhanced

Source: Clipper.lib

NETNAME()

Syntax: NETNAME()

Pass: Nothing

Return: < character expression >

Description: This function returns the text of the network station name in a 15-character string. If there is no network name, a null string is returned. In order to function properly, the IBM PC Local Area Network Program must be loaded.

Function: Clipper enhanced

Source: Clipper.lib

NEXTKEY()

Syntax: NEXTKEY()

Pass: Nothing

Return: < numeric expression >

Description: This function will read the next keystroke from the keyboard buffer without removing it; therefore, it may be used to process pending and future keystrokes.

Function: Clipper enhanced - Summer '87

Source: Extend.lib

Sample:

```
KEYBOARD CHR(13) + CHR(27) + "Q"
@ 10,10 PROMPT "Choice"
MENU TO Operat
IF NEXTKEY() = 27
   ? "Escape key is in the buffer.
ENDIF
```

OS()

Syntax: OS()

Pass: Nothing

Return: < character expression >

Description: The OS() function always returns "MS/PC-DOS."

Function: Clipper simulated - Autumn '86
Clipper enhanced - Summer '87

Source: Extenddb.prg - Autumn '86
Extend.lib - Summer '87

Autumn '86: In order to use this function, the EXTENDDB.PRG file must be compiled and linked in with your application and must appear in your link list with all other .OBJ files.

PCOL()

Syntax: PCOL()

Pass: Nothing

Return: < numeric expression >

Description: The PCOL() function returns the current column position of the print head on the printer.

Function: Standard

Source: Clipper.lib

Sample:

```
SET DEVICE TO PRINT
@ 1,10 SAY "This is a test"
STORE PCOL() TO test
@ 10,0 SAY "The previous line ended on column "
@ 10,PCOL() + 1 SAY test
```

PCOUNT()

Syntax: PCOUNT()

Pass: Nothing

Return: <numeric expression>

Description: This function returns the number of successful parameter matches issued. It can be used to test if the parameter name is "U" (undefined).

Function: Clipper enhanced

Source: Clipper.lib

Sample:

```
PARAMETERS a, b, c
DO CASE
CASE PCOUNT() = 3
? a
? b
? c
CASE PCOUNT() = 2
? a
? b
CASE PCOUNT() = 1
? a
OTHERWISE
? "No parameters were passed to this procedure/function"
ENDCASE
```

PROCLINE()

Syntax: PROCLINE()

Pass: Nothing

Return: < numeric expression >

Description: This function returns the source code line number of the currently running program or procedure.

Function: Clipper enhanced

Source: Clipper.lib

Notes: One warning with this function: the results may be unpredictable if used in conjunction with source code compiled without line numbers (the -l option on the compiler).

This function can be extremely useful when you want to the trace flow of operation through your program without the additional aid of DEBUG.OBJ.

Sample:

```
? "You are now at line "
?? PROCLINE()
?? " of your application"
```

PROCNAME()

Syntax: PROCNAME()

Pass: Nothing

Return: < expression string >

Description: This function returns the name of the program or procedure currently being executed.

Function: Clipper enhanced

Source: Clipper.lib

Notes: This function can be extremely useful in tracing the flow of operations through your program without the additional aid of

DEBUG.OBJ. It also can add to your application if certain prompts or messages are to appear in some areas and not in others. The name of the program or procedure may be tested and the prompt or message may or may not appear accordingly.

Sample:

```
IF PROCNAME() = "MAINMENU"
@ 23,10 SAY "You are running in the Main Menu"
ELSE
@ 23,10 SAY "You are NOT running in the Main Menu"
ENDIF
```

PROW()

Syntax: PROW()

Pass: Nothing

Return: < numeric expression >

Description: The PROW() function returns the current row position of the print head on the printer.

Function: Standard

Source: Clipper.lib

Sample:

```
SET DEVICE TO PRINT
@ 1,10 SAY "This is a test"
STORE PROW() TO test
@ 10,0 SAY "The previous was printed on row "
@ PROW(),PCOL() + 1 SAY test
```

RAT()

Syntax: RAT(<expC1>, <expC2>)

Pass: < character expression >, < character expression >

Return: < numeric expression >

Description: The RAT() function [Right AT()] searches through <expC2> for the last existence of <expC1>.

Function: Clipper enhanced - Summer '87

Source: Summer '87 - Extend.lib

Note: With the Summer '87 release, the maximum string capacity for this function is set to 64K in length.

Sample:

```
? "The current directory is " + ;
SUBSTR(CURDIR(), RAT("\", CURDIR()) - 1)
```

READEXIT()

Syntax: READEXIT([<expL>])

Pass: [<logical expression>]

Return: <logical expression>

Description: The READEXIT() function checks and toggles the Up and Down arrow keys as exit keys to a READ command.

The default mode for the Up and Down keys is a logical false (.F.)

Function: Clipper enhanced - Summer '87

Source: Clipper.lib

READINSERT()

Syntax: READINSERT([<expL>])

Pass: [<logical expression>]

Return: <logical expression>

Description: The READINSERT() function checks and toggles the status of INSERT KEY for all READs and the MEMOEDIT() function.

The default setting is logical false (.F.).

Function: Clipper enhanced - Summer '87

Source: Summer '87 - Clipper.lib

Sample: Please see Chapter 8, Memo Fileds.

READKEY()

Syntax: READKEY()

Pass: Nothing

Return: < numeric expression >

Description: This function returns a number representing the key pressed to exit from any full-screen mode.

Differences: There are some differences in what dBASE III will return as a value and what this simulated function will return:

Exit Key:	dBASE:	Clipper:
Backspace	0	no exit
^D, ^L	1	no exit
Lt arrow	2	no exit
Rt arrow	3	no exit
Up arrow	4	no exit
Dn arrow	5	no exit
PgUp	6	18
PgDn	7	3
Esc, ^Q	12	27 (Esc only)
^End, ^W	14	23 (^W only)
Type past end	15	ASCII of last char. typed
Enter	15	13
^Home	33	no exit
^PgUp	34	no exit
^PgDn	35	no exit
F1	36	no exit

Function: Clipper simulated - Autumn '86
Clipper enhanced - Summer '87

Source: Extenddb.prg - Autumn '86
Extend.lib - Summer '87

Autumn '86: In order to use this function, the EXTENDDB.PRG file must be compiled and linked in with your application and must appear in your link list with all other .OBJ files.

READVAR()

Syntax: READVAR()

Pass: Nothing

Return: <character expression>

Description: The READVAR() function returns the name of the variable pending in the current GET/MENU. If none is pending, a null string is returned.

Function: Clipper enhanced

Notes: This function is used either in conjunction with Clipper's HELP facility or a secondary procedure called by the SET KEY <expN> TO <procedure name>.

Sample:

```
CLEAR
STORE "Y" TO test
DO WHILE test = "Y"
  @  5,10 SAY "Please press F1"
  @ 10,10 SAY "Continue? (Y/N) " GET test ;
  PICT "!" VALID(test$"YN")
  READ
  @ 17,10 SAY "The current value is: "
  @ ROW(),COL() SAY READVAR()
ENDDO

*********************

PROCEDURE Help

  PARAMETERS p,l,v

  @ 12,10 SAY "The help says the current value is: "
  @ ROW(),COL() SAY READVAR()
  WAIT
```

RECCOUNT()

Syntax: RECCOUNT()

Pass: Nothing

Return: <numeric expression>

Description: The RECCOUNT() function returns the number of records present in the active database.

Function: Standard

Source: Clipper.lib

Autumn '86: For this release, use the LASTREC() function.

Notes: May be used in place of GO BOTTOM and STORing the RECNO() of the database to a temporary memory variable.

It is not dependent on an INDEX file being opened.

Sample:

```
USE Test
? "The number of records on file is "
?? RECCOUNT()
GO BOTTOM
STORE RECNO() TO testing
IF testing = RECCOUNT()
   ? "It is equal to the last record number"
ELSE
   ? "It is NOT equal"
ENDIF
```

RECNO()

Syntax: RECNO()

Pass: Nothing

Return: < numeric expression >

Description: The RECNO() function returns the position of the record pointer in the currently selected area.

Function: Standard

Source: Clipper.lib

Notes: If the database is empty, RECNO() will return a value of 1.

Sample:

```
USE File
ZAP
? RECNO()                  && Will return a 1
? EOF()                    && Will return .T.
```

```
APPEND FROM Another      && Appending 10 records
GO TOP
SKIP + 5
? RECNO()
STORE RECNO() + 1 TO test
?
? "The next record will be record # " + STR(test)
```

RECSIZE()

Syntax: RECSIZE()

Pass: Nothing

Return: < numeric expression >

Description: This function returns the number of bytes used by a single record in the currently selected and active database file.

Function: Clipper enhanced - Summer '87

Source: Autumn '86 - Extendc.obj
Summer '87 - Clipper.lib

Autumn '86: In order to use this function, the EXTENDC.OBJ file must be linked in with your application and must appear in your link list after CLIPPER.LIB.

Summer '87: With the Summer '87 release, this function was incorporated directly into the EXTEND.LIB file.

REPLICATE()

Syntax: REPLICATE(<expC>, <expN>)

Pass: < character expression >, < numeric expression >

Return: < character expression >

Description: The REPLICATE() function returns a string composed of <expN> repetitions of <expC>.

Function: Clipper enhanced

Source: Clipper.lib

Notes: Both parameters must be passed when calling this function, and they must follow the format of a character followed by a number.

Sample:
```
@ 10,10 SAY REPLICATE("-",20)
```

RESTSCREEN()

Syntax: RESTSCREEN(<expN1>, <expN2>, <expN3>, <expN4>, <expC1>)

Pass: <numeric expression>, <numeric expression>, <numeric expression>, <numeric expression>, <character expression>

Return: Nothing

Description: The RESTSCREEN() function restores the screen contents of <expC1> at window coordinates <expN1> - <expN4>.

Function: Clipper enhanced - Summer '87

Source: Summer '87 - Clipper.lib

Sample: Please see Chapter 16.

RIGHT()

Syntax: RIGHT(<expC>, <expN>)

Pass: <character expression>, <numeric expression>

Return: <character expression>

Description: The RIGHT() function returns the right-most <expN> characters of <expC>.

Function: Clipper enhanced

Source: Autumn '86 - Extenddb.prg
Summer '87 - Extend.lib

Autumn '86: In order to use this function, the EXTENDDB.PRG file must be compiled and linked in with your application and must appear in your link list with all other .OBJ files.

Summer '87: With the Summer '87 release, this function was incorporated directly into the Extend.lib file.

Note: With the Summer '87 release, the maximum string capacity for this function is set to 64K in length.

Sample:

```
? RIGHT("Hello There", 5) + " it is"  && Yields 'There it is'
```

RLOCK()

Syntax: RLOCK()/LOCK()

Pass: Nothing

Return: <logical expression>

Description: This function returns a logical true (.T.) on a successful attempt to lock a specific record in the currently active and selected file. This function will yield a false (.F.) if the file is currently locked or if the desired record is currently locked.

Function: Clipper enhanced

Source: Clipper.lib

ROUND()

Syntax: ROUND(<expN>,<expN>)

Pass: <numeric expression>,<numeric expression>

Return: <numeric expression>

Description: The ROUND() function rounds off the first <expN> to the number of decimal places specified by the second <expN>.

Function: Standard

Source: Clipper.lib

Sample:

```
? ROUND(12.422354, 2)   && prints 12.420000
? ROUND(164.23312, 3)   && prints 164.23300
```

ROW()

Syntax: ROW()

Pass: Nothing

Return: < numeric expression >

Description: The ROW() function returns the current cursor row location.

Function: Standard

Source: Clipper.lib

Sample:

```
CLEAR
@ 10,10 SAY "Hello"
?? SPACE(10)
?? ROW()
STORE ROW() + 10 TO down
@ down,10 SAY "Hello again..."
```

SAVESCREEN()

Syntax: SAVESCREEN(<expN1>, <expN2>, <expN3>, <expN4>)

Pass: < numeric expression >, < numeric expression >, < numeric expression >, < numeric expression >

Return: < character expression >

Description: The SAVESCREEN() function returns the screen contents in windowed area <expN1> - <expN4> as a string variable.

Function: Clipper enhanced - Summer '87

Source: Summer '87 - Clipper.lib

Sample: Please see Chapter 16.

SCROLL()

Syntax: SCROLL(<expN1>, <expN2>, <expN3>, <expN4>, <expN5>)

Pass: <numeric expression>, <numeric expression>, <numeric expression>, <numeric expression>, <numeric expression>

Return: Nothing

Description: The SCROLL() function either scrolls up or down or it wipes out a windowed screen portion at <expN1> - <expN4> coordinates.

<expN5> is the scrolling values. A positive number indicates the number of lines to scroll up within the windowed area, a negative number indicates the number of lines to scroll down within the windows area, and a value of 0 indicates the windowed area to be blanked out.

Function: Clipper enhanced - Summer '87

Source: Extend.lib

Sample:

```
*********************
* Name      Scr.prg
* Author    Stephen J. Straley
* Notice    Copyright (c) 1988 Stephen J. Straley & Associates
* Date      May 2, 1988
* Compile   Clipper Scr -m
* Release   Summer '87 Only
* Link      Plink86 fi scr lib clipper lib extend
* Note      This program shows how the SCROLL() function works
*           and it's versitility.
*
*********************

CLEAR SCREEN
SET CURSOR OFF
RUN Dir >Dostext.txt
@ 1,0 SAY "The scrolling will take place through "
@ 3,0 SAY "    This line ëëëëëëëëëëëëëëëëëëëëëëëëëëëëëëëëëëëëëëëëë"
@18,0 SAY "and this line ëëëëëëëëëëëëëëëëëëëëëëëëëëëëëëëëëëëëëëëëë"
@ 20,0 SAY "Key Strokes: Up / Dn / ENTER = Repaint / SPACE = Blank
out / ESC to Quit"
KEYBOARD CHR(13)
DO WHILE .T.
   INKEY(0)
   IF LASTKEY() = 27
      EXIT
```

```
      ELSEIF LASTKEY() = 13
         MEMOEDIT(MEMOREAD("Dostext.txt"), 4,10,17,70,.F.,.F.)
      ELSEIF LASTKEY() = 32
         SCROLL(4,1,17,70,0)
      ELSEIF LASTKEY() = 5
         SCROLL(4, 1, 17, 70, 1)
      ELSEIF LASTKEY() = 24
         SCROLL(4, 1, 17, 70, -1)
      ENDIF
   ENDDO
   SET CURSOR ON
   CLEAR SCREEN
```

SECONDS()

Syntax: SECONDS()

Pass: Nothing

Return: < numeric expression >

Description: The SECONDS() function returns a numeric value representing the number of seconds based on the current system time.

Function: Clipper enhanced

Source: Clipper.lib

Notes: The system time is considered to start at 0 (midnight); it continues up to 86,399 seconds. The value of the expression is displayed in both seconds and hundreds of seconds. This function can be useful in maintaining time logs. [See DAYS().]

Sample:

```
? "We are currently "
?? SECONDS()
?? " seconds past midnight"
```

SECS()

Syntax: SECS(< expC >)

Pass: < character expression >

Return: < numeric expression >

Description: This function yields a numeric expression that is the number of seconds based on a time string given in <expC>. See SECONDS() above.

Function: Clipper simulated - Autumn '86
Clipper enhanced - Summer '87

Source: Extenddb.prg - Autumn '86
Extend.lib - Autumn '87

Autumn '86: In order to use this function, the EXTENDDB.PRG file must be compiled and linked in with your application and must appear in your link list with all other .OBJ files.

SELECT()

Syntax: SELECT([<expC>])

Pass: [<character expression>]

Return: <numeric expression>

Description: The SELECT() function returns the numeric value of the currently selected area.

Function: Clipper enhanced

Source: Clipper.lib

Variance: With the Summer '87 release, the optional character expression is introduced. This allows the SELECT() function to check the existence of an alias or a file in use. If that alias name does not exist, the SELECT() function is a 0.

Notes: If used in conjunction with a user-defined HELP system, the HELP file can be placed in a separate database and toggled for use.

Sample:

```
********************
* Name        TEMPHELP.prg
* Date        August 6, 1986
* Notice      Copyright 1986, Stephen J. Straley
* Compile     Clipper.Temphelp
* Release     Autumn '86 or later
* Link        Plink86 fi Temphelp lib clipper;
* Note        This program shows the SELECT() function
```

```
*                  in direct use.
*********************

PARAMETERS p,l,v

IF p = "HELP" .OR. p = "VERIFY"
  RETURN
ENDIF

SAVE SCREEN
SET SCOREBOARD off
p = p + SPACE(10 - LEN(p))
v = v + SPACE(10 - LEN(v))
IF .NOT. FILE("HELP.DBF")
  @ 00,10,03,70 BOX scrframe
  @ 01,11 SAY "There is no HELP file available.   " + ;
              "Would you like a help "
  @ 02,27 SAY "file to be generated?"
  IF .NOT. VERIFY()
    RESTORE SCREEN
    RETURN
  ENDIF
  goback = SELECT()
  DO Dohelp
  tempgo = STR(goback)
  SELECT &tempgo
ENDIF

goback = SELECT()
SELECT 9
USE Help INDEX Help
SET FILTER TO search_p = p .AND. search_v = v
LOCATE FOR search_l = l
IF FOUND()
  ? helpscr
ELSE
  @ 23,10 SAY "Press Any key to Continue...."
ENDIF
qw = INKEY(0)
RESTORE SCREEN
tempgo = STR(goback)
SELECT &tempgo
RETURN
```

SETCANCEL()

Syntax: SETCANCEL([<expL>])

Pass: [<logical expression>]

Return: < logical expression >

Description: The SETCANCEL() function checks and toggles the Alt-C (termination key).

The default value is a logical false (.F.).

To toggle off the Alt-C key, a parameter value of logical false is required; toggling it on requires an logical true (.T.).

If a parameter is passed, the returned value is the previous setting; otherwise, it is the current setting.

Function: Clipper enhanced - Summer '87

Source: Summer '87 - Clipper.lib

SETCOLOR()

Syntax: SETCOLOR([< expC >])

Pass: [< character expression >]

Return: < character expression >

Description: The SETCOLOR() function returns the current color setting expressed as a character expression.

If a parameters is passed, that character expression must contain the standard SET COLOR TO expression in order for the SETCOLOR() function to set the color.

If a parameters is passed, the SETCOLOR() function returns the previous color setting; otherwise, the function returns the current color setting.

Only color-letter combinations are supported with the SETCOLOR() function.

Function: Clipper enhanced - Summer '87

Source: Summer '87 - Extend.lib

Sample:

```
old_color = SETCOLOR()
newcolor = W+/B
DO Errorsys
SET COLOR TO &old_color.
```

SETPRC()

Syntax: SETPRC(<expN>,<expN>)

Pass: <numeric expression>,<numeric expression>

Return: Nothing

Description: This function sets the internal PROW() and PCOL() values to the specified numeric expressions passed to this function. It is especially useful when issuing printer control codes without altering the values of PROW() or PCOL().

Function: Clipper enhanced

Source: Clipper.lib

Sample:

```
new_row = PROW()
new_col = PCOL()
SET PRINT ON
?? CHR(15)        && Condense print for some printers.
SETPRC(new_row, new_col)
```

SOUNDEX()

Syntax: SOUNDEX(<expC>)

Pass: <character expression>

Return: <character expression>

Description: This function yields a character expression that is derived from the given <expC>. This new <expC> will be a sound-like calculation based on the passed string. A code or simulation will be returned.

Function: Clipper simulated - Autumn '86
Clipper enhanced - Summer '87

Source: Extenddb.prg - Autumn '86
Extend.lib - Summer '87

Autumn '86: In order to use this function, the EXTENDDB.PRG file must be compiled and linked in with your application and must appear in your link list with all other .OBJ files.

Summer '87: With the Summer '87 release, this function was incorporated directly into the EXTEND.LIB file.

SPACE()

Syntax: SPACE(<expN>)

Pass: <numeric expression>

Return: <character expression>

Description: The SPACE() function generates a string consisting of <expN> blank spaces.

Function: Standard

Source: Clipper.lib

Note: With the Summer '87 release, the maximum string capacity for this function is set to 64K in length.

Sample:

```
? LEN(SPACE(10))
? '"' + SPACE(10) + '"'
? LEN(TRIM(SPACE(10)))
```

SQRT()

Syntax: SQRT(<expN>)

Pass: <numeric expression>

Return: <numeric expression>

Description: The SQRT() function returns the square root of <expN>.

Function: Standard

Source: Clipper.lib

Notes: Clipper does not support the square root of a negative number. The results of SQRT() are restricted to the amount the SET DECIMALS TO command has been set to.

Sample:

```
CLEAR
? SQRT(4)
? SQRT(5)
SET DECIMAL TO 8
? SQRT(4)
? SQRT(5)
```

STR()

Syntax: STR(expN,[,<length>[,[decimals>]])

Pass: <numeric expression>,<numeric expression>,<numeric expression>

Return: <character expression>

Description: This function converts any numeric expression (<expN>) into a character string. The second parameter sets the length of the string, and the third parameter sets the number of decimal places to be included.

Function: Standard

Source: Clipper.lib

Notes: If the second and third parameters are not given, the function returns a string with the length of 10 unless the number stipulated is longer than 10 significant places with or without decimals. If the length of 10 is assumed, note that the string returned from the function will have leading spaces.

Sample:

```
CLEAR
? STR(1)
? LEN(STR(1))
@ 10,10 SAY "|----|----|----|----|"
@ 11,10 SAY STR(1)
```

STRTRAN()

Syntax: STRTRAN(<expC1>, <expC2> [, <expC3> [, <expN1> [,<expN2>]]])

Pass: <character expression>, <character expression> [, <character expression> [, <numeric expression> [, <numeric expression>]]]

Return: <character expression>

Description: The STRTRAN() function searches for any occurrence of <expC2> in <expC1> and replaces it with <expC3>.

If <expC3> is not specified, a "" will be the replaced character.

If used, <expN1> dictates that the occurrence will be replaced. The default value is 1.

If used, <expN2> dictates how many occurrences to replace. The default value is all.

Function: Clipper enhanced - Summer '87

Source: Summer '87 - Extend.lib

Note: With the Summer '87 release, the maximum string capacity for this function is set to 64K in length.

STRZERO()

Syntax: STRZERO(<expN> [, <expN> [, <expN>]])

Pass: <numeric expression> [,<numeric expression> [,<numeric expression>]]

Return: <character expression>

Description: This function returns a string based on the given <expN> with leading 0s instead of blank spaces. The second <expN>, which is optional, is for the desired length of the returned <expC>. The third <expN>, which is also optional, is for the number of decimals to be included.

Function: Clipper simulated - Autumn '86
Clipper enhanced - Summer '87

Source: Extenddb.prg - Autumn '86
Extend.lib - Summer '87

Autumn '86: In order to use this function, the EXTENDDB.PRG file must be compiled and linked in with your application and must appear in your link list with all other .OBJ files.

STUFF()

Syntax: STUFF(<expC1>, <expN1>, <expN2>, <expC2>)

Pass: <character expression>, <numeric expression>, <numeric expression>, <character expression>

Return: <character expression>

Description: This function returns a character expression of <expC1> overlayed by <expC2>, starting at <expN1> character position and continuing on for <expN2>.

Function: Clipper simulated - Autumn '86
Clipper enhanced - Summer '87

Source: Extenddb.prg - Autumn '86
Extend.lib - Summer '87

Autumn '86: In order to use this function, the EXTENDDB.PRG file must be compiled and linked in with your application and must appear in your link list with all other .OBJ files.

Summer '87: With the Summer '87 release, this function was incorporated directly into the EXTEND.LIB file.

Note: With the Summer '87 release, the maximum string capacity for this function is set to 64K in length.

SUBSTR()

Syntax: SUBSTR(<expC1>,<expN1>[,<expN2>])

Pass: <character expression>,<numeric expression> [,<numeric expression>]>

Return: < character expression >

Description: The SUBSTR() function returns a character string composed of < expC, starting at the position < expN1 > and continuing for a length of < expN2 > characters.

Function: Standard

Source: Clipper.lib

Variance: In the Summer '87 release, if < expN2 > is a negative number, the SUBSTR() function will start from the right-most character of < expC1 >.

Notes: If the second numeric expression, which represents the number of characters to be returned, is left out, the SUBSTR() will continue its substring parse through the last character in the string.

With the Summer '87 release, the maximum string capacity for this function is set to 64K in length.

Sample:

```
CLEAR
STORE "Dave    Bill    Jim     Stephen JenniferAl      " TO a
STORE 1 TO pass
DO WHILE pass <> 7
  ?  "-> "
  ?? SUBSTR(a,pass * 8 - 7,8)
  pass = pass + 1
ENDDO
```

TONE()

Syntax: TONE(< expN1 >, < expN2 >)

Pass: < numeric expression >, < numeric expression >

Return: Nothing

Description: The TONE() function generates a tone through the speaker at a frequency of < expN1 > at a duration of < expN2 >. The duration is measured in increments of 1/18 of a second.

Table of Tones

Note	Freq. Value	Note	Freq. Value
C	130.80	Mid C	261.70
C#	138.60	C#	277.20
D	146.80	D	293.70
D#	155.60	D#	311.10
E	164.80	E	329.60
F	174.60	F	349.20
F#	185.00	F#	370.00
G	196.00	G	392.00
G#	207.70	G#	415.30
A	220.00	A	440.00
A#	233.10	A#	466.20
B	246.90	B	493.90
		C	523.30

Function: Clipper enhanced - Summer '87

Source: Summer '87 - Extend.lib

Sample:

```
*********************
* Name      Toneit.prg
* Author    Stephen J. Straley
* Notice    Copyright (c) 1988 Stephen J. Straley & Associates
* Date      May 2, 1988
* Compile   Clipper Toneit -m
* Release   Summer 87 Only
* Link      Plink86 fi toneit lib clipper lib extend
*
* Note      This program shows another way to use the TONE()
*           function
*           other than just with indexing and with errors.  Enjoy
*           running this program.
*********************

CLEAR SCREEN
TONE(PLAY("d"), PULSE("1/16"))
TONE(PLAY("d#"), PULSE("1/16"))
TONE(PLAY("e"), PULSE("1/16"))
TONE(PLAY("C"), PULSE("1/8"))
TONE(PLAY("e"), PULSE("1/16"))
TONE(PLAY("C"), PULSE("1/8"))
TONE(PLAY("e"), PULSE("1/16"))
TONE(PLAY("C"), PULSE("1/8"))
RESTNOTE(.2)
TONE(PLAY("C"), PULSE("1/16"))
TONE(PLAY("D"), PULSE("1/16"))
TONE(PLAY("D#"), PULSE("1/16"))
```

```
TONE(PLAY("E"), PULSE("1/16"))
TONE(PLAY("C"), PULSE("1/16"))
TONE(PLAY("D"), PULSE("1/16"))
TONE(PLAY("E"), PULSE("1/8"))
TONE(PLAY("b"), PULSE("1/16"))
TONE(PLAY("D"), PULSE("1/16"))
TONE(PLAY("C"), PULSE("1/8"))
RESTNOTE(.4)
TONE(PLAY("d"), PULSE("1/16"))
TONE(PLAY("d#"), PULSE("1/16"))
TONE(PLAY("e"), PULSE("1/16"))
TONE(PLAY("C"), PULSE("1/8"))
TONE(PLAY("e"), PULSE("1/16"))
TONE(PLAY("C"), PULSE("1/8"))
TONE(PLAY("e"), PULSE("1/16"))
TONE(PLAY("C"), PULSE("1/8"))
RESTNOTE(.2)
TONE(PLAY("a"), PULSE("1/16"))
TONE(PLAY("g"), PULSE("1/16"))
TONE(PLAY("f#"), PULSE("1/16"))
TONE(PLAY("a"), PULSE("1/16"))
TONE(PLAY("C"), PULSE("1/16"))
TONE(PLAY("E"), PULSE("1/8"))
RESTNOTE(.1)
TONE(PLAY("D"), PULSE("1/16"))
TONE(PLAY("D"), PULSE("1/16"))
TONE(PLAY("b"), PULSE("1/16"))
TONE(PLAY("D"), PULSE("1/8"))
RESTNOTE(.4)
TONE(PLAY("d"), PULSE("1/16"))
TONE(PLAY("d#"), PULSE("1/16"))
TONE(PLAY("e"), PULSE("1/16"))
TONE(PLAY("C"), PULSE("1/8"))
TONE(PLAY("e"), PULSE("1/16"))
TONE(PLAY("C"), PULSE("1/8"))
TONE(PLAY("e"), PULSE("1/16"))
TONE(PLAY("C"), PULSE("1/8"))
RESTNOTE(.2)
TONE(PLAY("C"), PULSE("1/16"))
TONE(PLAY("D"), PULSE("1/16"))
TONE(PLAY("D#"), PULSE("1/16"))
TONE(PLAY("E"), PULSE("1/16"))
TONE(PLAY("C"), PULSE("1/16"))
TONE(PLAY("D"), PULSE("1/16"))
TONE(PLAY("E"), PULSE("1/8"))
TONE(PLAY("b"), PULSE("1/16"))
TONE(PLAY("D"), PULSE("1/16"))
TONE(PLAY("C"), PULSE("1/8"))
RESTNOTE(.2)
TONE(PLAY("C"), PULSE("1/16"))
TONE(PLAY("D"), PULSE("1/16"))
TONE(PLAY("E"), PULSE("1/16"))
TONE(PLAY("C"), PULSE("1/16"))
```

```
TONE(PLAY("D"), PULSE("1/16"))
TONE(PLAY("E"), PULSE("1/16"))
RESTNOTE(.1)
TONE(PLAY("C"), PULSE("1/16"))
TONE(PLAY("D"), PULSE("1/16"))
TONE(PLAY("C"), PULSE("1/16"))
TONE(PLAY("E"), PULSE("1/16"))
TONE(PLAY("C"), PULSE("1/16"))
TONE(PLAY("D"), PULSE("1/16"))
TONE(PLAY("E"), PULSE("1/16"))
RESTNOTE(.1)
TONE(PLAY("C"), PULSE("1/16"))
TONE(PLAY("D"), PULSE("1/16"))
TONE(PLAY("C"), PULSE("1/16"))
TONE(PLAY("E"), PULSE("1/16"))
TONE(PLAY("C"), PULSE("1/16"))
TONE(PLAY("D"), PULSE("1/16"))
TONE(PLAY("E"), PULSE("1/8"))
TONE(PLAY("b"), PULSE("1/16"))
TONE(PLAY("D"), PULSE("1/16"))
TONE(PLAY("C"), PULSE())

********************

FUNCTION Restnote

   PARAMETERS restnote

   INKEY(restnote)
   RETURN("")

*********************

FUNCTION Pulse

   PARAMETERS note

   IF PCOUNT() = 0
      RETURN(18)
   ENDIF

   IF note= "1/64"
      RETURN(2.75/2)
   ELSEIF note= "1/32"
      RETURN(2.75)
   ELSEIF note= "1/16"
      RETURN(4.5)
   ELSEIF note= "1/8"
      RETURN(9)
   ELSEIF note= "1/4"
      RETURN(18)
   ELSEIF note= "1/2"
      RETURN(36)
```

```
    ELSEIF note= "3/4"
       RETURN(54)
    ELSEIF note= "1"
       RETURN(72)
    ELSEIF note= "2"
       RETURN(144)
    ELSEIF note= "3"
       RETURN(216)
    ELSE
       RETURN(288)
    ENDIF

*********************

FUNCTION Play

    PARAMETERS key

    IF key$"cc#"
       RETURN( IF( (key == "c"), 130.80, 138.60) )
    ELSEIF key$"dd#"
       RETURN( IF( (key == "d"), 146.80, 155.60) )
    ELSEIF key="e"
       RETURN( 164.80 )
    ELSEIF key$"ff#"
       RETURN( IF( (key == "f"), 174.60, 185.00) )
    ELSEIF key$"gg#"
       RETURN( IF( (key == "g"), 196.00, 207.70) )
    ELSEIF key$"aa#"
       RETURN( IF( (key == "a"), 220.00, 233.10) )
    ELSEIF key$"b"
       RETURN( 246.90 )
    ELSEIF key$"CC#"
       RETURN( IF( (key == "C"), 261.70, 277.20) )
    ELSEIF key$"DD#"
       RETURN( IF( (key == "D"), 293.70, 311.10) )
    ELSEIF key="E"
       RETURN( 329.60 )
    ELSEIF key$"FF#"
       RETURN( IF( (key == "F"), 349.20, 370.00) )
    ELSEIF key$"GG#"
       RETURN( IF( (key == "G"), 392.00, 415.30) )
    ELSEIF key$"AA#"
       RETURN( IF( (key == "A"), 440.00, 466.20) )
    ELSEIF key$"B"
       RETURN( 493.90 )
    ENDIF
```

TIME()

Syntax: TIME()

Pass: Nothing

Return: <character expression>

Description: This function returns the system time represented as a character string.

Function: Standard

Source: Clipper.lib

Sample:

```
CLEAR
? TIME()
? SUBSTR(TIME(),1,2)
```

TRANSFORM()

Syntax: TRANSFORM(<exp>, <expC>)

Pass: <character expression>/<numeric expression>,<picture expression>

Return: <character expression>

Description: This function returns <exp> in the format of the picture expression passed to the function as <expC>.

Function: Standard

Source: Clipper.lib

Notes: All picture options available in an @...SAY/GET command are also available with the TRANSFORM() function.

The <exp> can be either a numeric expression or a character expression.

This function is extremely useful for formatting output to alternate files to appear as the output would look on the screen or printer.

Sample:

```
? TRANSFORM(3242312.23, "$ ###,###,###.##)
```

TRIM()

Syntax: TRIM(<expC>)

Pass: <character expression>

Return: <character expression>

Description: This function returns <expC> with any trailing blank spaces removed.

Function: Standard

Source: Clipper.lib

Note: With the Summer '87 release, the maximum string capacity for this function is set to 64K in length.

Sample:

```
STORE "This is a test          " TO test
? LEN(test)
? test + "to see where the end is."
? LEN(TRIM(test))
? TRIM(test) + "to see where the end is."
*
* And now for proper format...
*
? TRIM(test) + " " + "to see where the end is."
```

TSTRING()

Syntax: TSTRING(<expN>)

Pass: <numeric expression>

Return: <character expression>

Description: This function yields a time string of <expN> seconds.

Function: Clipper simulated - Autumn '86
Clipper enhanced - Summer '87

Source: Extenddb.prg - Autumn '86
EXTEND.LIB - Summer '87

Autumn '86: In order to use this function, the EXTENDDB.PRG file must be compiled and linked in with your application and must appear in your link list with all other .OBJ files.

TYPE()

Syntax: TYPE(<expC>)

Pass: <character expression>

Return: <character expression>

Description: This function returns a single character code that indicates the data type of <expC> as follows:

```
Character   =   C
Numeric     =   N
Date        =   D
Logical     =   L
Memo        =   M
Array       =   A
Undefined   =   U
```

Function: Standard

Source: Clipper.lib

Variance: In the Summer '87 release, there are a few more added returned values for this function. They are as follows:

Returned Type	Meaning
UE	UE error (Syntactical Error)
UI	UI error (Indeterminate Error)

This allows the TYPE() function to test specified expressions as well as specific variable data types.

Notes: This function is used to test the existence of a variable field or expression.

If an array subscript is passed to the function, it returns the code for the type of that element.

Sample:

```
? TYPE("indate")
STORE DATE() TO indate
? TYPE("indate")
DECLARE indate[4]
```

```
? TYPE("indate")
? TYPE("indate[1]")
IF TYPE("outdate")="U"
  ? "outdate does not exist"
ELSE
  ? TYPE("outdate")
ENDIF
```

UPDATED()

Syntax: UPDATED()

Pass: Nothing

Return: < logical expression >

Description: This function tests if the last READ command changed any of the data associated with the appropriate GETs. If so, this function returns a logical true (.T.); otherwise, a false (.F.) is returned.

Function: Clipper enhanced

Source: Clipper.lib

Sample:

```
********************
* Name          UPSHOW.prg
* Date          August 6, 1986
* Notice        Copyright 1986, Stephen J. Straley
* Compile       Clipper Upshow
* Release       All versions
* Link          Plink86 fi Upshow lib clipper;
* Note          This program shows the use of the UPDATED()
*               function.
*
********************

CREATE Fire
USE Fire
APPEND BLANK
REPLACE field_name WITH "TEMP", field_type WITH "N"
REPLACE field_len WITH 10
USE
CREATE Ash FROM Fire
USE Ash
FOR x = 1 TO 30
   APPEND BLANK
   REPLACE temp WITH x
NEXT
STORE 1 TO whichone
```

```
DO WHILE .T.
CLEAR
    @ 10,20 SAY "Which Record to get ... " GET whichone RANGE 0,30
    READ
    IF whichone = 0
       EXIT
    ENDIF
    GO whichone
    @ 12,20 GET temp
 READ

    ******************************************************
    * The following is the actual demonstration of the *
    * use of the UPDATED() function.                   *
    ******************************************************

      IF UPDATED()
      @ 21,10 SAY "Now Indexing the File"
      INDEX ON temp TO Ash
   ELSE
      @ 21,10 SAY "No need to index ... not updated..."
   ENDIF

   WAIT
ENDDO
ERASE Ash.dbf
ERASE Ash.ntx
ERASE Fire.dbf
```

UPPER()

Syntax: UPPER(<expC>)

Pass: <character expression>

Return: <character expression>

Description: This function converts <expC> to uppercase characters.

Function: Standard

Source: Clipper.lib

Note: With the Summer '87 release, the maximum string capacity for this function is set to 64K in length.

Sample:

```
? UPPER("Nothing like 20 times faster!!")
```

USED()

Syntax: USED()

Pass: Nothing

Return: < logical expression >

Description: The USED() function returns a logical true (.T.) if the database file is in USE in the current work area.

Function: Clipper enhanced - Summer '87

Source: Clipper.lib

Note: This function was added to help with some networking difficulties.

VAL()

Syntax: VAL(< expC >)

Pass: < character expression >

Return: < numeric expression >

Description: This function converts any number previously defined as a character expression (< expC >) into a numeric expression.

Function: Standard

Source: Clipper.lib

Notes: Any nonnumeric character expression is evaluated as a zero (0). In Clipper, the VAL() function will also display the decimal portion of a number.

Sample:

```
? VAL("Clipper")
? VAL("390.9095")
? VAL("20")
```

VERSION()

Syntax: VERSION()

Pass: Nothing

Return: <character expression>

Description: This function always returns "Clipper, Autumn '86" for the Autumn '86 release and "Clipper, Summer '87" for the Summer '87 release.

Function: Clipper simulated - Autumn '86
Clipper enhanced - Summer '87

Source: Extenddb.prg - Autumn '86
Extend.lib - Summer '87

Autumn '86: In order to use this function, the EXTENDDB.PRG file must be compiled and linked in with your application and must appear in your link list with all other .OBJ files.

WORD()

Syntax: CALL <procedure> WITH WORD(<expN>)

Pass: <numeric expression>

Return: <character expression>

Description: This function converts a numeric parameter (<expN>), passed to a CALLed routine or procedure, from a data type DOUBLE to a type INT, thus reducing the CALLed routine's overhead.

Function: Clipper enhanced

Source: Clipper.lib

Notes: Keep in mind that if the value of <expN> does not fall within the range of -32K to +32K, there is no need to pass a larger parameter. **Do not use** WORD() if the variable is beyond this range!

YEAR()

Syntax: YEAR(<expD>)

Pass: <date expression>

Return: <numeric expression>

Description: The YEAR() function returns the numeric value for the year in <expD>.

Function: Standard

Source: Clipper.lib

Sample:

```
STORE DATE() TO indate
CLEAR
? YEAR(indate)
? YEAR(DATE() + 300)
```

CHAPTER SIX

DBEDIT(): List Box, Browsing, and More

While the Autumn '86 release added a new dimension to the core language with the DBU library, it still was too rough to manage simply and to incorporate into applications. Specifically, the DBEDIT() function gave programmers a crude ability to browse on open and active databases. However, with the Summer '87 release, the DBEDIT() function was greatly expanded and enhanced; it also incorporated everything, including new array functions, into one EXTEND.LIB file. Some of the basic differences between the Autumn '86 and Summer '87 releases of the DBEDIT() function are in the various "modes," user-defined functions accessible by DBEDIT(), and new window formatting techniques. Most of these enhancements, mainly pertaining to the use of the user-defined functions, can work with previous version of DBEDIT() in conjunction with the SET KEY TO command. Nevertheless, the Summer '87 version of DBEDIT() is not only easy to use, but it is functional and applicable in many ways and in many applications.

The first five parameters are basically the same in both versions: four window coordinates and an array containing the field names of the database being browsed. Creating that array and filling it with the appropriate values is relatively simple. First, open the desired database, then declare an array to be the size of the number of fields within that selected database. This is accomplished via the FCOUNT() function. Finally, fill the array with the names of the fields with the FIELDNAME() function. A sample code extract is as follows:

```
USE Clients
DECLARE dataset1[FCOUNT()]
FOR x = 1 TO FCOUNT()
   dataset1[x] = FIELDNAME(x)
NEXT
```

Using this in conjunction with the DBEDIT() function, a window area for the function may be generated by passing the top, left, bottom, right coordinates, along with the array of field descriptors. The actual call to the DBEDIT() function would look something like this:

```
DBEDIT(10,5,20,75,dataset1)
```

Scrolling through the database and across the fields is handled automatically by the DBEDIT() function. Additional parameters are accepted with the Summer '87 release.

The next allowed parameter is the name of a user-defined function that must be programmed for. Neither the parentheses nor any parameters are allowed to be included with this parameter. Only the root name of the function may be passed. Programming a function allows for many options. Keystrokes may be captured, file conditions checked, and field values cross-referenced and evaluated. Data entry also may be allowed.

Performing all of these operations will occur within the user-defined function so long as the function is adequately programed to handle all keystroke, field values, and database and mode conditions. Along with the root name of that user-defined function, DBEDIT() passes two parameters automatically to the function. The first parameter is the "mode" or status condition of the DBEDIT() function. The second parameter is the field number the DBEDIT() function is currently working on. Using this, the call to DBEDIT() would look like this:

```
DBEDIT(10,5,20,75,dataset1, "DBFUNC1")
```

And a sample extract of the user-defined function would look something like this:

```
**********************

FUNCTION Dbfunc1

  PARAMETERS pf1, pf2

  IF pf1 = 0          && Idle
    RETURN(1)
  ELSEIF pr1 = 3      && Database is empty
    RETURN(0)
  ENDIF

  keyval = LASTKEY()

  DO CASE
    CASE keyval = 5 .AND. pf1 = 1
      @ 18,00 SAY "Beginning of File"
      RETURN(1)
    CASE keyval = 23 .AND. pf1 = 2
      @ 18,00 SAY "End of File      "
      RETURN(1)
    CASE keyval = 27  && The ESC Key
      RETURN(0)
    CASE keyval = 13  && The RETURN Key
      temp = FIELDNAME(pf2)
      @ 23,00 SAY "Enter New Value => " GET &temp.
      READ
      RETURN(1)
    OTHERWISE
      @ 18,00 SAY "                 "
      RETURN(2)
  ENDCASE
```

The first parameter passed to the user-defined function is the status, or mode, of the DBEDIT() function. The following is a table of the values the user-defined function will expect to evaluate.

Mode (pf1 =)	Description
0	DBEDIT() is currently idle; all cursor key movements have been handled; no keystrokes are pending.
1	Attempt to cursor past BOF().
2	Attempt to cursor past EOF().
3	Database is empty.
4	Keystroke exception.

The other thing to keep in mind is the value DBEDIT() is expecting to be returned from the user-defined function. The RETURN values within the user-defined function may have three possible values. Listed below is a table of those possible values and their respective meanings.

RETURN (value)	Description
0	Quit DBEDIT().
1	Continue DBEDIT() as is.
2	Continue DBEDIT(), force data to be reread, and repaint the screen.
3	Append Mode, splits screen to allow data to be appended in windowed area. This is a system-wide toggle.

The user-defined function above tests to see if the key hit was the ENTER key and if so, it allows the user to enter new information pertaining to the field number in pf2. The reason the FIELDNAME(pf2) must be passed to a temporary variable **before** the GET command is because a macro cannot be performed directly on any function.

After the user-defined function, six more parameters may be passed to DBEDIT(); all are of array data types or of character data types. Some or these parameters may take an <expC> as a global meaning for all possible values in the array, if it were passed instead. A brief description on the meanings of those extra parameters follows.

The next parameter is an array containing the PICTURE format to be used for each displayed field. A global value may be passed instead of an array, which thus applies to all fields displayed. A string containing the global PICTURE string may be used instead of an array of PICTURE strings. To allow DBEDIT() to use default PICTURE string values, pass a null string ("") as this parameter. Using this parameter, the correct syntax would look something like this:

```
DBEDIT(10,5,20,75,dataset1, "DBFUNC1", "@B 999,999,999,999.99")
```

Specifying a numeric PICTURE string for a character field value will cause the displayed values to adhere to the numeric PICTURE format. Make sure that the passed PICTURE array or string corresponds to either each individual field value or all field values within the database.

Following this parameter is an array for the column headings for each field to be displayed. If not used, the actual name of the field will be used as the column heading. Using this parameter, the correct syntax would look something like this:

```
   DECLARE columns[FCOUNT()]
   FOR x = 1 TO FCOUNT()
      columns[x] = UPPER(SUBSTR(FIELDNAME(x), 1, 1)) + LOWER(SUBSTR(FIELDNAME(x),
2))
   NEXT
   DBEDIT(10,5,20,75,dataset1, "DBFUNC1", "@B 999,999,999,999.99", columns)
```

The next parameter that may be passed to the DBEDIT() function is either an array or <expC> containing the lines to separate the headings and the actual field displayed area. Using this parameter, the correct syntax would look something like this:

```
DBEDIT(10,5,20,75, dataset1, "DBFUNC1", "@B 999,999,999,999.99",;
columns, CHR(205))
```

Following this parameter is either an array or a character expression containing the characters to separate each displayed field. Again, if a specific <expC> is passed instead of an array, that string value will be used throughout the DBEDIT() function. Using this parameter, the correct syntax would look something like this:

```
DBEDIT (10,5,20,75, dataset1, "DBFUNC1", "@B 999,999,999,999.99",;
columns, CHR(205), " | ")
```

The next parameter that may be passed to the DBEDIT() function is either an array or <expC> containing the lines to separate the footings and the actual field displayed area. Using this parameter, the correct syntax would look something like this:

```
DBEDIT(10,5,20,75,dataset1, "DBFUNC1", "@B 999,999,999,999.99",;
columns, CHR(205), " | ", CHR(205))
```

Finally, the last possible parameter to pass to DBEDIT() is either an array or a character expression containing the footing text for each displayed field column. If the footing text is to carry onto more than one line, the array element or the <expC> must contain a semicolon where the line break is to occur.

Keep in mind that both the header text and the footer text will be placed within the designated windowed area for DBEDIT(). When using footer text and multiple-lined foot text, the text will take up the room otherwise used to display field information. In other words, if a footer takes up three lines, three lines will be set aside by DBEDIT() within the windowed area, and thus, three lines of field information will not be displayed.

Tips When Using DBEDIT()

Obviously, trial and error has been the method for developing a series of adequate tips when using the DBEDIT() function. Listed below are the just a few of those findings.

1. Make sure that the array containing the field names that is passed to the DBEDIT() function matches the currently selected and open database. Otherwise, an "unidentified macro" will occur at line 0, in the DBEDIT() function.

2. Normal screen handling methods do not apply to the DBEDIT() function. This means that the ROW() and COL() function will not return the last relative screen position of the cursor; rather, they return the bottom right corner of the screen.

3. There must be legitimate filled values for all array elements in the array containing the names of the fields. If a function or a user-defined function is desired and the array element is **not** filled with that functions name, like the name of a field, DBEDIT() will not work and will return a logical false. In the example below, if you remove the a1[1] = "RECNO()" command line and just call the DBEDIT() as specified, an error will occur.

4. There may be multiple calls for a DBEDIT() function; however, multiple calls to the user-defined function called by DBEDIT() will not work.

5. User-defined functions, as well as conventional functions, may be passed to DBEDIT() in the same way as a field name. Parameters for the function are allowed so long as they do not need to be individually evaluated. For example, VAL(FIELD(3)) is not allowed but VAL(A->str_amount) is permitted. In the case of a user-defined function, be sure that the function is defined in the application. Otherwise, a run-time error will occur.

6. Keystrokes may be individually captured and reset within the user-defined function called be the DBEDIT() function.

7. PROMPT and GET commands, embedded within the user-defined function, work as expected within the DBEDIT() function.

8. If using the APPEND MODE toggle, make sure that all keystrokes are properly programmed to handle this special condition and that upon completion of any appended operation, the toggle is set back to its default condition (off).

What Can DBEDIT() Really Do?

Below is a sample of the potential of the DBEDIT() function. Key areas to note are the RECNO() function being used, multiple calls to the DBEDIT() function, using the

SET RELATION command and multiple databases in conjunction with the DBEDIT() function, a GET within the DBEDIT(), and a few others as well.

```
**********************
* Name      Db_show.prg
* Author    Stephen J. Straley
* Notice    Copyright (c) 1988 Stephen J. Straley & Associates
* Date      February 29, 1988
* Compile   Clipper  Db_show -m
* Release   Summer '87
* Link      Mslink db_show,,,extend + clipper/se:1024,,;
* Note      This demonstration program shows all of the new advantages
*           of the new DBEDIT() function.
**********************

SET SCOREBOARD OFF
DO Makefiles
CLOSE ALL

SELECT 3
USE Statcode
INDEX ON status TO Statcode
GO TOP
DECLARE a3[FCOUNT()]
FOR x = 1 TO FCOUNT()
   a3[x] = FIELD(x)
NEXT

SELECT 2
USE Trans
INDEX ON account TO Trans
GO TOP

DECLARE a2[FCOUNT()]
FOR x = 1 TO LEN(a2)
   a2[x] = FIELD(x)
NEXT

SELECT 1
USE Clients
INDEX ON account TO Clients
SET RELATION TO account INTO trans, TO status INTO statcode
GO TOP

DECLARE a1[FCOUNT()+ 1], names[FCOUNT()+1], picture[FCOUNT()+1], footer[FCOUNT()+1]

AFILL(footer, "")
footer[1] = "This Field;Can not be;modified!"
a1[1] = "RECNO()"
names[1] = "Record #"

FOR x = 2 TO LEN(a1)
  a1[x] = field(x-1)
```

```
  names[x] = UPPERLOWER(field(x-1))
  names[x] = names[x] + SPACE(20 - LEN(names[x]))
NEXT
a1[2] = "C->DESCRIPT"
a1[16]= "ALOGIC()"
AFILL(picture, SPACE(30))
picture[11] = "$ 999,999,999,999.99          "
CLEAR SCREEN
@ 0, 2  SAY "Field Titles                Picture Strings"
FOR y = 2 TO LEN(names)
   @ y-1, 1 GET names[y] PICT "XXXXXXXXXXXXXXX"
   @ y-1, 25 GET picture[y]
NEXT
READ
FOR y = 2 TO LEN(names)
   names[y] = MESS_CENT(ALLTRIM(UPPERLOWER(names[y])), 20)
   picture[y] = ALLTRIM(picture[y])
NEXT
picture[1] = "@B"

CLEAR SCREEN
KEYBOARD CHR(19)

@ 0,0 SAY "Browse Client Account."
@ 0,63 SAY "F1 for Keystrokes"
@ 1,0 SAY REPLICATE("═", 80)
db_bottom = 12
DO WHILE .T.
   BEGIN SEQUENCE
   DBEDIT(2,1,db_bottom,79,a1, "func1", picture, names, "═", " │ ", "═", footer)
   EXIT
   END
ENDDO
CLEAR SCREEN

***************

FUNCTION Func1

   PARAMETERS p1, p2

   value = LASTKEY()

   IF p2 = 1
      KEYBOARD CHR(4)
   ENDIF

   DO CASE
      CASE value = -9
         SAVE SCREEN
         old_color = SETCOLOR()
         IF ISCOLOR()
            SET COLOR TO W/B
```

```
      ENDIF
      @ 7, 10 CLEAR TO 14, 60
      @ 7, 10 TO 14, 60
      IF p2 <> 2
         SELECT 2
         ret_rec = RECNO()
         SET FILTER TO B->account = A->account
         tally = 0.00
         SUM now_due TO tally
         @ 15,24 SAY "Total = " + TRANSFORM(tally, "999,999,999.99")
      ELSE
         SELECT 3
         ret_rec = RECNO()
      ENDIF
      DBEDIT(8, 11, 13, 59, IF(p1 = 2, "a3", "a2"), "func2")
      SET FILTER TO
      GOTO ret_rec
      SELECT 1
      RESTORE SCREEN
      SET COLOR TO &old_color.
      RETURN(1)

   CASE value = 27
      RETURN(0)
   CASE CHR(value)$"Rr"
      @ 24,00 SAY "Enter Bottom Row => " GET db_bottom VALID db_bottom > 7 .AND.
db_bottom <= 22
      READ
      @ 2,0 CLEAR
      BREAK
   CASE value = 28
      ttscrn = SAVESCREEN(8,12,20,67)
      @ 8,12 CLEAR TO 19,67
      @ 8,12 TO 19,67 DOUBLE
      @  9,15 SAY "ESC to Quit DBEDIT()"
      @ 11,15 SAY "F1   -  This screen"
      @ 12,15 SAY "F10 -  Another DBEDIT() / Detailed Information"
      @ 13,15 SAY "ALT A - Add Record to database"
      @ 14,15 SAY "ALT E - Edit Record currently selected by DBEDIT()"
      @ 15,15 SAY "ALT V - View Record currently selected by DBEDIT()"
      @ 16,15 SAY "ALT S - Search for a value"
      @ 17,15 SAY "All Arrow and Directional Keys default as expected"
      @ 18,15 SAY "R/r to Resize
      @ 19,13 SAY "Any Key to Continue..."
      INKEY(0)
      RESTSCREEN(8,12,20,67,ttscrn)
      CALL __cclr
      RETURN(1)
   CASE value = 287
      SET CURSOR ON
      search = SPACE(LEN(A->account))
      @ 24,00 SAY "Enter Account Number to go to => " GET search
      READ
```

```
      search = ALLTRIM(search)
      SEEK search
      @ 24,00 CLEAR
      SET CURSOR OFF
      RETURN(1)
   CASE value = 286
      @ 23,00 SAY "Would you like to Add a record? "
      IF VERIFY()
         SELECT 2
         APPEND BLANK
         SELECT 1
         APPEND BLANK
         SET CURSOR ON
         SAVE SCREEN
         old_color = SETCOLOR()
         IF ISCOLOR()
            SET COLOR TO W/GR
         ENDIF
         DO The_record WITH 3
         READ
         REPLACE B->account WITH A->account
         SET COLOR TO &old_color.
         SET CURSOR OFF
         RESTORE SCREEN
         CALL __cclr
      ENDIF
      @ 23,00 SAY "                                        "
      RETURN(2)
   CASE value = 274
      SAVE SCREEN
      SET CURSOR ON
      old_color = SETCOLOR()
      IF ISCOLOR()
         SET COLOR TO W/R
      ENDIF
      DO The_record WITH 2
      @ 24,00 SAY "Press ESC to Quit Edit Mode and to Return."
      READ
      SET COLOR TO &old_color.
      SET CURSOR OFF
      RESTORE SCREEN
      RETURN(2)
   CASE value = 303
      old_color = SETCOLOR()
      IF ISCOLOR()
         SET COLOR TO W+/RB
      ENDIF
      SAVE SCREEN
      DO The_record
      CLEAR GETS
      @ 24,00 SAY "Press ESC to Return to Browse Mode."
      DO WHILE INKEY(0) <> 27
      ENDDO
```

```
          SET COLOR TO &old_color.
          RESTORE SCREEN
          RETURN(1)
       CASE KEYS(value)

          DO CASE
             CASE value = 19          && The first field is OFF limits!
                IF p2 = 1
                   KEYBOARD CHR(4)
                ENDIF
             CASE (value = 5 .OR. value = 24)
                IF p1 = 1
                   @ 24,00 SAY " [ Top of File ]"
                ELSEIF p1 = 2
                   @ 24,00 SAY " [ Bottom of File ] "
                ELSE
                   @ 24,00 SAY "                       "
                ENDIF
          ENDCASE

          RETURN(1)

       OTHERWISE
          @ 23,00 SAY "Invalid Keystroke.  Any Key to Try Again..."
          @ 24,00 SAY value
          INKEY(0)
          @ 23,0 CLEAR
          return(1)
    ENDCASE

********************

FUNCTION Keys

   PARAMETERS the_val

   IF the_val = 5
      RETURN(.T.)
   ELSEIF the_val = 13
      RETURN(.T.)
   ELSEIF the_val = 4
      RETURN(.T.)
   ELSEIF the_val = 24
      RETURN(.T.)
   ELSEIF the_val = 19
      RETURN(.T.)
   ELSEIF the_val = 3
      RETURN(.T.)
   ELSEIF the_val = 18
      RETURN(.T.)
   ELSEIF the_val = 6
      RETURN(.T.)
   ELSEIF the_val = 1
```

```
      RETURN(.T.)
   ELSEIF the_val = 29
      KEYBOARD CHR(4)
      RETURN(.T.)
   ELSEIF the_val = 23
      RETURN(.T.)
   ELSE
      RETURN(.F.)
   ENDIF

*********************

PROCEDURE The_record

   PARAMETERS rec_way

   IF PCOUNT() = 0
      rec_way = 1
   ENDIF

   CLEAR SCREEN
   @ 1,0 TO 22,78 DOUBLE
   @ 1, 1 SAY "  " + IF(rec_way = 1, "View", IF(rec_way = 2, "Edit", "Add")) + " -
Only Mode  "
   FOR qaz = 1 TO FCOUNT()
       temp = FIELD(qaz)
       @ qaz+ IF((rec_way = 3), 1, 2) , RIGHT_JUST(UPPERLOWER(FIELD(qaz)), 20) SAY
UPPERLOWER(FIELD(qaz)) + " ë "  GET &temp.
   NEXT
   start_here = ROW()
   IF rec_way = 3   && Add mode, add to account file as well
      SELECT 2
      FOR y = 2 TO FCOUNT()
         temp = "B->" + FIELD(y)
         @ start_here + y, RIGHT_JUST(UPPERLOWER(FIELD(y)), 20) SAY UPPER-
LOWER(FIELD(y)) + " ë "  GET &temp.
      NEXT
      SELECT 1
   ENDIF

********************

FUNCTION Func2

   PARAMETERS q1, q2

   newvalue = LASTKEY()

   DO CASE
      CASE newvalue = 27
         CALL __cclr
         RETURN(0)
      CASE newvalue = 28
```

```
    ttscrn = SAVESCREEN(8,12,19,67)
    @ 8,12 CLEAR TO 19,67
    @ 8,12 TO 19,67 DOUBLE
    @  9,15 SAY "ESC to Quit DBEDIT()"
    @ 11,15 SAY "F1   -  This screen"
    @ 12,15 SAY "F10 -  Another DBEDIT() / Detailed Information"
    @ 13,15 SAY "ALT A - Add Record to database"
    @ 14,15 SAY "ALT E - Edit Record currently selected by DBEDIT()"
    @ 15,15 SAY "ALT V - View Record currently selected by DBEDIT()"
    @ 16,15 SAY "All Arrow and Directional Keys default as expected"
    @ 18,13 SAY "Any Key to Continue..."
    INKEY(0)
    RESTSCREEN(8,12,19,67,ttscrn)
    CALL __cclr
    RETURN(1)
 CASE newvalue = -8
    IF SELECT() = 3
       REPLACE A->status WITH C->status
       KEYBOARD CHR(27)
    ENDIF
    RETURN(1)
 CASE newvalue = 286
    @ 24,00 SAY "Would you like to Add a Record? "
    IF VERIFY()
       @ 24,00 SAY "                                          "
       APPEND BLANK
       SET CURSOR ON
       backscrn = SAVESCREEN(12,10,22,75)
       IF SELECT() = 3
          DO Codescr WITH "Add"
       ELSE
          REPLACE B->account WITH A->account, B->adate WITH DATE()
          DO Transscr WITH "Add"
       ENDIF
       READ
       RESTSCREEN(12,10,22,75,backscrn)
       IF SELECT() = 2
          tally = tally + B->now_due
          @ 15,24 SAY "Total = " + TRANSFORM(tally, "999,999,999.99")
       ENDIF
       SET CURSOR OFF
    ELSE
       @ 24,00 SAY "                                          "
    ENDIF
    KEYBOARD ""
    RETURN(2)
 CASE (value = 5 .OR. value = 24)
    IF q1 = 1
       @ 18,00 SAY " [ Top of File ]"
    ELSEIF q1 = 2
       @ 18,00 SAY " [ Bottom of File ] "
    ELSE
       @ 18,00 SAY "                    "
```

```
        ENDIF

      OTHERWISE
        CALL __cclr
        RETURN(1)
   ENDCASE

********************

FUNCTION Alogic

   RETURN(IF(A->paired, "Yes", "No "))

*********************

PROCEDURE Codescr

   PARAMETERS codeway

   @ 12, 20 CLEAR TO 16, 70
   @ 12, 20 TO 16, 70 DOUBLE
   @ 12, 22 SAY " &codeway. "
   FOR y = 1 TO FCOUNT()
      ntemp = FIELD(y)
      @ 13+y, RIGHT_JUST(FIELD(y), 37) SAY UPPERLOWER(FIELD(y)) + " => " GET
&ntemp.
   NEXT


********************

PROCEDURE Transscr

   PARAMETERS transway

   @ 14, 25 CLEAR TO 21, 65
   @ 14, 25 TO 21, 65 DOUBLE
   @ 14,27 SAY " &transway. "
   FOR y = IF(transway = "Add", 2, 1) TO FCOUNT()
      ntemp = FIELD(y)
      @ 15+y, RIGHT_JUST(FIELD(y), 38) SAY UPPERLOWER(FIELD(y)) + " = " GET
&ntemp.
   NEXT

*********************

PROCEDURE Makefiles

   CLEAR SCREEN
   ? "File One"
   CREATE Temp
   USE Temp
   DO Ap_it WITH "STATUS",  "C", 1,0
```

```
DO Ap_it WITH "ACCOUNT", "C", 6,0
DO Ap_it WITH "NAME",    "C",25,0
DO Ap_it WITH "ADDRESS1","C",20,0
DO Ap_it WITH "ADDRESS2","C",20,0
DO Ap_it WITH "CITY",    "C",15,0
DO Ap_it WITH "STATE",   "C", 2,0
DO Ap_it WITH "ZIP",     "C", 9,0
DO Ap_it WITH "CURRENT", "N",16,2
DO Ap_it WITH "DUE",     "N",16,2
DO Ap_it WITH "PHONE",   "C",14,0
DO Ap_it WITH "CONTACT", "C", 5,0
DO Ap_it WITH "INDATE",  "C", 6,0
DO Ap_it WITH "ACTIVE",  "C", 1,0
DO Ap_it WITH "PAIRED",  "L", 1,0
CREATE Clients FROM Temp
USE Clients
APPEND BLANK
REPLACE status WITH "3", account WITH "100000", name WITH "Nantucket Corporation
"
REPLACE address1 WITH "1255 Jefferson Blvd", city WITH "Los Angeles    ", state
WITH "CA"
REPLACE zip WITH "90066", current WITH 1000.00, due WITH 23.00, phone WITH "1-
800-231-1521"
REPLACE contact WITH "Ray", paired WITH .F.
APPEND BLANK
REPLACE status WITH "1", account WITH "200000", name WITH "Stephen Straley & As-
soc. "
REPLACE address1 WITH "319 Barrow Street", address2 WITH "Suite 7B"
REPLACE city WITH "Jersey City", state WITH "NJ", zip WITH "07302"
REPLACE current WITH 230000.00, due WITH 12.00, phone WITH "1-201-432-8189"
REPLACE contact WITH "Steve", paired WITH .F.
APPEND BLANK
REPLACE status WITH "6", account WITH "200001", name WITH "Falcon Software, Ltd.
"
REPLACE address1 WITH "319 Barrow - Ste 7B "
REPLACE city WITH "Jersey City", state WITH "NJ", zip WITH "07302"
REPLACE current WITH 200.00, due WITH 2.00, phone WITH "1-201-432-8189"
REPLACE contact WITH "Steve", paired WITH .T.
APPEND BLANK
REPLACE status WITH "1", account WITH "200010", name WITH "Number One Software"
REPLACE current WITH 2.00, due WITH 1221.00, paired WITH .F.
APPEND BLANK
REPLACE status WITH "3", account WITH "300000", name WITH "Ashton-Tate"
REPLACE current WITH 23.00, due WITH 13.00, paired WITH .F.
APPEND BLANK
REPLACE status WITH "1", account WITH "323333", name WITH "Lotus Development"
REPLACE current WITH 14525.00, due WITH 2313.00, paired WITH .T.
APPEND BLANK
REPLACE status WITH "1", account WITH "352231", name WITH "Microsoft, Corp."
REPLACE current WITH 7472374.00, due WITH 8482348.00, paired WITH .F.
APPEND BLANK
REPLACE status WITH "1", account WITH "400000", name WITH "IBM"
REPLACE current WITH 8237.00, due WITH 76674.00, paired WITH .F.
```

```
APPEND BLANK
REPLACE status WITH "2", account WITH "511001", name WITH "Panasonic"
REPLACE current WITH 1625.00, due WITH 95945.00, paired WITH .T.
APPEND BLANK
REPLACE status WITH "1", account WITH "610000", name WITH "Sony"
REPLACE current WITH 0.00, due WITH 0.00, paired WITH .T.
APPEND BLANK
REPLACE status WITH "2", account WITH "714442", name WITH "Tandy International"
REPLACE current WITH 0.00, due WITH 0.00, paired WITH .T.
APPEND BLANK
REPLACE status WITH "1", account WITH "740000", name WITH "Texaco Limited"
REPLACE current WITH 0.00, due WITH 0.00, paired WITH .F.
APPEND BLANK
REPLACE status WITH "4", account WITH "830000", name WITH "Magnus Production"
REPLACE current WITH 0.00, due WITH 0.00, paired WITH .F.
APPEND BLANK
REPLACE status WITH "1", account WITH "831000", name WITH "MacIntosh Corp."
REPLACE current WITH 0.00, due WITH 0.00, paired WITH .F.
APPEND BLANK
REPLACE status WITH "1", account WITH "845500", name WITH "Hayes MicroComputer"
REPLACE current WITH 0.00, due WITH 0.00, paired WITH .F.
APPEND BLANK
REPLACE status WITH "8", account WITH "860000", name WITH "Sharp Images"
REPLACE current WITH 0.00, due WITH 0.00, paired WITH .F.
APPEND BLANK
REPLACE status WITH "2", account WITH "900000", name WITH "Ford Motorcars"
REPLACE current WITH 0.00, due WITH 0.00, paired WITH .F.
APPEND BLANK
REPLACE status WITH "9", account WITH "910000", name WITH "Chrysler Corporation"
REPLACE current WITH 0.00, due WITH 0.00, paired WITH .F.
APPEND BLANK
REPLACE status WITH "9", account WITH "920000", name WITH "General Motors"
REPLACE current WITH 0.00, due WITH 0.00, paired WITH .F.
APPEND BLANK
REPLACE status WITH "9", account WITH "930000", name WITH "Nisan Motors"
REPLACE current WITH 0.00, due WITH 0.00, paired WITH .F.
APPEND BLANK
REPLACE status WITH "9", account WITH "931000", name WITH "Totyota"
REPLACE current WITH 0.00, due WITH 0.00, paired WITH .F.
APPEND BLANK
REPLACE status WITH "9", account WITH "933100", name WITH "Isuzu"
REPLACE current WITH 0.00, due WITH 0.00, paired WITH .F.
APPEND BLANK
REPLACE status WITH "9", account WITH "935000", name WITH "Honda Motocars"
REPLACE current WITH 0.00, due WITH 0.00, paired WITH .F.
APPEND BLANK
REPLACE status WITH "9", account WITH "939300", name WITH "Subaru"
REPLACE current WITH 0.00, due WITH 0.00, paired WITH .F.
APPEND BLANK
REPLACE status WITH "9", account WITH "940000", name WITH "ABC"
REPLACE current WITH 0.00, due WITH 0.00, paired WITH .F.
APPEND BLANK
REPLACE status WITH "9", account WITH "945000", name WITH "Fox Television "
```

```
    REPLACE current WITH 0.00, due WITH 0.00, paired WITH .F.
    APPEND BLANK
    REPLACE status WITH "9", account WITH "950000", name WITH "NBC"
    REPLACE current WITH 0.00, due WITH 0.00, paired WITH .F.
    APPEND BLANK
    REPLACE status WITH "9", account WITH "955000", name WITH "CBS"
    REPLACE current WITH 0.00, due WITH 0.00, paired WITH .F.
    USE
    ? "File Two"
    CREATE Temp
    USE Temp
    DO Ap_it WITH "ACCOUNT", "C", 6,0
    DO Ap_it WITH "ADATE",   "D", 8,0
    DO Ap_it WITH "NOW_DUE", "N",10,2
    DO Ap_it WITH "PAID",    "L", 1,0
    USE
    CREATE Trans FROM Temp
    USE Trans
    APPEND BLANK
    REPLACE account WITH "100000", adate WITH CTOD("02/18/88"), now_due WITH
25452.23, paid WITH .F.
    APPEND BLANK
    REPLACE account WITH "200000", adate WITH CTOD("02/18/88"), now_due WITH
54512.23, paid WITH .F.
    APPEND BLANK
    REPLACE account WITH "200001", adate WITH CTOD("02/18/88"), now_due WITH
545213.23, paid WITH .F.
    APPEND BLANK
    REPLACE account WITH "200010", adate WITH CTOD("02/18/88"), now_due WITH
5412.23, paid WITH .F.
    APPEND BLANK
    REPLACE account WITH "300000", adate WITH CTOD("02/18/88"), now_due WITH 512.23,
paid WITH .F.
    APPEND BLANK
    REPLACE account WITH "323333", adate WITH CTOD("02/18/88"), now_due WITH
5412.23, paid WITH .F.
    APPEND BLANK
    REPLACE account WITH "352231", adate WITH CTOD("02/18/88"), now_due WITH
5122.32, paid WITH .F.
    APPEND BLANK
    REPLACE account WITH "400000", adate WITH CTOD("02/18/88"), now_due WITH 2.33,
paid WITH .F.
    APPEND BLANK
    REPLACE account WITH "511001", adate WITH CTOD("02/18/88"), now_due WITH 52.36,
paid WITH .F.
    APPEND BLANK
    REPLACE account WITH "610000", adate WITH CTOD("02/18/88"), now_due WITH 3.54,
paid WITH .F.
    APPEND BLANK
    REPLACE account WITH "714442", adate WITH CTOD("02/18/88"), now_due WITH 1.25,
paid WITH .F.
    APPEND BLANK
    REPLACE account WITH "740000", adate WITH CTOD("02/18/88"), now_due WITH 0.01,
paid WITH .F.
```

```
    APPEND BLANK
    REPLACE account WITH "830000", adate WITH CTOD("02/18/88"), now_due WITH 221.22,
paid WITH .F.
    APPEND BLANK
    REPLACE account WITH "831000", adate WITH CTOD("02/18/88"), now_due WITH 84.50,
paid WITH .F.
    APPEND BLANK
    REPLACE account WITH "845500", adate WITH CTOD("02/18/88"), now_due WITH
7014.00, paid WITH .F.
    APPEND BLANK
    REPLACE account WITH "860000", adate WITH CTOD("02/18/88"), now_due WITH 21.00,
paid WITH .F.
    APPEND BLANK
    REPLACE account WITH "900000", adate WITH CTOD("02/18/88"), now_due WITH 7.01,
paid WITH .F.
    APPEND BLANK
    REPLACE account WITH "910000", adate WITH CTOD("02/18/88"), now_due WITH 10.25,
paid WITH .F.
    APPEND BLANK
    REPLACE account WITH "920000", adate WITH CTOD("02/18/88"), now_due WITH 2.50,
paid WITH .F.
    APPEND BLANK
    REPLACE account WITH "930000", adate WITH CTOD("02/18/88"), now_due WITH 6.00,
paid WITH .F.
    APPEND BLANK
    REPLACE account WITH "931000", adate WITH CTOD("02/18/88"), now_due WITH 10.00,
paid WITH .F.
    APPEND BLANK
    REPLACE account WITH "933100", adate WITH CTOD("02/18/88"), now_due WITH 0.01,
paid WITH .F.
    APPEND BLANK
    REPLACE account WITH "935000", adate WITH CTOD("02/18/88"), now_due WITH 24.12,
paid WITH .F.
    APPEND BLANK
    REPLACE account WITH "939300", adate WITH CTOD("02/18/88"), now_due WITH 15.24,
paid WITH .F.
    APPEND BLANK
    REPLACE account WITH "940000", adate WITH CTOD("02/18/88"), now_due WITH 0.12,
paid WITH .F.
    APPEND BLANK
    REPLACE account WITH "945000", adate WITH CTOD("02/18/88"), now_due WITH 5.21,
paid WITH .F.
    APPEND BLANK
    REPLACE account WITH "950000", adate WITH CTOD("02/18/88"), now_due WITH 48.21,
paid WITH .F.
    APPEND BLANK
    REPLACE account WITH "955000", adate WITH CTOD("02/18/88"), now_due WITH 4.21,
paid WITH .F.
    APPEND BLANK
    REPLACE account WITH "100000", adate WITH CTOD("02/18/88"), now_due WITH 47.21,
paid WITH .F.
    APPEND BLANK
    REPLACE account WITH "200000", adate WITH CTOD("02/18/88"), now_due WITH 4.21,
paid WITH .F.
```

```
   APPEND BLANK
   REPLACE account WITH "200001", adate WITH CTOD("02/18/88"), now_due WITH 42.65,
paid WITH .F.
   APPEND BLANK
   REPLACE account WITH "200010", adate WITH CTOD("02/18/88"), now_due WITH 2.21,
paid WITH .F.
   APPEND BLANK
   REPLACE account WITH "300000", adate WITH CTOD("02/18/88"), now_due WITH 4.84,
paid WITH .F.
   APPEND BLANK
   REPLACE account WITH "323333", adate WITH CTOD("02/18/88"), now_due WITH 5.21,
paid WITH .F.
   APPEND BLANK
   REPLACE account WITH "352231", adate WITH CTOD("02/18/88"), now_due WITH 2.14,
paid WITH .F.
   APPEND BLANK
   REPLACE account WITH "400000", adate WITH CTOD("02/18/88"), now_due WITH 78.21,
paid WITH .F.
   APPEND BLANK
   REPLACE account WITH "511001", adate WITH CTOD("02/18/88"), now_due WITH 43.26,
paid WITH .F.
   APPEND BLANK
   REPLACE account WITH "610000", adate WITH CTOD("02/18/88"), now_due WITH 32.12,
paid WITH .F.
   APPEND BLANK
   REPLACE account WITH "714442", adate WITH CTOD("02/18/88"), now_due WITH 34.21,
paid WITH .F.
   APPEND BLANK
   REPLACE account WITH "740000", adate WITH CTOD("02/18/88"), now_due WITH
3721.12, paid WITH .F.
   APPEND BLANK
   REPLACE account WITH "830000", adate WITH CTOD("02/18/88"), now_due WITH 34.71,
paid WITH .F.
   APPEND BLANK
   REPLACE account WITH "831000", adate WITH CTOD("02/18/88"), now_due WITH
29482.72, paid WITH .F.
   APPEND BLANK
   REPLACE account WITH "845500", adate WITH CTOD("02/18/88"), now_due WITH 31.43,
paid WITH .F.
   APPEND BLANK
   REPLACE account WITH "860000", adate WITH CTOD("02/18/88"), now_due WITH 273.13,
paid WITH .F.
   APPEND BLANK
   REPLACE account WITH "900000", adate WITH CTOD("02/18/88"), now_due WITH 243.13,
paid WITH .F.
   APPEND BLANK
   REPLACE account WITH "910000", adate WITH CTOD("02/18/88"), now_due WITH 234.73,
paid WITH .F.
   APPEND BLANK
   REPLACE account WITH "920000", adate WITH CTOD("02/18/88"), now_due WITH
2156.83, paid WITH .F.
   APPEND BLANK
   REPLACE account WITH "930000", adate WITH CTOD("02/18/88"), now_due WITH 22.09,
paid WITH .F.
```

```
   APPEND BLANK
   REPLACE account WITH "931000", adate WITH CTOD("02/18/88"), now_due WITH 542.56,
paid WITH .F.
   APPEND BLANK
   REPLACE account WITH "933100", adate WITH CTOD("02/18/88"), now_due WITH
4273.26, paid WITH .F.
   APPEND BLANK
   REPLACE account WITH "935000", adate WITH CTOD("02/18/88"), now_due WITH 4.32,
paid WITH .F.
   APPEND BLANK
   REPLACE account WITH "939300", adate WITH CTOD("02/18/88"), now_due WITH 36.14,
paid WITH .F.
   APPEND BLANK
   REPLACE account WITH "940000", adate WITH CTOD("02/18/88"), now_due WITH 5.78,
paid WITH .F.
   APPEND BLANK
   REPLACE account WITH "945000", adate WITH CTOD("02/18/88"), now_due WITH 4.95,
paid WITH .F.
   APPEND BLANK
   REPLACE account WITH "950000", adate WITH CTOD("02/18/88"), now_due WITH 1.23,
paid WITH .F.
   APPEND BLANK
   REPLACE account WITH "955000", adate WITH CTOD("02/18/88"), now_due WITH 64.51,
paid WITH .F.
   APPEND BLANK
   REPLACE account WITH "100000", adate WITH CTOD("02/18/88"), now_due WITH 24.20,
paid WITH .F.
   APPEND BLANK
   REPLACE account WITH "200000", adate WITH CTOD("02/18/88"), now_due WITH
2314.21, paid WITH .F.
   APPEND BLANK
   REPLACE account WITH "200001", adate WITH CTOD("02/18/88"), now_due WITH 0.15,
paid WITH .F.
   APPEND BLANK
   REPLACE account WITH "200010", adate WITH CTOD("02/18/88"), now_due WITH 4.26,
paid WITH .F.
   APPEND BLANK
   REPLACE account WITH "300000", adate WITH CTOD("02/18/88"), now_due WITH 1.23,
paid WITH .F.
   APPEND BLANK
   REPLACE account WITH "323333", adate WITH CTOD("02/18/88"), now_due WITH 1.24,
paid WITH .F.
   APPEND BLANK
   REPLACE account WITH "352231", adate WITH CTOD("02/18/88"), now_due WITH 7.25,
paid WITH .F.
   APPEND BLANK
   REPLACE account WITH "400000", adate WITH CTOD("02/18/88"), now_due WITH 8.14,
paid WITH .F.
   APPEND BLANK
   REPLACE account WITH "511001", adate WITH CTOD("02/18/88"), now_due WITH 0.26,
paid WITH .F.
   APPEND BLANK
   REPLACE account WITH "610000", adate WITH CTOD("02/18/88"), now_due WITH 7.19,
paid WITH .F.
```

```
   APPEND BLANK
   REPLACE account WITH "714442", adate WITH CTOD("02/18/88"), now_due WITH 8.23,
paid WITH .F.
   APPEND BLANK
   REPLACE account WITH "740000", adate WITH CTOD("02/18/88"), now_due WITH 47.20,
paid WITH .F.
   APPEND BLANK
   REPLACE account WITH "830000", adate WITH CTOD("02/18/88"), now_due WITH 47.21,
paid WITH .F.
   APPEND BLANK
   REPLACE account WITH "831000", adate WITH CTOD("02/18/88"), now_due WITH 7.23,
paid WITH .F.
   APPEND BLANK
   REPLACE account WITH "845500", adate WITH CTOD("02/18/88"), now_due WITH 47.51,
paid WITH .F.
   APPEND BLANK
   REPLACE account WITH "860000", adate WITH CTOD("02/18/88"), now_due WITH 8.32,
paid WITH .F.
   APPEND BLANK
   REPLACE account WITH "900000", adate WITH CTOD("02/18/88"), now_due WITH 47.22,
paid WITH .F.
   APPEND BLANK
   REPLACE account WITH "910000", adate WITH CTOD("02/18/88"), now_due WITH 1.00,
paid WITH .F.
   APPEND BLANK
   REPLACE account WITH "920000", adate WITH CTOD("02/18/88"), now_due WITH 23.32,
paid WITH .F.
   APPEND BLANK
   REPLACE account WITH "930000", adate WITH CTOD("02/18/88"), now_due WITH 8.00,
paid WITH .F.
   APPEND BLANK
   REPLACE account WITH "931000", adate WITH CTOD("02/18/88"), now_due WITH 0.23,
paid WITH .F.
   APPEND BLANK
   REPLACE account WITH "933100", adate WITH CTOD("02/18/88"), now_due WITH 0.32,
paid WITH .F.
   APPEND BLANK
   REPLACE account WITH "935000", adate WITH CTOD("02/18/88"), now_due WITH 0.32,
paid WITH .F.
   APPEND BLANK
   REPLACE account WITH "939300", adate WITH CTOD("02/18/88"), now_due WITH 5.32,
paid WITH .F.
   APPEND BLANK
   REPLACE account WITH "940000", adate WITH CTOD("02/18/88"), now_due WITH 0.32,
paid WITH .F.
   APPEND BLANK
   REPLACE account WITH "945000", adate WITH CTOD("02/18/88"), now_due WITH 3.32,
paid WITH .F.
   APPEND BLANK
   REPLACE account WITH "950000", adate WITH CTOD("02/18/88"), now_due WITH 3.32,
paid WITH .F.
   APPEND BLANK
   REPLACE account WITH "955000", adate WITH CTOD("02/18/88"), now_due WITH
334273.13, paid WITH .F.
```

```
   APPEND BLANK
   REPLACE account WITH "100000", adate WITH CTOD("02/18/88"), now_due WITH 2.73,
paid WITH .F.
   APPEND BLANK
   REPLACE account WITH "200000", adate WITH CTOD("02/18/88"), now_due WITH
2342.37, paid WITH .F.
   APPEND BLANK
   REPLACE account WITH "200001", adate WITH CTOD("02/18/88"), now_due WITH
32134.13, paid WITH .F.
   APPEND BLANK
   REPLACE account WITH "200010", adate WITH CTOD("02/18/88"), now_due WITH 27.43,
paid WITH .F.
   APPEND BLANK
   REPLACE account WITH "300000", adate WITH CTOD("02/18/88"), now_due WITH
2831314.32, paid WITH .F.
   APPEND BLANK
   REPLACE account WITH "323333", adate WITH CTOD("02/18/88"), now_due WITH
3382.34, paid WITH .F.
   APPEND BLANK
   REPLACE account WITH "352231", adate WITH CTOD("02/18/88"), now_due WITH 231.38,
paid WITH .F.
   APPEND BLANK
   REPLACE account WITH "400000", adate WITH CTOD("02/18/88"), now_due WITH 32.32,
paid WITH .F.
   APPEND BLANK
   REPLACE account WITH "511001", adate WITH CTOD("02/18/88"), now_due WITH 1.00,
paid WITH .F.
   APPEND BLANK
   REPLACE account WITH "610000", adate WITH CTOD("02/18/88"), now_due WITH 2.00,
paid WITH .F.
   APPEND BLANK
   REPLACE account WITH "714442", adate WITH CTOD("02/18/88"), now_due WITH 3.00,
paid WITH .F.
   APPEND BLANK
   REPLACE account WITH "740000", adate WITH CTOD("02/18/88"), now_due WITH 6.00,
paid WITH .F.
   APPEND BLANK
   REPLACE account WITH "830000", adate WITH CTOD("02/18/88"), now_due WITH 4.00,
paid WITH .F.
   APPEND BLANK
   REPLACE account WITH "831000", adate WITH CTOD("02/18/88"), now_due WITH 5.00,
paid WITH .F.
   APPEND BLANK
   REPLACE account WITH "845500", adate WITH CTOD("02/18/88"), now_due WITH 7.00,
paid WITH .F.
   APPEND BLANK
   REPLACE account WITH "860000", adate WITH CTOD("02/18/88"), now_due WITH 85.00,
paid WITH .F.
   APPEND BLANK
   REPLACE account WITH "900000", adate WITH CTOD("02/18/88"), now_due WITH 212.00,
paid WITH .F.
   APPEND BLANK
   REPLACE account WITH "910000", adate WITH CTOD("02/18/88"), now_due WITH 236.00,
paid WITH .F.
```

```
    APPEND BLANK
    REPLACE account WITH "920000", adate WITH CTOD("02/18/88"), now_due WITH 0.31,
paid WITH .F.
    APPEND BLANK
    REPLACE account WITH "930000", adate WITH CTOD("02/18/88"), now_due WITH
2323.00, paid WITH .F.
    APPEND BLANK
    REPLACE account WITH "931000", adate WITH CTOD("02/18/88"), now_due WITH 25.12,
paid WITH .F.
    APPEND BLANK
    REPLACE account WITH "933100", adate WITH CTOD("02/18/88"), now_due WITH 241.74,
paid WITH .F.
    APPEND BLANK
    REPLACE account WITH "935000", adate WITH CTOD("02/18/88"), now_due WITH 32.96,
paid WITH .F.
    APPEND BLANK
    REPLACE account WITH "939300", adate WITH CTOD("02/18/88"), now_due WITH 5.28,
paid WITH .F.
    APPEND BLANK
    REPLACE account WITH "940000", adate WITH CTOD("02/18/88"), now_due WITH 7.23,
paid WITH .F.
    APPEND BLANK
    REPLACE account WITH "945000", adate WITH CTOD("02/18/88"), now_due WITH
425412.36, paid WITH .F.
    APPEND BLANK
    REPLACE account WITH "950000", adate WITH CTOD("02/18/88"), now_due WITH
2475.92, paid WITH .F.
    APPEND BLANK
    REPLACE account WITH "955000", adate WITH CTOD("02/18/88"), now_due WITH 3.65,
paid WITH .F.
    APPEND BLANK
    REPLACE account WITH "100000", adate WITH CTOD("02/18/88"), now_due WITH 0.13,
paid WITH .F.
    APPEND BLANK
    REPLACE account WITH "200000", adate WITH CTOD("02/18/88"), now_due WITH 542.13,
paid WITH .F.
    APPEND BLANK
    REPLACE account WITH "200001", adate WITH CTOD("02/18/88"), now_due WITH 23.00,
paid WITH .F.
    APPEND BLANK
    REPLACE account WITH "200010", adate WITH CTOD("02/18/88"), now_due WITH 64.13,
paid WITH .F.
    APPEND BLANK
    REPLACE account WITH "300000", adate WITH CTOD("02/18/88"), now_due WITH 267.13,
paid WITH .F.
    APPEND BLANK
    REPLACE account WITH "323333", adate WITH CTOD("02/18/88"), now_due WITH 264.13,
paid WITH .F.
    APPEND BLANK
    REPLACE account WITH "352231", adate WITH CTOD("02/18/88"), now_due WITH 721.29,
paid WITH .F.
    APPEND BLANK
    REPLACE account WITH "400000", adate WITH CTOD("02/18/88"), now_due WITH
1542.73, paid WITH .F.
```

```
   APPEND BLANK
   REPLACE account WITH "511001", adate WITH CTOD("02/18/88"), now_due WITH
126437.13, paid WITH .F.
   APPEND BLANK
   REPLACE account WITH "610000", adate WITH CTOD("02/18/88"), now_due WITH 267.13,
paid WITH .F.
   APPEND BLANK
   REPLACE account WITH "714442", adate WITH CTOD("02/18/88"), now_due WITH
2642373.16, paid WITH .F.
   APPEND BLANK
   REPLACE account WITH "740000", adate WITH CTOD("02/18/88"), now_due WITH 2.31,
paid WITH .F.
   APPEND BLANK
   REPLACE account WITH "830000", adate WITH CTOD("02/18/88"), now_due WITH
3165.23, paid WITH .F.
   APPEND BLANK
   REPLACE account WITH "831000", adate WITH CTOD("02/18/88"), now_due WITH
16432.31, paid WITH .F.
   APPEND BLANK
   REPLACE account WITH "845500", adate WITH CTOD("02/18/88"), now_due WITH 9.03,
paid WITH .F.
   APPEND BLANK
   REPLACE account WITH "860000", adate WITH CTOD("02/18/88"), now_due WITH 121.24,
paid WITH .F.
   APPEND BLANK
   REPLACE account WITH "900000", adate WITH CTOD("02/18/88"), now_due WITH 37.12,
paid WITH .F.
   APPEND BLANK
   REPLACE account WITH "910000", adate WITH CTOD("02/18/88"), now_due WITH 31.13,
paid WITH .F.
   APPEND BLANK
   REPLACE account WITH "920000", adate WITH CTOD("02/18/88"), now_due WITH
27912.42, paid WITH .F.
   APPEND BLANK
   REPLACE account WITH "930000", adate WITH CTOD("02/18/88"), now_due WITH
7325.12, paid WITH .F.
   APPEND BLANK
   REPLACE account WITH "931000", adate WITH CTOD("02/18/88"), now_due WITH 14.72,
paid WITH .F.
   APPEND BLANK
   REPLACE account WITH "933100", adate WITH CTOD("02/18/88"), now_due WITH
331324.72, paid WITH .F.
   APPEND BLANK
   REPLACE account WITH "935000", adate WITH CTOD("02/18/88"), now_due WITH 38.53,
paid WITH .F.
   APPEND BLANK
   REPLACE account WITH "939300", adate WITH CTOD("02/18/88"), now_due WITH
4237.13, paid WITH .F.
   APPEND BLANK
   REPLACE account WITH "940000", adate WITH CTOD("02/18/88"), now_due WITH 24.72,
paid WITH .F.
   APPEND BLANK
   REPLACE account WITH "945000", adate WITH CTOD("02/18/88"), now_due WITH
312337.52, paid WITH .F.
```

```
   APPEND BLANK
   REPLACE account WITH "950000", adate WITH CTOD("02/18/88"), now_due WITH 3.15,
paid WITH .F.
   APPEND BLANK
   REPLACE account WITH "955000", adate WITH CTOD("02/18/88"), now_due WITH 67.22,
paid WITH .F.
   APPEND BLANK
   REPLACE account WITH "100000", adate WITH CTOD("02/18/88"), now_due WITH
3328.53, paid WITH .F.
   APPEND BLANK
   REPLACE account WITH "200000", adate WITH CTOD("02/18/88"), now_due WITH
21234.53, paid WITH .F.
   APPEND BLANK
   REPLACE account WITH "200001", adate WITH CTOD("02/18/88"), now_due WITH
28231.23, paid WITH .F.
   APPEND BLANK
   REPLACE account WITH "200010", adate WITH CTOD("02/18/88"), now_due WITH 825.12,
paid WITH .F.
   APPEND BLANK
   REPLACE account WITH "300000", adate WITH CTOD("02/18/88"), now_due WITH
35268.03, paid WITH .F.
   APPEND BLANK
   REPLACE account WITH "323333", adate WITH CTOD("02/18/88"), now_due WITH
1234.72, paid WITH .F.
   APPEND BLANK
   REPLACE account WITH "352231", adate WITH CTOD("02/18/88"), now_due WITH
31235.22, paid WITH .F.
   APPEND BLANK
   REPLACE account WITH "400000", adate WITH CTOD("02/18/88"), now_due WITH
38321.28, paid WITH .F.
   APPEND BLANK
   REPLACE account WITH "511001", adate WITH CTOD("02/18/88"), now_due WITH 32.12,
paid WITH .F.
   APPEND BLANK
   REPLACE account WITH "610000", adate WITH CTOD("02/18/88"), now_due WITH
37235.23, paid WITH .F.
   APPEND BLANK
   REPLACE account WITH "714442", adate WITH CTOD("02/18/88"), now_due WITH
423832.13, paid WITH .F.
   APPEND BLANK
   REPLACE account WITH "740000", adate WITH CTOD("02/18/88"), now_due WITH
21328.22, paid WITH .F.
   APPEND BLANK
   REPLACE account WITH "830000", adate WITH CTOD("02/18/88"), now_due WITH
31325.23, paid WITH .F.
   APPEND BLANK
   REPLACE account WITH "831000", adate WITH CTOD("02/18/88"), now_due WITH
1235.12, paid WITH .F.
   APPEND BLANK
   REPLACE account WITH "845500", adate WITH CTOD("02/18/88"), now_due WITH
3279513.22, paid WITH .F.
   APPEND BLANK
   REPLACE account WITH "860000", adate WITH CTOD("02/18/88"), now_due WITH 321.23,
paid WITH .F.
```

```
   APPEND BLANK
   REPLACE account WITH "900000", adate WITH CTOD("02/18/88"), now_due WITH 423.12,
paid WITH .F.
   APPEND BLANK
   REPLACE account WITH "910000", adate WITH CTOD("02/18/88"), now_due WITH
31564.23, paid WITH .F.
   APPEND BLANK
   REPLACE account WITH "920000", adate WITH CTOD("02/18/88"), now_due WITH
167232.13, paid WITH .F.
   APPEND BLANK
   REPLACE account WITH "930000", adate WITH CTOD("02/18/88"), now_due WITH 6.12,
paid WITH .F.
   APPEND BLANK
   REPLACE account WITH "931000", adate WITH CTOD("02/18/88"), now_due WITH 313.23,
paid WITH .F.
   APPEND BLANK
   REPLACE account WITH "933100", adate WITH CTOD("02/18/88"), now_due WITH 24.28,
paid WITH .F.
   APPEND BLANK
   REPLACE account WITH "935000", adate WITH CTOD("02/18/88"), now_due WITH 742.25,
paid WITH .F.
   APPEND BLANK
   REPLACE account WITH "939300", adate WITH CTOD("02/18/88"), now_due WITH 12.32,
paid WITH .F.
   APPEND BLANK
   REPLACE account WITH "940000", adate WITH CTOD("02/18/88"), now_due WITH
56412.23, paid WITH .F.
   APPEND BLANK
   REPLACE account WITH "945000", adate WITH CTOD("02/18/88"), now_due WITH
52141.23, paid WITH .F.
   APPEND BLANK
   REPLACE account WITH "950000", adate WITH CTOD("02/18/88"), now_due WITH 25.23,
paid WITH .F.
   APPEND BLANK
   REPLACE account WITH "955000", adate WITH CTOD("02/18/88"), now_due WITH 1.25,
paid WITH .F.
   APPEND BLANK
   REPLACE account WITH "100000", adate WITH CTOD("02/18/88"), now_due WITH 2.23,
paid WITH .F.
   APPEND BLANK
   REPLACE account WITH "200000", adate WITH CTOD("02/18/88"), now_due WITH 62.36,
paid WITH .F.
   APPEND BLANK
   REPLACE account WITH "200001", adate WITH CTOD("02/18/88"), now_due WITH 5.21,
paid WITH .F.
   APPEND BLANK
   REPLACE account WITH "200010", adate WITH CTOD("02/18/88"), now_due WITH 42.23,
paid WITH .F.
   APPEND BLANK
   REPLACE account WITH "300000", adate WITH CTOD("02/18/88"), now_due WITH 102.12,
paid WITH .F.
   APPEND BLANK
   REPLACE account WITH "323333", adate WITH CTOD("02/18/88"), now_due WITH 32.20,
paid WITH .F.
```

```
   APPEND BLANK
   REPLACE account WITH "352231", adate WITH CTOD("02/18/88"), now_due WITH 315.08,
paid WITH .F.
   APPEND BLANK
   REPLACE account WITH "400000", adate WITH CTOD("02/18/88"), now_due WITH 1.70,
paid WITH .F.
   APPEND BLANK
   REPLACE account WITH "511001", adate WITH CTOD("02/18/88"), now_due WITH 9.10,
paid WITH .F.
   APPEND BLANK
   REPLACE account WITH "610000", adate WITH CTOD("02/18/88"), now_due WITH 9.72,
paid WITH .F.
   APPEND BLANK
   REPLACE account WITH "714442", adate WITH CTOD("02/18/88"), now_due WITH
3084.02, paid WITH .F.
   APPEND BLANK
   REPLACE account WITH "740000", adate WITH CTOD("02/18/88"), now_due WITH
5137.13, paid WITH .F.
   APPEND BLANK
   REPLACE account WITH "830000", adate WITH CTOD("02/18/88"), now_due WITH 568.23,
paid WITH .F.
   APPEND BLANK
   REPLACE account WITH "831000", adate WITH CTOD("02/18/88"), now_due WITH 2.23,
paid WITH .F.
   APPEND BLANK
   REPLACE account WITH "845500", adate WITH CTOD("02/18/88"), now_due WITH 24.02,
paid WITH .F.
   APPEND BLANK
   REPLACE account WITH "860000", adate WITH CTOD("02/18/88"), now_due WITH 645.73,
paid WITH .F.
   APPEND BLANK
   REPLACE account WITH "900000", adate WITH CTOD("02/18/88"), now_due WITH
3426723.12, paid WITH .F.
   APPEND BLANK
   REPLACE account WITH "910000", adate WITH CTOD("02/18/88"), now_due WITH
3309725.31, paid WITH .F.
   APPEND BLANK
   REPLACE account WITH "920000", adate WITH CTOD("02/18/88"), now_due WITH
328321.02, paid WITH .F.
   APPEND BLANK
   REPLACE account WITH "930000", adate WITH CTOD("02/18/88"), now_due WITH
38235.13, paid WITH .F.
   APPEND BLANK
   REPLACE account WITH "931000", adate WITH CTOD("02/18/88"), now_due WITH
28322.13, paid WITH .F.
   APPEND BLANK
   REPLACE account WITH "933100", adate WITH CTOD("02/18/88"), now_due WITH 283.13,
paid WITH .F.
   APPEND BLANK
   REPLACE account WITH "935000", adate WITH CTOD("02/18/88"), now_due WITH
2832.13, paid WITH .F.
   APPEND BLANK
   REPLACE account WITH "939300", adate WITH CTOD("02/18/88"), now_due WITH
2831.03, paid WITH .F.
```

```
   APPEND BLANK
   REPLACE account WITH "940000", adate WITH CTOD("02/18/88"), now_due WITH 283.13,
paid WITH .F.
   APPEND BLANK
   REPLACE account WITH "945000", adate WITH CTOD("02/18/88"), now_due WITH 235.73,
paid WITH .F.
   APPEND BLANK
   REPLACE account WITH "950000", adate WITH CTOD("02/18/88"), now_due WITH 123.03,
paid WITH .F.
   APPEND BLANK
   REPLACE account WITH "955000", adate WITH CTOD("02/18/88"), now_due WITH
2137.30, paid WITH .F.
   APPEND BLANK
   REPLACE account WITH "100000", adate WITH CTOD("02/18/88"), now_due WITH 231.23,
paid WITH .F.
   APPEND BLANK
   REPLACE account WITH "200000", adate WITH CTOD("02/18/88"), now_due WITH
23023.00, paid WITH .F.
   APPEND BLANK
   REPLACE account WITH "200001", adate WITH CTOD("02/18/88"), now_due WITH
1543.23, paid WITH .F.
   APPEND BLANK
   REPLACE account WITH "200010", adate WITH CTOD("02/18/88"), now_due WITH 23.03,
paid WITH .F.
   APPEND BLANK
   REPLACE account WITH "300000", adate WITH CTOD("02/18/88"), now_due WITH
22354.03, paid WITH .F.
   APPEND BLANK
   REPLACE account WITH "323333", adate WITH CTOD("02/18/88"), now_due WITH
273123.00, paid WITH .F.
   APPEND BLANK
   REPLACE account WITH "352231", adate WITH CTOD("02/18/88"), now_due WITH
3231.30, paid WITH .F.
   APPEND BLANK
   REPLACE account WITH "400000", adate WITH CTOD("02/18/88"), now_due WITH 212.21,
paid WITH .F.
   APPEND BLANK
   REPLACE account WITH "511001", adate WITH CTOD("02/18/88"), now_due WITH 4.12,
paid WITH .F.
   APPEND BLANK
   REPLACE account WITH "610000", adate WITH CTOD("02/18/88"), now_due WITH 1.12,
paid WITH .F.
   APPEND BLANK
   REPLACE account WITH "714442", adate WITH CTOD("02/18/88"), now_due WITH 3.20,
paid WITH .F.
   APPEND BLANK
   REPLACE account WITH "740000", adate WITH CTOD("02/18/88"), now_due WITH 3.12,
paid WITH .F.
   APPEND BLANK
   REPLACE account WITH "830000", adate WITH CTOD("02/18/88"), now_due WITH 34.02,
paid WITH .F.
   APPEND BLANK
   REPLACE account WITH "831000", adate WITH CTOD("02/18/88"), now_due WITH 3.23,
paid WITH .F.
```

```
   APPEND BLANK
   REPLACE account WITH "845500", adate WITH CTOD("02/18/88"), now_due WITH 0.23,
paid WITH .F.
   APPEND BLANK
   REPLACE account WITH "860000", adate WITH CTOD("02/18/88"), now_due WITH 1.03,
paid WITH .F.
   APPEND BLANK
   REPLACE account WITH "900000", adate WITH CTOD("02/18/88"), now_due WITH 0.23,
paid WITH .F.
   APPEND BLANK
   REPLACE account WITH "910000", adate WITH CTOD("02/18/88"), now_due WITH 157.53,
paid WITH .F.
   APPEND BLANK
   REPLACE account WITH "920000", adate WITH CTOD("02/18/88"), now_due WITH 0.90,
paid WITH .F.
   APPEND BLANK
   REPLACE account WITH "930000", adate WITH CTOD("02/18/88"), now_due WITH 0.12,
paid WITH .F.
   APPEND BLANK
   REPLACE account WITH "931000", adate WITH CTOD("02/18/88"), now_due WITH 0.40,
paid WITH .F.
   APPEND BLANK
   REPLACE account WITH "933100", adate WITH CTOD("02/18/88"), now_due WITH 0.27,
paid WITH .F.
   APPEND BLANK
   REPLACE account WITH "935000", adate WITH CTOD("02/18/88"), now_due WITH 0.12,
paid WITH .F.
   APPEND BLANK
   REPLACE account WITH "939300", adate WITH CTOD("02/18/88"), now_due WITH 23.00,
paid WITH .F.
   APPEND BLANK
   REPLACE account WITH "940000", adate WITH CTOD("02/18/88"), now_due WITH 24.13,
paid WITH .F.
   APPEND BLANK
   REPLACE account WITH "945000", adate WITH CTOD("02/18/88"), now_due WITH
3212.42, paid WITH .F.
   APPEND BLANK
   REPLACE account WITH "950000", adate WITH CTOD("02/18/88"), now_due WITH
37231.42, paid WITH .F.
   APPEND BLANK
   REPLACE account WITH "955000", adate WITH CTOD("02/18/88"), now_due WITH 337.43,
paid WITH .F.
   USE
   ? "File Three"
   CREATE Temp
   USE Temp
   DO Ap_it WITH "STATUS",   "C", 1,0
   DO Ap_it WITH "DESCRIPT", "C",20,0
   USE
   CREATE Statcode FROM Temp
   USE Statcode
   ERASE Temp.dbf
   APPEND BLANK
```

```
   REPLACE status WITH "1", descript WITH "Normal Account"
   APPEND BLANK
   REPLACE status WITH "2", descript WITH "Inventory Account"
   APPEND BLANK
   REPLACE status WITH "3", descript WITH "Special"
   APPEND BLANK
   REPLACE status WITH "4", descript WITH "Fortune 500"
   APPEND BLANK
   REPLACE status WITH "5", descript WITH "Premire Account"
   APPEND BLANK
   REPLACE status WITH "6", descript WITH "Gold Card Member"
   APPEND BLANK
   REPLACE status WITH "7", descript WITH "Inventory Control"
   APPEND BLANK
   REPLACE status WITH "8", descript WITH "Unassigned"
   APPEND BLANK
   REPLACE status WITH "9", descript WITH "Development"
   APPEND BLANK
   REPLACE status WITH "A", descript WITH "Additional Account"
   APPEND BLANK
   REPLACE status WIT. "T", descript WITH "Tax Account"

********************
* The following functions and procedures are part of the Steve Straley Toolkit.
* Copyright (c) 1987, 1988 Stephen Straley & Associates
********************

********************

PROCEDURE Ap_it

   PARAMETERS apa, apb, apc, apd

   * apa = the field name
   * apb = the field data type
   * apc = the field length
   * apd = the field decimal

   IF PCOUNT() = 3
      apd = 0
   ENDIF

   APPEND BLANK
   IF apc > 255
      REPLACE field_name WITH apa, field_type WITH apb, field_len WITH INT(apc %
256), field_dec WITH INT(apc / 256)
   ELSE
      REPLACE field_name WITH apa, field_type WITH apb, field_len WITH apc,
field_dec WITH apd
   ENDIF

********************
```

```
FUNCTION Mess_cent

   PARAMETERS mess1, mess2

   the_len = LEN(mess1)
   half_space = INT((mess2/2) - the_len / 2)
   tot_len = mess2 - the_len - half_space
   RETURN(SPACE(half_space) + mess1 + SPACE(tot_len))

*********************

FUNCTION Upperlower

   PARAMETERS upla

   RETURN(UPPER(SUBSTR(upla, 1, 1)) + LOWER(SUBSTR(upla,2)))

*********************

FUNCTION Right_just

   PARAMETERS right_st, right_col

   IF PCOUNT() = 1
      right_col = 79
   ENDIF
   RETURN(IF(LEN(right_st) > right_col, right_st, right_col - LEN(right_st)))


*********************

FUNCTION Verify

   PARAMETERS comp, extra_key

   DO CASE
      CASE PCOUNT() = 0
         comp = "YyNn"
         extra_key = .F.
      CASE PCOUNT() = 1
         extra_key = .F.
   ENDCASE

   IF TYPE("scrpause") = "U"
      scrpause = 100
   ENDIF
   DO WHILE .T.
      the_var = ""
      inside = INKEY(0)
      DO CASE
      CASE inside = 4
         the_var = "Y"
      CASE inside = 19
```

```
        the_var = "N"
    OTHERWISE
        the_var = CHR(inside)
    ENDCASE
    IF the_var$comp
        EXIT
    ENDIF
ENDDO
IF the_var$SUBSTR(comp,1,2)
    ?? "Yes"
    IF extra_key
        INKEY(0)
    ELSE
        FOR qaz = 1 TO scrpause
        NEXT
    ENDIF
    RETURN(.T.)
ELSE
    ?? "No "
    IF extra_key
        INKEY(0)
    ELSE
        FOR qaz = 1 TO scrpause
        NEXT
    ENDIF
    RETURN(.F.)
ENDIF
```

CHAPTER SEVEN

Error Handling System

The error handling system is an added feature to the Summer '87 release. This system is based around a series of functions that classify different errors experienced by a Clipper application. These functions basically fall into six areas:

1. Database-related errors
2. Expression, type conflicts, and macro expansion errors
3. Miscellaneous errors
4. Printing errors
5. DOS and opening of file errors
6. Undefined errors

Two files are provided with the Clipper disks which may be linked into your application; they offer some support for these six areas. The two files are ERRORSYS.OBJ and ALTERROR.OBJ. Keep in mind that if you link in these two object modules, they are included **after** the main object file.

Now, before explaining the capabilities and possibilities of this feature, a clarification is in order. This feature does not automatically handle errors within an application, for example, as dBASE III does. Consider working at the dot prompt in dBASE and trying to USE a file that does not exist. dBASE prompts you if you need help and shows you the basic error. Never does an error of this type cause a message, including a "Q/A/I," to appear on the top line of the screen. These error utilities are not like the error handling routines in the interpreter. And because Clipper is a compiler, some errors, if encountered, may not be recoverable and thus, the application will not execute.

So what exactly is the error system? It is a series of function calls that have been allowed in the Clipper architecture that will be called if an error should occur. These function calls may be accessed by the programmer to customize an error trapping and recovery scheme. It is important to understand that the programmer, not Nantucket, is responsible for programming these functions properly, for structuring not only the user-interface but the recovery track as well. The error handling system is a means for you, the programmer, to do just that. If it is not used, the error system capabilities will be ignored and the Clipper application will generate familiar one-line messages across the top line of the screen along with the now existing message "Continue?"

All of the error functions have a basic parameter construct. If an error should occur and if there is an appropriate error function programmed to handle the error, use the following template below, as Clipper calls the errors, to see the various potential parameters Clipper may pass.

```
   ERRORFUNC(base_name, line_no, error_mess [, err_model [, _1 [, _2 [, _3 [, _4
[, _5]]]]]])
```

For example, consider the following two lines of code:

```
CLEAR SCREEN
   @ 2,0 SAY x
```

Clearly, the variable x has yet to be defined. Without an appropriate error function, the application would generate an "undefined identifier" message on the top line of the screen. However, programming an undefined error function to handle this might look something like this:

```
FUNCTION Undef_error

PARAMETERS base_name, line_no, error_mess, error_mode, _1

ret_row = ROW()
ret_col = COL()
errorscr = SAVESCREEN(17,10,24,70)
@ 17,12 SAY "◄ On-Line Error Experienced ►"
@ 19,12 SAY "An &a3. has occurred in program/function "
@ 20,12 SAY "module &a1..    In file " + PROCFILE() + " at line " +
ALLTRIM(STR(a2))
DO CASE
   CASE "UNDEFINED IDENTIFIER"$UPPER(a3)

   CASE "EXTERNAL"$UPPER(a3)

ENDCASE
RESTSCREEN(17,10,24,70, errorscr)
@ ret_row, ret_col SAY ""
RETURN(.F.)
```

There are plenty of options for the function, but there are several points to keep in mind as well. First, if the error is to be unrecoverable, the function should return a logical false (.F.). In the above example, the function always returns logical true. Next, the "error_mode" parameter yields the parameter (or parameters) in which the cause of the error is stored. For example in the above code extract, the "error_mode" has a value of _1. This is Clipper's notation that the cause of the error is in the parameter named _1. Looking to the value of the parameter _1, the value of x is found.

Note that this is true for the provided example: the cause of the error is the fact that the variable x had not been defined before the attempt to display it to the screen was made. The base_name parameter is the name of the function or the parameter in which the error took place. Additionally, the line_no parameter is a numeric parameter that contains the line number that the error occurred on. Note that if the program is compiled without line numbers (e.g., using the -l compiling switch), this value will always be 0. The error_mess parameter contains the actual message that would be displayed by the Clipper application if no error function was available. For example, in the above example, the variable x is yet to be defined and thus, the value of error_mess would be "undefined identifier." Note that the function actually tests to see if the value of error_mess is just that: UNDEFINED IDENTIFIER.

The second case is where a user-defined function or a misspelled function or procedure is present in the system and the compiled symbol is missing and EXTERNAL. This error is synonymous with the former UNDEFINED SYMBOL or MISSING EXTERNAL that is seen at the conclusion of linking. Below is a list of the basic errors that may be encountered, the class of error they are associated with, the internal function Clipper will call, whether the error is recoverable or not, the possible causes for the error, and a basic header for the function for you to use when programming.

1. Database Error

Error Class.: Database Error
Function called: DB_ERROR()
Recoverable: Possible
Reasons: "DATABASE REQUIRED" = Missing database or Invalid name given.
"EXCLUSIVE REQUIRED" = Generated if EXCLUSIVE USE is required for the database.
"FIELD NUMERIC OVERFLOW" = The number to be REPLACED into the field is too big for it.
"INDEX FILE CORRUPTED" = The index file is corrupted or the internal method of indexing is not the same as the file (e.g., the file is an .NDX file and the application is assuming .NTX).
"LOCK REQUIRED" = Attempting to work on a file or a record that requires a lock. This requirement affects both the file lock and the record lock.

Header:

```
*************************
FUNCTION Db_error()

PARAMETERS base_name, line_no, error_mess
```

2. Expression Error

Error Class: Expression Error
Function called: EXPR_ERROR()
Recoverable: Possible
Reasons: "EXPRESSION ERROR" = Attempting to expand a macro that contains an invalid or undefined value. An example of this would be a macro expression that refers to another variable; however, that variable has yet to be defined.

"TYPE MISMATCH" = The expression to be performed does not have the proper data types for the operation.
"SUBSCRIPT RANGE" = Attempting to manipulate a data element outside the range of the array as specified by the DECLARE or PUBLIC) command.
"ZERO DIVIDE" = Dividing any number by zero.

Header:
```
*************************
FUNCTION Expr_error()

PARAMETERS base_name, line_no, error_mess, ;
error_mode, _1, _2, _3
```

3. Miscellaneous Error

Error Class: Miscellaneous Error
Function Called: MISC_ERROR()
Recoverable: Possible
Reasons: "RUN ERROR" = This takes place when there is not enough memory to perform the RUN command or if COMMAND.COM is not available to be loaded.

"TYPE MISMATCH" = This type of "TYPE" error occurs when a REPLACE operation being performed is with the wrong data type.

Header:
```
********************
FUNCTION Misc_error

PARAMETERS base_name, line_no, error_mess,;
error_mode
```

Note: The error_mode parameter only contains some code fragment that represents the cause. It does not contain the common _1, _2, or _3 referring parameters.

4. Undefined Error

Error Class: Undefined Error
Function Called: UNDEF_ERROR()
Recoverable: Possible
Reasons: "UNDEFINED IDENTIFIER" = This takes place when there is a field, memory variable, or similar identifier **not** previously defined.

"NOT AN ARRAY" = A reference to an array element is made and that reference is not of array type.

"MISSING EXTERNAL" = A procedure or a function is not found while running. In some cases, this will be found at link time. Additionally, misspelled functions will also generate this error.

Header:

```
*********************
FUNCTION Undef_error

PARAMETERS base_name, line_no, error_mess,;
error_mode, _1
```

5. Open Error

Error Class: Open Error
Function Called: OPEN_ERROR()
Recoverable: Possible
Reasons: "OPEN ERROR" = This occurs when any file opening operation fails, other than those routines that involve the low-level functions added to the Summer '87 library.

Header:

```
*********************
FUNCTION Open_error

PARAMETERS base_name, line_no, error_mess,;
error_mode, _1
```

Note: The error_mode always will contain a code fragment yielding some indication of the reason for the error. The _1 parameter also contains the name of the file that the error place on.

6. Print Error

Error Class: Print Error
Function Called: PRINT_ERROR()
Recoverable: Possible
Reasons: "PRINT ERROR" = This takes place when there is any printing error, whether to disk or to the printer. If redirection is through a serial port and an error occurs, the OPEN_ERROR() is invoked.

Header:

```
*********************
FUNCTION Print_error

PARAMETERS base_name, line_no
```

It is not possible to recover from some errors. Here is a basic list of those errors:

1. **Disk Full:** When performing database operations and the disk becomes full.

2. **Internal Error:** Usually generated because of a corrupted index file. The application will terminate automatically when any key is pressed.

3. **Multiple Error:** An error occurs inside one of the above described error routines. The application will terminate automatically when any key is pressed.

4. **Not Enough Memory:** There is not enough available memory to begin the programmed operation. The application will terminate automatically when any key is pressed.

5. **Out of Memory:** There is not enough memory for the currently processing operation to continue. The application will terminate automatically when any key is pressed.

Having the basics down is one thing; applying the right interface is another. For example, missing externals should be noted, but the program should not continue to run. On the other hand, fields or variables that are mistyped need only to have the proper value assigned to them and the program can continue. Knowing these differences and building the proper interface is essential.

Additionally, there are some new functions and capabilities in the Summer '87 release that give the programmer the tools necessary to build a better mouse- (or bug) trap. The TONE() function is one such tool; ALTD() and DOSERROR() are others. And while it is not fully supported and functional, the PROCFILE() function may be handy to have. Along with these, the new BEGIN SEQUENCE command has larger ramifications outside the realm of error trapping and recovery. Finally, windowing and error logging is possible with these functions because the Summer '87 Clipper has partial screen saving and low-level file operations.

Using the windowing techniques and the low-level file functions adds a new dimension to these functions. For example, in the coded extract below, a pop-window is generated inside of the error function. Information regarding the error is asked and an attempt to recover from the error is made. The window is removed from the screen and the cursor is returned to the original row and column. Additionally, the TONE() function is used to signify the occurrence of an error.

```
********************
* Name      Error1.prg
* Date      March 9, 1988
* Notice    Copyright (c) 1988 Stephen J. Straley & Associates
* Note      This is a sample error tracking program.
* Compile   Clipper Error1 -m
```

```
* Release   Summer '87
* Link      Plink86 fi error1 lib extend lib clipper;
* Author    Stephen J. Straley
*********************

CLEAR SCREEN
@ 5,10 SAY x
@ 7,10 SAY "All Over"

*********************

FUNCTION Undef_error

   PARAMETERS a1, a2, a3, a4, a5

   ret_row = ROW()
   ret_col =COL()
   SOUNDERR()
   errorscr = SAVESCREEN(17,10,24,70)
   @ 17,10 CLEAR TO 24,70
   @ 17,10 TO 24,70 DOUBLE
   @ 17,12 SAY "◄ On-Line Error Experienced ►"
   @ 19,12 SAY "An &a3. has occurred in program/function "
   @ 20,12 SAY "module &a1..   In file " + PROCFILE() + " at line " +
ALLTRIM(STR(a2))
   DO CASE
      CASE "UNDEFINED IDENTIFIER"$UPPER(a3)
         DO WHILE .T.
            @ 23,12 SAY "Enter Data Type of &a5. (DNCL) "
            dataset = UPPER(CHR(INKEY(0)))
            IF dataset = "D"
               error = CTOD("  /  /  ")
               errpic= "99/99/99"
            ELSEIF dataset = "L"
               error = .F.
               errpic= ""
            ELSEIF dataset = "N"
               error = 1000000000.000000 - 1000000000.000000
               errpic = "999999999999.999999999999"
            ELSEIF dataset = "C"
               @ 23,12 SAY SPACE(LEN("Enter Data Type of &a5. (DNCL) "))
               error1 = 0
               @ 23,12 SAY "Enter length of string => " GET error1 VALID error1 >=
1 .AND. error1 < 3000
               READ
               @ 23,12 SAY "                                                        "
               error = SPACE(error1)
               errpic= IF(error1 > 20, "@S20", "@X")
            ELSE
               LOOP
            ENDIF
            EXIT
         ENDDO
```

```
            @ 23,12 SAY SPACE(LEN("Enter Data Type of &a5. (DNCL) "))
            @ 23,12 SAY "Enter new value for &a5. => " GET error PICT errpic
            READ
            PUBLIC &a5.
            STORE error TO &a5.
            IF dataset = "L"
               errmess = "STORE " + IF(error, ".T.", ".F.") + " TO &a5."
            ELSEIF dataset = "D"
               errmess = "STORE CTOD('" + ALLTRIM(STRVALUE(error)) + "') TO &a5."
            ELSEIF dataset = "C"
               errmess = "STORE [" + ALLTRIM(STRVALUE(error)) + "]  TO &a5."
            ELSE
               errmess = "STORE " + ALLTRIM(STRVALUE(error)) + "  TO &a5."
            ENDIF
      ENDCASE

      RESTSCREEN(17,10,24,70, errorscr)
      @ ret_row, ret_col SAY ""
      RETURN(.T.)

  *******************

  FUNCTION Sounderr

     TONE(700, 8)
     INKEY(.3)
     TONE(700, 8)
     INKEY(.3)
     TONE(700, 8)

 *
 * The following function is part of the Steve Straley Toolkit.
 * Copyright (c) 1988, Stephen J. Straley & Associates - All rights reserved
 *
 ********************

 FUNCTION Strvalue

    PARAMETERS showstring

    DO CASE
    CASE TYPE("showstring") = "C"
       RETURN(showstring)
    CASE TYPE("showstring") = "N"
       RETURN(STR(showstring))
    CASE TYPE("showstring") = "M"
       RETURN(" ")
    CASE TYPE("showstring") = "D"
       RETURN(DTOC(showstring))
    OTHERWISE
       RETURN(IF(showstring, "True", "False"))
    ENDCASE
* End of file
```

Additionally, the low-level file functions may be used to create, open, and write to an alternate error (.ERR) file. This technique allows the developer to run a program with errors, assign new values, and to log the errors to a file for retrieval purposes. This will save on the constant need to experience a bug, abort, fix, recompile, relink, and press on.

```
*********************
* Name      Error2.prg
* Date      March 9, 1988
* Notice    Copyright (c) 1988 Stephen J. Straley & Associates
* Note      This is a sample error tracking program.
* Compile   Clipper Error1 -m
* Release   Summer '87
* Link      Plink86 fi error1 lib extend lib clipper;
* Author    Stephen J. Straley
*
*********************

CLEAR SCREEN
@ 5,10 SAY x
@ 6,10 SAY y
@ 7,10 SAY newamount
@ 8,10 SAY "All Over"
WAIT
TYPE &errfile

*********************

FUNCTION Undef_error

   PARAMETERS a1, a2, a3, a4, a5

   ret_row = ROW()
   ret_col =COL()
   SOUNDERR()
   errorscr = SAVESCREEN(17,10,24,70)
   @ 17,10 CLEAR TO 24,70
   @ 17,10 TO 24,70 DOUBLE
   @ 17,12 SAY "◄ On-Line Error Experienced ►"
   @ 19,12 SAY "An &a3. has occurred in program/function "
   @ 20,12 SAY "module &a1..   In file " + PROCFILE() + " at line " +
ALLTRIM(STR(a2))
   DO CASE
      CASE "UNDEFINED IDENTIFIER"$UPPER(a3)
         DO WHILE .T.
            @ 23,12 SAY "Enter Data Type of &a5. (DNCL) "
            dataset = UPPER(CHR(INKEY(0)))
            IF dataset = "D"
               error = CTOD("  /  /  ")
               errpic= "99/99/99"
            ELSEIF dataset = "L"
               error = .F.
               errpic= ""
```

```
            ELSEIF dataset = "N"
               error = 1000000000.000000 - 1000000000.000000
               errpic = "999999999999.999999999999"
            ELSEIF dataset = "C"
               @ 23,12 SAY SPACE(LEN("Enter Data Type of &a5. (DNCL) "))
               error1 = 0
               @ 23,12 SAY "Enter length of string => " GET error1 VALID error1 >=
1 .AND. error1 < 3000
               READ
               @ 23,12 SAY "                                                        "
               error = SPACE(error1)
               errpic= IF(error1 > 20, "@S20", "@X")
            ELSE
               LOOP
            ENDIF
            EXIT
         ENDDO
         @ 23,12 SAY SPACE(LEN("Enter Data Type of &a5. (DNCL) "))
         @ 23,12 SAY "Enter new value for &a5. => " GET error PICT errpic
         READ
         PUBLIC &a5.
         STORE error TO &a5.
         IF dataset = "L"
            errmess = "STORE " + IF(error, ".T.", ".F.") + " TO &a5."
         ELSEIF dataset = "D"
            errmess = "STORE CTOD('" + ALLTRIM(STRVALUE(error)) + "') TO &a5."
         ELSEIF dataset = "C"
            errmess = "STORE [" + ALLTRIM(STRVALUE(error)) + "]  TO &a5."
         ELSE
            errmess = "STORE " + ALLTRIM(STRVALUE(error)) + "  TO &a5."
         ENDIF
         LOGERR(errmess)
   ENDCASE

   RESTSCREEN(17,10,24,70, errorscr)
   @ ret_row, ret_col SAY ""
   RETURN(.T.)

******************

FUNCTION Sounderr

   TONE(700, 8)
   INKEY(.3)
   TONE(700, 8)
   INKEY(.3)
   TONE(700, 8)

*****************

FUNCTION Logerr

   PARAMETERS logerror
```

```
   ret_line = "CHR(13) + CHR(10)"
   IF TYPE("errfile") = "U"
      PUBLIC errfile
      errfile = ALLTRIM(STR(INT(SECONDS())))+".ERR"
      IF !FILE(errfile)
         errhandle = FCREATE(errfile)
         FWRITE(errhandle, "The following is a list of errors experienced" +
&ret_line.)
         FWRITE(errhandle, "By Stephen J. Straley's on-line error trapping" +
&ret_line.)
         FWRITE(errhandle, "Utility Program." + &ret_line. + &ret_line.)
      ENDIF
   ELSE
      errhandle = FOPEN(errfile, 1)
      length = FSEEK(errhandle, 0, 2)
      FSEEK(errhandle, length)
   ENDIF
   FWRITE(errhandle, "Error:" + &ret_line.)
   FWRITE(errhandle, "        Discovered &a3. at line " + ALLTRIM(STR(a2)) + " in
module &a1. " + &ret_line.)
   FWRITE(errhandle, "        ------- " + &ret_line.)
   FWRITE(errhandle, "        Additional Information: " + a4 + "   " + a5 +
&ret_line. + &ret_line.)
   FWRITE(errhandle, "Solution:" + &ret_line.)
   FWRITE(errhandle, "           Add '" + logerror + "' TO LINE " + ALLTRIM(STR(a2 -
1)) + &ret_line. + &ret_line.)
   FCLOSE(errhandle)
   RETURN(.T.)

*
* The following function is part of the Steve Straley Toolkit.
* Copyright (c) 1988, Stephen J. Straley & Associates - All rights reserved
*
*********************

FUNCTION Strvalue

   PARAMETERS showstring

   DO CASE
   CASE TYPE("showstring") = "C"
      RETURN(showstring)
   CASE TYPE("showstring") = "N"
      RETURN(STR(showstring))
   CASE TYPE("showstring") = "M"
      RETURN(" ")
   CASE TYPE("showstring") = "D"
      RETURN(DTOC(showstring))
   OTHERWISE
      RETURN(IF(showstring, "True", "False"))
   ENDCASE
* End of file
```

Another feature added to the Summer '87 release of Clipper was the introduction of the BEGIN SEQUENCE ... END command construct. Mainly brought on to handle the error logic just described, the implied and embedded potential of this command is amazing. The explanation for this command is simple. First, determine a group of commands that are to be performed in a SEQUENCE. Surround that grouping with the BEGIN SEQUENCE command and terminate it with the END command. For example, this is a possibility:

```
   SET KEY -9 TO Bounceout
   r_time_err = .F.
   BEGIN SEQUENCE
   DO Enter_pay
   DO Calc_pay
   DO Print_pay
   END
   IF !(r_time_err)
      DO Adjustit
   ENDIF

**********************

PROCEDURE Bounceout

   PARAMETERS p, l, v

   r_time_err = .T.
   BREAK
```

In the above example, if the BREAK command was encountered in either Procedure Enter_pay, Calc_pay, or Print_pay by the F10 (the SET KEY TO procedure) key being pressed, the variable r_time_err would be set to logical true (.T.) and the IF command would be immediately processed. If the global flag r_time_err remains false, the procedure Adjustit would be executed. In the procedure Bounceout, the global flag is set and the BREAK command is issued. This tells the application to find the last BEGIN SEQUENCE...END construct on the stack, return to it, and to process the command after the END command. Note that the BREAK command may be in a lower procedure or function. The BREAK command may even appear in a validation field accessed via the VALID clause. Again, in the above example, the BREAK command is in a procedure that may be activated via the pressing of the hot key, the F10 (SET KEY TO -9) key. No matter the mode of operation, the BREAK command still applies.

However, be careful. The BEGIN SEQUENCE command follows the same construction as the DO WHILE, FOR, IF, and CASE commands. Nesting these commands is possible, but they must follow a specific order. For example, the following code extract is **not** valid.

```
BEGIN SEQUENCE
DO WHILE .T.
   <commands>
   END
ENDDO
```

You will get a sequence error when you compile this. Make sure that the END command is on the same level with the BEGIN SEQUENCE command.

The BEGIN SEQUENCE...END command enables such programming possibilities as RETURN TO MASTER, recursive programming, error recovery, and immediate escape routes. Listed below is another example of how to use the BEGIN SEQUENCE command, how to pop-off windows, and how to program for a RETURN TO MASTER situation.

```
*********************
* Name      Breakout.prg
* Date      March 9, 1988
* Notice    Copyright (c) 1988 Stephen J. Straley & Associates
* Note      This is just one sample on how to use the BEGIN SEQUENCE
*           command.
* Compile   Clipper Breakout -m
* Release   Summer '87
* Link      Plink86 fi breakout lib extend lib clipper;
* Author    Stephen J. Straley
*********************

CLEAR SCREEN
PUBLIC screens[5]
AFILL(screens, SPACE(4000))
SET KEY 27 TO Popup
SET KEY -9 TO Ret_master
SAVE SCREEN TO screens[1]
@ 2,5 TO 23,75 DOUBLE
@ 3,6 SAY PROCNAME()
@ 22,6 SAY "ESC to Pop Up a Level / F10 to Return to Master"
BEGIN SEQUENCE
DO WHILE .T.
   invar = " "
   @ 12,10 SAY "Press 'Y' to go to next level" GET invar
   READ
   IF invar$"Yy"
      DO Level1
   ENDIF
ENDDO
END
RESTORE SCREEN FROM screens[1]

*********************

PROCEDURE Level1

   SAVE SCREEN TO screens[2]
   @ 5,10 CLEAR TO 20,70
```

```
   @ 5,10 TO 20,70 DOUBLE
   @ 6,11 SAY PROCNAME()
   @ 19,11 SAY "ESC to Pop Up a Level / F10 to Return to Master"
   BEGIN SEQUENCE
   DO WHILE .T.
      invar = " "
      @ 12,15 SAY "Press 'Y' to go to the next level" GET invar
      READ
      IF invar$"Yy"
         DO Level2
      ENDIF
   ENDDO
   END
   RESTORE SCREEN FROM screens[2]

*********************

PROCEDURE Level2

   SAVE SCREEN TO screens[3]
   @ 7,15 CLEAR TO 18,65
   @ 7,15 TO 18,65 DOUBLE
   @ 8,16 SAY PROCNAME()
   @ 17,16 SAY "ESC to Pop Up a Level / F10 to Return to Master"
   BEGIN SEQUENCE
   DO WHILE .T.
      invar = " "
      @ 12,20 SAY "Press 'Y' to go to the next level" GET invar
      READ
      IF invar$"Yy"
         DO Level3
      ENDIF
   ENDDO
   END
   RESTORE SCREEN FROM screens[3]

*********************

PROCEDURE Level3

   SAVE SCREEN TO screens[4]
   @ 9,20 CLEAR TO 16, 60
   @ 9,20 TO 16, 60 DOUBLE
   @ 10,21 SAY PROCNAME()
   @ 15,21 SAY "ESC to Pop Up a Level / F10 to Master"
   BEGIN SEQUENCE
   DO WHILE .T.
      invar = " "
      @ 12,25 SAY "Press 'Y' to the next level" GET invar
      READ
      IF invar$"Yy"
         DO Level4
      ENDIF
```

```
   ENDDO
   END
   RESTORE SCREEN FROM screens[4]

********************

PROCEDURE Level4

   SAVE SCREEN TO screens[5]
   @ 11,25 CLEAR TO 14,55
   @ 11,25 TO 14,55 DOUBLE
   @ 13,26 SAY PROCNAME()
   @ 13,26 SAY "ESC to Pop Up / F10 to Master"
   BEGIN SEQUENCE
   DO WHILE .T.
      invar = " "
      @ 12,29 SAY "Any key remains here." GET invar
      READ
   ENDDO
   END
   RESTORE SCREEN FROM screens[5]

********************

PROCEDURE Popup

   PARAMETERS p, l, v

   BREAK

********************

PROCEDURE Ret_master

   PARAMETERS p, l, v

   KEYBOARD REPLICATE(CHR(27), VAL(SUBSTR(p, 6)))
* End of File.
```

The key to all of this is simple: the new built-in error system with the Summer '87 release not only adds new functions and versatility to Clipper applications, but adds user-friendly enchancements as well.

CHAPTER EIGHT

Memo Fields

INTRODUCTION TO MEMO FIELDS

The basic concept of the memo field is to provide a way to enter string information relative to a specific record without increasing the size of the master database file every time a record is APPENDed. Memo files are *dynamic:* they grow only when something is added, not when the record is APPENDed. It would be very inefficient to allow a 4K character field to exist in a database whether any information was there or not. It would be wasteful to use 4K for each record regardless of how much information is put in that field. For these reasons, memo fields are kept in a separate file.

This file has the same root name as the main database file, but it has a .DBT file extension. In the main database, the memo field is 10 characters in length and contains no more than a pointer tying that record to a record in the memo file. The memo file and fields are no more than an elongated string with a matching reference pointer.

Memo fields can be somewhat of a problem to work with in dBASE III. Many users ignore the word "memo" and treat the fields as description or short story fields. This use often pushes the product to its limit and invites disaster.

The memo field is just a note pad: a device by which short notes pertaining to a record can be added or viewed. One of the problems in dBASE III is that whenever a memo is worked on, the entire screen is given over to the memo field. This visually defeats the concept of the memo. Additionally, it is extremely difficult to port outside information into a memo field, especially text information longer than 255 bytes. Also it is impossible to use string functions on a memo field. Sometimes a note is best placed in a short character field directly in the database.

Clipper provides solutions to all these memo field problems.

CLIPPER AND MEMO FIELDS

In Clipper, memos can look like text: a small bordered, or windowed, area on the screen that can suddenly appear and disappear as desired. Using memo fields in Clipper has many advantages including direct cursor addressing of the area for editing, extended storage capabilities, and the ability to store memo information to character fields as well as to memory variables.

Memos can be added to or replaced using strings in Clipper. If strings are to be removed from the memo fields, the memo fields must first be stored to a temporary variable, and then the appropriate string is removed with the use of the AT() and the SUBSTR() functions.

The Summer '87 release contains a complete complement of memo functions, including a greatly enhanced MEMOEDIT() function. Below is a complete list of related functions. Those marked with an asterisk were added with the Summer '87 release.

	HARDCR():	This function replaces all soft carriage returns [CHR(141)] with hard carriage returns [CHR(13)].
	MEMOEDIT():	Displays and edits a memo field or string within the provided window area.
*	MEMOLINE():	Returns a formatted line from a memo field or string.
	MEMOREAD():	Reads the specified file to a character string.
*	MEMOTRAN():	Translates characters within a memo field or a character string.
	MEMOWRIT():	Writes a character string to specified file.
*	MLCOUNT():	Returns the number of lines in a memo field or character expression.
*	MLPOS():	Returns the position of a specified line number in a memo field or character string.

The function that was most expanded with the Summer '87 release was the MEMOEDIT() function. In the prior release, only six parameters were possible. With the Summer '87 release, up to 13 parameters are possible. The initial six remained the same, and are as follows:

```
MEMOEDIT(parameter1, parameter2, ... parameter6)
```

Parameter	Description
1.	The name of the memo field, variable, or character field
2.	The row coordinate of the top of the window to be used for the memo
3.	The column coordinate of the left side of the memo window
4.	The row coordinate of the bottom of the memo window

5. The column coordinate of the right side of the memo window
6. A logical flag indicating whether the memo is to be edited or merely displayed (.T. allows editing; .F. allows viewing)

When using the MEMOEDIT function, several rules must be followed to maintain system integrity:

1. If using the MEMOEDIT() function in conjunction with a memory variable, first set the value of the variable to a null string ("").

2. If using the MEMOEDIT() function in conjunction with a character field, first TRIM() the field to a null string ("").

   If there are values present in either the variable or character field, first store them to a temporary variable and then wipe out the contents of the original variable or field with a null string. After the edit, add the temporary variable either to the beginning or end of the edited field or variable.

3. Do not allow the user to access HELP.PRG while using MEMOEDIT().

   To accomplish this, you **must** issue this command prior to calling the MEMOEDIT() function:

   ```
   SET KEY 28 TO
   ```

   This will turn the F1 key [INKEY() value of 28] off. Once the MEMOEDIT() function had been completed, reinstate help with the command:

   ```
   SET KEY 28 TO Help
   ```

   Keep in mind that the MEMOEDIT() function can be used inside HELP.PRG.

4. Never allow an active key to do a procedure while using the MEMOEDIT() function.

   This is similar to rule number 3. Be sure to turn off any key that has been previously SET to a procedure. To do this, issue the following:

   ```
   SET KEY <expN> TO
   ```

   Then when finished with the MEMOEDIT() function, reset the key by entering:

   ```
   SET KEY <expN> TO <procedure>
   ```

   Again, the MEMOEDIT() function can be used within a procedure that was called by a key; however, all the rules still apply.

5. Avoid using the KEYBOARD command when using an active and open MEMOEDIT() function.

Although a routine will still work if rules 3, 4, and 5 have been violated, I have included them based on input from many users. It's better to be safe and follow these guidelines.

DISPLAYING A MEMO

A memo field can be sent to the screen, the printer, or an alternate file. Showing a memo on the screen is simple, but the others are not so easy. Let's take a brief look at displaying memo fields.

The area parameters we define for the memo field at the time of data entry are **not** permanent; they can be changed anytime the MEMOEDIT() function is called.

Let's look at a specific example:

```
REPLACE memo_field WITH MEMOEDIT(memo_field,5,5,20,75,.T.)
```

Now we change it to the following:

```
REPLACE memo_field WITH MEMOEDIT(memo_field,5,15,20,70,.F.)
```

Because the last parameter in the second example is set to false, the MEMOEDIT() function does not allow the memo field to be edited. However, what occurs is that the field is reformatted with the new border constraints. In order to adjust to varying column positions and for word-wrapping, the MEMOEDIT() function places soft carriage return markers inside the field. When a border approaches the middle of a word, the MEMOEDIT() places a CHR(141), instead of the customary hard carriage return CHR(13), in front of the word to be wrapped, and continues.

Using this high-bit graphic character allows the MEMOEDIT() to quickly reposition the contents to whatever row and column position is needed. The problem is that those high-bit characters remain inside the field. If we try to dump the contents directly out to the printer or to the screen by means other than the MEMOEDIT() function, we will be confronted with a startling discovery. This high-bit character plays havoc with form feeds and graphic characters on our printer. While these characters are not a problem for the screen, they can lock up the printer.

If we send the field contents to a file with the ALTERNATE command, we see all of the standard ASCII characters we typed into the memo field as well as all of the added CHR(141)s. The output problems remain both when using the MEMOEDIT() function and when not using it. We will discuss how to solve this problem later.

DISPLAYING MEMO FIELD CONTENTS USING MEMOEDIT()

Because MEMOEDIT() is a function, it returns a value that can be stored to a variable or to a field [e.g., STORE SUBSTR(a,1,3) TO x], or it can be tested for specific conditions [e.g., IF EOF()]. It would be a waste to store the value of the memo field [via MEMOEDIT()] to a memory variable if it were never to be used as a variable.

Here is a way, using the MEMOEDIT() function, to print the memo field to the screen in the desired area without assigning the value of the function to a memory variable:

```
IF "" = MEMOEDIT(memo_field,5,5,20,75,.F.)
ENDIF
```

The function will be called first and with the .F. (false) toggle, the memo field will be displayed in the given area. After expanding the MEMOEDIT() function, the value returned is actually the string of the memo field for the length of the given area. What occurs is that the memo field is displayed to the screen in the given area; after you leave the MEMOEDIT() function, the string is compared to a null string; since no other command is given within the IF...ENDIF command, the program flow continues.

Another major concern is how to treat a memo field that is larger than the prescribed window area on the screen. Because we used the false operator, the cursor is not in the memo field area; hence, we cannot page up or down within the MEMOEDIT() function. Only one full screen can be displayed. The answer to the problem lies **outside** the use of MEMOEDIT().

DISPLAYING MEMO FIELD CONTENTS WITHOUT USING MEMOEDIT()

In order to display a memo field that is larger than the screen, the MEMOEDIT() screen formatting high-order bit first must be stripped. The user-defined function BITSTRIP() will strip the field of these characters and replace them with hard carriage returns.

This function is discussed in a series of sample functions in Chapter 14, Designing User-Defined Functions. The procedure below shows the problems that will occur if a memo field is directly displayed to the screen when it is larger than one specific screen.

```
*********************
* Name         SHOWMEMO.prg
* Date         August 7, 1986
* Notice       Copyright 1986, Stephen J. Straley
* Note         This shows some of the problems
*              encountered using the MEMOEDIT function and
*              large memo fields.
*********************
```

```
STORE "Now is the time for all good men to come to the" TO mess
STORE mess + " aid of their country regardless of their" TO mess
STORE mess + " memo edit function --- or the word processor" TO   mess
STORE mess + " they happen to be using...." TO mess
CLEAR
@ 1,0 SAY "Now, here is the string for use...."
? mess
@ 7,0 SAY "Now here is a small screen of that...."
*******************************************************************
* The KEYBOARD() command shouldn't be used, but for demon-        *
* stration purposes, it becomes necessary!                        *
*******************************************************************
KEYBOARD CHR(23)
STORE MEMOEDIT(mess,18,20,20,60,.T.) TO mess
@ 24,0 SAY "Press Any Key to Continue..."
qw = INKEY(0)
@ 7,0 CLEAR
@ 7,0 SAY "Now here is the memo with the problems...."
? mess
@ 24,0 SAY "Press Any Key to Continue..."
qw = INKEY(0)
@ 15,0 CLEAR
@ 15,0 SAY "And here is the solution...."
? BITSTRIP(mess)

********************

FUNCTION Bitstrip

   PARAMETERS c

   outstring = ""
   DO WHILE .NOT. EMPTY(c)
      IF AT(CHR(141),c) = 0
         outstring = outstring + SUBSTR(c, 1, LEN(c))
         c = ""
      ELSE
         outstring = outstring + SUBSTR(c, 1, AT(CHR(141), c) - 1) + CHR(13)
         scan = AT(CHR(141), c) + 1
         c = SUBSTR(c, scan, LEN(c) - scan + 1)
      ENDIF
   ENDDO
   RETURN(outstring)
* End of File.
```

WHEN TO USE MEMO FIELDS

Memo fields can be useful tools for such things as notes for salespeople regarding special orders, contextual HELP, or even basic text information. If you are going to use memo fields, code just for the compiler rather than trying to make your code fit both environments; that usually won't work. Be careful of memory usage. MEMOEDIT()

is a memory-hungry function and saves the original memo field in memory as well as the edited version. For additional information on the use of the MEMOEDIT() function in an application, please review Chapter 15, Clipper HELP Utility.

The Summer '87 Abilities

The Summer '87 release gave seven new parameters to the MEMOEDIT() function including the ability to scroll horizontally and the ability to pass the name of a user-defined function to be activated every time a key is pressed within the MEMOEDIT() function. These two features, along with the other parameters, functions, and expanded string capacity opened new dimensions to the MEMO logic in Clipper. Before going into some of those possibilities, here is an in-depth look at the new MEMOEDIT() function:

```
MEMOEDIT([parameter1 ... parameter13])
```

Parameter Description

1. The name of the memo field or character string to be processed by MEMOEDIT().

2. The top row coordinate for the window area for MEMOEDIT().

3. The top column coordinate for the window area for MEMOEDIT().

4. The bottom row coordinate for the window area for MEMOEDIT().

5. The bottom column coordinate for the window area for MEMOEDIT()

6. A logical value to tell MEMOEDIT() to allow for editing (.T.) or to simply display the field contents (.F.).

7. The name of a user-defined function that will be executed whenever a key is pressed within MEMOEDIT().

8. The line length of the actual MEMODIT(). If this parameter is greater than the spacing between the two column parameters, the MEMOEDIT() function will horizontally scroll.

9. The size of the table spacing. The default spacing is four spaces.

10. The initial line in which the cursor is placed.

11. The initial column in which the cursor is placed.

12. The initial relative row position of the cursor in relation to the window position.

13. The initial relative column position of the cursor in relation to the window position.

The user-defined function opens up several possibilities including full word-processing capabilities and simulating GETs using the MEMOEDIT() function. Here are some rules to maintain with this version of the MEMOEDIT() function:

1. Using the .F. parameter option to display only a memo now requires that you issue a KEYBOARD CHR(27) before the MEMOEDIT() function is called. Otherwise, an additional logical parameter set to false must be passed in place of the user-defined function name.

```
MEMOEDIT(<expC>, <expN1 - 4>, .F., .F.)
```

2. The user-defined function is passed as a character string, without parentheses and parameter references.

3. The concept of "modes" is to tell the user-defined function, if specified, the general status of the MEMOEDIT() function. This must be one of the accepted parameters within the programmed user-defined function, along with the current row and column number within the MEMOEDIT() function.

SIMULATING A GET WITH THE MEMOEDIT()

The reason that this feature is more feasible with the Summer '87 release is because of the user-defined function capabilities in MEMOEDIT(). Since MEMOEDIT() passes to the function the current row and column number, the width of the GET area may be analyzed constantly.

```
********************
* Name      Fakeget.prg
* Date      March 12, 1988
* Notice    Copyright (c) 1988, Stephen J. Straley & Associates
* Author    Stephen J. Straley
* Compile   Clipper Fakeget -m
* Release   Summer '87
* Link      Tlink fakeget,,,extend + clipper
* Note      This program shows how to use the MEMOEDIT to simulate a GET
*           command.
********************

CLEAR SCREEN
SET SCOREBOARD OFF
```

```
new_val = ""
new_val = SIMGET(15,10,9,new_val)
? new_val
? LEN(new_val)

*********************

FUNCTION Simget

   PARAMETERS sim_row, sim_col, sim_len, simulate

   old_color = SETCOLOR()
   SETCOLOR(REVERSE(old_color))
    pass_back = MEMOEDIT(simulate, sim_row, sim_col, sim_row, sim_col + sim_len,
.T., "LIMITGET")
   SET COLOR TO &old_color.
   RETURN(pass_back)

*********************

FUNCTION Limitget

   PARAMETERS the_mode, the_line, the_col

   IF the_col = sim_len
      KEYBOARD CHR(23)
      RETURN(0)
   ENDIF

*
* The following function is part of the Steve Straley Toolkit.
* Copyright (c) 1988 by Stephen Straley & Associates, All rights reserved
*

*********************

FUNCTION Reverse

   PARAMETERS the_color

   the_say = STRTRAN(SUBSTR(the_color, 1, AT(",", the_color)-1), "+", "")
    RETURN(SUBSTR(the_say, AT("/", the_say)+1) + "/" + SUBSTR(the_say, 1, AT("/",
the_say)-1))
* End of file
```

LISTING A FILE WITHIN A MEMOEDIT()

The expanded abilities within the MEMOEDIT() function are numerous. One such discovery was the ability to call the MEMOEDIT() multiple times. In the Steve Straley Toolkit, the word processor was built around the MEMOEDIT() function. However, an added feature of the toolkit was to have an on-line table of contents, using another MEMOEDIT() to perform the actual display. Listed below is a simulation of that technology.

```
*********************
* Name     Listing.prg
* Date     March 12, 1988
* Notice   Copyright (c) 1988, Stephen J. Straley & Associates
* Author   Stephen J. Straley
* Compile  Clipper Listing -m
* Release  Summer '87
* Link     Tlink fakeget,,,extend + clipper
* Note     This program shows how to use the MEMOEDIT within a MEMOEDIT
*
*********************

CLEAR SCREEN
@ 21,10 SAY "Press F1 to List a file..."
@ 2,10 TO 20,70 DOUBLE
new_char = ""
MEMOEDIT(new_char, 3,11, 19, 69, .T., "Key1")

*********************

FUNCTION Key1

   PARAMETER keymode, keyline, keycol

   what_key = LASTKEY()
   IF what_key = 28
      listfile = SPACE(30)
      @ 24,00 SAY "Enter File to List => " GET listfile
      READ
      listfile = ALLTRIM(listfile)
      IF EMPTY(listfile)
         @ 24,00 CLEAR
      ELSE
         IF !FILE(listfile)
            @ 24,00 CLEAR
            @ 24,00 SAY "File not found.  Press Any key to return..."
            INKEY(0)
         ELSE
            filesize = FILESIZE(listfile)
            IF filesize >= (MEMORY(0) * 1024) .OR. filesize > 60000
               @ 24,00 CLEAR
               @ 24,00 SAY "You haven't enough room to load the file.  Any key..."
               INKEY(0)
            ELSE
               DO Listfile WITH listfile
            ENDIF
         ENDIF
      ENDIF
      @ 24,00 CLEAR
      RETURN(32)
   ENDIF
```

```
*********************

PROCEDURE Listfile

   PARAMETERS thefile

   intake = MEMOREAD(thefile)
   SAVE SCREEN
   @ 6,20 CLEAR TO 22, 60
   @ 6,20 TO 22,60 DOUBLE
   MEMOEDIT(intake, 7,21,21,59,.T.,"Key2", 132)
   RESTORE SCREEN

*********************

FUNCTION Key2

   PARAMETERS key2mode, key2line, key2col

   newkey = LASTKEY()
   IF newkey = 27
      RETURN(0)
   ELSEIF KEYS(newkey)
      RETURN(32)
   ELSE
      KEYBOARD CHR(27)
      RETURN(0)
   ENDIF

*********************

FUNCTION KEYS

   PARAMETERS testkey

   IF     testkey = 5
      RETURN(.T.)
   ELSEIF testkey = 13
      RETURN(.T.)
   ELSEIF testkey = 6
      RETURN(.T.)
   ELSEIF testkey = 1
      RETURN(.T.)
   ELSEIF testkey = 24
      RETURN(.T.)
   ELSEIF testkey = 19
      RETURN(.T.)
   ELSEIF testkey = 4
      RETURN(.T.)
   ELSEIF testkey = 18
      RETURN(.T.)
   ELSEIF testkey = 3
      RETURN(.T.)
```

```
   ELSE
      RETURN(.F.)
   ENDIF

*
* The following function is part of the Steve Straley Toolkit.
* Copyright (c) 1988 by Stephen Straley & Associates, All rights reserved
*

********************

FUNCTION Filesize

   PARAMETERS thefile

   thefile = UPPER(ALLTRIM(thefile))
   IF !FILE(thefile)
      RETURN(0)
   ENDIF

   **********************************************************
   * The following (commented out) code section works with *
   * the old Clipper and immediately after is the code for *
   * the new Clipper. *
   **********************************************************
   *
   *   SET CURSOR OFF
   *   RUN DIR &thefile >Lookatit
   *   nowthen = MEMOREAD("Lookatit")
   *   ERASE Lookatit
   *   SET CURSOR ON
   *    insidefil = FILL_OUT(SUBSTR(thefile, 1, AT(".", thefile) - 1), 9) + SUB-
STR(thefile, -3)
   *   RETURN(VAL(SUBSTR(nowthen, AT(insidefil, nowthen) + 12, 10)))
   *

   DECLARE fname[1], fsize[1]
   ADIR(thefile, fname, fsize)
   RETURN(fsize[1])
```

READING IN A FILE WITHIN A MEMOEDIT()

Again, while developing the Toolkit and the word processor within it, the need to read in a file and directly insert that file into the MEMOEDIT() became important. This technology was only available with the Summer '87 release. There are a couple of important factors to consider when trying to read the file and directly insert it into the MEMOEDIT() function.

1. Make sure that the amount of text to be inserted does not exceed the maximum string capacity of the Summer '87 release of Clipper. This value is now set at 64K.

2. Be aware that when stuffing the KEYBOARD with the characters from the file being read, some characters may seem to have been "dropped."

```
**********************
* Name      Readitin.prg
* Author    Stephen J. Straley
* Notice    Copyright (c) 1987, 1988 Stephen J. Straley & Associates
* Date      March 11, 1988
* Compile   Clipper Readitin -m
* Release   Summer '87
* Link      Plink86 fi readitin lib extend lib clipper
* Note      This program shows how to use the low-level file routines to
*           read in a file while in a MEMOEDIT() function.
*
**********************

CLEAR SCREEN
@ 21,10 SAY "Press F1 to Read in a file..."
@ 2,10 TO 20,70 DOUBLE
new_char = ""
MEMOEDIT(new_char, 3,11, 19, 69, .T., "Key1", 130)

**********************

FUNCTION Key1

   PARAMETER keymode, keyline, keycol

   what_key = LASTKEY()
   IF what_key = 28
      search_for = SPACE(25)
      filehandle = 0
      @ 22,00 CLEAR
      @ 23,01 SAY "Enter Name of File => " GET search_for PICT
"XXXXXXXXXXXXXXXXXXXXXXXXX" VALID TRY2OPEN(search_for, @filehandle)
      READ
      @ 22,00 CLEAR
      @ 23,01 SAY "Loading File Into Buffer..."
      IF EMPTY(search_for) .OR. LASTKEY() = 27
         @ 22,00 CLEAR
         RETURN(32)
      ENDIF
      IF FILESIZE(search_for) > 29000
         @ 23,00 CLEAR
         @ 23,01 SAY "File TOO large to bring into system.  Any Key to Continue"
         INKEY(0)
         @ 22,00 CLEAR
         RETURN(32)
      ENDIF
      REWIND(filehandle)   && reset the pointer position!
      read_amnt = 80
      byts_read = 80
      bffstring = SPACE(160)
```

```
      backout = ""
      DO WHILE byts_read == read_amnt
         byts_read = FREAD(filehandle, @bffstring, read_amnt)
         bffstring = STRTRAN(STRTRAN(ALLTRIM(bffstring), CHR(252),
CHR(13)+CHR(10)), CHR(251), CHR(13)+CHR(10))
         backout = backout + STRTRAN(bffstring, CHR(219), "")
         bffstring = SPACE(160)
      ENDDO
      FCLOSE(filehandle)
      @ 22,00 CLEAR
      KEYBOARD backout
      RETURN(32)
   ENDIF

*
* The following functions and proecdures are part of the Steve Straley Toolkit.
* Copyright (c) 1988 by Stephen Straley & Associates, All rights reserved
*

********************

FUNCTION Filesize

   PARAMETERS thefile

   thefile = UPPER(ALLTRIM(thefile))
   IF !FILE(thefile)
      RETURN(0)
   ENDIF

   ***********************************************************
   * The following (commented out) code section works with *
   * the old Clipper and immediately after is the code for *
   * the new Clipper.                                      *
   ***********************************************************
   *
   *   SET CURSOR OFF
   *   RUN DIR &thefile >Lookatit
   *   nowthen = MEMOREAD("Lookatit")
   *   ERASE Lookatit
   *   SET CURSOR ON
   *   insidefil = FILL_OUT(SUBSTR(thefile, 1, AT(".", thefile) - 1), 9) + SUB-
STR(thefile, -3)
   *   RETURN(VAL(SUBSTR(nowthen, AT(insidefil, nowthen) + 12, 10)))
   *

   DECLARE fname[1], fsize[1]
   ADIR(thefile, fname, fsize)
   RETURN(fsize[1])
```

```
**********************

FUNCTION Try2open

   PARAMETERS i_o_file, i_o_handle

   * i_o_handle is passed by REFERENCE!!
   IF EMPTY(i_o_file)
     RETURN(.F.)
   ENDIF
   i_o_handle = FOPEN(i_o_file)
   RETURN( ( FERROR() = 0 ) )

**********************

FUNCTION Rewind

   PARAMETERS r_handle

   FSEEK(r_handle, 0)
   RETURN(.T.)
* End of File
```

The key to remember with these functions is the new possibilities they, and all of the new features of the Summer '87 release, provide. The key to the MEMOEDIT() function is the user-defined function that can analyze and manipulate keystroke and character information while processing within the MEMOEDIT() function. This technology expands the Clipper horizons and moves from the world of "nice to have" to the world of reality.

CHAPTER NINE

Clipper Features, Utilities, and Expansions

The Summer '87 release not only introduced many new commands, functions, capabilities, and features, but a few new utilities as well. One of the most noticeable differences is the new enhanced DEBUG.OBJ. Listed below are the utility files that accompany the compiler. Those marked with an asterisk are either enhanced or added with the Summer '87 release.

	CREATE.EXE:	A program to create a dBASE III/Clipper compatible database (.DBF) file.
	REPORT.EXE:	A program to create a dBASE III/Clipper compatible form (.FM) file.
	LABEL.EXE:	A program to create a dBASE III/Clipper compatible label (.LBL) file.
*	RL.EXE	A Clipper compiled program that in the Summer '87 release replaces the REPORT.EXE and LABEL.EXE programs.
*	SWITCH.EXE:	A program to help chain program execution from one .COM or .EXE file to another
*	LINE.EXE:	A program to display a specific line number in a specified Clipper .PRG file.
*	MAKE.EXE:	A program to allow a predefined number of source code files with compiling and linking instructions.
*	DEBUG.OBJ:	An object file that can be linked with any application in order to help debug it.
*	NDX.OBJ:	An object file that, when linked with an application, will automatically generate and view dBASE III-compatible index files. If this file in not linked in, the default is to generate and view Clipper index files.
*	IBMANSI.OBJ	An ANSI object file that is IBM specific and that supports the functions keys and cursor keys of IBM PC machines.
*	PCBIOS.OBJ:	An object file that directs all screen I/O to the bios that allows the compiled application to run under such windowing environments as DeskView.
	ANSI.OBJ:	An object file that can be linked with any application in order to allow the application to run with the ANSI driver.

This includes any other screen driver provided it can be more machine specific (e.g., TIPRO.OBJ, WANG.OBJ, etc.). This driver does **not** support the cursor keys or the function keys of the IBM PC.

EXTEND.*: With versions prior to the Summer '87 release, this is a group of files containing functions that extend Clipper's capabilities to include dBASE III Plus commands and facilities.

These utilities were created to assist application developers in design, creation, and execution. Each utility program can be given to any end user without royalty or obligation to the Nantucket Corporation.

Some utilities are designed strictly for the execution of the application; that is, some utility programs either assist the program in running or assist the developer in finding problems with the application. Other utilities prepare certain conditions prior to the execution of the application. Each utility program is fully outlined in the following pages, and tips and hints on using them in the real world are included.

CREATE.EXE

Execution Syntax: CREATE <d:filename>

Notes: d: = drive and directory designator. If no drive designator is given, the current drive and directory are assumed.

<filename> = the name of the database file to be CREATED or MODIFY STRUCTUREd.

This program creates a new database file or modifies an existing one with the specified field names, field lengths, field types, and field decimal places. The CREATE program is similar to the CREATE command in dBASE III's interactive mode. Prompts are issued throughout this program and on-line help is available at any time by striking the F1 key.

Field names can have any combination of up to 10 characters with the following exceptions:

1. Spaces are not allowed in the middle of a field name.
2. Field names must start with an alphabetic character (A-Z, a-z).
3. Field names cannot contain hyphens.

Field types are represented by the following symbols:

1. C Character type
2. N Numeric type
3. L Logical type
4. D Date type
5. M Memo type

Field lengths (decimals not included):

1. Character fields: 37,343 characters.
2. Numeric fields: 15 characters.
3. Logical fields: 1 character.
4. Date field: 8 characters.
5. Memo field: 10 characters. (The memo file is dynamic: it will only increase as characters are added, not when blanks are APPENDed to the main file.)

Even with all of the database information necessary, there are a few drawbacks in this version of the CREATE utility program:

1. The file extension **must** be a .DBF extension. This prevents the developer from adapting his or her own descriptive style for tagging files with anything other than the .DBF extension. A viable way around this is to rename an existing file prior to running this program; then again rename the file after using CREATE.

2. The file extension cannot be given as part of the parameter. Since the file must have a .DBF extension, just pass the root name as the parameter to CREATE.

3. Make a copy of the file if records are present and you are going to modify the structure of the database. As in dBASE II, the utility program will not append the records from the old database to the new one.

Comments: This utility program is helpful when creating a file for testing or for meeting urgent schedules. For any total application, the ability to create databases should be coded into the application. In most cases, the user should not have access to a program that can alter the structure of a database (especially when that program could eliminate the records). The CREATE command in the Clipper Syntax Command Library gives applications the ability to self-generate database structures, thereby removing any possible need for this utility program. For further information regarding CREATing databases within an application, please refer to the CREATE and the INDEX commands in Chapter 2, Compiling.

REPORT.EXE

Execution Syntax: REPORT <d:filename>

Notes: d: = drive or directory designator. If no drive designator is given, the current drive or directory will be assumed.

<filename> = the name of the file that the REPORT utility program will generate. This file will have a .FRM extension.

This utility program creates a fresh report form or modifies an existing one. It does not react the same way as the report generator in dBASE III. Do not enter an extension, if you enter any at all, other than the expected .FRM. If you were to type

```
C>REPORT Test.new
```

you would see the following:

```
Clipper(tm) REPORT Generator, Winter '85
Copyright (c)  Nantucket Inc. 1985
Developed by: B. Russell / J. Rognerud

REPORT:  unable to open test.new.frm
```

After typing in the file name (in this case TEST), the following menu will appear:

```
Date: 04/21/86    Clipper(tm) Report Generator          New file:  TEST.frm

                        P A G E   H E A D I N G:


                   Enter page width..........  80
                   Enter left margin.........   8
                   Enter right margin........   0
                   Enter no. lines per page..  58
                   Double spaced report?.....   N
```

Under the title PAGE HEADING, a shaded area of four lines is provided for the actual heading for each page of the report. Under this are five parameters that can be changed for the report.

Warning: Any changes to these five parameters are not maintained when the report form is modified. The default values will always come up. If you change their values, make a note of them for future use.

After this page, a second screen of information is displayed:

```
Date: 04/21/86    Clipper(tm) Report Generator           New file:  TEST.frm

Group/subtotal on...........:


Summary report only? (Y/N) N                      Eject after each subtotal? (Y/N) N

Group/subtotal heading......:

Subgroup/subsubtotal on.....:


Subgroup/subsubtotal heading
```

The information required is self-explanatory.

Warning: If a field is specified for a subtotal or a subsubtotal, that field must be spelled exactly as it is in the database for which the report is being designed. Unlike the interpreter, REPORT does not have the capability to check the validity of a field's existence or spelling. If there is a misspelling or if there is no field with the specified name, a run-time error message will appear.

Finally, a third screen of information will appear. In this screen, each specific field to be included in the report must be entered. If TOTALS are to be included, answer "Y."

Warning: Again, the field names are not checked with the database for their existence and spelling. If a field listed in the report is not in the database or is misspelled, a run-time error will occur. Also, the lengths of the fields are not compared. Verify the lengths entered with the actual lengths.

Feature: One important feature of this utility program is that user-defined functions are allowed. However, as with fields, these functions must be defined somewhere within the application, otherwise a run-time error, "undefined symbol exists," will appear.

Example:

Subgroup/subsubtotal on.....:MYORDER(last_name)

```
Date: 04/21/86     Clipper(tm) Report Generator          New file:  TEST.frm
                                                         Field:    1

CONTENTS:

                          # decimal places    0  Totals? (Y/N) N


HEADER:   1
          2
          3
          4

Width:  10
```

Comments: REPORT.EXE is a quick utility program with some major loopholes. It would not be a good idea to give this utility program to a user inexperienced with dBASE III's report utility or with your program because column lengths are not totaled as you enter each field and field specs are not compared to what is entered. If you use this utility, be very careful and cross-check everything **before** running the report in a compiled application.

LABEL.EXE

Execution Syntax: LABEL <d:filename>

Notes: d: = drive and directory designator. If no drive designator is given, the current drive and directory will be assumed.

<filename> = the name of the file that the LABEL utility program generates. This file will have a .LBL extension.

This utility program is designed to create label format files with a .LBL extension to be used in conjunction with the Clipper LABEL command. If no extension is provided, the utility program adds the proper extension. If an extension is provided other than the expected .LBL (e.g., TEST.NEW), the LABEL program will not execute and the following message will appear:

```
Clipper(tm) LABEL Generator, Winter '85
Copyright (c)  Nantucket Inc. 1985
Developed by: B. Russell / J. Rognerud

LABEL:  unable to open test.new.lbl
```

The first screen of the LABEL program looks something like this:

```
Date: 04/21/85      Clipper(tm) Label Generator          New file: TEST.lbl



                    Enter width of label                 35
                    Enter height of label                 5
                    Enter left margin                     0
                    Enter lines between labels            1
                    Enter spaces between labels           0
                    Enter number of labels across         1
```

Comments: The six parameters above can be changed and are saved with the file (unlike the REPORT.EXE utility program).

Immediately following this screen, the final screen appears:

```
Date: 04/21/85               Label Contents:             New file: test.lbl


             1
             2
             3
             4
             5
```

If the height of the label, for example, is changed to 2, only two lines will appear on the second screen. A maximum of six lines is allowed.

Warning: Do not misspell the names of the fields to be used with the label file or use a field not associated with the selected database file at execution. If so, a run-time error appears.

Feature: User-defined functions are allowed in conjunction with the LABEL file.

Example:

```
                    Label Contents:

             1   CENTR(address_1)
             2   CENTR(address_2)
             3   CENTR(city)
             4   CENTR(state + "    " + zip)
             5
```

Comments: The LABEL.EXE utility program is perhaps the simplest utility program to use; however, it should not fall into the hands of an inexperienced user. Misspellings and nonexistent fields will be fatal. The developer should be in control of all output as well as all input. However, for quick labels without the aid of dBASE III, this utility program does the job.

RL.EXE

Execution Syntax: RL

Note: The RL.EXE program is a Clipper-compiled program for the Summer '87 release that takes the place of the REPORT and LABEL utility programs. Below is the list of .PRG files that make up the RL program, the compiling syntax, and the linking syntax.

Compile:

```
Clipper Rlfront -m
Clipper Rlback -m
Clipper Rldialog -m
```

Linking:

```
Tlink Rlfront + Rlback + Rldialog,Rl,,Extend + Clipper
```

Once compiled and linked, if executed, the main menu for this program would look something like this:

```
Report    Label    Quit
```

Choosing either REPORT or LABEL option, the following screen will appear:

```
Report    Label    Quit
```

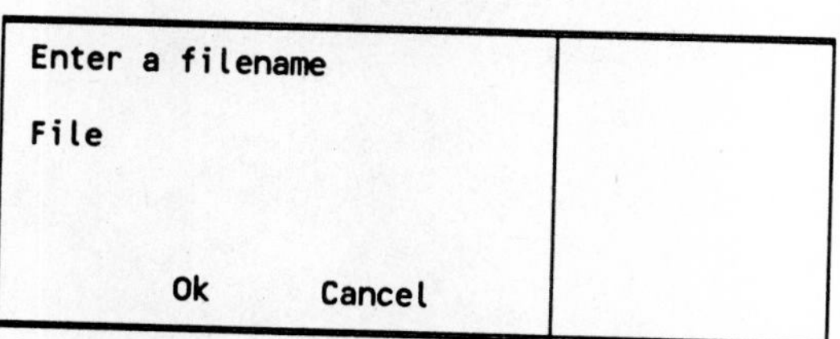

Choosing the REPORT option, this submenu will eventually appear.

```
F1      F2       F3      F4      F5      F6      F7     F10
Help    Layout   Groups  Fields  Delete  Insert  Go To  Exit
------------------------------------------------------------
                                             File STEVE.FRM
                                                  Field 1
                 — Field Definitions —            Total 1

Contents


Heading
      1
      2
      3
      4


Formatting
Width      10
Decimals    0
Totals     N
```

Choosing the LAYOUT option allows the standard REPORT.FRM page headings, margins, page widths, lines per page, double-spaced reports, page eject before and after printing, and report style (plain page).

For the LABEL submenu, the RL.EXE program will generate this screen:

```
F1     F2       F3                                 F10
Help   Toggle   Formats                            Exit
-------------------------------------------------------
                                         File STEVE.LBL
 Dimensions            Formatting
     Width      35           Margin        0
     Height      5           Lines         1
     Across      1           Spaces        0

     Remarks

            CONTENTS
Line 1─────────────────────────────────────────────────
```

Choosing the FORMAT submenu, the following options would then appear:

```
F1        F2        F3                                                F10
Help      Toggle    Formats                                           Exit
-------------------------------------------------------------------------
                                                          File STEVE.LBL
 Dimensions                         Formatting
      Width       35                      Margin          0
      Height       5                      Lines           1
      Across       1                      Spaces          0

      Remarks

             CONTE
Line 1 ---------        3 1/2 x 15/16 by 1              ---------------
                        3 1/2 x 15/16 by 2
                        3 1/2 x 15/16 by 3
                          4 x 17/16 by 1
                    3 2/10 x 11/12 by 3 (Cheshire)
```

LINE.EXE

Execution Syntax: LINE <filename> [<expN>]

Notes: The <filename> must include a .PRG file extension.

The <expN> is an optional numeric expression that, if passed, will display only a particular line number from the <filename>.

Comments: With some editors, the line number of a source program file is expressed in terms of total characters entered or even in terms of a page number, line number combination. The LINE.EXE program will take the <filename> and tag the lines with specific line numbers, which then can be traced back to any run-time errors.

It is suggested that during final debugging stages that the LINE.EXE program is redirected to a DOS file, which then can be printed.

SWITCH.EXE

Execution Syntax: SWITCH <main program> <program one> <program two> ... <program nine>

Definition: This program chains program execution from the <main program> to <program one>, from <program one> to <program two>, and so on up to <program nine>.

MAKE.EXE

Syntax: MAKE [/N] <script file>

Overview: The MAKE.EXE utility program is a program commonly used by most programmers who are used to programming with compilers. The theory behind the MAKE utility is to have a program that keeps track of the modules that make up an application, checks to see if any of them have been modified, recompiles only those that reflect recent changes, and automatically relinks the modules to make the executable program. Think of the MAKE as "make my program." The MAKE utility scans the disk for those modules defined to make up an application, recompiles only those that have changed, and links the modules together, with the proper libraries, in the proper order.

The MAKE program has to know what .PRG files to potentially compile, which .OBJ and .LIB files to link together to make up the compiled application, and the order in which to link them all together. This is accomplished with an accompanying "script" file. The script file is no more than a text file describing the basic construct of the application: from the link order to the compiling modules. To instruct MAKE to open the script file and follow the instructions, at the DOS prompt, the command would look something like this:

```
MAKE [/N] <script file>
```

There are two things to keep in mind with this command. First, the /N option tells the MAKE utility to display **only** the commands within the script file without actually invoking them. This is particularly useful when testing to see if the script file is built properly. Second, the file extension for the script file is not assumed. Normally, most script files will be made having a .MAK file extension; however, this is not mandatory.

The order in which commands are placed in the script file must follow some guidelines and rules. Additionally, some commands within the script file may be explicit or implied in nature. Again, the differences between the two types of command structures within the MAKE script file follow certain rules. First, you must define the target file for the ensuing commands and operations. For example, if an .OBJ file consists of four separate .PRG files, named EXAMPLE1.PRG through EXAMPLE4.PRG, the syntax in the script file would be as follows:

```
One.obj:Example1.prg Example2.prg Example3.prg Example4.prg
Clipper Example1
```

In this example, it is implied that EXAMPLE1.PRG will call (with a DO command) either EXAMPLE2.PRG through EXAMPLE4, and that any of these programs may call one of the other EXAMPLE?.PRGs. If any of the text or commands were to continue onto the next line, the "/" character would be required. Since Clipper will automatically compile referenced modules, only the top-most program file needs to be called. However, if this is not the case, then another possible MAKE command could be the following:

```
Example1.obj:Example1.prg
Clipper Example1 -m

Example2.obj:Example2.prg/
Clipper Example2 -m

Example3.obj:Example3.prg
Clipper Example3 -m

Example4.obj:Example4.prg
Clipper Example4 -m
```

This explicitly tells the MAKE program to MAKE an object module called ONE.OBJ that will consist of compiled modules EXAMPLE1.PRG through EXAMPLE4.PRG, with no other dependent modules. The same command construct in the script file holds true for the linking instructions as do for the compiling instructions. The targeted file is defined by the modules that make it up, followed by the command to actually do the operation. Using the above example, let's take the ONE.OBJ and make a NEW.EXE file consisting of the two main library files in the Summer '87 release. The text in the script file would look something like this:

```
New.exe:example1.obj example2.obj example3.obj example4.obj
Tlink example1 example2 example3 example4,New,,Extend + Clipper
```

Or, if using the Plink86 linker, the script file would then look like this:

```
New.exe:example1.obj example2.obj example3.obj example4.obj
Plink86 Fi example1 fi example2 fi example3 fi example4/
          Output New Lib Extend Lib Clipper;
```

Now, there is one important concept to remember: order. The order of these statements is extremely important. If a series of directions is out of order, the desired results may not happen. For example, if the linking command preceded the compiling commands in the MAKE script file, MAKE would first look at the date and time stamp of NEW.EXE and compare it with the date and time stamp of ONE.OBJ. Since they have not been updated, the command to link would not be executed. Following this, MAKE would then compare the date and time stamps of EXAM-

PLE1.PRG through EXAMPLE4.PRG, which make up ONE.OBJ. If one of these program files had been modified, MAKE would note this and look for the compiling instructions. However, since the linking instructions appeared in the script file before the compiling instructions, the executable file would not be modified. Therefore, order within the MAKE script file is important.

There are more possibilities with the MAKE utility program. Comments may be placed within the MAKE script file that help describe the contents of the script file. A comment is determined by the # character (the pound sign). For example, a comment labeling which commands within the script file are for linking and which are for compiling may be in order. To do this, the script file may look something like this:

```
# Compiling Instructions

Example1.obj:Example1.prg
Clipper Example1 -m

Example2.obj:Example2.prg/
Clipper Example2 -m

Example3.obj:Example3.prg
Clipper Example3 -m

Example4.obj:Example4.prg
Clipper Example4 -m

# Linking Instructions

New.exe:example1.obj example2.obj example3.obj example4.obj
Plink86 Fi example1 fi example2 fi example3 fi example4/
         Output New Lib Extend Lib Clipper;
```

Macros are also permitted within the MAKE script file. Think of them much like macros within the compiled application. A macro is defined by a dollar sign ($), parentheses [()] combination, but first it must be defined. For example, using the compiling instructions, a single macro may be assigned to represent all of the object files that comprise the ONE.OBJ. The script file would then look something like this:

```
# first define the macro
# Note that the linking commands are included in the macro

files = FI Example1 FI Example2 FI Example3 FI Example4

# now for the compiling instructions

Example1.obj:Example1.prg
Clipper Example1 -m

Example2.obj:Example2.prg/
Clipper Example2 -m
```

```
Example3.obj:Example3.prg
Clipper Example3 -m

Example4.obj:Example4.prg
Clipper Example4 -m

# Linking Instructions

New.exe:example1.obj example2.obj example3.obj example4.obj
Plink86 $(files) Output New Lib Extend Lib Clipper;
```

Finally, the last important concept to master with the MAKE utility is the rule pertaining to inference: performing a specific action on a set of files with one common file extension to produce another set of files with a different file extension. For example, the inference instructions within the script file would direct MAKE to produce a set of .OBJ files from a matching set of .PRG files. The syntax for the inference rule is as follows:

```
<source file extension><destination file extension>
<command>
```

To initiate the inference macro for the command, use the $ * (dollar sign, asterisk) character combination. The inference **must** be terminated with a colon; otherwise an error while running the MAKE utility will occur. For example, the compiling instructions in the script file may look something like this:

```
# Define the contents of the macro

files = FI Example1 FI Example2 FI Example3 FI Example4

# Now, the inference

.prg.obj:
Clipper $

-m -l -q

# This says to take the designated .prg files and make them
# .obj files by compiling them with Clipper using the -m, -l, and
# -q compiling switches.

# Now for the compiling instructions

Example1.obj:Example1.prg
Clipper Example1 -m

Example2.obj:Example2.prg/
Clipper Example2 -m

Example3.obj:Example3.prg
Clipper Example3 -m
```

```
Example4.obj:Example4.prg
Clipper Example4 -m

# Linking Instructions

New.exe:example1.obj example2.obj example3.obj example4.obj
Plink86 $(files) Output New Lib Extend Lib Clipper;
```

The MAKE file would know to take the following actions:

First, the meaning of the variable "files" is defined as containing the instructions for Plink86 to link object files EXAMPLE1 through EXAMPLE4.

Second, any .PRG file so defined within the script file will be inferred to the existence of a .OBJ file. To get the necessary .OBJ file, use Clipper to compile the .PRG files using switches m, l, and q.

Finally, create the executable file NEW.EXE from the linking command line.

It may at first appear to be a very complicated system. A good suggestion to follow would be to start out with small script files containing neither macro substitutions nor inferences. Just build a script file as you would think logically about how the system would be built. From this you can then add either the macro, the inference, or both as you become more accustomed to the way the MAKE utility works.

DEBUG.OBJ

Overview

One of the most difficult tasks in developing any application is making code error free. Even when applications work under the interpreter, there can be a hitch or two under the compiler. Error-free code on the first try is largely a fantasy. Invariably, bugs creep into code. The simplest bug is often the most difficult to locate. As a result, you should develop standard techniques that help you search for bugs. Techniques that work in interpretive environments may not be practical with compilers because of the need to recompile, relink, and try again.

Clipper has several commands that provide additional information and insight as an application runs. A small front-end module that can be invoked to test for certain conditions is necessary. This is precisely the function that DEBUG.OBJ provides.

The Debugger

The Summer '87 release contains a new, enhanced DEBUG.OBJ. It is completely different from the old DEBUG.OBJ, both in capability and in user interface. As can be expected, because of this vast improvement, the size of the debug object file, and the amount of required memory for it to run, is larger as well. The previous version's debugging utility file size was only 14,395 bytes; the Summer '87 release is 57,767 bytes. The correct date stamp for this file is 12-21-87. Linking procedures are still the same with this version. If the debugger is activated with the Alt-D key, the following new menu would come up:

```
Control  Display  Variable  Help  Break  Watch                   SSText Editor

 Go                                               Proc WORD1
 Go (animation)                                   Line    170
 Go (key)                                         Break points <off>
 Single Step
 DOS Shell
 Break Toggle
 Quit
```

From the CONTROL submenu, the options are listed above.

- The GO option continues program execution without the debugger intervening.
- The GO (animation) option is the same as the GO option except the "watch box" (in the upper right section of the screen display) is displayed with the name of the currently executed procedure and line number flashing by.
- The GO (key) option will execute after a key has been pressed. The debugger menu will reappear at a wait state (i.e., INPUT, ACCEPT, MENU TO, READ, or WAIT).
- The Step option allows the program to execute one line at a time; before each execution, the debugger will be automatically activated. To continue on in single-step mode, this option must be activated after each line of the program is executed.
- The DOS Shell option suspends the execution of the program temporarily while a DOS gateway is created. To return to the program from the DOS shell, the word "EXIT" must be typed in at the DOS prompt.
- The Break Toggle option toggles the evaluation of the break point on and off. The break point status is displayed in the watch box area.
- The Quit option simply exits both the debugger and the program.

The next submenu from the debugger is the Display option. Notice how the debugger now overlays the menu of the application that remains on the screen:

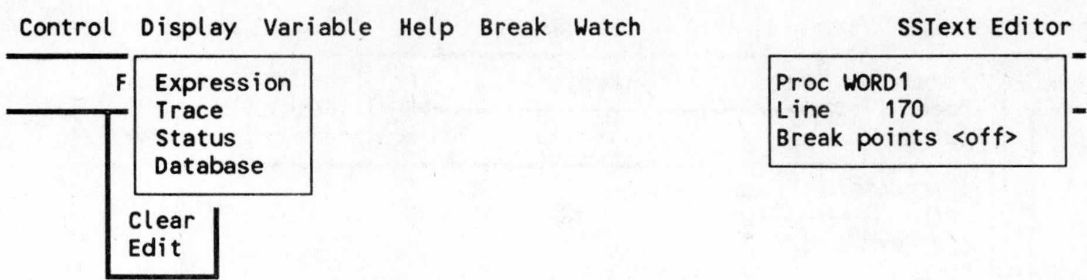

The Expression option allows an expression to be evaluted and displayed. Choosing this option from the debugger's menu, the expression to be evaluated may be typed in with the value at this menu:

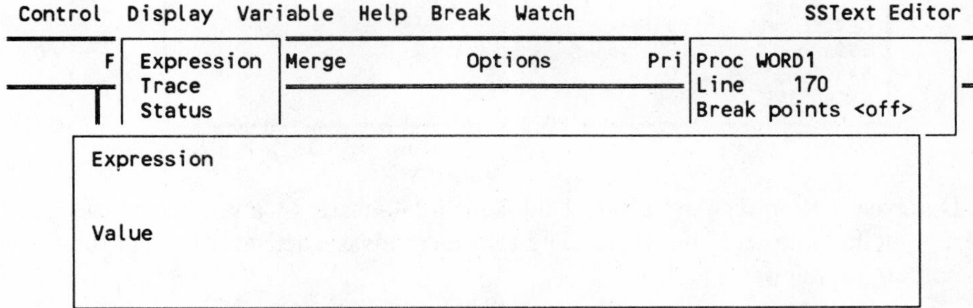

The Trace option shows that procedures have been executed in reverse activation order. This submenu would look something like this:

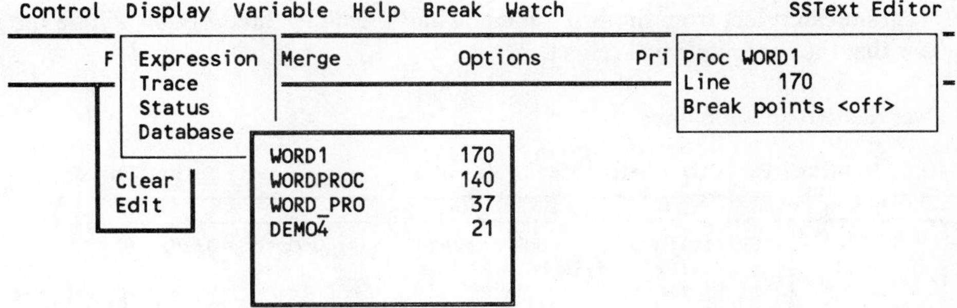

The Status option shows the status of all SET commands. Moving the down and/or up arrow keys will scroll through the status box, eventually showing all of the SET commands. That SET window area would look something like this:

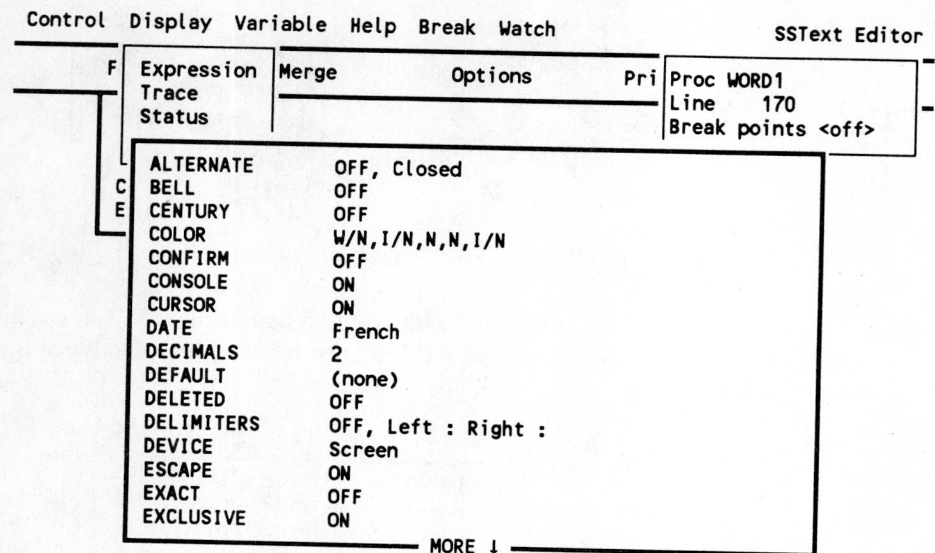

The Database option displays a list of the active databases, by alias, and allows four different methods to see these files. The four methods are activated by four function keys and are as follows:

```
F1 = The Overview Mode (the default option)
F2 = The Relations Mode
F3 = The Indexes Mode
F4 = The Structure Mode
```

The program can select from the first submenu and the highlighted option will be the database that the four mode will reflect.

The Overview Mode Submenu:

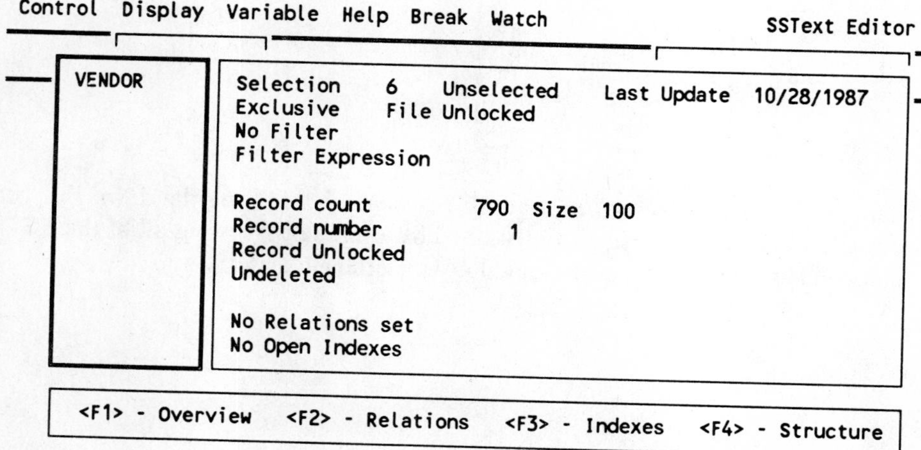

The Relations Mode Submenu:

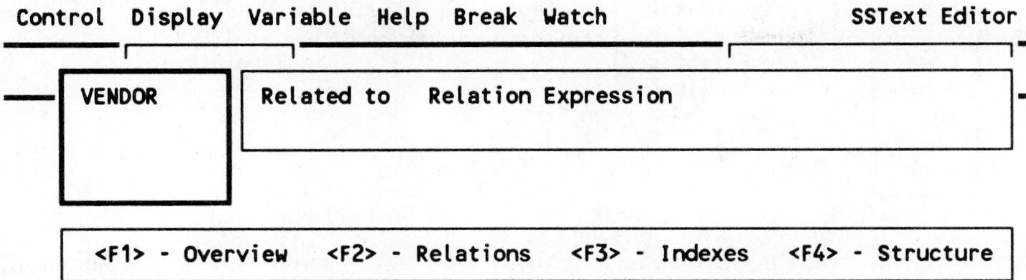

Indexes Mode Submenu:

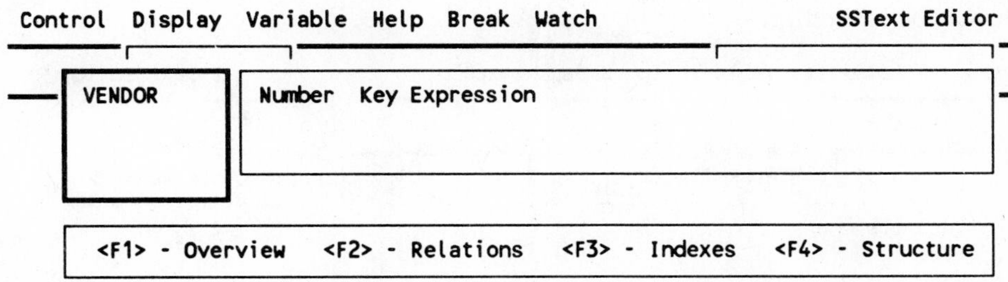

The Structure Mode Submenu:

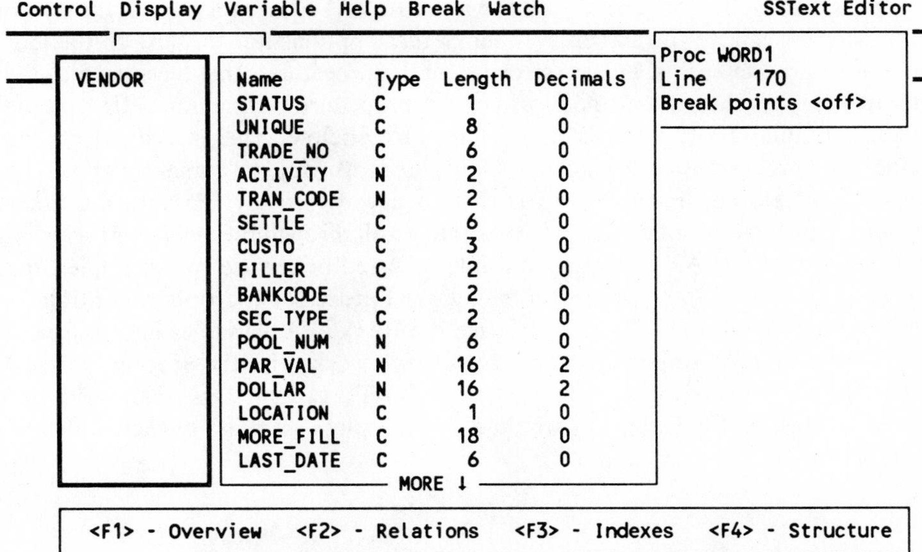

Next is the Variable menu option. From this menu variables, both PUBLIC and PRIVATE, may be assigned, manipulated, or displayed. The menu looks something like this:

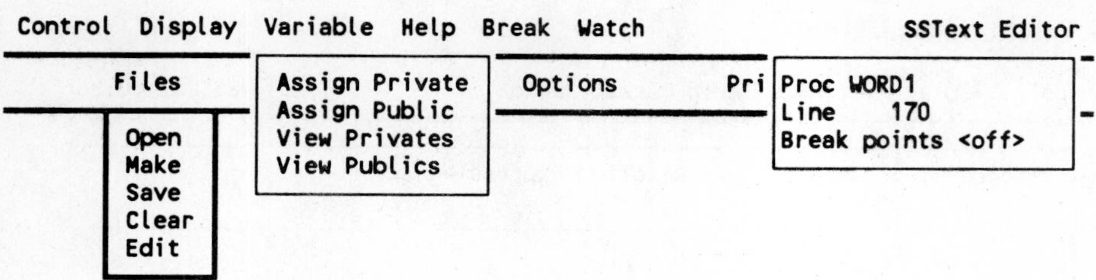

Assigned Private and Public variables are activated in the same manner. If selected, the window below will be shown. From here, type in the name of the PUBLIC or PRIVATE variable to be assigned or manipulated. If the variable is already known to Clipper, only the "New Value" may be entered; otherwise, the variable type and it's value may be entered.

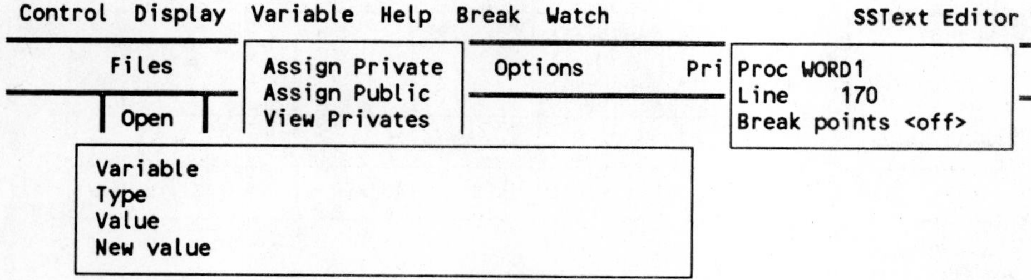

After these two options is the ability to view PRIVATE memory variables. Two windows are brought to the screen if either of these options are chosen. In the left-most column are the names, in reverse order, of the procedures that have been called or are active. This means that the most current procedure or function is first on the list, with the calling procedures listed in calling order below. The procedure that the "viewing" mode is currently working on is highlighted. Moving the cursor up and down this column selects which procedure you wish to view exclusively. Pressing the Enter key changes the window mode and allows you to scroll through the right-most window area, viewing all PRIVATE memory variables. Listed below are two examples; the first example works with the procedure in my word processor (part of Steve Straley's Toolkit) called "WORD1." To the right are the PRIVATE variables in that procedure. Followed by this screen is another screen that works with the procedure called "WORDPROC." Again, to the right are the PRIVATE variables associated with this procedure. Striking the Enter key would allow complete scrolling of the windowed area on the right.

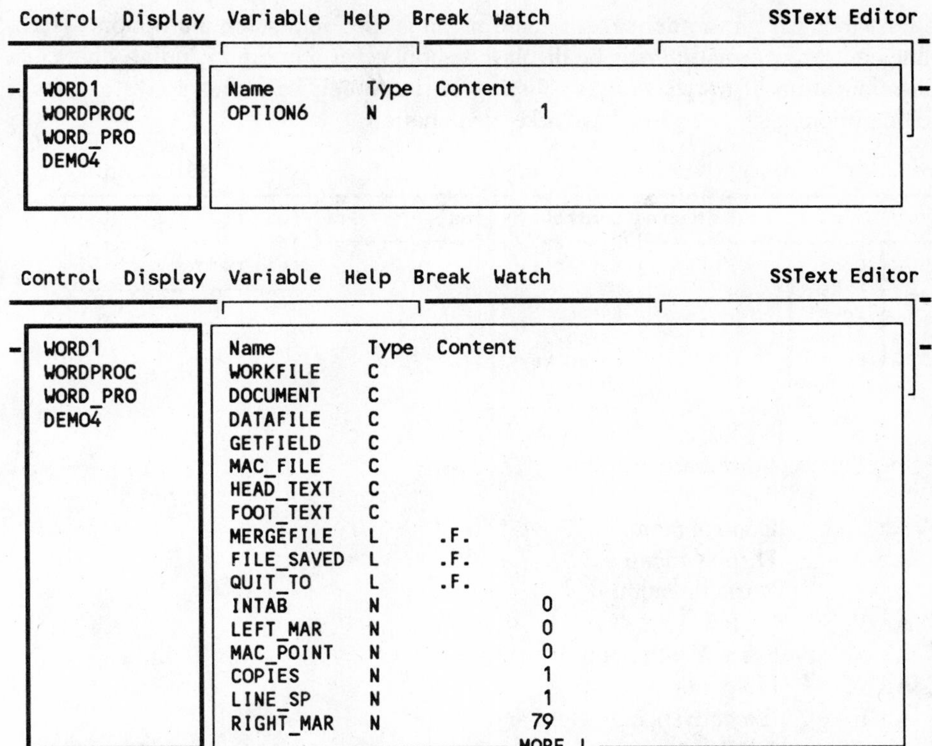

In viewing the PUBLIC variables in the system, a complete window area is displayed allowing the user to scroll through it. The displayed information is much like the PRIVATE viewing mode in that the name of the variable, the data type, and the current value is displayed. Here is what that windowed area would look like:

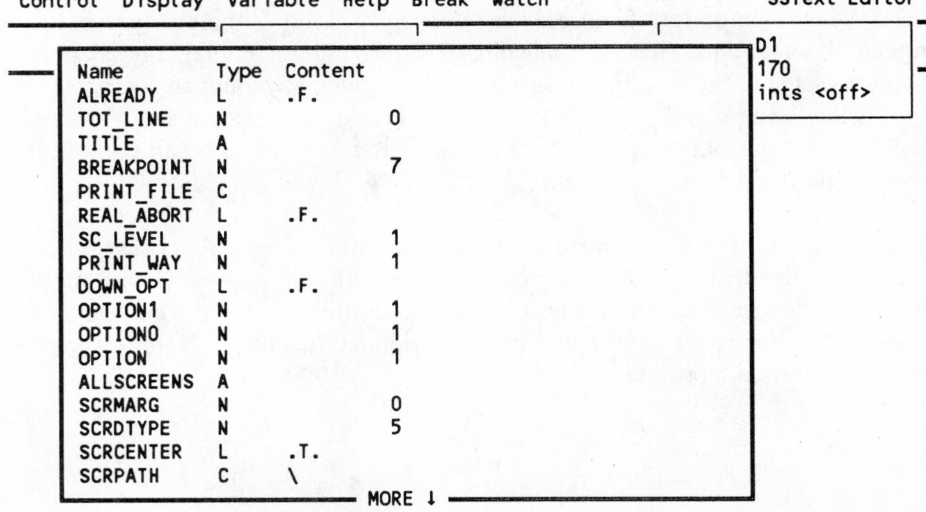

Control Display Variable Help Break Watch SSText Editor
D1
170
ints <off>
Name Type Content
ALREADY L .F.
TOT_LINE N 0
TITLE A
BREAKPOINT N 7
PRINT_FILE C
REAL_ABORT L .F.
SC_LEVEL N 1
PRINT_WAY N 1
DOWN_OPT L .F.
OPTION1 N 1
OPTIONO N 1
OPTION N 1
ALLSCREENS A
SCRMARG N 0
SCRDTYPE N 5
SCRCENTER L .T.
SCRPATH C \
MORE ↓

The next menu from the debugger's main menu is the Help submenu option. Here, on-line context information may be displayed about several items, including what each main-menu item offers as well as a listing of the Speed keys that activate certain specific options with just a two-keystroke combination.

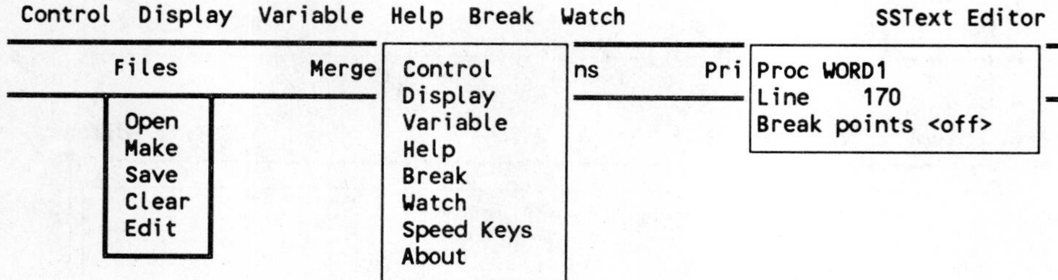

The Speed keys allowed are as follows:

Alt-Z	Control menu
Alt-X	Display menu
Alt-V	Variable menu
Alt-W	Watch menu
Alt-P	Set a Watch point and return
Alt-H	Help menu
Alt-F	Execute specific Help and return
Alt-B	Set Break point and return
Alt-S	Single step and return
Alt-G	Run program
Alt-A	Run program with animation
Alt-K	Run program with keystroke
Alt-Q	Quit

Perhaps the most important feature of any debugging utility is the ability to set and manipulate break points. With this new DEBUG.OBJ, up to 16 unique break points may be set. Some of the new enhancements to this include the ability to combine logical expressions and procedure (and function) line breaks, to toggle on and off a break point from the Control menu, and to watch the system status of a break point in the watch box windowed area.

A break point consists of a procedure name and either a logical expression or a specific line number. If the application is compiled with the -l option (removing line number), the line number will always be zero. Additionally, for the debugger, the name of a procedure may also be that of a user-defined function. Here is what the Break submenu would look like:

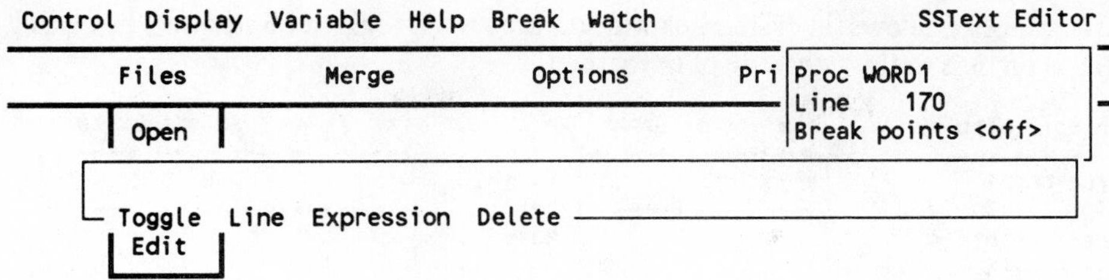

Below is the submenu for the Line option. Following that is the submenu for the Expression option. In either case, leave the Proc value as a blank default to the current working procedure or function. An expression can be a logical break point expression as well; for example: EMPTY(dollar). Finally, the Delete option actually removes a break point that is set in the system.

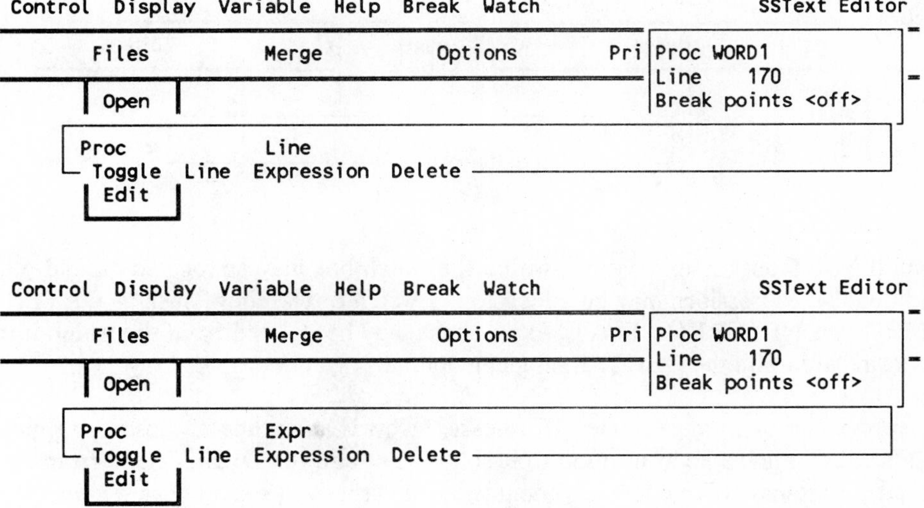

The watch box menu toggles the information and the windowed area for the watch box. It also contains current controlling information, such as the current working procedure and line number; up to 16 expressions may be displayed as well. For expressions containing character data types, only the first 20 characters will be displayed within the watch box window area.

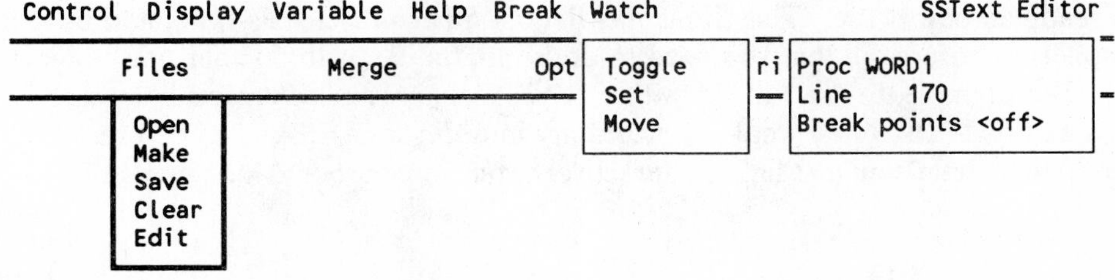

The first option allows the watch box window area to be toggled on or off. The default status is on; it is to the right side of the screen.

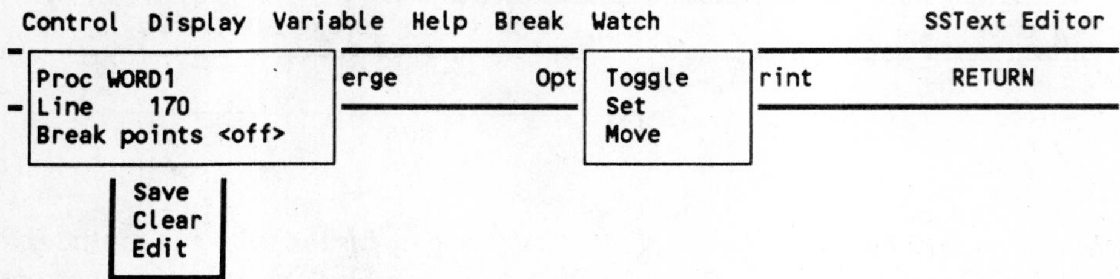

To move the window area of the watch box to the left side of the screen, select the Move option.

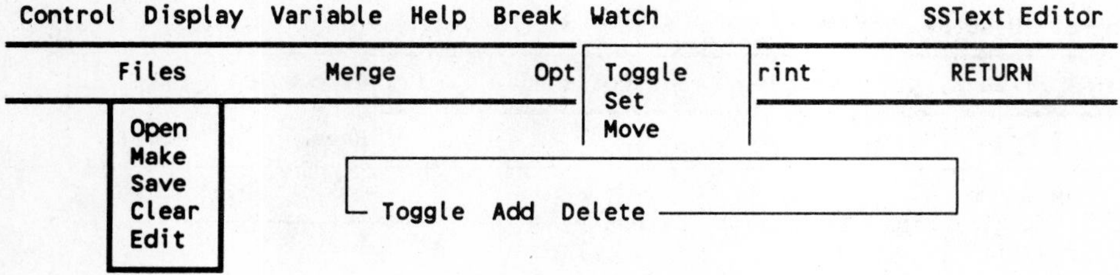

From the SET option, expressions within the watch box may be toggled on and off. Additionally, expressions may be added to the watch box window, such as DATE(), TIME() and NETERR(). Finally, expressions may be deleted from the watch box windowed area with the DELETE submenu option.

For versions prior to the Summer '87 release, below is an outline of those debugging capabilities. Please keep in mind that you cannot add the DEBUG.OBJ from the Summer '87 release to applications compiled with earlier versions. The new enhanced debugging utility will only work with application completely compiled and linked with the Summer '87 compiler and subsequent object and library files.

Make sure that the DEBUG.OBJ you are going to use is the correct debugger for the version of Clipper you are using. For the Winter '85 release, the proper DEBUG.OBJ file has a date stamp of 1-28-86 and a time stamp of 3:30a. Contrary to what the manual and documentation that comes with Clipper might say, the file DEBUG.OBJ is already an object file. This file is just like all other object files generated by the compiler; therefore, all that you need to do is link the file with all your other object files. For example, to use Plink86 with a LiNK file, an extra command line (e.g., FI <\directory\DEBUG>) would be necessary in order for DEBUG to be present in your application. Running Plink86 interactively, your screen should look like this:

```
C>plink86
PSA Linkage Editor (Nantucket Clipper) Version 1.46.c
Copyright (C) 1984 by Phoenix Software Associates Ltd.

=>fi GENMEN
=>fi \dbase\debug
=>lib \dbase\clipper
=>;
```

If you prefer the Microsoft Linker or DOS linker, the syntax is:

```
C>link
```

The following would then appear and you would enter the appropriate data:

```
Microsoft (R) 8086 Object Linker  Version 3.05
Copyright (C) Microsoft Corp 1983, 1984, 1985.  All rights reserved.

Object Modules [.OBJ]: GENMEN \dbase\debug
Run File [GENMEN.EXE]:
List File [NUL.MAP]:
Libraries [.LIB]: \dbase\/se:1024,,
```

or

```
C>link

IBM Personal Computer Linker
Version 2.20 (C) Copyright IBM Corp 1981, 1982, 1983, 1984

Object Modules [.OBJ]: GENMEN \dbase\debug
Run File [GENMEN.EXE]:
List File [NUL.MAP]:
Libraries [.LIB]: \dbase
```

The Can Do's and Can't Do's of DEBUG.OBJ

Before the DEBUG.OBJ command list is described in detail, you need to know what you can and cannot do with the debugger:

1. You can view and change memory variables.
2. You can display all SETs.
3. You can continue execution or step through the application line by line.
4. You can establish specific break points within the application that, when reached, will invoke the debugger.
5. You can evaluate expressions.
6. You can clear the screen.
7. You can trace all calling programs by name and by line number.
8. Depending on memory, you can leave the program temporarily and go to DOS.
9. You can direct output to the printer.
10. You cannot stop the debugger and fix code automatically.
11. You cannot DISPLAY STATUS for selected database or index files.

Using DEBUG.OBJ

You also need to know where to place the DEBUG object file in the listing of files and how to compile programs that are to be linked with the DEBUG.OBJ file:

1. The DEBUG object file
   a. They must be located in the main load module area (if using overlays) and not in an overlay (BEGINAREA...ENDAREA).
   b. They must not be the first file listed in your link list; the name of your program must be first.
2. **Do not** compile any program or module using the -l option (omit line numbers) if the debugger is to be used with it.

Once the debugger is linked in and you begin to execute your application, the first thing you will see is the debugger's message on the top line of your screen:

```
proc:GENMEN line:1  ([F1]-help,B,C,D,E,G,L,M,P,Q,R,S,T,V):
```

You can manually invoke the debugger at any time (without using the break-point scheme) by striking Alt-D. Even if an error occurs and the run-time message (Q/A/I) appears, the debugger can still be invoked by striking Alt-D a couple of times (or first type the letter "I," to ignore).

The Debug Commands

Press:	Command:	Description:
G	Go	Continues execution of the program.
S	Single step	Continues execution up to the next source line.
B	Break point	For break point 0, it specifies a conditional expression. With 1 to 9, it specifies a procedure and line number. The default procedure is the current one, and line numbers must match lines with commands (not blank lines).
Q	Quit	Stops execution, closes files, and returns to the system.
V	Variable Value	Enters the name of a memory variable. If it does not exist, a new PRIVATE variable is created. Its value is displayed and a new value is requested. Press <RETURN> to keep the old value.

R	Run	Runs a program from DOS.
T	Trace	Displays the names and line numbers of the procedures called to reach the current program line.
D	Display Status	Shows the status of the SET commands.
M	Memory Variables	Displays the PRIVATE memory variables for each procedure that has been called.
L	List Public	Lists all PUBLIC variables.
E	Expression Value	Enters an expression and prints its value.
P	Printer	Toggles PRINT ON and OFF.
C	Cls	Clears the screen.

CHAPTER TEN

Clipper Procedures

A procedure is a set of commands that perform a specific task. In general, procedures are created and used for small routines an application does repeatedly. To avoid having to recode those routines, dBASE III allows the routines to be pulled out and labeled separately. Whenever the routine is needed, the program files need only DO the procedure, much like DOing any other ordinary program file. A group of procedures can reside together in what dBASE III terms a "procedure file." This is the first real attempt to allow modular programming techniques within the dBASE III language.

Several benefits come from constructing procedure files. First, routines can be ported over from one application to the next, saving development time. Second, applications using well-developed procedure files become more polished and uniform in appearance. Finally, problems within procedures need only be corrected locally in order to cure system-wide dilemmas.

Clipper handles procedures somewhat differently, starting with the concept of the procedure itself. In Clipper, application code falls into one of two categories: *procedures* or *functions*. If a routine **does** something, it is a procedure; if a routine has a **value**, it is a function. Painting menu screens is a procedure, while converting a date to string representation is a function.

The more generic a procedure is (which normally means that there is more parameter passing), the better it will be able to service an entire application as well as other programs. This can all be summed up in five rules covering procedures:

1. There is no difference between a program and procedure.

   Clipper makes no distinction between a procedure and a program (.PRG) file. Technically, the compiler creates a symbol representing the name of a program file exactly as it does for a procedure.

2. There are no separate procedure files.

   Clipper places all code in one executable (.EXE) file. There is no need to worry about whether a procedure file is open or not. There is also no limit on the level of DO statements.

3. Procedure files cannot have the same name as a procedure being called.

4. Procedures can call other procedures as well as themselves.

   This is commonly referred to as program recursion.

5. Generalize to utilize.

   While procedures can be customized to closely fit a certain application, it is more practical to generalize procedures and have them react uniquely based on the parameters passed to them. By allowing for more parameter passing, applications can more strictly adhere to modular programming rules. The more modular the application, the easier it is to support, repair, and change.

PROCEDURES IN CLIPPER

Program files should be short, concise, and to the point. They should call other routines that, when combined, perform the overall operation. Procedures that are specialized to a single or a few limited operations should reside within the calling file and should not be placed in a master library or procedure file.

As a matter of fact, the SET PROCEDURE TO <filename> command in a program signals the compiler to go out to the directory and find the designated file and compile it with the main application. After that point, the command is treated as a remark line and is totally ignored. Therefore, procedure files can be exclusively compiled and linked intact without the recourse to the SET PROCEDURE TO <filename> command.

Procedure files under Clipper should be structured generically. If a routine is generic enough to be used often, it warrants being placed in a master procedure library file. A master file is one large .PRG file that contains many procedures that, like functions, can be called upon to serve specific needs of an application. Be careful about what goes in that master library file. If a procedure is common to only a couple of routines, do not place it in the master library file. Actually, you may want to establish a primary procedure file and a secondary file and use the secondary file for those routines limited to a subset of procedures or program files.

Avoid placing a procedure at the end of a file if it is already at the end of another program file. Clipper won't have a problem compiling the procedures separately, but a DUPLICATE error message (Warning 11) will appear when linking the files together. To avoid this, map out which files will contain the procedures common for all or establish a secondary procedure file. Here is an illustration to help you understand this point.

```
Program Files:          Procedures:

     A                       F
     B                       G
     C                       H
     D                       I
     E                       J
                             K
                             L
```

For this example, let's say all the program files require procedures F, G, and H at some time; but files A, B, and C also require procedures I, J, K, and L. Here are two possible ways of setting up the compilation:

Example 1:

```
Clip Files —>  A:                     B:                          C:

                 ┌ A                ┌ F                         ┌ I
Program          │ B   Procedures ──┤ G                         │ J
   Files ────────┤ C                └ H     Procedures ─────────┤ K
                 │ D                                            └ L
                 └ E
```

Compile @A, @B, @C

Linking A.OBJ + B.OBJ + C.OBJ + Clipper.lib = A.EXE

Example 2:

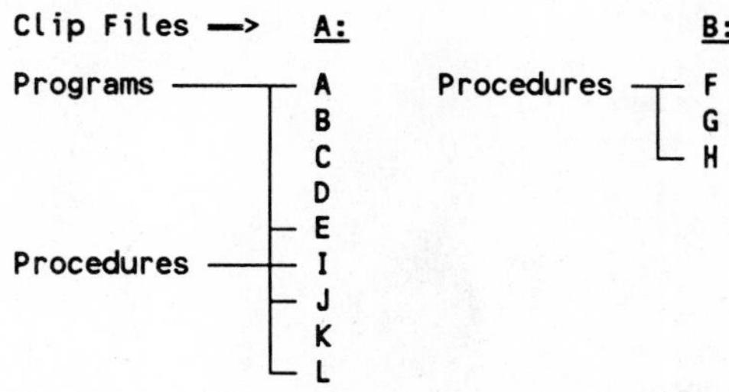

Compile @A, @B

Linking A.OBJ + B.OBJ + Clipper.lib = A.EXE

Example 1 has the advantage of having the second set of procedures (I, J, K, and L) in a secondary file for easy access and reference. The first set of procedures should always be in a separate file because they make up our master procedure library file, a file we port from application to application. However, this approach generates a larger .EXE file size, as compared to Example 2, because of the additional object file for the linker to handle.

There are other approaches to this problem, but the main question is, which one is right? The answer depends upon the environment and the situation surrounding the application itself. On the surface, however, both are correct.

Consider the following pieces of code. Both procedures do the same thing; the difference is in the way they do it.

Sample 1:

```
*********************
* Name          WHICHWY1.prg
* Date          August 7, 1986
* Notice        Copyright 1986, Stephen J. Straley & Associates
* Compile       Clipper Whichwy1 -m
* Release       Autumn '86 or later
* Link          Plink86 Fi Whichwy1 Lib Clipper
* Note          This demonstrates a specific procedure
*               approach.
*********************

PARAMETERS screenprnt, outfile

   frame = CHR(201) + CHR(205) + CHR(201) + CHR(186) + CHR(188) + CHR(205) +;
           CHR(200) + CHR(186) + CHR(32)
   @  7,10,14,40 BOX frame
   @  9,15 PROMPT " 1>  Print to Screen "
   @ 10,15 PROMPT " 2>  Print to Printer "
   @ 11,15 PROMPT " 3>  Print to File "
   @ 12,15 PROMPT " 0>  or Esc to RETURN "
   MENU TO screenprnt

   DO CASE
   CASE screenprnt = 4 .OR. screenprnt = 0
      RETURN
   CASE screenprnt = 3
      @ 7,10,14,40 BOX frame
      @  9,15 SAY "Enter File Name..."
      @ 11,15 SAY "--> " GET outfile PICT "!!!!!!!!!!!"
      READ
      IF LEN(TRIM(outfile)) = 0
         screenprnt = 1
      ELSE
         outfile = TRIM(outfile) + ".TXT"
      ENDIF
      * The two remaining options will be controlled by the
      * procedure calling WHICHWY1.
  ENDCASE
* End of File.
```

Sample 2:

```
*********************
* Name          WHICHWY2.prg
* Date          August 7, 1986
* Notice        Copyright 1986, Stephen J. Straley & Associates
* Compile       Clipper Whichwy2 -m
* Release       Autumn '86 or later
* Link          Plink86 Fi Whichwy2 Lib Clipper
* Note          This demonstrates a general procedure
*               approach.
*********************
```

```
PARAMETERS screenprnt, outfile, top, left

   frame = CHR(201) + CHR(205) + CHR(201) + CHR(186) + CHR(188) + CHR(205) +;
           CHR(200) + CHR(186) + CHR(32)
   @ top,left,top + 5, left + 40 BOX frame
   @ top + 1, left + 10 PROMPT " 1>  Print to Screen "
   @ top + 2, left + 10 PROMPT " 2>  Print to Printer "
   @ top + 3, left + 10 PROMPT " 3>  Print to File "
   @ top + 4, left + 10 SAY    "    Esc to RETURN"
   MENU TO screenprnt

   IF screenprnt = 3
      @ top + 1, left + 1, top + 4, left + 39 BOX SPACE(9)
      @ top + 1, left + 10 SAY "Enter File Name: "
      @ top + 3, left + 10 SAY "--> " GET outfile PICT "@!"
      READ
      screenprnt = IF(LEN(TRIM(screenprnt)) = 0, "", IF(AT(".",screenprnt) = ;
                   0, TRIM(SUBSTR(screenprnt,1,8)) + ".TXT", screenprnt))
         * The above line should be all on one line!
   ENDIF

   * Again, the first two options will be controlled by the
   * procedure calling WHICHWY2
* End of File
```

Notice the difference. By allowing the screen parameters to be passed in, the second sample procedure doesn't have to have the window in the same location every time it is called. Sometimes, the positioning of the box can overwrite an existing box or menu. The first procedure would have to be recoded for every situation that needed different screen positioning. In the second procedure, the screen position can be controlled by the calling program. By adding just two parameters, we have made the specific procedure more generic.

In doing so, we have saved six lines of code. Multiply this number by the number of times another routine requires a different screen position and the savings go up tremendously.

The point to all of this is to get you to use a modular approach to programming. One way to accomplish this is by coding efficiently using parameter passing. As you code, ask yourself if you will be doing this procedure again in the application and if it will work the way it is currently coded. If not, add a parameter or two and watch your procedures assume a more modular and efficient style.

The last technique to master is *recursive program calling*. There is, however, a practical limit on the number of levels of DOs: the internal memory stack that manages the level of DOs is a finite size and can be corrupted by too many DOs being pushed onto the stack and not popped. Popping a DO is accomplished by the RETURN command. With the advent of the BEGIN SEQUENCE command, clearing the stack for yet more recursive programming calling is possible. Again, this new technology is introduced with the Summer '87 release.

In theory at least, procedures can "DO" themselves as many times as necessary. Again, the more generic the procedure, the more likelihood of this happening. When you can get your procedures to be so generic that they call themselves with **different results**, you are approaching the ultimate goal: concise, modular, efficient code.

Listed below is an example of embedding procedures at the end of a program file and using recursive program calling. Compile and execute it to learn more about embedded procedures and recursive procedure calling.

```
********************
* Name          REPEAT.prg
* Date          March 15, 1988
* Notice        Copyright 1986, Stephen J. Straley & Associates
* Clipper       Clipper Repeat
* Release       Summer '87
* Link          Plink86 Fi Repeat Lib Clipper
* Note          This program file shows:
*               (a)  A procedure embedded in a program file
*               (b)  Recursive procedure calling
********************

SET SCORE OFF
CLEAR SCREEN
STORE 0 TO times
@ 11,15 SAY "How many times do you want to pass through? " GET times ;
        PICT "###" RANGE 0,100
@ 13,26 SAY "0 to exit - Maximum is 100"
READ
IF times = 0
   @ 15,25 SAY "Exiting to operating system..."
   QUIT
ENDIF
@ 15,22 SAY "Press any key to begin processing..."
input = INKEY(0)
CLEAR
DO Recurse WITH (times)

********************

PROCEDURE Recurse

   PARAMETERS through

   ?? through
   ?? SPACE(5)
   through = through - 1
   IF through = 0
      ?
```

```
        ? "Press any key to go back..."
        input = INKEY(0)
        DO Repeat
     ELSE
        DO Recurse WITH (through)
     ENDIF
  * End of File
```

Now, even though I showed this capability, keep in mind that with recursive procedure calling, the internal memory stack in Clipper is constantly pushed and never popped. Without returning to the preceding procedure in a normal fashion, a system memory fault will eventually appear and the application may crash.

It is important to remember to keep procedures small, direct, and simple. Huge program files are cumbersome. They should be broken up into several smaller procedures that collectively perform the same task.

PARAMETERS

Parameters Defined

A parameter is a set of one or more variables that is needed by the called procedure for the procedure to function properly. The parameters may be changed in value by the calling program or procedure and the new value passed to the called procedure. The called procedure will not run on its own because the value of the variable has not yet been established; that is the job of the calling procedure.

With proper parameter passing, procedures can be made more generic and thus more usable by other procedures. Assume, for example, that some data is to be displayed to the screen. This data must be displayed whether the operator is entering, scanning, editing, or deleting records. The small display is the same each time, yet it appears in different places on the screen depending upon the operation chosen by the operator. It would be foolish to recode this display four times, yet it is slightly different in each case. If we were to pass two parameters to a procedure, giving the row and the column at which we want the display to start, each operation could call the procedure with its own set of coordinates.

Under Clipper, parameters may be passed either by *reference* or by *value*.

Passing Parameters by Reference

Under most situations, parameters are passed by reference. The called procedure will refer to the parameter's value. In the compiler, a pointer to the address in memory that contains the value of the variable is passed to the called routine by the calling routine. This means that if the called procedure changes the value of the parameter, the address in memory that contains the variable's value is accessed and the data changed. The original value of that variable is lost. You should usually avoid using the PUBLIC command and initialize all variables in the top calling procedure file. This means that all variables can be referred to by the procedures below. This has the same effect as declaring the variables as public.

Even though a variable doesn't have to be passed to a specific procedure, if a lower procedure makes reference to a variable, that variable must be initialized at some prior point. Many times, however, for the sake of clarity, variables are renamed in subprocedures. In this case, the variable must be passed as a parameter by reference. Even though the variable name is different in the called procedure, the address of the original variable is maintained, which allows changes to the original variable to be made.

In order to pass a parameter by reference, only the name of the variable has to be coded in the calling routine.

Passing Parameters by Value

Parameters can also be passed to a called routine by value. The actual value of the variable is passed to the subroutine, not the address at which the value resides. This means that a parameter's value can be changed within the *called* routine without altering the original value of the variable in the *calling* routine. Many times variables global to a system are needed to operate a procedure, such as screen painting. As the procedure performs the task (panning down the screen, for example), the value of the row position is altered. Upon completion, the procedure returns to the calling routine, where the original starting row position is preserved. This eliminates the few extra steps needed to save the original value to another variable, altering the row variable, then restoring the row variable by storing the temporary variable to the row variable.

In order to pass a parameter to a routine by value only, the variable name must be placed within parentheses when it is passed by the calling routine.

Sample:

```
********************
* Name          PARAM.prg
* Date          August 7, 1986
* Notice        Copyright 1986, Stephen J. Straley & Associates
* Compile       Clipper Param
* Release       Winter '85 or greater
* Link          Plink86 Fi Param LIB Clipper
* Note          This program demonstrates differences in parameter
*               passing.  Involved are parameters passed by reference
*               and by value.
********************
```

```
DO WHILE .T.
   STORE "Today is Sunny!" TO name
   STORE 1 TO y
   STORE "Y" TO option
   CLEAR
   @ 2,20 SAY "Before the Routine"
   @ 2,60 SAY "After the Routine"
   @ 4,1 SAY "Name"
   @ 4,20 SAY name
   @ 6,1 SAY "Y"
   @ 6,20 SAY y
   @ 20,10 SAY "Are you ready for the passing (Y/N)? " GET option ;
      PICT "!" VALID(option$"YN")
   READ
   IF option = "N"
      QUIT
   ENDIF
   DO Sub_routin WITH (name), y
   @ 10,00 CLEAR
   @ 4,60 SAY name
   @ 6,60 SAY y
   @ 20,0 SAY "Press any key when finished comparing..."
   qw = INKEY(0)
ENDDO

********************

PROCEDURE Sub_routin

   PARAMETERS a,b

   @ 20,0 CLEAR
   @ 10,10 SAY "   What do you want the NAME to be? " GET a
   READ
   @ 12,10 SAY "                      How about Y? " GET b
   READ
   @ 24,0 SAY "Press Any key to go back..."
   qw = INKEY(0)
* End of File
```

Below is a sample program using arrays in parameter passing. If you do not have any experience in using arrays, you may want to read Chapter 12, Macros and Arrays, before studying the sample code below.

Sample:
```
*********************
* Name          PARA.prg
* Date          August 7, 1986
* Notice        Copyright 1986, Stephen J. Straley & Associates
* Compile       Clipper August
* Release       Winter '85 or later
* Link          Plink86 Fi Para Lib Clipper
* Note          This program demonstrates differences in parameter
*               passing.  Involved are parameters passed by
*               reference, by value, and arrays.
*
*********************

DECLARE z[5]      && This is an array to be passed as a parameter
FOR x = 1 TO 5
   STORE DATE() to z[x]
NEXT
DO WHILE .T.
   STORE " " to option
   STORE 1 TO x
   STORE "A" to y
   CLEAR
   @ 10,20 SAY "Before the Routine"
   @ 10,60 SAY "After the Routine"
   @ 12,1 SAY "X"
   @ 12,20 SAY x
   @ 14,1 SAY "Y"
   @ 14,20 SAY y
   FOR q = 1 TO 5
      @ 15+q,1 SAY "Date #"
      @ ROW(),COL() SAY q
      @ 15+q,20 SAY z[q]
   NEXT
   @ 5,10 SAY "Are you ready for the passing (Y/N)? " GET option ;
             PICT "!" VALID(option$"YN")
   READ
   IF option = "N"
      QUIT
   ENDIF
   DO Sub_routin WITH (x), y, "I am now here", z
   @ 12,60 SAY x
   @ 14,60 SAY y
   FOR q = 1 TO 5
      @ 15+q,60 SAY z[q]
   NEXT
   @ 24,0 SAY "Press Any key when finished comparing..."
   qw = INKEY(0)
ENDDO

*********************

PROCEDURE Sub_routin
```

```
PARAMETERS a,b,c,d

SAVE SCREEN
CLEAR
@ 10,10 SAY "   What do you want X to be: " GET a
READ
@ 12,10 SAY "                    How about y? " GET b
READ
@ 14,10 SAY "     What about this string? " GET c
READ
@ 16,10 SAY "Enter into the array these -> "
position = COL()
FOR q = 1 TO 5
   @ 15 + q, position GET d[q]
   READ
NEXT
@ 24,0 SAY "Press Any key to go back..."
qw = INKEY(0)
RESTORE SCREEN
* End of File
```

An entire array can be passed as a parameter to another routine by just passing the *identifier*, which is the array name without any subscripts. Please note that if this is done, the called routine has complete access to the array and can change values accordingly. Specific values in an array follow all other conventions described earlier.

Also, note that in this sample a literal was passed to the procedure that had no bearing on the original routine. There are cases where this is extremely important. A routine that prints a header, for example, needs only the name of the header. The header can vary from routine to routine and does not need to be placed in a variable and manipulated; in such a case just pass the string "as is" to the subroutine and print it.

A Final Thought

In all of this discussion there is one main point I have emphasized: modularizing. To take full advantage of Clipper's resources you must program in modules. Clipper allows programming methods to grow and develop. Procedures reduce entire applications to many single thoughts that, when combined, produce a unified whole.

CHAPTER ELEVEN

Extend Files

OVERVIEW

A few supplemental programs came with the Winter '85 and Autumn '86 releases of Clipper. Among these programs are a few written by Tom Rettig that provide an expanded command set that emulates dBASE III Plus. These programs were written in dBASE, C, and 8086 Assembler, using the user-defined functions facility in Clipper. These files are labeled with an EXTEND... beginning. Those UDFs written in dBASE syntax are located in Chapter 14, Designing User-Defined Functions (UDFs). The functions are contained in the following files that came with your compiler:

EXTENDDB.PRG	-	Functions in dBASE syntax
EXTENDA.ASM	-	Functions in 8086 Assembler
EXTENDC.C	-	Functions in C
EXTEND.H	-	The header file for EXTENDC.C

Using these files increases the size of the executable file by less than 6000 bytes. All of the added functions are listed at the end of this chapter.

The situation is drastically different for the Summer '87 release of Clipper. Many of the above-mentioned files are now incorporated in EXTEND.LIB. Additionally, since the Summer '87 release is now converted to Microsoft C 5.0 (from Lattice C), the internal extend system is drastically different. This difference has played havoc with many third-party developers when they are creating libraries to interface with the Clipper library.

Old routines written and compiled in ASM or in Lattice C are no longer compatible. This new extended structure change means that, using other tools like Codeview and Turbo C, writing and applying additional libraries are even easier. Because of the drastic change in the extend system and these ancillary files, I have divided this chapter into two sections. First will be a discussion on the pre-Summer '87 extend system and subsequent files. Following this will be a discussion of the Summer '87 extend system and all of the added files that come with that release. The Summer '87 section will also be split into two distinct parts. All assembly and C code covered in the first part of the second section will only work with version of Clipper prior to the Summer '87 release. There are added functions and utilities immediately following those routines that demonstrate the new extend system to the Summer '87 release. Do not mix these versions up.

PRE-SUMMER '87

EXTENDDB

This file has five sections: 1. functions that precisely emulate their dBASE III Plus counterparts, 2. dBASE III Plus functions that have embedded literal values or constants, 3. functions that are present in dBASE III Plus but have different names, 4. functions that do not exist in dBASE III Plus, and 5. functions that are EXTERNAL declarations for functions written in other languages that are linked separately.

EXTENDC.C

There is a module within Clipper that acts like an interface, which allows some of the internal functions to be extended to the developer. In this group of files, there are three important files written in the C language:

EXTEND.C
EXTEND.H
EXTENDC.C

EXTENDC.C includes the section of the compiler's source code, in C, that contains the parameter-passing function used by C programs that interfaces with normal Clipper applications. In EXTEND.C, the developer is allowed to write user-defined functions in C and to interface with applications.

The second file, EXTEND.H, is a header file to be used when compiling EXTEND.C. This file takes care of constant definitions and variable declarations.

There is a specific convention used when writing code that interfaces with the library. All functions internal to the compiler begin with an underscore, such as in saving screens with _SAVESCR or restoring screens with _RESTSCR. Also, dBASE III functions are listed in uppercase. In some cases, function names have been shortened in order not to conflict with key words in other languages, such as Lattice C.

PARAMETER PASSING

All parameters passed to a user-defined function are tested by the _parinfo() function that returns the number of parameters passed. The syntax is _parinfo(n) where n is the number of parameters as it appears in the user-defined function parameter list. EXTEND.H establishes several parameter-check macros that are used for parameter checking in the IF statements in the EXTENDC.C file. The other "_par" functions are *type specific* and are used to place the incoming user-defined function parameters appropriately in the *stack* internal to Clipper. For further information, please refer to the file entitled EXTEND.DOC on the same Clipper disk as the other EXTEND files. Each _par() function has an associated data type:

_parc()	=	character
_parl()	=	logical
_pards()	=	date (initially as string YYYYMMDD)
_parni()	=	numeric - integer

_parnl() = numeric - long
_parnd() = numeric - double

The functions beginning as "_ret" are functions for passing return values back to the compiler. One of these functions must be called prior to exiting from any C program in order to maintain the integrity of Clipper's internal stack.

_retc() = character
_retl() = logical
_retds() = date (initially as string YYYYMMDD)
_retni() = numeric from integer
_retnl() = numeric from long
_retnd() = numeric from double
_ret() = return to execution - no value passed

In order to maintain the stack with procedures that do not return a value, use the _ret() function.

EXTENDA.ASM

There are two basic functions in this file: ISCOLOR() and ISPRINTER(), neither of which requires a parameter. These functions have complete access to DOS, to the BIOS, and to the Clipper library. The same functions used by the EXTENDC.C file are now called as procedures to return values.

_RETC = character
_RETL = logical
_RETDS = date (initially a string YYYYMMDD -- > date type)
_RETNI = word as numeric
_RETNL = double word as numeric
_RETND = floating point as numeric

The value returned is the first value PUSHed onto the stack before calling the return value procedure, which then places it on the internal stack of the compiler. _RET is not required, which means a FAR return is required in order to maintain system integrity.

If more user-defined functions are added to the appropriate file, you need the IBM Macro Assembler to produce a new object file from EXTENDA.ASM. For the EXTENDC.C file, you must have Lattice C (preferably a version prior to version 3.0) or a Lattice-compatible version of C in order to produce a new object file. When using the Lattice compiler, three compiler options must be used: -ml, -v, and -n.

These symbols stand for the following: -ml = large model, -v = no stack checking, and -n = greater than eight characters in identifiers.

The extended functions add great capabilities and power to all Clipper applications, but if you intend to add to or modify this extended library, you should have a sound understanding of both Assembly language and Lattice C.

LIST OF FUNCTIONS IN THE EXTENDED LIBRARY

The following is a listing of the functions provided by the extended library. An asterisk denotes that the function was implemented directly into the Autumn '86 release of Clipper. For a complete description of each of the functions, please refer to Chapter 5, Functions.

Function:	**Description:**
* ABS()	Returns the absolute value of a number
* MAX()	Returns the higher of two numbers
* MIN()	Returns the lower of two numbers
ALLTRIM()	Trims leading and trailing blanks
AMPM()	Converts time to a 12-hour a.m. or p.m. format
DAYS()	Converts a number of seconds into days
DBF()	Returns the name of the selected and open database
DISKSPACE()	Returns the amount of remaining space on disk
ELAPTIME()	Calculates the number of seconds between two time strings
FKLABEL()	Returns the name of the <expN>th function key
FKMAX()	Returns 40, the number of function keys on an IBM XT
GETE()	Returns the environmental variables from operating system
HEADER()	Returns the size of a database header
ISALPHA()	Determines if the first character is alphabetic
ISCOLOR()	Determines if an active color card is found
ISPRINTER()	Determines if a parallel printer is on-line and ready
ISUPPER()	Determines if the first character is uppercase
LEFT()	Selects the left-most portion of a string
LENNUM()	Calculates the length of <expN>
LUPDATE()	Determines the date of the last update of a database file
MOD()	Returns the remainder of the first number divided by the second

NDX()	Returns the name of the index file in the <expN> position
OS()	Returns "MS/PC DOS"
RECSIZE()	Determines the size of a record in a database file
RIGHT()	Selects the right-most portion of a string
SECS()	Returns the number of seconds as a single numeric entity
SOUNDEX()	Creates a coded string that is based on a soundex algorithm
STRZERO()	Creates a string with leading zeros instead of blanks
STUFF()	Creates a string with a portion overlaid by a second string
TSTRING()	Creates a string based on a number of seconds
VERSION()	Returns the version of Clipper that contained this Extend library

SUMMER '87

ALTERROR.PRG	A sample file demonstrating the error system
DBU.PRG	Main module to view or browse a database
DBUCOPY.PRG	Copy module for Dbu.prg
DBUEDIT.PRG	Edit module for Dbu.prg
DBUHELP.PRG	Help module for Dbu.prg
DBUINDX.PRG	Indexing module for Dbu.prg
DBUSTRU.PRG	Create or modify database structure module for Dbu.prg
DBUUTIL.PRG	Utility module for Dbu.prg
DBUVIEW.PRG	View maintenance module for Dbu.prg
DOT.PRG	Crude pseudo-interpreter of some Clipper commands
ERRORSYS.PRG	Additional functions demonstrating error system
EXAMPLEP.PRG	Sample file containing some user-defined functions
KOPIPHIL.PRG	Sample file demonstrating some low-level routines
RLBACK.PRG	Component to RL.EXE
RLDIALOG.PRG	Functions for RL.EXE
RLFRONT.PRG	Component to RL.EXE
EXAMPLEA.ASM	Examples of Assembly routines for Summer '87
EXAMPLEC.C	Examples of C routines for Summer '87
EXTEND.DOC	Additional information of the extend system
EXTEND.H	Header file declaring externals for C programs
EXTENDA.INC	Extend system assembler macros
EXTENDA.MAC	Additional assembly routines
NANDEF.H	Additional header file for C programs

The Extend Functions

The new extend feature in Clipper treats C and ASM routines as other user-defined functions. This means that the CALL command is not necessary and your Clipper code can continue to be more function based than command and procedure based. Before discussing the internals and how it now interfaces to C and to the ASM file, here is a list of all the enhanced feature to the extend system:

Passing Information from Clipper through the Extend System

Character	_parc(int [, int])	__PARC
Date	_pards(int [,int])	__PARDS
Logical	_parl(int [, int])	__PARL
Numeric	_parni(int [, int])	__PARNI
Numeric	_parnl(int [, int])	__PARNL
Numeric	_parnd(int [, int])	__PARND
	_parclen(int [, int])	__PARCLEN
	_parcsiz(int [, int])	__PARCSIZ
	_parinfa(int, int)	__PARINFA
	_parinfo(int)	__PARINFO

Returning Information from the Extend System to Clipper

Character	_retc(char*)	__RETC
Date	_retds(char*)	__RETDS
Logical	_retl(int)	__RETL
Numeric	_retni(int)	__RETNI
Numeric	_retnl(long)	__RETNL
Numeric	_retnd(double)	__RETND
	_ret()	__RET
	_retclen(char*, int)	__RETCLEN

Compiling these outside routines also requires special parameters for their respective languages. For example, the proper syntax to compile outside C routines using Microsoft C version 5.0 would be:

```
CL /c /AL /Zl /Oalt /FPa /Gs <file>.c
```

For C programming, it is important to note that the C module or function that is to interface with Clipper must have the function name preceded by CLIPPER, as in the following example:

```
#include    <dos.h>
#indlude    <nandef.h>
#include    <extend.h>

CLIPPER Bootit()
{
  /* This reboots the computer;
     the function must have the CLIPPER
     name prefix! */
}
```

Linking these routines with Clipper is significantly different. For example, the proper method for linking an outside compile C routine with a Clipper application would be

```
Link /NOE <clipper file> <c file>,,,clipper;
```

If necessary, additional libraries may be added to the above example as well as other object modules. Make sure that the NOE switch is used. This prevents the linker from trying to bring in additional library files for the C routines that are already present in the Clipper library. Additionally, make sure the Microsoft linker, version 3.61 or later, is used to link the different object modules to the Clipper library. Finally, it may be necessary to specify the segment size for the linker. To set this linking switch, insert /SE:1024 following the /NOE switch. All linking switches are separated from each other and from file names by spaces.

Additionally, there is the ability to use some predefined interface macros for both C and ASM routines. These macros help generalize your user-defined functions in these other high-level languages. For example, the ability to check how many parameters are being received by a function is very useful to help generalize the function for an entire application. Many of Clipper's core functions have optional parameters. Below are two tables that explain the optional macros for their respective languages:

Macros for C

Macro	Defined As
PCOUNT	(_parinfo(<expN>))
ISCHAR(<expN>)	(_parinfo(<expN>))
ISNUM(<expN>)	(_parinfo(<expN>))
ISLOG(<expN>)	(_parinfo(<expN>))
ISDATE(<expN>)	(_parinfo(<expN>))
ISMEMO(<expN>)	(_parinfo(<expN>))
ISBYREF(<expN>)	(_parinfo(<expN>))
ISARRAY(<expN>)	(_parinfo(<expN>))
ALENGTH(<expN>)	(_parinfo(<expN>))

<expN> is defined as the parameter order number. So, if three parameters are passed to the C user-defined function, and the third parameter may be of character data type or of numeric data type, ISCHAR(3) will be logical true (.T.) for the character data type and ISNUM(3) will be logical true (.T.) for the numeric data type. If a parameter is passed by reference (using the @ sign on the Clipper side of the program), use the ISBYREF() function.

Macros for ASM

Macro	Defined As
GET_PCOUNT	Number of parameters passed in AX register
GET_PTYPE	Type of parameters passed in AX
GET_CHAR	Address of a string in AX:BX
GET_INT	Integer in AX register
GET_LONG	Long integer in AX:BX
GET_DBL	Double in AX:BX:CX:DX
GET_DATESTR	Address of a date sting in AX:BX
GET_LOGICAL	Logical in AX register
RET_CHAR	Returns string pointed to
RET_INT	Returns integer value
RET_LONG	Returns long integer
RET_DBL	Returns double
RET_DATESTR	Returns date string
RET_LOGICAL	Returns logical value

These macros are defined in EXTENDA.MAC. When creating assembly-level functions for Clipper, make sure that Microsoft MASM 5.0 (or later) is used.

Finally, there are two functions for C programs that directly interface with the internal memory tables in Clipper. One function frees allocated memory and reallocates it for the Clipper-compiled application. The other grabs extra memory for the Clipper program. These two functions, defined in EXTEND.H, are as follows

FUNCTION: **_exmback(<expC1>, <expN2>)**

Parameters: <expC1> is an unsigned character pointer and <expN1> is the number of bytes grabbed by the _exmgrab() function.

Returns: Nothing.

Description: The _exmback() function releases the memory allocated by the _exmgrab() function. It is important to note that the same pointer and requested memory size in bytes used by the _exmgrab() function must be passed as parameters to this function.

FUNCTION: **_exmgrab(<expN>)**

Parameters: <expN> is the number of bytes of memory to grab and allocate.

Returns: A character pointer referring to the allocated memory position.

Description: The _exmgrab() functions attempts to allocate an amount of memory in bytes. If it is successful, it will return a character pointer to that allocated space. If it is not successful, the function will return a NULL. Memory allocated by this function should be freed with the _exmback() function.

Sample using these two functions:

To allocate 190K of memory, use the following format.

```
#include    <nandef.h>
#include    <extend.h>

int mem_size ;
char *buffer ;

mem_size = 190 * 1024

buffer = _exmgrab(mem_size) /* This gets 190K of memory and places the unsigned
character pointer to 'buffer */

if (buffer = !NULL)
   {
   /* perform task */
   }

_exmback( buffer, mem_size ) /* This release the grabbed 190K of memory. */

/* end of example */
```

Remember that if the attempt to allocate extra memory for an operation is **not** successful, the contents of the buffer pointer will be NULL.

Passing Parameters in C

FUNCTION: **_parc()**

Headers: <nandef.h>
<extend.h>

Syntax: _parc(<expN1> [, <expN2>)

Description: The _parc() function is used to get character parameters from Clipper. The <expN1> represents the actual parameter placement in the list, and the option <expN2> represents the array element index pointer.

The _parc() does not make a copy of the passed parameter.

Samples:

Clipper Code:

```
SENDCHAR("Logon")
```

C Code:

```
CLIPPER Sendchar()
{
   static char words[40] ;
   strcpy( _parc(1), words ) ;
   iitype( words ) ;
   _ret()
}
```

FUNCTION: **_parclen()**

Headers: <nandef.h>
<extend.h>

Syntax: _parclen(<expN1> [, <expN2>])

Description: The _parclen() function determines the length of a given string. The <expN1> represents the actual parameter placement within the list, while <expN2> is the array element index pointer. This was established because of the slight difference between a null byte and CHR(0). It checks for the length of the string, checking for embedded CHR(0) characters. And it gets the length of the string without counting the null terminator.

FUNCTION: **_parcsiz()**

Headers: <extend.h>
<nandef.h>

Syntax: _parcsiz(<expN1> [, <expN2>])

Description: The _parcsiz() returns the number of bytes allocated in memory for that string. This calculation includes the null terminator. <expN1> represents the actual parameter placement within the list, while <expN2> is the array element index pointer. This calculation does not work on constants; therefore _parsize() would yield a 0. Additionally, if you are assigning a value to a variable that exceeds the allocated memory size for that variable, that variable will write over other memory areas.

FUNCTION: **_pards()**

Headers: <nandef.h>
<extend.h>

Syntax: _pards(<expN1> [, <expN2>])

Description: The _pards() function receives a date parameter from Clipper and yields a pointer in the format of "YYYMMDD," which is the normal method Clipper stores dates internally. The first <expN1> represents the actual parameter placement within the list, while <expN2> is the array element index pointer. Keep in mind that there is only one pointer on the stack and it **must** copy the results to a variable using C's strcpy() function. The pointer may not be passed.

Samples:

Clipper Code:

```
SENDDATE(DATE())
```

C Code:

```
CLIPPER Senddate()
{
   char the_date[9] ;
   sprintf( _pards(1), "%.8s/0", the_date) ;
}
```

FUNCTION: **_parinfa()**

Headers: <nandef.h>
<extend.h>

Syntax: _parinfa(<expN1> [, <expN2>])

Description: The _parinfa() function returns the data type of an array element and may be used for parameter data type-checking. The first <expN> represents the actual parameter placement within the list, while <expN2> is the array element index pointer. Keep in mind that each array element must be individually tested before it is used since Clipper allows arrays to have mixed data types. Additionally, _parinfa(<expN1>, 0) yields the number of elements in the array.

FUNCTION: **_parinfo()**

Headers: <nandef.h>
<extend.h>

Syntax: _parinfo(<expN1>)

Description: This _parinfo(<expN1>) function may be used to test the data type of a parameter. The first <expN> represents the actual parameter placement within the list.

Using the _parinfo() like Clipper's INKEY() function, _parinfo(0) returns the number of parameters passed.

The value returned by the function, which is defined in <extend.h>, may be one of the following values:

Undefined Variables	0
Character Data	1
Numeric Data	2
Logical Data	4
Date Data	8
MPTR Data	32 (or with type when passed by reference)
Memo data	65
Array Data	512

If a parameter is passed by reference, add MPTR(32) to the type value and test for that summation. Below is a table of the basic values for data types that are passed by reference (using the @ sign) rather than by value:

Undefined Reference Variable	32
Character Reference Data	33
Numeric Reference Data	34
Logical Reference Data	36
Date Reference Data	40

FUNCTION: **_parl()**

Headers: <nandef.h>
<extend.h>

Syntax: _parl(<expN1> [, <expN2>])

Description: The _parl() function receives a logical parameter from Clipper and converts it to an integer. The first <expN> represents the actual parameter placement within the list, while <expN2> is the array element index pointer. A logical true (.T.) value will receive a value of 1 and a logical false (.F.) will receive a value of 0.

Samples:

Clipper Code:
```
SENDLOGIC(ISPRINTER())
```

C Code:
```
CLIPPER Sendlogic()
{


}
```

FUNCTION: **_parni()**

Headers: <nandef.h>
<extend.h>

Syntax: _parni(<expN1> [, <expN2>])

Description: The _parni() function receives a numeric parameter from Clipper and converts it to an integer value. The first <expN> represents the actual parameter placement within the list, while <expN2> is the array element index pointer.

Samples:

Clipper Code:
```
SENDINT(2)
```

C Code:
```
CLIPPER Sendint()
{
   int the_number ;
   the_number = _parni(1) ;
}
```

FUNCTION: **_parnd()**

Headers: <nandef.h>
<extend.h>

Syntax: _parnd(<expN1> [, <expN2>])

Description: The _parnd() function receives a numeric parameter from Clipper and converts it to a double value. The first <expN> represents the actual parameter placement within the list, while <expN2> is the array element index pointer.

FUNCTION: _parnl()

Headers: <nandef.h>
<extend.h>

Syntax: _parnl(<expN1> [, <expN2>])

Description: The _parnl() function receives a numeric parameter from Clipper and converts it to a long data type. The first <expN> represents the actual parameter placement within the list, while <expN2> is the array element index pointer.

Samples:

Clipper Code: SENDLONG(13.2837432)

C Code:

```
CLIPPER Sendlong()
{
  long the_number ;
  the_number = _parl(1) ;
}
```

RECEIVING PARAMETERS TO CLIPPER FROM C

FUNCTION: _ret()

Headers: <nandef.h>
<extend.h>

Syntax: _ret()

Description: The _ret() function has no value. This allows the function in C to be called via the DO command, which Clipper will then treat as a regular procedure.

Samples:

Clipper Code: `SENDCHAR("Logon")`

C Code:

```
CLIPPER Sendchar()
{
   static char words[40] ;
   strcpy( _parc(1), words ) ;
   iitype( words ) ;
   _ret() ;
}
```

FUNCTION: **_retc()**

Headers: <nandef.h>
<extend.h>

Syntax: _retc(<expC>)

Description: The _retc() function returns to Clipper a character pointer to the string for the application to use, where <expC> is the character pointer in C.

Samples:

Clipper Code: `newstr = GETSCREEN()`

C Code:

```
CLIPPER Getscreen()
{
   static buffer[2000] ;
   iirdfld( 0, buffer, sizeof(buffer) ) ;
   _retc(buffer) ;
}
```

FUNCTION: **_retclen()**

Headers: <nandef.h>
<extend.h>

Syntax: _retclen(<expC>, <expN>)

Description: The _retclen() function returns a string pointer that is a specified length. This function accounts for embedded CHR(0) characters while the _retc() function does not. The <expC> represent the character pointer in C where the <expN> value represents the length of the string.

FUNCTION: **_retds()**

Headers: <nandef.h>
<extend.h>

Syntax: _retds(<expC>)

Description: This function returns to Clipper a date data type that is represented in C by <expC> and as a character pointer in the standard format "YYYYMMDD."

Samples:

Clipper Code:

```
DATE() - GETDATE()
```

C Code:

```
CLIPPER Getdate()
{
   _retds("19880101") ;
}
```

FUNCTION: **_retl()**

Headers: <nandef.h>
<extend.h>

Syntax: _retl(<exp>)

Description: The _retl() function returns a logical value to Clipper for the boolean value or flag represented as <exp>. These values treat a Clipper true (.T.) as 1 and a Clipper false (.F.) as 0

Samples:

Clipper Code:

```
IF ISFATAL()
   ? "Irma Failure.   Exiting Program"
   QUIT
ENDIF
```

C Code:

```
CLIPPER Isfatal()
   {
      if (iifatal() ) _retl(1) ;
      else _retl(0) ;
   }
```

FUNCTION: **_retnd()**

Headers: <nandef.h>
<extend.h>

Syntax: _retnd(<expN>)

Description: The _retnd() function returns to Clipper a number for a C double type represented as <expN>.

FUNCTION: **_retnl()**

Headers: <nandef.h>
<extend.h>

Syntax: _retnl(<expN>)

Description: The _retnl() function returns to Clipper a number for a C long type represented as <expN>.

Samples:

Clipper Code:

```
newnumb = GETNUMB()
```

C Code:

```
CLIPPER Getnumb()
{
   long the_number ;
   /* process the number */
   _retnl(the_number) ;
}
```

FUNCTION: **_retni()**

Headers: <nandef.h>
<extend.h>

Syntax: _retni(<expN>)

Description: The _retni() function returns to Clipper a number for a C integer type represented as <expN>.

Samples:

Clipper Code:

```
field_no = FIELD_NUMB()
```

C Code:

```
CLIPPER Field_numb()
{
    int the_number ;
    the_number = iiscreen() ;
    _retni( the_number ) ;
}
```

Parameters to Assembly

When interfacing Clipper to Assembly, remember that all parameters are passed as C data types. This is because Clipper's internals are written in C. There are 11 general rules to follow whenever passing parameters to an assembly subroutine.

1. Move the parameter number to be obtained into a register.
2. Push the register.
3. Call the appropriate function for the data type of the parameter.
4. The parameter is received in the registers either by value or by pointer reference.
5. Restore the stack.
6. Declare all Assembly routines as PUBLIC.
7. Declare the extend function to be as EXTRN and FAR or INCLUDE EXTENDA.INC. This file makes the necessary declarations.
8. Define your data segments, grouped together with Clipper's internal DGROUP. If you do not do this, DS must point to DGROUP before you call any Extend function.
9. Class data segments as DATA.
10. Class code segments as CODE. This was previously classed as PROG for the Autumn '86 release.
11. If no parameters are passed back to Clipper, use the _RET before any Assembly routine concludes.

FUNCTION: _PARC

Usage for String:

```
mov   ax, <expN1>
push      ax
call  _PARC
add   sp, 2
```

Usage for String in Array Parameter:

```
mov   ax, <expN1>
push  bx, <expN2>
push  bx
push  ax
call  _PARC
```

```
add  sp, 4
```

Arguments:

<expN1> - parameter placement order in list.
<expN2> - index of array element to be accessed.

Description:

This function places the address of a Clipper character string in registers DX:AX where DX contains the segment and AX contains the offset.

FUNCTION: _PARCLEN

Usage for String:

```
mov  ax, <expN1>
push ax
call _PARCLEN
add  sp, 2
```

Usage for String in Array Parameter:

```
mov  ax, <expN1>
mov  bx, <expN2>
push bx
push ax
call _PARCLEN
add  sp, 4
```

Arguments:

<expN1> - parameter placement order in list.
<expN2> - index of array element to be accessed.

Description:

This function returns the length of a given string in the AX register. It will check for the length of a string with embedded CHR(0) characters. It will also get the length of a string without counting the null terminator.

FUNCTION: _PARCSIZ

Usage for String:

```
mov  ax, <expN1>
push ax
call _PARCSIZ
add  sp, 2
```

Usage for String in Array Parameter:

```
mov  ax, <expN1>
mov  bx, <expN2>
push bx
```

```
push ax
call __PARCSIZ
add sp, 2
```

Arguments: <expN1> - parameter placement order in list.
<expN2> - index of array element to be accessed.

Description: This routine returns the number of bytes in memory allocated for the specified string, including the null terminator. It is located in the AX register. All constants have a value of 0 with __PARCSIZ.

FUNCTION: __PARDS

Usage for String:

```
mov ax, <expN1>
push ax
call __PARDS
add sp, 2
```

Usage for String in Array Parameter:

```
mov ax, <expN1>
mov bx, <expN2>
push bx
push ax
call __PARDS
add sp, 2
```

Arguments: <expN1> - parameter placement order in list.
<expN2> - index of array element to be accessed.

Description: This routine places the address of a Clipper date in the DX:AX register where DX is the segment and AX is the offset. This date is stored in a string form of "YYYYMMDD."

FUNCTION: __PARINFA

Usage for Array Length:

```
mov ax, <expN1>
mov bx, 0
push bx
push ax
call __PARINFA
add sp, 2
```

Usage for Elements in array:

```
mov  ax, <expN1>
mov  bx, <expN2>
push bx
push ax
call __PARINFA
add  sp, 4
```

Arguments:

<expN1> - parameter placement order in list.
<expN2> - index of array element to be checked for data type.

Description:

If <expN2> is 0, _PARINFA places the length of the array passed in register AX. If the value of <expN2> is greater than 0, __PARINFA places the type of the specified parameter in the AX register. Use the following table:

Data Type	AX Register Value	
Undefined	0	
Character	1	
Numeric	2	
Logical	4	
Date	8	
By reference	32	(or with type)
Memo	65	
Array	512	

FUNCTION: __PARINFO

Usage for number of parameters:

```
mov  ax, 0
push ax
call __PARINFO()
add  sp, 2
```

Usage for type of parameter:

```
mov  ax, <expN>
push ax
call __PARINFO
add  sp, 2
```

Arguments:

<expN> - parameter placement order in list.

Description: If <expN> is 0, this routine places the number of parameters passed in the AX register. If <expN> is greater than 0, __PARINFO places the type of the specified parameter in the AX register using the following table:

Undefined Variables	0	
Character Data	1	
Numeric Data	2	
Logical Data	4	
Date Data	8	
MPTR Data	32	(or with type when passed by reference)
Memo Data	65	
Array Data	512	

If a parameter is passed by reference, add MPTR(32) to the type value and test for that summation. Below is a table of the basic values for data types that are passed by reference (using the @ sign) rather than by value

Undefined Reference Variable	32
Character Reference Data	33
Numeric Reference Data	34
Logical Reference Data	36
Date Reference Data	40

FUNCTION: __PARL

Usage for Logical:

```
mov  ax, <expN1>
push ax
call __PARL
add  sp, 2
```

Usage for Logical in Array Parameter:

```
mov  ax, <expN1>
mov  bx, <expN2>
push bx
push ax
call __PARL
add  sp, 4
```

Arguments: <expN1> - parameter placement order in list.
<expN2> - index of array element to be accessed.

Description: This routine places the word of a Clipper logical value in the AX register. A logical true (.T.) is represented with a 1 and a logical false (.F.) is represented as a 0.

FUNCTION: _PARND

Usage for Double:

```
mov  ax, <expN1>
push ax
call _PARND
add  sp, 2
```

Usage for Double in Array Parameter:

```
mov  ax, <expN1>
mov  bx, <expN2>
push ax
push ax
call _PARND
add  sp, 4
```

Arguments: <expN1> - parameter placement order in list.
<expN2> - index of array element to be accessed.

Description: This function places the address of a double value passed from a Clipper numeric data type in the DX:AX registers, where the DX register contains the segment and the AX register contains the offset.

FUNCTION: _PARNI

Usage for Integer:

```
mov  ax, <expN1>
push ax
call _PARNI
add  sp, 2
```

Usage for Integer in Array Parameter:

```
mov  av, <expN1>
mov  bx, <expN2>
push bx
push ax
call _PARNI
add  sp, 4
```

Arguments: <expN1> - parameter placement order in list.

<expN2> - index of array element to be accessed.

Description: The _PARNI routine receives a number from Clipper and places it as an integer in the AX register.

FUNCTION: _PARNIL

Usage for Numeric Long:

```
mov  ax, <expN1>
push ax
call _PARNL
add  sp, 2
```

Usage for Numeric Long in Array Parameter:

```
mov  ax, <expN1>
mov  bx, <expN2>
push bx
push ax
call _PARNL
add  sp, 4
```

Arguments: <expN1> - parameter placement order in list.
<expN2> - index of array element to be accessed.

Description: This routine receives a number from Clipper, passes it as a long number, and stores the value in registers DX:AX.

Receiving Parameters from ASM

FUNCTION: _RET

Syntax: call _RET

Arguments: None.

Description: This routine prevents internal stack corruption and, if used, allows the ASM function to be called as a DO <function> and to tell Clipper to treat it as a procedure.

FUNCTION: _RETC

Syntax:

```
mov <regester 1>, <expN1>
mov <register 2>, <expN2>
push <register 1>
push <register 2>
call _RETC
add sp, 4
```

Arguments: Where <expN1> is the segment address of the string and <expN2> is the offset address of the string.

Description: This routine passes back to Clipper a character string that is pointed to via <register 1> and <register 2>.

FUNCTION: _RETCLEN

Syntax:

```
mov <register 1>, <expN1>
mov <register 2>, <expN2>
mov <register 3>, <expN3>
push <register 3>
push <register 1>
push <register 2>
call _RETCLEN
add sp, 6
```

Arguments:
<expN1> is the segments address of the string.
<expN2> is the offset address of the string.
<expN3> is the length of the string to be returned to the Clipper application.

Description: This routine passes back to Clipper a string of characters pointed to by registers <1> and <2>. It passes it with a specified length, thus allowing the string to have embedded CHR(0) characters.

FUNCTION: _RETDS

Syntax:

```
mov <register 1>, <expN1>
mov <register 2>, <expN2>
push <register 1>
push <register 2>
call _RETDS
add sp, 4
```

Argument: <expN1> is the segments address of a date string.
<expN2> is the offset address of a date string.

Description: This routines passes back to Clipper a date that was in the string in the form of "YYYMMDD."

FUNCTION: _RETL

Syntax:

```
mov  <register 1>,  <expN1>
push <register 1>
call _RETL
add  sp, 2
```

Argument: <expN1> is either 1 or 0 depending on if Clipper is to receive a logical true (.T.) or a logical false (.F.).

Description: This routine passes to Clipper a logical value from a word value.

FUNCTION: _RETND

Syntax:

```
mov  <register 1>,  <expN1>
mov  <register 2>
mov  <register 3>
mov  <register 4>
push <register 1>
push <register 2>
call _RETND
add  sp, 8
```

Argument: <expN1> is the value returned to Clipper.

Description: This routine passes a double number back to Clipper as a number.

FUNCTION: _RETNI

Syntax:

```
mov  <register 1>,  <expN1>
push <register 1>
call _RETNI
add  sp, 2
```

Argument: <expN1> is the value to be returned as an integer.

Description: This routine passes back to Clipper a number stored in <register 1> as a numeric value.

FUNCTION: __RETL

Syntax:

```
mov  <register 1>, <expN1>
mov  <register 2>
push <register 1>
push <register 2>
call __RETNL
add  sp, 4
```

Argument: <expN1> is a long value to be returned to Clipper.

Description: This routine passes back a number to Clipper that is stored as a long integer in registers <register 1>:<register 2>.

ASSEMBLY AND C ROUTINES AND THE CALL COMMAND

THE CALL COMMAND

Clipper by itself can deal with most of the data management and screen handling situations you will face. There are, however, some tasks for which Clipper needs to use routines programmed in other languages. The CALL command allows you to program in C or in Assembler those routines the compiler is unable to handle directly. These routines then can be linked in with the rest of the application and CALLed as required. For details on the specific restrictions, please review the section on command syntax under CALL in Chapter 4, Commands.

The uniqueness of the Summer '87 release now allows most of the outside routines to be treated as though they are part of the internals of the Clipper library. For example, now most functions in C can be called as if they are regular Clipper functions, and with the introduction of __RET (for assembly) and _ret() (for C), functions can be treated as procedures. This ability allows head programmers and project leaders to develop C and Assembly routines while others access them in normal Clipper-like fashion.

Because of the differences to the internals of the Clipper library, the first section of this chapter will work only with the Autumn '86 release of the compiler. These routines will **not** work with the Summer '87 release, so keep that in mind when trying to apply these additions. Following these samples will be a complete section of subroutines specifically designed to work only with the Summer '87 release. All routines perform distinct tasks, normally machine or operating-system specific. A good rule to follow is if Clipper cannot perform the task, it probably requires a C or Assembly routine to be written and added. The routines below are specifically defined and documented, and they include examples that demonstrate their use.

Autumn '86 release

BOOT.ASM	This routine warm-boots the computer. It can be used to chain two large applications together through the use of the AUTOEXEC.BAT file.
LOCK.ASM	This routine checks if the Insert, Caps Lock, Scroll Lock, and Num Lock keys are on or off.
CURSOR.ASM	This routine toggles the cursor on and off.
DRSTATUS.ASM	This routine checks the status of a drive.
NODRIVES.ASM	This routine checks the number of drives in the system.
PRSTATUS.ASM	This routine checks the printer status.

BOOT.ASM

```
***********************
* Name          BOOT.asm
* Date          August 10, 1986
* Note          Contributed by Fred Ho, this is the Assembly
*               routine that reboots the computer upon command.
********************
;
public  BOOTIT                          ; warm boot
;
_prog  segment byte                     ; byte aligned
assume cs:_prog
;
BOOTIT proc     far
       push     bp
       mov      bp,sp

       int      19h

       pop      bp
       ret
```

```
BOOTIT  endp
;
_prog  ends
       end
;
;End of File
```

LOCK.ASM

```
********************
* Name          LOCKASM.asm
* Date          August 10, 1986
* Note          Contributed by David Dodson, this is to be used for
*               IBM PCs or absolutely 100 percent compatibles.
*               This routine checks the status of the four keys:
*               Caps, Insert, Num Lock, and Scroll Lock.  If the values
*               returned are in capital letters, the keys are ON,
*               otherwise, they are OFF.
*
*               Call LCKTAB with any four-character field
********************

;
public LCKSTAT
;
datasg segment para    'DATA'

LCKTAB db      'icnS'
       db      'icNs'
       db      'icNS'
       db      'iCns'
       db      'iCnS'
       db      'iCNs'
       db      'iCNS'
       db      'Icns'
       db      'IcNs'
       db      'IcNs'
       db      'IcNS'
       db      'ICns'
       db      'ICnS'
       db      'ICNs'
       db      'ICNS'
;
NUMB1  db      10h
FOUR   db      04h
;
datasg ends
;
;

_prog  segment byte    ; byte aligned
assume cs:_prog,ds:datasg,es:datasg
```

```
;
LCKSTAT proc    far
        push    bp
        mov     bp,sp
        push    ds
        push    es
        sub     ax,ax
        push    ax
        mov     ax,datasg
        mov     es,ax
        mov     ds,ax

        mov     ah,02
        int     16h
        xor     bx,bx
        mov     bl,al

        mov     ax,bx
        div     NUMB1
        lea     si,LCKTAB
        dec     al
        mul     FOUR
        add     si,ax
        cld
        les     di,[bp + 6]
        mov     cx,04
        rep     movsb

        stosb
        pop     ax
        pop     es
        pop     ds
        pop     bp
        ret
LCKSTAT endp
;
;
_prog   ends
        end
```

PRNTLOCK.PRG

```
********************
* Name          PRNTLOCK.prg
* Date          August 10, 1986
* Notice        Copyright 1986, 1987, 1988, Stephen J. Straley & Associates
* Note          Uses an Assembly routine to check to see if the Insert,
*               Caps Lock, Num Lock, and Scroll Lock keys are
*               set on or off.
*
********************
```

```
a = "abcd"
DO WHILE .T.
   CLEAR
   CALL Lckstat WITH a
   ?
   ? "The INSERT KEY is set " + IF(ISUPPER(SUBSTR(a,1,1)), "ON", "OFF")
   ?
   ? "The CAPS LOCK KEY is set " + IF(ISUPPER(SUBSTR(a,2,1)), "ON", "OFF")
   ?
   ? "The NUM LOCK KEY is set " + IF(ISUPPER(SUBSTR(a,3,1)), "ON", "OFF")
   ?
   ? "The SCROLL LOCK KEY is set " + IF(ISUPPER(SUBSTR(a,4,1)), "ON", "OFF")
   ?
   ?
   WAIT
ENDDO

********************

FUNCTION Isupper

   PARAMETERS a

   RETURN a $ [ABCDEFGHIJKLMNOPQRSTUVWXYZ]
```

CURSOR.ASM

```
********************
* Name          CURSOR.asm
* Date          August 10, 1986
* Note          Contributed by Fred Ho, this is to be used for IBM PCs or
*               100 percent compatibles that allow direct video mapping.
*               This routine acts as a toggle; it will
*               turn the cursor on or off whenever called.
*********************

PUBLIC  cursw
;
video           EQU     10h
curlin          EQU     01h
offlin          EQU  0FF00h
colcur          EQU   0A0Bh
eqpchk          EQU     11h
off             EQU    0FFh
on              EQU     00h
bw              EQU     30h
;
_PROG   SEGMENT BYTE
        ASSUME  CS:_PROG
;
cursw   PROC    FAR
        push    bp
```

```
        mov     bp,sp
        push    ds
        push    es
        cld
        cmp     byte ptr cs:[fstpas],0
        jnz     docurs
        mov     byte ptr cs:[fstpas],1
        int     eqpchk
        and     ax,bw
        cmp     ax,bw
        jnz     docurs
        mov     word ptr cs:[onlin],colcur
docurs:
        mov     ah,curlin
        lds     si,dword ptr [bp + 6]
        mov     bx,si
        push    cs
        pop     es
        mov     di,offset cs:oncmd
        mov     cx,3
        rep     cmpsb
        jnz     offtst
        mov     byte ptr cs:[curflg],off
        mov     cx,cs:[onlin]
        jmp     short curon
offtst:
        mov     si,bx
        mov     di,offset cs:offcmd
        mov     cx,4
        rep     cmpsb
        jnz     switch
        mov     byte ptr cs:[curflg],on
        mov     cx,offlin
        jmp     short curon
switch:
        mov     cx,cs:[onlin]
        cmp     byte ptr cs:[curflg],off
        jz      curon
        mov     cx,offlin
curon:
        int     video
        not     byte ptr cs:[curflg]
        pop     es
        pop     ds
        pop     bp
        ret
cursw   ENDP
;
curflg          DB      00h
fstpas          DB      00h
oncmd           DB      'ON',0
offcmd          DB      'OFF',0
onlin           DW      0707h
```

```
;
_PROG   ENDS
        END

; End of File
```

SAMPCURS.PRG

```
*********************
* Name          SAMPCURS.prg
* Date          August 10, 1986
* Notice        Copyright 1986, 1987, 1988, Stephen J. Straley & Associates
* Note          This program, linked in with the CURSOR.obj file,
*               demonstrates how the cursor can be turned on or off.
*********************

X = " "
DO WHILE x <> "X" .AND. x <> "x"
    CLEAR
    CALL CURSW
    WAIT "CURSOR IS NOW OFF...." TO x
    CALL CURSW
    WAIT "CURSOR IS NOW ON....." TO x
ENDDO
X = " "
DO WHILE x <> "X" .AND. x <> "x"
    CLEAR
    CALL CURSW WITH "OFF"
    WAIT "CURSOR OFF (WITH <param>)...." TO x
    CALL CURSW WITH "ON"
    WAIT "CURSOR ON (WITH <param>)....." TO x
ENDDO
* End of File
```

DRSTATUS.ASM

```
**********************
* Name          DRSTATUS.asm
* Date          August 10, 1986
* Notice        Copyright 1986-8, Stephen J. Straley & Associates
* Note          Contributed by David Dodson, this is to be
*               used for IBM PCs or 100 percent compatibles.
*               This routine needs a single-byte parameter in
*               capital letters only: the drive designator. The returned
*               value will be in the following format:
*
*               0  |    DRIVE READY - READ / WRITE
*               1  |    DRIVE READY - WRITE PROTECTED
*               2  |    DRIVE NOT READY - DOOR OPEN
*               3  |    DRIVE NOT READY - NON - DOS DISK
*               4  |    DRIVE NOT READY - MISC. ERROR
**********************
;
```

```
PUBLIC  drstat
;
dskint          EQU     13h
read            EQU     02h
write           EQU     03h
dskrst          EQU     00h
wrprot          EQU     03h
door            EQU     80h
nondos          EQU     02h
;
_PROG   SEGMENT BYTE
        ASSUME  CS:_PROG
;
drstat  PROC    FAR
        push    bp
        mov     bp,sp
        push    es
        push    ds
        lds     si,dword ptr [bp + 6]
        push    cs
        pop     es
        mov     bx,offset cs:buffer
        lodsb
        sub     al,'A'
        mov     dl,al
        mov     dh,0
        mov     cx,1
        mov     al,1
        mov     ah,read
        int     dskint
        jc      error
        mov     ah,write
        mov     al,1
        int     dskint
        jc      error
        mov     al,'0'
        jmp     done
error:
        mov     al,'1'
        cmp     ah,wrprot
        jz      reset
        inc     al
        cmp     ah,door
        jz      reset
        inc     al
        cmp     ah,nondos
        jz      reset
        inc     al
reset:
        push    ax
        mov     ah,dskrst
        int     dskint
        pop     ax
```

```
done:
        les     di,dword ptr [bp + 10]
        stosb
        pop     ds
        pop     es
        pop     bp
        ret
drstat  ENDP
;
buffer  DB      1024 DUP(0)
;
_PROG   ENDS
        END
; End of File
```

DRVESTAT.PRG

```
********************
* Name          DRVESTAT.prg
* Date          August 10, 1986
* Notice        Copyright 1986-8, Stephen J. Straley & Associates
* Notes         This program shows the status of the disk drive.
********************

STORE " " TO x, st
CLEAR
DO WHILE UPPER(x) <> "X"
     IF ROW() > 20
        CLEAR
     ENDIF
     which = " "
     WAIT "Which drive? " TO which
     CALL DRSTAT WITH which, st
     DO CASE
     CASE st = "0"
        ?? " <= Drive is ready in READ/WRITE mode"
     CASE st = "1"
        ?? " <= Drive is ready but is write protected"
     CASE st = "2"
        ?? " <= Drive is NOT ready; the door is open"
     CASE st = "3"
        ?? " <= Drive is NOT ready; it is NOT a DOS disk"
     OTHERWISE
        ?? " <= Drive is NOT ready because of a miscellaneous error"
     ENDCASE
     ?
     WAIT "    ENTER X TO EXIT OR ANY OTHER KEY TO CONTINUE....  " TO x
     ?
ENDDO
* End of File
```

NODRIVES.ASM

```
*********************
* Name          NODRIVES.asm
* Date          August 10, 1986
* Notice        Copyright 1986-8, Stephen J. Straley & Associates
* Note          Contributed by David Dodson, this is to be
*               used for IBM PCs or 100 percent compatibles.
*               This routine returns the number of logical drives available
*               on the machine in question.  A call with a 2-byte string, returns
*               an ASCII 2-digit value equal to the number of logical drives.
*               Use VAL() to convert to numeric.
**********************
;
PUBLIC  numdsk
;
dos             EQU     21h
seldsk          EQU     0Eh
curdsk          EQU     19h
;
_PROG   SEGMENT BYTE
        ASSUME  CS:_PROG
;
numdsk  PROC    FAR
        push    bp
        mov     bp,sp
        push    es
        cld
        les     di,dword ptr [bp + 6]
        mov     ah,curdsk
        int     dos
        mov     dl,al
        mov     ah,seldsk
        int     dos
        mov     ah,0
        aam
        add     ax,3030h
        xchg    ah,al
        stosw
        pop     es
        pop     bp
        ret
numdsk  ENDP
_PROG   ENDS
        END
; End of File
```

NUMBDRVS.PRG

```
*********************
* Name          NUMBDRVS.prg
* Date          August 10, 1986
* Notice        Copyright 1986-8, Stephen J. Straley & Assocaites
* Note          This program tests the number of drives available.
*********************

ndrv = "  "
CALL NUMDSK WITH ndrv
n = VAL(ndrv)
? n
* End of File
```

PRSTATUS.ASM

```
**********************
* Name          PRSTATUS.asm
* Date          August 10, 1986
* Note          Contributed by David Dodson, this is to be used
*               for IBM PCs or 100 percent compatibles.
*               This routine is to be CALLed to determine the current status
*               of the parallel printer on IBM compatibles. This routine is a
*               simple go or no-go status report.  Its usefulness stems from
*               the fact that program termination to the operating system can
*               be avoided; i.e., instead of a DOS error message, provide
*               an internal program error message if the printer is not
*               available.  The program will then return to the
*               application instead of DOS.  Call with a single-byte string
*               as a parameter. Returned in this string will be:
*
*                           0 = ON LINE, READY
*                           1 = PRINTER OFF LINE OR NOT READY
*
*               This routine assumes parallel port 1.
*********************

PUBLIC  prstat
;
CHECK   EQU     2                       ; status check command
PNUM    EQU     0                       ; parallel port 1
PRNT    EQU     17h                     ; bios printer interrupt
REDY    EQU     90h                     ; printer ready
;
_PROG   SEGMENT BYTE
        ASSUME  CS:_PROG
;
prstat  PROC    FAR
        push    bp                      ; standard setup, param's
        mov     bp,sp                   ;
        push    es                      ;
```

```
        les     di,dword ptr [bp + 6]     ; address of return status byte
        mov     ah,CHECK                  ; status check
        mov     dx,PNUM                   ; port 1
        int     PRNT                      ;
        mov     al,'0'                    ; returned if O.K.
        cmp     ah,REDY                   ; ready ?
        jz      done                      ; yes
        inc     al                        ; ascii 1
done:
        stosb                             ; place return byte
        pop     es                        ; restore state
        pop     bp                        ;
        ret
prstat  ENDP
_PROG   ENDS
        END
; End of File
```

PRINTSTT.PRG

```
*********************
* Name          PRINTSTT.prg
* Date          August 10, 1986
* Notice        Copyright 1986-8, Stephen J. Straley & Associates
* Note          This program reports the status of the printer.
*********************

STORE " " TO is_ready
CALL Prstat WITH is_ready
CLEAR
? "The printer is "
?? IF(is_ready = "0", "ready!", "not ready")
* End of File
```

Summer '87 Release

All of the examples below are written in Microsoft C 5.0. Following these descriptions will be the source code for each function. For simplicity, all functions are coded in a file labeled SUMMER_C.C. After this will be a sample Clipper program that will demonstrate these special routines.

BOOTIT()	Reboots the computer
NUM_DRIVES()	Returns the ASCII value for the last drive designated on the computer
THE_MEM()	Returns the number of bytes of memory installed on the computer

C_DRIVE()	Returns the ASCII value for the letter of the currently logged drive
RS_STAT()	Returns a logical true if the Right-Shift key is pressed
LS_STAT()	Returns a logical true if the Left-Shift key was pressed
INS_STAT()	Returns a logical true if the Insert key is toggled on
NUMLOCK_ST()	Returns a logical true if the Num Lock key is toggled on
SCR_LCK_ST()	Returns a logical true if the Scroll Lock key is toggled on
CAP_LCK_ST()	Returns a logical true if the Caps Lock key is toggled on
AL_STAT()	Returns a logical true if either Alt key is pressed
AL_LS_STAT()	Returns a logical true if the Alt-Left Shift key is pressed
AL_RS_STAT()	Returns a logical true if the Alt-Right Shift key is pressed

All of these routines should be compiled using the following sequence of commands:

```
   CL /c /AL /Oalt /Zl /FPa /Gs Summer_c.c
```

```
********************
* Name      Summer_c.c
* Author    Stephen J. Straley
* Notice    Copyright (c) 1988 Stephen J. Straley & Associates
* Date      April 2, 1988
* Compile   cl /c /AL /Oalt /Zl /FPa /Gs Summer_c.c
* Release   Microsoft C 5.0
* Note      This file contains several special routines that
*           will work with Clipper.
*********************

#include <dos.h>
#include <nandef.h>
#include <extend.h>

CLIPPER Bootit()
{
   union REGS r ;
   int86(0x19, &r, &r) ;
   _ret() ;
}
```

```
CLIPPER Num_drives()
{
   union REGS r ;
   int no_drives ;
   int cur_drive ;

   r.h.ah = 25 ;
   int86(0x21, &r, &r ) ;
   cur_drive = r.h.al ;

   r.h.ah = 14 ;
   r.h.dl = cur_drive ;
   int86(0x21, &r, &r ) ;
   no_drives = r.h.al ;
   _retni(no_drives + 64) ;
}

CLIPPER The_mem()
{
   union REGS r ;
   int av_memory ;

   int86(0x12, &r, &r ) ;
   av_memory = r.x.ax ;
   _retni(av_memory) ;
}

CLIPPER C_drive()
{
   union REGS r ;
   int cur_d_rive ;

   r.h.ah = 25 ;
   int86(0x21, &r, &r ) ;
   cur_d_rive = r.h.al ;
   _retni(cur_d_rive + 65) ;
}

CLIPPER rs_stat()
{
   union REGS r;

   r.h.ah = 2 ;
   int86(0x16, &r, &r) ;

   if (r.h.al & 1) _retl(1) ;
   else _retl(0) ;
}

CLIPPER ls_stat()
{
   union REGS r;
```

```
   r.h.ah = 2 ;
   int86(0x16, &r, &r) ;

   if (r.h.al & 2) _retl(1) ;
   else _retl(0) ;
}

CLIPPER ctrl_stat()
{
   union REGS r;

   r.h.ah = 2 ;
   int86(0x16, &r, &r) ;

   if (r.h.al & 4) _retl(1) ;
   else _retl(0) ;
}

CLIPPER ins_stat()
{
   union REGS r;

   r.h.ah = 2 ;
   int86(0x16, &r, &r) ;

   if ( r.h.al & 128 ) _retl(1) ;
   else _retl(0) ;
}

CLIPPER numlock_st()
{
   union REGS r;

   r.h.ah = 2 ;
   int86(0x16, &r, &r) ;

   if (r.h.al & 32) _retl(1) ;
   else _retl(0) ;
}

CLIPPER scr_lck_st()
{
   union REGS r;

   r.h.ah = 2 ;
   int86(0x16, &r, &r) ;

   if (r.h.al & 16) _retl(1) ;
   else _retl(0) ;
}

CLIPPER cap_lck_st()
{
```

```
   union REGS r;

   r.h.ah = 2 ;
   int86(0x16, &r, &r) ;

   if (r.h.al & 64) _retl(1) ;
   else _retl(0) ;
}

CLIPPER al_stat()
{
   union REGS r;

   r.h.ah = 2 ;
   int86(0x16, &r, &r) ;

   if (r.h.al & 8) _retl(1) ;
   else _retl(0) ;
}

CLIPPER al_ls_stat()
{
   union REGS r;

   r.h.ah = 2 ;
   int86(0x16, &r, &r) ;

   if (r.h.al & 10) _retl(1) ;
   else _retl(0) ;
}

CLIPPER al_rs_stat()
{
   union REGS r;

   r.h.ah = 2 ;
   int86(0x16, &r, &r) ;

   if (r.h.al & 9) _retl(1) ;
   else _retl(0) ;
}

CLIPPER d_stat()
{
   union REGS r;
   int look_drive, the_status ;

   look_drive = _parni(1) ;
   r.h.dl = 2 ;
   r.h.dl = look_drive ;
   int86(0x13, &r, &r) ;

   the_status = r.h.ah ;
```

```
   _retni(the_status) ;
}
```

To make these routines work properly, you must link in with EXTEND.LIB and CLIPPER.LIB the **large library model** from Microsoft. This file is labeled LLIBC.LIB.

The Link line for these routines would be the following, using Microsoft's 3.61 linker:

```
LINK /NOE /SE:1024 <filename> Summer_c,,,LLIBC + CLIPPER
```

CHAPTER TWELVE

Macros and Arrays

THE WORLD OF MACRO SUBSTITUTION

A *macro* is a symbol that tells the compiler to look for the associated definition for that symbol and to act upon those values accordingly.

Generally the programmer places a series of command verbs in a macro. When it is executed, the macro is expanded and the true representation of the macro is evaluated and executed. For example, a dBASE developer may program an application so that the user can choose which fields to LIST and the order in which they are to be LISTed. A simple LIST command followed by a macro (&) could refer to as few as one field or as many as all of the fields. In Clipper, this would have to be coded differently. Although macros have many advantages, there are restrictions on their use in the compiler environment.

SOME GUIDELINES FOR USING MACROS

1. Macros are allowed in DO WHILE...ENDDO and FOR...NEXT loops.
2. Macros can be used in conjunction with arrays.
3. Macros cannot contain any part of the syntactical structure of a command.
4. Macros can contain operators.
5. Macros can have up to 16 parses.

MACROS IN A DO WHILE

The ability to have macro substitution in a DO WHILE...ENDDO loop, a valuable tool for programming introduced in dBASE II, was initially abandoned in dBASE III. The abandonment of this feature in dBASE III brought widespread disappointment. However, Clipper allows macro substitution in DO WHILE...ENDDO and in FOR... NEXT loops.

USING MACROS AND ARRAYS

With the advent of arrays in Clipper, macros assumed a new importance. Especially necessary for developing matrixes, macro substitution with arrays can build complex memory structures. Consider the following:

```
DECLARE database[15]
FOR x = 1 TO 15
   temp = LTRIM(STR(x))
```

```
    * There will be a new array established for each database
    * name present.  These new arrays (name1[], name2[], name3[],
    * ... name15[] are built relating to each database
    * (database[1], database[2], database[3], ... database[15].
    * The macro varies as the loop executes, which in turn
    * varies the name of the array.

    DECLARE name&temp[99]
    DECLARE type&temp[99]
    DECLARE len&temp[99]
    DECLARE dec&temp[99]
    DECLARE indx&temp[7]
NEXT
```

A series of arrays is established in this example, each with a unique root name with common numbered extensions and based on a main array. As the array named DATABASE pans down through its elements ([]), the corresponding subscript number is converted to a string and placed in a macro. This then points to the next appropriate array pertaining to that subscript number. Further information will be found later in this chapter in the section on arrays.

MACROS AND THE STRUCTURE OF A COMMAND

At compile time, the commands that are in a macro are not defined as such; the macro is defined but not the contents. If, for example, a user is allowed to choose to LIST one field or five fields, the compiler must know in advance which case will occur, one field or five. Normally, the command structure looks like this:

```
STORE SPACE(40) TO list_input
@ 01,01 SAY "Enter Field to List: " GET list_input
READ
LIST &list_input
```

An interpreter finds this satisfactory, but a compiler does not. At the time of compiling, the macro has no value assigned to it. The value comes at run-time. The compiler establishes a symbol that is referenced for expansion when the application is executed. Therefore, the compiler doesn't know whether one field is to be listed or five. When establishing the code for the LIST command, the compiler must know how many fields to list. This is determined by the comma, which in turn is part of the syntactical structure of the LIST command. In order to call upon the necessary library routines to make the command work, the compiler must have all of the necessary information before execution. Consider the following:

```
STORE "CLEAR" TO com_line
&com_line
```

The compiler has no problem with the first line. The string "CLEAR" is stored to the symbol defined as com_line. The compiler sees the second line as a macro expansion;

it establishes another symbol to hold the expanded value of com_line. The compiler does not know what command will be in the expanded macro; in this case what should be established is a symbol that will CLEAR the screen. To do this, the compiler has to interpret the previous command, which is what dBASE III does and which is precisely what slows down applications running under interpreters.

To sum up, remove command syntax from macros and, if applicable, establish multiple macros for the varying parts of the command. Otherwise, hard code any commands that you might have put in a macro.

OPERATORS IN A MACRO

Even though command syntax is not legal in macros, operators are. Mathematical operators (i.e., +, -, *, /) and logical operators (i.e., .OR., .NOT., .AND.) are not considered as part of the syntactical structure of the command and are allowed in a macro.

PARSING A MACRO

In the compiler, a macro is parsed into logical sections. Each section is then given a representing token (please see Chapter 2, Compiling) and is linked accordingly. In Clipper, macros may only be parsed 16 times. If too many parses have occurred, the following error message will normally appear at the top of the screen when the application is executing:

```
MACRO EXPANSION ERROR
```

To avoid this error, you should limit your macros to separate entities. However, it can be difficult to plan what is a separate entity and what is not. The basic rule is that the following are entities:

1. Functions
2. Field and variable names
3. Mathematical operators
4. Conditional operators (.AND., .NOT., .OR.)

Consider the following:

Sample 1:

```
USE Multy
STORE "INT(RECNO()/2) = RECNO()/2 .AND. " TO show
STORE show + "(LEN(TRIM(proc_name)) > 0 .AND. top > 0 " TO show
STORE show + ".AND. left > 0 .AND. bottom > 0 .AND. " TO show
STORE show + "right > 0) .OR. (row_mess > 0 .AND. " TO show
STORE show + "col_mess > 0 .AND. row_esc > 0 .AND. " TO show
```

```
STORE show + "col_esc > 0) .OR.  (LEN(TRIM(STR(search))) > 0 " TO show
STORE show + ".AND.  LEN(TRIM(variable)) > 0)" TO show
SET FILTER TO &show
GO TOP
LIST
```

This extensive macro causes a Macro Expansion Error on the line with the SET FILTER TO command. The problem is that all the code in the macro is necessary for the application. If too much is being parsed, break the macro into separate macros and use both macros on the SET FILTER TO command. Now consider the following variation on the above code fragment:

Sample 2:

```
USE Multy
STORE "INT(RECNO()/2) = RECNO()/2 .AND. " TO show1
STORE show1 + "(LEN(TRIM(proc_name)) > 0 .AND. top > 0 " TO show1
STORE show1 + ".AND. left > 0 .AND. bottom > 0 .AND. " TO show1

STORE "right > 0) .OR. (row_mess > 0 .AND. " TO show2
STORE show2 + "col_mess > 0 .AND. row_esc > 0 .AND. " TO show2
STORE show2 + "col_esc > 0) .OR.  (LEN(TRIM(STR(search))) > 0 " TO show2
STORE show2 + ".AND.  LEN(TRIM(variable)) > 0)" TO show2

SET FILTER TO &show1. &show2
GO TOP
LIST
```

In the first sample there were too many parses in one macro. In the second sample the macro was broken up into two separate macros. Remember that each macro can be parsed up to 16 times.

You can also get a Macro Expansion Error message if there isn't sufficient parsing of the macro, causing a problem with the macro syntax. For example:

```
STORE "LEN(TRIM(proc_name)) > 0 " TO show
STORE show + "row + col > 0" TO show
SET FILTER TO &show
GO TOP
LIST
```

This yields a Macro Expansion Error because there is no conditional operator either at the end of the first or the beginning of the second STORE TO command that separates the two operations.

The above guidelines may indicate that macros do not perform the same functions in the compiler as they do in the interpreter. That is not exactly the case, but it **is** true that programmers have to pay more attention to code structure when working with compilers than with interpreters.

If an application is "macro intensive," look at how you use the macros before frustrating yourself with the compiler. If the syntax of command is spelled out as a literal and not in a macro, your chances for success are high. If you run into problems with macros and the way they are expanded, remember that there is always more than one way to code any given situation.

Tips on Using Macros

One of the undocumented features to Clipper's macro capability is the use of a macro and a UDF (user-defined function). While I was developing a database generator in Steve Straley's Toolkit, I found a way to have the name of a user-defined function within a macro variable. In this case, the VALIDation clause changed as the user entered the data type of the field that was being worked on. For example, consider having an extensive CASE statement that branches to the same type of GET command, each with different validation clause. It may look something like this:

```
DO CASE
   CASE TYPE("data") = "C"
      @ 10,10 SAY "Enter Length: " GET input;
                              VALID CHAR(input)
   CASE TYPE("data") = "N"
      @ 10,10 SAY "Enter Length: " GET input;
                              VALID NUMB(input)
   CASE TYPE("data") = "D"
      @ 10,10 SAY "Enter Length: " GET input;
                              VALID DATEIN(input)
   CASE TYPE("data") = "L"
      @ 10,10 SAY "Enter Length: " GET input;
                              VALID LOGIC(input)
   CASE TYPE("data") = "M"
      @ 10,10 SAY "Enter Length: " GET input;
                              VALID MEMO(input)
ENDCASE
READ
```

Each function tests the user for the proper length to be entered based on the type of data previously set by the user. Clipper's macro logic will allow a small code table to be built if we change the logic flow of the program to look like this:

```
DO CASE
   CASE TYPE("data") = "C"
      in_func = "CHAR(input)"
   CASE TYPE("data") = "N"
      in_func = "NUMB(input)"
   CASE TYPE("data") = "D"
      in_func = "DATEIN(input)"
   CASE TYPE("data") = "L"
      in_func = "LOGIC(input)"
   CASE TYPE("data") = "M"
```

```
        in_func = "MEMO(input)"
    ENDCASE
    @ 10,10 SAY "Enter Length: " GET input ;
                VALID &in_func.
    READ
```

The reason this code extract will yield a smaller code size is that there is only one "@ SAY...GET" as opposed to five. This reduction may not seem significant; however, if it is applied to an application that is pushing the memory boundaries of the machine and the size of the executable load module of the application, this ability may prove to be important.

Another type of macro is with the use of parentheses. These tell Clipper to expand the variable within the parentheses and then treat the contents as a literal; in other words, they may replace all command/function options which have literal values placed in the code. For example, to use a file, the file name may be typed in the program in the following manner:

```
USE people
```

The literal here is PEOPLE – the name of a database. We can tell it is a literal because it is in the code **without** the use of quotation marks. A *variable* containing the name of the desired database may be used as well, with the assistance of macro substitution. This code example would look like this:

```
variable = "People"
USE &variable
```

The Summer '87 release allows parentheses to be used for the literal portion of the command. The code would look like this:

```
variable = "People"
USE (variable)
```

This convention, however, will **not** work inside a function as a parameter which requires expressions rather than literals. For example, the FILE() function requires a string parameter which is denoted with the use of quotation marks within the function. Also, variables, if used, are not passed by macro substitution. Their reference value is passed internally and Clipper does the rest. So in these cases, parentheses are not necessary.

Other examples of the use of parentheses in macro substitution include such commands as the SELECT option, most SET commands, and the SET KEY TO command.

ARRAYS AND MATRIXES

An array is a database made up of only one field and is held in memory. The name of the array is also the name of the field, and the subscript is used as the record pointer. In the Summer '87 version of Clipper, there is a complete set of array-based functions; in addition the capability of the internal logic of an array has been enhanced. The asterisk in the list below notes a new Summer '87 function. All of these functions include:

*	ACHOICE():	Executes a list box using array elements of character data type as the displayed values in the window.
*	ACOPY():	Copies elements from one array to another.
	ADEL():	Deletes an array element from an array.
	ADIR():	Files an array with file information from the directory.
*	AFIELDS():	Files an array with field definition information.
	AFILL():	Fills an array with one value.
	AINS():	Inserts a new subscript position into an array.
	ASCAN():	Searches for a specific value within an array.
*	ASORT():	Sorts an array in ascending order. If the name of an array is the same as a field name in an open database, the array will not be sorted. Change the name of the array if this happens.

Before discussing the purpose and use of arrays, let's first examine the syntax used to declare an array in Clipper:

```
DECLARE array_name[x]
```

or

```
PUBLIC array_name[x]
```

DECLARE: The Clipper command that initializes the array. With all versions of Clipper, this command only initializes PRIVATE arrays.

PUBLIC: The Clipper command that initializes the array. PUBLIC arrays are only allowed with the Summer '87 version.

array_name: The name of the array; also known as the identifier.

[x]: The subscript; in a declaration statement (either with DECLARE or PUBLIC) this sets the number of elements contained in the array.

The following guidelines pertaining to array will help in your planning:

1. An array without any elements takes up approximately 2K of memory space.

2. The amount of variable space (the V variable with the SET CLIPPER = to command) affects the number of arrays allowed.

3. Each element in an array takes up additional memory space dependent on the size of that element type and whether or not it can fit in the preallocated space.

4. Memo fields cannot be stored directly in an array. Since the contents of a memo field are character data with a length dependent on the length of the string, a memo field can be stored first as a string variable and then placed in the array.

5. An array can contain mixed data types.

6. With versions prior to the Summer '87 release, arrays have been always PRIVATE. Now, with the PUBLIC command, an array may be PUBLIC as well.

7. Arrays cannot be directly SAVEd to memory files.

8. A memory variable assigned to the same name as an array destroys the array and all elements contained in it and also releases corresponding memory.

9. The TYPE(array_name) function returns an "A" representing the array if only the array name (without brackets) is used with this function. If specific elements are pointed to with the TYPE() function, such as TYPE("array_name[pointer]"), the TYPE() function performs as expected on that element of the array.

10. The LEN(array_name) function returns the number of elements the array has been declared to hold. The number is obtained if only the array name (without brackets) is used. If specific elements are pointed to with the LEN() function, such as LEN(array_name[pointer]), the LEN() function performs as expected on that element of the array.

11. Macros can be used in conjunction with an array; however, macros cannot be used to declare (with DECLARE or PUBLIC) the array if the command syntax is in the macro.

Wrong:

```
temp = "array_name[10]"
DECLARE &temp.
```

Right:

```
temp = "array_name"
DECLARE &temp.[10]
temp = "array_name[10]"
STORE 1 TO &temp.
? &temp.
```

12. Using an array with context sensitive HELP will not precisely work. Using arrays with the READ command in conjunction with either Clipper's internal HELP or any SET KEY TO procedure means only the array name will be passed to the procedure and not the array name with subscript pointer. Therefore, applying direct context-sensitive HELP referring to a specific array element may not be accomplished without special programming techniques (e.g., using global variables with the HELP and the array).

AN ILLUSTRATION OF AN ARRAY

The array automatically establishes 14 bytes per element. (NOTE: There were 22 bytes in the Autumn '86 release.) The full size of the array is dependent on the number of elements called for by the DECLARE command.

If, for example, 1000 elements are DECLAREd in an array named "legions," the actual size of legions[] is 14 bytes times 1000, or roughly 14K. If a string 30 characters long is stored in the array, an address is stored that points to the actual position in memory. The array then indirectly consumes an additional 30 bytes for that string. This is what the code looks like:

```
STORE "HI" to temp
STORE 7 TO top
DECLARE legions[5]
STORE "This is a test" TO legions[1]
STORE .T. TO legions[2]
STORE 43 TO legions[3]
STORE CTOD("09/08/86") TO legions[4]
STORE "now is the time for all good men to come to the aid of ";
     TO legions[5]
```

```
Pre-Allocated Memory

   Memvar top           [7       ]
          temp          [HI      ]
          legions       [BDEFA   ] — which points to ┐
                                                     │
                         ┌───────────────────────────┘
                         V
            [<------14 bytes------>]  BDEFA

            ["This is a test"......]  <- position 1
            [.T....................]  <- position 2
            [43....................]  <- position 3
            [09/08/86..............]  <- position 4
            [address A6EFF.........]  <- position 5
                         │
                         │
                         │  that points in memory to that
                         │  address
                         │
                         V
  A6EFF ["now is the time for all good men to come to the aid of "]
```

A SMALL SAMPLE

Let's say we wish to STORE 25 numbers to an array.

```
DECLARE choice[25]          && Line 1
FOR x = 1 TO 25             && Line 2
   choice[x] = x * 2        && Line 3
NEXT                        && Line 4
```

Line 1 establishes an array called choice[] that has 25 elements. Any previous memory variable or array with that name is destroyed. Immediately after the DECLARE command is the beginning of a FOR...NEXT loop with 25 iterations, 1 through 25. Line 3, therefore, will be executed 25 times with the variable x incrementing by 1 on each pass. The value stored to the array at position x is 2 times x. The first pass points to the first position in the array and STOREs 2 to the array at position 1, the second pass STOREs 4 to the array at position 2, and so on until the twenty-fifth pass, which STOREs 50 to the array at position 25.

ARRAYS AND PROCEDURES

Arrays, as well as specific elements in the array, can be passed to procedures. Since arrays are always PRIVATE, they must be passed to procedures by reference. This is done by passing only the array identifier or name to the procedure. Any change made to the array in the called procedure changes values in the array in the calling procedure. Specific elements in an array can be passed by value to a procedure as long as the subscript is used in conjunction with the identifier and the subscript points to the correct element in the array.

The following procedure demonstrates some of the many uses of an array as well as some of the functions (e.g., LEN() and TYPE()) that can be used on an array. It also shows how arrays are passed as parameters.

```
*********************
* Name          SAMPARRY.prg
* Date          August 4, 1986
* Notice        Copyright 1986-1988, Stephen J. Straley
* Compile       Clipper Samparry -m
* Release       Autumn '86
* Link          Plink86 fi samparry lib dbu lib clipper;
* Note          This program initializes the months and the
*               days of the week to two memory variables and
*               passes them to procedures.
*********************

DECLARE month_a[12], day_a[7], date_a[50], numb_a[25], hodge_a[100]

*******************************************
* The following initializes the arrays. *
*******************************************

FOR x = 1 TO 50
   DO CASE
      CASE x <= 7
         day_a[x]   = CDOW(DATE() + (1 *x))
         month_a[x] = CMONTH(DATE() + (30 * x))
         numb_a[x]  = x * 324
         date_a[x]  = DATE() + x * 84
      CASE x > 7 .AND. x <= 12
         month_a[x] = CMONTH(DATE() + (30 * x))
         numb_a[x]  = x * 324
         date_a[x]  = DATE() + x * 84
      CASE x > 12 .AND. x <= 25
         numb_a[x]  = x * 324
         date_a[x]  = DATE() + x * 84
      CASE x > 25
         date_a[x]  = DATE() + x * 84
   ENDCASE
NEXT
CLEAR
```

```
*****************************************************
* This section displays the values of the arrays. *
*****************************************************

@ 01,05 SAY "Days of the week are ... "
FOR x = 1 TO 7
   ? day_a[x]
   hodge_a[x] = day_a[x]
NEXT
WAIT
CLEAR

@ 01,05 SAY "Months of the year are ... "
FOR x = 1 TO 12
   ? month_a[x]
   hodge_a[x + 7] = month_a[x]
NEXT
WAIT
CLEAR

STORE 1 TO temp_col
STORE 3 TO temp_row

@ 01,05 SAY "A random set of 25 numbers are ... "
FOR x = 1 TO 25
   @ temp_row, temp_col SAY numb_a[x]
   DO Chngescr
   hodge_a[x + 19] = numb_a[x]
NEXT
WAIT
CLEAR

STORE 1 TO temp_col
STORE 3 TO temp_row

@ 01,05 SAY "A random of 50 dates are ... "
FOR x = 1 TO 50
   @ temp_row, temp_col say date_a[x]
   DO Chngescr
   hodge_a[x + 44] = date_a[x]
NEXT
WAIT
CLEAR

STORE 1 TO temp_col
STORE 3 TO temp_row

@ 01,05 SAY "The total is ... "
FOR x = 1 TO 100
   @ temp_row, temp_col SAY hodge_a[x]
   DO Chngescr
NEXT
WAIT
CLEAR
```

```
*************************************************************
* The following displays information using the LEN() and *
* TYPE() functions.                                      *
*************************************************************

@ 10,15 SAY "The following will show the depth of each array ... "
@ 12,10 SAY "The number of elements in the Month Array   "
?? LEN(month_a)
@ 13,10 SAY "The number of elements in the Day Array     "
?? LEN(day_a)
@ 14,10 SAY "The number of elements in the Number Array  "
?? LEN(numb_a)
@ 15,10 SAY "The number of elements in the Date Array    "
?? LEN(date_a)
@ 16,10 SAY "The number of elements in Hodge Podge Array "
?? LEN(hodge_a)
@ 20,10 SAY "The type of the arrays are ...              "
?? TYPE("month_a")
WAIT
CLEAR
STORE "" TO in_temp

*******************************************************************
* This section passes an array element to a procedure by value. *
*******************************************************************

DO Passarry WITH month_a[3]
@ 14,10 SAY "Month_a[3] is out of the procedure and equal to: "
@ 14,60 SAY month_a[3]
WAIT

*********************************************************
* This section passes the array element by value and *
* shows how to reassign the value to the array.      *
*                                                    *
*********************************************************

DO Passarry WITH month_a[3]
month_a[3] = in_temp
@ 14,10 SAY "Month_a[3] is out of the procedure and equal to: "
@ 14,60 SAY month_a[3]
WAIT

*************************************************************
* This section passes the entire array to a procedure by *
* reference.                                             *
*************************************************************

DO Anotarry WITH numb_a
CLEAR

STORE 3 TO temp_row
STORE 1 TO temp_col
```

```
@ 01,05 SAY "The numbers are now set to ... "
FOR x = 1 TO 25
   @ temp_row, temp_col SAY numb_a[x]
   DO Chngescr
NEXT

*********************

PROCEDURE Passarry

   PARAMETERS in_val

   CLEAR
   @ 04,23 SAY "The value of the passed array is ... "
   @ 04,60 SAY in_val
   @ 06,23 SAY "Let us change the value ... " GET in_val
   READ
   @ 08,23 SAY "The new value is ... "
   @ 08,60 SAY in_val
   @ 10,20 SAY ""
   in_temp = in_val
   WAIT

*********************

PROCEDURE Anotarry

   PARAMETERS b

   CLEAR
   temp_col = 1
   temp_row = 3
   @ 01,05 say "You may edit this Number Array ... "
   FOR x = 1 TO 25
      @ temp_row, temp_col GET b[x]
      DO Chngescr
   NEXT
   READ

*********************

PROCEDURE Chngescr

   temp_col = temp_col + 15
   IF temp_col > 65
      temp_col = 1
      temp_row = temp_row + 1
   ENDIF
* End of File
```

ARRAYS AND MATRIXES

Arrays in Clipper are one dimensional. In some languages, more than one subscript can be passed to the array, in which case it is referred to as a two-dimensional array, or the beginnings of a matrix. A matrix is a multidimensional array in which the elements are interwoven and tied to one another.

To illustrate the structure of an array, let's say we want to establish up to 10 individual databases, each with 99 possible field names, field types, field lengths, and, if applicable, field decimal places. The field descriptors must in some way relate to the appropriate database much like a relation established between databases. However, since this all needs to be entirely in memory, the SET RELATION TO command does not work. As each database is given a name, the pointer for that name must somehow refer to other arrays that will carry the detailed information; however, each detailed array has many pieces of information. In other languages, such as BASIC, the array declaration would look something like this:

```
DIM array_name(2,4)
```

This tells the computer that there will be four y elements for each element of x and that there are two x elements. Graphically, this is:

```
x       y
1       1,2,3,4
2       1,2,3,4
```

Since this is not legal in Clipper, we must somehow simulate it.

Simulating a Matrix: Part 1

The following procedures establish in memory 15 database structures including database names, field names, field type, their lengths, and the number of decimal places to be used. Only 99 field names, types, etc., are allowed because of memory restrictions. Users can employ this routine to create structures interactively without any other utility programs. This code demonstrates the use of arrays in conjunction with macros.

```
********************
* Name          CREATEIT.prg
* Date          August 10, 1986
* Notice        Copyright 1986, Stephen J. Straley
* Compile       Clipper Createit
* Release       Autumn '86
* Link          Plink86 fi Createit lib dbu lib clipper;
* Note          This procedure creates several databases
*               in memory (15 maximum) as well as the structures
*               for each.  This is done using arrays and macros
*               to simulate matrixes.  Then the actual .DBF file
*               is written with the CREATEIT command.
********************
```

```
SET CONFIRM ON
SET SCOREBOARD OFF
CLEAR
scrframe = CHR(201) + CHR(205) + CHR(187) + CHR(186) + ;
           CHR(188) + CHR(205) + CHR(200) + CHR(186) + CHR(32)
DECLARE database[15]
FOR x = 1 TO 15
   temp = LTRIM(STR(x))

   ***********************************************************
   * Below, a separate array is created based on the        *
   * database[] array.  The idea is that as the pointer     *
   * in database[] advances, and the subscript pointer      *
   * in essence points to the four arrays that contain the *
   * detailed information on the database[] array.          *
   ***********************************************************

   DECLARE name&temp[99], type&temp[99], len&temp[99], dec&temp[99]
NEXT
@ 0,0,23,79 BOX SUBSTR(scrframe,1,8)
@ 0,30 SAY " Create Databases "
FOR x = 1 TO 15
   STORE SPACE(12) TO database[x]
   @ 2,3 SAY "Enter Database Name: " GET database[x] PICT "@!"
   READ
   IF !EMPTY(database[x])
      temp = LTRIM(STR(x))
      trow = 8
      tcol = 0
      FOR y = 1 TO 99
         STORE SPACE(10) TO name&temp[y]
         STORE SPACE(1) TO type&temp[y]
         STORE 0 TO len&temp[y], dec&temp[y]
         @ 3,3 SAY "   Enter Field Name: " GET name&temp[y] PICT "@!"
         @ 4,3 SAY "               Type: " GET type&temp[y] PICT "!" ;
               VALID(type&temp[y]$"NCLDM ")
         @ 5,3 SAY "             Length: " GET len&temp[y] PICT "####" ;
               RANGE 0, 255
         @ 6,3 SAY "           Decimals: " GET dec&temp[y] PICT "##"
               RANGE 0,15
         READ
         IF EMPTY(name&temp[y])
            y = 100
         ELSE
            DO CASE
            CASE type&temp[y] = "D"
               len&temp[y] = 8
               dec&temp[y] = 0
            CASE type&temp[y] = "L"
               len&temp[y] = 1
               dec&temp[y] = 0
            CASE type&temp[y] = "M"
               len&temp[y] = 10
               dec&temp[y] = 0
```

```
            CASE type&temp[y] = "N"
               IF len&temp[y] > 15
                  len&temp[y] = 15
               ENDIF
            OTHERWISE
               dec&temp[y] = 0
            ENDCASE
            IF trow > 22
               trow = 8
               FOR steve = 8 TO 22
                  @ steve,3 SAY SPACE(47)
               NEXT
            ENDIF
            @ trow,5 SAY name&temp[y]
            @ trow,COL() + 2 SAY type&temp[y]
            @ trow,COL() + 2 SAY len&temp[y]
            @ trow,COL() + 2 SAY dec&temp[y]
            trow = trow + 1
         ENDIF
      NEXT
      FOR steve = 1 TO 22
         @ steve, 3 SAY SPACE(47)
      NEXT
      @ x, 52 SAY LTRIM(STR(x)) + "-> "
      @ x, COL() SAY database[x]
   ELSE
      x = 17
   ENDIF
NEXT
@ 0,0,23,79 BOX scrframe
@ 10,26 SAY "Now Creating the Databases....."
x = 1
DO WHILE !EMPTY(database[x])
   z = LTRIM(STR(x))
   CREATE Temp
   USE Temp
   FOR y = 1 TO 99
      APPEND BLANK
      REPLACE field_name WITH name&z[y]
      REPLACE field_type WITH type&z[y]
      REPLACE field_len WITH len&z[y]
      REPLACE field_dec WITH dec&z[y]
      IF EMPTY(name&z[y+1])
         y = 100
      ENDIF
   NEXT
   USE
   temp_name = database[x]
   CREATE &temp_name FROM Temp
   ERASE Temp.dbf
   CLOSE DATABASES
   x = x + 1
ENDDO
CLEAR
* End of File
```

Simulating a Matrix: Part 2

There is another way to simulate a matrix condition. Because an array can contain a mixture of any data types (except for the memo type), it is possible to write a user-defined function that will take two numbers (the two numbers normally found in a matrix statement) and generate a single number that points to a position in a one-dimensional array that is **equivalent** to a given element from a two-dimensional array.

To better understand this technique, think of a card file in the library. Each file box (an array) has index cards (the x dimension) with several cards on individual books behind each of them (the y dimension). If every index card had the same number of book cards behind it, it would be simple to come up with a formula to tell the user what absolute position in the card file yields the *yth* card in the *xth* index.

The example DIMEN.PRG below is a simulation of this technique. Keep in mind that the formula for a three-dimensional array is similar to but more complex than that for a two-dimensional array.

```
********************
* Name          DIMEN.prg
* Date          August 10, 1986
* Notice        Copyright 1986, Stephen J. Straley
* Compile       Clipper Dimen
* Release       Autumn '86
* Link          Plink86 fi dimen lib dbu lib clipper;
* Note          This program is designed to simulate a multidimensional
*               array construct using macros to simulate the condition.
*               A user-defined function was created to point to the proper
*               position in the one-dimensional array.
********************

DO WHILE .T.
   STORE 0 TO x,y
   CLEAR
   @ 5,10 SAY "What is x range? " GET x PICT "###" RANGE 0,999
   @ 7,10 SAY "What is y range? " GET y PICT "###" RANGE 0,999
   READ
   IF EMPTY(x) .OR. EMPTY(y)
      EXIT
   ENDIF
   ********************************************
   *  The maximum number of elements in the   *
   *  array will always be the value of x     *
   *  times the value of y.                   *
   ********************************************
   DECLARE master[(x*y)]
   DECLARE names[x]
   FOR outside = 1 TO x
      STORE SPACE(30) TO names[outside]
      @ 10,10 SAY "Enter Name Number " + TRANSFORM(outside, "99") + ;
```

```
            " => " GET names[outside]
      READ
      *
      *  By TRANSFORMing the 'outside' variable, users will know which
      *  subscript value they are working with while entering in information
      *
      FOR inside = 1 TO y
         ****************************************************
         *  Outside is the current xth position while inside *
         *  is the current yth position.                     *
         ****************************************************
         STORE 0 TO master[DIM(outside, inside)]
         @ 11 + inside,10 SAY "Enter number: " ;
           GET master[DIM(outside, inside)]
         READ
      NEXT
      WAIT
      @ 10,0 CLEAR
   NEXT
   WAIT "Now for the list:"
   @ 10,0 CLEAR
   FOR outside = 1 TO x
      ? names[outside]
      ? SPACE(5)
      FOR inside = 1 TO y
         ?? master[DIM(outside, inside)]
      NEXT
   NEXT
   WAIT "This is it ..."
ENDDO

********************

FUNCTION Dim

    PARAMETERS a, b

    ******************************************************************
    *  A is only a private variable with the value of OUTSIDE as passed, *
    *  B is only a private variable with the value of INSIDE as passed,  *
    *  and the Y value is looked at publicly in order to determine the   *
    *  limits of the calculations.  Otherwise, the Y value would         *
    *  have to be passed as a parameter, thus altering the look of the   *
    *  two-dimensional function, or the user-defined function must       *
    *  be hard coded to fit the Y value.                                 *
    ******************************************************************

    temp = ((a * y) - y) + b
    RETURN(temp)
```

Storing and Restoring Arrays to and from Disk

This was another technique I developed while putting together Steve Straley's Toolkit. In exploring the many possibilities of array logic and manipulation, I found a pressing need for one application to create a series of arrays with undetermined length, and another application to use those same arrays. The trick I found was in the MEMOREAD() function. I found that this function, if used on a memory file (.MEM) yielded the name of the first element saved in the file. This meant that I could not only save the array to disk, but I could save the array's length embedded in the name of the first element. This way, the length of the array can be determined and DECLAREd before the array is brought into the system from the disk. Below is a sample of how that can be accomplished.

```
*********************
* Name     Savethem.prg
* Author   Stephen J. Straley
* Notice   Copyright (c) 1988 Stephen J. Straley & Associates
* Date     February 7, 1988
* Compile  Clipper Savethem -m
* Release  Autumn '86
* Link     Mslink Savethem,,,extend + clipper
* Note     This demonstrates saving arrays to disk and restoring them.
*          This discovery can be found in Steve Straley's Toolkit.
*********************

CLEAR SCREEN
DECLARE dataset1[23]

FOR x = 1 TO 23
   dataset1[x] = x * 3
   @ x, 1 SAY dataset1[x]
NEXT
WAIT

DO Savearray WITH "DATASET1", dataset1
CLEAR SCREEN
@ 3,0 SAY "Press Any Key to Clear ALL MEMORY..."
INKEY(0)

CLEAR ALL
CLOSE ALL
RELEASE ALL
CLEAR
@ 0,0 SAY "Now, reinitializing an array to the exact number of elements in
DATASET1"

DECLARE new_array[DEC_ARRAY("DATASET1")]

DO Restarray WITH "DATASET1", new_array
```

```
FOR x = 1 TO LEN(new_array)
   @ 3+x, 1 SAY new_array[x]
NEXT
WAIT

*********************

PROCEDURE Savearray

   PARAMETERS arr_file, arr_name

   IF EMPTY(AT(".", arr_file))
      arr_file = arr_file + ".ARR"
   ENDIF

   ext = ALLTRIM(STR(LEN(arr_name)))
   STORE "" TO AAAA&ext.
   FOR qaz = 1 TO LEN(arr_name)
      ext = ALLTRIM(STR(qaz))
      STORE arr_name[qaz] TO AAAB&ext.
   NEXT
   SAVE ALL LIKE AAA* TO &arr_file.

*********************

FUNCTION Dec_array

   PARAMETERS arr_file

   IF EMPTY(AT(".", arr_file))
      arr_file = arr_file + ".ARR"
   ENDIF

   IF !FILE(arr_file)
      RETURN(0)
   ELSE
      RETURN(VAL(SUBSTR(MEMOREAD(arr_file), 5)))
   ENDIF

*********************

PROCEDURE Restarray

   PARAMETERS arr_file, arr_name

   IF EMPTY(AT(".", arr_file))
      arr_file = arr_file + ".ARR"
   ENDIF

   RESTORE FROM &arr_file. ADDITIVE

   FOR qaz = 1 TO LEN(arr_name)
      ext = ALLTRIM(STR(qaz))
```

```
      STORE AAAB&ext. TO arr_name[qaz]
   NEXT
   RELEASE ALL LIKE AAA*
* End of File
```

The additional functions in Clipper's array logic allow several new features and possibilities. Displaying a database structure now is simple and easy. Also, for compatibility purposes, Clipper can now simulate some of the features some interpreters have, such as GATHER and SCATTER. Below are two samples of how to use some of the new capabilities with arrays.

```
*********************
* Name      Pickdisp.prg
* Author    Stephen J. Straley
* Notice    Copyright (c) 1988 Stephen J. Straley & Associates
* Date      February 7, 1988
* Compile   Clipper Pickdisp -m
* Release   Summer '87
* Link      Plink86 fi Pickdisp lib extend lib clipper;
* Note      This shows how to use the ASORT(), ADIR(), and AFIELDS()
*           functions.
*********************

DECLARE thefiles[ADIR("*.DBF")]
ADIR("*.DBF", thefiles)
ASORT(thefiles)

CLEAR SCREEN
FOR x = 1 TO LEN(thefiles)
   ? thefiles[x]
NEXT
?
?
y = SPACE(8)
@ 24,00 SAY "Enter name > " GET y PICT "XXXXXXXX"
READ
IF EMPTY(y) .OR. LASTKEY() = 27 .OR. !FILE(ALLTRIM(y) + ".DBF")
   QUIT
ENDIF

thefiles = ALLTRIM(y) + ".DBF"
USE &thefiles.
DECLARE fields[FCOUNT()], types[FCOUNT()], sizes[FCOUNT()], dec[FCOUNT()]
AFIELDS(fields, types, sizes, dec)
CLEAR SCREEN
@ 0,0 SAY thefiles
@ 0,25 SAY "Last Updated: "
?? LUPDATE()
@ 1,0 SAY "Name          Type          Length          Decimals"
FOR x = 1 TO FCOUNT()
   ? fields[x]
   ?? SPACE(10)
```

```
   ?? types[x]
   ?? SPACE(10)
   ?? sizes[x]
   ?? SPACE(10)
   ?? dec[x]
NEXT
WAIT
* End of File
```

The following simulates another interpreter's command of GATHER and SCATTER.

```
*********************
* Name      Gat_scat.prg
* Author    Stephen J. Straley
* Notice    Copyright (c) 1988 Stephen J. Straley & Associates
* Date      February 8, 1988
* Compile   Clipper Gat_scat -m
* Release   Autumn '86
* Link      Plink86 fi gat_scat lib extend lib clipper;
* Note      This program shows how to simulate the GATHER/SCATTER
*           capabilities.
*
*           This logic was developed while compiling Steve Straley's Toolkit.
*           by Four Seasons Pub., Inc. and SJS & Associates.
*********************

   IF !FILE("PEOPLE.DBF")
      DO Make_peo
   ENDIF
   USE People
   DECLARE dataset1[ARRAY_SIZE("A")]
   DECLARE dataset2[ARRAY_SIZE("A", "SEC", 5)]
   DECLARE dataset3[ARRAY_SIZE("A", "POOL")]
   CLEAR SCREEN

   DO Barray WITH dataset1, "A"
   DO Barray WITH dataset2, "A", "SEC", 5
   DO Barray WITH dataset3, "A", "POOL"

   FOR x = 1 TO LEN(dataset1)
      @ x, 1 GET dataset1[x]
   NEXT
   FOR y = 1 TO 5
      @ y, 40 GET dataset2[y]
   NEXT
   z = ROW() + 1
   FOR xx = 1 TO LEN(dataset3)
      @ z + xx, 40 GET dataset3[xx]
   NEXT
   READ

   CLEAR SCREEN
   DO Rarray WITH dataset1, "A", 1
```

```
@ 0,0 SAY "Field Name      Phase One            " + ;
  "      Phase Two        Phase three"

FOR x = 1 TO FCOUNT()
   temp_get = FIELDNAME(x)
   @ x+1, 1 SAY temp_get + ":"
   @ x+1,13 GET &temp_get.
NEXT
CLEAR GETS

@ 23,00 SAY "Any key for phase two..."
INKEY(0)
@ 23,00 CLEAR
DO Rarray WITH dataset2, "A", 1, "SEC", 5
FOR x = 1 TO FCOUNT()
   temp_get = FIELDNAME(x)
   @ x+1,35 GET &temp_get.
NEXT
CLEAR GETS
@ 23,00 SAY "Any key for phase three.."
INKEY(0)
@ 23,00 CLEAR
DO Rarray WITH dataset3, "A", 1, "POOL"
FOR x = 1 TO FCOUNT()
   temp_get = FIELDNAME(x)
   @ x+1,55 GET &temp_get.
NEXT
CLEAR GETS
@ 23,00 SAY "Any key for the next step.."
INKEY(0)
@ 23,00 CLEAR

RELEASE ALL
DECLARE dataset1[ARRAY_SIZE("A")]
DECLARE dataset2[ARRAY_SIZE("A", "SEC", 5)]
DECLARE dataset3[ARRAY_SIZE("A", "POOL")]

CLEAR SCREEN
DO Sarray WITH dataset1, "A"
DO Sarray WITH dataset2, "A", 1, "SEC", 5
DO Sarray WITH dataset3, "A", 1, "POOL"
FOR x = 1 TO LEN(dataset1)
   @ x, 1 GET dataset1[x]
NEXT
FOR y = 1 TO 5
   @ y, 40 GET dataset2[y]
NEXT
z = ROW() + 1
FOR xx = 1 TO LEN(dataset3)
   @ z + xx, 40 GET dataset3[xx]
NEXT
READ
```

```
*********************

PROCEDURE Barray

   PARAMETERS the_array, the_file, the_field, the_length

   ret_area = STR(SELECT())
   STORE 1 TO start_at, blanka
   IF LEN(the_file) = 1
      SELECT &the_file
   ELSE
      SELECT 0
      USE &the_file.
   ENDIF

   IF PCOUNT() < 4
      the_length = LEN(the_array)
   ELSE
      IF the_length > LEN(the_array)
         the_length = LEN(the_array)
      ENDIF
   ENDIF

   IF PCOUNT() > 2
      b_fields = ""
      FOR now_go = 1 TO FCOUNT()
         b_fields = b_fields + FILL_OUT(FIELDNAME(now_go), 10)
      NEXT
      start_at = (AT(UPPER(FILL_OUT(the_field, 10)), b_fields) + 9) / 10
      the_length = INT(the_length + start_at - 1)
   ELSE
      start_at = 1
   ENDIF

   IF start_at <= 1
      start_at = 1
   ENDIF

   start_at = INT(IF(start_at <= 1, 1, start_at))
   incremen = 1
   FOR blanka = start_at TO the_length STEP 1
      temp_blank = FIELDNAME(blanka)
      the_array[incremen] = MAKE_EMPTY(&temp_blank)
      * IF TYPE("the_array[incremen]") = "N"
      *    WAIT LEN(STR(the_array[incremen]))
      * ENDIF
      incremen = incremen + 1
   NEXT

   IF LEN(the_file) > 1
      CLOSE DATABASE
   ENDIF
   SELECT &ret_area.
```

```
********************

PROCEDURE Rarray

   PARAMETERS the_array, the_file, the_rec, the_field, the_length

   DO CASE
      CASE PCOUNT() = 4
         the_length = 0
      CASE PCOUNT() = 3
         the_field = ""
         the_length = 0
      CASE PCOUNT() = 2
         the_rec = 0
         the_field = ""
         the_length = 0
   ENDCASE

   ret_area = STR(SELECT())

   IF LEN(the_file) = 1
      SELECT &the_file
   ELSE
      SELECT 0
      USE &the_file.
   ENDIF

   IF LASTREC() < the_rec .OR. the_rec = 0
      GO BOTTOM
      APPEN BLANK
   ELSE
      GOTO the_rec
   ENDIF

   IF EMPTY(the_length)
      the_length = LEN(the_array)
   ELSE
      IF the_length > LEN(the_array)
         the_length = LEN(the_array)
      ENDIF
   ENDIF

   old_length = the_length

   IF !EMPTY(the_field)
      b_fields = ""
      FOR now_go = 1 TO FCOUNT()
         b_fields = b_fields + FILL_OUT(FIELDNAME(now_go), 10)
      NEXT
      start_at = (AT(UPPER(FILL_OUT(the_field, 10)), b_fields) + 9) / 10
      the_length = INT(the_length + start_at - 1)
   ELSE
      start_at = 1
   ENDIF
```

```
   start_at = INT(IF(start_at <= 1, 1, start_at))

   increment = 1
   FOR blanka = start_at TO the_length
      temp_blank = FIELDNAME(blanka)
      REPLACE &temp_blank WITH the_array[increment]
      increment = increment + 1
   NEXT

   IF LEN(the_file) > 1
      CLOSE DATABASE
   ENDIF
   SELECT &ret_area.

********************

PROCEDURE Sarray

   PARAMETERS the_array, the_file, the_rec, the_field, the_length

   DO CASE
      CASE PCOUNT() = 4
         the_length = 0
      CASE PCOUNT() = 3
         the_field = ""
         the_length = 0
      CASE PCOUNT() = 2
         the_rec = 0
         the_field = ""
         the_length = 0
   ENDCASE

   ret_area = STR(SELECT())

   IF LEN(the_file) = 1
      SELECT &the_file
   ELSE
      SELECT 0
      USE &the_file.
   ENDIF

   IF LASTREC() < the_rec .OR. the_rec = 0
      GO BOTTOM
   ELSE
      GOTO the_rec
   ENDIF

   IF EMPTY(the_length)
      the_length = LEN(the_array)
   ELSE
      IF the_length > LEN(the_array)
         the_length = LEN(the_array)
      ENDIF
   ENDIF
```

```
   old_length = the_length

   IF !EMPTY(the_field)
      b_fields = ""
      FOR now_go = 1 TO FCOUNT()
         b_fields = b_fields + FILL_OUT(FIELDNAME(now_go), 10)
      NEXT
      start_at = (AT(UPPER(FILL_OUT(the_field, 10)), b_fields) + 9) / 10
      the_length = INT(the_length + start_at - 1)
   ELSE
      start_at = 1
   ENDIF

   start_at = INT(IF(start_at <= 1, 1, start_at))

   increment = 1
   FOR blanka = start_at TO the_length
      temp_blank = FIELDNAME(blanka)
      IF TYPE(temp_blank) = "N"
         the_array[increment] = MAKE_EMPTY(&temp_blank)
      ENDIF
      STORE &temp_blank TO the_array[increment]
      increment = increment + 1
   NEXT

   IF LEN(the_file) > 1
      CLOSE DATABASE
   ENDIF
   SELECT &ret_area.

*******************

FUNCTION Array_size

   PARAMETERS array_a, array_b, array_c

   ret_area = STR(SELECT())
   start_at = 1
   IF LEN(array_a) = 1
      SELECT &array_a.
   ELSE
      SELECT 0
      IF !FILE(array_a)
         SELECT &ret_area.
         RETURN(0)
      ENDIF
      USE &array_a.
   ENDIF

   array_numb = 1
   DO CASE
      CASE PCOUNT() = 1          && Only the file area/name
         array_numb = FCOUNT()
```

```
      CASE PCOUNT() = 3
         array_numb = array_c
      OTHERWISE
         IF TYPE("array_b") = "C"    && IF a field name ELSE a field number
            b_fields = ""
            FOR now_go = 1 TO FCOUNT()
               b_fields = b_fields + FILL_OUT(FIELDNAME(now_go), 10)
            NEXT
            start_at = (AT(UPPER(FILL_OUT(array_b, 10)), b_fields) + 9) / 10
            IF start_at <= 1
               start_at = 1
            ENDIF
         ELSE
            start_at = array_b
         ENDIF

         array_numb = FCOUNT() - start_at + 1

   ENDCASE
   IF LEN(array_a) > 1
      CLOSE DATABASE
   ENDIF
   SELECT &ret_area.
   RETURN(array_numb)

********************

FUNCTION Fill_out

   PARAMETERS fill_a, fill_b

   * fill_a = the string to be filled out
   * fill_b = the lenght to fill out the string to

   IF PCOUNT() = 1
      fill_b = 80
   ELSE
      IF TYPE("fill_b") = "C"
         fill_b = VAL(b)
      ENDIF
      fill_b = IIF(fill_b <= 1, 80, fill_b)
   ENDIF

   IF fill_b <= LEN(fill_a)
      RETURN(fill_a)
   ENDIF
   RETURN(fill_a + SPACE(fill_b - LEN(fill_a)))

********************

FUNCTION Make_empty

   PARAMETERS in_field, in_name
```

```
   IF PCOUNT() = 1
      in_name = ""
   ENDIF

   DO CASE
   CASE TYPE("in_field") = "C"
      RETURN(SPACE(LEN(in_field)))
   CASE TYPE("in_field") = "N"
      RETURN(VAL(STR(in_field)))
   CASE TYPE("in_field") = "D"
      RETURN(CTOD("  /  /  "))
   OTHERWISE
      RETURN(.F.)
   ENDCASE

*********************

PROCEDURE Make_peo

   ret_to = ALLTRIM(STR(SELECT()))
   SELECT 1
   CREATE Template
   USE Template
   DO Ap_it WITH [STATUS],   [C],  1, 0
   DO Ap_it WITH [UNIQUE],   [C],  8, 0
   DO Ap_it WITH [TRADE],    [C],  6, 0
   DO Ap_it WITH [ACTIVITY], [N],  2, 0
   DO Ap_it WITH [TRAN],     [N],  2, 0
   DO Ap_it WITH [SETTLE],   [C],  6, 0
   DO Ap_it WITH [CUSTO],    [C],  3, 0
   DO Ap_it WITH [FILLER],   [C],  2, 0
   DO Ap_it WITH [BANK],     [C],  2, 0
   DO Ap_it WITH [SEC],      [C],  2, 0
   DO Ap_it WITH [POOL],     [N],  6, 0
   DO Ap_it WITH [PAR],      [N], 11, 2
   DO Ap_it WITH [DOLLAR],   [N],  9, 4
   DO Ap_it WITH [LOCATION], [C],  1, 0
   DO Ap_it WITH [MORE],     [C], 13, 0
   DO Ap_it WITH [L_DATE],   [C],  6, 0
   DO Ap_it WITH [STAT],     [C],  1, 0
   DO Ap_it WITH [PARIED],   [L],  1, 0
   USE
   CREATE People.dbf FROM Template
   ERASE Template.dbf
   USE People.dbf
   SELECT 1

*********************

PROCEDURE Ap_it

   PARAMETERS apa, apb, apc, apd
```

```
   * apa = the field name
   * apb = the field data type
   * apc = the field length
   * apd = the field decimal

   IF PCOUNT() = 3
      apd = 0
   ENDIF

   APPEND BLANK
   IF apc > 255
      REPLACE field_name WITH apa, field_type WITH apb, field_len WITH;
      INT(apc % 256), field_dec WITH INT(apc / 256)
   ELSE
      REPLACE field_name WITH apa, field_type WITH apb, field_len WITH;
      apc, field_dec WITH apd
   ENDIF
* End of File
```

LAST WORDS ON ARRAYS

The importance of the previous examples is that they show the limitations of some of Clipper's extended features and demonstrate some conditions where using an array may be more useful than using a disk file. Keep in mind that arrays have limitations. When you use an array construct to build a database rather than using the disk (increasing speed of execution by avoiding constant disk I/O), you are limited by available memory. You still have to consider disk space because at some time you probably will need to write the information in memory out to the disk.

CHAPTER THIRTEEN

Low-Level File Logic

A NEW DIMENSION TO CLIPPER PROGRAMMING

LOW-LEVEL FILE FUNCTIONS

The low-level file functions not only enhance the basic Clipper language, but they revolutionize it as well. These function and routines are intended to only work with the Summer '87, or later, release of Clipper. In past versions, especially with the language being viewed from the interpretive point of view, the only basic file manipulation involves .DBF, .NTX/.NDX, or .MEM files. Even though the rest of the DOS world could handle all types of files, only these pertaining to database management were accessible by the compiler. Clipper then approached basic ASCII text files and opened the concept of memos, long character strings, and a more generic file and text approach. To complete the cycle and round out the language, Clipper may now look at and handle all types of file formats. To the development community this now means that Clipper applications, by themselves, can interact with other types of files and formats including larger ASCII text files, worksheets and spreadsheet files, and binary files. Clipper evolved into a more complete language set, like C, and as a result, your applications may now evolve into more sophisticated and structured systems.

The entire file logic revolves around a concept that is familiar to most C programmers. With these functions, a file is opened, closed, and read via an associated *file handle*. This means that a file is no longer just a drive and directory name, a root name, and an extension; it is number that DOS assigns to that file. Any operation performed with that file must be done with the file handle and **not** the file name. This number is assigned by the operating system and cannot be assigned by the programmer. For example, the FOPEN() and FCREATE() functions either open or create a file, but they return the file handle associated with that file. Any reading or writing from or to that file must be done with this file handle.

Another thing to keep in mind as you try to use these functions is the file pointer. Nothing is automatic in using these functions. Think about reading a record: if you read a record, the record pointer does not move. Internally, after Clipper gives you the information in the record (i.e., field information), it automatically repositions itself to the beginning character of that record. Otherwise, the file pointer would still be located at the very end of the record just read. This means that Clipper performs this character scan throughout a record for you. Using the low-level function, this task must be programmed by you if you try to use these functions in your applications.

In this section I have outlined these basic functions and their general purposes and I have offered a few possible suggestions on "when" and "how" to use them in your applications. Many of these ideas came to me while acting as a beta test site for Nantucket and developing the Stephen Straley Toolkit. If you choose to try some of these ideas, be sure to include the EXTEND.LIB in your link list.

NAME	PURPOSE
FCLOSE()	Will close a DOS file associated with the handle.
FCREATE()	Creates a new DOS file or sets an existing DOS file to a file length of zero.
FERROR()	Returns a DOS error code after a terminated file function.
FOPEN()	Opens a DOS file.
FREAD()	Reads characters from a DOS file and stores them into a memory variable.
FREADSTR()	Reads characters from a DOS file.
FSEEK()	Moves the file pointer to a new position in the DOS file.
FWRITE()	Write the contents of a variable to a DOS file.
BIN2I()	Converts a character string that is a 16-bit signed integer to a numeric value.
BIN2L()	Converts a character string that is a 32-bit signed long integer to a numeric value.
BIN2W()	Converts a character string that is a 16-bit unsigned integer to a numeric value.
I2BIN()	Converts an integer numeric value to a character string that is formatted as an unsigned integer.
L2BIN()	Converts an integer numeric value to a character string that is formatted as a 32-bit signed integer.

Chaining a file attribute byte using the binary function is relatively easy. Listed below are two sample programs that will demonstrate this new capability in Clipper. In the section listed as UDF, I have modified these procedures to be functions and they are listed there as well. As you try these extracts, keep in mind one small problem I discovered. When you try to use the FSEEK() function to obtain the file length (e.g., FSEEK(<file handle>, 0, 2), be sure to rewind the file pointer back to the beginning of the file with a FSEEK(<file handle>, 0). Otherwise, if you try to FREAD() or FREADSTR() any characters, the results will be a null string because the file pointer is at the end of file marker.

```
********************
* Name      Hidefile.prg
* Author    Stephen J. Straley
* Notice    Copyright (c) 1988 Stephen J. Straley & Associates
* Date      February 5, 1988
* Compile   Clipper  Hidefile -m
* Release   Summer '87
* Link      Plink86 fi hidefile lib extend lib clipper;
* Note      This shows some of the binary file logic.
*
*           There is a similar UDF called HIDEAFILE() in Chapter 14, which
*           pertains to my special user-defined functions.
********************

PARAMETERS the_file

IF PCOUNT() = 0
   QUIT
ENDIF

CLEAR SCREEN

backup = SUBSTR(the_file, 1, AT(".", the_file) - 1) + "$$$"
RENAME &the_file. TO &backup.

fhandle = FCREATE(the_file, 2)
nhandle = FOPEN(backup)
length = FSEEK(nhandle, 0, 2)   && Obtain file length

FSEEK(nhandle, 0 )      && You must rewind the file pointer to the top
NOTE                       or this example will not work!

FWRITE(fhandle, FREADSTR(nhandle, length))
FCLOSE(fhandle)
FCLOSE(nhandle)

ERASE &backup.

RUN TYPE &the_file.
?
?
?
?
WAIT "The file is hidden!   Any key to continue."
* End of file: Hidefile.prg
```

And now to regain the hidden file:

```
********************
* Name      Getfile.prg
* Author    Stephen J. Straley
* Notice    Copyright (c) 1988 Stephen J. Straley & Associates
* Date      February 5, 1988
```

```
* Compile  Clipper Getfile -m
* Release  Summer '87
* Link     Plink86 fi getfile lib extend lib clipper;
* Note     This shows some of the binary file logic.
*
*          There is a similary UDF called GETFILE() in Chapter 14, which
*          pertains to my special user-defined functions.
********************

PARAMETERS the_file

IF PCOUNT() = 0
   QUIT
ENDIF

CLEAR SCREEN

fhandle = FCREATE("NEW_FILE.$$$", 0)
nhandle = FOPEN(the_file)
length  = FSEEK(nhandle, 0, 2)
FSEEK(nhandle, 0)
FWRITE(fhandle, FREADSTR(nhandle, length))
FCLOSE(fhandle)
FCLOSE(nhandle)

FCREATE(the_file, 0)
ERASE &the_file
RENAME New_file.$$$ TO &the_file.
ERASE New_file.$$$
* End of file: Getfile.prg
```

With the new binary file functions, you can design the application to check to see if the file requested by the user is a legitimate .DBF file. Additionally, you can check to see if the .DBF file has an associated .DBT (memo) file. This is very handy when you have a generic backup and restore procedure and you want to know if the file you are backing up has an associated memo file.

```
********************
* Name     Chkfiles.prg
* Author   Stephen J. Straley
* Notice   Copyright (c) 1988 Stephen J. Straley & Associates
* Date     February 6, 1988
* Compile  Clipper Chkfiles -m
* Release  Summer '87
* Link     Mslink Chkfiles,,,extend + clipper/se:1024,,;
* Note     This checks to see if the file is a .DBF file or an .NTX file, and if
*          it is a .DBF file, it checks if there is an associated .DBT file.
********************

PARAMETERS the_file

IF PCOUNT() = 0
   QUIT
ENDIF
```

```
CLEAR SCREEN

fhandle = FOPEN(the_file)
*
* An error condition will exist if either FERROR() <> 0 or if the file
* handle returned from FOPEN() = 0.
*
IF FERROR() <> 0
   ? "The file is not available.  Any key to continue."
   INKEY(0)
   QUIT
ENDIF

IF IF_DBF(fhandle)
   ? "The file is a standard Clipper database file."
   ?
   ? "There is " + IF(IF_DBT(fhandle), "", "NOT") + ;
     " an associated memo file."
ELSEIF IF_NTX(fhandle)
   ? "This is a Clipper .NTX file!"
ELSE
   ? "The file you entered is neither a database file or a"
   ? "Clipper index file."
ENDIF

*********************

FUNCTION If_dbf

   PARAMETERS dbf_handle

   REWIND(dbf_handle, 0)
   dbf_char = ASC(FREADSTR(dbf_handle, 1))
   FSEEK(dbf_handle, -1, 1)
   RETURN( ( dbf_char = 3 .OR. dbf_char = 131 ) )

*********************

FUNCTION If_ntx

   PARAMETERS ntx_handle

   REWIND(ntx_handle, 0)
   ntx_char = ASC(FREADSTR(ntx_handle, 1))
   FSEEK(ntx_handle, -1, 1)
   RETURN( ntx_char = 6 )

*********************

FUNCTION If_dbt

   PARAMETERS dbf_handle
```

```
   REWIND(dbf_handle, 0)
   dbf_char = ASC(FREADSTR(dbf_handle, 1))
   FSEEK(dbf_handle, -1, 1)
   RETURN( (dbf_char = 131) )

********************

FUNCTION Rewind

   PARAMETERS r_handle

   FSEEK(r_handle, 0)
   RETURN(.T.)
* End of File
```

Another capability opened up by the low-level logic functions is the ability to look at record in a flat file format. There have been occasions where a specific record in a SDF file is needed. On those occasions it always seemed to be a bit of a nuisance to bring the entire SDF file into a database file just to pull one record. Now with these low-level functions and file logic, this simple request becomes a simple reality.

```
********************
* Name     Sdf_pull.prg
* Author   Stephen J. Straley
* Notice   Copyright (c) 1988 Stephen J. Straley & Associates
* Date     February 7, 1988
* Compile  Clipper Sdf_pull -m
* Release  Summer '87
* Link     Mslink Sdf_pull,,,extend + clipper/se:1024,,;
* Note     This program shows how a single record in a SDF file
*          can be obtained.
********************

PARAMETERS the_file

IF PCOUNT() = 0
   ?
   ? "Sdf_pull <filename>"
   QUIT
ENDIF

length = REC_LENGTH(the_file)
? "Here's the record..."
?
wait GET_REC(the_file, length, 6)

********************

FUNCTION Rec_length

   PARAMETERS afile

   fhandle = FOPEN(afile)
   counter = 0
```

```
   DO WHILE .T.
      the_char = FREADSTR(fhandle, 1)
      IF ASC(the_char) = 13
         new_char = FREADSTR(fhandle, 1)
         FSEEK(fhandle, 1, -1)
         IF ASC(new_char) = 10
            FCLOSE(fhandle)
            RETURN(counter)
         ENDIF
      ELSEIF ASC(the_char) = 0   && End of file condition
         RETURN(0)
      ENDIF
      counter = counter + 1
   ENDDO

**********************

FUNCTION Get_rec

   PARAMETERS get_file, get_len, get_rec

   fhandle = FOPEN(get_file)
   IF get_rec > 1
      FOR counter = 1 TO get_rec - 1
         FSEEK(fhandle, get_len + 2, 1) && adding 2 for CHR(13)+CHR(10)
      NEXT
   ENDIF
   ret_chr = FREADSTR(fhandle, get_len)
   FCLOSE(fhandle)
   RETURN(ret_chr)
* End of File
```

Another possibility with the low-level file logic was found when I implemented the ability to read in a file while inside of my word processor in Steve Straley's Toolkit. The idea was simple: while inside of a MEMOEDIT() (emulating a text editor), hit a hot key and start reading in characters in a file using the FREADSTR() function and stuffing the KEYBOARD with those same characters. I also found that not only did the binary file functions and KEYBOARD command work as expected but so did a GET and a READ command.

```
*********************
* Name      Readin.prg
* Author    Stephen J. Straley
* Notice    Copyright (c) 1988 Stephen J. Straley & Associates
* Date      February 7, 1988
* Compile   Clipper  Readin -m
* Release   Summer '87
* Link      Mslink Readin,,,extend + clipper/se:1024,,;
* Note      This example was taken in part from my Stephen Straley Toolkit,
*           published by Four Seasons and Stephen J. Straley & Associates.
*********************
```

```
CLEAR SCREEN
textin = ""
@ 1,0 SAY "Press ATL R to read in a file!        CTRL W to Exit"
@ 2,0 TO 22,79 DOUBLE
SET KEY 275 TO Readitin
textin = MEMOEDIT(textin, 3,1,21,78,.T.)
CLEAR SCREEN
? textin
WAIT

********************

PROCEDURE Readitin

   PARAMETERS p, l, v

   pop_row = ROW()
   pop_col = COL()
   filehandle = 0
   search_for = SPACE(25)
   @ 23,00 CLEAR
   @ 23,01 SAY "Enter Name of File => " GET search_for ;
           PICT "XXXXXXXXXXXXXXXXXXXXXXXXX" VALID ;
           TRY2OPEN(search_for, @filehandle)
   READ
   @ 23,00 CLEAR
   @ 23,01 SAY "Loading File Into Buffer..."
   IF EMPTY(search_for) .OR. LASTKEY() = 27
      @ 23,00 CLEAR
      @ pop_row, pop_col SAY ""
      RETURN
   ENDIF
   REWIND(filehandle)   && reset the pointer position!
   read_amnt = 80
   byts_read = 80
   bffstring = SPACE(160)
   backout = ""
   DO WHILE byts_read == read_amnt
      byts_read = FREAD(filehandle, @bffstring, read_amnt)
      bffstring = STRTRAN(STRTRAN(ALLTRIM(bffstring), CHR(252),
CHR(13)+CHR(10)), CHR(251), CHR(13)+CHR(10))
      backout = backout + STRTRAN(bffstring, CHR(219), "")
      bffstring = SPACE(160)
   ENDDO
   FCLOSE(filehandle)
   KEYBOARD backout
   @ pop_row, pop_col SAY ""
   RETURN

********************

FUNCTION Try2open

   PARAMETERS i_o_file, i_o_handle
```

```
      * i_o_handle is passed by REFERENCE!!
      IF EMPTY(i_o_file)
         RETURN(.F.)
      ENDIF
      i_o_handle = FOPEN(i_o_file)
      RETURN( ( FERROR() = 0 ) )

   ********************

   FUNCTION Rewind

      PARAMETERS r_handle

      FSEEK(r_handle, 0)
      RETURN(.T.)
   * End of File.
```

Finally, a last possibility came to me while I was shipping the Steve Straley Toolkit. With the distribution disks and the self-extracting .EXE files, I wanted to tag the files with the appropriate serial number of each distribution disk. Using some of the low-level routines and some basic DOS capabilities, I was able to not only tag those executable files but read and verify them as well.

```
********************
* Name      Serializ.prg
* Author    Stephen J. Straley
* Notice    Copyright (c) 1988 Stephen J. Straley & Associates
* Date      February 24, 1988
* Compile   Clipper Serializ -m
* Link      Tlink serializ,,,extend + clipper
* Note      This sample file shows how to serialize an executable file
*           and how to read those serial numbers at a later time.
********************

CLEAR SCREEN
file   = SPACE(8)
serial = SPACE(15)
fhandle = 0
DO WHILE .T.
   @ 5,5 SAY "Enter .EXE file name (no extension) => " GET file PICT "!!!!!!!!"
   READ
   IF EMPTY(file) .OR. LASTKEY() = 27
      QUIT
   ENDIF
   file = ALLTRIM(file) + ".EXE"
   IF !FILE(file)
      @ 7, 5 SAY "File can not be found"
   ELSE
      EXIT
   ENDIF
ENDDO
@ 7, 0 CLEAR
```

```
@ 7, 5 SAY "Enter Serial Number to tag to &file. " GET serial PICT "@X"
READ

IF SERIAL(file, serial)
   @ 9, 5 SAY "Serial Number tagged to &file. "
ELSE
   @ 9, 5 SAY "Error in writing to the file.  File now closed."
   QUIT
ENDIF

fhandle = FOPEN(file)
the_number = GETSERIAL(fhandle, LEN(serial))

@ 11, 5 SAY "One moment to get serial number! " + the_number
?
WAIT

********************

FUNCTION Serial

   PARAMETERS f_file, f_serial

   MEMOWRIT("SERIAL.TXT", f_serial)
   RUN COPY /b &f_file. + Serial.txt &f_file. >NUL
   RETURN((ERRORLEVEL() = 0))

********************

FUNCTION Getserial

   PARAMETERS f_handle, s_length

   backtrack = (s_length + 1) * -1
   FSEEK(f_handle, backtrack, 2)
   oldstr = FREADSTR(f_handle, s_length)
   RETURN(oldstr)
* End of File
```

Finally, there is an additional series of binary functions that convert 16-byte characters and 32-byte characters into character strings. Additionally, there are functions that convert character strings into 16- and 32-byte characters. These functions are exceedingly useful when trying to access and read information not normally stored as straight ASCII text. For example, in the file header of a standard .DBF file, the second byte is a 16-byte character that represents the year the .DBF file was last updated. For example, if the .DBF file was last updated in the year 1988, that byte would look like a 58. Converting this hexadecimal value would give 88 [(5 X 16) + 8 = 88]. Now, the BIN2I function converts this byte automatically into a readable number.

Below is a sample program that shows how some of these new functions work directly on a database file.

```
*********************
* Name      Look_dbf.prg
* Author    Stephen J. Straley
* Notice    Copyright (c) 1988 Stephen J. Straley & Associates
* Date      March 17, 1988
* Compile   Clipper Look_dbf -m
* Link      Plink86 fi look_dbf lib extend lib clipper
* Note      This program shows how to use the new binary functions in
*           conjunction with the low-level functions to look at a .DBF file.
*********************

PARAMETERS thefile

IF PCOUNT() = 0
   ? "Repair <filename>"
   ?
   QUIT
ENDIF

DECLARE bytes[32]
AFILL(bytes, "")
bytes[5] = 0
CLEAR SCREEN
fhandle = FOPEN(thefile)
IF fhandle = -1
   ? "Can't Open File!"
   ?
   QUIT
ENDIF

bytes[1] = BIN2I( FREADSTR(fhandle, 1) )  && 0  /  The dBASE Identifier
bytes[2] = BIN2I( FREADSTR(fhandle, 1) )  && 1  /  The Year of the Last Update
bytes[3] = BIN2I( FREADSTR(fhandle, 1) )  && 2  /  The Month of the Last Update
bytes[4] = BIN2I( FREADSTR(fhandle, 1) )  && 3  /  The Day of the Last Update

bytes[5] = BIN2L( FREADSTR(fhandle, 4) )  && 4 - 7  /  Number of records in the
database
bytes[6] = BIN2W( FREADSTR(fhandle, 2) )  && 8 - 9  /  Length of Header in bytes
bytes[7] = BIN2W( FREADSTR(fhandle, 2) )  && 10 - 11 / Length of each record
bytes[8] = FREADSTR(fhandle,20)  && 12 - 31          / Reserved bytes...

FOR x = 1 to 7
   ? bytes[x]
NEXT

?
? "The Date of the last update was " + ALLTRIM(STR(bytes[3])) + "/" +
ALLTRIM(STR(bytes[4])) + "/" + ALLTRIM(STR(bytes[2]))
?
WAIT

CLEAR SCREEN
fieldnumb = 1
frow = 1
fcol = 1
```

```
DO WHILE ( FSEEK(fhandle, 0, 1) < bytes[6]-31 )
   IF fcol > 70
      frow = frow + 7
      fcol = 5
   ENDIF
   IF frow > 20
      @ 1,0 CLEAR
      frow = 1
      fcol = 1
   ENDIF
   @ frow+1, fcol SAY "Field Number " + ALLTRIM(STR(fieldnumb))
   @ frow+2, fcol SAY "     Name is " + FREADSTR(fhandle, 11)   && Name of field
   @ frow+3, fcol SAY "      Type = " + FREADSTR(fhandle, 1)    && type

   BIN2L(FREADSTR(fhandle, 4))   && Address

   @ frow+4, fcol SAY "    Length = " + ALLTRIM(STR(BIN2I(FREADSTR(fhandle, 1))))
&& field length
   decimals = BIN2I(FREADSTR(fhandle, 1))    && dec. length
   IF decimals > 20 .OR. decimals < 0
      @ frow+5, fcol SAY "  Decimals = 0"
   ELSE
      @ frow+5, fcol SAY "  Decimals = " + ALLTRIM(STR(decimals))
   ENDIF

   FREADSTR(fhandle, 14)
   fieldnumb = fieldnumb + 1
   INKEY(1)
   fcol = fcol + 25
ENDDO
@ 23,00 SAY ""
WAIT "Press Any Key for display of Records..."
CLEAR SCREEN
@ 0,0 SAY "\" + CURDIR() + "\" + UPPER(thefile)
?
FSEEK( fhandle, 0 )
FSEEK( fhandle, bytes[6], 1)
FOR x = 1 TO bytes[5]
  disp = FREADSTR(fhandle, bytes[7])
  IF !EMPTY(AT(CHR(26), disp))
     EXIT
  ENDIF
  ? SUBSTR(disp, 1, 79)
  IF ROW() = 21
     SCROLL(2,0,22,79,1)
     @ 20, 00 SAY ""
  ENDIF
  INKEY(.1)
  IF LASTKEY() = 27
     EXIT
  ENDIF
NEXT
FCLOSE(fhandle)
* End of file
```

CHAPTER FOURTEEN

Designing User-Defined Functions (UDFs)

One of Clipper's most powerful features is that it gives you the ability to create a set of commonly used routines and treat them as functions. User-defined functions (UDFs) can be great programming time savers and can also reduce system maintenance time. When you fix or modify a user-defined function, all applications using that function can be changed by recompiling the function file and relinking that new file with all other relevant files. And these features were enhanced in the Summer '87 release.

Some examples of commonly needed features that lend themselves well to user-defined functions are error messages, screen formats, password generation and verification, and check conversion routines (taking numbers and converting them into words). Once you develop a set of user-defined functions, system development and maintenance is drastically reduced. When designing your own functions, you should strive for consistency and unity, especially if they will be used by others.

Functions often are said to have a *value*. The value of the function is the value that the function returns to the calling program. If a function returns either a .T. or an .F., the function is said to have a *logical* value. Added to this basic structure is the concept of parameters by reference. In the Summer '87 release of Clipper, not only does a function have a value, but it manipulates the value of the parameters passed to it. This gives the concept of user-defined functions even greater flexability.

SYNTAX OF UDFS

While functions can appear at the end of program files, it's advisable to keep all generic functions together in one file to be compiled separately and later linked in with the other object files. But whether you append your functions to a program file or keep them all in one library, they must be defined in the same way.

Syntax:

```
FUNCTION <Function name>

PARAMETERS <variables>          && This is optional

[Body of function]

RETURN(<value or variable>)
```

If a parameter is passed by reference (use the @ sign preceding the parameter name), any manipulation on that parameter within the body of the function will modify the value of that parameter.

SAMPLE FUNCTIONS

The following is a list of functions for which I have provided source code in this chapter. In some cases, sample code in an application environment is also provided for clarity. Some of the functions are small versions of similar functions in the Steve Straley Toolkit (tm).

Any function in the following list that is marked with an asterisk is featured in the Steve Straley Toolkit (tm) published by Four Seasons Publishing Co., Inc.

* Apop():	An easy function to display an array in a pop-up window. Autumn '86 compatible.
* Attribute():	Returns the attribute byte at a specific row, column coordinate.
Bitstrip():	Strips all of the high-order bits set for word processing in a memo field.
Center():	Centers a string in a given screen width.
Centr():	Used in conjunction with the MESSAGE (Autumn '86 release or earlier) clause in the SET MESSAGE. TO/PROMPT commands. This function centers the prompt on the row.
Chkamnt():	Returns the word value for any numeric value. Useful in check-writing routines.
Chkpass():	Checks that the string passed to it equals the proper value for the password generated by GENPASS().
* Cosin():	Return the cosine of an angle.
Chng_prmpt() Scan_prmpt() Delt_prmpt():	These three functions are used for scrolling through a database, depending upon whether the operation calls for a CHANGE, a SCAN, or a DELETION.
Day_Word():	Returns the name of the day. If a number is passed to the function rather than a date, the function will convert that number to a string representation.
Denial():	Returns a word description for action on a data field.
* Decryption():	Goes with the encryption logic to convert those strings back into readable characters.

Divide0(): Traps for and avoids Divide by Zero run-time errors; this is especially useful when running REPORT FORM commands.

Dltrim(): Returns a string with leading and trailing blank spaces deleted.

Endfield(): Returns the number of fields in any given database.

* Encrypt(): An encryption routine that helps to encrypt any string.

Expand(): Used for report generation, this function expands a given string with spaces.

* Explodec(): Shows how to perform a UDF on a PICTURE clause, which specifically makes Clipper characters go right to left.

Fill_array(): Fills an array with the field values of a database.

Fill_out(): Returns a string padded with spaces. To be used in conjunction with the CENTR() function, for report formatting, and for the SET MESSAGE TO command.

* Fox_date(): Returns a date value based on the conclusion of cursor key manipulation.

Genpass(): Generates a numeric value for any string given to it. Used for generating passwords, it can be modified for each application or use.

Goodfile(): Tests whether a file is a dBASE III database file. This function can be modified to test for the value of the other related files.

* Good_env(): Tests the environment based on passed values.

Got(): Works in conjunction with POP(). It yields the value for a specific file, field, and rcord number.

Great_zero(): Similar to MUST_FILL() in that the number being checked must be greater than zero.

Last_day(): Returns the last day of the month.

Lookup(): Demonstrates the usefulness of a UDF in conjunction with the VALID clause.

Make_empty(): Makes an empty value depending on the data type involved. This function may be used independently; however, it was designed to work in conjunction with GOT().

Must_fill(): Used for a field that **must** be filled. Optional parameters are the row and column positions for the message.

*Multiple_of(): Returns a logical true (.T.) if a number is a multiple of another.

*Occurrence(): Returns the number of occurrences of a string within another.

Percent(): Yields a string in percent format from the two numbers passed to it.

Pop(): In conjunction with GOT(), returns the record number of a set of valid choices (such as zip codes) that may be located in another file or in the current file. It will also display the values in a pop-up window and will allow the cursor keys to move through the window and choose the correct information.

Prntdate(): Converts the printed date format based on a pointer passed to the function along with the date to be converted.

Prnttime(): Generates the time in standard format, designates a.m. or p.m., converts military time to standard time, and offers the option of including seconds in the output.

Qwait(): Designed for user interface, this function checks to see if the "Q" was input and returns a .T. or .F.. This function is quite like verify; however, with this function, options like "Q to Quit" can be checked instead of "Y for Yes." Both functions [Verify() and Qwait()] can be modified and combined.

* Randomize(): Returns a random number.

* Reverse(): Returns the reverse colors based on a color string.

* Rewind(): Moves the file pointer to the top of the file. To be used with all low-level functions.

* Right_just(): Helps right-justify a string to a specific column coordinate.

Roundit(): Specifically designed for two-digit numeric input. It is better than the existing rounding features in Clipper.

* Shadow(): Generates a shadow line for a list box.

* Show_rec(): Shows the record currently being processed; it also allows the Esc key to be pressed.

* Sin():	Returns the sine value for an angle.
* Tangent():	Returns the tangent value for an angle.
* Try2open():	Tries to open a file using the low-level functions.
Upperlower():	Returns a string with the first character in uppercase and all others in lowercase.
Verify():	Checks for true and false conditions and returns the proper value.

APOP()

Syntax: APOP(<expN1>, <expN2>, <expN3>, <expN4>, <expC1> [<expL1> [, <expC2> [, <expL2>]]])

Pass: <top-row coordinate>, <top-column coordinate>, <number down>, <number over>, <array name> [, <with prompts> [,<message> [, <with shadow>]]]

Description: This function is a much simplified version of the new ACHOICE() function. It will display a pop-up window based on the top left coordinate of <expN1> and <expN2>. The windowed area will continue on for <expN3> rows and <expN4> columns. The array elements to be displayed will be stored in array <expC1>. If the array is to be in display-only mode, <expL1> should be set to logical false. Otherwise it will be set to logical true, which will allow the array elements to be picked from the array. If a special message is to be displayed, that message will be contained in <expC2>. If a shadow line is to accompany the list box, <expL2> should be set to logical true. The default is set to logical false (.F.).

Function: User-defined function.

Code:

```
*********************
* Notice: Copyright 1988, Stephen J. Straley & Associates

FUNCTION Apop

   PARAMETERS atop, aleft, adown, aover, the_array, ;
              prompt_it, pop_mess, pop_shad

   DO CASE
      CASE PCOUNT() = 5
         prompt_it = .T.
         pop_mess = ""
```

```
      pop_shad = .F.
   CASE PCOUNT() = 6
      pop_mess = ""
      pop_shad = .F.
   CASE PCOUNT() = 7
      pop_shad = .F.
ENDCASE

SAVE SCREEN
@ atop, aleft CLEAR TO atop+adown, aleft+aover
@ atop, aleft TO atop+adown, aleft+aover DOUBLE
IF pop_shad
   SHADOW(atop, aleft,atop+adown, aleft+aover)
ENDIF

IF !EMPTY(pop_mess)
   @ atop, aleft + 2 SAY pop_mess
ENDIF

STORE 1 TO screen_no, posit, sim_rec
STORE .F. TO up, down

per_screen = adown - 4
ending = LEN(the_array)
spacing= adown - 1
beg_set = 1
DO WHILE .T.
   SCROLL(atop+1, aleft+1, atop+adown-1, aleft+aover-2, 0 )
   * Blanks the screen

   IF prompt_it
      SET KEY 18 TO Pan_up
      SET KEY  3 TO Pan_down
   ENDIF

   STORE 1 TO starting, opt

   posit = (screen_no * per_screen) - (per_screen - 1)

   FOR the_choice = posit TO (per_screen * screen_no)

      IF prompt_it
         @ atop + starting, aleft + 1 PROMPT " " + ;
           FILL_OUT(the_array[the_choice], aover-2)
      ELSE
         @ atop + starting, aleft + 1 SAY " " + ;
           IF(LEN(the_array[the_choice]) >aover-2, ;
           SUBSTR(the_array[the_choice], 1, aover-2), ;
           the_array[the_choice])
      ENDIF
      starting = starting + 1

      IF the_choice >= ending    && simulate an EOF() condition
```

```
            EXIT
         ENDIF
      NEXT
      @ atop+adown-2, aleft+1 SAY "ESC to Quit"
      @ atop+adown-1, aleft+1 SAY "PgUp / PgDn"

      IF prompt_it
         MENU TO opt
         SET KEY 18 TO
         SET KEY  3 TO
      ELSE
         INKEY(0)
         DO CASE
            CASE LASTKEY() = 27
               opt = 0
            CASE LASTKEY() = 18
               up = .T.
               opt = 0
            CASE LASTKEY() = 3
               down = .T.
               opt = 0
            OTHERWISE
               opt = 1
         ENDCASE

      ENDIF

      IF opt = 0
         DO CASE
            CASE up .AND. !down
               up = .F.
               screen_no = IF(screen_no=1, screen_no, ;
                                   screen_no - 1)
            CASE down .AND. !up
               down = .F.
               screen_no = screen_no + 1
               IF screen_no > INT(LEN(the_array)/per_screen)+1
                  screen_no = screen_no - 1
               ENDIF
            OTHERWISE
               EXIT
         ENDCASE
      ELSE
         opt = (opt + (per_screen * screen_no)) - per_screen
         EXIT
      ENDIF
   ENDDO
   RESTORE SCREEN
   RETURN(opt)

********************

PROCEDURE Pan_up
```

```
    PARAMETERS p, l, v

    KEYBOARD CHR(27)
    up = .T.

********************

PROCEDURE Pan_down

    PARAMETERS p, l, v

    KEYBOARD CHR(27)
    down = .T.
```

ATTRIBUTE()

Syntax: ATTRIBUTE(<expN1>, <expN2>)

Pass: <row coordinate>, <column coordinate>
Return: <numeric expression>

Description: This function returns the ASCII value of the attribute byte at the expressed row and column coordinates.

Code:

```
********************
* Notice: Copyright 1988, Stephen J. Straley & Associates
********************

FUNCTION Attribute

    PARAMETERS att_row, att_col

    att_screen = SPACE(4000)
    SAVE SCREEN TO att_screen
    att_screen = SUBSTR(att_screen, (att_row * 160), 160)
    att_char = SUBSTR(att_screen,((att_col * 2) + 3), 1)
    RELEASE att_screen
    RETURN(ASC(att_char))
```

BITSTRIP()

Syntax: BITSTRIP(<expC> [, <expN>])

Pass: <character expression> [, <numeric expression>]
Return: <character expression>

Description: The BITSTRIP() function strips the high-order bits that help wrap words around inside a memo field or long string variable. The returned value is the string representation of the memo field with hard returns [CHR(13)] replacing soft returns [CHR(141)].

This function will not work directly with an @...SAY/GET command: the graphic symbols for carriage return and line feed will display.

Function: User-defined function.

Autumn '86 Code:

```
*********************
* Notice:  Copyright 1988, Stephen J. Straley & Associates
*********************

FUNCTION Bitstrip

PARAMETERS c, padding

IF TYPE("padding") = "U"
  padding = 0
ENDIF
outstring = ""
DO WHILE !EMPTY(c)
   IF AT(CHR(141),c) = 0
      outstring = outstring + SUBSTR(c, 1, LEN(c))
       c = ""
   ELSE
      outstring = outstring + ;
      SUBSTR(c, 1, AT(CHR(141), c) - 1) + CHR(13)
      outstring = outstring + SPACE(padding)
      scan = AT(CHR(141), c) + 1
      c = SUBSTR(c, scan, LEN(c) - scan + 1)
  ENDIF
ENDDO
RETURN(outstring)
```

Summer '87 Code:

```
*********************
* Notice:  Copyright 1988, Stephen J. Straley & Associates
*********************
FUNCTION Bitstrip

PARAMETERS bitc, padding

IF PCOUNT() = 1
   padding = 0
ENDIF
RETURN(STRTRAN(bitc,CHR(141),SPACE(padding)+CHR(13)+;
       CHR(10)+SPACE(padding)))
```

Usage:

```
USE Database
GO TOP
SET PRINT ON
DO WHILE .NOT. EOF()
?BITSTRIP(memo_field)
SET PRINT OFF
WAIT
? SPACE(10) + BITSTRIP(memo_field,10)
WAIT
SET PRINT ON
ENDDO
SET PRINT OFF
```

CENTER()

Syntax: CENTER(<expC>)

Pass: <character expression>
Return: <numeric expression>

Description: The CENTER() function was designed to help center strings within a given area. If no length is given, the function assumes a width of 80.

Function: User-defined function.

Code:

```
**********
* Notice:  Copyright 1988, Stephen J. Straley & Associates
**********

FUNCTION Center

  PARAMETERS in_string, in_length

  IF TYPE("in_length") = "U"
     in_length = 80
  ENDIF
  RETURN(in_length/2 - LEN(in_string)/2)
```

Usage:

```
@ 23,CENTER(EXPAND("The End")) SAY EXPAND("The End")
```

CENTR()

Syntax: CENTR(<expC>)

Pass: <character expression>
Return: <character expression>

Description: The CENTR() function works in conjunction with the SET MESSAGE TO and the PROMPT command. The CENTR() function centers the character expression found in the MESSAGE clause for each PROMPT command by padding the front of the expression with blank spaces.

Function: User-defined function.

Code:

```
**********
* Notice:  Copyright 1988, Stephen J. Straley & Associates
**********

FUNCTION Centr

    PARAMETERS a

    temp = 40 - INT(LEN(a)/2)
    RETURN(SPACE(temp) + a)
```

Usage:

```
@ 4, 8, 15, 72 BOX SUBSTR(scrframe,1,8)
SET MESSAGE TO 24
@ 3, 29 SAY "Legal Billing Main Menu"
@ 6, 10 PROMPT " 1>  Client Information "  ;
   MESSAGE CENTR("Basic Information on Clients")
@ 8, 14 PROMPT " 2>  Matter Information "  ;
   MESSAGE CENTR("Matter Information Based on Client")
@ 10, 18 PROMPT " 3>  Transactions "  ;
   MESSAGE CENTR("Transactions Based on Matter Information")
@ 11, 18 PROMPT " 4>  Disbursements "  ;
   MESSAGE CENTR("Disbursements Based on Matter Information")
@ 12, 18 PROMPT " 5>  Payments "  ;
   MESSAGE CENTR("Payments Based on Matter Information")
@ 6, 48 PROMPT " 6>  Codes "  ;
   MESSAGE CENTR("Disbursements/Attorney/Matter Type Codes")
@ 8, 48 PROMPT " 7>  Reports "  ;
   MESSAGE CENTR("Print Lists and Reports")
@ 10, 48 PROMPT " 8>  EOP Processing "  ;
   MESSAGE CENTR("End Of Period Processing")
@ 12, 48 PROMPT " 9>  Utilities "  ;
   MESSAGE CENTR("File and Program Utilities")
@ 14, 31 SAY "ESC to Exit Program"
MENU TO option
```

CHKAMNT()

Syntax: CHKAMNT(<expN>)

Pass: <numeric expression>
Return: <character expression>

Description: The CHKAMNT() function is designed to give the word value for any two-decimal positive numeric value. Specifically applicable in writing checks or vouchers. This function also calls upon another function, GRP_EXPAND(), to further narrow down the value of the input.

Function: User-defined function.

Code:

```
**********
* Notice:  Copyright 1988, Stephen J. Straley & Associates
**********
FUNCTION Chkamnt

PARAMETERS figure

   final = ""
   IF figure < 0
      final = "Unable to Print"
      RETURN(final)
   ELSE
      cents = SUBSTR(STR(figure, 15, 2), 14, 2)
      new = INT(figure)
   ENDIF

   ***********************
   * Check for BILLIONS *
   ***********************
   temp = INT(new/1000000000)
   IF temp > 0
      final = final + GRP_EXPAND(temp_ + " Billion "
      new = new - (temp * 1000000000)
   ENDIF

   ***********************
   * Check for MILLIONS *
   ***********************
   temp = INT(new/1000000)
   IF temp > 0
      final = final + GRP_EXPAND(temp) + " Million "
      new = new - (temp * 1000000)
   ENDIF

   ************************
   * Check for THOUSANDS *
   ************************
   temp = INT(new/1000)
   IF temp > 0
      final = final + GRP_EXPAND(temp) + " Thousand "
      new = new - (temp * 1000)
   ENDIF
   temp = new
```

```
   ********************
   * Check for UNITS *
   ********************
   IF temp > 0
      final = final + GRP_EXPAND(temp)
   ENDIF

   IF SUBSTR(final,1,3) = "One" .AND. LEN(final) = 3
      final = final + " Dollar and " + cents + "/100"
   ELSE
      final = final + " Dollars and " + cents + "/100"
   ENDIF

RETURN(final)
```

GRP_EXPAND()

Syntax: GRP_EXPAND(<expN>)

Pass: <numeric expression>
Return: <character expression>

Description: The GRP_EXPAND() function is the second half of the CHKAMNT() function.

Function: User-defined function.

Code:

```
**********
* Notice:  Copyright 1988, Stephen J. Straley & Associates
**********
FUNCTION Grp_expand

 PARAMETERS group_val

 one_unit=         "One      Two      Three    Four     Five     "
 one_unit=one_unit+"Six      Seven    Eight    Nine     Ten      "
 one_unit=one_unit+"Eleven   Twelve   Thirteen Fourteen Fifteen  "
 one_unit=one_unit+"Sixteen  SeventeenEighteen Nineteen"
 ten_unit = "Twenty Thirty Forty  Fifty  Sixty  "
 ten_unit = ten_unit + "SeventyEighty Ninety "
 group_str = ""

   IF group_val > 99
   new1 = INT(group_val/100)
   group_str = group_str + TRIM(SUBSTR(one_unit, (new1*9_-8,9))
   group_val = group_val - (new1 * 100)
   group_str = group_str + " Hundred "
   ENDIF
   IF group_val > 19
```

```
      new1 = INT(group_val/10)-1
      group_str = group_str + TRIM(SUBSTR(ten_unit,(new1*7)-6,7))
      new1 = INT(group_val/10)*10
         group_val = group_val - new1
         IF group_val > 0
            group_str = group_str + "-"
         ENDIF
      ENDIF
      IF group_val > 0
         group_str = group_str + ;
         TRIM(SUBSTR(one_unit,(group_val*9)-8,9))
      ENDIF

      RETURN(group_str)
```

Usage:

```
amount = 735.45
@ 10,10 SAY CHKAMNT(amount)
```

CHKPASS()

Syntax: CHKPASS(<expN1>, <expN2>)

Pass: <numeric expression>, <numeric expression>
Return: <logical expression>

Description: The CHKPASS() function displays a window at the positions given, along with the prompt in the proper location. Available for reference to the function are the following variables:

scrtimes	(the number of times to execute the function)
scrframe	[the outline of the chosen frame for BOX()]
scrpass	[the value of the password generated by GENPASS()]

If the input given passes the CHKPASS() function, the function returns a .T. value; otherwise it will be .F. (false). If passwords are not wanted, scrtimes is set to 0.

Function: User-defined function.

Code:

```
**********
* Notice:  Copyright 1988, Stephen J. Straley & Associates
**********
FUNCTION Chkpass

   PARAMETERS row, col
```

```
   IF scrtimes = 0
      RETURN(.T.)
   ENDIF
   FOR x = 1 TO scrtimes
      in_pass = SPACE(15)
      IF TYPE("scrframe") = "U"
         @ row-3, col-5 CLEAR TO row+3, col+34
         @ row-3, col-5 TO row+3, col+34 DOUBLE
      ELSE
         @ row-3, col-5, row+3, col+34 BOX scrframe
      ENDIF
      @ row,col SAY "Password --> " ;
      GET in_pass PICT "XXXXXXXXXXXXXXX"
      READ
      IF !EMPTY(in_pass)
         temp_count = GENPASS(in_pass)
         IF temp_count = scrpass
            RETURN(.T.)
         ENDIF
      ENDIF
   NEXT

   RETURN(.F.)
```

Usage:

```
CASE option = 7
   IF CHKPASS(20,5)
      DO Subopt
   ELSE
      @ 17,0,23,39 BOX scrframe
      @ 19, 3 SAY "Attempt to Access Utility Submenu"
      @ 20, 3 SAY "    without proper access code."
      @ 21, 3 SAY "      Any Key to Continue ...."
      INKEY(0)
   ENDIF
ENDCASE
```

COSIN()

Syntax: COSIN(<expN1>, <expC1>)

Pass: <numeric expression>, <character expression>

Return: <numeric expression>

Description: This function returns the cosine value for the numeric expression passed to it. That expression may be either in the form of degrees or radians. To toggle for radian calculation, the value of <expC1> must be something other than "D."

Code:

```
**********
* Notice:  Copyright 1988, Stephen J. Straley & Associates
*
* Written and contributed by ESSOR MASO
*
* For the input argument in the first circle,
* degrees -360 <=arg <=360.
* The error ABS(e(arg)) <= 2*10^(-9); the value 2 is returned if
* either the argument or the D or R is missing, or the
* ABS(arg) > 360.
*
* Correct form: COSIN(arg,'D')
*
* National Bureau of Standards Handbook of Mathematical Functions
**********

FUNCTION Cosin

PARAMETERS cos_work, cos_deg

SET DECIMAL TO 10

PRIVATE cos_int,cos_squ

cos_sign = ( cos_work < 0)
IF ABS(IIF(UPPER(cos_deg)#'D',cos_work,;
       cos_work*1.5707963268/90))>6.2831853072 .OR. PCOUNT()#2
   RETURN(2)
ENDIF

cos_work=ABS(IIF(UPPER(cos_deg)#'D',cos_work,cos_work*1.5707963268
/90))
cos_int=MOD(INT(cos_work/1.5707963268),4)
cos_work=MOD(cos_work,1.5707963268)
IF cos_int=1.OR.cos_int=3
   cos_work=1.5707963268-cos_work
ENDIF
STORE cos_work*cos_work TO cos_work,cos_squ
cos_work=.0000247609-.0000002605*cos_squ
cos_work=-.0013888397+cos_work*cos_squ
cos_work=.0416666418+cos_work*cos_squ
cos_work=-.4999999963+cos_work*cos_squ
cos_work=ROUNDTHEM(1+cos_work*cos_squ,8)
IF cos_int=1.OR.cos_int=2
   cos_work=-cos_work
ENDIF
RETURN(cos_work)

********************

FUNCTION Roundthem

   PARAMETERS the_numb, no_places
```

```
    SET DECIMAL TO no_places

    RETURN(IIF(the_numb < 0, INT(the_numb *;
            10^no_places-.5),INT(the_numb*;
            10^no_places+.5))/10^no_places)
```

CHNG_PRMPT()
SCAN_PRMPT()
DELT_PRMPT()

Syntax: CHNG_PRMPT(<expN>)
SCAN_PRMPT(<expN>)
DELT_PRMPT(<expN>)

Pass: <numeric expression>
Return: <numeric expression>

Description: These three functions are used to help pan through a database based on the desired operation. The number passed to the functions is the row number for the choices to appear on. What makes them unique is that while they perform a task, their values can be tested and appropriate action can be taken based on the answer.

Function: User-defined function.

Sample:

```
**********
* Notice:  Copyright 1988, Stephen J. Straley & Associates
**********
FUNCTION Chng_prmpt

* This is the MENU prompt at the passed
* coordinates for CHANGE information.

   PARAMETERS a_row

   temp_var = 3
   @ a_row,10 SAY ;
     "< >ext - < >revious - < >dit - < >hoose Again - < >uit"
   @ a_row,11 PROMPT "N"
   @ a_row,20 PROMPT "P"
   @ a_row,33 PROMPT "E"
   @ a_row,42 PROMPT "C"
   @ a_row,59 PROMPT "Q"
   MENU TO temp_var
   RETURN(temp_var)

********************
```

```
FUNCTION Scan_prmpt

   * This is the MENU prompt at the passed
   * coordinates for SCAN information.

   PARAMETERS a_row

   temp_var = 1
   @ a_row, 17 SAY ;
      "< >ext - < >revious - < >hoose Again - < >uit"
   @ a_row, 18 PROMPT "N"
   @ a_row, 27 PROMPT "P"
   @ a_row, 40 PROMPT "C"
   @ a_row, 57 PROMPT "Q"
   MENU TO temp_var
   RETURN(temp_var)

********************

FUNCTION Delt_prmpt

   * This is the MENU prompt at the passed
   * coordinates for DELETE information.

   PARAMETERS a_row

   temp_strng = "< >ext - < >revious - < >" + ;
                IF(DELETED(), "ecall", "elete") + ;
                " - < >hoose Again - < >uit"
   temp_var = 3
      @ a_row,10 SAY temp_strng
   @ a_row,11 PROMPT "N"
   @ a_row,20 PROMPT "P"
   @ a_row,33 PROMPT IF(DELETED(), "R", "D")
   @ a_row,44 PROMPT "C"
   @ a_row,61 PROMPT "Q"
   MENU TO temp_var
   RETURN(temp_var)
```

Usage:

```
USE Multy
GO TOP
DO WHILE .T.
   DO Paint_it
   which_way = DELT_PRMPT(18)
   DO CASE
      CASE which_way = 1
         SKIP
      CASE which_way = 2
         SKIP -1
      CASE which_way = 3
         DO Delt_it
      CASE which_way = 4
         EXIT
```

```
      OTHERWISE
         KEYBOARD CHR(13)
      EXIT
   ENDCASE
   DO Adjust
ENDDO
```

DAY_WORD()

Syntax: DAY_WORD(<exp>)

Pass: <date expression> or <numeric expression>
Return: <character expression>

Description: The DAY_WORD() function returns the string of any date variable or field with the value of the 1st, the 2nd, the 3rd, the 4th, etc.

Function: User-defined function.

Code:

```
**********
* Notice:  Copyright 1988, Stephen J. Straley & Associates
**********
FUNCTION Dayword

PARAMETERS in_date

IF TYPE("in_date") = "D"
   in_day = STR(DAY(in_date),2)
   in_val = VAL(in_day)
ELSE
   in_day = STR(in_date, 2)
   in_val = in_date
ENDIF

IF in_val > 3 .AND. in_val < 21
   in_day = in_day + "th"
ELSE
   in_val = VAL(SUBSTR(in_day,2,1))
   in_day = in_day + ;
   SUBSTR("thstndrdthththththth"), (in_val * 2) + 1, 2)
ENDIF
RETURN(in_day)
```

Usage:

```
wording = DAY_WORD(DATE())
   ? "Today is the " + wording
```

DENIAL()

Syntax: DENIAL(<expN>)

Pass: <numeric expression>
Return: <character expression>

Description: This function helps label an entry screen with the appropriate display message. For example, if menu option 1 is pressed, this normally means "ENTER"; menu option 2 means "CHANGE"; menu option 3 means "SCAN"; and menu option 4 means "DELETE".

Function: User-defined function.

Code:

```
**********
* Notice:  Copyright 1986, Stephen J. Straley
**********
FUNCTION Denial

PARAMETERS decision

RETURN(DLTRIM(SUBSTR("Enter ChangeScan  Delete", ;
  (decision * 6) - 5, 6)))
```

Usage:

```
@ 10,10 PROMPT " Enter  "
@ 11,10 PROMPT " Change "
@ 12,10 PROMPT " Scan   "
@ 13,10 PROMPT " Delete "
MENU TO option
IF !EMPTY(option)
   @ 0,0 CLEAR
   @ 1,0 SAY DENIAL(option) + " Information"
   ext = DLTRIM(STR(option))
   DO Data&ext.
ENDIF
```

DECRYPTION()

Syntax: DECRYPTION(<expC>)

Pass: <character expression>
Return: <character expression>

Description: This function was designed to decrypt those character fields or string that were encrypted via the ENCRYPTION() function.

Function: User-defined function.

Code:

```
**********
* Notice:  Copyright 1986, Stephen J. Straley
**********
FUNCTION Decrypt

PARAMETERS to_do

padback = LEN(to_do)
done    = ""
to_do   = DLTRIM(to_do)
FOR qaz = LEN(to_do) TO 1 STEP -1
   done = done + CHR(ASC(SUBSTR(to_do, qaz, 1)) - 104)
NEXT
RETURN(FILL_OUT(done, padback))
```

DIVIDE0()

Syntax: DIVIDE0(<expN1>, <expN2>)

Pass: <numeric expression>, <numeric expression>

Return: <numeric expression>

Description: The DIVIDE0() function returns the results of <expN1> (the numerator) divided by <expN2> (the divisor), or 0 if <expN2> is equal to 0.

Function: User-defined function.

Code:

```
**********
* Notice:  Copyright 1988, Stephen J. Straley & Associates
**********
FUNCTION Divide0

PARAMETERS top_numb, bot_numb

IF bot_numb == 0
   RETURN(0)
ENDIF
RETURN(top_numb / bot_numb)
```

Usage:

```
in  = 7
out = 0
? "The results are as follows:  " + STR(DIVIDE0(in, out))
```

DLTRIM()

Syntax: DLTRIM(<expC>)

Pass: <character expression>
Return: <character expression>

Description: The DLTRIM() function is primarily used immediately after a numeric field or variable has been converted to a string. In Clipper, as in dBASE III, numbers converted to strings are padded with blank spaces to concatenate the string for indexing purposes. However, in most cases a TRIM() or an LTRIM() will not suffice; the spaces have to be completely removed from the string.

In the Summer '87 release, the ALLTRIM() function is equivalent; however, that function resides in EXTEND.LIB, not in CLIPPER.LIB.

Function: User-defined function.

Code:

```
**********
* Notice:  Copyright 1988, Stephen J. Straley & Associates
**********
FUNCTION Dltrim

   PARAMETER in_string

   RETURN(LTRIM(TRIM(in_string)))
```

Usage:

```
x = 4
*
* Here x is initialized to a numeric value to make it easier
* to show how the STR() function puts in preceding blanks
* and DLTRIM() eliminates them.
*
findit = last_name + DLTRIM(STR(x)) + phone_num
SEEK findit
```

ENDFIELD()

Syntax: ENDFIELD(<expC>)

Pass: <character expression>
Return: <numeric expression>

Description: The ENDFIELD() function returns the number of fields in the given database. This function does a binary search to determine the position of the last field in the database. This is equivalent to the FCOUNT() function.

Function: User-defined function.

Code:

```
**********
* Notice:  Copyright 1988, Stephen J. Straley & Associates
**********
FUNCTION Last_field

PARAMETERS Filename

USE &filename
first  = 1
last   = 1024
middle = INT(last/2)

* The basis of a binary search is to take a beginning (first)
* and an ending (last) and find the midpoint (middle).
* Once done, the actual search is to check if the value in
* question is above or below the midpoint value.  Depending
* upon the outcome of the test, the first, last, and middle are
* adjusted accordingly.  Once the value in question is equal to
* the midpoint, the value is found.  The purpose of a binary
* search is simple: to search for a value by taking the halves of
* the extremes.  Binary searches are one of the fastest types of
* searches used: if a database being searched doubles in size,
* the binary search still has only one additional pass to make.

DO WHILE first <> last
   * Check the length of the field at the middle position.
   * IF the value is 0, there is no field at position middle:
   *   make the value of last equal to middle.
   * ELSE, there is a value at position middle: make the value
   *   of first equal to middle.  Then recalculate the value of
   *   middle based on the new values of first and last.

   IF EMPTY(FIELDNAME(middle))
      last = middle
   ELSE
      first = middle
   ENDIF
   middle = first + INT((last - first)/2)
   IF !EMPTY(FIELDNAME(middle)) .AND. ;
      EMPTY (FIELDNAME(middle + 1))
      last  = middle
      first = middle
   ENDIF
ENDDO
RETURN(last)
```

Usage:

```
howmany = ENDFIELD("MULTY")
? "There are " + TRANSFORM(howmany, "9999) + "fields "
?? "in Multy.dbf"
```

ENCRYPT()

Syntax: ENCRYPT(<expC>)

Pass: < character expression >
Return: < character expression >

Description: This function actually takes each character in <expC> and converts it in value up 104 ASCII() positions. It also reverses the order the string, meaning that the original front character will be the last character. This is useful when wanting to encrypt a unique password so that when looking at the string or field via an interpeter or DOS, the meaning of the field will not be revealed.

Function: User-defined function.

Code:

```
***********
* Notice:  Copyright 1988, Stephen J. Straley & Associates
***********
FUNCTION Encrypt

PARAMETERS to_do

padback = LEN(to_do)
done = ""
to_do = DLTRIM(to_do)
FOR qaz = LEN(to_do) TO 1 STEP -1
   done = done + CHR(ASC(SUBSTR(to_do, qaz, 1)) + 104)
NEXT
RETURN(FILL_OUT(done, padback))
```

Usage:

```
@ 10,10 SAY "Enter Secret Password: " GET M->password ;
   VALID "@X"
READ
IF LASTKEY() <> 27 .AND. UPDATED()
   REPLACE A->password WITH ENCRYPT(M->password)
ENDIF
```

EXPAND()

Syntax: EXPAND(<expC>)

Pass: <character expression>
Return: <characer expression>

Description: The EXPAND() function is designed for screen formatting as well as for report generation. It expands a string with a blank space between each character.

Function: User-defined function.

Code:

```
**********
* Notice:  Copyright 1986-8, Stephen J. Straley & Associates
**********
FUNCTION Expand

PARAMETER in_string

length  = LEN(in_string)
counter = 1
out_str = ""

DO WHILE counter <= length
   out_str = out_str + SUBSTR(in_string, counter,1) + " "
   counter = counter + 1
ENDDO
RETURN(TRIM(out_str))
```

Usage:

```
@ 2,23 SAY EXPAND("Enter Customer")
```

EXPLODEC()

Syntax: EXPLODEC(<expC1>, @<expC2>)

Pass: <formatted PICTURE string>, by reference <character expression>
Return: <formatted PICTURE string>

Description: This function is specifically part of the Steve Straley Toolkit (tm) and will only work with the Summer '87 release of Clipper. It is a function that, when placed on a PICTURE clause, will interrupt the natural flow of the GET command and cause the letters to flow right to left rather than left to right. This also shows how Clipper will accept user-defined functions in a PICTURE clause.

Function: User-defined function.

Code:

```
***********
* Notice:  Copyright 1988, Stephen J. Straley & Associates
***********
FUNCTION Explodec

   PARAMETERS a, the_char

   b = ROW()
   c = COL()
   go_for = LEN("&a")
   astring = SPACE(go_for)
   @ b,c GET astring PICT "&a"
   CLEAR GETS
   disp = ""
   at_what = c + go_for - 1
   @ b,at_what + 1 SAY ""
   how_many = 1

   DO WHILE INKEY(0) <> 13
      DO CASE
      CASE LASTKEY() = 27
         EXIT
      CASE (LASTKEY() >= 32 .AND. LASTKEY() <= 126)

         disp = disp + CHR(LASTKEY())
         how_many = how_many + 1

         @ b,at_what GET disp PICT "&a"

         IF at_what > c
            at_what = at_what - 1
         ENDIF
      CASE LASTKEY() = 19 .OR. LASTKEY() = 8 .OR. LASTKEY() = 7
         disp = SPACE(go_for - LEN(disp) + 1) + ;
                SUBSTR(disp, 1, LEN(disp) - 1)
         how_many = how_many - 1
         @ b,c GET disp PICT "&a"
         disp = LTRIM(disp)
         IF at_what >= c + go_for - 1
            at_what = c + go_for - 1
         ELSE
            at_what = at_what + 1
         ENDIF

      ENDCASE

      CLEAR GETS

   ENDDO

   IF LASTKEY() = 27
      KEYBOARD CHR(27)
```

```
   ELSE
      KEYBOARD CHR(13)
   ENDIF

   front_sp = SPACE(go_for - LEN(disp))
   the_char = front_sp + disp

   @ b,c SAY ""

   RETURN("&a")
```

Usage:

```
wait_st = SPACE(40)
@ 4,10 SAY "BACKSPACE and Left Arrow Keys " + ;
   "WORK!!!    Press ESC to Exit!"
@ 2, 5 SAY "Enter a File Name => " GET wait_st PICT ;
   EXPLODEC("XXXXXXXXXXXXXXXXXXXXXXXXXXXXXXXXXXXXXXXX", @wait_st)
READ
```

FILL_ARRAY()

Syntax: FILL_ARRAY(<expC1>, <expN1>, <expN2>, <expC2>, <expN3> [, <expC3>])

Pass: <character expression>, <numeric expression>, numeric expression>, <character expression>, expression numeric [, <character expression>]

Return: <logical expression>

Description: The FILL_ARRAY() function was designed to load a range of fields from a database into an array. The array must be DECLARED prior to the issuance of the function and must be set to the maximum number of possible elements. <expC1> is the name of the array; <expN1> is the starting counter within the array; <expN2> is the ending counter within the array; <expC2> is for the name of the database; <expN3> is for the field number to be used; and <expC3>, which is optional, is any filter condition to be placed on the newly selected and active database. You may alter the values of the beginning and ending counters in order to fill an array only partially with field values. If you do, the function will still start at the top of the file and replace the values accordingly.

Function: User-defined function.

Code:

```
**********
* Notice:  Copyright 1988, Stephen J. Straley & Associates
**********
```

```
FUNCTION Fill_array

PARAMETERS the_array, start, end_at, the_file, the_field, the_filt

go_back = SELECT()
IF !FILE(the_file)
   RETURN(.F.)
ENDIF
SELECT 9
USE &the_file
IF TYPE("the_filt") <> "U"
   SET FILTER TO &the_filt.
ENDIF
GO TOP
temp_val = FIELDNAME(the_field)
DO WHILE !EOF()
   the_array[start] = &temp_val.
   start = start + 1
   IF start > end_at
      EXIT
   ENDIF
   SKIP
ENDDO
return_to = DLTRIM(STR(go_back))
SELECT &return_to.

RETURN(.T.)
```

Usage:

```
********************
* Name        FILLIT.prg
* Date        March 25, 1988
* Notice      Copyright 1988, Stephen J. Straley & Associates
* Compile     Clipper Fillit
* Release     Autumn '86 or later
* Link        Autumn '86: Plink86 fi fillit lib dbu lib clipper
*             Summer '87: Plink87 fi fillit lib extend lib clipper
* Note        This program shows how to use the FILL_ARRAY()
*             function.  Notice that the same database is
*             opened twice.  This is allowed in Clipper.
*             The ramifications of this are numerous,
*             including the use of data-dictionaries and
*             Clipper SQL routines with immediate cross-
*             checking.
********************

USE Client
DECLARE mast_list[LASTREC()]
IF FILL_ARRAY(mast_list, 1, LASTREC(), "Client.dbf", 3)
   CLEAR
   FOR x = 1 TO LEN(mast_list)
      ? mast_list[x]
   NEXT
ELSE
```

```
   ? "File Not Found!!"
ENDIF

*********************

FUNCTION Fill_array

PARAMETERS the_array, start, end_at, the_file, the_field, the_filt

go_back = SELECT()
IF !FILE(the_file)
   RETURN(.F.)
ENDIF
SELECT 9
USE &the_file
IF TYPE("the_filt") <> "U"
   SET FILTER TO &the_filt.
ENDIF
GO TOP
temp_val = FIELDNAME(the_field)
DO WHILE !EOF()
   the_array[start] = &temp_val.
   start = start + 1
   IF start > end_at
      EXIT
   ENDIF
   SKIP
ENDDO
return_to = DLTRIM(STR(go_back))
SELECT &return_to.
RETURN(.T.)
* End of File
```

FILL_OUT()

Syntax: FILL_OUT(<expC> [,<expN>])

Pass: <character expression> [,<numeric expression>]
Return: <character expression>

Description: The FILL_OUT() function is designed for screen and report formatting. It fills out the given string with blank spaces, defaulting to a width of 79. It may be used in conjunction with the CENTR() function to properly center a message for the SET MESSAGE TO / PROMPT...MESSAGE commands for versions of Clipper prior to Summer '87. With later versions, this function may be used to fill-out prompt bars in order to simulate pull-down style menus.

Function: User-defined function.

Code:

```
**********
* Notice:  Copyright 1988, Stephen J. Straley & Associates
**********
FUNCTION Fill_out

PARAMETERS a, b

IF TYPE("b") = "U"
   b = 79
ENDIF
c = b - LEN(a)
RETURN(a + SPACE(c))
```

Usage:

```
@ 2,23 PROMPT " 1> Chart of Accounts " ;
MESSAGE CENTR(FILL_OUT("This is for the Chart of Accounts"))
```

FOX_DATE()

Syntax: FOX_DATE(<expD> [, <expN1> [, <expN2>]])

Pass: <date expression> [, <row coordinate> [, <column coordinate>]]

Return: <date expression>

Description: In answer to a challenge, this function shows the versatility of the concept of user-defined functions where this function will manipulate a date variable or field using the cursor keys. Option parameters are the row and column coordinates to have this function activate on. This function should be used with the Summer '87 release of Clipper.

Function: User-defined function.

Code:

```
**********
* Notice:  Copyright 1988, Stephen J. Straley & Associates
**********
FUNCTION Fox_date

   PARAMETERS g_d_date, g_d_row, g_d_col

    IF PCOUNT() = 1
       g_d_row = ROW()
       g_d_col = COL()
    ENDIF

    g_d_level = 2
    SET CURSOR OFF
    DO WHILE .T.
       @ g_d_row, g_d_col GET g_d_date
```

```
      CLEAR GETS
      dummy = INKEY(0)
      DO CASE
      CASE dummy = 13 .OR. dummy = 27 .OR. ;
          dummy = 23 .OR. dummy = 3
         EXIT
      CASE CHR(dummy) $ "Mm"
         g_d_level = 1
      CASE CHR(dummy) $ "Dd"
         g_d_level = 2
      CASE CHR(dummy) $ "Yy"
         g_d_level = 3
      CASE CHR(dummy) $ "+-"
         gd1 = MONTH(g_d_date)
         gd2 = DAY(g_d_date)
         gd3 = YEAR(g_d_date)
         DO CASE
         CASE g_d_level = 1
            gd1 = gd1 + IF(CHR(dummy) = "+", 1, -1)
            gd1 = IF(gd1 < 1, 12, IF(gd1 > 12, 1, gd1))
            IF EMPTY(CTOD(STR(gd1) + "/" + STR(gd2) + ;
               "/" + SUBSTR(STR(gd3), 3)))
               gd2 = 1
            ENDIF
         CASE g_d_level = 2
            gd2 = gd2 + IF(CHR(dummy) = "+", 1, -1)
            NOTE - Go to top of day for month
            IF gd2 < 1
               gd2 = LAST_DAY(gd1, gd3)
            ELSE
               NOTE - Check to see if good date in month's range
               IF gd2 > 27
                  IF EMPTY(CTOD(STR(gd1) + "/" + ;
                     STR(gd2) + "/" + SUBSTR(STR(gd3), 3)))
                     gd2 = 1
                  ENDIF
               ENDIF
            ENDIF
         OTHERWISE
            gd3 = gd3 + IF(CHR(dummy) = "+", 1, -1)
         ENDCASE
         g_d_date = CTOD(STR(gd1) + "/" + STR(gd2) + ;
                  "/" + SUBSTR(STR(gd3), 3))

      ENDCASE
   ENDDO
   SET CURSOR ON
   RETURN(g_d_date)
```

Usage: `indate = DATE()`

GENPASS()

Syntax: GENPASS(<expC>)

Pass: < character expression >
Return: < numeric expression >

Description: The GENPASS() function provides a password-generation scheme for any application. It may be modified to any extreme for protection purposes. It returns a numeric value for any string, based on the ASCII value of each character multiplied by its relative position in the string.

Function: User-defined function.

Code:

```
**********
* Notice:  Copyright 1988, Stephen J. Straley & Associates
**********
FUNCTION Genpass

PARAMETERS in_string

count = LEN(TRIM(in_string))
final = 0
FOR beginning = 1 to (count + 1)
   final = final + ;
      ASC(SUBSTR(in_string, beginning, 1)) * beginning
NEXT
RETURN(final)
```

Usage:

```
password = SPACE(15)
@ 10, 3 SAY "What Password do you wish to use?  " ;
              GET password PICT "XXXXXXXXXXXXXXX"
READ
scrpass = GENPASS(password)
```

GOODFILE()

Syntax: GOODFILE(<expC>)

Pass: < character expression >
Return: < logical expression >

Description: The GOODFILE() function determines if the file is a legitimate dBASE III file. It may be modified to search for an ASCII 83, which would signal that the file is not only a dBASE III database but that it contains a memo field. This may be useful when copying files to be sure the memo file gets copied. Additionally, with the Summer '87 release, there are other ways to check the validity of the file. For those functions, please refer to Chapter 13, Low-Level File Logic.

Function: User-defined function.

Code:

```
***********
* Notice:  Copyright 1988, Stephen J. Straley & Associates
***********
FUNCTION Goodfile

PARAMETERS file

CREATE Temp
USE Temp
APPEND BLANK
REPLACE field_name WITH "HEADER", ;
        field_type WITH "C", field_len WITH 32
USE
CREATE Header FROM Temp
CLOSE DATABASE
ERASE Temp.dbf
USE Header
APPEND FROM &file SDF
GO TOP
DO WHILE ASC(SUBSTR(header,1,1)) == 3 .OR. ;
         ASC(SUBSTR(header,1,1)) == 83
   x = ASC(SUBSTR(header,3,1))
   IF x > 12
      EXIT
   ENDIF
   x = ASC(SUBSTR(header,4,1))
   IF x > 32
      EXIT
   ENDIF
   USE
   ERASE Header.dbf
   RETURN(.T.)
ENDDO
USE
ERASE Header.dbf

RETURN(.F.)
```

Usage:

```
*********************
* Name      GOOD.prg
* Date      March 25, 1988
* Notice    Copyright 1988, Stephen J. Straley & Associates
* Compile   Clipper Good
* Release   Winter '85 or later
```

```
* Link        Plink86 fi good lib clipper
* Note        This program shows how to use a function like GOOD-
*             FILE().  This can also be used to test if a data-
*             base file has a .DBT file with it (the first byte
*             will be an 83, not a 3).  If it is, when using
*             the COPY TO command, you can be sure to copy the
*             memo file with it.
*********************

DO WHILE .T.
   CLEAR
   STORE SPACE(12) TO lookfor
   @ 6,10 SAY "Enter ? for directory..."
   @ 8,10 SAY "Enter name of file with extension: " ;
          GET lookfor PICT "@!" VALID(DODIR())
   READ
   @ 9,0 CLEAR
   IF EMPTY(lookfor)
      QUIT
   ENDIF
   IF AT(".",lookfor) = 0
      WAIT " Please enter an extension..."
      LOOP
   ENDIF
   lookfor = LTRIM(lookfor)
   lookfor = TRIM(lookfor)
   IF .NOT. FILE(lookfor)
     WAIT "Enter a good file name, or leave blank to quit.."
      LOOP
   ENDIF
   @ 11,10 SAY "That file "
   ?? IF(GOODFILE(lookfor), "IS", "IS NOT") + " a dBASE III file"
   ?
   WAIT "Press any key for next entry..."
ENDDO

*********************

FUNCTION Dodir

   IF SUBSTR(lookfor,1,1) = "?"
      ?
      RUN DIR /W
      RETURN(.F.)
   ENDIF
   RETURN(.T.)

*********************

FUNCTION Goodfile

PARAMETERS file
```

```
CREATE Temp
USE Temp
APPEND BLANK
REPLACE field_name WITH "HEADER", ;
        field_type WITH "C", field_len WITH 32
    USE
CREATE Header FROM Temp
CLOSE DATABASE
ERASE Temp.dbf
USE Header
APPEND FROM &file SDF
GO TOP
DO WHILE ASC(SUBSTR(header,1,1)) == 3 .OR. ;
         ASC(SUBSTR(header,1,1)) == 83
   x = ASC(SUBSTR(header,3,1))
   IF x > 12
      EXIT
   ENDIF
   x = ASC(SUBSTR(header,4,1))
   IF x > 32
      EXIT
   ENDIF
   USE
   ERASE Header.dbf
   RETURN(.T.)
ENDDO
USE
ERASE Header.dbf
RETURN(.F.)
* End of File
```

GOOD_ENV()

Syntax: GOOD_ENV(<expN1>, <expN2>, <expN3>, <expN4>, <expN5>, <expN6>)

Pass: <numeric expression>, <numeric expression>, <numeric expression>, <numeric expression>, <numeric expression>, <numeric expression>

Return: <logical expression>

Description: This function tests to see if the current environmental conditions check out. If used in the front of an application, this can be used to test to see if there is enough basic memory and reserved memory to continue to run the application. This function was designed to be used with the Summer '87 release of the compiler.

Function: User-defined function.

Code:

```
**********
* Notice:  Copyright 1988, Stephen J. Straley & Associates
**********
FUNCTION Good_env

   PARAMETERS gooda, goodb, goodc, goodd, goode, goodf

   did_pass = .T.
   the_env = UPPER(GETE("CLIPPER"))

   FOR qaz = 1 TO 6
      the_let = SUBSTR("VREXFS", qaz, 1)
      the_par = "good" + CHR(96 + qaz)

      IF !EMPTY(&the_par.)
         did_pass = (&the_par. <= VAL(SUBSTR(the_env, ;
                    AT(the_let, the_env) + 1, 3)))
         IF !did_pass
            RETURN(.F.)
         ENDIF
      ENDIF
   NEXT
   RETURN(did_pass)
```

Usage:

```
STORE 0 TO numba, numbb, numbc, numbd, numbe, numbf
@  3, 1 SAY "The V option => " GET numba
@  3,41 SAY "The R option => " GET numbb
@  4, 1 SAY "The E option => " GET numbc
@  4,41 SAY "The X option => " GET numbd
@  5, 1 SAY "The F option => " GET numbe
@  5,41 SAY "The S option => " GET numbf
READ
IF LASTKEY() = 27
   EXIT
ENDIF
IF GOOD_ENV(numba, numbb, numbc, numbd, numbe, numbf)
   @ 7,10 SAY "Environment Status Checks Out..."
ELSE
   @ 7,10 SAY "Environment Parameters Do Not Check Out!"
ENDIF
```

GOT()

Syntax: GOT(<expC>, <expN1>, <expN2>)

Pass: <character expression>, <numeric expression>, <numeric expression>

Return: <expression>

Description: The GOT() function was created to give the user a chance to view valid choices (such as zip codes) that may be located in another file or in the current file. <expC> is the name of the file to be used; <expN1> is the field to focus on within the file; and <expN2> is the specific record number this function will look at. This function was designed to be used with the POP() and MAKE_EMPTY() functions.

Function: User-defined function.

Code:

```
**********
* Notice:  Copyright 1988, Stephen J. Straley & Associates
**********
FUNCTION Got

PARAMETERS file, field_no, record

ret_area = STR(SELECT())

IF LEN(file) = 1
   SELECT &file.
ELSE
   SELECT 0
   USE &file
ENDIF

IF field_no > FCOUNT()
   RETURN("")
ENDIF

IF record = 0 .OR. LASTREC() = 0
   GO TOP
   in_betw = FIELDNAME(field_no)
   give_it = &in_betw
   SELECT &ret_area.
   RETURN(MAKE_EMPTY(give_it))
ELSE
   GO record
ENDIF
in_betw = FIELDNAME(field_no)
output = &in_betw
SELECT &ret_area.
RETURN(output)
```

Usage: Sample code is in the section entitled "Using GOT(), POP(), and MAKE_EMPTY()" at the end of Chapter 14, Designing User-Defined Functions.

GREAT_ZERO()

Syntax: GREAT_ZERO(<expN1>, <expN2>, <expN3>)

Pass: <numeric expression>, <numeric expression>, <numeric expression>

Return: <logical expression>

Description: The GREAT_ZERO() function returns a .T. if the field or variable expressed in <expN3> is greater than 0. <expN1> and <expN2> are the row and column position on which to put an error message if <expN3> fails the test.

Function: User-defined function.

Code:

```
**********
* Notice:  Copyright 1988, Stephen J. Straley & Associates
**********
FUNCTION Great_zero

PARAMETERS arow, acol, value

IF value < 0
   arow, acol SAY "Number is too low!"
   RETURN(.F.)
ENDIF
arow, acol SAY SPACE(20)
RETURN(.T.)
```

LOOKUP()

Syntax: LOOKUP()

Pass: Nothing

Return: <logical expression>

Description: The LOOKUP() function demonstrates how to use a user-defined function in conjunction with the VALID clause. The concept, rather than the actual code, is important.

Function: User-defined function.

Code:

```
**********
* Notice:  Copyright 1988, Stephen J. Straley & Associates
**********
FUNCTION Lookup
* This function is designed to always return a .T.
* so that if the zip code is found, the state variable
```

```
* will be manipulated by the function; otherwise, it is
* left alone and may be manipulated by the operator.

DO CASE
CASE inzip = "98234"
   instate = "CA"
CASE inzip = "76233"
   instate = "GA"
CASE inzip = "12009"
   instate = "NY"
ENDCASE
RETURN(.T.)
```

Usage:

```
DO WHILE .T.
   STORE SPACE(2) TO instate
   STORE SPACE(5) TO inzip
   CLEAR
   TEXT

    Try entering either your own zip code or one of the following
choices:

   98234  -   (CA)
   76233  -   (GA)
   12009  -   (NY)

   ENDTEXT
   @ 12,10 SAY "Enter Zip Code: " GET inzip VALID(LOOKUP())
   @ 14,10 SAY "         State: " GET instate PICT "!!"
   READ
   @ 18,10 SAY "Do you want to continue? "
   IF !VERIFY()
      QUIT
   ENDIF
   ENDDO
```

MAKE_EMPTY()

Syntax: MAKE_EMPTY(<exp>)

Pass: <expression>

Return: <expression>

Description: The MAKE_EMPTY() function will evaluate an expression, determine its data type, and return an empty value of that type. This function can be used to initialize an array based on a database. It was originally designed to be used with the GOT() and POP() functions to allow a user to escape out of the pop-menu and yield a null answer to GOT().

Function: User-defined function.

Code:

```
**********
* Notice:  Copyright 1988, Stephen J. Straley & Associates
**********
FUNCTION Make_empty

PARAMETERS in_field, in_name

IF PCOUNT() = 1
   in_name = ""
ENDIF

DO CASE
CASE TYPE("in_field") = "C"
   RETURN(SPACE(LEN(in_field)))
CASE TYPE("in_field") = "N"
   RETURN(VAL(STR(in_field)))
CASE TYPE("in_field") = "D"
  RETURN(CTOD("  /  /  "))
OTHERWISE
   RETURN(.F.)
ENDCASE
```

Usage: Sample code is in the section entitled "Using GOT(), POP(), and MAKE_EMPTY()" at the end of the User-Defined Function section.

MUST_FILL()

Syntax: MUST_FILL(<expC> [, <expN1>, <expN2>])

Pass: <character expression> [, <numeric expression>, <numeric expression>]

Return: <logical expression>

Description: The MUST_FILL() function returns a logical .T. if the name of the field or variable expressed in <expC> has something in it. If the field is EMPTY(), an error message is displayed and a false is returned. If <expN1> (the row), and <expN2> (the column) are given, the error message appears at that position; otherwise, the error message appears on the same row as the GET.

Function: User-defined function.

Code:

```
**********
* Notice:  Copyright 1988, Stephen J. Straley & Associates
**********
FUNCTION Must_fill
```

```
PARAMETERS mustfa, mustfb, mustfc

IF LASTKEY() = 5
   IF TYPE("mustfb") = "U"
      ?? SPACE(26)
   ELSE
      @ mustfb, mustfc SAY SPACE(26)
   ENDIF
   RETURN(.T.)
ENDIF
IF EMPTY(mustfa)
   IF TYPE("mustfb") = "U"
      ?? "This field MUST be filled"
   ELSE
      @ mustfb, mustfc SAY "This field MUST be filled"
   ENDIF
   RETURN(.F.)
ELSE
   IF TYPE("mustfb") = "U"
      ?? SPACE(26)
   ELSE
      @ mustfb, mustfc SAY SPACE(26)
   ENDIF
   RETURN(.T.)
ENDIF
```

Usage:

```
STORE SPACE(12) TO filename
@ 10,10 SAY "Enter File Name => " GET filename ;
  VALID(MUST_FILL(filename))
READ
STORE 0 TO age
@ 12,10 SAY "Now enter your age => " GET age;
  VALID(MUST_FILL(age,14,25))
READ
```

MULTPLE_OF()

Syntax: MULTPLE_OF(<expN1>, <expN2>)

Pass: <numeric expression>, <numeric expression>
Return: <logical expression>

Description: This function returns a logical true (.T.) if <expN1> is a multiple of <expN2>. It is helpful when calculating row and page numbers.

Function: User-defined function.

Code:

```
**********
* Notice:  Copyright 1988, Stephen J. Straley & Associates
**********
FUNCTION Multple_of
```

```
PARAMETERS the_number, the_base

RETURN(IF(the_number / the_base = INT(the_number / the_base),;
        .T., .F.))
```

Usage:

```
@ 0,0 CLEAR
DO WHILE !EOF()
   ? RECNO()
   IF MULTIPLE_OF(ROW(), 19)
      WAIT
      @ 0,0 CLEAR
      @ 1,0 SAY ""
   ENDIF
   SKIP
ENDDO
```

OCCURENCE()

Syntax: OCCURENCE(<expC1>, <expC2>)

Pass: <character expression>, <character expression>
Return: <numeric expression>

Description: This functions tells how many times <expC1> appears in <expC2>.

Function: User-defined function.

Code:

```
**********
* Notice:  Copyright 1988, Stephen J. Straley & Associates
**********
FUNCTION Occurence

   PARAMETERS astring, bstring

   return_cnt = 0
   DO WHILE !EMPTY(AT(astring, bstring))
      return_cnt = return_cnt + 1
      bstring = SUBSTR(bstring, AT(astring, bstring)+1)
   ENDDO
   RETURN(return_cnt)
```

PERCENT()

Syntax: PERCENT(<expN1>, <expN2>)

Pass: <numeric expression>, <numeric expression>
Return: <character expression>

Description: The PERCENT() function returns a character string in the format of a percentage. The calculation is based on <expN1> divided by <expN2> (the divisor). The function also traps for a zero in the divisor (<expN2>).

Function: User-defined function.

Code:

```
**********
* Notice:  Copyright 1988, Stephen J. Straley & Associates
**********
FUNCTION Percent

PARAMETERS pertop, perbot

DO CASE
   CASE PCOUNT() = 0
      RETURN("")
   CASE perbot = 0
      RETURN("")
ENDCASE

RETURN(TRANSFORM(pertop/perbot, "###.##%"))
```

Usage:

```
CLEAR
USE Vendor
lastrec = LASTREC()
DO WHILE !EOF()
   @ 10,10 SAY PERCENT(RECNO(), lastrec)
   SKIP
ENDDO
```

POP()

Syntax: POP (<expN1>, <expN2>, <expN3>, <expN4>, <expC1>, <expN5> [,<expC2>]

Pass: <numeric expression>, <numeric expression>, <numeric expression>, <numeric expression>, <character expression>, <numeric expression> [, <character expression>]

Return: <numeric expression>

Description: The POP() function will return the record number of a set of valid choices (e.g., zip codes) that may be located in another file or in the current file. <expN1> is the top row coordinate for the pop menu; <expN2> is the top column coordinate; <expN3> is the number of rows down from the top left coordinate the pop menu should use; <expC1> is the name of the file to use (this may be the currently active file, as well); <expN5> is the field number to focus on in the selected database; and finally, <expC2> which is optional, may be used to set a specific filter on the file to be used. The field number may be a different number from the field number in the GOT() function. This will allow the developer to display code names for the user while the GOT() will yield the actual code value. This function was designed to be used with the GOT() and MAKE_EMPTY() functions.

Function: User-defined function.

Code:

```
**********
* Notice:  Copyright 1988, Stephen J. Straley & Associates
**********
FUNCTION Pop

PARAMETERS top, left, down, over, file, field_no, filt

ret_area = STR(SELECT())
DECLARE pointer[down]
STORE SPACE(4000) TO backscr, frontscr
SAVE SCREEN TO backscr
scrframe = CHR(201) + CHR(205) + CHR(187) + CHR(186) + ;
           CHR(188) + CHR(205) + CHR(200) + CHR(186) + CHR(32)
   @ top, left, top+down, left+over BOX scrframe
SAVE SCREEN TO frontscr
   IF LEN(file) = 1
      SELECT &file.
   ELSE
      SELECT 8
      USE &file.
   ENDIF

   IF LASTREC() = 0
      SELECT &ret_area.
      SET KEY 18 TO
      SET KEY  3 TO
      RETURN(0)
   ENDIF

IF TYPE("filt") = "U"
   SET FILTER TO
ELSE
   SET FILTER TO &filt
ENDIF
GO TOP
hit_bottom = .T.
starting = RECNO()
option = 1
screen_no = 1
DO WHILE .T.
```

```
RESTORE SCREEN FROM frontscr
beg_set = RECNO()
FOR x = 1 TO down - 3
   pointer[x] = RECNO()
   inbetw = FIELDNAME(field_no)
   showit = &inbetw
   IF LEN(showit) >= over-2
      showit = SUBSTR(showit, 1, over-3)
   ENDIF
   @ top+x, left+1 PROMPT " " + FILL_OUT(showit,over-2)
   SKIP
   IF EOF()
      hit_bottom = .T.
      x = down - 2
   ENDIF
NEXT
next_set = RECNO()
DO CASE
CASE EOF()                          && Last Screen Full
   IF screen_no > 1                 && Not the first screen
      IF over <= 8
         top+down+1, left+2 SAY "Esc for UP"
      ELSE
         @ top+down-2, left+2 SAY "Esc for UP"
      ENDIF
   ENDIF
OTHERWISE                           && Somewhere else
   IF screen_no  > 1                && Not the first screen
      IF over <= 8
         @ top+down+1, left+2 SAY "Esc for UP"
         @ top+down+2, left+2 PROMPT "Down Page"
      ELSE
         @ top+down-2, left+2 SAY "Esc for UP"
         @ top+down - 1, left+2 PROMPT "Down Page"
      ENDIF
   ELSE
      IF over <= 8
         @ top+down + 2, left+2 PROMPT "Down Page"
      ELSE
         @ top+down - 1, left+2 PROMPT "Down Page"
      ENDIF
   ENDIF
ENDCASE

GO starting
MENU TO option
DO CASE
CASE option = 0
   IF hit_bottom
      hit_bottom = .F.
   ENDIF
   IF screen_no > 1
      screen_no = screen_no - 1
```

```
            GO beg_set
            backward = (down - 3) * -1
            SKIP backward
         ELSE
            SELECT &ret_to.
            RETURN(0)
         ENDIF
      CASE option = down - 2
         option = 1
         GO next_set
         screen_no = screen_no + 1
      OTHERWISE
         pass_to = pointer[option]
         RESTORE SCREEN FROM backscr
         STORE SPACE(4000) TO backscr, frontscr
         SELECT &ret_to.
         RETURN(pass_to)
      ENDCASE
   ENDDO
```

Usage: Sample code is in the section entitled "Using GOT(), POP(), and MAKE_EMPTY()" at the end of the User-Defined Function section.

PRNTDATE()

Syntax: PRNTDATE(<expD>, <expN>)

Pass: <date expression>, <numeric expression>
Return: <character expression>

Description: The PRNTDATE() function converts a date to a string in a special format that is mainly used in report writing. The <expN> determines which string format will be returned:

<expN>:	Date Format:
1	February 7th, 1987
2	Saturday, the 7th of February, 1987
3	Saturday, the 7th of February
4	The 7th of February, 1987
5	Saturday, February 7, 1987
6	February 7, 1987
7	1987-02-07
other	02/07/87

Function: User-defined function.

Code:

```
**********
* Notice:  Copyright 1988, Stephen J. Straley & Associates
**********
FUNCTION Printdate

PARAMETERS in_date, date_opt

DO CASE
CASE date_opt = 1
   out_str = CMONTH(in_date) + " " + DAYWORD(in_date) + ;
             ", " + DLTRIM(STR(YEAR(in_date)))
CASE date_opt = 2
   out_str = CDOW(in_date) + ", the " + DAYWORD(in_date) +;
             " of " + CMONTH(in_date) + ", " + ;
             DLTRIM(STR(YEAR(in_date)))
CASE date_opt = 3
   out_str = CDOW(in_date) + ", the " + DAYWORD(in_date) +;
             " of " + CMONTH(in_date)
CASE date_opt = 4
   out_str = "The " + dayword(in_date) + " of " + ;
             CMONTH(in_date) + ", " + ;
             DLTRIM(STR(YEAR(in_date)))
CASE date_opt = 5
   out_str = CDOW(in_date) + ", " + CMON(in_date) + " "
   out_str = out_str + DLTRIM(STR(DAY(in_date),2)) + ;
             ", " + STR(YEAR(in_date),4)
CASE date_opt = 6
   out_str = CMONTH(in_date) + " " + ;
             DLTRIM(STR(DAY(in_date))) + ", " + ;
             DLTRIM(STR(YEAR(in_date)))
CASE date_opt = 7
   out_str = SUBSTR(DTOS(in_date),1, 4) + "-" + ;
             SUBSTR(DTOS(in_date), 5,2) + "-" + ;
             SUBSTR(DTOS(in_date),7)
OTHERWISE
   out_str = DTOC(in_date)
ENDCASE
RETURN(out_str)
```

Usage:

```
? PRINTDATE(DATE(), 1)
```

PRNTTIME()

Syntax: PRNTTIME(<expL>)

Pass: <logical expression>
Return: <character expression>

Description: The PRNTTIME() function returns the system time as a string. It converts military (24-hour) time to standard time and designates a.m.

or p.m. If <expL> is .T., the seconds are returned as well; otherwise, the string does not contain the seconds.

Function: User-defined function.

Code:

```
**********
* Notice:  Copyright 1988, Stephen J. Straley & Associates
**********
FUNCTION Prnttime

PARAMETERS with_secs

temptime = SECONDS()
hours    = INT(temptime / 3600)
minutes  = INT((temptime - hours * 3600) / 60)
secs     = INT(temptime - (hours * 3600) - (minutes * 60))

DO CASE
CASE hours = 0 .AND. minutes = 0
   comptime = "Midnight"
CASE hours = 12 .AND. minutes = 0
   comptime = "Noon"
OTHERWISE
   hours    = IF(hours > 12, hours - 12, hours)
   comptime = LTRIM(STR(hours)) + ":" + ;
              IF(minutes < 10, "0", "") + ;
              LTRIM(STR(minutes)) + " " + ;
              IF(hours > 11, "Pm", "Am")
ENDCASE
IF with_secs
   comptime = comptime + " and " + ;
              LTRIM(STR(secs)) + " seconds"
ENDIF
RETURN(comptime)
```

Usage:

```
FOR y = 1 TO 100
   CLEAR
   out_flag = IF(y/2 = INT(y/2), .T., .F.)
   @ 12,10 SAY "The current time is: " + PRNTTIME(out_flag)
   FOR x = 1 TO 200
   NEXT
NEXT
```

QWAIT()

Syntax: QWAIT()

Pass: nothing

Return: <logical expression>

Description: The QWAIT() function is similar to VERIFY() except that this one checks for the letter Q rather than the letter Y.

Function: User-defined function.

Code:

```
**********
* Notice:  Copyright 1988, Stephen J. Straley & Associates
**********
FUNCTION Qwait
   PARAMETERS qwa
   IF PCOUNT() = 0
      qwa = ""
   ENDIF
   IF TYPE ("scrpause") = "U"
      scrpause = 100
   ENDIF
   SET CONSOLE OFF
   WAIT TO intemp
   SET CONSOLE ON
   IF EMPTY (qwa)
      FOR qaz = 0 to scrpause
      NEXT
      RETURN (.T.)
   ELSE
      IF UPPER (intempt) = qwa
         FOR qaz = 0 TO scrpause
         NEXT
         RETURN (.T.)
      ELSE
         FOR qaz = 0 TO scrpause
         NEXT
         RETURN (.F.)
      ENDIF
   ENDIF
```

Usage:

```
@ 10,10 SAY "Press Any Key to Continue or Q to QUIT"
IF QWAIT
   EJECT
   RETURN
ENDIF
```

RANDOMIZE()

Syntax: RANDOMIZE(<expN>)

Pass: <numeric expression>
Return: <numeric expression>

Description: This function returns a random number based on the base number passed to it.

Code:

```
**********
* Notice:  Copyright 1988, Stephen J. Straley & Associates
**********
FUNCTION Randomize

   PARAMETERS random

   negative = (random < 0)
   IF random = 0
      RETURN(0)
   ENDIF

   random = ABS(random)
   ttx = SECONDS()/100
   ttj = (ttx - INT(ttx)) * 100
   tty = LOG(SQRT(SECONDS()/100))
   ttk = (tty - INT(tty)) * 100
   ttl = ttj * ttk
   ttz = ttl - INT(ttl)
   tts = random * ttz
   ttt = ROUND(tts, 2)
   rett = INT(ttt) + IF(INT(ttt)+1 < random+1, 1, 0)
   RETURN(rett * IF(negative, -1, 1))
```

Usage:

```
FOR x = 1 TO 10
   ? RANDOMIZE(x)
NEXT
```

REVERSE()

Syntax: REVERSE(<expC>)

Pass: <color string>
Return: <color string>

Description: This function returns a color string with reverse color parameters. It is to be used to reverse the video to display a list box. Only use it with the Summer '87 release.

Function: User-defined function.

Code:

```
**********
* Notice:  Copyright 1986, Stephen J. Straley
**********
FUNCTION Reverse

PARAMETERS the_color
```

```
the_say = STRTRAN(SUBSTR(the_color, 1, AT(",", ;
        the_color)-1), "+", "")
RETURN(SUBSTR(the_say, AT("/", the_say)+1) + "/" + ;
     SUBSTR(the_say, 1, AT("/", the_say)-1))
```

Usage:

```
SAVE SCREEN
old_color = SETCOLOR()
SETCOLOR( REVERSE( SETCOLOR() ) )
@ 10,10 CLEAR TO 20,70
@ 10,10 TO 20,70 DOUBLE
@ 23,00 SAY ""
WAIT
SETCOLOR(old_color)
RESTORE SCREEN
```

REWIND()

Syntax: REWIND(<expN>)

Pass: <file handle>
Return: Nothing.

Description: This function moves the file pointer of the file handle expressed as <expN> and places it at the beginning of the file. This function only works with the Summer '87 release.

Function: User-defined function.

Code:

```
**********
* Notice:  Copyright 1988, Stephen J. Straley & Associates
**********
FUNCTION Rewind

PARAMETERS r_handle

FSEEK(r_handle, 0)
RETURN(.T.)
```

RIGHT_JUST()

Syntax: RIGHT_JUST(<expC> [, <expN>])

Pass: <character expression> [, <numeric expression>]
Return: <numeric expression>

Description: This function takes a string expression and returns a column position that, if used, would right-justify the string to the <expN>th column position. If not used, the default value for <expN> will be 79.

Function: User-defined function.

Code:

```
**********
* Notice:  Copyright 1986, Stephen J. Straley
**********
FUNCTION Right_just

PARAMETERS right_st, right_col

IF PCOUNT() = 1
   right_col = 79
ENDIF
RETURN(IF(LEN(right_st) > right_col, right_st, ;
       right_col - LEN(right_st)))
```

Usage:

```
@ 0,0 CLEAR
@ 0,RIGHT_JUST("Release 1.0") SAY "Release 1.0"
```

ROUNDIT()

Syntax: ROUNDIT(<expN>)

Pass: <numeric expression>
Return: <numeric expression>

Description: The ROUNDIT() function was created because it is more predictable and consistent than the ROUND() function in Clipper.

Function: User-defined function.

Code:

```
**********
* Notice:  Copyright 1988, Stephen J. Straley & Associates
**********
FUNCTION Roundit

PARAMETER in_amount

in_amount = INT(in_amount * 100 + .5) / 100.00
RETURN(in_amount)
```

Usage:

```
 x = 10.756 / 11.234
answer = ROUNDIT(x)
```

SHADOW()

Syntax: SHADOW(<expN1>, <expN2>, <expN3>, <expN4>)

Pass: <top row coordinate>, <top column coordinate>, <bottom row coordinate>, <bottom column coordinate>

Return: Nothing.

Description: This function is used to display a shadow around a list box or menu area drawn by either the BOX command or the @...SAY...DOUBLE command. This function may be used only with the Summer '87 release of Clipper.

Function: User-defined function.

Code:

```
**********
* Notice:  Copyright 1988, Stephen J. Straley & Associates
**********
FUNCTION Shadow

PARAMETERS shada, shadb, shadc, shadd

shad_color = SETCOLOR()
SETCOLOR( STRTRAN( shad_color, "+", "" ) )

FOR shadx = shada+1 TO shadc+1
   @ shadx, shadd+1 SAY CHR(177)
NEXT
@ shadx-1,shadb+1 SAY REPLICATE(CHR(177), shadd-shadb)

SETCOLOR( shad_color )
RETURN(.F.)
```

Usage:

```
@ 10,10 CLEAR TO 20, 30
@ 10,10 TO 20,30 DOUBLE
SHADOW(10,10,20,30)
```

SHOW_REC()

Syntax: SHOW_REC([<expN1> [, <expN2>]])

Pass: [<row coordinate> [, <column coordinate>]]

Return: <logical expression>

Description: This function simply displays the current record number at the current screen location or the specified screen location. If the Esc key is pressed while this function is processed, a logical false (.F.) will be returned; otherwise, a logical true (.T.) will be returned.

Function: User-defined function.

Code:

```
**********
* Notice:  Copyright 1988, Stephen J. Straley & Associates
**********
FUNCTION Show_rec

PARAMETERS show_row, show_col

IF PCOUNT() = 0
   show_row = ROW()
   show_col = COL()
ELSE
   IF PCOUNT() = 1
      show_col = COL()
   ENDIF
ENDIF

@ show_row, show_col SAY RECNO() PICT "@B"
RETURN((INKEY() = 27))
```

Usage:

```
REPORT FORM Testing WHILE SHOW_REC(24,60)
DELETE ALL WHILE SHOW_REC(24,60)
```

SIN()

Syntax: SIN(<expN>, <expC>)

Pass: <numeric expression>, <character expression>

Return: <numeric expression>

Description: This function returns the sine value for the numeric expression passed to it. That expression may be either in the form of degrees or radians. To toggle for radian calculation, the value of <expC1> must be something other than "D."

Function: User-defined function.

Code:

```
**********
* Notice:  Copyright 1988, Stephen J. Straley & Associates
* Written and contributed by ESSOR MASO
*
* For the input argument in the first circle,
* degrees -360 <=arg <=360.
*
* The error ABS(e(arg)) <= 2*10^(-9).  The value 2 is returned
* if either the argument or the D or R is missing
* or the ABS(arg) > 360.
*
```

```
* Correct form: SIN(arg,'D')
*
* National Bureau of Standards Handbook of Mathematical Functions
**********

FUNCTION Sin


PARAMETERS sin_work, sin_deg

SET DECIMAL TO 10

IF ABS(IIF(UPPER(sin_deg)#'D', sin_work, sin_work * ;
   1.5707963268/90))>6.2831853072 .OR. PCOUNT()#2
   RETURN(2)
ENDIF
RETURN(COSIN(IIF(sin_deg # 'D',1.5707963268,90) - ;
       sin_work, sin_deg))
```

TANGENT()

Syntax: TANGENT(<expN>, <expC>)

Pass: <numeric expression>, <character expression>
Return: <numeric expression>

Description: This function returns the tangent value for the numeric expression passed to it. That expression may be either in the form of degrees or radians. To toggle for radian calculation, the value of <expC1> must be something other than "D."

Function: User-defined function.

Code:

```
**********
* Notice:  Copyright 1988, Stephen J. Straley & Associates
* Written and contributed by ESSOR MASO
*
* For the input argument in the first eighth of a circle,
* degrees -45 <=arg <=45
*
* The error ABS(e(arg)) <= 2*10^(-8)
* The value 2 is returned if either the argument or the
* D or R is missing
* or the ABS(arg) > 45.
*
* Correct form: TANGENT(arg,'D')
*
* National Bureau of Standards Handbook of Mathematical Functions
**********
```

```
FUNCTION Tangent

PARAMETERS tan_work, tan_deg

SET DECIMAL TO 10

PRIVATE tan_first, tan_squ, tan_sign

tan_sign = (tan_work < 0.000)

IF ABS(IIF(UPPER(tan_deg)#'D',tan_work,tan_work * ;
   1.5707963268/90))>.7853981634 .OR. PCOUNT()#2
   RETURN(2)
ENDIF

STORE IIF(UPPER(tan_deg)#'D',ABS(tan_work),ABS(tan_work) *;
      1.5707963268/90) TO tan_first
STORE VAL(STR(tan_first*tan_first,12,10)) TO tan_work,tan_squ
tan_work = .0029005250 + .0095168091 * tan_squ
tan_work = .0245650893 + tan_work * tan_squ
tan_work = .0533740603 + tan_work * tan_squ
tan_work = .1333923995 + tan_work * tan_squ
tan_work = .3333314036 + tan_work * tan_squ
tan_work = 1 + tan_work * tan_squ
tan_work = ROUNDTHEM(tan_first*tan_work,8)
RETURN(IIF(tan_sign, -tan_work, tan_work))

********************

FUNCTION Roundthem

PARAMETERS the_numb, no_places

SET DECIMAL TO no_places

RETURN(IIF(the_numb < 0, INT(the_numb *;
        10^no_places-.5),INT(the_numb*;
        10^no_places+.5))/10^no_places)
```

TRY2OPEN()

Syntax: TRY2OPEN(<expC>, @<expN>)

Pass: <file name>, @<numeric expression>

Return: <logical expression>

Description: This function tries to open the specified file and if it is successful, not only will the function return a logical true (.T.), but the file handle will be returned via <expN>, which has to be passed by reference. If there is an error when trying to open the file, the function will return a logical false. This function will only work with the Summer '87 release.

Function: User-defined function.

Code:

```
**********
* Notice:  Copyright 1988, Stephen J. Straley & Associates
**********
FUNCTION Try2open

PARAMETERS i_o_file, i_o_handle

* i_o_handle is passed by REFERENCE!!
IF EMPTY(i_o_file)
    RETURN(.F.)
ENDIF
i_o_handle = FOPEN(i_o_file)
RETURN( ( FERROR() = 0 ) )
```

UPPERLOWER()

Syntax: UPPERLOWER(<expC>)

Pass: <character expression>
Return: <character expression>

Description: The UPPERLOWER() function reformats any character string with the first character capitalized and the rest lowercase.

Function: User-defined function.

Code:

```
**********
* Notice:  Copyright 1988, Stephen J. Straley & Associates
**********
FUNCTION Upperlower

PARAMETERS a

front = SUBSTR(a,1,1)
back  = SUBSTR(a,2)

RETURN(UPPER(front)+LOWER(back))
```

Usage:

```
@ 10,10 SAY UPPERLOWER("mr. ") + UPPERLOWER("SMITH")
```

VERIFY()

Syntax: VERIFY([<expC> [, <expL>]])

Pass: [<character expression> [, <logical expression>]]
Return: <logical expression>

Description: The VERIFY() function is used for checking the console for either a "Yy" or a "Nn" response to a question. If any other four characters are to be tested, those characters are passed as <expC>. If the display is to remain on the screen until another key is pressed, <expL> should be set to a logical true (.T.). The default value is a logical false.

Function: User-defined function.

Code:

```
**********
* Notice:  Copyright 1988, Stephen J. Straley & Associates
**********
FUNCTION Verify

PARAMETERS comp, extra_key

DO CASE
   CASE PCOUNT() = 0
      comp = "YyNn"
      extra_key = .F.
   CASE PCOUNT() = 1
      extra_key = .F.
ENDCASE

IF TYPE("scrpause") = "U"
   scrpause = 100
ENDIF
DO WHILE .T.
   the_var = ""
   inside = INKEY(0)
   DO CASE
   CASE inside = 4
      the_var = "Y"
   CASE inside = 19
      the_var = "N"
   OTHERWISE
      the_var = CHR(inside)
   ENDCASE
   IF the_var$comp
      EXIT
   ENDIF
ENDDO
IF the_var$SUBSTR(comp,1,2)
```

```
            ?? "Yes"
            IF extra_key
               INKEY(0)
            ELSE
               FOR qaz = 1 TO scrpause
               NEXT
            ENDIF
            RETURN(.T.)
         ELSE
            ?? "No "
            IF extra_key
               INKEY(0)
            ELSE
               FOR qaz = 1 TO scrpause
               NEXT
            ENDIF
            RETURN(.F.)
         ENDIF
```

Usage:

```
@ 10,10 SAY DATE()
@ 13,10 SAY "Is this the correct date? (Y/N) "
IF VERIFY()
   DO Rest_of_prog
ELSE
   DO Change_Date
ENDIF
```

USING GOT(), POP(), and MAKE_EMPTY()

Below is a program that will generate two databases, fill one database with valid choices, and leave the other empty. Then a data entry screen will appear. If you enter either an invalid code or a "?" in the CODE field, a pop-up menu will appear to the right with all of the valid choices for that field, based on the CODE.DBF previously established. The GOT() function assigns the GET variable the value of the field in the CODE.DBF file based on the RECNO() that was passed back from the POP() function. The POP() function displays the pop-up menu in the bordered area and allows direct cursor control through the CODES.DBF over the desired fields. The MAKE_EMPTY() function makes an EMPTY() GET variable if the user should escape completely out of the pop-up menu.

```
*********************
* Name          GOT_POP.prg
* Date          March 25, 1988
* Notice        Copyright 1988, Stephen J. Straley & Associates
* Compile       Clipper Got_pop
* Release       Autumn '86 or later
* Link          Autumn '86: Plink86 fi got_pop lib dbu lib clipper
*               Summer '87: Plink86 fi got_pop lib extend lib clipper
* Note          This program demonstrates the use of the user-defined functions
*               POP(), GOT(), MAKE_EMPTY(), and FILL_OUT().
*********************
```

```
* Creating Dummy Information

CREATE Template
USE Template
APPEND BLANK
REPLACE field_name WITH "CODES", field_type WITH "C", field_len WITH 5
APPEND BLANK
REPLACE field_name WITH "STATE", field_type WITH "C", field_len WITH 2
USE
CREATE Codes FROM Template
USE Codes
APPEND BLANK
REPLACE codes WITH "90350", state WITH "CA"
APPEND BLANK
REPLACE codes WITH "06854", state WITH "CT"
APPEND BLANK
REPLACE codes WITH "10017", state WITH "NY"
APPEND BLANK
REPLACE codes WITH "40047", state WITH "GA"
APPEND BLANK
REPLACE codes WITH "10376", state WITH "NJ"
APPEND BLANK
REPLACE codes WITH "98765", state WITH "OE"
USE
CREATE Template
USE Template
APPEND BLANK
REPLACE field_name WITH "CCODES", field_type WITH "C", field_len WITH 5
APPEND BLANK
REPLACE field_name WITH "CSTATE", field_type WITH "C", field_len WITH 2
APPEND BLANK
REPLACE field_name WITH "CNAME", field_type WITH "C", field_len WITH 10
USE
CREATE Client FROM Template
USE
ERASE Template.dbf
USE Client

* A Dummy Data Entry Screen

DO WHILE .T.
   CLEAR
   temp_code = SPACE(5)
   temp_state = SPACE(2)
   @ 5,5 SAY "        Enter State Zip Code => " GET temp_code PICT "XXXXX"
VALID(GOOD_STATE(temp_code))
   @ 7,5 SAY "      Press Esc to Escape"
   READ
   IF LASTKEY() = 27 .OR. EMPTY(temp_code)
      EXIT
   ENDIF
   SELECT 1
   APPEND BLANK
```

```
   REPLACE ccodes WITH temp_code, cstate WITH temp_state
   CLEAR
   @ 5,5 SAY "            State Zip Code => " GET ccodes
   CLEAR GETS
   @ 7,5 SAY "                State Code => " GET cstate PICT "!!"
   @ 9,5 SAY "               Client Name => " GET cname PICT "@X"
   READ
ENDDO

********************

FUNCTION Good_state

PARAMETER in_temp

IF EMPTY(in_temp) .AND. LASTKEY() = 27
   RETURN(.T.)
ENDIF
SAVE SCREEN
SELECT 2
USE Codes
LOCATE FOR codes = in_temp
IF FOUND()
   @ 7, 40 SAY "                         "
   temp_code = codes
   temp_state = state
   RETURN(.T.)
ELSE
   @ 7, 40 SAY "Move Cursor keys for Codes"
   a_file = "CODES.DBF"
   temp_code = GOT(a_file, 1, POP( 9, 45, 10, 9, a_file, 1))
   IF !EMPTY(temp_code)
      KEYBOARD CHR(13)
   ELSE
      RESTORE SCREEN
   ENDIF
   RETURN(.F.)
ENDIF

********************

FUNCTION Got

   PARAMETERS file, field_no, record

   ret_area = STR(SELECT())

   IF LEN(file) = 1
      SELECT &file.
   ELSE
      SELECT 0
      USE &file
   ENDIF
```

```
   IF field_no > FCOUNT()
      RETURN("")
   ENDIF

   IF record = 0 .OR. LASTREC() = 0
      GO TOP
      in_betw = FIELDNAME(field_no)
      give_it = &in_betw
      SELECT &ret_area.
      RETURN(MAKE_EMPTY(give_it))
   ELSE
      GO record
   ENDIF
   in_betw = FIELDNAME(field_no)
   output = &in_betw
   SELECT &ret_area.
   RETURN(output)

********************

FUNCTION Make_empty

   PARAMETERS in_field, in_name

   IF PCOUNT() = 1
      in_name = ""
   ENDIF

   DO CASE
      CASE TYPE("in_field") = "C"
         RETURN(SPACE(LEN(in_field)))
      CASE TYPE("in_field") = "N"
         RETURN(VAL(STR(in_field)))
      CASE TYPE("in_field") = "D"
        RETURN(CTOD("  /  /  "))
      OTHERWISE
         RETURN(.F.)
   ENDCASE

********************

FUNCTION Pop

PARAMETERS top, left, down, over, file, field_no, filt

    PARAMETERS top, left, down, over, file, field_no, filt

    ret_area = STR(SELECT())
    DECLARE pointer[down]
    STORE SPACE(4000) TO backscr, frontscr
    SAVE SCREEN TO backscr
    scrframe = CHR(201) + CHR(205) + CHR(187) + CHR(186) + ;
               CHR(188) + CHR(205) + CHR(200) + CHR(186) + CHR(32)
       @ top, left, top+down, left+over BOX scrframe
    SAVE SCREEN TO frontscr
```

```
   IF LEN(file) = 1
      SELECT &file.
   ELSE
      SELECT 8
      USE &file.
   ENDIF

   IF LASTREC() = 0
      SELECT &ret_area.
      SET KEY 18 TO
      SET KEY  3 TO
      RETURN(0)
   ENDIF
 IF TYPE("filt") = "U"
   SET FILTER TO
ELSE
   SET FILTER TO &filt
ENDIF
GO TOP
hit_bottom = .T.
starting = RECNO()
option = 1
screen_no = 1
DO WHILE .T.
   RESTORE SCREEN FROM frontscr
   beg_set = RECNO()
   FOR x = 1 TO down - 3
      pointer[x] = RECNO()
      inbetw = FIELDNAME(field_no)
      showit = &inbetw
      IF LEN(showit) >= over-2
         showit = SUBSTR(showit, 1, over-3)
      ENDIF
      @ top+x, left+1 PROMPT " " + FILL_OUT(showit,over-2)
      SKIP
      IF EOF()
         hit_bottom = .T.
         x = down - 2
      ENDIF
   NEXT
   next_set = RECNO()
   DO CASE
   CASE EOF()                         && Last Screen Full
      IF screen_no > 1                && Not the first screen
         IF over <= 8
            top+down+1, left+2 SAY "Esc for UP"
         ELSE
            @ top+down-2, left+2 SAY "Esc for UP"
         ENDIF
      ENDIF
   OTHERWISE                           && Somewhere else
      IF screen_no  > 1                && Not the first screen
         IF over <= 8
            @ top+down+1, left+2 SAY "Esc for UP"
            @ top+down+2, left+2 PROMPT "Down Page"
         ELSE
```

```
            @ top+down-2, left+2 SAY "Esc for UP"
            @ top+down - 1, left+2 PROMPT "Down Page"
         ENDIF
      ELSE
         IF over <= 8
            @ top+down + 2, left+2 PROMPT "Down Page"
         ELSE
            @ top+down - 1, left+2 PROMPT "Down Page"
         ENDIF
      ENDIF
   ENDCASE

   GO starting
   MENU TO option
   DO CASE
   CASE option = 0
      IF hit_bottom
         hit_bottom = .F.
      ENDIF
      IF screen_no > 1
         screen_no = screen_no - 1
         GO beg_set
         backward = (down - 3) * -1
         SKIP backward
      ELSE
         SELECT &ret_to.
         RETURN(0)
      ENDIF
   CASE option = down - 2
      option = 1
      GO next_set
      screen_no = screen_no + 1
   OTHERWISE
      pass_to = pointer[option]
      RESTORE SCREEN FROM backscr
      STORE SPACE(4000) TO backscr, frontscr
      SELECT &ret_to.
      RETURN(pass_to)
   ENDCASE
ENDDO

********************

FUNCTION Fill_out

PARAMETERS a, b

IF TYPE("b") = "U"
   b = 79
ENDIF
c = b - LEN(a)
RETURN(a + SPACE(c))
* End of File
```

CHAPTER FIFTEEN

Clipper's HELP Utility

A BRIEF SYNOPSIS OF HELP

The compiler contains a way to build a tool that's useful both for developers and their customers of applications compiled with Clipper: *on-line help.*

No matter how much time and energy is spent in designing the ultimate user-friendly system, no matter how many error trapping routines are provided, regardless of how clear, helpful, and extensive the documentation may be, end users usually fit one or more of the following descriptions:

1. They always get confused, bewildered, lost, and frustrated.

2. They always manage to break a system regardless how hard you have tried to prevent this from happening.

3. They never read the documentation.

The entire purpose of on-line HELP is to provide a means by which the developer may provide assistance to the program user even if the documentation never gets read. A developer should know that **no matter** how clear the program, how extensive the manual, or how involved the training, that cry for HELP eventually arrives. Context-sensitive on-line HELP doesn't always prevent this from occurring, but it doesn't hurt.

The idea behind the HELP scheme in Clipper is that you can build a structured CASE statement that tests for the program name, variable name, and line number when the F1 key is struck. If help is needed on a variable or field, the user can press F1 and get specific information on that element. Thus, at every question, field input, and menu item displayed, the user can be guided through the system by the system. Of course, all of this is only possible if you have built a file called HELP.PRG.

HELP.PRG

Clipper has a default that looks for a procedure marked HELP whenever the F1 Key is pressed. If no file is present in the executable file, nothing will happen. Therefore, the first thing to do is to create a file named HELP.PRG.

Because this file is not directly referenced by any other programs, it must be compiled separately. If you do not compile this file separately, Clipper will not see it when F1 is pressed and your HELP scheme will not work. Once compiled, HELP.PRG must be linked into your application as a separate object file: if you neglect this step, no help will be available. Finally, don't compile any program with the **-l** option. If no line numbers are generated with the object files, HELP will not have anything to use for the second parameter it needs (as described in the following section).

The basic construct of the file is one massive DO CASE...ENDDO structure where each branch of the CASE is a separate test and may then branch for further testing.

P, L, V - MORE THAN JUST THREE LETTERS

The HELP procedure needs to have a PARAMETER command as the very first command line. Three parameters are automatically passed to HELP, regardless of the type of HELP designed. These three parameters are:

1. P = program or procedure name of the routine calling HELP; this is of character type.

2. L = the line number of the source code line number calling HELP; this is of numeric type. It is the line number of the READ command associated with the corresponding GET command.

3. V = variable name in the routine calling HELP; this is of character type.

Remember that these three variables need not be initialized in any routine or declared PUBLIC in order to function. They are PRIVATE variables germane only to the HELP file and are released upon RETURN from HELP. In addition, these three variables are not restricted to these names: P, L, and V are used for clarity and simplicity within this document. Follow basic coding techniques when choosing a name appropriate for you.

With the Summer '87 release, these three parameters need not be passed. The internal stack of Clipper will not be corrupted if you choose not to pass these three parameters. In previous versions, these three parameters **must** be passed to HELP, but they do not have to be evaluated or tested within the program. Obviously, the more specific the HELP generated, the more extensive the evaluation on these variables has to be. Keep in mind that if you do *not* accept any parameters in HELP.PRG (or any SET KEY TO procedure), those values otherwise available may not be evaluated.

GLOBAL POINTER VARIABLES

HELP is just another procedure, except it is called by a key rather than a specific command in the program. All variables initialized prior to the HELP routine can be accessed by it. Many times, a global variable is immediately initialized to an empty value. This value will be accessed at some time by the HELP procedure. These global variables can be used to help direct or control the information displayed by the HELP procedure far better than just the variables P, L, and V.

Generalized HELP is based on the idea that one variable used in different programs can refer to the same piece of helpful information. If this is true in your application, a more generalized HELP is in order rather than a context-sensitive one. This method of HELP is treated further in the section entitled "Generalized Help"; however, the basic technique is to use global variables only when the three variables passed to the HELP procedure are not adequate or are too cumbersome to use effectively. Just make sure that the variables accessed by the HELP procedure have been established previously. Otherwise, an undefined symbol message will appear at run-time.

TOPIC-ORIENTED HELP

A concept introduced with the Steve Straley Toolkit and the Summer '87 release, the idea of topic-oriented HELP is to use the PROMPT command inside of the HELP.PRG, allowing the user to choose a general category of HELP. From this choice, additional information may be displayed. Using this in conjunction with saving text and arrays to disk, it is now possible to save your entire user documentation and make it available via the HELP.PRG. Consider each chapter in a table of contents as a choice on the PROMPT menu, from which the actual chapter contents are displayed.

HELP INSIDE OF HELP

Basic to the concept of the HELP feature is the idea that the user is free to use the HELP procedure at any time. But what happens if the user should press the F1 key while inside the HELP procedure? The system may be able to keep track of things on one or two levels with only a minor glitch on the screen; however, system integrity is jeopardized. Anything past one or two levels is taking an unwarranted risk. More than likely, the application will generate an error, such as a System Memory Error. The developer must prevent this from happening. There are two ways to accomplish this task.

First, you can test to see if the calling program's name is HELP; if it is, simply go back to the calling program, which in this case is HELP. To do this, insert these three lines of code immediately after the PARAMETER statement:

```
IF p = "HELP"
   RETURN
ENDIF
```

The other method is to simply deactivate the F1 key. Immediately after the PARAMETER command, type this command:

```
SET KEY 28 TO
```

This follows the SET KEY TO command syntax and turns off the F1 key. When the execution of the program is returned to the original calling procedure, remember to turn on the HELP facility with the following command:

```
SET KEY 28 TO Help
```

HELP NEEDING HELP

If you decide that you need some additional help for HELP, a minor modification is needed to the SET KEY TO solution. Simply redirect the F1 key to another procedure (e.g., let's say HELPHELP) that could be a HELP procedure for the HELP procedure. To do this, issue the following command immediately after the PARAMETER command in the first HELP procedure:

```
SET KEY 28 TO Helphelp
```

All of the same rules will apply to HELPHELP. At this point, it may be a good idea to turn off the F1 key to keep from going any further. Keep track of the current level of the application and SET the F1 key accordingly. If this step is not taken, at some point in the application HELP may be turned off unexpectedly.

MEMOEDIT() AND HELP

The MEMOEDIT() function is a convenient feature to use in conjunction with the HELP procedure. MEMOEDIT() allows quick windowing techniques for displaying text information. However, the F1 key **must** be turned **off** prior to the use of the MEMOEDIT() function. If it is not, the user could edit the HELP information while inside the HELP routine. Once the MEMOEDIT() function has returned its value, the F1 key may be reinstated. With the new Summer '87 release of Clipper, the F1 key may be evaluated within the MEMOEDIT() function. This is accomplished with the new user-defined function option passed as a parameter to MEMOEDIT(). To see an example of this capability, please see the Chapter 8, Memo Fields. One other new concept with this release of Clipper is the ability to store ASCII text in a file and simply read it in via the MEMOREAD() function. HELP can then be created external to the program and without any special file format. The idea here is to simply type in with your text editor the text you want to display to the screen when HELP is called upon. Use the MEMOREAD() function to read in the text, followed by the MEMOEDIT() function to display it and to restrict certain key values. Again, for additional information on how this should be coded, please see Chapter 8, Memo Fields.

HELP TEXT: IN THE PROGRAM OR A FILE?

As you will see in the sample code later on in this section, the text information for HELP can reside either in the program or in a file on the disk. Each method has an advantage and a disadvantage. If you design HELP to reside in the program itself, you need to keep a close watch on the amount of memory required by the application without HELP. If the application is small enough, the HELP information can be coded in and compiled with the rest of the application. The advantage of this method is in execution speed. Since the HELP information is resident in memory with everything else, access to the information is virtually instantaneous.

If memory space is a problem, the text for on-line HELP should be in a database file on the disk. This saves memory and compiling time; however, access time to the specific information increases dramatically. Review your application without HELP and consider the environment in which it will be running before deciding which of the two methods is best for your application.

HELP IN AN OVERLAY

HELP is needed at all times. Regardless of the procedure that is being used, the user will eventually look for HELP. It is possible to place the HELP object file in a separate overlay section to be loaded into the system whenever it is called. The problem with this is that there is sure to be more than one overlay area. Since the rules of overlaying dictate that no section in an overlay can call any other section in that same overlay, this can cause major problems. In most situations, the programmer decides which files belong where. However, since the developer cannot foresee when the HELP utility will be used, this file must be accessible to all procedures at all times. If the HELP procedure is called by another section within the same overlay, an EXEC SEQUENCE ERROR is sure to follow. For this reason alone, HELP should never be placed in an overlay section.

Always avoid placing the HELP file anywhere but in the main load module.

THE CLEAR COMMAND IN HELP

Never use the CLEAR command by itself to clear the screen when using the HELP facility, whether it is context-sensitive or general HELP. When you use CLEAR, all GETS are also cleared, which means that when the HELP returns control to the calling program, your application goes past the variable you were inquiring about. This may disrupt an application's entire execution scheme. This is true for **any** procedure called by the SET KEY <expN> TO <procedure>, since the calling of HELP is no more than a SET KEY 28 TO Help. To circumvent this, instead of using CLEAR by itself, add an appropriate @ SAY command such as:

```
@ 0,0 CLEAR
```

This clears the entire screen and positions the cursor to the top-left corner of the screen, but it does **not** clear the GETS in the system. An additional clause was added to the CLEAR command in the Summer '87 release. If you are using this version of the compiler, use the follow command syntax to clear the screen within your HELP system:

```
CLEAR SCREEN
```

This is equivalent to the @ 0,0 CLEAR command.

SAVE SCREEN IN HELP

In order to take full advantage of the HELP system, use the SAVE SCREEN command to save the screen prior to displaying any HELP information. Then, once the information is displayed, RESTORE the SCREEN to its original display and continue with the execution of the program. The SAVE SCREEN command should be the first command prior to any structured DO CASE...ENDCASE statements or IF...ENDIF command other than the IF...ENDIF command that tests for the HELP procedure.

CONSTRUCTING CONTEXT-SENSITIVE HELP

Context-specific HELP provides information on specific variables and fields throughout your application. Operational flow may be described best in a manual, but specific HELP on variables and user input is handled best by on-line HELP.

In using this technique, it is advisable to develop the application first and then use these lines of code:

```
PROCEDURE Help

PARAMETERS p, l, v

SET KEY 28 TO
SAVE SCREEN
@ 10,10 SAY "The calling program is:  "
?? p
@ 12,10 SAY "The source code line is: "
?? l
@ 14,10 SAY "The variable is:         "
?? v
?
?
?
WAIT
SET KEY 28 TO Help
RESTORE SCREEN
```

Then, at every variable for which you want to write specific HELP, just press the F1 key and jot down the three values displayed on the screen. Once you have all of the values you need, construct the DO CASE...ENDCASE command as follows:

1. Group all of the P values together and build the initial level of DO CASE...ENDCASE. Establish an OTHERWISE statement to display a message informing the user that "No Help Is Available."

2. Group all of the V values together and build a secondary, nested DO CASE...ENDCASE structure. Establish an OTHERWISE statement to display a message informing the user that "No Help Is Available."

3. Only if absolutely necessary (normally this occurs with memory variables in the main application rather than fields) group the L values together and test them. If applicable, build a third nested DO CASE...END-CASE structure or an IF...ENDIF structure. Additionally establish an OTHERWISE or ELSE statement to display a message informing the user that "No Help Is Available."

The following sample code demonstrates these principles:

```
*********************
* Name          SHOWHELP.prg
* Date          March 15, 1988
* Notice        Copyright 1988, Stephen J. Straley & Associates
* Compile       Clipper Showhelp -m
* Release       Autumn '86 or later
* Link          Plink86 fi showhelp lib clipper
* Note          This program shows how context-sensitive HELP works,
*               how a database pertaining to HELP works, and how
*               to create your own HELP "on-the-fly."
*********************

CLEAR
TEXT

   A series of screens and variables will appear, as well as a menu
   choice.  Choose a menu option, build a HELP screen for each level,
   and note the coding techniques involved.

   Please press any key to begin demonstration ...
ENDTEXT
INKEY(0)
DO WHILE .T.
   CLEAR
   option1 = 0
   @ 4, 8 TO 12, 72 DOUBLE
   @ 3, 29 SAY "Legal Billing Main Menu"
   @ 6, 10 PROMPT " 1>  Client Information "
   @ 8, 14 PROMPT " 2>  Matter Information "
```

```
   @ 6, 48 PROMPT " 3>  Codes "
   @ 8, 48 PROMPT " 4>  Reports "
   @ 10, 31 SAY "ESC to Exit Program"
   MENU TO option1
   IF option1 = 0
      QUIT
   ELSE
      off = TRANSFORM(option1, "9")
      DO Branch&off.
   ENDIF
ENDDO

********************

PROCEDURE Branch1

   CLEAR
   STORE 1 TO this, that
   @ 10, 0 SAY "Enter in ages or F1 => " GET this
   @ 11, 0 SAY "                       " GET that
   READ

********************

PROCEDURE Branch2

   CLEAR
   @ 10,10 SAY "A new procedure for the same variable"
   @ 12,10 SAY "                 Enter a new value => " GET option1
   READ

********************

PROCEDURE Branch3

   CLEAR
   @ 10,10 SAY "Press any key to go to Branch2 "
   INKEY(0)
   DO Branch2

********************

PROCEDURE Branch4

   CLEAR
   STORE .T. TO yes
   @ 10,10 SAY  "This option should yield 'No Help Available' .. " GET yes
   READ

********************

PROCEDURE Help

   PARAMETERS p,l,v
```

```
SET KEY 28 TO
SAVE SCREEN
IF v = "YES"
   @ 00,10 CLEAR TO 03,70
   @ 00,10 TO 03,70 DOUBLE
   @ 01,15 SAY "There is no help available!  Any Key to continue..."
   INKEY(0)
   RESTORE SCREEN
   RETURN
ENDIF
SET SCOREBOARD OFF
IF .NOT. FILE("HELP.DBF")
   @ 00,10 CLEAR TO 03,70
   @ 00,10 TO 03,70 DOUBLE
   @ 01,11 SAY "There is no HELP file available.    Would you like a help "
   @ 02,11 SAY "              file to be generated? "
   IF !VERIFY()
      RESTORE SCREEN
      SET KEY 28 TO Help
      RETURN
    ENDIF
    DO Dohelp
 ENDIF
 SELECT 9
 USE Help INDEX Help
 search = SUBSTR(p,1,10) + SUBSTR(v,1,10) + TRANSFORM(l, "9999")
 SEEK search
 IF FOUND()
    @ top,left TO bottom,right DOUBLE
    IF "" = MEMOEDIT(helpscr,top+1,left+1,bottom-1,right-1,.F.)
    ENDIF
    * With the Summer '87 Clipper, the above command should read like this:
    * MEMOEDIT(helpscr, top+1, left+1, bottom-1, right-1, .F., .F.)
    @ bottom-1,left+1 SAY "Any Key to Continue..."
 ELSE
    @ 00,10 CLEAR TO 03,70
    @ 00,10 TO 03,70 DOUBLE
    @ 01,11 SAY "There is no HELP for this section.  Would you like to make"
    @ 02,11 SAY "              a HELP screen for this? "
    IF !VERIFY()
       RESTORE SCREEN
       SET KEY 28 TO Help
       RETURN
    ENDIF
    APPEND BLANK
    REPLACE lookit WITH SUBSTR(p,1,10) + SUBSTR(v,1,10) +;
            TRANSFORM(l,"9999")
    STORE SPACE(4000) TO in_help, full_scr
    SAVE SCREEN TO full_scr
    * In the Summer '87 release of Clipper,
    * the _scrsave, _scrrest, and _cclr had
    * an extra underscorse placed in front
    * of there symbol calls because Clipper
```

```
* was compiled in Microsoft C 5.0.  In
* previous versions, "CALL _scrsave WITH full_scr"
* is now "CALL __scrsave with full_scr"
*
STORE 0 TO temp_top, temp_left, temp_bot, temp_right
DO WHILE .T.
   RESTORE SCEEN FROM full_scr
   @ 00,10 CLEAR TO 03,70
   @ 00,10 TO 03,70 DOUBLE
   @ 01,20 SAY "Position cursor with arrow for TOP, LEFT corner."
   cursor = 0
   newcur = CHR(201)
   SAVE SCREEN TO in_help
   @ 12,40 SAY newcur
   trow = 12
   tcol = 40
   DO WHILE.T.
      cursor = INKEY(0)
      DO CASE
      CASE cursor = 5
         IF trow - 1 > 0
            trow = trow - 1
         ENDIF
      CASE cursor = 4
         IF tcol + 1 < 79
            tcol = tcol + 1
         ENDIF
      CASE cursor = 19
         IF tcol - 1 > 0
            tcol = tcol - 1
         ENDIF
      CASE cursor = 24
         IF trow + 1 < 24
            trow = trow + 1
         ENDIF
      CASE cursor = 13 .OR. cursor = 27
         EXIT
      ENDCASE
      RESTORE SCREEN FROM in_help
      @ trow, tcol SAY newcur
   ENDDO
   STORE trow TO temp_top
   STORE tcol TO temp_left
   @ 00,10 CLEAR TO 03,70
   @ 00,10 TO 03,70 DOUBLE
   @ 01,14 SAY "Position cursor with arrow for BOTTOM, RIGHT corner."
   cursor = 0
   SAVE SCREEN TO in_help
   newcur = CHR(188)
   trow = temp_top + 2
   tcol = temp_left + 5
   @ trow, tcol SAY newcur
   DO WHILE.T.
```

```
        cursor = INKEY(0)
        DO CASE
        CASE cursor = 5
           IF trow - 1 > temp_top
              trow = trow - 1
           ENDIF
        CASE cursor = 4
           IF tcol + 1 < 79
              tcol = tcol + 1
           ENDIF
        CASE cursor = 19
           IF tcol - 1 > temp_left + 3
              tcol = tcol - 1
           ENDIF
        CASE cursor = 24
           IF trow + 1 < 24
              trow = trow + 1
           ENDIF
        CASE cursor = 13 .OR. cursor = 27
           EXIT
        ENDCASE
        RESTORE SCREEN WITH in_help
        @ trow, tcol SAY newcur
     ENDDO
     STORE trow TO temp_bot
     STORE tcol TO temp_right
     SAVE SCREEN TO in_help
     DO Temphelp
     @ 00,10 CLEAR TO 03,70
     @ 00,10 TO 03,70 DOUBLE
     @ 02,25 SAY "Is this what you wanted?  "
     IF !VERIFY()
        RESTORE SCREEN FROM in_help
        LOOP
     ELSE
        @ 00,10 CLEAR TO 03,70
        @ 00,10 TO 03,70 DOUBLE
        @ 01,20 SAY "      Ctrl-W to SAVE / Ctrl-Q to Abandon"
     ENDIF
     REPLACE top WITH temp_top, bottom WITH temp_bot, left WITH temp_left,;
     right WITH temp_right
     EXIT
  ENDDO
  DO WHILE .T.
     @ top,left CLEAR TO bottom,right
     @ top,left TO bottom, right DOUBLE
     REPLACE helpscr WITH MEMOEDIT(helpscr,top+1,left+1,bottom-1,right-1,.T.)
     @ top,left,bottom,right BOX scrframe
     IF "" = MEMOEDIT(helpscr,top+1,left+1,bottom-1,right-1,.F.)
     * For the Summer '87 release of Clipper, this function should read:
     * MEMOEDIT(helpscr,top+1,left+1,bottom-1,right-1,.F.,.F.)
     ENDIF
     @ bottom-1,left+1 SAY "IS THIS CORRECT?   "
```

```
            IF !VERIFY()
               LOOP
            ENDIF
            EXIT
         ENDDO
         @ bottom-1,left+1 SAY "Press Any key to Continue...."
      ENDIF
      INKEY(0)
      RESTORE SCREEN
      SET KEY 28 TO Help
      RETURN

*********************

PROCEDURE Dohelp

   PARAMETER p1, l1, v1

   SELECT 9
   CREATE Temp
   USE Temp
   APPEND BLANK
   REPLACE field_name WITH "LOOKIT", field_type WITH "C", field_len WITH 24
   APPEND BLANK
   REPLACE field_name WITH "TOP", field_type WITH "N", field_len WITH 2
   APPEND BLANK
   REPLACE field_name WITH "LEFT", field_type WITH "N", field_len WITH 2
   APPEND BLANK
   REPLACE field_name WITH "BOTTOM", field_type WITH "N", field_len WITH 2
   APPEND BLANK
   REPLACE field_name WITH "RIGHT", field_type WITH "N", field_len WITH 2
   APPEND BLANK
   REPLACE field_name WITH "HELPSCR", field_type WITH "M", field_len WITH 10
   USE
   CREATE Help FROM Temp
   ERASE Temp
   USE Help
   INDEX ON lookit TO Help

*********************

PROCEDURE Temphelp

   SET COLOR TO W*
   @ temp_top, temp_left, temp_bot, temp_right BOX SUBSTR(scrframe,1,8)
   SET COLOR TO 7

*********************

FUNCTION Verify

   SET CONSOLE OFF
   STORE "" TO inertemp
```

```
   DO WHILE .NOT. inertemp$"YyNn"
      WAIT TO inertemp
   ENDDO
   SET CONSOLE ON
   IF UPPER(inertemp) = "Y"
      ?? "Yes"
      te = INKEY(.25)
      RETURN(.T.)
   ENDIF
   ?? "No "
   te = INKEY(.25)
   RETURN(.F.)
* End of File
```

SAMPLE OF CONTEXT-SENSITIVE HELP

The following program demonstrates one way to design a HELP scheme that is specific to the calling program's name, the variable name, and the line number. Note that this information is kept in the program file, increasing its overall size.

```
********************
* Name          DOMENU1.prg
* Date          March 15, 1988
* Notice        Copyright 1988, Stephen J. Straley & Associates
* Compile       Clipper Domenu1
* Release       Autumn '86 release or later
* Link          Plink86 fi domenu1 lib clipper
* Note          This program demonstrates how context-specific
*               HELP can be implemented.
********************

CLEAR
DO Domen1

********************

PROCEDURE Domen1

   DO WHILE .T.
      CLEAR
   scrframe =  CHR(201) + CHR(205) + CHR(187) + CHR(186) + ;
               CHR(188) + CHR(205) + CHR(200) + CHR(186) + CHR(32)
      STORE SPACE(4000) TO ascreen, bscreen, cscreen
      STORE 0 TO option
      @ 6, 1, 17, 75 BOX SUBSTR(scrframe,1,8)
      @ 5, 30 SAY "M A I N    M E N U"
      @ 8, 7 PROMPT " 1> Chart of Accounts "
      @ 10, 7 PROMPT " 2> Transactions "
      @ 12, 7 PROMPT " 3> Posting / Balancing "
      @ 14, 7 PROMPT " 4> Print Listings "
      @ 8, 48 PROMPT " 5> Print Reports "
      @ 10, 48 PROMPT " 6> Transfers "
```

```
      @ 12, 48 PROMPT " 7> Utilities "
      @ 14, 48 PROMPT " 8> End of Period "
      @ 16, 33 SAY "ESC to RETURN"
      MENU TO option
      SAVE SCREEN TO ascreen
      DO CASE
      CASE option = 0
         @ 18, 15 SAY "All Files Closed, Returning to Operating System"
         QUIT
      CASE option = 1
         DO Domen11
      OTHERWISE
         **************************
         * Do subprocedure here. *
         **************************
      ENDCASE
   ENDDO

*********************

PROCEDURE Domen11

   DO WHILE .T.
      IF !EMPTY(bscreen)
         RESTORE SCREEN FROM bscreen
      ENDIF
      STORE 0 TO option1
      @ 9, 39, 22, 64 BOX scrframe
      @ 10, 46 SAY "COA Sub-Menu"
      @ 12, 43 PROMPT " 1> Enter Account "
      @ 14, 43 PROMPT " 2> Edit Account "
      @ 16, 43 PROMPT " 3> Scan Accounts "
      @ 18, 43 PROMPT " 4> Delete Accounts "
      @ 21, 46 SAY "ESC to RETURN"
      MENU TO option1
      SAVE SCREEN TO bscreen
      DO CASE
      CASE option1 = 0
         EXIT
      CASE option1 = 1
         STORE SPACE(10) TO in_name, in_descpt
         STORE 0 TO in_bal, in_accnt
         @ 14,5,20,75 BOX scrframe
         @ 16,10 SAY "Enter Account Number: " GET in_accnt PICT "#####.##"
         @ 18,10 SAY "        Account Name: " GET in_name PICT "@X" ;
                 VALID(!EMPTY(in_name))
         @ 16,46 SAY "    Balance: $" GET in_bal PICT "###,###,###.##"
         @ 18,46 SAY "Description: " GET in_descpt
         READ
      OTHERWISE
         **************************
         * Do subprocedure here. *
         **************************
      ENDCASE
   ENDDO
```

```
**********************

PROCEDURE Help

   PARAMETERS p, l, v

      SET KEY 28 TO
      SAVE SCREEN
      DO CASE
      CASE p == "DOMEN1"
         DO CASE
         CASE v == "OPTION"
           @ 18, 7,23,72 BOX scrframe
           @ 19,12 SAY "This is the MAIN MENU.  Choose the menu item with the"
           @ 20,12 SAY "cursor keys, striking the RETURN key or first character"
           @ 21,12 SAY "string for immediate response.  Otherwise, the ESCape"
           @ 22,12 SAY "will return to Operating System."
           hrow = ROW()
           hcol = COL() + 1
         OTHERWISE
           @ 0,0,4,79 BOX scrframe
           @ 2,5 SAY "No Help is Available.  "
           hrow = ROW()
           hcol = 40
         ENDCASE
      CASE p == "DOMEN11"
         DO CASE
         CASE v == "OPTION1"
            @ 18, 7,23,72 BOX scrframe
            @ 19,12 SAY "This is the submenu for the CHART OF ACCOUNTS. Move"
            @ 20,12 SAY "cursor keys for appropriate item, or first character"
            @ 21,12 SAY "string for immediate response.  Otherwise, the ESCape"
            @ 22,12 SAY "will return to the Main Menu. "
            hrow = ROW()
            hcol = COL() + 1
         CASE v == "IN_ACCNT"
            @ 1,5,5,75 BOX scrframe
            @ 2,11 SAY "Please enter the Account Number being entered into the"
            @ 3,11 SAY "Chart of Accounts.   To exit this routine, strike the"
            @ 4,11 SAY "PgDn Key when returned."
            hrow = ROW()
            hcol = COL() + 1
         CASE v == "IN_NAME"
            @ 1,5,5,75 BOX scrframe
            @ 2,11 SAY "Please enter the Account Name for the entered Account"
            @ 3,11 SAY "Number.  This field MUST contain a value."
            hrow = ROW() + 1
            hcol = 17
         CASE v == "IN_BAL"
            @ 1,5,5,75 BOX scrframe
            @ 2,11 SAY "Please enter the Account Balance for the entered Account"
            @ 3,11 SAY "Number.  Leave blank for empty balance."
            hrow = ROW()
```

```
        hcol = COL() + 2
      CASE v == "IN_DESCPT"
        @ 1,5,5,75 BOX scrframe
        @ 2,11 SAY "Please enter the Description for the entered Account"
        @ 3,11 SAY "Number.  Leave blank for an empty field"
        hrow = ROW()
        hcol = COL() + 5
      OTHERWISE
        @ 0,0,4,79 BOX scrframe
        @ 2,5 SAY "No Help is Available.  "
        hrow = ROW()
        hcol = 40
      ENDCASE
    OTHERWISE
      @ 0,0,4,79 BOX scrframe
      @ 2,5 SAY "No Help is Available.  "
      hrow = ROW()
      hcol = 40
    ENDCASE
    @ hrow, hcol SAY "[Any Key to RETURN]"
    STORE INKEY(0) TO tempkey
    RESTORE SCREEN
    SET KEY 28 TO Help
* End of File
```

GENERAL HELP

General HELP is designed to provide the user with a sense of the flow of operation of the program rather than with specific information on the fields or variables.

In order to establish general HELP, a global variable is set at the very top-level procedure. This variable, call it "help_code," is initialized as available to all subprocedures, including HELP. As you proceed through the application, change the value of help_code. Then, inside HELP, test only for the value of the help_code and build the HELP screen accordingly.

One approach would be to initialize help_code to a value of zero in the first routine of the application. Inside HELP, if the value of help_code equals 0, display the "No Help Is Available" message.

Whatever HELP scheme you choose, make sure to:

1. Initialize the global variable at the very top level of the program or procedure.
2. Still pass the parameters.
3. SAVE the screen prior to execution and RESTORE it when leaving the routine.

4. Disengage the F1 key before entering HELP and reinstate it upon leaving, or test for calling program = "HELP."

SAMPLE OF GENERAL HELP

The following program is a sample implementation of general HELP.

```
********************
* Name          DOMENU2.prg
* Date          March 18, 1988
* Notice        Copyright 1986, Stephen J. Straley & Associates
* Compile       Clipper Domenu2
* Release       Autumn '86 or later
* Link          Plink86 fi domenu2 lib clipper
* Note          This program demonstrates how generalized HELP
*               can be implemented.
********************

CLEAR
DO Domen1

********************

PROCEDURE Domen1

DO WHILE .T.
   CLEAR
   scrframe =  CHR(201) + CHR(205) + CHR(187) + CHR(186) + ;
               CHR(188) + CHR(205) + CHR(200) + CHR(186) + CHR(32)
   STORE SPACE(4000) TO ascreen, bscreen, cscreen
   STORE 0 TO option, help_code
   @ 6, 1, 17, 75 BOX scrframe
   @ 5, 30 SAY "M A I N    M E N U"
   @ 8, 7 PROMPT " 1> Chart of Accounts "
   @ 10, 7 PROMPT " 2> Transactions "
   @ 12, 7 PROMPT " 3> Posting or Balancing "
   @ 14, 7 PROMPT " 4> Print Listings "
   @ 8, 48 PROMPT " 5> Print Reports "
   @ 10, 48 PROMPT " 6> Transfers "
   @ 12, 48 PROMPT " 7> Utilities "
   @ 14, 48 PROMPT " 8> End of Period "
   @ 16, 33 SAY "ESC to RETURN"
   MENU TO option
   SAVE SCREEN TO ascreen
   DO CASE
   CASE option = 0
      @ 18, 15 SAY "All Files Closed, Returning to Operating System"
      QUIT
   CASE option = 1
      DO Domen11
```

```
   OTHERWISE
      **************************
      * Do subprocedure here. *
      **************************
   ENDCASE
ENDDO

********************

PROCEDURE Domen11

DO WHILE .T.
   IF !EMPTY(bscreen)
      RESTORE SCREEN FROM bscreen
   ENDIF
   @ 9, 39, 22, 64 BOX scrframe
   STORE 0 TO option1
   @ 10, 46 SAY "COA Sub-Menu"
   @ 12, 43 PROMPT " 1> Enter Account "
   @ 14, 43 PROMPT " 2> Edit Account "
   @ 16, 43 PROMPT " 3> Scan Accounts "
   @ 18, 43 PROMPT " 4> Delete Accounts "
   @ 21, 46 SAY "ESC to RETURN"
   MENU TO option1
   SACE SCREEN TO bscreen
   DO CASE
   CASE option1 = 1
      STORE SPACE(10) TO in_name, in_descpt
      STORE 0 TO in_bal, in_accnt
      STORE 1 TO help_code
      @ 14,5,20,75 BOX scrframe
      @ 16,10 SAY "Enter Account Number: " GET in_bal  PICT "#####.##"
      @ 18,10 SAY "         Account Name: " GET in_name PICT "@X" ;
              VALID(!EMPTY(in_name))
      @ 16,46 SAY "    Balance: $" GET in_bal PICT "###,###,###.##"
      @ 18,46 SAY "Description: " GET in_descpt
      READ
   CASE option1 = 2
      **************************
      * Do subprocedure here. *
      **************************
   CASE option1 = 3
      **************************
      * Do subprocedure here. *
      **************************
   CASE option1 = 4
      **************************
      * Do subprocedure here. *
      **************************
   CASE option1 = 0
      EXIT
   ENDCASE
ENDDO
```

```
*********************

PROCEDURE Help

PARAMETERS p, l, v

   SET KEY 28 TO
   SAVE SCREEN
   DO CASE
   CASE help_code = 0
      @ 18, 7,23,72 BOX scrframe
      @ 19,12 SAY "Move the cursor to the proper menu option, then strike the"
      @ 20,12 SAY "RETURN key, or strike the first character in the menu"
      @ 21,12 SAY "string for immediate response.  Otherwise, the ESCape will"
      @ 22,12 SAY "Return to the Main Menu."
      hrow = ROW()
      hcol = COL() + 1
   CASE help_code = 1
      @ 3,10,10,70 BOX scrframe
      @ 5,12 SAY "This is the ENTER ACCOUNT INFORMATION submenu...."
      @ 7,12 SAY "     Enter in the appropriate information and strike the"
      @ 8,12 SAY "     RETURN key to complete the entry."
      hrow = ROW()
      hcol = COL() + 1
   OTHERWISE
      @ 0,0,4,79 BOX scrframe
      @ 2,5 SAY "No Help Is Available.  "
      hrow = ROW()
      hcol = 40
   ENDCASE
   @ hrow, hcol SAY "[Any Key to RETURN]"
   STORE INKEY(0) TO tempkey
   RESTORE SCREEN
   SET KEY 28 TO Help
* End of File
```

USING MEMOEDIT() AND A DISK FILE

There is another way to approach the subject of on-line HELP: using disk files. As more and more information is added to the HELP procedure, the size of your executable file increases and, in some cases, becomes too big to manage. In the technique shown in this example, the HELP procedure is larger than any of the other examples, but the program file will not increase further, regardless of the amount of information recorded for HELP.

Another feature of this technique is the use of the MEMOEDIT() function. In this example, the user can design a custom HELP screen based on the variable or program involved. This type of HELP is more like an on-line notepad.

The following code demonstrates context-specific HELP using a disk file:

```
*********************
* Name          DOMENU3.prg
* Date          March 15, 1988
* Notice        Copyright 1988, Stephen J. Straley & Associates
* Compile       Clipper Domenu3 -4
* Release       Autumn '86 or later
* Link          Plink86 fi domenu lib clipper
* Note          This program demonstrates how specific HELP
*               can be instituted in conjunction with the MEMOEDIT()
*               function and writing the context-specific HELP to a
*               disk file.
*********************

CLEAR
DO Domen1

*********************

PROCEDURE Domen1

   DO WHILE .T.
      CLEAR
      scrframe = CHR(201) + CHR(205) + CHR(187) + CHR(186) + ;
                 CHR(188) + CHR(205) + CHR(200) + CHR(186) + CHR(32)
      STORE SPACE(4000) TO ascreen, bscreen, cscreen
      STORE 0 TO option
      SET FUNCTION 10 TO CHR(23)   && This is to write the memo
      @ 6, 1, 17, 75 BOX SUBSTR(scrframe,1,8)
      @ 5, 30 SAY "M A I N    M E N U"
      @ 8, 7 PROMPT " 1> Chart of Accounts "
      @ 10, 7 PROMPT " 2> Transactions "
      @ 12, 7 PROMPT " 3> Posting / Balancing "
      @ 14, 7 PROMPT " 4> Print Listings "
      @ 8, 48 PROMPT " 5> Print Reports "
      @ 10, 48 PROMPT " 6> Transfers "
      @ 12, 48 PROMPT " 7> Utilities "
      @ 14, 48 PROMPT " 8> End of Period "
      @ 16, 33 SAY "ESC to RETURN"
      MENU TO option
      SAVE SCREEN TO ascreen
      DO CASE
      CASE option = 0
         @ 18, 15 SAY "All Files Closed. Returning to Operating System"
         QUIT
      CASE option = 1
         DO Domen11
      OTHERWISE
         *************************
         * Do subprocedure here. *
         *************************
      ENDCASE
   ENDDO
```

```
********************

PROCEDURE Domen11

   DO WHILE .T.
      IF !EMPTY(bscreen)
         RESTORE SCREEN FROM bscreen
      ENDIF
      STORE 0 TO option1
      @ 9, 39, 22, 64 BOX scrframe
      @ 10, 46 SAY "COA Sub-Menu"
      @ 12, 43 PROMPT " 1> Enter Account "
      @ 14, 43 PROMPT " 2> Edit Account "
      @ 16, 43 PROMPT " 3> Scan Accounts "
      @ 18, 43 PROMPT " 4> Delete Accounts "
      @ 21, 46 SAY "ESC to RETURN"
      MENU TO option1
      SAVE SCREEN TO bscreen
      DO CASE
      CASE option1 = 0
         EXIT
      CASE option1 = 1
         STORE SPACE(10) TO in_name, in_descpt
         STORE 0 TO in_bal, in_accnt
         @ 14,5,20,75 BOX scrframe
         @ 16,10 SAY "Enter Account Number: " GET in_accnt PICT "#####.##"
         @ 18,10 SAY "        Account Name: " GET in_name PICT "@X"
                 VALID(!EMPTY(in_name))
         @ 16,46 SAY "    Balance: $" GET in_bal PICT "###,###,###.##"
         @ 18,46 SAY "Description: " GET in_descpt
         READ
      OTHERWISE
         *************************
         * Do subprocedure here. *
         *************************
      ENDCASE
   ENDDO

********************

PROCEDURE Help

   PARAMETERS p, l, v

      SET KEY 28 TO
      SAVE SCREEN
      SET SCOREBOARD OFF
      scrframe = CHR(201) + CHR(205) + CHR(187) + CHR(186) + ;
                 CHR(188) + CHR(205) + CHR(200) + CHR(186) + CHR(32)
      IF !FILE("HELP.DBF")
         @ 00,10,03,70 BOX scrframe
         @ 01,11 SAY "There is no HELP file available. Would you like a help"
         @ 02,27 SAY "file to be generated? "
```

```
      IF !VERIFY()
         RESTORE SCREEN
         SET KEY 28 TO Help
         RETURN
      ENDIF

      NOTE If a data base is open, its selected area must be noted
      goback = SELECT()
      DO Dohelp
      NOTE Once the help has been performed, the previously selected area
      NOTE is reselected.
      tempgo = STR(goback)
      SELECT &tempgo

   ENDIF
   goback = SELECT()
   SELECT 9
   USE Help INDEX Help
   search = SUBSTR(p,1,10) + SUBSTR(v,1,10) + TRANSFORM(l, "9999")
   SEEK search
   IF FOUND()
      @ top,left,bottom,right BOX scrframe
      IF "" = MEMOEDIT(helpscr,top+1,left+1,bottom-1,right-1,.F.)
      * For the Summer '87 release, this line should read:
      * MEMOEDIT(helpscr,top+1,left+1,bottom-1,right-1,.F.,.F.)
      ENDIF
      @ bottom-1,left+1 SAY "Any Key to Continue..."
   ELSE
      @ 00,10,03,70 BOX scrframe
      @ 01,11 SAY "There is no HELP for this section.  Would you like to make"
      @ 02,28 SAY "a HELP screen for this? "
      IF .NOT. VERIFY()
         RESTORE SCREEN
         SET KEY 28 TO Help
         RETURN
      ENDIF
      APPEND BLANK
      REPLACE lookit WITH SUBSTR(p,1,10) + SUBSTR(v,1,10) + TRANSFORM(l,"9999")
      STORE SPACE(4000) TO in_help, full_scr
      STORE 0 TO temp_top, temp_left, temp_bot, temp_right
      SAVE SCREEN TO full_scr
      DO WHILE .T.
         RESTORE SCREEN FROM full_scr
         @ 00,10,03,70 BOX scrframe
         @ 01,20 SAY "Position cursor with arrow for TOP, LEFT corner."
         cursor = 0
         newcur = CHR(201)
         SAVE SCREEN TO in_help
         trow = 12
         tcol = 40
         @ trow, tcol SAY newcur
         * For the Summer '87 release
         * SET CURSOR OFF
```

```
        DO WHILE.T.
           cursor = INKEY(0)
           loop_again = MOVECURS()
           IF !loop_again
              EXIT
           ENDIF
           RESTORE SCREEN FROM in_help
           @ trow, tcol SAY newcur
        ENDDO
        STORE trow TO temp_top
        STORE tcol TO temp_left
        @ 00,10,03,70 BOX scrframe
        @ 01,14 SAY "Position cursor with arrow for BOTTOM, RIGHT corner."
        cursor = 0
        SAVE SCREEN TO in_help
        newcur = CHR(188)
        trow = temp_top + 2
        tcol = temp_left + 5
        @ trow, tcol SAY newcur
        DO WHILE.T.
           cursor = INKEY(0)
           loop_again = MOVECURS()
           IF !loop_again
              EXIT
           ENDIF
           RESTORE SCREEN FROM in_help
           @ trow, tcol SAY newcur
        ENDDO
        * For the Summer '87 release
        * SET CURSOR ON
        STORE trow TO temp_bot
        STORE tcol TO temp_right
        RESTORE SCREEN FROM in_help
        DO Temphelp
        @ 00,10,03,70 BOX scrframe
        @ 02,25 SAY "Is this what you wanted?  "
        IF .NOT. VERIFY()
           RESTORE SCREEN FROM in_help
           LOOP
        ELSE
           EXIT
        ENDIF
     ENDDO
     @ 00,10,03,70 BOX scrframe
     @ 01,15 SAY "Enter in HELPful information.   Keep to ONE screen"
     @ 02,15 SAY "      of text.  Press F10 when finished."
     REPLACE top WITH temp_top, bottom WITH temp_bot
     REPLACE left WITH temp_left, right WITH temp_right
     DO WHILE .T.
        @ top,left,bottom,right BOX scrframe
        REPLACE helpscr WITH MEMOEDIT(helpscr,top+1,left+1,;
        bottom-1,right-1,.T.)
        @ top,left,bottom,right BOX scrframe
```

```
         IF "" = MEMOEDIT(helpscr,top+1,left+1,bottom-1,right-1,.F.)
         * For the Summer '87 release, the MEMOEDIT() should read
         * MEMOEDIT(helpscr,top+1,left+1,bottom-1,right-1,.F.,.F.)
         ENDIF
         @ bottom-1,left+1 SAY "IS THIS CORRECT?   "
         IF .NOT. VERIFY()
            LOOP
         ENDIF
         EXIT
      ENDDO
      @ bottom-1,left+1 SAY "Press Any key to Continue..."
   ENDIF
   INKEY(0)
   RESTORE SCREEN
   tempgo = STR(goback)
   SELECT &tempgo
   SET KEY 28 TO Help
   RETURN

 *********************

 PROCEDURE Dohelp

   SELECT 9
   CREATE Temp
   USE Temp
   APPEND BLANK
   REPLACE field_name WITH "LOOKIT", field_type WITH "C", field_len WITH 24
   APPEND BLANK
   REPLACE field_name WITH "TOP", field_type WITH "N", field_len WITH 2
   APPEND BLANK
   REPLACE field_name WITH "LEFT", field_type WITH "N", field_len WITH 2
   APPEND BLANK
   REPLACE field_name WITH "BOTTOM", field_type WITH "N", field_len WITH 2
   APPEND BLANK
   REPLACE field_name WITH "RIGHT", field_type WITH "N", field_len WITH 2
   APPEND BLANK
   REPLACE field_name WITH "HELPSCR", field_type WITH "M", field_len WITH 10
   USE
   CREATE Help FROM Temp
   USE
   ERASE Temp
   USE Help
   INDEX ON lookit TO Help

*********************

PROCEDURE Temphelp

  SET COLOR TO W*
  @ temp_top, temp_left, temp_bot, temp_right BOX SUBSTR(scrframe,1,8)
  SET COLOR TO 7
```

```
******************************

FUNCTION VERIFY

   SET CONSOLE off
   WAIT TO inertemp
   SET CONSOLE on
   IF UPPER(inertemp) = "Y"
      ?? "Yes"
      te = INKEY(.25)
      RETURN(.T.)
   ENDIF
   ?? "No "
   te = INKEY(.25)
   RETURN(.F.)

*********************

FUNCTION Movecurs

   DO CASE
   CASE cursor = 5
      IF trow - 1 > 0
         trow = trow - 1
      ENDIF
   CASE cursor = 4
      IF tcol + 1 < 79
         tcol = tcol + 1
      ENDIF
   CASE cursor = 19
      IF tcol - 1 > 0
         tcol = tcol - 1
      ENDIF
   CASE cursor = 24
      IF trow + 1 < 24
         trow = trow + 1
      ENDIF
   CASE cursor = 13 .OR. cursor = 27
      RETURN(.F.)
   ENDCASE
   RETURN(.T.)
* End of File
```

A NEW WAY TO USE MEMOEDIT() IN Summer '87

The new capabilities of the MEMOEDIT() function are explored in the sample program below. It is now possible to have a submenu within HELP, to have the program generate all HELP files automatically, to have a window area in reverse color and to scroll within that window area using the cursor keys, and to return to the main menu when the HELP is finished.

```
*********************
* Name          DOMENU4.prg
* Date          March 15, 1988
* Notice        Copyright 1988, Stephen J. Straley & Associates
* Compile       Clipper Domenu4 -4
* Release       Autumn '86 or later
* Link          Plink86 fi domenu lib clipper
* Note          This program demonstrates how specific HELP
*               can be instituted in conjunction with the MEMOEDIT()
*               function and writing the context-specific HELP to a
*               disk file.
*********************

CLEAR
DO M_helpfile
DO Domen1

*********************

PROCEDURE Domen1

   SET WRAP ON
   scrframe = CHR(201) + CHR(205) + CHR(187) + CHR(186) + ;
              CHR(188) + CHR(205) + CHR(200) + CHR(186) + CHR(32)
   STORE 0 TO option, help_opt
   DO WHILE .T.
      CLEAR SCREEN
      STORE SPACE(4000) TO ascreen, bscreen, cscreen
      SET FUNCTION 10 TO CHR(23)   && This is to write the memo
      @ 6, 1 TO 17, 75 DOUBLE
      @ 5, 30 SAY "M A I N    M E N U"
      @ 8, 7 PROMPT " 1> Chart of Accounts "
      @ 10, 7 PROMPT " 2> Transactions "
      @ 12, 7 PROMPT " 3> Posting or Balancing "
      @ 14, 7 PROMPT " 4> Print Listings "
      @ 8, 48 PROMPT " 5> Print Reports "
      @ 10, 48 PROMPT " 6> Transfers "
      @ 12, 48 PROMPT " 7> Utilities "
      @ 14, 48 PROMPT " 8> End of Period "
      @ 16, 33 SAY "ESC to RETURN"
      MENU TO option
      SAVE SCREEN TO ascreen
      DO CASE
      CASE option = 0
         @ 18, 15 SAY "All Files Closed. Returning to Operating System."
         QUIT
      CASE option = 1
         DO Domen11
     OTHERWISE
         *************************
         * Do subprocedure here. *
         *************************
      ENDCASE
   ENDDO
```

```
*********************

PROCEDURE Domen11

   DO WHILE .T.
      IF !EMPTY(bscreen)
         RESTORE SCREEN FROM bscreen
      ENDIF
      STORE 0 TO option1
      @ 9, 39, 22, 64 BOX scrframe
      @ 10, 46 SAY "COA Sub-Menu"
      @ 12, 43 PROMPT " 1> Enter Account "
      @ 14, 43 PROMPT " 2> Edit Account "
      @ 16, 43 PROMPT " 3> Scan Accounts "
      @ 18, 43 PROMPT " 4> Delete Accounts "
      @ 21, 46 SAY "ESC to RETURN"
      MENU TO option1
      SAVE SCREEN TO bscreen
      DO CASE
      CASE option1 = 0
         EXIT
      CASE option1 = 1
         STORE SPACE(10) TO in_name, in_descpt
         STORE 0 TO in_bal, in_accnt
         @ 14,5,20,75 BOX scrframe
         @ 16,10 SAY "Enter Account Number: " GET in_accnt PICT "#####.##"
         @ 18,10 SAY "        Account Name: " GET in_name PICT "@X"
                 VALID(!EMPTY(in_name))
         @ 16,46 SAY "    Balance: $" GET in_bal PICT "###,###,###.##"
         @ 18,46 SAY "Description: " GET in_descpt
         READ
      OTHERWISE
         **************************
         * Do subprocedure here. *
         **************************
      ENDCASE
   ENDDO

*********************

PROCEDURE Help

   PARAMETERS p, l, v

      SET KEY 28 TO
      SAVE SCREEN
      @ 5,30 CLEAR TO 13,50
      @ 5,30 TO 13,50 DOUBLE
      @  7,33 PROMPT "  Regular Help  "
      @  9,33 PROMPT "  Diskfile Help "
      @ 11,33 PROMPT "     Return     "
      MENU TO help_opt
      IF help_opt = 3 .OR. EMPTY(help_opt)
```

```
      SET KEY 28 TO Help
      RESTORE SCREEN
      RETURN
   ELSEIF help_opt = 2
      DO Helpfile
      SET KEY 28 TO Help
      RESTORE SCREEN
      RETURN
   ENDIF

   SET SCOREBOARD OFF
   scrframe = CHR(201) + CHR(205) + CHR(187) + CHR(186) + ;
              CHR(188) + CHR(205) + CHR(200) + CHR(186) + CHR(32)
   IF !FILE("HELP.DBF")
      @ 00,10,03,70 BOX scrframe
      @ 01,11 SAY "There is no HELP file available. Would you like a HELP"
      @ 02,27 SAY "file to be generated? "
      IF !VERIFY()
         RESTORE SCREEN
         SET KEY 28 TO Help
         RETURN
      ENDIF

      NOTE If a database is open, its selected area must be noted
      goback = SELECT()
      DO Dohelp
      NOTE Once the HELP has been performed, the previously selected area
      NOTE is reselected.
      tempgo = STR(goback)
      SELECT &tempgo

   ENDIF
   goback = SELECT()
   SELECT 9
   USE Help INDEX Help
   search = SUBSTR(p,1,10) + SUBSTR(v,1,10) + TRANSFORM(l, "9999")
   SEEK search
   IF FOUND()
      @ top,left,bottom,right BOX scrframe
      MEMOEDIT(helpscr,top+1,left+1,bottom-1,right-1,.F.,.F.)
      @ bottom-1,left+1 SAY "Any Key to Continue..."
   ELSE
      @ 00,10,03,70 BOX scrframe
      @ 01,11 SAY "There is no HELP for this section.  Would you like to make"
      @ 02,28 SAY "a HELP screen for this? "
      IF .NOT. VERIFY()
         RESTORE SCREEN
         SET KEY 28 TO Help
         RETURN
      ENDIF
      APPEND BLANK
      REPLACE lookit WITH SUBSTR(p,1,10) + SUBSTR(v,1,10) + TRANSFORM(l,"9999")
      STORE SPACE(4000) TO in_help, full_scr
```

```
STORE 0 TO temp_top, temp_left, temp_bot, temp_right
SAVE SCREEN TO full_scr
DO WHILE .T.
   RESTORE SCREEN FROM full_scr
   @ 00,10,03,70 BOX scrframe
   @ 01,20 SAY "Position cursor with arrow for TOP, LEFT corner."
   cursor = 0
   newcur = CHR(201)
   SAVE SCREEN TO in_help
   trow = 12
   tcol = 40
   @ trow, tcol SAY newcur
   SET CURSOR OFF
   DO WHILE.T.
      cursor = INKEY(0)
      loop_again = MOVECURS()
      IF !loop_again
         EXIT
      ENDIF
      RESTORE SCREEN FROM in_help
      @ trow, tcol SAY newcur
   ENDDO
   STORE trow TO temp_top
   STORE tcol TO temp_left
   @ 00,10,03,70 BOX scrframe
   @ 01,14 SAY "Position cursor with arrow for BOTTOM, RIGHT corner."
   cursor = 0
   SAVE SCREEN TO in_help
   newcur = CHR(188)
   trow = temp_top + 2
   tcol = temp_left + 5
   @ trow, tcol SAY newcur
   DO WHILE.T.
      cursor = INKEY(0)
      loop_again = MOVECURS()
      IF !loop_again
         EXIT
      ENDIF
      RESTORE SCREEN FROM in_help
      @ trow, tcol SAY newcur
   ENDDO
   SET CURSOR ON
   STORE trow TO temp_bot
   STORE tcol TO temp_right
   RESTORE SCREEN FROM in_help
   DO Temphelp
   @ 00,10,03,70 BOX scrframe
   @ 02,25 SAY "Is this what you wanted?  "
   IF .NOT. VERIFY()
      RESTORE SCREEN FROM in_help
      LOOP
   ELSE
      EXIT
```

```
            ENDIF
         ENDDO
         @ 00,10,03,70 BOX scrframe
         @ 01,15 SAY "Enter in HELPful information.   Keep to ONE screen"
         @ 02,15 SAY "       of text.  Press F10 when finished."
         REPLACE top WITH temp_top, bottom WITH temp_bot
         REPLACE left WITH temp_left, right WITH temp_right
         DO WHILE .T.
            @ top,left,bottom,right BOX scrframe
            REPLACE helpscr WITH MEMOEDIT(helpscr,top+1,left+1,;
            bottom-1,right-1,.T.)
            @ top,left,bottom,right BOX scrframe
            IF "" = MEMOEDIT(helpscr,top+1,left+1,bottom-1,right-1,.F.)
            * For the Summer '87 release, the MEMOEDIT() should read
            * MEMOEDIT(helpscr,top+1,left+1,bottom-1,right-1,.F.,.F.)
            ENDIF
            @ bottom-1,left+1 SAY "IS THIS CORRECT?   "
            IF .NOT. VERIFY()
               LOOP
            ENDIF
            EXIT
         ENDDO
         @ bottom-1,left+1 SAY "Press Any key to Continue..."
      ENDIF
      INKEY(0)
      RESTORE SCREEN
      tempgo = STR(goback)
      SELECT &tempgo
      SET KEY 28 TO Help
      RETURN

*********************

PROCEDURE Dohelp

   SELECT 9
   CREATE Temp
   USE Temp
   APPEND BLANK
   REPLACE field_name WITH "LOOKIT", field_type WITH "C", field_len WITH 24
   APPEND BLANK
   REPLACE field_name WITH "TOP", field_type WITH "N", field_len WITH 2
   APPEND BLANK
   REPLACE field_name WITH "LEFT", field_type WITH "N", field_len WITH 2
   APPEND BLANK
   REPLACE field_name WITH "BOTTOM", field_type WITH "N", field_len WITH 2
   APPEND BLANK
   REPLACE field_name WITH "RIGHT", field_type WITH "N", field_len WITH 2
   APPEND BLANK
   REPLACE field_name WITH "HELPSCR", field_type WITH "M", field_len WITH 10
   USE
   CREATE Help FROM Temp
   USE
```

```
   ERASE Temp
   USE Help
   INDEX ON lookit TO Help

*********************

PROCEDURE Temphelp

   SET COLOR TO W*
   @ temp_top, temp_left, temp_bot, temp_right BOX SUBSTR(scrframe,1,8)
   SET COLOR TO 7

*********************

FUNCTION Movecurs

   DO CASE
   CASE cursor = 5
      IF trow - 1 > 0
         trow = trow - 1
      ENDIF
   CASE cursor = 4
      IF tcol + 1 < 79
         tcol = tcol + 1
      ENDIF
   CASE cursor = 19
      IF tcol - 1 > 0
         tcol = tcol - 1
      ENDIF
   CASE cursor = 24
      IF trow + 1 < 24
         trow = trow + 1
      ENDIF
   CASE cursor = 13 .OR. cursor = 27
      RETURN(.F.)
   ENDCASE
   RETURN(.T.)

*********************

PROCEDURE Helpfile

   portscr = SAVESCREEN(15,0,21,70)
   old_color = SETCOLOR()
   @ 15,0 CLEAR TO 21,70

   SETCOLOR ( REVERSE(old_color) )
   @ 15,0 TO 21,70 DOUBLE
   SETCOLOR( old_color )
   SET CURSOR ON
   MEMOEDIT(MEMOREAD("HELPFILE.TXT"), 16,1,20,69,.T.,"RESTRICT", 130)
   SET CURSOR OFF
   RESTSCREEN(15,0,21,70,portscr)
```

```
********************

FUNCTION Restrict

   PARAMETERS the_mode, the_line, the_col

   rest_key = LASTKEY()

   IF rest_key = 27
      RETURN(0)
   ELSEIF rest_key = 24
      RETURN(32)
   ELSEIF rest_key = 5
      RETURN(32)
   ELSEIF rest_key = 6
      RETURN(32)
   ELSEIF rest_key = 118 .OR. rest_key = 86
      RETURN(0)
   ELSEIF rest_key > 31 .AND. rest_key < 500
      KEYBOARD CHR(27)
      RETURN(101)
   ENDIF
   RETURN(0)

*********************

PROCEDURE M_helpfile

   carriage = "CHR(13) + CHR(10)"
   hlp_str = &carriage. + &carriage. + "   This is a Help screen"
   hlp_str = hlp_str + "read off of disk via the MEMOREAD() function." + &carriage.
   hlp_str = hlp_str + &carriage. + "   This file can be created in many "
   hlp_str = hlp_str + "ways, either by the program itself like" + &carriage.
   hlp_str = hlp_str + "                          this example, or via a text-editor."
   hlp_str = hlp_str + &carriage. + &carriage. + "   The purpose of this is to show
"
   hlp_str = hlp_str + "just another way to store and to " + &carriage
   hlp_str = hlp_str + "   retrive a help file from disk." + &carriage. + &car-
riage.
   hlp_str = hlp_str + "Press ESC Key to Continue...."
   MEMOWRIT("HELPFILE.TXT", hlp_str)

* The following functions are part of the Steve Straley Toolkit.
* Copyright 1988 (c) by Stephen J. Straley & Associates - All Rights Reserved

*********************

FUNCTION Verify

   PARAMETERS comp, extra_key

   DO CASE
      CASE PCOUNT() = 0
```

```
         comp = "YyNn"
         extra_key = .F.
      CASE PCOUNT() = 1
         extra_key = .F.
   ENDCASE

   IF TYPE("scrpause") = "U"
      scrpause = 100
   ENDIF
   DO WHILE .T.
      the_var = ""
      inside = INKEY(0)
      DO CASE
      CASE inside = 4
         the_var = "Y"
      CASE inside = 19
         the_var = "N"
      OTHERWISE
         the_var = CHR(inside)
      ENDCASE
      IF the_var$comp
         EXIT
      ENDIF
   ENDDO
   IF the_var$SUBSTR(comp,1,2)
      ?? "Yes"
      IF extra_key
         INKEY(0)
      ELSE
         FOR qaz = 1 TO scrpause
         NEXT
      ENDIF
      RETURN(.T.)
   ELSE
      ?? "No "
      IF extra_key
         INKEY(0)
      ELSE
         FOR qaz = 1 TO scrpause
         NEXT
      ENDIF
      RETURN(.F.)
   ENDIF

*********************

FUNCTION Reverse

   PARAMETERS the_color

   the_say = STRTRAN(SUBSTR(the_color, 1, AT(",", the_color)-1), "+", "")
   RETURN(SUBSTR(the_say, AT("/", the_say)+1) + "/" + SUBSTR(the_say, 1, AT("/",
the_say)-1))
* End of File
```

MULTIPLE LEVEL HELP, EVERYTHING AT ONCE

The following example is the expanded version of the HELP utility. Basically, it is everything at once, including multiple levels of HELP. Notice the ability to inquire for more HELP within the HELP procedure. A second level of HELP is established and the appropriate key (the F1 Key) is set accordingly.

```
********************
* Name          DOMENU5.prg
* Date          March 15, 1988
* Notice        Copyright 1986, Stephen J. Straley & Associates
* Compile       Clipper Domenu4
* Release       Autumn 86 or greater
* Link          Plink86 fi domenu4 lib clipper
* Note          This program demonstrates how HELP can
*               have another level of HELP in it.
*               Also, this example shows practically
*               every aspect of the Clipper HELP facility.
********************

CLEAR
DO Domen1

********************

PROCEDURE Domen1

   DO WHILE .T.
      CLEAR
      scrframe = CHR(201) + CHR(205) + CHR(187) + CHR(186) + ;
                 CHR(188) + CHR(205) + CHR(200) + CHR(186) + CHR(32)
      STORE SPACE(4000) TO ascreen, bscreen, cscreen
      STORE 0 TO option
      SET FUNCTION 10 TO CHR(23)   && This is to write the memo
      @ 6, 1, 17, 75 BOX SUBSTR(scrframe,1,8)
      @ 5, 30 SAY "M A I N    M E N U"
      @ 8, 7 PROMPT " 1> Chart of Accounts "
      @ 10, 7 PROMPT " 2> Transactions "
      @ 12, 7 PROMPT " 3> Posting / Balancing "
      @ 14, 7 PROMPT " 4> Print Listings "
      @ 8, 48 PROMPT " 5> Print Reports "
      @ 10, 48 PROMPT " 6> Transfers "
      @ 12, 48 PROMPT " 7> Utilities "
      @ 14, 48 PROMPT " 8> End of Period "
      @ 16, 33 SAY "ESC to RETURN"
      MENU TO option
      SAVE SCREEN TO ascreen
      DO CASE
      CASE option = 0
         @ 18, 15 SAY "All Files Closed. Returning to Operating System"
         QUIT
      CASE option = 1
```

```
         DO Domen11
      OTHERWISE
         **************************
         * Do subprocedure here. *
         **************************
      ENDCASE
   ENDDO

********************

PROCEDURE Domen11

   DO WHILE .T.
      IF !EMPTY(bscreen)
         RESTORE SCREEN FROM bscreen
      ENDIF
      STORE 0 TO option1
      @ 9, 39, 22, 64 BOX scrframe
      @ 10, 46 SAY "COA Sub-Menu"
      @ 12, 43 PROMPT " 1> Enter Account "
      @ 14, 43 PROMPT " 2> Edit Account "
      @ 16, 43 PROMPT " 3> Scan Accounts "
      @ 18, 43 PROMPT " 4> Delete Accounts "
      @ 21, 46 SAY "ESC to RETURN"
      MENU TO option1
      SAVE SCREEN TO bscreen
      DO CASE
      CASE option1 = 0
         EXIT
      CASE option1 = 1
         STORE SPACE(10) TO in_name, in_descpt
         STORE 0 TO in_bal, in_accnt
         @ 14,5,20,75 BOX scrframe
         @ 16,10 SAY "Enter Account Number: " GET in_accnt PICT "#####.##"
         @ 18,10 SAY "        Account Name: " GET in_name PICT "@X" ;
                 VALID(!EMPTY(in_name))
         @ 16,46 SAY "    Balance: $" GET in_bal PICT "###,###,###.##"
         @ 18,46 SAY "Description: " GET in_descpt
         READ
      OTHERWISE
         **************************
         * Do subprocedure here. *
         **************************
      ENDCASE
   ENDDO

********************

PROCEDURE Help

   PARAMETERS p, l, v

      SET KEY 28 TO Help2
      SAVE SCREEN
```

```
STORE 0 TO level
@ 18,20,23,60 BOX scrframe
@ 19,25 PROMPT "1> Design Custom Help"
@ 20,25 PROMPT "2> Take Pre-designed Help"
@ 22,25 SAY    "ESC Key to RETURN TO SYSTEM"
MENU TO level
RESTORE SCREEN
IF level = 0
   RETURN
   ELSE
   IF level = 1
      DO Help3
      RETURN
   ENDIF
ENDIF
SAVE SCREEN
DO CASE
CASE p == "DOMEN1"
   DO CASE
  CASE v == "OPTION"
      @ 18, 7,23,72 BOX scrframe
      @ 19,12 SAY "This is the MAIN MENU.  Choose the menu item with the "
      @ 20,12 SAY "cursor keys, striking the RETURN key or first character"
      @ 21,12 SAY "in the string for immediate response.  Otherwise, EScape"
      @ 22,12 SAY " will return to Operating System. "
      hrow = ROW()
      hcol = COL() + 1
   OTHERWISE
      @ 0,0,4,79 BOX scrframe
      @ 2,5 SAY "No Help Is Available.  "
      hrow = ROW()
      hcol = 40
   ENDCASE
CASE p == "DOMEN11"
   DO CASE
   CASE v == "OPTION1"
      @ 18, 7,23,72 BOX scrframe
      @ 19,12 SAY "This is the submenu for the CHART OF ACCOUNTS.  Move the"
      @ 20,12 SAY "cursor keys for appropriate item, or first character"
      @ 21,12 SAY "in the string for immediate response.  Otherwise, EScape"
      @ 22,12 SAY "will return to the Main Menu. "
      hrow = ROW()
      hcol = COL() + 1
   CASE v == "IN_ACCNT"
      @ 1,5,5,75 BOX scrframe
      @ 2,11 SAY "Please enter the Account Number being entered into the"
      @ 3,11 SAY "Chart of Accounts.   To exit this routine, strike the"
      @ 4,11 SAY "PgDn Key when returned."
      hrow = ROW()
      hcol = COL() + 1
   CASE v == "IN_NAME"
      @ 1,5,5,75 BOX scrframe
      @ 2,11 SAY "Please enter the Account Name for the entered Account"
```

```
            @ 3,11 SAY "Number.  This field MUST contain a value."
            hrow = ROW() + 1
            hcol = 17
         CASE v == "IN_BAL"
            @ 1,5,5,75 BOX scrframe
            @ 2,11 SAY "Please enter the Account Balance for the entered Account"
            @ 3,11 SAY "Number.  Leave blank for empty balance."
            hrow = ROW()
            hcol = COL() + 2
         CASE v == "IN_DESCPT"
            @ 1,5,5,75 BOX scrframe
            @ 2,11 SAY "Please enter the Description for the entered Account"
            @ 3,11 SAY "Number.  Leave blank for an empty field"
            hrow = ROW()
            hcol = COL() + 5
         OTHERWISE
            @ 0,0,4,79 BOX scrframe
            @ 2,5 SAY "No Help is Available.  "
            hrow = ROW()
            hcol = 40
         ENDCASE
      OTHERWISE
         @ 0,0,4,79 BOX scrframe
         @ 2,5 SAY "No Help is Available."
         hrow = ROW()
         hcol = 40
      ENDCASE
      @ hrow, hcol SAY "[Any Key to RETURN]"
      STORE INKEY(0) TO tempkey
      RESTORE SCREEN
      SET KEY 28 TO Help

*********************

PROCEDURE Help2

   PARAMETERS p2, l2, v2
   SET KEY 28 TO
   STORE SPACE(4000) TO screen2
   SAVE SCREEN TO screen2
   SET COLOR TO W*+
   @ 0,5 SAY "Design Help will allow users to custom their HELP for the system"
   @ 2,5 SAY "Predesigned HELP is just that ... help already configured for system"
   @ 4,5 SAY "Press any key to return to Menu Choice...."
   INKEY(0)
   SET COLOR TO
   SET KEY 28 TO Help2
   RESTORE SCREEN FROM screen2

*********************

PROCEDURE Help3

   PARAMETERS p3, l3, v3
```

```
SET KEY 28 TO
SAVE SCREEN
SET SCOREBOARD OFF
IF .NOT. FILE("HELP.DBF")
   @ 00,10,03,70 BOX scrframe
   @ 01,11 SAY "There is no HELP file available.   Would you like a HELP "
   @ 02,27 SAY "file to be generated? "
   IF .NOT. VERIFY()
      RESTORE SCREEN
      SET KEY 28 TO Help
      RETURN
   ENDIF

   NOTE If a database is open, its selected area must be noted
   goback = SELECT()
   DO Dohelp
   NOTE Once the help has been performed, the selected area is
   NOTE reselected.
   tempgo = STR(goback)
   SELECT &tempgo

ENDIF
goback = SELECT()
SELECT 9
USE Help INDEX Help
search = SUBSTR(p,1,10) + SUBSTR(v,1,10) + TRANSFORM(l, "9999")
SEEK search
IF FOUND()
   @ top,left,bottom,right BOX scrframe
   IF "" = MEMOEDIT(helpscr,top+1,left+1,bottom-1,right-1,.F.)
   * For the Summer '87 release, the MEMOEDIT() function should be:
   * MEMOEDIT(helpscr,top+1,left+1,bottom-1,right-1,.F.,.F.)
   ENDIF
   @ bottom-1,left+1 SAY "Any Key to Continue..."
ELSE
   @ 00,10,03,70 BOX scrframe
   @ 01,11 SAY "There is no HELP for this section.  Would you like to make"
   @ 02,28 SAY "a HELP screen for this? "
   IF .NOT. VERIFY()
      RESTORE SCREEN
      SET KEY 28 TO Help
      RETURN
   ENDIF
   APPEND BLANK
   REPLACE lookit WITH SUBSTR(p,1,10) + SUBSTR(v,1,10) + TRANSFORM(l,"9999")
   STORE SPACE(4000) TO in_help, full_scr
   STORE 0 TO temp_top, temp_left, temp_bot, temp_right
   SAVE SCREEN TO full_scr
   DO WHILE .T.
      RESTORE SCREEN FROM full_scr
      @ 00,10,03,70 BOX scrframe
      @ 01,20 SAY "Position cursor with arrow for TOP, LEFT corner."
      cursor = 0
```

```
newcur = CHR(201)
SAVE SCREEN TO in_help
@ 12,40 SAY newcur
trow = 12
tcol = 40
* For the Summer '87 release
* SET CURSOR OFF
DO WHILE.T.
   cursor = INKEY(0)
   loop_again = MOVECURS()
   IF !loop_again
      EXIT
   ENDIF
   RESTORE SCREEN FROM in_help
   @ trow, tcol SAY newcur
ENDDO
STORE trow TO temp_top
STORE tcol TO temp_left
@ 00,10,03,70 BOX scrframe
@ 01,14 SAY "Position cursor with arrow for BOTTOM, RIGHT corner."
cursor = 0
SAVE SCREEN TO in_help
newcur = CHR(188)
trow = temp_top + 2
tcol = temp_left + 5
@ trow, tcol SAY newcur
DO WHILE.T.
   cursor = INKEY(0)
   loop_again = MOVECURS()
   IF !loop_again
      EXIT
   ENDIF
   RESTORE SCREEN FROM in_help
   @ trow, tcol SAY newcur
ENDDO
* For the Summer '87 rlease
* SET CURSOR ON
STORE trow TO temp_bot
STORE tcol TO temp_right
SAVE SCREEN TO in_help
DO Temphelp
@ 00,10,03,70 BOX scrframe
@ 02,25 SAY "Is this what you wanted?  "
IF .NOT. VERIFY()
   RESTORE SCREEN FROM in_help
   LOOP
ELSE
   EXIT
ENDIF
```
```
ENDDO
@ 00,10,03,70 BOX scrframe
@ 01,15 SAY "Enter in HELPful information.   Keep to ONE screen"
@ 02,15 SAY "      of text.  Press F10 when finished."
```

```
         REPLACE top WITH temp_top, bottom WITH temp_bot
         REPLACE left WITH temp_left, right WITH temp_right
         DO WHILE .T.
            @ top,left,bottom,right BOX scrframe
            REPLACE helpscr WITH MEMOEDIT(helpscr,top+1,left+1,;
            bottom-1,right-1,.T.)
            @ top,left,bottom,right BOX scrframe
            IF "" = MEMOEDIT(helpscr,top+1,left+1,bottom-1,right-1,.F.)
            * For the Summer '87 release, the MEMOEDIT() function should be:
            * MEMOEDIT(helpscr,top+1,left+1,bottom-1,right-1,.F.,.F.)
            ENDIF
            @ bottom-1,left+1 SAY "IS THIS CORRECT?   "
            IF .NOT. VERIFY()
               LOOP
            ENDIF
            EXIT
         ENDDO
         @ bottom-1,left+1 SAY "Press Any key to Continue...."
      ENDIF
      INKEY(0)
      RESTORE SCREEN
      tempgo = STR(goback)
      SELECT &tempgo
      SET KEY 28 TO Help
      RETURN

********************

PROCEDURE Dohelp

   SELECT 9
   CREATE Temp
   USE Temp
   APPEND BLANK
   REPLACE field_name WITH "LOOKIT", field_type WITH "C", field_len WITH 24
   APPEND BLANK
   REPLACE field_name WITH "TOP", field_type WITH "N", field_len WITH 2
   APPEND BLANK
   REPLACE field_name WITH "LEFT", field_type WITH "N", field_len WITH 2
   APPEND BLANK
   REPLACE field_name WITH "BOTTOM", field_type WITH "N", field_len WITH 2
   APPEND BLANK
   REPLACE field_name WITH "RIGHT", field_type WITH "N", field_len WITH 2
   APPEND BLANK
   REPLACE field_name WITH "HELPSCR", field_type WITH "M", field_len WITH 10
   USE
   CREATE Help FROM Temp
   USE
   ERASE Temp
   USE Help
   INDEX ON search_p + search_v TO Help
```

```
********************

PROCEDURE Temphelp

  SET COLOR TO W*
  @ temp_top, temp_left, temp_bot, temp_right BOX SUBSTR(scrframe,1,8)
  SET COLOR TO 7

***************************

FUNCTION VERIFY

   SET CONSOLE off
   WAIT TO inertemp
   SET CONSOLE on
   IF UPPER(inertemp) = "Y"
      ?? "Yes"
      te = INKEY(.25)
      RETURN(.T.)
   ENDIF
   ?? "No "
   te = INKEY(.25)
   RETURN(.F.)

********************

FUNCTION Movecurs

   DO CASE
   CASE cursor = 5
      IF trow - 1 > 0
         trow = trow - 1
      ENDIF
   CASE cursor = 4
      IF tcol + 1 < 79
         tcol = tcol + 1
      ENDIF
   CASE cursor = 19
      IF tcol - 1 > 0
         tcol = tcol - 1
      ENDIF
   CASE cursor = 24
      IF trow + 1 < 24
         trow = trow + 1
      ENDIF
   CASE cursor = 13 .OR. cursor = 27
      RETURN(.F.)
   ENDCASE
   RETURN(.T.)
* End of File
```

FINAL CONSIDERATIONS ON HELP FILES

Here are the file sizes for each of the HELP files we have studied:

1. General Help - 5K
2. Specific Help - 7K
3. Help to a File - 9K
4. Everything - 13K

The first two HELP files increase in size as more information is appended to the procedure. In large applications, where disk space and memory space is always a concern, these two examples may not be viable options.

The third example relies totally on the disk. The main disadvantage is speed (because of disk I/O), but speed may be a reasonable price to pay for virtually unlimited on-line HELP.

The last example is a combination of HELP files written both in the procedure and to the disk. The main advantage to this approach is that for most HELP routines the user or developer can write most of the information out to the disk. However, for additional information, especially for MUST FILL fields and variables, it may be best to write specific information directly in the procedure or to write a general HELP as a guide to operations.

Finally, remember it is crucial to applications using an overlay memory format to keep the HELP.PRG file in the main load module at all times.

CHAPTER SIXTEEN

Programming Structure and Application Layout

This chapter outlines rules of programming, guides to developing applications, and considerations about user support. Because of the nature of the subject, sample coding is sparse in this section; the information is more about Clipper as a language than about tricks in using Clipper. Additional information regarding special windowing techniques in relation to the Summer '87 release is also included.

GUIDELINES FOR GOOD PROGRAMMING

There are several rules of programming listed below. They are practical principles to follow when programming. These rules are not inviolate, but they can lend some structure to an often confusing job.

If you are familiar with these principles, review them again. If you are not, study the examples and the rules and judge your coding techniques against them. In either case, look on these rules as merely guides and remember that they may be broken to accomplish some worthwhile point. The problem is distinguishing between valid violations and just common sloppiness. The ability to make this judgment well comes with experience.

KEEP THE USER IN MIND

This refers to backup support. Your application is only good if your user base can work with it. The best way to accomplish this is with careful screen handling and meticulous control.

Keep in mind that the proper screen actually should be determined by the user. In some cases, the proper screen can require as much as 70 percent custom coding and 30 percent generic code. In other cases, the opposite is true. The point is to know your audience!

Clipper saves time and code with certain screen routines, especially with the SAVE SCREEN, BOX, and MENU...PROMPT commands. However, it still takes ingenuity to make the best use of these features. The use of color adds to applications; it enhances the final results and eases user interfacing. If color is used, allow an additional 10 percent in development time. Give the user as many options as possible to alter the basics of the application, including setting the screen border, the data delimiter, forcing a carriage return for every field, ringing a bell for every filled field, and similar customized settings.

The following code provides a screen and system initialization generator that can become a standard tool for your future applications.

```
********************
* Name          SCRINIT.prg
* Date          March 15, 1988
* Notice        Copyright 1988, Stephen J. Straley & Associates
* Compile       Clipper Scrinit
* Release       Autumn '86 or greater
* Link          Plink86 fi scrinit lib clipper
* Notes         This is an initialization menu for items that
*               pertain to the screen.  It writes a file named
*               SCREEN.SYS; all variables inside that file
*               pertaining to screen control begin with the
*               letters "scr."
********************

SET SCOREBOARD OFF

CLEAR
scrleft_1   = "Copyright (c) 1988 - Stephen J. Straley & Associates"
scrleft_2   = "All Rights Reserved"
right_1     = "Terminal/System Setup Program"
right_2     = "Version 3.00"
tscreen     = SPACE(4000)
scrframe    = CHR(201) + CHR(205) + CHR(187) + CHR(186) + CHR(188) + ;
              CHR(205) + CHR(200) + CHR(186)
center      = "Drive Assignment Setup"
@ 0,0 SAY scrleft_1
@ 1,0 SAY scrleft_2
@ 0,RIGHT_JUST(right_1) SAY right_1
@ 1,RIGHT_JUST(right_2) SAY right_2
@ 3,CENTER(center) SAY center
@ 4,0,23,79 BOX scrframe
SAVE SCREEN TO tscreen
IF .NOT. FILE("SCREEN.SYS")
   STORE "C:" TO scrprog, scrdata
   STORE .F. TO scrconfirm, scrdelim, scrcolor, scrinten, scrbell, scrshow,;
             scrtype
   STORE "" TO scrframe, scrbar, scrlin
   STORE "::" TO scrdelimto
   STORE 1 TO option, scrtimes, scrpass
   STORE .T. scrsys
ELSE
   RESTORE FROM Screen.sys ADDITIVE
   STORE 1 TO option
ENDIF

DO WHILE .T.

   RESTORE SCREEN FROM tscreen

   @  7, 5 PROMPT " 1> System Configured for " + ;
                  IF(scrsys, "Hard", "Floppy") + " Disk "
   @  7,45 PROMPT " 2> Program Drive Set to " + scrprog + " "
   @  8,45 PROMPT " 3> Data Drive Set to " + scrdata + " "
```

```
@ 10, 5 PROMPT " 4> Confirm is " + IF(scrconfirm, "ON ", "OFF ")
@ 11, 5 PROMPT " 5> Delimiters are " + IF(scrdelim, "ON ", "OFF ")
@ 12, 5 PROMPT " 6> Delimiters SET to " + scrdelimto + " "
@ 13, 5 PROMPT " 7> Screen " + IF(scrcolor, "Bright ", "Normal ")
@ 14, 5 PROMPT " 8> Field Color is " + IF(scrinten, "ON ", "OFF ")
@ 15, 5 PROMPT " 9> Bell " + IF(scrbell, "WILL", "WILL NOT") + " ring "
@ 10,40 PROMPT " A> Password " + IF(scrshow, "WILL", "WILL NOT") +;
               " echo to screen "
@ 12,40 PROMPT " B> Change Password "
@ 14,40 PROMPT " C> " + DLTRIM(STR(scrtimes)) + " tries at the Password "
@ 16,40 PROMPT " D> " + IF(scrtype, "Engage", "Disengage") +;
               " Type-Ahead Feature "
@ 18,33 PROMPT " 0> Save Values "
MENU TO option
DO CASE
CASE option = 1
   scrsys = !scrsys
   IF .NOT. scrsys
      KEYBOARD option = 2
   ENDIF
CASE option = 2
      @ 21,10 SAY "Enter Program Drive: " GET scrprog PICT "!";
                 VALID(SUBSTR(scrprog,1,1) $"ABCDEFGHIJKLMNOP")
      READ
      IF .NOT. scrsys
      IF scrprog = scrdata
            @ 21,10 SAY SPACE(50)
            @ 22,10 SAY "Data Drive and Program Drive NOT EQUAL " +;
                      " for Floppy System"
            @ 21,10 SAY "Enter Data Drive: " GET scrdata PICT "!";
                      VALID(SUBSTR(scrdata,1,1) $"ABCDEFGHIJKLMNOP";
                      .AND.  scrprog <> scrdata)
            READ
      ENDIF
   ENDIF
CASE option = 3
   @ 21,10 SAY "Enter Data Drive: " GET scrdata PICT "!";
             VALID(SUBSTR(scrdata,1,1) $"ABCDEFGHIJKLMNOP")
   READ
        IF .NOT. scrsys
        IF scrprog = scrdata
           @ 21,10 SAY SPACE(50)
           @ 22,10 SAY "Program Drive and Data Drive NOT EQUAL for " +;
                     "Floppy System"
           @ 21,10 SAY "Enter Program Drive: " GET scrprog PICT "!";
                     VALID(SUBSTR(scrprog,1,1) $"ABCDEFGHIJKLMNOP";
                     .AND.  scrdata <> scrprog)
        ENDIF
      ENDIF
CASE option = 4
        scrconfirm = !scrconfirm  && This means IF(scrconfirm, .F., .T.)
CASE option = 5
        scrdelim = !scrdelim
```

```
   CASE option = 6
            STORE " " TO choice
            @ 21,10 SAY "Set Left Delimiter:   " GET choice PICT "X"
            READ
            STORE choice TO scrdelimto
            STORE " " TO choice
            @ 21,10 SAY "Set Right Delimiter:  " GET choice PICT "X"
            READ
            STORE scrdelimto + choice TO scrdelimto
   CASE option = 7
      scrcolor = !scrcolor
   CASE option = 8
      scrinten = !scrinten
   CASE option = 9
      scrbell = !scrbell
   CASE option = 10
      scrshow = !scrshow
   CASE option = 11
      STORE SPACE(15) TO password
      @ 21,10 SAY "What Password do you want to use? " GET password;
               PICT "XXXXXXXXXXXXXXX"
      READ
      scrpass = GENPASS(password)
   CASE option = 12
      @ 21,10 SAY "How may tries for a correct password? " GET scrtimes;
              PICT "##" range 0,99
      READ
   CASE option = 13
      scrtype = !scrtype
   OTHERWISE
      EXIT
   ENDCASE

ENDDO
RESTORE SCREEN FROM tscreen
@ 3,3 SAY SPACE(60)
@ 3,29 SAY "Installing the Border"
SAVE SCREEN TO tscreen
in_choice = 4
prmpt_4 = scrframe
prmpt_5 = REPLICATE(CHR(177), 8) + " "
prmpt_6 = CHR(218) + CHR(196) + CHR(191) + CHR(179) + ;
          CHR(217) + CHR(196) + CHR(192) + CHR(179) + CHR(32)
prmpt_7 = CHR(222) + CHR(223) + CHR(221) + CHR(221) + ;
          CHR(221) + CHR(220) + CHR(222) + CHR(222) + CHR(32)
prmpt_9 = REPLICATE(CHR(15), 8) + " "
DO WHILE .T.
   RESTORE SCREEN FROM tscreen
   @ 6,5   PROMPT  " 1>   ********* "
   @ 6,32  PROMPT  " 2>   ========= "
   @ 6,59  PROMPT  " 3>   --------- "
   @ 8,5   PROMPT  " 4>   &prmpt_4. "
   @ 8,32  PROMPT  " 5>   &prmpt_5. "
```

```
@ 8,59  PROMPT  " 6>   &prmpt_6. "
@ 10,5  PROMPT  " 7>   &prmpt_7. "
@ 10,32 PROMPT  " 8>      "
@ 10,59 PROMPT  " 9>   &prmpt_9. "
@ 13,20 SAY "Move Cursor to choose preferred border"
MENU TO in_choice

DO CASE
CASE in_choice = 1
   scrframe = "******** "
   scrbar   = REPLICATE("*",80)
   scrlin   = "*"
CASE in_choice = 2
   scrframe = "======== "
   scrbar   = REPLICATE("=",80)
   scrlin   = "="
CASE in_choice = 3
   scrframe = "-------- "
   scrbar   = REPLICATE("-",80)
   scrlin   = "|"
CASE in_choice = 4
   scrframe = CHR(201) + CHR(205) + CHR(187) + CHR(186) + CHR(188) + ;
              CHR(205) + CHR(200) + CHR(186) + CHR(32)
   scrbar   = CHR(204) + REPLICATE(CHR(205), 78) + CHR(185)
   scrlin   = CHR(186)
CASE in_choice = 5
   scrframe = REPLICATE(CHR(177), 8) + " "
   scrbar   = REPLICATE(CHR(177),80)
   scrlin   = CHR(177)
CASE in_choice = 6
   scrframe = CHR(218) + CHR(196) + CHR(191) + CHR(179) + CHR(217) + ;
              CHR(196) + CHR(192) + CHR(179) + CHR(32)
   scrbar   = CHR(195) + REPLICATE(CHR(196), 78) + CHR(180)
   scrlin   = CHR(179)
CASE in_choice = 7
   scrframe = CHR(222) + CHR(223) + CHR(221) + CHR(221) + CHR(221) + ;
              CHR(220) + CHR(222) + CHR(222) + CHR(32)
   scrbar   = CHR(222) + REPLICATE(CHR(220),78) + CHR(221)
   scrlin   = CHR(222)
CASE in_choice = 8
   scrframe = " "
   scrbar   = REPLICATE("",80)
   scrlin   = ""
CASE in_choice = 9
   scrframe = REPLICATE(CHR(15), 8) + " "
   scrbar   = REPLICATE(CHR(15), 80)
   scrlin   = CHR(15)
ENDCASE
RESTORE SCREEN FROM tscreen
@ 8,10,16,69 BOX SUBSTR(scrframe,1,8)
@ 12,10 SAY SUBSTR(scrbar,1,1) + SUBSTR(scrbar,2,58) + SUBSTR(scrbar,80,1)

@ 19,25 SAY "Is this the border you want?  "
```

```
    IF VERIFY()
       EXIT
    ENDIF

ENDDO
writefile = scrprog + "SCREEN.SYS"
@ 22,24 SAY "Now Saving parameters to " + writefile
SAVE ALL LIKE scr* TO &writefile
RESTORE SCREEN FROM tscreen
@ 12,18 SAY  "Finished with Terminal/System Initialization"
@ 24,00 SAY ""
QUIT

*****************

FUNCTION Genpass

   PARAMETERS in_string

   COUNT = LEN(TRIM(in_string))
   final = 0
   FOR beginning = 1 TO (COUNT + 1)
      final = final + ASC(SUBSTR(in_string,beginning,1)) * beginning
   NEXT

   RETURN(final)

********************

FUNCTION Verify

   * This is for 'Is this Correct? (Y/N)' *

   SET CONSOLE OFF
   STORE "" TO verify_var
   DO WHILE .NOT. verify_var$"YyNn"
      WAIT TO verify_var
   ENDDO
   SET CONSOLE ON
   IF UPPER(verify_var) = "Y"
      ?? "Yes"
      RETURN(.T.)
   ENDIF
   ?? "No "
   RETURN(.F.)

********************

FUNCTION Dltrim

   PARAMETERS a

   RETURN(LTRIM(TRIM(a)))
* End of File
```

BE MODULAR (ONLY ONE SCREEN AT A TIME)

Requiring the user to scroll up another screen to get more information thwarts the flow of action. If a particular action in your program extends beyond the scope of one screen, you have set up road blocks to smooth running and introduced user frustration. Cut the code down by being more modular. Force yourself to keep things in one coherent screen and you will have happier users and more effective, cleaner, and tighter code.

Clipper has several techniques that facilitate modular coding. One such feature is that procedures can call one another. Procedures that are recursive in nature reduce the basic code size a great deal. Another example of modular programming is in the implementation of user-defined functions. However, if you use some of Clipper's extended features, remember that they are only available in the compiled environment and not under the interpreter.

BUILD A LIBRARY

You save time by developing code for the future. Spend a little time now for future projects and assemble a function and procedure library. No matter what industry you are programming for, many routines are always the same. For example, a check always requires numeric values to be converted to character string output.

When you have an extensive library, repetitive coding becomes a thing of the past. When repetitive coding is eliminated, many simple errors (the most frustrating kind) disappear. A well-developed function library supports the concepts of modular programming. If you find a bug in a library function, recode the function and relink it to all other applications calling it.

KEEP IT SIMPLE

There is often a strong tendency to develop applications in an overly complicated fashion. Remember that coding applications is very much like writing for a newspaper. Write clearly, say what you mean, keep to the point, and be as simple as you can. Do not try to be too clever and sacrifice clarity for fancy routines that only muddle your application.

In line with the rule of simplicity, choose the names you use carefully. Consider the variable names in the following example:

```
STORE .T. TO hel_fr_ovr
DO WHILE hel_fr_ovr
   <commands>
ENDDO
```

This is cute, but the variable name would make more sense if it were labeled something like "top_loop" or "looping." Naming variables is a question of style and technique, but the point is that variables should have names that either describe their location or operation. This makes code maintenance much easier. For the sake of reducing the size of an application, try using constants whenever possible rather than variables. Not only will this reduce the size of the executable code, but the program will run faster as well.

THE TELEPHONE TECHNIQUE

The telephone technique helps to keep code (1) clear and easy to read, (2) compact and concise, and (3) true to the overall structure of the application. The telephone technique is very simple. Take a section of your code and see if you can read it to someone over a telephone, line by line, command by command. If the person on the other side of the line can understand what you are trying to accomplish in your procedure and what the major branches, tests, and values are, your code is understandable and direct, and it adheres to many of the fundamental rules of good programing.

If the person on the other end of the conversation does not understand your code and your intent, the code may be too verbose, cryptic, vague, or simply may miss the point. If your code has any of these problems, do not patch it, rewrite it.

Make sure that for each section of your code you know what you are trying to accomplish and what steps are necessary in order to get you there. Speaking out loud while you program may also be helpful. Use some means of communication to test the validity of your code. If it fails these simple tests, it will surely fail in the computer.

The telephone technique tests the strength of your code. If there are too many problems with it, start over and try again.

AVOID EXCESS BRANCHING ON IF

This rule is difficult to adhere to because no one starts out intending to use branching excessively. The main point is one of control. If an IF branch is necessary [and the IF() function is inappropriate], keep control of it. One simple IF command can easily lead to another embedded IF command, which in turn yields a few more embedded IF commands. Sooner or later, if you use proper indenting, your code will wander off the right side of the screen.

If there is a situation that generates several testing conditions, break up the IF...ENDIF commands into a more structured DO CASE...ENDCASE followed by the necessary IF... ENDIF command. Nesting several layers of IF commands only complicates your code. The basic structure for the IF...ELSE...ENDIF command is two branches, one for a true condition and one for a false one. If multiple logical testing conditions exist and you do not wish to use a DO CASE...ENDCASE structure, use nested IF() function calls.

DO NOT PATCH; REWRITE

Programmers often get too attached to their code and, in an attempt to save some faulty part, keep sticking in more lines of code. What normally evolves is a quilted pattern of several halfhearted attempts at one major thought, none of which ever seems to get the job done.

Bad code comes from bad design. Go back to the beginning and rework the design to improve the code. **Do not try to patch bad code**! Too much time is wasted on code with bad technique or design.

ESTIMATE 3 TIMES MORE TIME

This is more of a rule of planning than a rule of coding. Always estimate 3 times more time for application development than you think you need. Developers invariably leave out time for bad coding, revisions, modifications, and, of course, documentation. There are several variables that need to be figured into the time equation, including working with the compiler, working in a different environment, testing, and planning. Generally speaking, you should establish a time schedule, multiply that figure by 3, and you will be closer to the truth.

CODING AND CUTENESS DON'T MIX

Developing clever or cute routines is wonderful on the surface, but it invariably has a cost in clarity. Even if you document your code heavily, cute code is confusing months later when you have to make modifications. In addition, cute code tends to restrict alterations. Write code clearly and concisely with enough comments to maintain readability. Write enough code to get the job done.

If you code for yourself as well as for your customers, you will save countless hours in debugging, recoding, and in alterations.

FOLLOW A LOGICAL FLOW

Computers are based on logic, specifically Boolean logic. Programs should flow logically as well. In some languages where line numbers are allowed, it is easy to get caught in a spaghetti mush of GOTO and GOSUB statements. Many applications look like they started with a clear basic idea, then were given a quick addition here and there, including a few interfacing routines and a couple of slapped together functions, and then released. The application may work, but it is still sloppy.

Programming should flow from one distinct module to another without confusion or ambiguity.

AVOID SENSELESS ERRORS

The time spent on careful planning is almost always less than time spent fixing mistakes that result from rushing through the coding for an application. Some mistakes are inevitable, but the goal is to cut down on the mistakes that happen because of carelessness.

COMMENTS AND NOTATIONS

Whenever you are programming, assume that someone else will eventually read your code. You can help that reader by writing clearly. However, no matter how well you label variables, plan the program flow, and define your structure, code alone isn't enough. Use comments and internal notations to explain structural elements, important variables, calling routines, and functions. Comment lines are not compiled, so the execution of the generated object file will not be slowed down by commented information.

Treat comments like the code; be direct and to the point.

Finally, do not comment bad code; rewrite it!

ELEVEN RULES FOR SUCCESS IN PROGRAMMING

1. Write first in easy-to-understand pseudo-code, then translate into Clipper code.
   - Do not stop with your first draft.
   - Do not patch bad code; rewrite it.
   - Do not strain to reuse code; just reorganize it.
   - Make sure special cases are really special cases.
   - Write and test a big program in small pieces.
   - Do not stop at one bug; find others.
   - Watch out for off-by-one errors:
     - 10.0 times 0.1 is hardly ever 1.0: test to make sure that calculations are correct.
     - Do not compare floating point numbers just for equality.
   - Be in control. Measure the effect of any change before making the change for the sake of efficiency.

2. Write clearly.

   - Do not be too clever.
   - Make your programs read from top to bottom.
   - Let the data structure the program.
   - Do not diddle with code to make it faster; find a better algorithm.
   - Format a program to help the reader understand it.
   - Indent code to show the logical structure of a program.

3. Say what you mean, simply and directly.

   - Make sure your code "does nothing" gracefully. Too often developers, when asked what their routine does, say "it does nothing." If this is the case, check it again. "Does nothing" code has a tendency to do plenty!
   - Program defensively.
   - Make it right before making it faster.
   - Keep it right when making it faster.
   - Make it clearer before making it faster.
   - Do not sacrifice clarity for small gains in "efficiency."
   - Keep it simple to make it faster.

4. Modularize.

   - Use subroutines.
   - Make the coupling between modules clearly visible.
   - Each module should do one thing and do it **well**.
   - Use recursive procedures for recursively defined structures.

5. Use library functions.

   - Replace repetitive expressions with calls to a common function.

6. Avoid too many temporary variables.

   - Choose variable names that cannot be confused.
   - Choose procedure names that describe their basic purpose.
   - Choose function names that describe their basic purpose.
   - Choose field names that make the program simple.
   - Use variable names that mean something.
   - Create labels that mean something.

7. Let the machine and language do the dirty work.

8. Avoid unnecessary branches.

   - Do not use conditional branches as a substitute for a logical expression.
   - Use IF...ELSE...ENDIF to emphasize that only one of two actions is to be performed.

- Use the fundamental control flow constructs.
- Follow each division and its associated action as closely as possible.
- Avoid multiple exits from loops.
- Use the good features of the language and avoid the bad ones.
- Use data arrays to avoid repetitive control sequences.

9. Use DO WHILE and indenting to delimit groups of statements.
   - Use DO and DO WHILE to emphasize the presence of loops.
   - Use DO CASE to implement multiway branches.

10. Initialize all variables before use.

11. Make sure comments and code agree.
   - Do not just echo the code with comments. Make the comments count!
   - Do not comment bad code; rewrite it!
   - Do not overcomment.

A STRUCTURED FORM FOR APPLICATION DEVELOPMENT

One of the most difficult things to do is to estimate the amount of time it takes to create an application. It's human to expect to devote far less time than reality demands. This is especially true for consultants who base their livelihood on the time they bill out for projects.

Getting clients and projects is based in part on reputation and in part on the ability to bid a project properly and then to bring in the project on time and on budget. To control time and budgeting, good developers should use a checklist of items that includes all of the features that make up an application.

DEVELOPMENT CHECKLIST:

Hours | Cost

1. System Environment Generation
    a. Screen Design
        i. Help
        ii. Color
        iii. Menus
    b. Application Parameters
        i. Passwords
        ii. Borders
        iii. Check Numbers
        iv. Miscellaneous
2. Creating Databases and Indexes
    a. Fields
    b. Memos (If Applicable)
    c. Key Fields
    d. Relations
3. Data Control
    a. Entering
    b. Editing
    c. Viewing
    d. Deleting (If Applicable)
4. Calculation
    a. Totaling
    b. Summing and Averaging
    c. Balancing
5. Reporting and Listing
    a. Screen
    b. Printer
    c. File
6. System Maintenance
    a. Sorting and Reindexing
    b. Backing up and Restoring Data
    c. Data Cleanup
    d. Reconfiguring System
    e. Miscellaneous
7. Data Interface (If Applicable)
    a. Importing
    b. Exporting
    c. Across Systems
8. Multiuser Control (If Applicable)
9. Testing
10. Documentation

SCREEN DESIGN AND LAYOUT IN CLIPPER

SCREEN DESIGN THEORY

The most sophisticated programs can be worth absolutely nothing if screens are designed and handled poorly. An application's screens are the programmer's way of interacting cohesively, progressing logically, and eliminating confusion for the user. The following are not absolutes but rather are guidelines and suggestions for screen design.

Several user-interfacing techniques have come to light in the microcomputer world. One example is the surface-sensitive device commonly known as a *mouse*. This device is a small peripheral attached to the computer that is either controlled by a roller ball underneath or is sensitive to a special pad. When the mouse is moved, a corresponding arrow on the screen moves in the same direction. Choices or options are selected by pushing a button on the mouse. The mouse guides users both visually and physically. Another method designed to increase user understanding is the *pull-down menu*. After the user chooses an option from a command line, a new frame or *window* shows up on the screen with further choices or options. This technique can give the user a sense of progress as he or she goes through each screen. The user gets the feeling that the computer is doing something as each window is pulled-down from the command line.

The next method is similar to pull-down menus. The user is presented with only one menu at a time, and an item chosen from one menu brings up another menu with additional selections. The user is never confronted with too many choices and can slowly work through the program. This is an old technique, but it is still effective if it is used well.

Now we come to the introduction to true window management with the Summer '87 Clipper. Several new features in this release make screen manipulation efficient on memory and easy to code. Included in this section are a few examples explored in the Steve Straley Toolkit, which bases everything on the pull-down style of menus. What makes this version of Clipper more applicable to pull-down windows is the introduction of PUBLIC arrays, portions of the screen saved and recalled from memory variables (rather than the entire screen), and new enhanced functions.

There are many variations on the use of windows. You can take a dull menu and make it far more effective by just highlighting the previously selected menu item. Keeping previous menus visible while overlapping new menus also adds clarity to the program and maintains a sense of progress. The construction of menus and windows is covered in the next section of this chapter. The principles of interfacing with users are universal, however, no matter what method you employ.

THE PRINCIPLES OF USER INTERFACING

Keep a Standard Format for Screens and Prompts

Consistency is extremely important. Menus should read top to bottom, then left to right; numbers are also better than letters. Whatever your preference, decide upon one method of screen layout and stick to it. This simple but important rule of screen consistency is ignored much too often. If you decide that the number 0 is used to exit from the application, the number 0 should also be used to exit from all submenus to higher menus. If numbers are used to select menu options, maintain that format and never switch to letters.

Prompts and messages, as well as menu headers if used, should be kept uniform from menu to menu. Normally, headers are used to contain the developing company's name, the name of the company using the product, a company logo, copyright declaration and date, the product name and possibly its developer, and the current version number. Again, be consistent. If the main menu title is centered on line 5 of the screen, all menu titles should follow suit. Users get accustomed to looking at the same places on the screen for certain pieces of information. Users are creatures of habit out of necessity. Time lost searching for the "right" option on a screen is time wasted.

Many Menus, Few Options

Group similar options together to make submenus. Group general items as options that lead to submenus.

Many developers try to fit as many options on one screen as possible. The user cannot absorb all of that information at one time. Even though it may seem more convenient to add just one or two more options to a higher-level menu screen rather than take the time to program an entire new screen, it's worth the extra programming time. Users can follow the logic of the program far more easily if menus have only the minimum number of choices.

Show the Progression of Options

Inform the users of the current level of operation, how they got there, and what is going to happen next.

Users are left too often with screens that have no indication of what preceded or what follows, leading to confusion and getting lost in the application. Highlighting previous choices is a good practice, as is leaving the higher menu on the screen while drawing the next submenu in a smaller section on the screen with the new choices and standard prompt. This method shows previous screens, preventing a user from getting lost, especially if selected items are highlighted, and it shows the next steps in a clear, concise manner. Pull-down menus are similar in that previous choices are expanded into new frames and new choices appear.

Keep the Wording Simple

Unnecessary use of big words adds to confusion and confusion adds to lost time.

Maintain a Sense of Operation

Whenever the computer is doing something, show it. Don't let the user assume that something is going on when there could be a problem or, conversely, that there is a problem when none exists.

All too often, the user is left in the dark when the computer is doing something that takes time. Relying on the disk drive light is not effective, as most operations are performed in memory before going to the disk drive. The use of a benevolent "One Moment Please" message on the screen that stays there for several hours is not sufficient because it doesn't reflect the actual operation taking place.

Maintain Easy Escape Methods

Allow the user to escape from wrong choices without having to wait for an operation to complete. Keep in mind that the user may make a mistake in choosing an item from a menu. Users poke and plod through menu choices, looking for the right path or the right menu. Allow this to happen. Getting into the system is important, but getting out is equally important. Choose an escape key or method and stick to it throughout the application.

Provide as Much Help as Possible

The key to providing effective user help is to give as much information as possible without cluttering the screen.

Use Clipper's HELP.PRG facility. Remember that users generally do not read manuals. Take the time to set up on-line HELP whenever possible. While doing so, remember there is a fine line between sufficient help and too much clutter.

The type of help that should be on the screen at all times with the menus either shows the user how to get more help or how to move between menus.

There are two ways of approaching the development of HELP.PRG. One way is to create HELP.PRG with all of the text information that you will provide with your application. This is easy to develop, but takes space. The other way to develop HELP screens is to have them available separately, yet maintain the option for the user to invoke them at any time.

WINDOWING WITH CLIPPER

Using the Box Command to Draw Boxes

Syntax: @ <t,l,b,r> BOX <string>

The BOX command is no more than two separate @...SAY or @...GET statements combined. The first two coordinates <t,l> are the top-left positions for the box. The following two numbers are the bottom-right coordinates. The top and bottom coordinates must be in the range of 0 to 24, and the left and right coordinates must be in the 0 to 79 range. The <string> portion of the command is the section where you specify the design of the border of the box as well as the "fill" character. These characters must be in the following order:

1. The top-left corner character
2. The character used across the top
3. The top-right corner character
4. The character down the right side
5. The bottom-right corner character
6. The character across the bottom
7. The bottom-left corner character
8. The character up the left side
9. The character used to fill the box.

Generally, in designing menus, the fill character will be the space [CHR(32)]. In the following sample, the fill character, as well as all of the other characters comprising the frame, are from the IBM graphic character set.

Sample:

```
frame = CHR(201) + CHR(205) + CHR(187) + CHR(186) +;
        CHR(188) + CHR(205) + CHR(200) + CHR(186) +;
        CHR(176)

@ 0,0,23,79 BOX frame
```

The screen is surrounded by a frame and filled with graphic blocks.

Here's a tip: to clear the BOXed area quickly, use the BOX command with a null string in place of the character set, and the area specified by the four coordinates will be cleared.

Sample:

```
@ 0,0,23,79 BOX ""
```

Sample Code Using the BOX Command:

```
*********************
* Name          DRAWBOX.prg
* Date          March 15, 1988
* Notice        Copyright 1986, Stephen J. Straley & Associates
* Compile       Clipper Drawbox
* Release       All Release
* Link          Plink86 fi drawbox lib clipper
* Note          This shows the use of boxes on the screen and
*               how they can be incremented and decremented.  The
*               last screen takes advantage of the fill character
*               whereas all other BOXes are just frames.
*********************

STORE CHR(218) + CHR(196) + CHR(191) + CHR(179) + CHR(217) +;
      CHR(196) + CHR(192) + CHR(179) + CHR(176) TO frame

CLEAR
STORE 1 TO counter, top, left
STORE 23 to bottom
STORE 78 to right
DO WHILE counter <> 11

   @ top, left, bottom, right BOX SUBSTR(frame,1,8)

   STORE top + 1 TO top
   STORE left + 3 TO left
   STORE bottom - 1 TO bottom
   STORE right - 3 TO right
   STORE counter + 1 to counter
ENDDO

@ top, left, bottom, right BOX frame
@ top + (bottom - top) / 2, left + (right - left) / 2 - 3 SAY ;
   "Finished"
STORE 1 TO counter
DO WHILE counter <> 500
   STORE counter + 1 TO counter
ENDDO
@ 23,00 SAY ""
* End of File
```

Windows for Menus and Submenus

When developing menus and submenus, set a style and always use it. In many of my applications, for example, I use the zero (0) to exit from submenus to higher-level menus and to exit the application. The escape method does not change from menu to menu and the user feels more at ease. Also state menu options clearly, limiting the number of options on the screen and panning from top to bottom and left to right.

Overlap submenus, with the background (usually the main menu) overlapped by submenus, which overlap each other. An additional technique is to have previous menu choices remain on screen in inverse video. Screens should be saved as the operator goes down through the application and the user should have the option to "pop" up to the previous menu without going back to the main menu. The following sample code shows other ways of using screen saving with arrays, MENU...PROMPT commands, and the BOX command.

Sample Code for Windowing Menus:

```
*********************
* Name          DRAWMEN1.prg
* Date          March 15, 1988
* Notice        Copyright 1988, Stephen J. Straley & Associates
* Compile       Clipper Drawmen1
* Release       Winter '85 or later
* Link          Plink86 fi drawmen1 lib clipper
* Note          This sample code shows how to develop menus as
*               they move down to more specific options, how screens
*               can be saved and recalled (especially in conjunction
*               with arrays), and how BOXes are drawn.
*********************

STORE CHR(201) + CHR(205) + CHR(187) + CHR(186) + ;
      CHR(188) + CHR(205) + CHR(200) + CHR(186) + " " TO scrframe
SET INTENS on
SET DELIM off
prompt  = "Enter Choice:  "
disp0_1 = " 1>    Chart Of Accounts "
disp0_2 = " 2>    Transactions "
disp0_3 = " 3>    Posting & Balancing "
disp0_4 = " 4>    Transfers "
disp0_5 = " 5>    Print Lists or Checks "
disp0_6 = " 6>    Print Reports "
disp0_7 = " 7>    Utilities "
disp0_8 = " 8>    End of Period "
disp0_0 = " 0>    Exit Program "
disp1_1 = " 1>   Enter an Account "
disp1_2 = " 2>   Edit an Account "
disp1_3 = " 3>   Examine Accounts "
disp1_4 = " 4>   Delete an Account "
disp1_0 = " 0>   Return to Main Menu "
disp2_1 = " 1>  Enter Transaction "
disp2_2 = " 2>  Edit Transaction "
disp2_3 = " 3>  Delete Transaction "
disp2_0 = " 0>  Return to Main Menu "
disp5_1 = " 1>   Chart of Account Info. "
disp5_2 = " 2>   Print or Reprint Checks "
disp5_3 = " 3>   Transaction Information "
disp5_4 = " 4>   Heading Listings "
disp5_0 = " 0>   Return to Main Menu "
DO WHILE .T.
```

```
option = "0"
@ 0,0 CLEAR
@ 5,0,20,79 BOX SUBSTR(scrframe,1,8)
@  4,33 SAY "M A I N   M E N U"
@  7,10 SAY "1>    Chart Of Accounts"
@ 10,10 SAY "2>    Transactions"
@ 13,10 SAY "3>    Posting & Balancing"
@ 16,10 SAY "4>    Transfers"
@  7,50 SAY "5>    Print Lists or Checks"
@ 10,50 SAY "6>    Print Reports"
@ 13,50 SAY "7>    Utilities"
@ 16,50 SAY "8>    End of Period"
@ 18,30 SAY "0>    Exit Program"
@ 22,30 SAY prompt GET option PICT "9" VALID(option $"012345678")
READ
DO CASE
CASE option = "1"
   @ 7,9 GET disp0_1
   CLEAR GETS
   @ 12,37,22,76 BOX scrframe
   @ 13,44 SAY "Chart of Accounts SubMenu"
   @ 15,46 SAY "1>   Enter an Account"
   @ 16,46 SAY "2>   Edit an Account"
   @ 17,46 SAY "3>   Examine Accounts"
   @ 18,46 SAY "4>   Delete an Account"
   @ 19,46 SAY "0>   Return to Main Menu"
   @ 21,47 SAY prompt GET option PICT "9" VALID(option $"0")
   READ

CASE option = "3"
   STORE "0" TO option
   @ 13, 9 GET disp0_3
   CLEAR GETS
   @ 10,37,18,76 BOX scrframe
   @ 11,47 SAY "Post or Balance Submenu"
   @ 13,45 SAY "1>  Post Transactions"
   @ 14,45 SAY "2>  Balance Accounts"
   @ 15,45 SAY "0>  Return to Main Menu"
   @ 17,47 SAY prompt GET option PICT "9" VALID(option $"0")
   READ

CASE option = "5"
   STORE "0" TO option, suboption
   @  7,49 GET disp0_5
   CLEAR GETS
   @ 9,3,19,43 BOX scrframe
   @ 10,11 SAY "Print Lists or Checks Submenu"
   @ 12,10 SAY "1>   Chart of Account Info."
   @ 13,10 SAY "2>   Print or Reprint Checks"
   @ 14,10 SAY "3>   Transaction Information"
   @ 15,10 SAY "4>   Heading Listings"
   @ 16,10 SAY "0>   Return to Main Menu"
   @ 18,12 SAY prompt GET option PICT "9" VALID(option $"01234")
```

```
READ
DO CASE
CASE option = "0"
   @ 16,09 GET disp5_0
   CLEAR GETS
   LOOP
CASE option = "1"
   @ 12, 9 GET disp5_1
   CLEAR GETS
   @ 6,40,16,77 BOX scrframe
   @  7,46 SAY " Printing Chart of Accounts"
   @  9,49 SAY "1>  Account Listing"
   @ 10,49 SAY "2>  Account History"
   @ 11,49 SAY "3>  Budget Listing"
   @ 12,49 SAY "0>  Return to Main Menu"
   @ 14,49 SAY prompt GET suboption PICT "9" VALID(suboption $"0123")
   READ

CASE option = "2"
   @ 13, 9 GET disp5_2
   CLEAR GETS
   @ 6,37,15,76 BOX scrframe
   @ 7, 43 SAY "        Reprint or Print Checks"
   @ 9, 45 SAY "1>  Print Checks"
   @ 10,45 SAY "2>  Reprint Checks"
   @ 11,45 SAY "3>  Print Check Register"
   @ 12,45 SAY "0>  Return to Main Menu"
   @ 14,46 SAY Prompt GET suboption PICT "9" VALID(suboption $"0123")
   READ

CASE option = "3"
   @ 14, 9 GET disp5_3
   CLEAR GETS
   @ 6,37,17,76 BOX scrframe
   @  7,43 SAY "       Print Transaction List"
   @  9,45 SAY "1>  By Transaction Code"
   @ 10,45 SAY "2>  By Transaction Source"
   @ 11,45 SAY "3>  By Date of Transaction"
   @ 12,45 SAY "4>  By Account Order"
   @ 13,45 SAY "5>  All Transactions"
   @ 14,45 SAY "0>  Return to Main Menu"
   @ 16,48 SAY prompt GET suboption PICT "9" VALID(suboption $"012345")
   READ

CASE option = "4"
   @ 15, 9 GET disp5_4
   CLEAR GETS
   @ 6,37,15,76 BOX scrframe
   @  7,42 SAY "  List General Headings Submenu"
   @  9,42 SAY "1>  List Master or Submasters"
   @ 10,42 SAY "2>  List Subheadings or Subtotals"
   @ 11,42 SAY "3>  List All"
   @ 12,42 SAY "0>  Return to Submenu"
```

```
        @ 14,45 SAY prompt GET suboption PICT "9" VALID(suboption $"0123")
        READ

     ENDCASE

  CASE option = "7"

  CASE option = "2"
     STORE "0" TO option
     @ 10, 9 GET disp0_2
     CLEAR GETS
     @ 8,37,17,76 BOX scrframe
     @  9,47 SAY "Transaction Submenu"
     @ 11,45 SAY "1>  Enter Transaction"
     @ 12,45 SAY "2>  Edit Transaction"
     @ 13,45 SAY "3>  Delete Transaction"
     @ 14,45 SAY "0>  Return to Main Menu"
     @ 16,48 SAY prompt GET option PICT "9" VALID(option $"0")
     READ

  CASE option = "4"
     STORE "0" TO option
     @ 16, 9 GET disp0_4
     CLEAR GETS
     @ 9,37,22,76 BOX scrframe
     @ 10,47 SAY "Transfer Data Submenu"
     @ 12,41 SAY "1>   Transfer Accounts Receivable"
     @ 13,41 SAY "2>   Transfer Payroll"
     @ 14,41 SAY "3>   Transfer Accounts Payable"
     @ 15,41 SAY "4>   Transfer Inventory"
     @ 16,41 SAY "5>   Transfer Other Systems"
     @ 17,41 SAY "6>   Transfer Outside Systems"
     @ 18,41 SAY "7>   Post Transfers"
     @ 19,41 SAY "0>   Return to Main Menu"
     @ 21,45 SAY prompt GET option PICT "9" VALID(option $"0")
     READ

  CASE option = "6"
     STORE "0" TO option
     @ 10,49 GET disp0_6
     CLEAR GETS
     @  9,3,18,43 BOX scrframe
     @ 10,12 SAY "Print Reports Submenu"
     @ 12, 8 SAY "1>   Print Trial Balance"
     @ 13, 8 SAY "2>   Print Statement of Income"
     @ 14, 8 SAY "3>   Print Balance Sheet"
     @ 15, 8 SAY "0>   Return to Main Menu"
     @ 17,11 SAY prompt GET option PICT "9" VALID(option $"0")
     READ

  CASE option = "8"
     STORE "0" TO option
     @ 16,49 GET disp0_8
```

```
        CLEAR GETS
        @ 7,2,17,38 BOX scrframe
        @  8, 8 SAY "End of Period Processing"
        @  9,16 SAY "Submenu"
        @ 11,10 SAY "1>  End of Month"
        @ 12,10 SAY "2>  End of Quarter"
        @ 13,10 SAY "3>  End of Year"
        @ 14,10 SAY "0>  Return to Main Menu"
        @ 16,11 SAY prompt GET option PICT "9" VALID(option $"0123")
        READ

     CASE option = "0"
        @ 18,29 GET disp0_0
        CLEAR GETS
        CLOSE
        @ 22,17 SAY "All Files Closed.  Returning to Operating System."
        QUIT
     ENDCASE
  ENDDO
  * End of File
```

SCREEN SAVING

The ability to save screens carries the responsibility of monitoring the size of an application. Two questions arise:

1. How many screens should one save?
2. Does saving screens really help the user?

The answer to the second question is, without a doubt, yes! But menus aren't the only things that should be saved. In many applications, previous data entry screens are more important to save than the menus. Don't forget that the bottom line to saving screens is saving time. If data entry and data processing are performed 65 percent of the time, saving data-entry screens would be more beneficial than saving menus.

Why not save both? It would be nice to save all screens, but the reality is that it takes 4K of memory per screen. It would be nice to be able to save 20 screens (menus, processing screens, and help screens) in an application, but with a total of 80K in additional overhead to the system many applications can't afford that luxury!

Sample Code for Windowing Menus

To illustrate the windowing techniques in conjunction with saving screens and using arrays, the previous windowing example is elaborated upon in the following code. Notice that this program uses a lot of memory. Even though the .EXE program is relatively small, the total amount of RAM required is about 384K.

```
********************
* Name          DRAWMEN2.prg
* Date          March 15, 1988
* Notice        Copyright 1988, Stephen J. Straley & Associates
* Compile       Clipper Drawmen2
* Release       Autumn '86 or later
* Link          Plink86 fi drawmen2 lib clipper
* Note          Shows how menus are created in conjunction with
*               saving screens and the use of arrays.  This is
*               developed from DRAWMEN1.prg.
********************

STORE CHR(201) + CHR(205) + CHR(187) + CHR(186) + CHR(188) +;
      CHR(205) + CHR(200) + CHR(186) + CHR(32) TO scrframe
SET INTENS on
SET DELIM off

***************************************************************
* The following arrays are established for all of the         *
* possible screens to follow.  The "shown[x]" array is        *
* used to test if the submenu has been shown before.          *
* If it has, shown[x] is true and the appropriate screen      *
* will be called back from the screen[x] array.  If not,      *
* the BOX command and the proper displays are drawn; the      *
* screen is saved to screen[x], and shown[x] is set to true. *
***************************************************************

DECLARE screen[15], shown[15]
FOR x = 1 TO 15
   STORE .F. TO shown[x]
NEXT

STORE "Enter Choice:" TO prompt
STORE SPACE(4000) TO tempscreen

***********************************************************
* The following are the menu variables for inverse video. *
***********************************************************

disp0_1 = " 1>   Chart Of Accounts "
disp0_2 = " 2>   Transactions "
disp0_3 = " 3>   Posting & Balancing "
disp0_4 = " 4>   Transfers "
disp0_5 = " 5>   Print Lists or Checks "
disp0_6 = " 6>   Print Reports "
disp0_7 = " 7>   Utilities "
disp0_8 = " 8>   End of Period "
disp0_0 = " 0>   Exit Program "
disp1_1 = " 1>   Enter an Account "
disp1_2 = " 2>   Edit an Account "
disp1_3 = " 3>   Examine Accounts "
disp1_4 = " 4>   Delete an Account "
disp1_0 = " 0>   Return to Main Menu "
```

```
disp2_1 = " 1>   Enter Transaction "
disp2_2 = " 2>   Edit Transaction "
disp2_3 = " 3>   Delete Transaction "
disp2_0 = " 0>   Return to Main Menu "
disp5_1 = " 1>   Chart of Account Info. "
disp5_2 = " 2>   Print or Reprint Checks "
disp5_3 = " 3>   Transaction Information "
disp5_4 = " 4>   Headings Listings "
disp5_0 = " 0>   Return to Main Menu "
option = "0"

**********************************
* Now for the actual operation. *
**********************************

CLEAR
@ 5,0,20,79 BOX SUBSTR(scrframe,1,8)
@ 4,33 SAY "M A I N   M E N U"

DO WHILE .T.

   **********************************
   * This section is the main menu. *
   **********************************
   IF shown[15]
      RESTORE SCREEN FROM screen[15]
   ELSE
      @  7,10 SAY "1>    Chart Of Accounts"
      @ 10,10 SAY "2>    Transactions"
      @ 13,10 SAY "3>    Posting & Balancing"
      @ 16,10 SAY "4>    Transfers"
      @  7,50 SAY "5>    Print Lists or Checks"
      @ 10,50 SAY "6>    Print Reports"
      @ 13,50 SAY "7>    Utilities"
      @ 16,50 SAY "8>    End of Period"
      @ 18,30 SAY "0>    Exit Program"
      SAVE SCREEN TO tempscreen
      * Do NOT save the screen directly to an array element. First save it
      * to a memory variable, and then STORE that to the array element.
      STORE tempscreen TO screen[15]
      STORE .T. TO shown[15]
   ENDIF
   @ 22,30 SAY prompt GET option PICT "9" VALID(option $"012345678")
   READ

   DO CASE

   CASE option = "1"

      ******************************
      * This is the first submenu. *
      ******************************
      STORE "0" TO option
      IF shown[1]
         RESTORE SCREEN FROM screen[1]
```

```
     ELSE
        @  7, 9 GET disp0_1
        CLEAR GETS
        @ 12,37,22,76 BOX scrframe
        @ 13,44 SAY "Chart Of Accounts Submenu"
        @ 15,46 SAY "1>   Enter an Account"
        @ 16,46 SAY "2>   Edit an Account"
        @ 17,46 SAY "3>   Examine Accounts"
        @ 18,46 SAY "4>   Delete an Account"
        @ 19,46 SAY "0>   Return to Main Menu"
        SAVE SCREEN TO tempscreen
        STORE tempscreen TO screen[1]
        STORE .T. TO shown[1]
     ENDIF
     @ 21,47 SAY prompt GET option PICT "9" VALID(option $"0")
     READ

  CASE option = "2"

     ********************************
     * This is the second submenu. *
     ********************************
     STORE "0" TO option
     IF shown[2]
        RESTORE SCREEN FROM screen[2]
     ELSE
        @ 10, 9 GET disp0_2
        CLEAR GETS
        @ 8,37,17,76 BOX scrframe
        @  9,47 SAY "Transaction Submenu"
        @ 11,45 SAY "1>  Enter Transaction"
        @ 12,45 SAY "2>  Edit Transaction"
        @ 13,45 SAY "3>  Delete Transaction"
        @ 14,45 SAY "0>  Return to Main Menu"
        SAVE SCREEN TO tempscreen
        STORE tempscreen TO screen[2]
        STORE .T. TO shown[2]
     ENDIF
     @ 16,48 SAY prompt GET option PICT "9" VALID(option $"0")
     READ

  CASE option = "3"

     *******************************
     * This is the third submenu. *
     *******************************
     STORE "0" TO option
     IF shown[3]
        RESTORE SCREEN FROM screen[3]
     ELSE
        @ 13, 9 GET disp0_3
        CLEAR GETS
        @ 10,37,18,76 BOX scrframe
```

```
        @ 11,47 SAY "Post or Balance Submenu"
        @ 13,45 SAY "1>  Post Transactions"
        @ 14,45 SAY "2>  Balance Accounts"
        @ 15,45 SAY "0>  Return to Main Menu"
        SAVE SCREEN TO tempscreen
        STORE tempscreen TO screen[3]
        STORE .T. TO shown[3]
     ENDIF
     @ 17,47 SAY prompt GET option PICT "9" VALID(option $"0")
     READ

  CASE option = "4"

     *********************************
     * This is the fourth submenu. *
     *********************************
     STORE "0" TO option
     IF shown[4]
           RESTORE SCREEN FROM screen[4]
        ELSE
           @ 16, 9 GET disp0_4
           CLEAR GETS
           @ 9,37,22,76 BOX scrframe
           @ 10,47 SAY "Transfer Data Submenu"
           @ 12,41 SAY "1>   Transfer Accounts Receivable"
           @ 13,41 SAY "2>   Transfer Payroll"
           @ 14,41 SAY "3>   Transfer Accounts Payable"
           @ 15,41 SAY "4>   Transfer Inventory"
           @ 16,41 SAY "5>   Transfer Other Systems"
           @ 17,41 SAY "6>   Transfer Outside Systems"
           @ 18,41 SAY "7>   Post Transfers"
           @ 19,41 SAY "0>   Return to Main Menu"
           SAVE SCREEN TO tempscreen
           STORE tempscreen TO screen[4]
           STORE .T. TO shown[4]
        ENDIF
        @ 21,45 SAY prompt GET option PICT "9" VALID(option $"0")
        READ

  CASE option = "5"

     ********************************
     * This is the fifth submenu. *
     ********************************
     DO WHILE .T.

        STORE "0" TO option, suboption
        IF shown[5]
           RESTORE SCREEN FROM screen[5]
        ELSE
           @  7,49 GET disp0_5
           CLEAR GETS
           @ 9,3,19,43 BOX scrframe
```

```
    @ 10,11 SAY "Print Lists or Checks Submenu"
    @ 12,10 SAY "1>   Chart of Account Info."
    @ 13,10 SAY "2>   Print or Reprint Checks"
    @ 14,10 SAY "3>   Transaction Information"
    @ 15,10 SAY "4>   Headings Listings"
    @ 16,10 SAY "0>   Return to Main Menu"
    SAVE SCREEN TO tempscreen
    STORE tempscreen TO screen[5]
    STORE .T. TO shown[5]
ENDIF
@ 18,12 SAY prompt GET option PICT "9" VALID(option $"01234")
READ

DO CASE

CASE option = "0"
     @ 16,09 GET disp5_0
     CLEAR GETS
     EXIT

CASE option = "1"
   IF shown[10]
      RESTORE SCREE FROM screen[10]
   ELSE
      @ 12, 9 GET disp5_1
      CLEAR GETS
      @ 6,40,16,77 BOX scrframe
      @  7,46 SAY " Printing Chart of Accounts"
      @  9,49 SAY "1>  Account Listing"
      @ 10,49 SAY "2>  Account History"
      @ 11,49 SAY "3>  Budget Listing"
      @ 12,49 SAY "0>  Return to Submenu"
      SAVE SCREEN TO tempscreen
      STORE tempscreen TO screen[10]
      STORE .T. TO shown[10]
   ENDIF
   @ 14,49 SAY prompt GET suboption PICT "9" VALID(suboption $"0")
   READ

CASE option = "2"
   IF shown[11]
      RESTORE SCREEN FROM screen[11]
   ELSE
      @ 13, 9 GET disp5_2
      CLEAR GETS
      @ 6,37,15,76 BOX scrframe
      @ 7, 43 SAY "        Re/Print Checks"
      @ 9, 45 SAY "1>  Print Checks"
      @ 10,45 SAY "2>  Reprint Checks"
      @ 11,45 SAY "3>  Print Check Register"
      @ 12,45 SAY "0>  Return to Submenu"
      SAVE SCREEN TO tempscreen
      STORE tempscreen TO screen[11]
```

```
            STORE .T. TO shown[11]
         ENDIF
         @ 14,46 SAY Prompt GET suboption PICT "9" VALID(suboption $"0")
         READ

      CASE option = "3"
         IF shown[12]
            RESTORE SCREEN FROM screen[12]
         ELSE
            @ 14, 9 GET disp5_3
            CLEAR GETS
            @ 6,37,17,76 BOX scrframe
            @  7,43 SAY "      Print Transaction List"
            @  9,45 SAY "1>  By Transaction Code"
            @ 10,45 SAY "2>  By Transaction Source"
            @ 11,45 SAY "3>  By Date of Transaction"
            @ 12,45 SAY "4>  By Account Order"
            @ 13,45 SAY "5>  All Transactions"
            @ 14,45 SAY "0>  Return to Submenu"
            SAVE SCREEN TO tempscreen
            STORE tempscreen TO screen[12]
            STORE .T. TO shown[12]
         ENDIF
         @ 16,48 SAY prompt GET suboption PICT "9" VALID(suboption $"0")
         READ

      CASE option = "4"
         IF shown[13]
            RESTORE SCREEN FROM screen[13]
         ELSE
            @ 15, 9 GET disp5_4
            CLEAR GETS
            @ 6,37,15,76 BOX scrframe
            @  7,42 SAY "  List General Headings Submenu"
            @  9,42 SAY "1>  List Master or Submasters"
            @ 10,42 SAY "2>  List Subheadings or Subtotals"
            @ 11,42 SAY "3>  List All"
            @ 12,42 SAY "0>  Return to Submenu"
            SAVE SCREEN TO tempscreen
            STORE tempscreen TO screen[13]
            STORE .T. TO shown[13]
         ENDIF
         @ 14,45 SAY prompt GET suboption PICT "9" VALID(suboption $"0")
         READ
      ENDCASE
   ENDDO

CASE option = "6"

   ******************************
   * This is the sixth submenu. *
   ******************************
   STORE "0" TO option
   IF shown[6]
      RESTORE SCREEN FROM screen[6]
```

```
         ELSE
            @ 10,49 GET disp0_6
            CLEAR GETS
            @  9,3,18,43 BOX scrframe
            @ 10,12 SAY "Print Reports Submenu"
            @ 12, 8 SAY "1>   Print Trial Balance"
            @ 13, 8 SAY "2>   Print Statement of Income"
            @ 14, 8 SAY "3>   Print Balance Sheet"
            @ 15, 8 SAY "0>   Return to Main Menu"
            SAVE SCREEN TO tempscreen
            STORE tempscreen TO screen[6]
            STORE .T. TO shown[6]
         ENDIF
         @ 17,11 SAY prompt GET option PICT "9" VALID(option $"0")
         READ

      CASE option = "7"

      CASE option = "8"

         *********************************
         * This is the eighth submenu. *
         *********************************
         STORE "0" TO option
         IF shown[8]
            RESTORE SCREEN FROM screen[8]
         ELSE
            @ 16,49 GET disp0_8
            CLEAR GETS
            @ 7,2,17,38 BOX scrframe
            @  8, 8 SAY "End of Period Processing"
            @  9,16 SAY "Submenu"
            @ 11,10 SAY "1>  End of Month"
            @ 12,10 SAY "2>  End of Quarter"
            @ 13,10 SAY "3>  End of Year"
            @ 14,10 SAY "0>  Return to Main Menu"
            SAVE SCREEN TO tempscreen
            STORE tempscreen TO screen[8]
            STORE .T. TO shown[8]
         ENDIF
         @ 16,11 SAY prompt GET option PICT "9" VALID(option $"0")
         READ

      OTHERWISE

         @ 18,29 GET disp0_0
         CLEAR GETS
         CLOSE
         @ 22,17 SAY "All Files Closed.  Returning to Operating System"
         QUIT

      ENDCASE
   ENDDO
   * End of File
```

ADDING PROMPTS TO THE WINDOW PICTURE

What follows should give you an added picture of saving menu screens and processing screens for better user interaction. Not every screen has been developed, only enough of them to give an overall view of the final picture.

The code listed below builds on the sample menus drawn before. In this sample, we take advantage of the PROMPT command. Following this sample is a final sample of how to develop menus, which incorporates all of the techniques previously mentioned.

```
*****************
* Sample Menu  *
*****************

CLEAR
STORE SPACE(4000) TO mainscreen, listscreen
STORE CHR(201) + CHR(205) + CHR(187) + CHR(186) + CHR(188) + ;
      CHR(205) + CHR(200) + CHR(186) + " " TO scrframe
center = "M A I N    M E N U"
message = " <ESC> Key for Main Menu "
@ 5,0,20,79 BOX SUBSTR(scrframe,1,8)
SAVE SCREEN TO mainscreen

DO WHILE .T.
   ********
   *  Set up the environment
   ********
   RESTORE SCREEN FROM mainscreen
   @  7,10 PROMPT " 1>    Chart Of Accounts "
   @ 10,10 PROMPT " 2>    Transactions "
   @ 13,10 PROMPT " 3>    Posting & Balancing "
   @ 16,10 PROMPT " 4>    Transfers "
   @  7,50 PROMPT " 5>    Print Lists or Checks "
   @ 10,50 PROMPT " 6>    Print Reports "
   @ 13,50 PROMPT " 7>    Utilities "
   @ 16,50 PROMPT " 8>    End of Period "
   @ 18,30 SAY    "Press <Esc> to Exit"
   MENU TO option
   STORE 1 TO sub_option

   DO CASE
   CASE option = 1
      @ 8,38,22,77 BOX scrframe
      @ 10,45 SAY "Chart Of Accounts Submenu"
      @ 12,47 PROMPT " 1>   Enter an Account "
      @ 14,47 PROMPT " 2>   Edit an Account "
      @ 16,47 PROMPT " 3>   Examine Accounts "
      @ 18,47 PROMPT " 4>   Delete an Account "
      @ 20,47 SAY message
      MENU TO sub_option
      IF sub_option = 0
         LOOP
      ENDIF
```

```
CASE option = 3
   @ 12,38,22,77 BOX scrframe
   @ 14,48 SAY "Post/Balance Submenu"
   @ 16,45 PROMPT " 1>  Post Transactions "
   @ 18,45 PROMPT " 2>  Balance Accounts "
   @ 20,45 SAY message
   MENU TO sub_option

CASE option = 5
   @ 8,2,23,42 BOX scrframe
   @ 10,12 SAY "Print Lists or Checks Submenu"
   @ 12, 9  PROMPT " 1>   Chart of Account Info. "
   @ 14, 9  PROMPT " 2>   Print or Reprint Checks "
   @ 16, 9  PROMPT " 3>   Transaction Information "
   @ 18, 9  PROMPT " 4>   Headings Listings "
   @ 20, 9  SAY message
   MENU TO sub_option

CASE option = 7

CASE option = 2
   @  6,38,18,77 BOX scrframe
   @  8,48 SAY "Transaction Submenu"
   @ 10,46 PROMPT " 1>  Enter Transaction "
   @ 12,46 PROMPT " 2>  Edit Transaction "
   @ 14,46 PROMPT " 3>  Delete Transaction "
   @ 16,46 SAY message
   MENU TO sub_option

CASE option = 4
   @ 7,38,18,77 BOX scrframe
   @  8,48 SAY "Transfer Data Submenu"
   @ 10,40 PROMPT " 1>   Transfer Accounts Receivable "
   @ 11,40 PROMPT " 2>   Transfer Payroll "
   @ 12,40 PROMPT " 3>   Transfer Accounts Payable "
   @ 13,40 PROMPT " 4>   Transfer Inventory "
   @ 14,40 PROMPT " 5>   Transfer Other Systems "
   @ 15,40 PROMPT " 6>   Post Transfers "
   @ 16,43 SAY message
   MENU TO sub_option

CASE option = 6
   @ 11,2,22,42 BOX scrframe
   @ 12,11 SAY "Print Reports Submenu"
   @ 14, 7 PROMPT " 1>   Print Trial Balance "
   @ 16, 7 PROMPT " 2>   Print Statement of Income "
   @ 18, 7 PROMPT " 3>   Print Balance Sheet "
   @ 20, 7 SAY message
   MENU TO sub_option
   IF sub_option = 0
      LOOP
   ENDIF
   row = 16
   col = 45
   screenprnt = 0
```

```
         outfile = SPACE(10)
         DO Whichway WITH screenprnt, outfile
         IF screenprnt = 0
            LOOP
         ENDIF

      CASE option = 8
         @ 7,2,22,42 BOX scrframe
         @  9,10 SAY "End of Period Processing"
         @ 10,18 SAY "Submenu"
         @ 12,12 PROMPT " 1>  End of Month "
         @ 14,12 PROMPT " 2>  End of Quarter "
         @ 16,12 PROMPT " 3>  End of Year "
         @ 18,12 SAY    " <Esc> Key for Main Menu "
         MENU TO sub_option
         IF sub_option = 4
            LOOP
         ENDIF

      OTHERWISE
         CLOSE
         @ 22,17 SAY "All Files Closed.  Returning to Operating System."
         QUIT
      ENDCASE
   ENDDO

   *********************

   PROCEDURE Whichway

      PARAMETERS screenprnt, outfile

      @ row, col, row + 7, col + 30 BOX scrframe

      @ row+2, col+5 PROMPT " 1>  Print to Screen "
      @ row+3, col+5 PROMPT " 2>  Print to Printer "
      @ row+4, col+5 PROMPT " 3>  Print to File "
      @ row+5, col+5 SAY    "   RETURN to Menu "
      MENU TO screenprnt

      DO CASE
      CASE screenprnt = 0
         RETURN
      CASE screenprnt = 3
         @ row, col, row + 7, col + 30 BOX scrframe
         @ row+2,col+5 SAY "Enter File Name.."
         @ row+4,col+5 SAY "--> " GET outfile PICT "!!!!!!!!!!"
         READ
         IF LEN(TRIM(outfile)) = 0
            screenprnt = 1
         ELSE
            outfile = TRIM(outfile) + ".TXT"
         ENDIF
      ENDCASE
   * End of Program
```

GOING ONE STEP FURTHER

The following code incorporates all the techniques we have studied up to now. This code was basically generated by GENMEN.PRG (see Appendix I) and then modified and commented further.

```
********************
* Name          DRAWMEN3.prg
* Date          March 15, 1988
* Notice        Copyright 1988, Stephen J. Straley & Associates
* Compile       Clipper Drawmen3
* Release       Autumn '86 or later
* Link          Plink86 fi drawmen3 lib clipper
* Note          This is a sample of a menu generated by the menu
*               generator.
********************

 CLEAR
 DO Domen1

********************

PROCEDURE Domen1

   DO WHILE .T.
      CLEAR
      *RESTORE FROM Screen.sys
      * Since there is no screen file 'SCREEN.SYS', the following
      * are the codes for the frame.
      STORE CHR(201) + CHR(205) + CHR(187) + CHR(186) + CHR(188) +;
            CHR(205) + CHR(200) + CHR(186) + CHR(32) TO scrframe
      SET INTENS on
      SET DELIM off
       STORE SPACE(4000) TO ascreen, bscreen, cscreen, dscreen, escreen,
     fscreen
      *DO Setup
      STORE 0 TO option
      @ 5, 0, 20, 77 BOX SUBSTR(scrframe,1,8)
      @ 4, 30 SAY "M A I N    M E N U"
      @ 8, 7 PROMPT " 1>    Chart of Accounts "
      @ 11, 7 PROMPT " 2>    Transactions "
      @ 14, 7 PROMPT " 3>    Posting & Balancing "
      @ 17, 7 PROMPT " 4>    Transfers "
      @ 8, 43 PROMPT " 5>    Print Lists or Checks "
      @ 11, 43 PROMPT " 6>    Print Reports "
      @ 14, 43 PROMPT " 7>    Utilities "
      @ 17, 43 PROMPT " 8>    End of Period "
      @ 19, 33 SAY "Esc to RETURN"
      MENU TO option
      SAVE SCREEN TO ascreen
      *
      * Another acceptable method would be as follows:
      * DO CASE
```

```
        * CASE option = 0
        *    @ 21, 18 SAY "All Files Closed, Returning to Operating System"
        *    QUIT
        * OTHERWISE
        *    branch = TRANSFORM(option, "9")
        *    DO Domen1&branch.
        * ENDCASE
        *
        DO CASE
        CASE option = 1
           DO Domen11
        CASE option = 2
           DO Domen12
        CASE option = 3
           DO Domen13
        CASE option = 4
           DO Domen14
        CASE option = 5
           DO Domen15
        CASE option = 6
           DO Domen16
        CASE option = 7
           **************************
           * Do subprocedure here. *
           **************************
        CASE option = 8
           DO Domen18
        CASE option = 0
           @ 21, 18 SAY "All Files Closed, Returning to Operating System."
           QUIT
        ENDCASE
ENDDO

********************

PROCEDURE Domen11

   DO WHILE .T.
      IF !EMPTY(bscreen)
         RESTORE SCREEN FROM bscreen
      ENDIF
      STORE 0 TO option1
      @ 7, 39, 24, 73 BOX scrframe
      @ 8, 43 SAY "Chart of Accounts Submenu"
      @ 11, 44 PROMPT " 1>  Enter an Account "
      @ 14, 44 PROMPT " 2>  Edit an Account "
      @ 17, 44 PROMPT " 3>  Examine an Account "
      @ 20, 44 PROMPT " 4>  Delete an Account "
      @ 23, 50 SAY "Esc to RETURN"
      MENU TO option1
      SAVE SCREEN TO bscreen
      DO CASE
      CASE option1 = 0
```

```
         EXIT
      OTHERWISE
         **************************
         * Do subprocedure here. *
         **************************
      ENDCASE
   ENDDO

********************

PROCEDURE Domen12

   DO WHILE .T.
      IF !EMPTY(bscreen)
         RESTORE SCREEN FROM bscreen
      ENDIF
      STORE 0 TO option1
      @ 8, 39, 22, 72 BOX scrframe
      @ 9, 46 SAY "Transaction Submenu"
      @ 12, 44 PROMPT " 1>  Enter Transaction "
      @ 15, 44 PROMPT " 2>  Edit Transaction "
      @ 18, 44 PROMPT " 3>  Delete Transactions "
      @ 21, 49 SAY "Esc to RETURN"
      MENU TO option1
      SAVE SCREEN TO bscreen
      DO CASE
      CASE option1 = 0
         EXIT
      OTHERWISE
         **************************
         * Do subprocedure here. *
         **************************
      ENDCASE
   ENDDO

   ********************

   PROCEDURE Domen13

   DO WHILE .T.
      IF !EMPTY(bscreen)
         RESTORE SCREEN FROM bscreen
      ENDIF
      STORE 0 TO option1
      @ 12, 39, 22, 71 BOX scrframe
      @ 13, 45 SAY "Post or Balance Submenu"
      @ 15, 43 PROMPT " 1>  Post Transactions "
      @ 18, 43 PROMPT " 2>  Balance Accounts "
      @ 21, 49 SAY "Esc to RETURN"
      MENU TO option1
      SAVE SCREEN TO bscreen
      DO CASE
      CASE option1 = 0
```

```
        EXIT
    OTHERWISE
        ***************************
        * Do subprocedure here. *
        ***************************
    ENDCASE
ENDDO

********************

PROCEDURE Domen14

DO WHILE .T.
    IF !EMPTY(bscreen)
        RESTORE SCREEN TO bscreen
    ENDIF
    STORE 0 TO option1
    @ 6, 38, 24, 67 BOX scrframe
    @ 7, 42 SAY "Transfer Data Submenu"
    @ 9, 41 PROMPT " 1>  Accounts Receivable "
    @ 11, 41 PROMPT " 2>  Payroll "
    @ 13, 41 PROMPT " 3>  Accounts Payable "
    @ 15, 41 PROMPT " 4>  Inventory "
    @ 17, 41 PROMPT " 5>  Other Systems "
    @ 19, 41 PROMPT " 6>  Outside Systems "
    @ 21, 41 PROMPT " 7>  Post Transfers "
    @ 23, 46 SAY "Esc to RETURN"
    MENU TO option1
    SAVE SCREEN TO bscreen
    DO CASE
    CASE option1 = 0
        EXIT
    OTHERWISE
        ***************************
        * Do subprocedure here. *
        ***************************
    ENDCASE
ENDDO

********************

PROCEDURE Domen15

DO WHILE .T.
    IF !EMPTY(bscreen)
        RESTORE SCREEN FROM bscreen
    ENDIF
    STORE 0 TO option1
    @ 9, 5, 21, 44 BOX scrframe
    @ 10, 12 SAY "Print Lists or Checks Submenu"
    @ 12, 11 PROMPT " 1>  Chart of Accounts Info. "
    @ 14, 11 PROMPT " 2>  Print or Reprint Checks "
    @ 16, 11 PROMPT " 3>  Transaction Information "
```

```
   @ 18, 11 PROMPT " 4>  Heading's Listings "
   @ 20, 19 SAY "Esc to RETURN"
   MENU TO option1
   SAVE SCREEN TO bscreen
   DO CASE
   CASE option1 = 1
      DO Domen151
   CASE option1 = 2
      DO Domen152
   CASE option1 = 3
      DO Domen153
   CASE option1 = 4
      DO Domen154
   CASE option1 = 0
      EXIT
   ENDCASE
   STORE SPACE(4000) TO cscreen
ENDDO

*********************

PROCEDURE Domen151

DO WHILE .T.
   IF !EMPTY(cscreen)
      RESTORE SCREEN FROM cscreen
   ENDIF
   STORE 0 TO option2
   @ 13, 40, 23, 73 BOX scrframe
   @ 14, 44 SAY "Printing Chart of Accounts"
   @ 16, 46 PROMPT " 1>  Account Listing "
   @ 18, 46 PROMPT " 2>  Account History "
   @ 20, 46 PROMPT " 3>  Budget Listing "
   @ 22, 51 SAY "Esc to RETURN"
   MENU TO option2
   SAVE SCREEN TO cscreen
   DO CASE
   CASE option2 = 0
      EXIT
   OTHERWISE
      **************************
      * Do subprocedure here. *
      **************************
   ENDCASE
ENDDO

*********************

PROCEDURE Domen152

DO WHILE .T.
   IF !EMPTY(cscreen)
      RESTORE SCREEN FROM cscreen
```

```
   ENDIF
   STORE 0 TO option2
   @ 11, 42, 22, 74 BOX scrframe
   @ 12, 50 SAY "Reprint or Print Checks"
   @ 14, 46 PROMPT " 1>  Print Checks "
   @ 16, 46 PROMPT " 2>  Reprint Checks "
   @ 18, 46 PROMPT " 3>  Print Check Register "
   @ 21, 52 SAY "Esc to RETURN"
   MENU TO option2
   SAVE SCREEN TO cscreen
   DO CASE
   CASE option2 = 0
      EXIT
   OTHERWISE
      **************************
      * Do subprocedure here. *
      **************************
   ENDCASE
ENDDO

********************

PROCEDURE Domen153

DO WHILE .T.
   IF !EMPTY(cscreen)
      RESTORE SCREEN FROM cscreen
   ENDIF
   STORE 0 TO option2
   @ 10, 42, 24, 75 BOX scrframe
   @ 11, 48 SAY "Print Transaction List"
   @ 13, 46 PROMPT " 1>  By Transaction Code "
   @ 15, 46 PROMPT " 2>  By Transaction Source "
   @ 17, 46 PROMPT " 3>  By Date of Transaction "
   @ 19, 46 PROMPT " 4>  By Account Order "
   @ 21, 46 PROMPT " 5>  All Transactions "
   @ 23, 53 SAY "Esc to RETURN"
   MENU TO option2
   SAVE SCREEN TO cscreen
   DO CASE
   CASE option2 = 0
      EXIT
   OTHERWISE
      **************************
      * Do subprocedure here. *
      **************************
   ENDCASE
ENDDO

********************

PROCEDURE Domen154
```

```
DO WHILE .T.
   IF !EMPTY(cscreen)
      RESTORE SCREEN FROM cscreen
   ENDIF
   STORE 0 TO option2
   @ 12, 41, 22, 75 BOX scrframe
   @ 13, 43 SAY "List General Headings Submenu"
   @ 15, 43 PROMPT " 1> List Master or Submasters "
   @ 17, 43 PROMPT " 2> List Subheadings or Subtotals "
   @ 19, 43 PROMPT " 3> List All "
   @ 21, 52 SAY "Esc to RETURN"
   MENU TO option2
   SAVE SCREEN TO cscreen
   DO CASE
   CASE option2 = 0
      EXIT
   OTHERWISE
      **************************
      * Do subprocedure here. *
      **************************
   ENDCASE
ENDDO

********************

PROCEDURE Domen16

DO WHILE .T.
   IF !EMPTY(bscreen)
      RESTORE SCREEN FROM bscreen
   ENDIF
   STORE 0 TO option2
   @ 9, 4, 21, 42 BOX scrframe
   @ 11, 13 SAY "Print Report Submenu"
   @ 13, 8 PROMPT " 1>  Print Trial Balance "
   @ 15, 8 PROMPT " 2>  Print Statement of Income "
   @ 17, 8 PROMPT " 3>  Print Balance Sheet "
   @ 19, 17 SAY "Esc to RETURN"
   MENU TO option2
   SAVE SCREEN TO bscreen
   DO CASE
   CASE option2 = 0
      EXIT
   OTHERWISE
      **************************
      * Do subprocedure here. *
      **************************
   ENDCASE
ENDDO

********************

PROCEDURE Domen18

DO WHILE .T.
   IF !EMPTY(bscreen)
```

```
            RESTORE SCREEN FROM bscreen
         ENDIF
         STORE 0 TO option1
         @ 9, 6, 19, 38 BOX scrframe
         @ 10, 12 SAY "End of Period Submenu"
         @ 12, 12 PROMPT " 1>  End of Month "
         @ 14, 12 PROMPT " 2>  End of Quarter "
         @ 16, 12 PROMPT " 3>  End of Year "
         @ 18, 17 SAY "Esc to RETURN"
         MENU TO option1
         SAVE SCREEN TO bscreen
         DO CASE
         CASE option1 = 0
            EXIT
         OTHERWISE
            **************************
            * Do subprocedure here. *
            **************************
         ENDCASE
      ENDDO
   * End of File
```

PUTTING THE WHOLE THING TOGETHER

The final menu below puts everything together, including the new possibilities in the Summer '87 release. Many of the techniques below were created exclusively for the Steve Straley Toolkit, where I focus on pull-down menus, quick escape routes, saving only portions of screens, small procedures and functions, public arrays, and much more. Indeed, there is plenty going on in the code sample below and it is strongly suggested that you take the time necessary to understand each line of code and what impact it has on the entire scheme.

```
********************
* Name          DRAWMEN5.prg
* Date          March 15, 1988
* Notice        Copyright 1988, Stephen J. Straley & Associates
* Compile       Clipper Drawmen5
* Release       Summer 87 only
* Link          Plink86 fi drawmen5 lib clipper
* Note          Shows how menus are created in conjunction with
*               saving screens and the use of arrays.   This is
*               developed from DRAWMEN1.prg.
********************

PUBLIC sc_level, allscreens[20]
AFILL(allscreens, "")
sc_level = 1
options = 1
SET INTENS on
SET WRAP ON
SET DELIM off
```

```
SET KEY -9 TO Breakout          && This Simulates RETURN TO MASTER
CLEAR SCREEN
KEYBOARD CHR(13)                && This pulls down the first menu automatical-
     ly
@  0, 0 SAY "Main Menu"
@  0,69 SAY "Release 1.0"
@ 24,0 SAY "Press F10 for Top Menu or Esc to Move Up 1 Level"
DO Pushscreen WITH 0,0,24,79    && Save the base screen

DO Pushscreen WITH 1,0,3,79,.T.,.F.
DO WHILE .T.
   BEGIN SEQUENCE
      DO Totalkeyoff
      @ 2, 1 PROMPT " Accounts "
      @ 2,12 PROMPT " Transactions "
      @ 2,27 PROMPT " Post or Balance "
      @ 2,42 PROMPT " Lists or Reports "
      @ 2,58 PROMPT " Utilities "
      @ 2,70 PROMPT " EOP "
      MENU TO options
      DO Totalkeyon
      IF options = 0
         EXIT
      ELSE
         ext = ALLTRIM(STR(options))
         DO Menu&ext.
      ENDIF
   END
ENDDO
DO Popscreen WITH 1,0,3,79
@ 4,0 SAY " All Files Closed.   Returning to Operating System. "
QUIT

********************

PROCEDURE Menu1

   opt1 = 1
   DO Pushscreen WITH 3, 1, 11,10,.T.,.T.
   DO WHILE .T.
      @  4,2 PROMPT " Enter  "
      @  5,2 PROMPT " Change "
      @  6,2 PROMPT " Scan   "
      @  7,2 PROMPT " Delete "
      @  8,2 PROMPT " Finder "
      @ 10,2 PROMPT " Quit   "
      MENU TO opt1
      IF opt1 = 0
         EXIT
      ELSEIF opt1 = 6
         KEYBOARD CHR(27) + CHR(27)
         EXIT
      ELSEIF opt1 = 5
```

```
          DO Finder
          *
       ENDIF
    ENDDO
    DO Popscreen WITH 3, 1, 11,10

*********************

PROCEDURE Menu2

    opt = 1
    DO Pushscreen WITH 3,12,10,24,.T.,.T.
    DO WHILE .T.
       @  4,13 PROMPT " Enter     "
       @  5,13 PROMPT " Change    "
       @  6,13 PROMPT " Scan      "
       @  7,13 PROMPT " Delete    "
       @  9,13 PROMPT " Transfers "
       MENU TO opt1
       IF opt1 = 0
          EXIT
       ELSEIF opt1 = 5
          DO Menu22
       ELSE
          DO Menu21 WITH opt1
       ENDIF
    ENDDO
    DO Popscreen WITH 3,12,10,24

*********************

PROCEDURE Menu21

    PARAMETERS row_no

    opt2 = 1
    DO Pushscreen WITH 4+row_no,14,12+row_no,32,.T.,.T.
    DO WHILE .T.
       @  5+row_no,15 PROMPT " General Journal "
       @  6+row_no,15 PROMPT " Receivables     "
       @  7+row_no,15 PROMPT " Payables        "
       @  8+row_no,15 PROMPT " Payroll         "
       @  9+row_no,15 PROMPT " Inventory       "
       @ 10+row_no,15 PROMPT " Operator Error  "
       @ 11+row_no,15 PROMPT " User Defined    "
       MENU TO opt2
       IF opt2 = 0
          EXIT
       ELSE
          *
       ENDIF
    ENDDO
    DO Popscreen WITH 4+row_no,14,12+row_no,32
```

```
********************

PROCEDURE Menu22

   opt2 = 1
   DO Pushscreen WITH 10,14,19,36,.T.,.T.
   DO WHILE .T.
      @ 11,15 PROMPT " Accounts Receivable "
      @ 12,15 PROMPT " Payroll             "
      @ 13,15 PROMPT " Accounts Payable    "
      @ 14,15 PROMPT " Inventory           "
      @ 15,15 PROMPT " Other Systems       "
      @ 16,15 PROMPT " Outside Systems     "
      @ 18,15 PROMPT " Post Transfers      "
      MENU TO opt2
      IF opt2 = 0
         EXIT
      ELSE
         *
      ENDIF
   ENDDO
   DO Popscreen WITH 10,14,19,36

********************

PROCEDURE Menu3

   opt1 = 1
   DO Pushscreen WITH 3,27,7,46,.T.,.T.
   DO WHILE .T.
      @ 4,28 PROMPT " Post Transfers   "
      @ 5,28 PROMPT " Post Regulars    "
      @ 6,28 PROMPT " Balance Accounts "
      MENU TO opt1
      IF opt1 = 0
         EXIT
      ELSE
         *
      ENDIF
   ENDDO
   DO Popscreen WITH 3,27,7,46

********************

PROCEDURE Menu4

   opt1 = 1
   DO Pushscreen WITH 3,42,12,69,.T.,.T.
   DO WHILE .T.
      @  4,43 PROMPT " Chart of Account Info.  "
      @  5,43 PROMPT " Print or Reprint Checks    "
      @  6,43 PROMPT " Transaction Information "
      @  7,43 PROMPT " Headings Listings       "
```

```
      @  9,43 PROMPT " Trial Balance          "
      @ 10,43 PROMPT " Statement of Income    "
      @ 11,43 PROMPT " Balance Sheet          "
      MENU TO opt1
      IF     opt1 = 0
         EXIT
      ELSE
         ext2 = ALLTRIM(STR(opt1))
         DO Menu4&ext2.
      ENDIF
   ENDDO
   DO Popscreen WITH 3,42,12,69

********************

PROCEDURE Menu41

   opt3 = 1
   DO Pushscreen WITH 5,44,9,62,.T.,.T.
   DO WHILE .T.
      @ 6,45 PROMPT " Account Listing "
      @ 7,45 PROMPT " Account History "
      @ 8,45 PROMPT " Budget Listing  "
      MENU TO opt3
      IF opt3 = 0
         EXIT
      ELSE
         *
      ENDIF
   ENDDO
   DO Popscreen WITH 5,44,9,62

********************

PROCEDURE Menu42

  opt3 = 1
  DO Pushscreen WITH 6,44,10,68,.T.,.T.
  DO WHILE .T.
     @ 7,45 PROMPT " Print Checks         "
     @ 8,45 PROMPT " Reprint Checks       "
     @ 9,45 PROMPT " Print Check Register "
     MENU TO opt3
     IF opt3 = 0
        EXIT
     ELSE
        *
     ENDIF
  ENDDO
  DO Popscreen WITH 6,44,10,68
```

```
********************

PROCEDURE Menu43

   opt3 = 1
   DO Pushscreen WITH 7,44,13,70,.T.,.T.
   DO WHILE .T.
      @  8,45 PROMPT " By Transaction Code    "
      @  9,45 PROMPT " By Transaction Source  "
      @ 10,45 PROMPT " By Date of Transaction "
      @ 11,45 PROMPT " By Account Order       "
      @ 12,45 PROMPT " All Transactions       "
      MENU TO opt3
      IF opt3 = 0
         EXIT
      ELSE
         *
      ENDIF
   ENDDO
   DO Popscreen WITH 7,44,13,70

********************

PROCEDURE Menu44

   opt3 = 1
   DO Pushscreen WITH 8,44,12,73,.T.,.T.
   DO WHILE .T.
      @  9,45 PROMPT " List Master or Submasters    "
      @ 10,45 PROMPT " List Subheadings or Subtotals "
      @ 11,45 PROMPT " List All                     "
      MENU TO opt3
      IF opt3 = 0
         EXIT
      ELSE
         *
      ENDIF
   ENDDO
   DO Popscreen WITH 8,44,12,73

********************

PROCEDURE Menu45

********************

PROCEDURE Menu46

********************

PROCEDURE Menu47
```

```
********************

PROCEDURE Menu5

   opt1 = 1
   DO Pushscreen WITH 3,39,16,69,.T.,.T.
   DO WHILE .T.
      @  4,40  PROMPT " 1> Change Passwords          "
      @  5,40  PROMPT " 2> Change Screen Parameters "
      @  6,40  PROMPT " 3> Browse All Records        "
      @  7,40  PROMPT " 4> Remove Marked Records     "
      @  8,40  PROMPT " 5> Unmark Tagged Records     "
      @  9,40  PROMPT " 6> Rebuild Indexes           "
      @ 10,40  PROMPT " 7> Recreate Databases        "
      @ 11,40  PROMPT " 8> Change System Date        "
      @ 12,40  PROMPT " 9> Word Processing           "
      @ 13,40  PROMPT " A> Report Writing            "
      @ 14,40  PROMPT " B> Design Check Format       "
      @ 15,40  PROMPT " C> Design Report Format      "
      MENU TO opt1
      IF opt1 = 0
         EXIT
      ELSE
         *
      ENDIF
   ENDDO
   DO Popscreen WITH 3,39,16,69

********************

PROCEDURE Menu6

   opt1 = 1
   DO Pushscreen WITH 3,59,7,76,.T.,.T.
   DO WHILE .T.
      @ 4,60 PROMPT " End of Month   "
      @ 5,60 PROMPT " End of Quarter "
      @ 6,60 PROMPT " End of Year    "
      MENU TO opt1
      IF opt1 = 0
         EXIT
      ELSE
         *
      ENDIF
   ENDDO
   DO Popscreen WITH 3,59,7,76

********************

PROCEDURE Finder

   old_color = SETCOLOR()
   SET COLOR TO N/W
```

```
    DO Pushscreen WITH 9,6,19,58,.T.,.T.,.T.,.T.
    SETCOLOR( old_color )
    @ 10,7 SAY SPACE(50)
    @ 11,7 SAY FILL_OUT(" This is the Finder", 50)
    @ 12,7 SAY SPACE(50)
    @ 13,7 SAY FILL_OUT("   This Windowing technique developed in Clipper", 50)
    @ 14,7 SAY FILL_OUT("         by Stephen J. Straley & Assocaites", 50)
    @ 15,7 SAY FILL_OUT("   It is featured in the Steve Straley Toolkit &", 50)
    @ 16,7 SAY FILL_OUT("                        The Yacht( tm)", 50)
    @ 17,7 SAY SPACE(50)
    @ 18,7 SAY FILL_OUT( " Press Any Key to Return...", 50)
    INKEY(0)
    DO Popscreen WITH 9,6,19,58,.T.

********************

PROCEDURE Breakout

    PARAMETERS p, l, v

    @ 4,0 CLEAR
    sc_level = 3                                  && Reset the screen level
    KEYBOARD CHR(27)                              && Clear the MENU TO command
    DO Pushscreen WITH 1,0,3,79,.F.,.T.,.T.   && Redraw Border
    @ 24,0 SAY "Press F10 for Top Menu or Esc to Move Up 1 Level"
    BREAK
* End of File

* NOTE:
* All Functions and Procedures below are part of the Steve Straley Toolkit
* Copyright (c) 1988 by Stephen J. Straley & Associates - All Rights Reserved

********************

FUNCTION Reverse

    PARAMETERS the_color

    the_say = STRTRAN(SUBSTR(the_color, 1, AT(",", the_color)-1), "+", "")
    RETURN(SUBSTR(the_say, AT("/", the_say)+1) + "/" + SUBSTR(the_say, 1,
      AT("/", the_say)-1))

********************

FUNCTION Fill_out

    PARAMETERS fill_a, fill_b

    * fill_a = the string to be filled out
    * fill_b = the Length to fill out the string to

    IF PCOUNT() = 1
       fill_b = 80
```

```
   ELSE
      IF TYPE("fill_b") = "C"
         fill_b = VAL(b)
      ENDIF
      fill_b = IIF(fill_b <= 1, 80, fill_b)
   ENDIF

   IF fill_b <= LEN(fill_a)
      RETURN(fill_a)
   ENDIF
   RETURN(fill_a + SPACE(fill_b - LEN(fill_a)))

********************

PROCEDURE Pushscreen

    PARAMETERS push1, push2, push3, push4, pushsave, pushscr, pushbord, push-
      shad

   DO CASE
      CASE PCOUNT() = 4  && 4 parameters means No border, No Frame, Just save
      the area
         pushsave = .T.
         pushscr = .T.
         pushbord = .F.
         pushshad = .F.
      CASE PCOUNT() = 5  && 5 parameters mean Save area without border logic
         pushscr = .T.
         pushbord = .F.
         pushshad = .F.
      CASE PCOUNT() = 6
         pushbord = .T.
         pushshad = .F.
      CASE PCOUNT() = 7
         pushshad = .F.
   ENDCASE

   IF pushsave
      push_temp = ""
      IF pushshad
         allscreens[sc_level] = SAVESCREEN(push1, push2, push3 + 1, push4 + 1)
      ELSE
         allscreens[sc_level] = SAVESCREEN(push1, push2, push3, push4)
      ENDIF
      sc_level = IF(sc_level = 20, sc_level, sc_level + 1)
   ENDIF

   IF pushbord                                             && Yes, I want a bor-
     der!
      IF !pushscr                                          && No, I Just want a
      frame, hold the filling
         @ push1, push2 TO push3, push4 DOUBLE
      ELSE
```

```
         @ push1, push2 CLEAR TO push3, push4
         @ push1, push2 TO push3, push4 DOUBLE
      ENDIF
      IF pushshad
         SHADOW(push1, push2, push3, push4)
      ENDIF
   ENDIF

*********************

PROCEDURE Popscreen

   PARAMETERS pop1, pop2, pop3, pop4, popshad

   IF PCOUNT() = 4
      popshad = .F.
   ENDIF
   sc_level = IF(sc_level = 1, sc_level, sc_level - 1)
   pop_temp = allscreens[sc_level]
   IF popshad
      RESTSCREEN(pop1, pop2, pop3+1, pop4+1, pop_temp)
   ELSE
      RESTSCREEN(pop1, pop2, pop3, pop4, pop_temp)
   ENDIF

*********************

PROCEDURE Clear_area

   PARAMETERS clear1, clear2, clear3, clear4

   DO CASE
   CASE (clear3 - clear1 > 1) .AND. (clear4 - clear2 > 1)
      SCROLL(clear1 + 1, clear2 + 1, clear3 - 1, clear4 - 1,0)
   CASE (clear3 - clear1 > 1) .AND. !(clear4 - clear2 > 1)   && 1 column
      FOR c_area = clear1+1 TO clear3-1
         @ c_area,clear2+1 SAY " "
      NEXT
   CASE !(clear3 - clear1 > 1) .AND. (clear4 - clear2 > 1)   && 1 Row
      @ clear1+1,clear2 SAY SPACE(LEN(clear4-clear2)-2)
   ENDCASE

*********************

FUNCTION Shadow

   PARAMETERS shada, shadb, shadc, shadd

   shad_color = SETCOLOR()
   SETCOLOR( STRTRAN( shad_color, "+", "" ) )

   FOR shadx = shada+1 TO shadc+1
      @ shadx, shadd+1 SAY CHR(177)
```

```
   NEXT
   @ shadx-1,shadb+1 SAY REPLICATE(CHR(177), shadd-shadb)

   SETCOLOR( shad_color )
   RETURN(.F.)

*********************

PROCEDURE Totalkeyon

   SET KEY  4 TO Rside
   SET KEY 19 TO Lside
   SET KEY 24 TO

*********************

PROCEDURE Totalkeyoff

   SET KEY  4 TO
   SET KEY 19 TO

*********************

PROCEDURE Rside

   PARAMETERS p, l, v

   KEYBOARD CHR(27) + CHR(4) + CHR(13)

*********************

PROCEDURE Lside

   PARAMETERS p, l, v

   KEYBOARD CHR(27) + CHR(19) + CHR(13)

*********************

PROCEDURE Dside

   PARAMETERS p, l, v

   KEYBOARD CHR(13)
* End of File
```

WINDOWING BUT NOT MENUS

The ability to create and manipulate windows in Clipper offers a powerful tool to the developer. Imagination and creativity are the only limits to the uses you can put this to. In the following code, we have opened a window that allows the display of some text and then scrolls it backward.

```
*********************
* Name          WINDOW.prg
* Date          March 15, 1988
* Notice        Copyright 1988, Stephen J. Straley & Associates
* Compile       Clipper Window
* Release       Autumn '86 or later
* Link          Plink86 fi window lib clipper
* Note          This program shows how the screen can be parsed and
*               manipulated and made to scroll backward.  Though this routine
*               as it's written has no real purpose, it shows the ability of
*               Clipper to handle windowing without the aid of another
*               language.  In other words, this routine simulates windowing
*               with no Assembly required.
*
*               It should also be noted that the SUBSTR() function is parsing
*               the screen in 160 character sections.  That is to allow for
*               the 80 characters on each line and each accompanying attribute
*               byte.   An attribute byte is a character that tells the
*               computer to throw the next character displayed into a specific
*               mode, such as red, blue, bright, underlining, or flashing.
*********************

STORE SPACE(4000) TO temp
SAVE SCREEN TO temp
FOR x = 25 TO 1 STEP - 1
   window  = SUBSTR(temp,3841,160)
   partial = window + temp
   temp    = SUBSTR(partial,1,4000)
   RESTORE SCREEN FROM temp
NEXT
* End of file
```

FORMATTING FOR HARD COPY

CONSIDERATIONS ON OUTPUT

Screen handling is just one part of an application. Data input to get information into the system and data manipulation to crunch numbers and arrange or modify the information are also necessary. Output is the final concern of application building.

All output considerations should include three destinations: the screen, the printer, and the disk drive. Many systems fail to allow output to an alternative file. By porting the information to a disk file, the user can use that data later.

You need to decide whether to use the REPORT form utility or to design custom reports. It gets to be a problem to constantly port over .FRM and .LBL files from a master floppy disk. Also, a lot of code must be added to check that the files are available on the disk. Finally, there is the problem of security: the .FRM and .LBL files can be altered by the user. This defeats one purpose of the compiler, which is to protect the developers ideas and code from the rest of the world. Should the user have access to the output code or should the output generator be embedded in the rest of the application? This is a serious question that must be addressed completely.

Below is a brief synopsis of three ways to output information.

SCREEN REPORTS

The two main considerations for all reports to the screen are the amount of space available and the amount of information required. The two are often in conflict. There are many times when the limit in the screen's capacity restricts the amount of information that can be given. If too much information is included, the screen becomes unreadable. Be careful to send only vital information to the screen. Screen output should be for quick reference and verification, not for complete reports. Balances are fine for screen reports, for example, but complete invoice detail is probably excessive. Each system's requirements change, but keep the restrictions of the screen and the purpose of the report in mind.

Allow an easy escape back to some entry or menu point. The user-defined function QWAIT(), which we discussed earlier, was designed for this specific purpose. It allows the user to press any key for the next screen of information or the letter Q to go back. This function can be made standard for all screen reports. For example:

```
USE Temp
SET FILTER TO .NOT. posted
GO TOP
DO WHILE .NOT. EOF()
   @ 6,1,22,78 BOX SPACE(9)
   @  8, 5 SAY "Name of account:  " GET accnt_name
   @  9, 5 SAY "          Number:  " GET accnt_numb
   @ 11,12 SAY "Current Balances"
   @ 11,52 SAY "Previous Balances"
   @ 13, 2 SAY "  Month-> "
   @ 14, 2 SAY "Quarter-> "
   @ 15, 2 SAY "   Year-> "
   @ 13,12 GET current_m
   @ 14,12 GET current_q
   @ 15,12 GET current_y
   @ 13,47 GET previous_m
   @ 14,47 GET previous_q
   @ 15,47 GET previous_y
   CLEAR GETS
   @ 18,10 SAY "Press any key to continue or 'Q' to Quit..."
   IF QWAIT()
      QUIT
   ENDIF
ENDDO
```

```
*********************

FUNCTION Qwait

   SET CONSOLE OFF
   WAIT TO intemp
   SET CONSOLE ON
   IF UPPER(intemp) = "Q"
      RETURN(.T.)
   ENDIF
   RETURN(.F.)
```

As with the design of menus, be consistent with screen report formats.

PRINTER REPORTS

You should also understand and work within the limits of the hard-copy format. Some printers can produce condensed print. For example, to condense the print on an Epson printer, use the following set of commands (which you could put into a user-defined function in your library file along with a Reset function):

```
SET PRINT ON
SET CONSOLE OFF
?? CHR(15)
SET PRINT OFF
SET CONSOLE ON
```

As with screen control, you should allow an easy escape route. Users change their minds; with the compiler's added features it's very easy to provide for these changes. For example, the application should allow for single sheet or continuous paper reports, as well as normal-sized or condensed print reports. As another option, the program might be designed to ask the user to press any key for the next page after each page of printout. However, if there are quite a few pages to print, this option shouldn't be used. Additionally, the program should allow the user to abort printing. Below is a simple printing control routine:

```
DO WHILE .T.
   CLEAR
   FOR x = 1 To 200
      @ 10,10 SAY x
   NEXT
   IF LASTKEY() <> ASC("c") .OR. LASTKEY() = ASC("C")
      WAIT "Esc to Abort - 'C' to continue - or any key..."
   ENDIF
   IF NO_PRINT()
      @ 20,20 SAY "All complete"
      QUIT
   ENDIF
ENDDO
```

```
*********************

FUNCTION No_print

   IF LASTKEY() = 27
      RETURN(.T.)
   ENDIF
   RETURN(.F.)
```

FILE REPORTS

In printing out reports to an alternate file, several obstacles vanish immediately. Format, pausing for a change of paper, and escape routines are no longer problems. One new problem to be concerned with is disk space.

Possible options may be to allow for a few notes to be entered before or after the report, as well as a change of the default drive for the report. In either case, be consistent. Make all options available for all reports, not just for a few. The user will have trouble remembering which reports allow certain features and which do not. If possible, use the TRANSFORM() function universally for screen, paper, and file reports.

OUTPUT USING .FRM AND .LBL FILES

One of the big disadvantages with Clipper was the inability to stop a report or label from printing when using .FRM and .LBL files. In the interpreter version, it had been expected that if the Esc key was pressed while the report, for example, was printing, dBASE would stop execution of the report. In Clipper, the same effect can be achieved with a little extra coding. First, in the REPORT or LABEL command, add a user-defined function as part of the WHILE clause. For example:

```
REPORT FOR Stattax FOR A->state = "CA" WHILE ABORT()
```

Next, program the function to always return a logical true (.T.) unless the Escape key is pressed. That code section would look something like this:

```
********************

FUNCTION Abort

   RETURN( INKEY() <> 27 )
```

This code can be made more elaborate, for example, by testing for the Escape key (27) and prompting users to see if they are sure before returning a logical false. In any event, the scheme behind this is simple. If the Escape key is pressed while the function call is being made by Clipper, INKEY() will equal 27 and the expression in ABORT will be false. This will be returned to the WHILE clause in the REPORT command, which in turn will stop the command from processing. Otherwise, Clipper will always return a logical true (.T.) to the WHILE clause and the report will continue to print.

Another interesting possibility with user-defined functions and the REPORT command is to embed directly into the .FRM file the names of user-defined functions. This will not work under the interpreter; however, it is perfectly acceptable in the compiled environment. For example, a date field is in Julian date-like format (YYYYMMDD) and the output in the .FRM file should be in standard date format. It is simple to create a user-defined function that will take a Julian date-like string and convert it into a Gregorian date string.

```
*********************

FUNCTION Disp_date

   PARAMETERS the_date

   ret_val = SUBSTR(the_date, 5,2) + "/" + ;
             SUBSTR(the_date, 7, 2) + "/" + ;
             SUBSTR(the_date, 3,2)
   RETURN(ret_val)
```

The only thing to keep in mind is getting the function call into the report form. dBase will not allow this since it will check the validity of the function name during input. So the only solution is to use the REPORT.EXE utility program and modify the report to accept this function call. The field name in the report would look something like this:

```
DISP_DATE(field_date)
```

Keep in mind that several restrictions apply. First, if you want to carry this technology over to numeric data and the display is to contain dollar signs and commas, it is possible to get it in the display using the TRANSFORM() function or a user-defined function. However, be careful **not** to total on these fields. Since they will be converted to string data types, the ability to total and subtotal on these fields will be lost. Finally, do not try to manipulate the head of the printer with elaborate user-defined functions in the report or label forms. While it may seem to work, Clipper actually has a special internal counter that keeps track of the row and column numbers; resetting the printer with a SETPRC() or PROW(), PCOL() function will not work. This best thing to do in such cases is to try a couple of tests before beginning a major project.

A FINAL WORD ON OUTPUT

In many cases the REPORT utilities of both dBASE III and Clipper are not sufficient. With the added ability of multiple-child relations as well as user-defined functions, the REPORT utility program almost becomes obsolete. Judge the system size carefully as well. Applications grow with each report. It may be adequate to allow for some standard REPORT forms as well as some additional customized reports.

Study the following code as a sample of code that outputs to the printer. The code outputs a text file stored on your disk. It breaks for pages as designated and generates line numbers.

```
********************
* Name          OUTPUT.prg
* Date          March 15, 1988
* Notice        Copyright 1988, Stephen J. Straley & Associates
* Compile       Clipper Output
* Release       Autumn '86 or greater
* Link          PLINK86 FI OUTPUT LIB CLIPPER
* Note          This program prints out any text file to the printer,
*               prompting the user for page numbers, line numbers,
*               pauses, file extension, and program name.
********************

CREATE Temp
APPEND BLANK
REPLACE field_name WITH "LINEPUT", field_type WITH "C", field_len WITH 132
USE
CREATE Reading FROM Temp
USE Reading
ERASE Temp
DO WHILE .T.
   CLEAR
   STORE SPACE(35) TO drive
   STORE SPACE(40) TO input
   @ 10,10 SAY "Name of File to Print => " GET input PICT "@!"
   READ
   IF LEN(TRIM(input)) = 0
      CLOSE DATABASES
      ERASE Reading
      QUIT
   ENDIF
   @ 12, 5 SAY "What drive/direcrtory to look on => " GET drive PICT "@!"
   @ 14, 5 SAY "Leave blank for logged drive/directory default"
   READ
   IF AT(".",input) = 0
      input = TRIM(input) + ".PRG"
   ENDIF
   the_file = TRIM(drive) + input
   IF .NOT. FILE(the_file)
      @ 19,CENTER(the_file) SAY the_file
      @ 20,CENTER("is not present on disk.  Please choose again, or") ;
           SAY "is not present on disk.  Please choose again, or"
      @ 21,CENTER("leave blank to exit program...") ;
           SAY "leave blank to exit program..."
      LOOP
   ENDIF
```

```
@ 14, 5 SAY SPACE(69)
@ 20,10 SAY SPACE(69)
@ 21,10 SAY SPACE(69)
GO TOP
@ 24,10 SAY "Now Reading Information...."
APPEND FROM &the_file. SDF
@ 24,10 SAY SPACE(69)
STORE 0 TO times
DO WHILE times = 0
   @ 14,10 SAY "Number of lines per page to print?? " GET times PICT "##"
   READ
   IF times > 66
      STORE 0 TO times
      @ 22,10 SAY "Only 66 lines per page are allowed.  Please reenter!!!"
      LOOP
   ENDIF
ENDDO
@ 14,00 CLEAR
@ 18,10 SAY "Do you wish to PAUSE after each page? "
pause = VERIFY()
@ 19,10 SAY "Do you wish to print page numbers? "
pages = VERIFY()
IF pages
   times = times - 4
ENDIF
@ 20,10 SAY "Do you wish to print line numbers? "
lprint = VERIFY()
amount = 1
@ 0,0,24,79 BOX SPACE(9)
@ 12,10 SAY "Press Any Key to Begin Printing... or Q to Quit..."
IF QWAIT()
   LOOP
ENDIF
@ 12,10 SAY "          Now Printing.  One Moment Please...        "
down = 0
SET DEVICE TO PRINT
GO TOP
DO WHILE .NOT. EOF()
   IF lprint
      @ down,00 SAY RECNO() PICT "@B"
      @ down,10 SAY TRIM(lineput)
   ELSE
      @ down,0 SAY TRIM(lineput)
   ENDIF
   IF RECNO()/times = INT(RECNO()/times)
      IF pages
         @ down + 2,0 SAY "Page"
         @ PROW(),PCOL()+2 SAY amount PICT "@B"
      ENDIF
      EJECT
      amount = amount + 1
      down = 1
      IF pause
```

```
            SET DEVICE TO SCREEN
            @ 12,10 SAY "Press Any Key to Begin Printing... or Q to Quit..."
            IF QWAIT()
               EXIT
            ENDIF
            @ 12,10 SAY "        Now Printing.  One Moment Please...        "
            SET DEVICE TO PRINT
         ENDIF
      ENDIF
      down = down + 1
      SKIP
   ENDDO
   EJECT
   SET DEVICE TO SCREEN
   ZAP
   CLEAR
ENDDO

********************************

FUNCTION pause
* This function pauses for a given length of time as specified and returns
* a null value.

PARAMETERS i

FOR x = 0 TO i
   mtime = TIME()
   DO WHILE mtime = TIME()
   ENDDO
NEXT

RETURN("")

********************

FUNCTION Qwait

   SET CONSOLE OFF
   WAIT TO intemp
   SET CONSOLE ON
   IF UPPER(intemp) = "Q"
      RETURN(.T.)
   ENDIF
   RETURN(.F.)

********************

FUNCTION Verify

   SET CONSOLE OFF
   STORE "" TO verify_var
   DO WHILE .NOT. verify_var$"YyNn"
```

```
      WAIT TO verify_var
   ENDDO
   SET CONSOLE ON
   IF UPPER(verify_var) = "Y"
      ?? "Yes"
      IF INKEY(0) = 0
      ENDIF
      RETURN(.T.)
   ENDIF
   ?? "No "
   IF INKEY(0) = 0
   ENDIF
   RETURN(.F.)

********************

FUNCTION Center

   PARAMETERS a

   result = INT(LEN(a)/2)
   RETURN(40-result)
* End of File
```

LIST-BOX TECHNOLOGY

Use Clipper to push an application, to make it interact with the end user. There are many ways to do this, both in the new and old version of the compiler. The topics listed below are designed to give you a few new ideas about how to view the use of the language, some practical examples, and easy to follow coding extracts. Not all of these ideas may apply to your situation; you are the best judge of that. However, you can assess the value of some of this information and apply it whenever and wherever applicable. Some of the topics covered are:

- List-box technology
- Using SET KET TO in an application
- Creating batches, indexes, and databases from within an application
- Adding GETs on the fly

List-Box Technology

The concept of a list box is growing with importance as end users of applications begin to experience this more and more. Initially, list-box technology was hindered either by the machine's abilities, the limitations of the language, or end-user apprehension. This apprehension began to fade as languages and machines increased in strength and power. Now with the Summer '87 release of Clipper, mastering this technique, along with pull-down menus, is simple. Now, your applications will attain a status never before imagined.

List-box technology is simple: it lists correct and valid responses to a data entry point in a specified windowed area, and it allows the user to "point and shoot" from that list. Point and shoot means to scroll through the windowed area, viewing all choices, and being able to pick a choice and have that choice entered as the original data entry point. For example, consider entering in invoice information, but the computer operator forgets the part number for one of the line items on the invoice. While attempting to enter in an invalid part number, a windowed area near the data field would appear and in it would be all of the part numbers and descriptions valid for that field being entered. The operator would then be allowed to scan through the window screen, viewing all of the valid choices. Pressing a special key (usually the Enter key) chooses the right part number and stores that value in the original invoice entry field.

There are several ways to accomplish this in Clipper. One is with the DBEDIT() function, listing information directly from a database. The other is with the ACHOICE() function, which lists information from an array list. Finally, a technique I developed long before either of these functions made their way into the language is to use the GOT() and MPOP() functions.

Using ACHOICE() as a list box means that the validating information for a particular field is contained within the array passed to ACHOICE(). This means that if the data entry field is to be verified against a database (i.e., a "CODE" database), the information in that database would be stored first into the array. Once the information is in the array, scanning and searching is extremely fast. However, storing all of a database into an array may not only be time consuming, but impossible as well because of the restrictions on memory. Nevertheless, it is possible to do it, and it is quite efficient with small amounts of information. Whenever the data being entered is to be verified against a database, I generally use GOT() and MPOP().

Setting up a GET for a list-box window is simple. First, identify the field with which you want to have a list box associated. Next, use the VALID() clause to assign a user-defined function to that particular GET. For example, a code extract may look something like this:

```
@ 10,10 SAY "Enter State => " GET state VALID GOODSTATE()
```

There are of course variations on this. For example, the variable "state" could be passed as a parameter to GOODSTATE(). In the Summer '87 release of Clipper, this parameter could be passed by reference rather than by value by preceding "state" with an "@." For this, the same code extract would look something like this:

```
@ 10,10 SAY "Enter State => " GET state ;
  VALID GOODSTATE(@state)
```

Now the list-box and validation capabilities will be handled in the GOODSTATE() function. In that function, several techniques are worth noting. First, plan for an escape path. This means to test to see if either the variable is empty or if the last key pressed was the Esc key; in either case, return a logical true value. This value would then be passed to the VALID clause, which in turn would complete the GET and move onto the next variable. In the case of testing for the Esc key, this means that all GETS within the READ would be completed and thus the READ would be completed. Additionally, if this particular GET is within a stream of GETS, it may be very important to test for the up arrow key [LASTKEY() = 5] and to allow the user to go back to previous variables in case an error was made. A sample coded extract of this would look something like this:

```
FUNCTION Goodstate

  PARAMETERS astate

  IF LASTKEY() = 5 .OR. LASTKEY() = 27 .OR.;
     EMPTY(astate)
     RETURN(.T.)
  ENDIF
```

The next step is to test if the variable "state" has a legal response. In the following example, the test will be performed on a previously opened and indexed database in select area 4, while the current GET is performed on a database in select area 1. A simple SEEK command would test to see if the entered information is valid. Continuing with the code extract, the function would then look something like this:

```
FUNCTION Goodstate

  PARAMETERS astate

  IF LASTKEY() = 5 .OR. LASTKEY() = 27 .OR.;
     EMPTY(astate)
     RETURN(.T.)
  ENDIF
  SELECT D
  SEEK astate
  IF FOUND()
     SELECT A
     RETURN(.T.)
  ELSE
     SELECT A
     * Perform listbox
     RETURN(.F.)
  ENDIF
```

With the Summer '87 release, testing an expression with the FOUND() function from another selected area is possible. For example, instead of having two "SELECT A" command lines, only one would be needed. And the FOUND() function would be slightly modified to include the alias area letter. Thus the same code extract would look something like this:

```
FUNCTION Goodstate

   PARAMETERS astate

   IF LASTKEY() = 5 .OR. LASTKEY() = 27 .OR.;
      EMPTY(astate)
      RETURN(.T.)
   ENDIF
   SELECT D
   SEEK astate
   SELECT A
   IF (D->FOUND())
      RETURN(.T.)
   ELSE
      * Perform listbox
      RETURN(.F.)
   ENDIF
```

It is important to note that parentheses are required around the expression "D=>FOUND()" in order for it to work properly.

Now for the list-box technology. If the variable to be validated is **not** passed to the function or if it is passed by value (not by reference or by using the Summer '87 release), the function must directly assign a value to the variable. Otherwise, the function assigns the value to the parameter passed to the function, which in turns sets the value of the calling variable simply because the original variable (state) was passed by reference. I use two functions to help with this. The GOT() function simply gets the value of a field based on the name of the database (or area it is opened in), the field number, and the record number. This function gets that specific value. The MPOP() function draws a windowed area based on four coordinates, the name of the database to be opened or selected, a list of fields to be displayed within the window area, an optional FILTER expression, and an optional logical value that tells MPOP() to only display unique information within the windowed area. The function returns the record number of the choice selected. Thus, MPOP() is the list-box function and, like DBEDIT(), it returns the record number of the selected item. Using MPOP() may prove to be easier than using DBEDIT() only because of an easier construction of required parameters.

The reason there are two functions is mainly because of the observation that a user may want the displayed information to be different from the obtained information. For example, going back to the invoice problem mentioned before, what if the part numbers were coded in an unusual manner, or what if the data operator is new and not familiar with the codes? It would be quite apparent that the displayed information may be different from the obtained information. Maybe the descriptions of the code would be more adequate for the list box, which in turn points to the desired part number. This is simple using the MPOP() function.

Using these two functions together will give the necessary list box. Finally, after the selection is made, the KEYBOARD should be stuffed with a carriage return, which will cause the newly found value for the variable "state" to be automatically tested again through the function as if the user typed in valid information to begin with. Combining all of this, the function would finally look something like this:

```
FUNCTION Goodstate

  PARAMETERS astate

  IF LASTKEY() = 5 .OR. LASTKEY() = 27 .OR.;
     EMPTY(astate)
     RETURN(.T.)
  ENDIF
  SELECT D
  SEEK astate
  SELECT A
  IF (D->FOUND())
     RETURN(.T.)
  ELSE
     @ 3,45 SAY "Pick the Correct State"
     astate = GOT("D", 1, MPOP(4,40,10,20,"D", "2+1+3")
     KEYBOARD CHR(13)
     RETURN(.F.)
  ENDIF
```

Of course, these list-box functions may be coded to be more generic. For example, by adding another parameter passed to the user-defined function, it is possible to have the same function work for data entry as well as in the data edit mode.

SET KEY TO

There are many advantages in using this command. Some situations call for immediate escape logic while others call for an immediate change in the data scanning criteria. In either case, the SET KEY TO command can solve the problem. With the introduction of the BEGIN SEQUENCE command, a procedure containing the BREAK clause will emulate a RETURN TO MASTER command. For example, consider the following code extract:

```
sc_level = 1

SET KEY -9 TO Breakout          && This Simulates RETURN TO MASTER

DO Pushscreen WITH 1,0,3,79,.T.,.F.
DO WHILE .T.
   BEGIN SEQUENCE
      @ 2, 1 PROMPT " Accounts "
      @ 2,12 PROMPT " Transactions "
      @ 2,27 PROMPT " Post/Balance "
```

```
      @ 2,42 PROMPT " Lists/Reports "
      @ 2,58 PROMPT " Utilities "
      @ 2,70 PROMPT " EOP "
      MENU TO options
      IF options = 0
         EXIT
      ELSE
         DO Menu1
      ENDIF
   END
ENDDO
@ 1,0 CLEAR
@ 4,0 SAY " All Files Closed.   Returning to Operating System. "
QUIT

********************

PROCEDURE Menu1

   opt1 = 1
   DO Pushscreen WITH 3, 1, 11,10,.T.,.T.
   DO WHILE .T.
      @  4,2 PROMPT " Enter  "
      @  5,2 PROMPT " Change "
      @  6,2 PROMPT " Scan   "
      @  7,2 PROMPT " Delete "
      @  8,2 PROMPT " Finder "
      @ 10,2 PROMPT " Quit   "
      MENU TO opt1
      IF opt1 = 0
         EXIT
      ELSEIF opt1 = 6
         KEYBOARD CHR(27) + CHR(27)
         EXIT
      ELSEIF opt1 = 5
         DO Finder
         *
      ENDIF
   ENDDO
   DO Popscreen WITH 3, 1, 11,10

********************

PROCEDURE Breakout

   PARAMETERS p, l, v

   @ 4,0 CLEAR
   sc_level = 1
   KEYBOARD CHR(27)
   BREAK
* End of Code Extract
```

The thing to note here is the KEYBOARD command in PROCEDURE Breakout. The reason that this command is necessary is simple. Follow the logical flow of the application: the first menu calls the second and so on. However, the special key (SET KEY -9 TO Breakout) may be struck while processing one of the MENU TO commands. The BREAK command in the Breakout procedure will take effect **after** the completion of the MENU TO command. So in the above extract, if the F10 key is struck while processing the MENU TO command in PROCEDURE Menu2, PROCEDURE Breakout will be called. The screen will be cleared at the proper coordinates to remove the window, the window variable ("sc_level") will be reset to a proper value, and the KEYBOARD will be stuffed with a keystroke that will terminate the MENU TO command. Once the MENU TO command has finished processing, the BREAK command will the take effect and send the program to the last active END command, which in this example, is to the top-level menu.

Obviously another possibility is to use the SET KEY TO command to emulate familiar features in many other packages such as DOS Gateway or a Pop-Up Calendar. These capabilities are easy to code for any application. However, another possibility is using the SET KEY TO command to change the criteria of a SEEK condition. For this, consider the following code extract:

```
*********************
* Name      Chg_get.prg
* Author    Stephen J. Straley
* Notice    Copyright (c) 1988 Stephen J. Straley & Associates
* Date      March 21, 1988
* Compile   Clipper Chg_get -m
* Release   Autumn '86 or later
* Link      Mslink chg_get,,,clipper/se:1024,,;
* Note      This demonstration program shows how to change the GET and
*           to search criteria with the SET KEY TO logic.
*********************

SET SCOREBOARD OFF
DO Makefiles
CLOSE ALL

SELECT 1
USE Statcode INDEX Statcd1, Statcd2

DO WHILE .T.

   @ 0,0 CLEAR

   field1 = " "
   field2 = SPACE(20)

   SET KEY 9 TO Changeit     && This is the TAB key

   @ 2,10 SAY "Enter Code Value => " GET field1 PICT "X"
   @ 4,10 SAY "Press TAB to Change Criteria"
```

```
   @ 5,10 SAY "      Esc to Quit"

   READ
   IF LASTKEY() = 27
      EXIT
   ENDIF

   IF !EMPTY(field1)
      SEEK field1
   ENDIF

   IF FOUND()
      @ 7,20 SAY "Record Was Found.   Any Key to Try Again..."
   ELSE
      @ 7,20 SAY "Record NOT present.   Press Any Key..."
   ENDIF
   INKEY(0)

ENDDO

CLEAR SCREEN

*********************

PROCEDURE Changeit

   PARAMETERS p, l, v

   SET KEY 9 TO
   CLEAR GETS
   @ 2,10 CLEAR
   @ 2,10 SAY "Enter Description => " GET field2 PICT "@X"
   @ 5,10 SAY "      Esc to Quit"
   READ
   SET ORDER TO 2
   search = TRIM(field2)
   SEEK search
   field1 = status
   SET ORDER TO 1

**********************

PROCEDURE Makefiles

   CLEAR SCREEN
   CREATE Temp
   USE Temp
   DO Ap_it WITH "STATUS",   "C", 1,0
   DO Ap_it WITH "DESCRIPT", "C",20,0
   USE
   CREATE Statcode FROM Temp
   USE Statcode
   ERASE Temp.dbf
```

```
   APPEND BLANK
   REPLACE status WITH "1", descript WITH "Normal Account"
   APPEND BLANK
   REPLACE status WITH "2", descript WITH "Inventory Account"
   APPEND BLANK
   REPLACE status WITH "3", descript WITH "Special"
   APPEND BLANK
   REPLACE status WITH "4", descript WITH "Fortune 500"
   APPEND BLANK
   REPLACE status WITH "5", descript WITH "Premire Account"
   APPEND BLANK
   REPLACE status WITH "6", descript WITH "Gold Card Member"
   APPEND BLANK
   REPLACE status WITH "7", descript WITH "Inventory Control"
   APPEND BLANK
   REPLACE status WITH "8", descript WITH "Unassigned"
   APPEND BLANK
   REPLACE status WITH "9", descript WITH "Development"
   APPEND BLANK
   REPLACE status WITH "A", descript WITH "Additional Account"
   APPEND BLANK
   REPLACE status WITH "T", descript WITH "Tax Account"
   INDEX ON status TO Statcd1
   INDEX ON descript TO Statcd2

********************
* The following functions and procedures are part of the Steve Straley Toolkit
* Copyright (c) 1987, 1988 Stephen Straley & Associates.
********************

********************

PROCEDURE Ap_it

   PARAMETERS apa, apb, apc, apd

   * apa = the field name
   * apb = the field data type
   * apc = the field length
   * apd = the field decimal

   IF PCOUNT() = 3
      apd = 0
   ENDIF

   APPEND BLANK
   IF apc > 255
      REPLACE field_name WITH apa, field_type WITH apb, field_len WITH INT(apc %
256), field_dec WITH INT(apc / 256)
   ELSE
      REPLACE field_name WITH apa, field_type WITH apb, field_len WITH apc,
field_dec WITH apd
   ENDIF
```

```
* End of File
```

Note that the Tab key is the special key in this example. The user has the choice of finding the record via the first key ("status"), or, by pressing the TAB key, the GET is cleared and the record may now be searched for via the second key ("descript"). Adding list-box technology to this enhanced feature means a full-service browse capability.

Creating Batch, Databases, and Indexes WITHIN the Application

In some cases, a Clipper application will interact with a mainframe. In these cases, special programs to download the data will be executed within the compiled program. Sometimes, batch files are made to run the Clipper program, then to run the downloading software, only to run another Clipper application that actually works with the information just obtained from the mainframe. All of these are extra work, when in fact the Clipper application can create the necessary batch files, run them, then continue processing with the newly obtained data. This saves on load time and on disk space, not to mention on keeping track of the flow of data. Here is such an example:

```
*********************
* Name      Newdemo.prg
* Author    Stephen J. Straley
* Notice    Copyright (c) 1988 Stephen J. Straley & Associates
* Date      May 2, 1988
* Compile   Clipper Newdemo -m
* Release   Summer '87 Only
* Link      Plink86 Fi Newdemo Lib Clipper Lib Extend;
* Note      This program is in part an extract from Steve Straley's
*           Toolkit published by Four Season's Pubishing Co., Inc.
*           and demonstrates how to make databases on the fly, how the
*           EMPTY() can work in other ways, and how to write a batch
*           file within Clipper to run, new ways to use DBEDIT(),
*           using VALID to look up things within the files, and testing
*           with the GETE() function.
*********************

   * This section checks the environment using the GETE() funciton
   * and if incorrect, writes a batch file that will correct the
   * problem.   Check GOOD_ENV() and PROCEDURE Reset_env for code
   * eamples.

   IF !GOOD_ENV(020, 000, 000, 000, 020, 000)
      DO Reset_env WITH "SETDEMO.BAT", "020", "000", ;
                        "000", "000", "020", "000"
      CLEAR SCREEN
      @ 0,0 SAY "Please type in SETDEMO to reset the system!"
      QUIT
   ELSE
```

```
      ERASE Setdemo.bat
   ENDIF
   CLEAR SCREEN
   IF FILE("Ontap.dbf")
      USE Ontap
      start = 0
      DO WHILE .T.
         startsec = SECONDS()
         *
         * Display, using the LOCATE command, all records which have
         * 1000000.00 == the field par_val.  This uses the EMPTY()
         * function as the trick.
         *
         LOCATE FOR EMPTY(sizes) .AND. RECNO() > start
         IF FOUND()
            ? RECNO()
            ?? "  "
            ?? sizes
            ?? "  "
            ?? files
            ?? "  "
            ?? SECONDS() - startsec
            start = RECNO()
         ELSE
            EXIT
         ENDIF
      ENDDO
      WAIT
   ENDIF
   DO Nextstep

*******************

PROCEDURE Nextstep

   DO Creatdbf  && This Procedure makes the databases on the fly!
   DO Makearry  && This creates PUBLIC arrays.
   DO Mainmenu  && This is the beginning of the Newdemo program.

*******************

PROCEDURE Mainmenu

   CLEAR SCREEN
   SET WRAP ON
   SET SCOREBOARD OFF
   @  0,0 SAY "Demo for dbug(tm)"
   @  0,RIGHTJUST("HJS Research", 80) SAY "HJS Research"
   @  1,0 SAY "Contributed by:"
    @  1,RIGHTJUST("Steve Straley & Associates", 80) SAY "Steve Straley & Associa-
tes"
   @ 24,0 SAY "Press ESC to Quit"
   option = 1
```

```
   screen = SPACE(4000)
   DO WHILE .T.
      IF EMPTY(screen)
         @ 4,10 TO 20,70 DOUBLE
         SAVE SCREEN TO screen
      ELSE
         RESTORE SCREEN FROM screen
      ENDIF
      @  7,20 PROMPT " 1>  Scan for a File in Database         "
      @ 10,20 PROMPT " 2>  Generate Listing of Files to Screen  "
      @ 13,20 PROMPT " 3>  Add Speical Notation to Files        "
      @ 16,20 PROMPT " 4>  Pop Out to DOS for a second....      "
      MENU TO option
      IF option = 0
         EXIT
      ELSEIF option = 1
         DO Scanfiles
      ELSEIF option = 2
         DO Showfiles
      ELSEIF option = 3
         DO Addnote
      ELSEIF option = 4
         DO Fakedos
      ENDIF
   ENDDO
   CLEAR SCREEN

********************

PROCEDURE Addnote

   USE Ontap INDEX Ontap
   SAVE SCREEN
   lookup = SPACE(13)
   @ 9,15 CLEAR TO 13,65
   @ 9,15 TO 13,65 DOUBLE
   @ 11,20 SAY "Enter Name of file => " GET lookup ;
         PICT "@!" VALID ONFILE(lookup)
   READ
   IF LASTKEY() = 27 .OR. EMPTY(lookup)
   ELSE
      @ 9,15 CLEAR TO 13,65
      @ 9,15 TO 13,65 DOUBLE
      @ 9,17 SAY "< Enter Note >"
      @ 13,48 SAY "< F8 TO Save >"
      SET FUNCTION 8 TO CHR(23)
      oldcolor = SETCOLOR()
      SETCOLOR(REVERSE(SETCOLOR()))
      REPLACE notes WITH STRTRAN(STRTRAN( ;
              MEMOEDIT(notes, 10,17,12,63, .T.), CHR(10), ""), ;
              CHR(13), "")
      COMMIT
      SETCOLOR(oldcolor)
```

```
   ENDIF
   RESTORE SCREEN
   CLOSE ALL

*******************

PROCEDURE Scanfiles

   USE Ontap INDEX Ontap
   SAVE SCREEN
   lookup = SPACE(13)
   @ 9,15 CLEAR TO 13,65
   @ 9,15 TO 13,65 DOUBLE
   @ 11,20 SAY "Enter Name of file => " GET lookup PICT "@!" ;
           VALID ONFILE(lookup)
   READ
   IF LASTKEY() = 27 .OR. EMPTY(lookup)
   ELSE
      @ 9,15 CLEAR TO 13,65
      @ 9,15 TO 13,65 DOUBLE
      @ 10,20 SAY "File Name" GET files
      @ 10,45 SAY "Size " GET sizes PICT "@B99999999"
      @ 11,20 SAY "     Date" GET datestamp
      @ 11,45 SAY "Time " GET times
      partnote = SUBSTR(notes, 1, 25)
      @ 12,20 SAY " Notation" GET partnote
      CLEAR GETS
      @ 13,50 SAY "< Any Key >"
      INKEY(0)
   ENDIF
   RESTORE SCREEN
   CLOSE ALL

*******************

FUNCTION Onfile

   PARAMETERS search

   IF EMPTY(search)
      RETURN(.T.)
   ENDIF
   search = LTRIM(TRIM(search))
   SEEK search
   IF FOUND()
      RETURN(.T.)
   ELSE
      @ 12,20 SAY "That's NOT on File...."
      RETURN(.F.)
   ENDIF

*******************
```

```
PROCEDURE Showfiles

   USE Ontap
   DECLARE dispit[1]
   dispit[1] = "SHOWITEMS()"
   header = "Files on Disk..."
   SAVE SCREEN
   @ 11,0 CLEAR TO 20,79
   @ 11,0 TO 20,79 DOUBLE
   DBEDIT(12,1,19,78,dispit, "INPUTIT", .F., header)
   RESTORE SCREEN
   CLOSE ALL

********************

FUNCTION Inputit

   PARAMETERS instat

   whatkey = LASTKEY()
   IF whatkey = 27
      RETURN(0)
   ENDIF

   IF instat = 2
      KEYBOARD CHR(31)
   ELSEIF instat = 1
      KEYBOARD CHR(30)
   ENDIF
   RETURN(1)

********************

FUNCTION Showitems

   RETURN(files  + " SIZE=" + TRANSFORM(sizes, "@B999,999,999") + ;
          " DATE=" + DTOC(datestamp) + " TIME=" + times )

********************

PROCEDURE Creatdbf

   DIR *.DBF
   WAIT "Press Any Key to Make the Database"
   CREATE Template
   USE Template
   APPEND BLANK
   REPLACE field_name WITH "files", field_type WITH "C", ;
           field_len WITH 12, field_dec WITH 0
   APPEND BLANK
   REPLACE field_name WITH "sizes", field_type WITH "N", ;
           field_len WITH 12, field_dec WITH 0
   APPEND BLANK
```

```
   REPLACE field_name WITH "datestamp", field_type WITH "D", ;
           field_len WITH 8, field_dec WITH 0
   APPEND BLANK
   REPLACE field_name WITH "times", field_type WITH "C", ;
           field_len WITH 8, field_dec WITH 0
   APPEND BLANK
   REPLACE field_name WITH "notes", field_type WITH "M", ;
           field_len WITH 10, field_dec WITH 0
   USE
   CREATE Ontap FROM Template
   ERASE Template.dbf
   DIR *.DBF
   WAIT "Now Compare!  Any Key to Continue!"

********************

PROCEDURE Makearry

   how_many = ADIR("*.*")
   DECLARE afiles[how_many], asizes[how_many], adate[how_many], ;
           atimes[how_many]
   ADIR("*.*", afiles, asizes, adate, atimes)
   USE Ontap
   INDEX ON files TO Ontap
   FOR x = 1 TO how_many
      APPEND BLANK
      REPLACE files WITH afiles[x], sizes with asizes[x], ;
              datestamp WITH adate[x], times WITH atimes[x]
   NEXT
   USE

************************** Special Notation **************************
*                                                                    *
* The following three functions are part of Steve Straley's Toolkit. *
*                                                                    *
*                             Release 1.0                            *
**********************************************************************

********************

FUNCTION Reverse

   PARAMETERS the_color

   the_say = STRTRAN(SUBSTR(the_color, 1, AT(",", the_color)-1), "+", "")
   RETURN(SUBSTR(the_say, AT("/", the_say)+1) + "/" + ;
          SUBSTR(the_say, 1, AT("/", the_say)-1))

********************

FUNCTION Rightjust

   PARAMETERS right_st, right_col
```

```
   IF PCOUNT() = 1
      right_col = 79
   ENDIF
   RETURN(IF(LEN(right_st) > right_col, right_st, right_col - ;
            LEN(right_st)))

********************

PROCEDURE Fakedos

   SET CURSOR ON
   pop_row = ROW()
   pop_col = COL()
   old_color = SETCOLOR()
   SAVE SCREEN
   @ 0,0 CLEAR
   @ 1,0 SAY "Enter EXIT to Return to Program Control...."
   RUN Command
   RESTORE SCREEN
   SET COLOR TO &old_color.
   @ pop_row, pop_col SAY ""

********************

FUNCTION Good_env

   PARAMETERS gooda, goodb, goodc, goodd, goode, goodf

   did_pass = .T.
   the_env = UPPER(GETE("CLIPPER"))

   FOR qaz = 1 TO 6
      the_let = SUBSTR("VREXFS", qaz, 1)
      the_par = "good" + CHR(96 + qaz)

      IF !EMPTY(&the_par.)
         did_pass = (&the_par. <= ;
             VAL(SUBSTR(the_env, AT(the_let, the_env) + 1, 3)))
         IF !did_pass
            RETURN(.F.)
         ENDIF
      ENDIF
   NEXT
   RETURN(did_pass)

********************

PROCEDURE Reset_env

   PARAMETERS the_batch, the_v, the_r, the_e, the_x, the_f, the_s

   r1 = "Echo Off" + CHR(13) + CHR(10) + "CLS" + CHR(13) + ;
```

```
        CHR(10) + "SET CLIPPER= "
   r2 = IF(!EMPTY(VAL(the_v)), "v" + FILL_ZEROS(the_v) + ";", "")
   r3 = IF(!EMPTY(VAL(the_r)), "r" + FILL_ZEROS(the_r) + ";", "")
   r4 = IF(!EMPTY(VAL(the_e)), "e" + FILL_ZEROS(the_e) + ";", "")
   r5 = IF(!EMPTY(VAL(the_x)), "x" + FILL_ZEROS(the_x) + ";", "")
   r6 = IF(!EMPTY(VAL(the_f)), "f" + FILL_ZEROS(the_f) + ";", "")
   r7 = IF(!EMPTY(VAL(the_s)), "s" + FILL_ZEROS(the_s) + ";", "") + ;
        CHR(13) + CHR(10)
   r8 = "CLS" + CHR(13) + CHR(10) + "echo DOS has now been set.  " + ;
        "Please Start your Program Over again!" + ;
        CHR(13) + CHR(10) + CHR(13) + CHR(10)
   MEMOWRIT(the_batch, r1+r2+r3+r4+r5+r6+r7+r8)

********************

FUNCTION Fill_zeros

   PARAMETER clipnumb, zeros

   IF PCOUNT() = 1
      zeros = 3
   ENDIF
   zeros = IF(zeros < 1, 1, zeros)

   newnumb = ALLTRIM(TRANSFORM(clipnumb,"999"))
   DO WHILE LEN(newnumb) <> zeros
      newnumb = "0" + newnumb
   ENDDO
   RETURN(newnumb)
```

Another feature within the compiler is the ability to create databases within an application. This means that an application can be distributed as one executable file and that file will generate the proper databases and indexes if a "start-up" condition exists.

The idea of writing a batch file is not new, but doing so within a Clipper application and then running that batch file from the application is new. This is very useful if many C-compiled program need to be executed that require special parameters passed to them. For example, a Clipper application contains all of the names and passwords of legitimate people to log onto the mainframe computer. The log-on routine, written in C, requires two parameters and these two parameters are picked from within the Clipper application. Once the log-on procedures are accomplished, a special file transfer program downloads the information and then it copies back into the Clipper application. It would be extremely cumbersome to write a batch file that ran the entire process, including the Clipper application. However, if your application wrote the batch file, processed the commands, and then returned to the program to bring in the information, the awkwardness of batch files would be eliminated. Additionally, it would all be external to the end user. Consider the following code extract:

```
   carriage = "CHR(13) + CHR(10)"
   astr = "ECHO OFF" + &carriage. + "CLS" + &carriage.
```

```
bstr = "IF NOT EXIST *.FAL GOTO DONE" + &carriage. + ;
       "DEL *.FAL >NUL" + &carriage. + ;
       "GOTO DONE" + &carriage.
cstr = ":DONE" + &carriage. + "VM " + ;
      ALLTRIM(A->user_id) + " " + ALLTRIM(A->password) +;
      " " + &carriage.
dstr = "FTCMS/R/V/D/N AFILE.FAL " +;
       "MAINFRAM FILE A1 PCFILE" +; &carriage.
estr = "LOGOFFVM" + &carriage. + ;
       "REN AFILE.FAL PCFILE.FAL >NUL" + &carriage.
fstr = "ECHO Adjusting File for Proper " +;
       "Transfer" + &carriage. +"ADJUST2" + &carriage.
gstr = "REN FAIL_TOD.FAL AFILE.FAL >NUL" + &carriage. +;
       "DEL FAILDOWN.FAL >NUL" + &carriage.

aastr = astr + bstr + cstr + dstr + estr + fstr + gstr

MEMOWRIT("DOBATCH.BAT", aastr)
RUN Dobatch
ERASE Dobatch.bat
```

The MEMOWRIT() function is used to write the batch file DOBATCH.BAT. After this is accomplished, the batch file is then executed. Inside the batch file, four separate programs are executed: VM.EXE, FTCMS.EXE, LOGOFF.EXE, and ADJUST.EXE. These are just some examples of specialized programs to log onto a mainframe, transfer data from a mainframe, log off the mainframe, and then adjust the data for Clipper. The sequence and the necessary information to run the programs is created by the application that eventually will use the information processed. This way, users do not have to worry about this extra step.

Outside of batch files, databases may be generated **within** the application. This allows the developer to distribute applications knowing that once the program is installed, the application, if it is so programmed, will generate the databases on the fly. Throughout this text there are plenty of examples of using the CREATE command and generating databases as you go.

Adding Fields to a READ While Processing

One of the earliest discoveries was the ability to use the SET KEY TO command to add GET fields to a pending READ stack. Particularly useful in multiple data entry conditions, specific fields can be grouped together into a separate procedure. That procedure may be called **while** actually entering data. Clipper would just add those GETs to the READ stack and process them in order. This order is not based on screen locations; rather it is based on calling order. For example, here is a sample, using the Tab key as the special hot key:

```
SET KEY 9 TO Addgets
```

```
@ 10,10 GET name
@ 11,10 GET company
@ 12,10 GET address1
@ 13,10 GET address2
READ

********************

PROCEDURE Addgets

   PARAMETERS p, l, v

   @  9,10 GET code
   @ 14,10 GET phone
   @ 15,10 GET due
```

Note that if the Tab key is pressed, the three additional GETs in Procedure Addgets will be processed. The order of the GET will be in a continuous stream; that is to say that the "code" field will be processed **after** the "address2" field, followed then by the "phone" and "due" fields. The point to keep in mind is that the screen location may not follow program flow; if this feature is implemented, this point should be kept in mind.

APPENDIX A

DOS Errors

Listed below is a table of the DOS error codes and messages.

Error Number	Description
1	Invalid function number
2	File not found
3	Path not found
4	Too many open files (no file handles left)
5	Access denied
6	Invalid handle
7	Memory control blocks destroyed
8	Insufficient memory
9	Invalid memory block address
10	Invalid environment
11	Invalid format
12	Invalid access code
13	Invalid data
14	Reserved
15	Invalid drive was specified
16	Attempt to remove the current directory
17	Not same device
18	No more file
19	Attempt to write on write-protected disk
20	Unknown unit
21	Drive not ready
22	Unknown command
23	Data error (CRC)
24	Bad request structure length
25	Seek error
26	Unknown media type
27	Sector not found
28	Printer out of paper
29	Write fault
30	Read fault
31	General failure
32	Sharing violation
33	Lock violation
34	Invalid disk change
35	FCB unavailable
36	Sharing buffer overflow
37	Reserved
38	Reserved
39	Reserved
40	Reserved
41	Reserved
42	Reserved

43	Reserved
44	Reserved
45	Reserved
46	Reserved
47	Reserved
48	Reserved
49	Reserved
50	Network request not supported
51	Remote computer not listening
52	Duplicate name on network
53	Network name not found
54	Network busy
55	Network device no longer exists
56	Network BIOS command limit exceeded
57	Network adapter hardware error
58	Incorrect response from network
59	Unexpected network error
60	Incompatible remote adapter
61	Print queue full
62	Not enough space for print file
63	Print file deleted (not enough space)
64	Network name deleted
65	Access denied
66	Network device type incorrect
67	Network name not found
68	Network name limit exceeded
69	Network BIOS session limit exceeded
70	Temporarily paused
71	Network request not accepted
72	Print or disk redirection paused
73	Reserved
74	Reserved
75	Reserved
76	Reserved
77	Reserved
78	Reserved
79	Reserved
80	File already exists
81	Reserved
82	Cannot make directory entry
83	Fall on INT 24H
84	Too many redirections
85	Duplicate redirection
86	Invalid password
87	Invalid parameter
88	Network device fault

APPENDIX B

Command Syntax

The following is a quick reference to all of the Clipper commands, the proper syntax, and the associated clauses and phrases. All listed commands reflect the Summer '87 release of Clipper.

MATHEMATICAL, RELATIONAL, AND LOGICAL OPERATIONS

Operation Desired	Operator	Syntax	Special Notes
Addition or concatenation.	+	<exp> + <exp>	
Subtraction	-	<exp> - <exp>	
Multiplication	*	<expN> * <expN>	
Division	/	<expN> / <expN>	
Exponentiation	**	<expN> ** <expN>	
Modulus	%	<expN> % <expN>	
Less Than	<	<exp> < <exp>	
Greater Than	>	<exp> > <exp>	
Equal	=	<exp> = <exp>	Not to be used with !
Not Equal	# or <>	<exp> # <exp>	
Less Than or Equal To	<=	<exp> <= <exp>	
Greater Than or Equal To	>=	<exp> >= <exp>	
Evaluate Variables	==	<exp> == <exp>	SET EXACT ON has effect
And	.AND.	<exp>.AND.<exp>	Both <exp>'s MUST be true
Not	.NOT. or !	.NOT.<exp> or !<exp>	<exp> must NOT be true. Not to be used with =.
Or	.OR.	<exp> .OR. <exp>	One <exp> MUST be true.

Below is a *truth table*. Given the following possibilities within a command line with two separate conditions, the tables below show how each condition should be viewed in relation to the operator being used.

.AND.	Y	!Y
X :	True	False
!X :	False	False

If the X condition is .T. .AND. the Y condition is .T., only then is the expression evaluated to a .T. condition.

.OR.	Y	!Y
X :	True	True
!X :	True	False

If either the Y condition is .T. .OR. the X condition is .T., .OR. BOTH conditions evaluate to .T., the .OR. evaluates to a .T. Only when both X and Y are .F. will the .OR. expression evaluate to .F.

DATA DISPLAY OPERATIONS

Operation Desired	Command	Syntax
Display to Screen/Printer	@	@ <row,column> [SAY<exp> [PICTURE <clause>]] [GET<exp> [PICTURE <clause>]] [RANGE<exp,exp> [VALID <exp>]] [CLEAR]

	* @	* @ <row,column>[CLEAR] TO<row2, col2>[DOUBLE]
	?	? <expression list>
	??	?? <expression list>
Print Labels	LABEL	LABEL FORM <filename> [<scope>][SAMPLE] [TO PRINT] [FOR/WHILE <condition>] [TO FILE <filename>]
Print Report	REPORT FORM	REPORT FORM <filename> [<scope>] [FOR <condition>] [WHILE <condition>] [PLAIN][HEADING <expC>][NOEJECT] [TO PRINT][TO FILE <filename>]
Show Fields/Records	DISPLAY	DISPLAY [OFF][scope] FIELDS <field list> [FOR/WHILE <condition>]
	LIST	LIST [OFF] [scope]<field list>[FOR<condition>] [WHILE <condition>] [TO PRINT/TO FILE <filename>]
Show Text	TEXT	TEXT [TO PRINT/TO FILE <filename>] <text> ENDTEXT
Type File	TYPE	TYPE <filename> [TO PRINT] [TO FILE<filename>]

ADDITION/CHANGING OF DATA

Operation Desired	Command	Syntax
Change Data	REPLACE	REPLACE [<scope>] <field> WITH <exp> [, <field> WITH <exp>...] [FOR <condition>] [WHILE <condition>]
Input Data	ACCEPT	[<prompt message>] TO <memvar>
	INPUT	INPUT [<expC>] TO <memvar>

DATABASE MANIPULATION

Operation Desired	Command	Syntax
Choose Work Area	SELECT	SELECT <expN> SELECT <expC>
Close Files	CLOSE	CLOSE <file type>
Copy Records from a Database	APPEND FROM	APPEND [scope][FIELDS <field list>] FROM <filename> [FOR/WHILE <condition>] [SDF/Delimited]
Create File	CREATE	CREATE <database filename>
	CREATE FROM	CREATE <newfile> FROM <structure extended file>
Flush Buffer Information to Disk	COMMIT	COMMIT
Join Databases	JOIN	JOIN WITH <alias> TO <new filename> FOR <condition> [FIELDS <field list>]

Open a database	USE	USE [<filename>][INDEX <index list>] [ALIAS <expC>]
Reconstruct Index	REINDEX	REINDEX
Remove Data Marked for deletion	PACK	PACK
Sort Database	SORT	SORT <scope> TO [<newfile>] ON <field> [/A][/C][/D] [,<field2>] [/A][/C][/D][FOR <condition>] [WHILE <condition>]
Unlock a database	UNLOCK	UNLOCK [ALL]
Unmark Data Marked for deletion	RECALL	RECALL <scope> [FOR]/ [WHILE] <condition>]
Update fields	UPDATE ON	UPDATE ON <key field> FROM <Alias> REPLACE <field> WITH <exp> [,<field2> WITH <exp>...]
Wipe out Data in file	ZAP	ZAP

MANIPULATING MEMORY VARIABLES

Operation Desired	Command	Syntax
Change contents of memory variable	STORE	STORE <expression> TO <memory variable> [, <memory variable list>]
Clear Memory	CLEAR MEMORY RELEASE	CLEAR MEMORY RELEASE <memory variable> RELEASE <memory variable list> RELEASE ALL [LIKE / EXCEPT <skeleton>]
Clear Open GETS on Active READ	CLEAR GETS	CLEAR GETS
Compute Average of values	AVERAGE	AVERAGE <field list> TO <memvar list> [FOR/WHILE <condition>]
Count values	COUNT	COUNT [<scope>][FOR/WHILE <condition>] TO <memvar>
Establish Array	DECLARE	DECLARE <memvar> [<expN>][,<array list>]
Establish Variables	PUBLIC	PUBLIC Clipper
Recover Memory File	RESTORE FROM	RESTORE FROM <filename> [ADDITIVE]
Sum of values	SUM	SUM <field list> TO <memvar list> [FOR/WHILE <condition>]
Total of fields/values	TOTAL ON	TOTAL ON <key field> TO <newfile> [<scope>] FIELDS <field list> [FOR <condition>] [WHILE <condition>] RANDOM

POSITIONING WITHIN DATABASE

Operation Desired	Command	Syntax
Find Record: Literal	FIND	FIND <expC>/<expN>
Condition	LOCATE	LOCATE [<scope>] FOR <condition> [WHILE <condition>]
Variable	SEEK	SEEK <expression>

Move Record Pointer	SKIP	SKIP [expN] [ALIAS <expN><expC>]
Position Record Pointer	GO / GOTO	GO / GOTO <exp>/TOP/BOTTOM
Resume Searching After Locate	CONTINUE	CONTINUE

MANIPULATING RECORDS

Operation Desired	Command	Syntax
Add Blank Records to Database	APPEND BLANK	APPEND BLANK
Mark Record for Deletion	DELETE	DELETE [<scope>][FOR <condition>] [WHILE <condition>]

CREATION/MANIPULATION OF FILES

Operation Desired	Command	Syntax
Build Index File	INDEX	INDEX ON <key expression> TO <filename>
Copy File	COPY FILE	COPY FILE <filename> TO <filename>
Copy File Structure	COPY STRUCTURE	COPY STRUCTURE TO <filename> [FIELDS <field list>]
	COPY STRUCTURE	COPY TO <filename> STRUCTURE EXTENDED
Erase File	ERASE	ERASE <filename>
Rename File	RENAME	RENAME <filename> TO <filename>
Save Memory File	SAVE TO	SAVE TO <filename> [ALL LIKE / EXCEPT <skeleton>]

PROGRAM CONTROL

Operation Desired	Command	Syntax
Branch for Multiple Testing	DO CASE	DO CASE CASE <condition> <commands> CASE <condition> <commands> OTHERWISE <commands> ENDCASE
Call outside program	CALL	CALL <process> [WITH <parameter list>]
Complete a GET	READ	READ
Declare a Procedure/Function Outside Current program name	EXTERNAL	EXTERNAL <procedure list> (May not be in the procedure list)
Define Code as FUNCTION	FUNCTION	FUNCTION <name> [PARAMETERS <expC>] <commands> RETURN(<value>)
Define Condition	IF	IF <condition> <commands>

		[ELSE] <commands> ENDIF
Establish Process	PROCEDURE	PROCEDURE <procedure name>
Go Back to Calling Program	RETURN	RETURN
Group a series of commands for immediate break	BEGIN SEQUENCE...END	BEGIN SEQUENCE...END
Jump to top of DO WHILE	LOOP	LOOP
Menu Options	MENU TO PROMPT... MESSAGE	MENU TO <memvar> @ <row>,<col> PROMPT <expC> [MESSAGE <expC>]
Notation	NOTE, *, &&	NOTE / * <text> <command line> && <text>
Pass Values to Procedures	PARAMETERS	PARAMETERS <parameter list>
Pause	WAIT	WAIT [<expC>][TO <memvar>]
Perform Task	DO	DO <file name> [WITH <parameter(s)>]
Premature Terminate of DO WHILE	EXIT	EXIT
Repeat Task	DO WHILE	DO WHILE <condition> <commands> ENDDO
	FOR...NEXT	FOR <memvar> = <expN> TO <expN> [STEP <expN>] <commands> NEXT
Run another program	RUN / (!)	RUN <filename> ! <filename>
Stop Processing	CANCEL QUIT	CANCEL QUIT
Stuff the Keyboard	KEYBOARD	KEYBOARD <expC>
Terminate a set of commands grouped by the BEGIN SEQUENCE...END construct	BREAK	BREAK

SYSTEM CONTROL PARAMETERS

Operation Desired	Command	Syntax
SET System Conditions	SET ALTERNATE	SET ALTERNATE TO [<filename>] SET ALTERNATE TO SET ALTERNATE ON/OFF
	SET COLOR TO	SET COLOR TO [<standard>[,<enhanced> [<border>]]]
	SET CONFIRM	SET CONFIRM ON/OFF
	SET CONSOLE	SET CONSOLE ON/OFF
	SET CENTURY	SET CENTURY ON/OFF

	SET CURSOR	SET CURSOR ON/OFF
	SET DECIMALS TO	SET DECIMALS TO <expN>
	SET DEFAULT TO	SET DEFAULT TO <disk drive>
	SET DELETED	SET DELETED ON/OFF
	SET DELIMITERS	SET DELIMITERS ON/OFF SET DELIMITERS TO [<expC>] [DEFAULT]
	SET DEVICE	SET DEVICE TO <PRINT/SCREEN>
	SET ESCAPE	SET ESCAPE ON/OFF
	SET EXACT	SET EXACT ON/OFF
	SET EXCLUSIVE	SET EXCLUSIVE ON/OFF
	SET FILTER TO	SET FILTER TO [<expression>]
	SET FIXED	SET FIXED ON/OFF
	SET FORMAT TO	SET FORMAT TO <file name>
	SET FUNCTION	SET FUNCTION <expN> TO <expC>
	SET INDEX	SET INDEX TO [<file list>]
	SET INTENSITY	SET INTENSITY ON/OFF
	SET KEY TO	SET KEY <expN> TO [<proc.]
	SET MARGIN TO	SET MARGIN TO <expN>
	SET MESSAGE TO	SET MESSAGE TO <expN>
	SET ORDER TO	SET ORDER TO [<expN>]
	SET PATH TO	SET PATH TO <expC>
	SET PRINT	SET PRINT ON/OFF
	SET PRINTER TO	SET PRINTER TO [<device>/<filename>]
	SET PROCEDURE TO	SET PROCEDURE TO <filename>
	SET RELATION TO	SET RELATION TO <key exp> / RECNO() / <expN> INTO <alias> [,TO <key exp> / RECNO() / <expN> INTO <alias>...]
	SET SOFTSEEK	SET SOFTSEEK ON/OFF
	SET TYPEAHEAD	SET TYPEAHEAD <expN>
	SET UNIQUE	SET UNIQUE ON/OFF
	SET WRAP	SET WRAP ON/OFF

SCREEN HANDLING OPERATIONS

Operation Desired	Command	Syntax
Draw Window on Screen	BOX	@ <top,left,bottom,right> BOX <string>
Clear the Screen	CLEAR	CLEAR
Clear the System	CLEAR ALL	CLEAR ALL
Recover Screen	RESTORE SCREEN	RESTORE SCREEN
Save Screen	SAVE SCREEN	SAVE SCREEN

MISCELLANEOUS

Operation Desired	Command	Syntax
Directory	DIR	DIR [<drive>] [<path>] [<skeleton>]
Issue Page Eject	EJECT	EJECT

APPENDIX C

Functions

The following pages contain a quick reference to all of the Clipper functions, their proper syntax, and the data type returned. Included with this list are all proper definitions of syntax words and operators. The functions are grouped by category. This list reflects the Summer '87 release of Clipper.

MATHEMATICAL FUNCTIONS

Operation	Function	Syntax	Value Returned
Absolute Value of a Number	ABS()	ABS(<expN>)	Numeric
Exponential of number	EXP()	EXP(<expN>)	Numeric
Logarithm of number	LOG()	LOG(<expN>)	Numeric
Remainder of two numbers	MOD()	MOD(<expN>, <expN>)	Numeric
Round off numeric value	ROUND()	ROUND(<expN>,<expN>)	Numeric
Square Root	SQRT()	SQRT(<expN>)	Numeric

OPERATING SYSTEM FUNCTIONS

Operation	Function	Syntax	Value Returned
Amount of available memory	MEMORY(0)	MEMORY(0)	Numeric
Current Working Directory	CURDIR()	CURDIR()	Character
Available Disk Space	DISKSPACE()	DISKSPACE(<expN>)	Numeric
Date of last update to database	LUPDATE()	LUPDATE()	Date
DOS error level	DOSERROR()	DOSERROR()	Numeric
Executes debugger or enables/disables Alt-D	ALTD()	ALTD()	Nothing
File Existence	FILE()	FILE(<expC>)	Logical
Last key pressed at console	LASTKEY()	LASTKEY()	Numeric
Length of a database header	HEADER()	HEADER()	Numeric
Name of the function key label	FKLABEL()	FKLABEL(<expN>)	Character
Name of the operating system	OS()	OS()	Character
Number of maximum function keys available	FKMAX()	FKMAX()	Numeric
Read the value of the last key pressed	READKEY()	READKEY()	Numeric
Set DOS error level	ERRORLEVEL()	ERRORLEVEL(<expN>)	Numeric
Toggles the Alt-C on or off for termination	SETCANCEL()	SETCANCEL()	Nothing
Value of environmental variable	GETE()	GETE(<expC>)	Character
Waiting for keyboard input	INKEY()	INKEY() or INKEY(<expN>)	Numeric

STRING FUNCTIONS

Operation	Function	Syntax	Value Returned
ASCII value of character string	ASC()	ASC(<expC>)	Numeric
Blank space	SPACE()	SPACE(<expN>)	Character
Character representation of ASCII value	CHR()	CHR(<expN>)	Character
Convert character type to numeric type	VAL()	VAL(<expC>)	Numeric
Convert numeric zero to string	STRZERO()	STRZERO(<expN> [, <expN> [, <expN>]])	Character
Delete all leading and trailing blanks	ALLTRIM()	ALLTRIM(<expC)	Character
Display expression with specified picture	TRANSFORM()	TRANSFORM(<exp>,<expC>)	Character
Length of a number	LENNUM()	LENNUM(<expN>)	Numeric
Length of a string	LEN()	LEN(<expC>)	Numeric
Lowercase the string or character	LOWER()	LOWER(<expC>)	Character
Left trim the string	LTRIM()	LTRIM(<expC>)	Character
Left-most portion of a string	LEFT()	LEFT(<expC>, <expN>)	Character
Position in main string of substring	AT()	AT(<expC>, <expC>)	Numeric
Repeat a character expression x times	REPLICATE()	REPLICATE(<expC>,<expN>)	Character
Replace portion of string with another	STUFF()	STUFF(<expC>, <expN>, <expN>, <expC>)	Character
Replace contents of string with another string value	STRTRAN()	STRTRAN(<expC>, <expC>, <expC>)	Character
Replace soft carriage returns for hard	HARDCR()	HARDCR(<expC>)	Character
Right-most portion of a string	RIGHT()	RIGHT(<expC>, <expN>)	Numeric
Search contents of string with substring	RAT()	RAT(<expC1>, <expC2>)	Numeric
Substring selection	SUBSTR()	SUBSTR(<expC>,<expN> [,<expN>])	Character
Test for alphabetic character	ISALPHA()	ISALPHA(<expC>)	Logical
Test for lowercase character	ISLOWER()	ISLOWER(<expC>)	Logical
Test for uppercase character	ISUPPER()	ISUPPER(<expC>)	Logical
Trim blank spaces from string	TRIM()	TRIM(<expC>)	Character
Uppercase the string or character	UPPER()	UPPER(<expC>)	Character

DATABASE FUNCTIONS

Operation	Function	Syntax	Value Returned
Alias name of a work area	ALIAS()	ALIAS(<expN>)	Character
Check to see if file is being used in work area	USED()	USED()	Logical
Field name in database	FIELDNAME()	FIELDNAME(<expN>)	Character
Found record after locate, seek, or find	FOUND()	FOUND()	Logical
Index in descending order	DESCEND()	DESCEND(<exp>)	Expression
Key expression in active index	INDEXKEY()	INDEXKEY(<expN>)	Character
Last read changed any data in GETs	UPDATED()	UPDATED()	Logical
Last record number in active database	LASTREC()	LASTREC()	Numeric
Name of active filter expression	DBFILTER()	DBFILTER()	Character
Name of active relation expression	DNRELATION()	DBRELATION()	Character
Name of current or selected database	DBF()	DBF()	Character
Name of the index position	NDX()	NDX(<expN>)	Character
Number of fields in active database	FCOUNT()	FCOUNT()	Numeric
Record number at current position	RECNO()	RECNO()	Numeric
Record positioned is marked for deletion	DELETED()	DELETED()	Logical
Record positioned at beginning of file	BOF()	BOF()	Logical
Record positioned at end of file	EOF()	EOF()	Logical
Selected area currently open	SELECT()	SELECT()	Numeric
Size of record in selected database	RECSIZE()	RECSIZE()	Numeric
Sound-like interpretation of character	SOUNDEX()	SOUNDEX(<expC>)	Character
Target work area of active relation	DBRSELECT()	DBRSELECT()	Numeric

DATE AND TIME FUNCTIONS

Operation	Function	Syntax	Value Returned
Calendar Month	CMONTH()	CMONTH(<expD>)	Character
Character to Date conversion	CTOD()	CTOD(<expC>)	Date
Convert numeric seconds to time string	TSTRING()	TSTRING(<expN>)	Character
Date to Character conversion	DTOC()	DTOC(<expD>)	Character
Date to String conversion	DTOS()	DTOS(<expD>)	Character
Date of system	DATE()	DATE()	Date

Operation	Function	Syntax	Value Returned
Day of the Week	DOW()	DOW(<expD>)	Numeric
Day of Week	CDOW()	CDOW(<expD>)	Character
Day of the Month	DAY()	DAY(<expD>)	Numeric
Elapsed Days passed	DAYS()	DAYS(<expN>)	Numeric
Elapsed Time passed	ELAPTIME()	ELAPTIME(<expC>, <expC>)	Character
Month of the Year	MONTH()	MONTH(<expD>)	Numeric
Number of seconds from time string	SECS()	SECS(<expC>)	Numeric
System time as seconds or hundreds	SECONDS()	SECONDS()	Numeric
Time of system	TIME()	TIME()	Character
Worded time expression	AMPM()	AMPM(<expC>)	Character
Year	YEAR()	YEAR(<expD>)	Numeric

NETWORKING FUNCTIONS

Operation	Function	Syntax	Value Returned
Availability to share file	NETERR()	NETERR()	Logical
Lock a File	FLOCK()	FLOCK()	Logical
Lock a Record	RLOCK()	RLOCK()	Logical
Name of the network work station	NETNAME()	NETNAME()	Character

MEMO FIELD FUNCTIONS

Operation	Function	Syntax	Value Returned
Character replacement of memo field	MEMOTRAN()	MEMOTRAN(<expC> [,<expC>] [, <expC>]	Character
Determines position of specified line in memo field	MPLOS()	MLPOS(<expC>, <expN1>, <expN2>)	Numeric
Memo edit and display in a given area	MEMOEDIT()	MEMOEDIT(<exp>,<expN1>, <expN2>,<expN3>, <expN4>, [<expL1> [,<expC2> [, <expN5> [, <expN6> [,<expN7> [<expN8> [<expN9> [<expN10>]]]]]]]])	Character
Number of lines in memo field	MLCOUNT()	MLCOUNT(<expC> [,<expN1> [,<expN2> [,<expL>]]])	Numeric
Read a file from disk to character string	MEMOREAD()	MEMOREAD(<expC>)	Character
Returns a formatted line from memo field	MEMOLINE()	MEMOLINE(<expC> [, <expN1>	Character

Operation	Function	Syntax	Value Returned
		[,<expN2> [,<expN3> [,<expL>]]]])	
Write a memo field or character string to disk	MEMOWRIT()	MEMOWRIT(<expC>, <expC>)	Logical

DISPLAY AND PRINTER FUNCTIONS

Operation	Function	Syntax	Value Returned
Column position of printer	PCOL()	PCOL()	Numeric
Column position of screen	COL()	COL()	Numeric
Current color setting of monitor	SETCOLOR()	SETCOLOR(<expC>)	Character
Test for on-line or ready printer status	ISPRINTER()	ISPRINTER()	Logical
Restore screen contents from memory variable	RESTSCREEN()	RESTSCREEN (<expN1>, <expN2>, <expN3>, <expN4>, <expC>)	None
Row position of printer	PROW()	PROW()	Numeric
Row position of screen	ROW()	ROW()	Numeric
Save screen contents to memory variable	SAVESCREEN()	SAVESCREEN(<expN1>, <expN2>, <expN3>, <expN4>)	Character
Scroll screen contents	SCROLL()	SCROLL(<expN1>, <expN2>, <expN3>, <expN4>, <expN5>)	None
Set the printer row and column position	SETPRC()	SETPRC(<expN>, <expN>)	--------

ARRAY FUNCTIONS

Operation	Function	Syntax	Value Returned
Copy elements from one array to another	ACOPY()	ACOPY()	None
Deleting an element from an array	ADEL()	ADEL(<expC>, <expN>)	--------
Fill an array with a specific element	AFILL()	AFILL(<expC>,<exp> [,<expN>[,<expN>]])	--------
Fill array with field information	AFILL()	AFILL()	
Insert an element into an array	AINS()	AINS(<expC>, <expN>)	--------
List box based on array contents	ACHOICE()	ACHOICE()	Numeric
Look for an element in an array	ASCAN()	ASCAN(<expC>, <exp> [,<expN> [,<expN>]])	Numeric
Sorts an array in ascending order	ASORT()	ASORT()	
Store DIRectory pattern or names in an array	ADIR()	ADIR(<expC> [,<expC>])	Numeric

PROGRAMMING FUNCTIONS

Operation	Function	Syntax	Value Returned
Allows Up and Down Arrow keys to exit a READ	READEXIT()	READEXIT(<expL>)	Logical
Convert numeric double type to integer type	WORD()	WORD(<expN>)	Numeric
Empty field or variable	EMPTY()	EMPTY(<exp>)	Logical
If testing of two conditions	IF()	IF(<exp>,<exp>,<exp>)	<expression list>
Key expression of index	INDEXKEY()	INDEXKEY()	Character
Line number of program, procedure, or function	PROCLINE()	PROCLINE()	Numeric
Name of current index file extension	INDEXEXT()	INDEXEXT()	Character
Name of current GET/MENU variable	READVAR()	READVAR()	Character
Name of program, procedure. or function	PROCNAME()	PROCNAME()	Character
Number of parameters passed	PCOUNT()	PCOUNT()	Numeric
Order number of current active index	INDEXORD()	INDEXORD()	Numeric
Sound a speaker tone	TONE()	TONE(<expN1>, <expN2>)	None
Toggles insert key on and off	READINSERT()	READINSERT(<expL>)	None
Type of variable or field	TYPE()	TYPE(<exp>)	Character
Version of program	VERSION()	VERSION()	Character

LOW-LEVEL FUNCTIONS

Operation	Function	Syntax	Value Returned
Convert 16-byte string to integer	BIN2I()	BIN2I(<expC>)	Numeric
Convert 32-byte string to integer	BIN2L()	BIN2L(<expC>)	Numeric
Convert 16-byte unsigned integer to numeric	BIN2W()	BIN2W(<expC>)	Numeric
Convert integer to character string	I2BIN()	I2BIN(<expN>)	Character
Convert integer to character string	L2BIN()	L2BIN(<expN>)	Character
Closes an open file	FCLOSE()	FCLOSE(<expN>)	Logical
Create a new file	FCREATE()	FCREATE(<expC> [, <expN>])	Numeric
Open a file	FOPEN()	FOPEN(<expC> [, <expN>])	Numeric
Read characters from a file	FREAD()	FREAD(<expN1>,@<memvarC>,<expN2>)	Numeric
Read characters from a file	FREADSTR()	FREADSTR(<expN1>, <expN2>)	Numeric
Set file point	FSEEK()	FSEEK(<expN1>,<expN2>[,<expN2>])	Numeric
Tests for DOS error	FERROR()	FERROR()	Numeric
Write buffer contents to file	FWRITE()	FWRITE(<expN1>,<expC>[,<expN2>])	Numeric

APPENDIX D

Error Messages

Each version of Clipper has had different error messages. To document all of the possible error messages from all of the versions would be a momentous task. Below, therefore, is a brief look at the possible error conditions (and where applicable, the error messages). Try to find your problem on the list. The errors are broken into three categories: *compiling, linking,* and *execution* errors.

Compiling error messages are normally straight-forward. If an error occurs during compiling, treat it according to the message displayed. Sometimes the messages are a bit cryptic, but in time their meaning will become clearer. If multiple errors occur, fix the first error before all others. Often one error will generate three or four subsequent error messages.

Linking errors are much like compiling errors; once you get the hang of it, they make perfect sense. Unfortunately, it can seem to take an eternity to understand them. Most linking errors are caused by one or more of the following three reasons:

1. Mismatching compiler and library versions
2. Linking duplicate procedures
3. Misspelling function names

Execution errors are more difficult to figure out than compiling or linking errors. Any number of factors may be the cause of the problem, ranging from the subtle differences between the environment of an interpreter and that of the compiler to hardware inconsistencies to problems with the code, the compiler, or both.

If you have a problem, first link in the DEBUGger with the rest of your application. Try to pinpoint the line on which the error is occurring. If the line number is far greater than any line number in your application, look for the last reasonable line number you recognize before the error. These large line numbers are caused by calls to the Clipper library.

If the problem persists, try to duplicate the problem outside your application. Small test programs specifically designed to isolate a problem are good DEBUGging techniques. Finally, if, **after** trying all logical methods (which include reading all "READ_ME" files and the documentation), you still can't locate the error, call Nantucket. You may have a problem with the compiler and their additional insight and current information may get to the root of the matter.

One word of advice: **never** say "But it works in dBASE..." It is understood that most people are converting existing dBASE III code into Clipper. Because of that, the technicians approach all problems as problems attributable to the differences between a compiler and an interpreter. If, however, there is a problem with the compiler, the technicians are the first to test, document, and admit to the problem.

Your best bet is probably never to assume that the problem you are experiencing is caused by the compiler. Arrange your questions or problems as specifically as you can and always note all error messages and whether they are compile, link, or execution error messages.

COMPILING ERRORS

TOO MANY CONSTANTS - NEGATIVE CONSTANTS IN TABLE - TOO MANY PROCS

Since the compiler tries to pull in all associated program, procedure, and format files, the constant table may have exceeded its capacity. Currently, only 32K worth of constants can be assigned in one compilation. In older versions, if the constant table was overloaded, the message "TOO MANY CONSTANTS" appeared and the compiled code would be incomplete. Linking the object module and execution yielded unpredictable results.

In an attempt to increase the size of all of the tables, the error message was taken out, but the table space for the code, the symbols, and the constants remained at 32K. However, in the reference, if the constant table did become overloaded during the compile, in the end it would generate an object file with a negative constant table size (i.e., -35738 symbols).

The solution remains: break down the amount of source code that the compiler is looking at one time. In order to facilitate this, the use of CLiP files is necessary.

TOO MANY LABELS - TOO MANY SYMBOLS - TOO MANY PROCS

As with the TOO MANY CONSTANTS problem, there is a specific size for the symbol and code tables. If too many procedures or functions are called, eventually, the appropriate tables overload. Again, just as with the constant table situation, if this should occur, the only solution is to break up the amount of a compile into smaller sections and then to link them back together.

ASSIGNMENT ERRORS

A variable has been assigned an improper value. An example is the following:

```
STORE x TO "This is a test"
```

This is an ASSIGNMENT ERROR because it is impossible to give the string "This is a test" the value of x.

Another possible cause of an ASSIGNMENT ERROR is the use of a semicolon in a string. In dBASE III, the semicolon tells the interpreter that the remaining characters for this command line are on the following line. This can be in the middle of a string. For example:

```
CLEAR
STORE "Now is the time for all good men to come to the aid of their ;
country!" TO x
? x
```

In dBASE III, here is the result:

```
. ? x
Now is the time for all good men to come to the aid of their country!
```

But in Clipper, if you tried to compile the same code, the following would occur:

```
C>clipper test
The Clipper Compiler, Winter '85
Copyright (c) 1985, 1986 Nantucket Inc., All Rights Reserved.

Compiling TEST.PRG
line     7:  missing 2nd quote
STORE "Now is the time for all good men to come to the aid of their ;

line     7:  STORE error
STORE

line     8:  ASSIGNMENT error
country!" TO x

line     8:  ASSIGNMENT error
country
4 errors detected
Code size:31    Symbols:64    Constants:112

C>
```

In Clipper, the workaround would be to split up the sentence and assign it to two separate variables and then add them together later.

Another possible error, similar to the previous example, is with command lines that have the wraparound character (soft carriage return) in them. This high-bit character cannot be in any program file to be compiled. The compiler acts the same way as it did with the semicolon. The solution is to remove those characters.

UNBALANCED PARENTHESES

This message is precise: too many parentheses are in a line. Be careful if you use parentheses to separate conditions for clarity. Also, if using multiple functions, the same problem may arise: too many or too few parentheses are in the command line. The compiler gives a little help by flagging the area where the extraneous parenthesis appears. Consider the following example:

```
? SUBSTR(DTOC(DATE(),1,2) + SUBSTR(DTOC(DATE(),7,2))
```

This causes two major error messages, a TOO MANY ARGUMENTS error and a UNBALANCED PARENTHESIS error. Both would eventually yield a FATAL AT 0 - invalid code error.

In the first function, the DTOC() function only requires one parameter, yet by the structure of the command line, it appears that three parameters are being passed. Because of this, the whole sequence of parentheses is unbalanced, which yields the second error. And the final error is caused by no code being generated at all, ending at line 0 (the top of the program file) because nothing makes sense to the compiler. In order to correct the problem, go through the command line character by character. If you have to, start from the innermost function and work your way out. In our example, the correct structure is:

```
. ? SUBSTR(DTOC(DATE()),1,2)+SUBSTR(DTOC(DATE()),7,2)
```

PROBLEMS WITH DO, IF, DO CASE, FOR...NEXT, and BEGIN SEQUENCE

The compiler is **very** strict with the use of these commands. Not only must there be a proper number of terminators for them (ENDDO, ENDIF, ENDCASE, END), but they must also be balanced properly.

Just because you may get a "enddo w/o while" does not necessarily mean that there is a problem with your DOs and your ENDDOs.

There is a special stack table inside the compiler. Every time a DO, an IF, FOR, or a DO CASE appear, a marker is placed on the stack. Each marker is unique and the compiler keeps track of what it was that caused this counter to be placed on the stack. Every time the compiler sees an ENDDO, ENDIF, NEXT, ENDCASE, or an END, it removes a marker from the stack. The marker that is removed from the stack must coincide with the command that placed the marker on the stack in the first place. If there is an imbalance between the number of commands that placed markers on the stack, and the number of commands that removed markers from the stack, an error will occur. Additionally, if a marker is removed by an improper matching command, the series of markers that follows will not match correctly, which will cause an UNBALANCED or MISSING error message.

The compiler is very precise in finding these errors, but it only tells you that an imbalance exists. Check all of the markers and make sure that they are properly offset by the corresponding command. dBASE is tolerant of some of these errors because only

1K worth of source code is really kept in memory; if an UNBALANCED error exists, but its marker would have been more than 5K of source code away, dBASE III will not find it! Clipper, as you may learn to your dismay, allows no such sloppiness.

STRUCTURE ERROR

This error is specific to the Summer '87 release in that it means an unbalanced condition exists between either a DO WHILE, a FOR NEXT, a DO CASE, or a BEGIN SEQUENCE command. Treat this error as described in the previous heading.

FATAL AT < > - ILLEGAL SYMBOL MODE

Normally this messages appears in conjunction with a PHASE ERROR. It means that when it tried to compile the code at the second pass, the compiler couldn't understand the symbolic tokens. The line number given often indicates the general area of the problem, but don't count on it. The best way to decipher this error is to break down your application into specific programs and try to compile them separately, thus narrowing down the possible choices.

FATAL AT < > - ILLEGAL SYMBOL MODE

Check to make sure that the procedure list in your EXTERNAL command does not include the name of the procedure being compiled. You cannot tell the compiler that it is **not** to compile the very program it is compiling!

FATAL AT 0 - End of File

While Clipper was attempting to compile the program, either in creating the temporary file or the final object file, the disk drive became full.

PHASE ERRORS

Most PHASE ERRORS are brought on by one or more previously found FATAL ERRORS. If this is not the case, remember that Clipper is a two-pass compiler: on the first pass the compiler turns the source code into representing tokens, and on the second pass, it tries to turn the tokens into machine-level object code. Somehow, the tokens generated by the first pass are not decipherable by the second pass. This out-of-sync symptom causes a phase error. If the problem does not go away after a recompile, call for technical assistance.

INVALID PARAMETERS

The number of parameters passed to a function is not right. For an example, please refer to the example above on Unbalanced Parenthesis. Make sure that you are passing exactly as many parameters as are required by the function--no more and no less.

HYPHENS AND NUMBERS IN PROGRAM NAMES

Many application generators and programs use hyphens in the name of the program or procedure in order to better identify its purpose. Although this practice is allowed in dBASE III, it isn't allowed in Clipper. The reason for this is that the same routine that checks for the validity of field names also checks for program names as well.

FORMAT FILES AND CLIP FILES

If CLiP files are being used, FORMAT files are ignored. With CLiP files, all that will be looked at are files with a .PRG extension. Since FORMAT files have a .FMT extension, the compiler will not even attempt to locate them. What needs to be done if CLiP files are used is to rename all FORMAT file extensions from .FMT to .PRG and to change the code in the procedures that calls them from SET FORMAT TO <Filename> to DO <Filename>.

LINKING ERRORS

UNDEFINED SYMBOLS IN A WEIRD MODULE (NORMALLY BEGINNING WITH I/O)

This indicates that the version of Clipper you are using is not compatible with the library the linker is referring to. Make sure that you are using the right version of the library. With the Winter '85 version of the compiler, only two libraries may be used, one dated 01-29-86 and one dated 05-01-86. If you are using the Autumn '86 compiler, the date stamp of the appropriate library should 10-31-86.

If you are using the correct libraries, check the version of the compiler you are using. To do this, just type in Clipper at the DOS prompt and note the version statement that appears.

With the Summer '87 release, one more possible hurdle needs to be tackled. If linking in outside C object modules written in Microsoft C 5.0 (or later), make sure that the /NOE switch is used. Additionally, **only** use Microsoft's linker 5.61 or later to link the object modules together with the libraries. The /NOE switch tells the linker that the required library files for the extra object module (the C object file) is within the CLIPPER.LIB or the EXTEND.LIB. This prevents extra erroneous messages from appearing when linking the files together.

Finally, make sure that no object file being linked in has been compiled with an older version. Once you use a new version of the compiler (not the library) on **any** program, procedure, format, or function file, then **all** program, procedure, format, and function files must be recompiled in order to maintain system-wide integrity.

The error codes listed below are in reverse numerical order:

Error 59

This is like Error 58. If you get this message, please refer to the section in this text pertaining specifically to Plink86 Error Messages.

Error 58

This is saying that the amount of one object module is too large for the linker to handle. The maximum stack segment (roughly half the size of the object module being linked in) is 64K bytes.

Error 57

You have a problem with the OVERLAY.LIB file. Make sure that the correct version of this library is being linked in with the appropriate version of Plink86. If you are using PLINK86.EXE (64,320 bytes) with a date stamp of 01-29-86, you should be using the OVERLAY.LIB file (23,040 bytes) with a date stamp also of 01-29-86. This version was used for versions prior to the Autumn '86 release. With the Autumn '86 release, the proper date stamp for Plink86 (78,688 bytes) should be 10-31-86 and the corresponding date stamp for the OVERLAY.LIB (6,932 bytes) is 10-31-86.

Error 54

This says that there is not enough available memory to load and run Plink86. The minimum requirement for Plink86 is 256K bytes.

Error 52

A symbol (a function call, a procedure name, or a memory variable) used in an object module is "self-defined." In other words, the DEFINE command was used to define a symbol that is relative to another symbol. This defining process can continue until eventually the original symbol is reached in this cycle.

Error 51

Normally, this is brought on with the use of the BUILD and DEFINE commands, which are not supported in the special version of Plink86 provided with the Clipper compiler.

Error 50

This says that Plink86 can not create the memory map on the disk. Check to see if the disk is full or if it is write protected.

Error 49

Again, this error pertains to the disk. It simply means that Plink86 cannot close the designated output file. Either the disk is write protected or there is a general hardware error.

Error 48

A fatal disk read error was detected in the output file. This was probably caused by an irrecoverable hardware error.

Error 47

A fatal disk write error has occurred in the output file. Possibly the disk is full or write protected, or there has been some other type of hardware-related error.

Error 46

This says that an invalid output file type has been specified. If one is given, it must either be .EXE or .CMD (for CP/M 86 machines).

Error 45

A general error that detects that Plink86 cannot create the output disk file. Check to see if the disk directory is full or if the disk is write protected.

Error 43

The object module specified in the link list could not be located. Check to see if indeed the file is located on the designated directory path or if you have spelled the name of the object file correctly.

Error 42

A fatal read error in the object file was detected.

Error 41

A premature end of file was detected. This is usually preceded with an "Unknown record type 7." Basically, the linker is attempting to link nonobject files with the Clipper library. This is usually brought on when the CL.BAT batch file is used and the .PRG is passed along with the file name as a parameter. Clipper assumes that procedure files have the extension .PRG, so the .PRG is redundant. However, when the linking process starts, the .PRG is still passed as a parameter into the linker. When the linker tries to link the .PRG file, and not the .OBJ file, it chokes. To get around this, don't pass the file extension if you use CL.BAT.

EXECUTION ERRORS

SCREEN DISPLAYS IN THE WRONG PLACE

This error is caused by a bad compile. The only solution is to recompile. If the problem persists, add a few remark lines and try again. If that does not solve the problem, call technical support.

VALUES DO NOT EQUAL

Because of a rounding problem internal to Lattice C, Clipper also has an internal rounding problem. This means that in many cases, values that should equal one another, do not. This is especially true when the ROUND() or INT() functions are used or math-intensive calculations are performed. To get around this, either use the user-defined ROUNDIT() function in Chapter 13, be more specific in the INT() function, or use the double equal sign (= =) whenever possible.

CLIPPER ERROR MESSAGES

The standard Q/A/I error message was changed for the Summer '87 release. For prior versions, the Q/A/I message is issued by Clipper at run-time when Clipper or DOS finds an unrecoverable error when it tries to execute a command or function. It means:

Q - Quit the program, closing all files properly and return to DOS.
A - Abort to DOS immediately.
I - Ignore error, and try to continue with the program.

The user must enter either Q, A, or I from the keyboard in order to continue. If "I" is entered, keep in mind that the system integrity may be corrupted.

For the Summer '87 release, there are several types of error messages. One is "Continue?, " which requires either a "Y" for yes or an "N" for no. Other types of error will bring a "Retry?, " which again requires either a "Y" or a "N" response. In both of these cases, the "N" response will terminate the program. These error messages are documented in Chapter 7, Using the Error System.

INDEX ERROR READ/WRITE

This error normally means one of two things:

1. The mother board is set for 640K of RAM while the expansion board is set for 256K of RAM.

2. The disk is full.

INDEX ERROR UPDATE

Make sure that you are using a library dated 05-01-86 when using Winter '85 release. If you have not received this error with the library date stamp of 01-29-86 when using the Winter '85 release, it is not necessary to acquire the 05-01-86 library. Otherwise, contact Nantucket for this library. The updated library resolves this problem.

DOS ERROR 0

This error is **not** an error from DOS. Whenever the application experiences an error during execution that the internal mechanisms installed by Clipper cannot understand, it attempts to go to the operating system and to find the cause of the problem. If it cannot find the associated DOS error to the problem, it assigns a 0 error code.

More than likely, the cause of this error is an object file with a negative-sized constant table. If that is the case, check the section on COMPILING ERRORS AND NEGATIVE CONSTANTS earlier in this section for the solution.

A complete listing of the DOS error messages are available in Appendix A.

This error is only known to occur in the Winter '85 version of the compiler.

DOS ERROR 2

This means that the file you are trying to use, find, or do something with cannot be found. If you are using macro substitution for file names, make sure that the macros have the proper dot terminators and that their values are what you expect them to be.

DOS ERROR 3

This error indicates that the path designated and passed to DOS was invalid. If you are using macro substitution for the path, make sure that the macros have the proper dot terminators and that their values are what you expect them to be. Also, make sure that the path really exists.

DOS ERROR 4

This message means that you have tried to open too many files for DOS to handle. If this error appears, check the CONFIG.SYS file. Remember, the CONFIG.SYS should be set to at least the following number of files and buffers:

```
FILES   = 20
BUFFERS = 8
```

Once you've fixed the CONFIG.SYS file, reboot the system and try again. If the problem persists, contact the technical support staff.

PROGRAM TOO BIG TO FIT INTO MEMORY or "NOT ENOUGH MEMORY"

This message is quite literal and is generated by the operating system, not by Clipper. It means what it says, the program you are trying to load is too big to fit properly into memory. Even though it may seem that there is plenty of room for the program, Clipper has additional requirements (please see the section on memory requirements) and these restrictions may be part of the problem.

Another possible cause for this problem is when the computer's *mother board* is set for 640K of RAM while the expansion board is set for 256K. Make sure that all internal hardware configurations are set properly.

Finally, with the Summer '87 release, if the "Not Enough Memory" error should appear, also check the status of the SET CLIPPER= value. You can do this directly from DOS by typing in "SET". If either the V, R, E, or X parameters are too large or too small for the application to load in, this error will be generated. To clear the currently SET value for Clipper, just type SET CLIPPER= followed by the carriage return. If the error remains, the problem lies in previously discussed area.

MACRO EXPANSION ERROR

This error is one of the most difficult to trap, decipher, and solve. A Macro Expansion Error occurs when the macro library is trying to expand an expression beyond its means. All macros are limited to 16 parses. This means that an expression can have only 16 logical parts for the macro library to understand at one time. Symbols, operators, and expressions are all items for the macro library to parse and interpret.

IF an ALIAS is used, a macro can only handle 9 parses.

In some cases this error occurs on lines where no macro exists. The reason for this is commands that pertain to REPORTS, LABELS, or INDEXing are processed through the macro library.

In either case, try to break up the amount of information being processed on the command line. For normal macros, split the one macro into two separate macros. For all others, use a combination of other commands to help set database conditions, scopes, and ranges on separate command lines.

MAC RELEASE ERROR

Like the Macro Expansion Error, the MAC Release Error indicates that the macro library is trying to release an expression that is not a macro or is not understood by the macro library. Think of it as trying to release a CLEAR command. How does one go about releasing a CLEAR command? This type of conflict disrupts the compiler at run-time. Link in the DEBUGger and step through the application to the command line just prior to the occurrence of the error. Double check the validity of all variables and fields. If everything appears satisfactory, try to duplicate the error in a smaller test environment. If you are able to duplicate the error, contact the Technical Support Staff with the problem. If the problem disappears in the test, go back to the original code and recode the problem area a little differently, combining a couple of commands, or separating one command into a couple. If a macro is involved, try hard coding a portion of the macro or evaluating the macro in the DEBUGger.

JOIN WITH A WHILE CLAUSE

It's an error because this combination is not allowed.

CURSOR AND FUNCTION KEYS WITH ANSI.OBJ

Whenever using an application with the ANSI driver (or any other driver), the cursor keys and function keys will not work. Be careful because keys that were taken for granted (e.g., F1 for HELP and Ctrl-C to break out of a routine) will not work. In some cases, the SET KEY TO procedure may work, but only one key at a time. They may be redefined via your operating system; however, be careful not to define a key to a value of another key. You could lock yourself out of a solution and into a problem. Please consult your DOS manual for proper instructions.

Additionally, the Summer '87 release of Clipper has a special object module that allows the cursor keys to work. Instead on ANSI.OBJ, link in IBMANSI.OBJ for the correct results.

DIVIDE OVERFLOW

This is a message interrupt from DOS that signals that the integrity of the command processor is in question. Link in the DEBUG object file and step through the application to pinpoint the line on which the error occurs. If that yields no help or further indications, call for technical assistance.

DIVIDE BY ZERO

Because Clipper is a compiler, the error trapping routines inside dBASE (the interpreter) are not present. In many REPORTs, massive divisions are globally enacted, even on fields where the denominator is zero. Division by zero is not allowed. Build a routine or user-defined function to avoid this problem.

SYSTEM ERROR MEMORY ERROR OR FAULT

Normally, one of two things can cause this problem. The first involves using the MEMOEDIT() function and trying to access HELP or any other SET KEY TO procedure. In order to avoid any problem that may creep up if this function is used, set all keys off including the HELP key. To turn off the HELP key, type in SET KEY 28 TO. After the MEMOEDIT() function has completed its operation, reset HELP with SET KEY 28 TO Help. Follow the same procedures for all other SET KEY TO commands.

The other situation that can cause this error message to appear also concerns the SET KEY TO and the HELP functions. If the three PARAMETERS (p, l, and v) are not passed to the procedure, regardless of their use, the stack is eventually corrupted and an error occurs. Make sure that the procedures being called by the SET KEY TO command have the proper PARAMETERS.

GETS AND READS IN CALLING PROGRAM ARE CLEARED

This normally occurs when implementing context-sensitive HELP with all SET KEY TO procedures. If the CLEAR command is issued to clear the screen, it will also CLEAR the GETS/READs as well, even those on the calling end of the application. In order to CLEAR the screen and keep all GETs and READs active, the following workaround must be used:

```
@ 0,0 CLEAR
```

DATA OFF ONE POSITION

This problem is normally caused by either dBASE II database files having been converted to dBASE III via dCONVERT or by using the Summer '85 version of Clipper on databases created under dBASE III Plus. In either case, if the data is being displayed offset by one character, rewrite the headers of the databases for true dBASE III files, either under version 1.0/1.1 or Plus. Keep in mind that if the files are rewritten under PLUS, the Winter '85 version (or later versions) of the compiler **must** be used to get proper results. To rewrite the headers, use dBASE and USE the data files, then COPY TO a new file. Delete the old database from the disk and rename the new file to the name of the old file. This will ensure that the file has the proper dBASE III header.

CANNOT FIND/SEEK DATA ELEMENTS

There are two possible reasons for this message:

First, if the indexes were created from databases that were either dCONVERTed or created under dBASE III PLUS (and you are not using the Winter '85 version), the FIND/SEEK commands will probably not work properly. To remedy this, rewrite the headers properly (please see the section on Data Displaying off one character) and rebuild the indexes.

Second, if the indexes were built from fields that were TRIMmed, the FIND/SEEK commands will not work properly. In Clipper, indexes are generated based on a blank record. TRIMming a blank record would generate a null byte for the index space. A space is required to allow the FIND/SEEK command to work and to allow the proper index key structure. Consider the following:

```
last_name     C   20
first_name    C   20
mid_init      C   1

USE File
INDEX ON TRIM(last_name) + ", " + TRIM(first_name) + " " + mid_init
```

The index key is generated with enough space for four characters: two for the ", ", one for the second " ", and one for the middle initial. To open up enough space for the fields being TRIMmed, you must use the SPACE() function to pad the index key. The new syntax would look like this:

```
USE File
INDEX ON TRIM(last_name) + ", " + TRIM(first_name) + " " + ;
      mid_init + SPACE(LEN(last_name) + LEN(first_name))
```

If the FIND or SEEK still does not work, especially if the file is a secondary file, refer to Chapter 4 for specific examples on using the INDEX command with a SUBSTR(TRIM()) combination.

This is also true for the INDEX ON CMONTH(date). In order to get it to INDEX and FIND or SEEK properly, the proper number of blank spaces must be added:

```
USE File
INDEX ON SUBSTR(CMONTH(datefield) + SPACE(10)) 1, 10)
```

PROBLEMS WITH SUM OR TOTAL

If TOTALs are not coming out quite right or if fields are not being APPENDED properly, this is probably caused by the lack of a FIELDs list. These commands require that a FIELDs list be included with the command. In some cases where the entire database is being SUMmed or TOTALed, all fields cannot be listed on the same command line. Macro substitution is the best solution for this problem.

ONLY ONE FIELD LISTING

Check to see if you are LISTing with a macro substitution that contains a comma in the string. If so, remember that syntactical structures of commands cannot be placed inside a macro; they must be in place as a literal. During compilation, no comma is seen; therefore the compiler only allows the first field in the macro list to be printed.

EXECUTION IS SLOWER THAN IN DBASE

Most of the time this is caused by the poor use of macro substitution. Consider the following:

```
instead_of = "state = 'CA' .AND. SUBSTR(zip,1,2) = '91'"
SET FILTER TO &instead_of
DO WHILE .NOT. EOF()
   DO Printit
ENDDO
```

As each record in the database is looked at in the Printit procedure, it is tested against the FILTERed condition. With each test to the FILTER, the macro is completely expanded. This sequence would speed up greatly if the macro were hard coded.

If any part of a macro is being expanded repetitively, find some means to change those command clauses as literals in a command line, thus leaving the rest for a macro.

EXEC SEQUENCE ERROR

This is caused by a section in one overlay directly or indirectly calling another section in the same overlay. The problem is in the way the linker maintains control of the operation; the calling procedure is wiped out of memory as the second procedure comes into operation. Once the called procedure is finished, it tries to go back to the original procedure. The EXEC SEQUENCE ERROR pops up at this time, when the program realizes that it does not know where to go.

UNDEFINED IDENTIFIER

This message is specific to the Summer '87 release in that it used to be known as an "unknown symbol." This basically means that the variable was not previously initialized, or that a function call was made and the function is not available in the application. Make sure that the variable is initialized or, if passing field information, that the alias area is used in conjunction with the field name. Also, make sure that the function is available to the program. This is also detectable when linking. It will generate an "Unresolved External" or "Unknown Symbol" message from most linkers.

A FEW THINGS TO WATCH OUT FOR...

USING THE STR() FUNCTION

If a string conversion on a numeric value is performed, an extra placement must be allowed for the integer to the left of the decimal place.

For example, consider the following:

```
STORE .9823615 TO temp_var
@ 3, 5 SAY STR(temp_var,8,7)
```

The results would be a complete string of asterisks (********).

To work around this problem, make the length of the string one greater:

```
@ 3, 5 SAY STR(temp_var,9,7)
```

DISPLAY COMMAND

Rather than being an error, this is more of a difference. Nevertheless, the DISPLAY command acts like the LIST command and will not stop to prompt the user that the screen is full.

APPENDIX E

Clipper and Networking

NETWORKING VERSUS MULTITASKING

There is a big difference between multiuser and multitasking software. Back in the days of CP/M and MP/M, the concepts of multiuser and multitasking seemed to coexist. In that era, nothing was truly multitasking. This meant that the main computer, or server, could only perform different tasks one at a time, or serially, by sharing time among the different tasks. These multitasking systems' most serious restriction was their inability to have true *file locking* and *record locking*. This concept allows many users to **simultaneously** access the same files (normally data-base files). If a record becomes altered or "updated," the change should be immediately reflected as such to all users on the system. With multitasking systems, this was simulated by having multiple files on many drives and collating the data at the end of work day. A true PC-based multiuser system was yet to come.

Today, both concepts are possible. There are several packages available that attach many computer terminals to a main computer called a "server." This computer services all the file handling needs for the users. However, no two users can access a file at the same time. Even on multiuser systems, the files must be locked, preventing other users from gaining access to the system. With multiuser-based systems, the server can *lock* specific files, records, and fields from other users. These routines are normally handled by a secondary software package, residing in memory, between DOS and the application. When software is called upon, for example, to lock a record, it goes "out to DOS" and invokes the necessary interrupts to perform the task, via the operating system.

In reality, neither the application nor the operating system "talks" to one another to perform these operations. Software packages like Novell and PC Net reside in memory and handle all of the locking for the developer and the user. The trick is to call the necessary Assembly or C routines that do the trick.

Since Clipper's open architecture allows user-defined functions and outside routines, written in Assembly or C, to be brought into the application, the implementation of file, record, and field locking is quite simple. Many who know both the Novell software and Assembly language have made libraries in Assembler that activate the necessary file, record, and field locking commands. These libraries are then linked into applications. On the application side, user-defined functions (like RLOCK(), FLOCK(), and FDLOCK()) are created that have the proper CALL commands that go out to the Assembly routines, which in turn go to the operating system. Throughout the application, once the functions have been established and the library CALLs linked in, the developer needs only to issue simple dBASE-like commands to activate a multiuser application.

The Autumn '86 release of Clipper has those library routines built-in as well as the functions predefined in the instruction set. However, additional libraries may be obtained and added to Clipper to yield even more power and flexibility in a networking environment. One such library is offered by Neil Weicher of Communication Horizon. Neil helped Brian Russell develop some of the library calls in the next Clipper and has a library ready made for the current version. An additional feature Clipper developers may take advantage of is the ability to lock MEM, REPORT, LABEL, and even text files. Additionally, buffers can be flushed at will and active databases will be reread.

The Summer '87 release only saw a few new functions added to the library. For example, NETNAME() and NETERROR() are now supported.

Make sure that the network software is not engaged while trying to install the compiler.

Listed below are a few companies and individuals with third-party software and information concerning networking and Clipper:

Novell Netware Information

Neil Weicher - Communication Horizon Software
701 7th Ave., - 9th Floor
New York, NY 10036

3COM Ethernet

Donald Radle - Radle Computer Systems
5751 Darrow Road
Hudson, OH 44236

Neil Weicher - Communication Horizon Software
701 7th Ave., - 9th Floor
New York, NY 10036

APPENDIX F

Screen Drivers and the ANSI.OBJ File

One of the ways Clipper increases speed is the manner in which it displays information on the screen. The compiler calls the video RAM directly. Video RAM is the internal video addressing for IBM and fully compatible computers. Computers that follow this standard have no problem running an application that was compiled with Clipper.

There are some computers, however, that require a specific screen driver to handle the video addressing. A driver is like a converter: a video driver converts the code for direct video mapping into escape-sequence based code. This code emulates the video addressing normally performed by the computer. Because of this additional processing step before the information is displayed to the screen, the output appears to execute more slowly.

One sequence of escape codes, the ANSI (American National Standards Institute) codes, established a specific sequence of characters to display information to the screen. Most PCs that can't handle IBM video mapping can use the ANSI codes if the following command line is present in the CONFIG.SYS file in root directory:

```
DEVICE = [d:][path/]ANSI.SYS
```

The file ANSI.SYS (which comes with DOS) must be available in the root directory or in the PATH. The ANSI.OBJ file, which was provided with your copy of Clipper, must be linked into your application just as if it were any other object file compiled by Clipper. Remember not to link in the ANSI object file in an overlay area. This object file must reside in the main load module.

If the ANSI.OBJ file is used, the cursor keys and other related keys will not work unless they have been redefined by the operating system before running the application. There are specific DOS commands and utility programs that allow you to do this. Please refer to your DOS manual for the appropriate syntax.

Some computers don't follow the standards of the ANSI sequence but have their own screen driver sequences. The ANSI.OBJ file will not work with these computers even if DEVICE was set to ANSI in the CONFIG.SYS file. Special screen drivers need to be created in order for applications to work with these computers. The developer needs to keep in mind that if an application is to be installed on a WANG computer, for example, the object files of the application need to be relinked with a WANG screen driver. Applications need to be linked with drivers for the proper environment, and this responsibility rests with the developer. Currently, there are drivers available from Nantucket for the standard ANSI computers, TI Professional, WANG, and DEC Rainbow.

For the summer '87 release, there are now three separate screen drivers. The standard ANSI.OBJ remains the same, while the other two files are just variations.

The IBMANSI.OBJ allows for the ANSI standard screen handling routines to work as well as the IBM-specific cursor keys and function keys. Do not try to use this object module on machines that are anything other than 100 percent IBM PC compatable.

Finally, the PCBIOS.OBJ file was created to allow the Clipper application to run under programs like Desqview. This driver writes specifically to the BIOS of the IBM PC that allow the Clipper program to still function while the window-like program remain in control. Again, this is screen driver issues IBM-specific calls and should not be linked into applications other than those applications that are to run under program like Desqview and only on 100 percent IBM PC or compatable machines.

APPENDIX G

Simulating dBASE III Commands

Many dBASE III commands are intended for the interpretive environment and are not included in the Clipper language. However, there are times when they would be useful to have. Using the built-in power of Clipper, they can be simulated. The following simulations use user-defined functions and customized procedures found in previous chapters. It is possible to take those functions and procedures and create a separate SIMULATE.PRG file for all of these simulations. Then, after compiling that file separately, link it with the examples listed below. The alternative method is to compile each simulation as is.

DISPLAY STRUCTURE

```
********************
* Name          DISPSTRU.prg
* Date          March 20, 1988
* Notice        Copyright 1988, Stephen J. Straley & Associates
* Compiler      Clipper Dispstru
* Release       Winter '85 or later
* Link          Plink86 fi dispstru lib clipper
* Note          A Procedure that simulates dBASE III's
*               Display Structure command in Clipper.
********************

   PARAMETERS Infile

      IF EMPTY(infile)
         infile = SPACE(30)
         @ ROW(),0 SAY "No data base in USE.  Enter filename: " GET infile
         READ
         IF EMPTY(infile)
            QUIT
         ENDIF
      ENDIF
      *****
      * Check to see if the clause 'TO PRINT' is added to the simulation
      *****
      search = AT("TO PRINT",UPPER(infile))  && <= Check for the words...
      IF search <> 0                         && <= There is no clause
         toggle = .T.
         infile = SUBSTR(infile,1,search-1)  && <= There is the clause
      ELSE
         toggle = .F.
      ENDIF
      search = AT(".",infile)                && check for file extension
      IF search = 0
         infile = TRIM(infile) + ".DBF"
      ENDIF
      IF !FILE(infile)
         ? "File Not Found"
         QUIT
      ENDIF
```

```
RUN DIR &infile > Tempfile.txt
CREATE Temp
USE Temp
APPEND BLANK
REPLACE field_name WITH "LINE", field_type WITH "C", field_len WITH 80
USE
CREATE Template FROM Temp
USE Template
ERASE Temp
APPEND FROM Tempfile.txt SDF
ERASE Tempfile.txt
GO 3
search = AT("of ",line)
direct = SUBSTR(line,search+3)
GO 5
search = AT("-",line)
datein = SUBSTR(line,search - 2,8)
USE &infile
ERASE Template
COPY STRUCTURE EXTENDED TO Template
USE Template
record = STR(LASTREC())
count  = 1
IF toggle
   SET PRINTER ON          && Turn printer on due to PRINT clause
ENDIF
? "Structure for database: " + TRIM(direct) + "\" + infile
? "Number of data records: " + record
? "Date of Last update   : " + datein
? "Field       Name       Type       Width       Dec"
GO TOP
DO WHILE .NOT. EOF()
   ?  RECNO()
   ?? SPACE(3)
   ?? field_name
   ?? SPACE(5)
   ?? TYPENAME()
   ?? SPACE(5)
   ?? field_len
   ?? SPACE(5)
   IF field_dec > 0
      ?? field_dec
   ENDIF
   SKIP
   count = count + 1
   IF count > 16       && Allowing only 16 fields to be displayed
      count = 1        && before the WAIT message appears
      WAIT
   ENDIF
ENDDO
USE
ERASE Template.dbf
ERASE Temp.dbf
```

```
      IF toggle               && Turn the printer off
         SET PRINT OFF
      ENDIF
**********************
* Function Typename *
**********************

FUNCTION Typename

DO CASE
CASE field_type = "N"
   RETURN("Numeric  ")
CASE field_type = "D"
   RETURN("Date     ")
CASE field_type = "M"
   RETURN("Memo     ")
CASE field_type = "C"
   RETURN("Character")
CASE field_type = "L"
   RETURN("Logical  ")
ENDCASE
RETURN("Undefined")
* End of file
```

RETURN TO MASTER

There are two ways to simulate the RETURN TO MASTER command with version of Clipper prior to the Summer '87 release. With the Summer '87 release, there is an additional way to RETURN TO MASTER, using the BEGIN SEQUENCE command. The first involves using the KEYBOARD command to stuff the keyboard with the keystrokes that would come from a sub-level, one at a time.

The other method is to treat everything as a procedure, including the top level program. When the top level of the program is desired, the procedure is called directly. The problem with this approach is that as procedures are placed onto the internal memory stack (pushed), they are never removed from the stack (popped). Eventually, once the stack is full, a system memory error occurs.

1. STUFFING THE KEYBOARD

```
********************
* Name        MASTER1.prg
* Date        March 20, 1988
* Notice      Copyright 1988, Stephen J. Straley & Assocaites
* Compile     Clipper Master1
* Release     Winter '85 or later
* Link        Plink86 fi master1 lib clipper
* Note        This procedure simulates RETURN TO MASTER.
********************
```

```
DO WHILE .T.
   CLEAR
   STORE 1 TO option
   @ 0,0 SAY "This is the top menu..."
   @ 1,0 PROMPT " 1> Go Down to the Next Level "
   @ 2,0 PROMPT " 0> Exit to Operating System "
   MENU TO option
   IF option = 2
      QUIT
   ENDIF
   DO Level2
ENDDO

PROCEDURE Level2

   DO WHILE .T.
      @ 3,0 CLEAR
      STORE 1 TO subopt
      @ 4,5 PROMPT " 1>  Go Down to the Next Level "
      @ 5,5 PROMPT " 0>  Go Up a Level "
      MENU TO subopt
      IF subopt = 2
         RETURN
      ENDIF
      DO Level3
   ENDDO

PROCEDURE Level3

   DO WHILE .T.
      @ 6,0 CLEAR
      STORE 1 TO subopt2
      @ 7,10 PROMPT " 1> Go down yet another level "
      @ 8,10 PROMPT " 2> Go up one level "
      @ 9,10 PROMPT " 3> RETURN TO MASTER "
      MENU TO subopt2
      DO CASE
      CASE subopt2 = 1
         DO Level4
      CASE subopt2 = 2
         RETURN
      OTHERWISE
         KEYBOARD "0"
         RETURN
      ENDCASE
   ENDDO

PROCEDURE Level4

   DO WHILE .T.
      @ 10,0 CLEAR
      STORE 1 TO subopt3
      @ 11,15 PROMPT " 1> Go Up a Level "
```

```
         @ 12,15 PROMPT " 0> Go to top "
         MENU TO subopt3
         IF subopt3 = 2
            KEYBOARD "3"
          ENDIF
         RETURN
      ENDDO
   * End of MASTER1.prg
```

2. EVERYTHING IS A PROCEDURE

```
********************
* Name          MASTER2.prg
* Date          March 20, 1988
* Notice        Copyright 1988, Stephen J. Straley & Associates
* Compile       Clipper Master2
* Release       Winter '85 or later
* Link          Plink86 fi master2 lib clipper
* Note          This procedure simulates RETURN TO MASTER.
********************

   DO Level1

   PROCEDURE Level1

      DO WHILE .T.
         CLEAR
         STORE 1 TO option
         @ 0,0 SAY "This is the top menu..."
         @ 1,0 PROMPT " 1> Go Down to the Next Level "
         @ 2,0 PROMPT " 0> Exit to Operating System "
         MENU TO option
         IF option = 2
            QUIT
         ENDIF
         DO Level2           && Go down to the next procedure
      ENDDO

   PROCEDURE Level2

      DO WHILE .T.
         @ 3,0 CLEAR
         STORE 1 TO subopt
         @ 4,5 PROMPT " 1>  Go Down to the Next Level "
         @ 5,5 PROMPT " 0>  Go Up a Level "
         MENU TO subopt
         IF subopt = 2      && This "pops" the stack by going back
            RETURN
         ENDIF
         DO Level3          && Going down to the next level
      ENDDO
```

```
PROCEDURE Level3

    DO WHILE .T.
       @ 6,0 CLEAR
       STORE 1 TO subopt2
       @ 7,10 PROMPT " 1> Go down yet another level "
       @ 8,10 PROMPT " 2> Go up one level "
       @ 9,10 PROMPT " 3> RETURN TO MASTER "
       MENU TO subopt2
       DO CASE
       CASE subopt2 = 1
          DO Level4          && "Push" down yet another level
       CASE subopt2 = 2
          RETURN             && "Pop" up to another level
       OTHERWISE
          DO Level1          && Go directly to the top, "pushing"
       ENDCASE               && another level onto the stack
    ENDDO

PROCEDURE Level4

    DO WHILE .T.
       @ 10,0 CLEAR
       STORE 1 TO subopt3
       @ 11,15 PROMPT " 1> Go Up a Level "
       @ 12,15 PROMPT " 0> Go to top "
       MENU TO subopt3
       IF subopt3 = 2
          DO Level1    && This "pushes" another procedure onto the stack
       ENDIF
       RETURN          && This "pops" the stack one level
    ENDDO
* End of MASTER2.prg
```

CREATE STRUCTURE

```
*********************
* Name          CREATE.prg
* Date          March 20, 1988
* Notice        Copyright 1988, Stephen J. Straley & Associates
* Compile       Clipper Create
* Release       Autumn '86 or later
* Link          Autumn '86: Plink86 fi create lib dbu lib clipper
*               Summer '87: Plink86 fi create lib extend lib clipper
* Note          This procedure creates several databases (15 maximum)
*               as well as the structures for each, all in memory.
*               This is done using arrays and macros to simulate
*               matrixes.
*********************
```

```
SET CONFIRM ON
SET SCOREBOARD OFF
CLEAR
DECLARE database[15]
FOR x = 1 TO 15
   temp = LTRIM(STR(x))
   ********************************************************
   * Below, a separate array is created based on the      *
   * database[] array.  The idea is that as the pointer   *
   * in the database[] array passes down, the subscript   *
   * pointer will point to the appropriate                *
   * four arrays that contain the detailed information    *
   * on the database[] array.                             *
   ********************************************************

   **********************************************************
   * Below, the arrays are set to 99 because of a restric- *
   * tion in memory.  Since most databases do not use more *
   * than just a few fields, 99 should suffice.            *
   **********************************************************

   DECLARE name&temp[99], type&temp[99], len&temp[99], dec&temp[99]
NEXT
scrframe = CHR(201) + CHR(205) + CHR(187) + CHR(186) + ;
           CHR(188) + CHR(205) + CHR(200) + CHR(186) + CHR(32)
@ 0,0,23,79 BOX SUBSTR(scrframe,1,8)
@ 0,30 SAY " Create Databases "
FOR x = 1 TO 15
   STORE SPACE(12) TO database[x]
   @ 2,3 SAY "Enter Database Name: " GET database[x] PICT "@!"
   READ
   IF AT(".", database[x]) = 0
      database[x] = TRIM(SUBSTR(database[x],1,8)) + ".DBF"
   ENDIF
   IF EMPTY(database[x])
      temp = LTRIM(STR(x))
      trow = 8
      tcol = 0
      FOR y = 1 TO 99
         STORE SPACE(10) TO name&temp[y]
         STORE SPACE(1) TO type&temp[y]
         STORE 0 TO len&temp[y], dec&temp[y]
         @ 3,3 SAY "   Enter Field Name: " GET name&temp[y] PICT "@!"
         @ 4,3 SAY "                Type: " GET type&temp[y] PICT "!" ;
              VALID(type&temp[y]$"NCLDM ")
         @ 5,3 SAY "   Length: " GET len&temp[y] PICT "####" RANGE 0, 3000
         @ 6,3 SAY " Decimals: " GET dec&temp[y] PICT "##" RANGE 0,15
         READ
         IF LEN(TRIM(name&temp[y])) = 0     && This is equal to the EMPTY()
            y = 100                         && function. If it is,
         ELSE                               && increment the FOR counter
            DO CASE                         && beyond the range.
            CASE type&temp[y] = "D"
```

```
                    len&temp[y] = 8
                    dec&temp[y] = 0
                 CASE type&temp[y] = "L"
                    len&temp[y] = 1
                    dec&temp[y] = 0
                 CASE type&temp[y] = "M"
                    len&temp[y] = 10
                    dec&temp[y] = 0
                 CASE type&temp[y] = "N"
                    IF len&temp[y] > 15
                       len&temp[y] = 15
                    ENDIF
                 OTHERWISE
                    dec&temp[y] = 0
                 ENDCASE
                 IF trow > 22
                    trow = 8
                    ************************************************************
                    * The BOX command (@ 8,3,22,50 BOX " ") could have been    *
                    * used in place of the following FOR...NEXT loop.  This    *
                    * loop is here because in an older version of the compiler*
                    * the BOX command would clear an area in a spiral motion  *
                    * rather than just straight down from top to bottom       *
                    ************************************************************
                    FOR steve = 8 TO 22
                       @ steve,3 SAY SPACE(47)
                    NEXT
                 ENDIF
                 @ trow,5 SAY name&temp[y]
                 @ trow,COL() + 2 SAY type&temp[y]
                 @ trow,COL() + 2 SAY len&temp[y]
                 @ trow,COL() + 2 SAY dec&temp[y]
                 trow = trow + 1
              ENDIF
           NEXT
           FOR steve = 1 TO 22
              @ steve, 3 SAY SPACE(47)
           NEXT
           @ x, 52 SAY LTRIM(STR(x)) + "-> "
           @ x, COL() SAY database[x]
        ELSE
           x = 17
        ENDIF
     NEXT
     @ 0,0,23,79 BOX scrframe
     @ 10,26 SAY "Now Creating the Databases....."
     x = 1
     DO WHILE LEN(TRIM(database[x])) <> 0
        z = LTRIM(STR(x))
        CREATE Temp
        USE Temp
        FOR y = 1 TO 99
           APPEND BLANK
```

```
         REPLACE field_name WITH name&z[y], field_type WITH type&z[y]
         REPLACE field_len WITH len&z[y], field_dec WITH dec&z[y]
         IF LEN(TRIM(name&z[y+1])) = 0
            y = 100
         ENDIF
      NEXT
      USE
      temp_name = database[x]
      CREATE &temp_name FROM Temp
      ERASE Temp.dbf
      CLOSE DATABASES
      x = x + 1
   ENDDO
   CLEAR
   * End of CREATE.prg
```

BROWSE

```
********************
* Name          BROWSE.prg
* Date          March 20, 1988
* Notice        Copyright 1988, Stephen J. Straley & Associates
* Compile       Clipper Browse
* Release       Autumn '86 or later
* Link          Plink86 FI Browse FI Dbu Lib Memo Lib Clipper
* Notes         This program tries to emulate the BROWSE feature or function
*               of dBASE III.  Cursor movement moves the display bar around.
*               However, to edit a record that the display bar is on,
*               the "B" key first must be pressed.
********************

PARAMETER file

IF AT("." file) = 0
   file = UPPER(TRIM(file)) + ".DBF"
ENDIF
DO Openfile
frame = CHR(201) + CHR(205) + CHR(187) + CHR(186) + ;
        CHR(188) + CHR(205) + CHR(200) + CHR(186) + CHR(32)
STORE SPACE(4000) TO tempscr, screen
DO Drawbord
SAVE SCREEN TO screen
* Summer '87 can be CALL __scrave WITH screen
* Autumn '86 can be CALL _scrsave WITH screen
SET FUNCTION 10 TO CHR(23)
DO Startup

********************

PROCEDURE Startup

**************************************************************************
* Setting Up the variables:
```

```
*
*
*  ending      :   the number of fields available in given file.
*  current     :   current record number of database
*
*  col_count   :   column position of the cursor on screen
*
*  row_count   :   row position of the cursor on screen
*
*  position    :   the field number BROWSE currently is resting on in
*                  CURRENT record of used FILE.
*
*  redraw      :   logical flag for a redraw of records on screen
*
*  advance     :   logical flag to allow for advancement of record number
*
*  last_posit  :   the field number allowed to be shown in the last
*                  column position
*
*  frst_posit  :   the field number allowed to be shown in the first
*                  column position
*
*  in_val      :   the name of the field at any given position
*
*  in_command  :   the variable to store the INKEY()
*
*****************************************************************************

   ending     = ENDFIELD(file)
   current    = RECNO()
   bottom_rec = LASTREC()
   col_count  = 2
   position   = 1
   row_count  = 9
   redraw     = .F.
   advance    = .F.
   last_posit = 0
   frst_posit = 1
   in_val     = ""

   **********************************************
   * Setting the variables to the file given *
   **********************************************
   last_posit = HOWMANY()
   DO Colmdraw
   DO Redraw
   GO current
   DO Fieldsho

   DO WHILE .T.
      @ 0,15 SAY RECNO() PICT "@B"
      in_command = 0
      in_command = INKEY()
```

```
DO CASE
 CASE in_command = ASC("q") .OR. in_command = ASC("Q") .OR. in_command =
     65 .OR. in_command = 97
   @ 24,00 SAY ""
   CLOSE DATABASES
   QUIT

CASE in_command = 29                         && Go to top of the file
   GO TOP
   DO Startup

CASE in_command = 4                          && For the Right arrow key
   IF position < ending
      IF position < last_posit
         position = position + 1
         DO U_feldlt
      ELSE
         frst_posit = last_posit
         last_posit = HOWMANY()
         DO Colmdraw
         DO Redraw
         GO current
         col_count = 4 + FIELD_LEN(FIELDNAME(frst_posit))
         position = position + 1
         row_count = 9
      ENDIF
      DO Fieldrt
   ENDIF

CASE in_command = 19                         && For the left arrow key
   IF position  > 1
      IF position > frst_posit
         position = position - 1
         DO U_feldrt
      ELSE
         frst_posit = frst_posit - 1
         last_posit = HOWMANY()
         position = position - 1
         DO Colmdraw
         DO Redraw
         col_count = FIELD_LEN(FIELDNAME(frst_posit)) + 4
         col_count = 2
         row_count = 9
      ENDIF
      DO Fieldlt
   ENDIF

CASE in_command = 89 .OR. in_command = 121
   in_val = FIELDNAME(position)
   temp   = FIELD_LEN(in_val)
   DO CASE
   CASE TYPE(in_val) = "C"
      REPLACE &in_val WITH SPACE(temp)
```

```
    CASE TYPE(in_val) = "N"
       REPLACE &in_val WITH 0.00
    CASE TYPE(in_val) = "D"
       REPLACE &in_val WITH CTOD("  /  /  ")
    CASE TYPE(in_val) = "L"
       REPLACE &in_val WITH .F.
    ENDCASE
    DO Fieldsho
 CASE in_command = 18                             && For screen up
    IF current > 7
       row_count = row_count - 7
       DO Upsevrl
       SKIP - 7
       current = RECNO()
       DO Showrec
       DO Fieldsho
    ENDIF

 CASE in_command=ASC("B") .OR. in_command=ASC("b")     && Begin to Edit
    IF TYPE(in_val) <> "M"                             && the highlighted
       @ row_count, col_count SAY &in_val              && field/record
       @ 23,0 SAY SPACE(159)
       @ 23,0 GET &in_val
       READ
       tempin = FIELDNAME(position)
       REPLACE &tempin WITH &in_val
       @ row_count, col_count GET &in_val
       CLEAR GETS
       @ 23,0 CLEAR
    ELSE
       SAVE SCREEN
       @ row_count, col_count SAY "memo"
       STORE &in_val TO editing
       tempin = FIELDNAME(position)
       @ 20,5,24,75 BOX frame
       REPLACE &tempin WITH MEMOEDIT(editing,21,6,23,74,.T.)
       RESTORE SCREEN
    ENDIF

 CASE in_command = 3                                  && For down screen
    IF current + 7 < bottom_rec
       row_count = row_count + 7
       DO Dwnsevrl
       SKIP + 7
       current = RECNO()
       DO Showrec
       DO Fieldsho
    ENDIF

 CASE in_command = 85 .OR. in_command = 117     && To delete a record
    IF DELETED()
       RECALL
       @ row_count,0 SAY " "
```

```
        ELSE
           DELETE
           @ row_count,0 SAY "*"
        ENDIF

     CASE in_command = 1
        GO TOP
        current = RECNO()
        DO Redraw
        row_count = 9
        GO current
        DO Showrec
        DO Fieldsho

     CASE in_command = 6                     && Go to bottom of the screen
        current = bottom_rec
        GO current
        DO Redraw
        row_count = 9
        GO current
        DO Showrec
        DO Fieldsho

     CASE in_command = 24                     && Go Down one record
        SKIP
        IF EOF()
           SKIP - 1
        ELSE
           SKIP - 1
           row_count = row_count + 1
           DO Downrec
           SKIP
           current = RECNO()
           DO Showrec
           DO Fieldsho
        ENDIF

     CASE in_command = 5                       && Go up one record
        SKIP - 1
        IF BOF()
           GO current
        ELSE
           SKIP + 1
           row_count = row_count - 1
           DO Uprec
           SKIP - 1
           current = RECNO()
           DO Showrec
           DO Fieldsho
        ENDIF
     ENDCASE

  ENDDO
```

```
****************

PROCEDURE Openfile

  ***************************************************************************
  * This procedure opens the file entered.  If none, the expected message *
  * is displayed.                                                          *
  ***************************************************************************

  IF file = "."
     file = SPACE(14)
     @ ROW(),0 SAY "No database is in USE.  Enter file name: ";
              GET file PICTURE "@!"
     READ
     file = TRIM(file)
     x = AT(".",file)
     IF X = 0
        file = file + ".DBF"
     ENDIF
  ENDIF
  IF .NOT. FILE("&file")
     ? file + " not found"
     WAIT
     QUIT
  ENDIF
  USE &file
  CLEAR
  SET SCOREBOARD OFF
  GO TOP
  RETURN

****************

PROCEDURE Drawbord

  *********************************************
  * Draw the border of BROWSE and HELP menu. *
  *********************************************

  @ 0,1 SAY "Record No. "
  @ 0,50 SAY TRIM(file)
  @ 1,0,6,79 BOX frame
  FOR aa = 20 to 60 STEP 20
     @ 1,aa SAY CHR(203)
     @ 6,aa SAY CHR(202)
  NEXT
  FOR aa = 2 to 5
     @ aa,20 SAY CHR(186)
     @ aa,40 SAY CHR(186)
     @ aa,60 SAY CHR(186)
  NEXT
  @ 2,2 SAY "CURSOR <--   -->"
  @ 3,2 SAY "Char:  <-    ->"
```

```
    @ 4,2 SAY "Field: <-    ->"
    @ 2,22 SAY "      UP   DOWN"
    @ 3,22 SAY "Rec:     " + CHR(24) + "    " + CHR(25)
    @ 4,22 SAY "Page: PgUp  PgDn"
    @ 5,22 SAY "File: Home  End"
    @ 2,42 SAY "        DELETE"
    @ 3,42 SAY "Char:   DEL"
    @ 4,42 SAY "Field:    Y"
    @ 5,42 SAY "Record:  U"
    @ 2,62 SAY "       BROWSE"
    @ 3,62 SAY "Begin:       B"
    @ 4,62 SAY "Save/Quit    Q"
    @ 5,62 SAY "Abort:       A"
    RETURN

*************

PROCEDURE COLMDRAW

    ************************************************************************
    * Colmdraw draws the field names of the file in use                    *
    *          just below the menu.                                        *
    ************************************************************************
    * temp     :  a temporary variable to start the draw of colmdraw out   *
    *             at the TEMP position                                     *
    *                                                                      *
    * start    :  a FOR - NEXT counter to move across the fields in a      *
    *             file within the parameters of frst_posit and last_posit *
    ************************************************************************
    temp = 2
    RESTORE SCREEN FROM screen
    * Summer '87 this can be CALL __scrrest WITH screen
    * Autumn '86 this can be CALL _scrrest WITH screen
    FOR start = frst_posit TO last_posit
       in_val = FIELDNAME(start)
       IF TYPE(in_val) = "M"
          @ 7,temp SAY SUBSTR(in_val,1,4)
          temp = temp + 6
       ELSE
          @ 7,temp SAY in_val
          temp = temp + FIELD_LEN(in_val)+2
       ENDIF
    NEXT
    @ 8,0 SAY REPLICATE("-",80)
    RELEASE temp, start
    RETURN
```

```
**************

PROCEDURE Redraw

   ***************************************************************************
   * Redraw redraws the screen for the fields or records of the file in use  *
   *        between the rows of 9 and 20 inclusive,for the number of fields  *
   *        allowed by HOWMANY().                                            *
   * starthere  : the starting field position for the draw.  Does not        *
   *              change the value of position                               *
   * down       : a temporary variable to start the drawing of the rows      *
   *              between 9 and 20                                           *
   * across     : a temporary variable to start the drawing of the columns   *
   *              between 2 and the value of HOWMANY()                       *
   * start      : the counter to go across the screen                        *
   ***************************************************************************
   starthere = position
   FOR down = 9 TO 20
      across = 2
      IF DELETED()
         @ down,0 SAY "*"
      ENDIF
      FOR start = frst_posit TO last_posit
         in_val = FIELDNAME(start)
         IF TYPE(in_val) = "M"
            @ down,across SAY "memo"
         ELSE
            @ down,across SAY &in_val
         ENDIF
         across = across + 2 + FIELD_LEN(in_val)
      NEXT
      starthere = starthere +1
      IF starthere > LASTREC()
         down = 21
      ELSE
         SKIP
      ENDIF
   NEXT
   SKIP - 12
   RETURN

********************

PROCEDURE FIELDSHO

   ***********************************************************************
   * Fieldsho is a procedure that GETS the field at position and         *
   * displays it accordingly to the screen at row_count and col_count.   *
   ***********************************************************************
   in_val = FIELDNAME(position)
   IF TYPE(in_val) = "M"
      tempit = "memo"
      @ row_count,col_count GET tempit
   ELSE
      @ row_count,col_count GET &in_val
   ENDIF
   CLEAR GETS
```

```
    RETURN

 ***************

 PROCEDURE Downrec

    *****************************************************************
    * Downrec gets things ready to go down and then goes ahead. *
    *****************************************************************
    IF row_count > 20
       RESTORE SCREEN FROM screen
       * Summer '87 this can be CALL __scrrest WITH screen
       * Autumn '86 this can be CALL _scrrest WITH screen
       DO Colmdraw
       SKIP
       DO Redraw
       GO current
       row_count = 9
    ELSE
       IF TYPE(in_val) = "M"
          @ row_count-1,col_count SAY "memo"
       ELSE
          @ row_count-1,col_count SAY &in_val
       ENDIF
    ENDIF
    RETURN

 *************

 PROCEDURE Uprec

    *****************************
    * Uprec goes up a record. *
    *****************************
    IF row_count < 9
       RESTORE SCREEN FROM screen
       * Summer '87 this can be CALL __scrrest WITH screen
       * Autumn '86 this can be CALL _scrrest WITH screen
       DO Colmdraw
       SKIP - 1
       DO Redraw
       GO current
       row_count = 9
    ELSE
       IF TYPE(in_val) = "M"
          @ row_count+1,col_count SAY "memo"
       ELSE
          @ row_count+1,col_count SAY &in_val
       ENDIF
    ENDIF
    RETURN
 ***************
```

```
PROCEDURE Showrec

   ****************************************************************
   * Showrec displays the current record number to the screen. *
   ****************************************************************
   @ 0,15 SAY SPACE(8)
   @ 0,15 SAY current PICT "@B"
   RETURN

****************

PROCEDURE Upsevrl

   ************************************
   * Upsevrl goes up seven records. *
   ************************************
   IF row_count < 9
      RESTORE SCREEN FROM screen
      * Summer '87 this can be CALL __scrrest WITH screen
      * Autumn '86 this can be CALL _scrrest WITH screen
      DO Colmdraw
      SKIP - 7
      DO Redraw
      GO current
      row_count = 9
   ELSE
      IF TYPE(in_val) = "M"
         @ row_count+7,col_count SAY "memo"
      ELSE
         @ row_count+7,col_count SAY &in_val
      ENDIF
   ENDIF
   RETURN

****************

PROCEDURE Dwnsevrl

   **************************************************************************
   * Dwnsevrl gets things ready to go down seven records and goes ahead. *
   **************************************************************************
   IF row_count > 20
      RESTORE SCREEN FROM screen
      * Summer '87 this can be CALL __scrrest WITH screen
      * Autumn '86 this can be CALL _scrrest WITH screen
      DO Colmdraw
      SKIP + 7
      DO Redraw
      GO current
      row_count = 9
   ELSE
      IF TYPE(in_val) = "M"
         @ row_count-7,col_count SAY "memo"
      ELSE
         @ row_count-7,col_count SAY &in_val
      ENDIF
   ENDIF
```

```
RETURN

*******************

PROCEDURE U_feldlt

   ************************************************
   * U_FELDLT will unshow a field to the left. *
   ************************************************
   IF TYPE(in_val) = "M"
      @ row_count, col_count SAY "memo"
      col_count = col_count + 6
   ELSE
      @ row_count,col_count SAY &in_val
      col_count = col_count + 2 + FIELD_LEN(in_val)
   ENDIF
   RETURN

***************

PROCEDURE Fieldrt

   ***********************************************
   * FIELDRT will GET the field to the right. *
   ***********************************************
   in_val = FIELDNAME(position)
   IF TYPE(in_val) = "M"
      tempit = "memo"
      @ row_count,col_count GET tempit
   ELSE
      @ row_count,col_count GET &in_val
   ENDIF
   CLEAR GETS
   RETURN

*************

PROCEDURE U_feldrt

   *********************************************
   * U_FELDRT will show field to the right. *
   *********************************************
   IF TYPE(in_val) = "M"
      @ row_count, col_count SAY "memo"
   ELSE
      @ row_count,col_count SAY &in_val
   ENDIF
   in_val = FIELDNAME(position)
   col_count = col_count - 2 - FIELD_LEN(in_val)
   RETURN

****************
```

```
PROCEDURE Fieldlt

   ***********************************************
   * FIELDLT will GET the field to the left. *
   ***********************************************
   in_val = FIELDNAME(position)
   IF TYPE(in_val) = "M"
      tempit = "memo"
      @ row_count,col_count GET tempit
   ELSE
      @ row_count,col_count GET &in_val
   ENDIF
   CLEAR GETS
   RETURN

****************

FUNCTION Endfield

   ****************************************************
   * This function determines the number of the last *
   * field in database given, using a binary search  *
   * algorithm.                                       *
   ****************************************************

   PARAMETERS File

   Use &File
   x = 1
   y = 1024
   z = int(y/2)
   DO WHILE X <> Y
      IF LEN(FIELDNAME(z)) = 0
         y = z
      ELSE
         x = z
      ENDIF
      z = x + int((y-x)/2)
      IF LEN(FIELDNAME(z)) > 0 .AND. LEN(FIELDNAME(z+1)) = 0
         y = z
         x = z
      ENDIF
   ENDDO
   RETURN(Y)

********************

FUNCTION Howmany

   ***********************************************************
   * Determines how many fields can be shown on the screen. *
   ***********************************************************
```

```
    length = 0
    FOR rover = position TO ending
       in_val = fieldname(rover)
       IF TYPE(in_val) = "M"
          length = length + 6
       ELSE
          length = length + FIELD_LEN(in_val)+2
       ENDIF
       IF length > 77
          RETURN(rover - 1)
       ENDIF
    NEXT
    * The remaining fields all fit on the screen
    RETURN(rover)

****************

FUNCTION Fieldshow

    IF advance
       @ row_count, col_count SAY &in_val
       col_count = col_count + 2 + FIELD_LEN(in_val)
       position = position + 1
       IF col_count > 80
          col_count = 2
          @ 9,0,20,79 BOX SPACE(9)
          col_count = REDRAW()
       ENDIF
    ENDIF
    in_val = FIELDNAME(position)
    @ row_count, col_count GET &in_val
    CLEAR GETS
    RETURN("")

*****************

FUNCTION Fieldminus

    IF advance
       @ row_count,col_count SAY &in_val
       col_count = col_count - 2 - FIELD_LEN(in_val)
       IF col_count < 2
          position = position - 1
          col_count = COLMDRAW()
          col_count = REDRAW()
       ENDIF
       position = position - 1
       in_val = fieldname(position)
       @ row_count,col_count GET &in_val
       CLEAR GETS
    ENDIF
    RETURN("")
```

```
*****************

FUNCTION Nowait

   SET CONSOLE OFF
   WAIT
   SET CONSOLE ON
   RETURN("")

*****************

FUNCTION FIELD_LEN

   ****************************************
   * Field_len function                   *
   *                                      *
   * Returns LEN() for character strings *
   * Returns LEN(STR()) for numeric       *
   * Returns 1 for logical                *
   * Returns 8 for date                   *
   * Returns 4 for memo                   *
   ****************************************
   PARAMETER field_name

   IF TYPE(field_name) = "C"
      IF LEN(field_name) > LEN(&field_name)
         RETURN(LEN(field_name))
      ELSE
         RETURN(LEN(&field_name))
      ENDIF
   ENDIF
   IF TYPE(field_name) = "N"
      RETURN(LEN(STR(&field_name)))
   ENDIF
   RETURN( AT(TYPE(field_name), "L  M   D") )
   * Logical type returns an "L", since it is in the 1st position AT returns 1
   * Memo type returns an "M", since it is in the 4th position AT returns 4
   * Date type returns an "D", since it is in the 8th position AT returns 8

* End of BROWSE.prg
```

EDIT

```
*********************
* Name          EDIT.prg
* Date          March 20, 1988
* Notice        Copyright 1988, Stephen J. Straley & Associates
* Compile       Clipper Edit
* Release       Autumn '86 or later
* Link          Autumn '86: Plink86 fi edit lib dbu lib clipper
*               Summer '87: Plink86 di edit lib extend lib clipper
* Note          This program emulates the EDIT command of dBASE III.
*               One exception is on a field larger than the width
*               of the screen: this program will allow a window
*               in which the edit can take place.
*
*               A limitation to this program is that it will only work
*               with 15 or fewer fields.   However, minor modifications
*               can be made allowing it to accept databases with
*               more fields.
*
*               Additionally, the way Memos and lengthy string fields
*               are handled are a bit different in this simulation from
*               dBASE III/Plus.
*********************

PARAMETER file

file = UPPER(TRIM(file)) + ".DBF"
DO Openfile
frame = CHR(201) + CHR(205) + CHR(187) + CHR(186) + ;
        CHR(188) + CHR(205) + CHR(200) + CHR(186) + CHR(32)
DO Drawbord

**********************************************************************
* Variable Declaration                                               *
*                                                                    *
*   howmany   = the number of fields in database                    *
*   screens   = the number of screens                               *
*   pan       = this variable was set up to test for which screen   *
*               position.                                            *
*   recnumb   = was initialized to store the current record number  *
*   good_time = a logical variable to allow for an update or not    *
*   nullstr   = a null string variable that is to be global and     *
*               used for multiple-purposes                           *
**********************************************************************

howmany = ENDFIELD()
* The operator is an addition that shows the modulus of 2.
* numbers
screens = INT(IF(howmany % 15 > 0, howmany / 15 + 1, howmany / 15))
recnumb = 1
pan     = 1
nullstr = ""
```

```
good_time = .T.

SET KEY 28 TO                           && Turns off On-Line Help
SET KEY -1 TO Deltit
SET KEY -9 TO Quitit
SET KEY  5 TO Upit
SET KEY 24 TO Dwit
DECLARE tempdata[15]                    && This array holds the data for one
*                                       && screen
GO TOP
STORE SPACE(4000) TO newscr
SAVE SCREEN TO newscr
DO WHILE .T.
   DO Adjust
    RESTORE SCREEN FROM newscr
   * Summer '87 this can be CALL __scrrest WITH newscr
   * Autumn '86 this can be CALL _scrrest WITH newscr
   DO Dispstat
   DO Scrnstat
   x = 1
   DO WHILE x <= 15
      good_time = .T.
      intemp   = FIELDNAME(x)
      tempdata[x] = &intemp
      IF EMPTY(intemp)
         EXIT
      ENDIF
      DO CASE
      CASE TYPE(intemp) = "M"
         @ 6+x,12 SAY ""
         tempvar = INKEY(0)
            IF tempvar = 5
               x = x - 1
               LOOP
            ENDIF
         good_time = .F.

      CASE TYPE(intemp) = "C"
         IF LEN(tempdata[x]) > 60
            @ 6+x,12 SAY ""
            tempvar = INKEY(0)
            IF tempvar = 5
               x = x - 1
               LOOP
            ENDIF
            good_time = .F.
         ELSE
            @ 6+x,12 GET tempdata[x]
            READ
         ENDIF

       CASE TYPE(intemp) = "D"
          dat_disp = DTOC(tempdata[x])
```

```
         @ 6+x,12 GET dat_disp PICT "99/99/99" VALID(GOOD_DATE())
         READ
         tempdata[x] = CTOD(dat_disp)

      OTHERWISE
         @ 6+x,12 GET tempdata[x]
         READ
      ENDCASE
      IF good_time
         REPLACE &intemp WITH tempdata[x]
      ENDIF
      DO CASE
      CASE LASTKEY() = 3
         x = 15
      CASE LASTKEY() = 18
         x = 15
         SKIP - 1
      CASE LASTKEY() = 27 .OR. LASTKEY() = 17
         @ 24,00 SAY ""
         QUIT
      CASE LASTKEY() = 29
           IF TYPE(intemp) = "M" .OR. (TYPE(intemp) = "C" .AND.
          LEN(tempdata[x]) > 60)
            newtemp = &intemp
            DO Editit
            REPLACE &intemp WITH newtemp
         ENDIF
      CASE LASTKEY() = 5
         x = x - 1
      ENDCASE

      x = x + 1

   ENDDO
   DO CASE
   CASE LASTKEY() = 13 .OR. LASTKEY() = 24 .OR. LASTKEY() = 3
      SKIP
   CASE LASTKEY() = 5
      SKIP - 1
   ENDCASE

ENDDO

********************

PROCEDURE Scrnstat

   FOR y = 1 TO 15

      intemp    = FIELDNAME(y)
      tempdata[y] = &intemp

      IF EMPTY(intemp)          && check to see if the field
```

```
      RETURN                      && is actually there.  If not,
   ENDIF                          && then return to calling proc

   @ 6+y,00 SAY FIELDNAME(y)
   SET COLOR TO 0/7
   DO CASE
   CASE TYPE(intemp) = "M"
      @ 6+y,12 SAY "memo"
   CASE TYPE(intemp) = "C"
      IF LEN(tempdata[y]) > 60
         @ 6+y,12 SAY "string"
      ELSE
         @ 6+y,12 SAY tempdata[y]
      ENDIF
   CASE TYPE(intemp) = "D"
      dat_disp = DTOC(tempdata[y])
      @ 6+y,12 SAY dat_disp
   OTHERWISE
      @ 6+y,12 SAY tempdata[y]
   ENDCASE
   SET COLOR TO

NEXT

********************

FUNCTION GOOD_DATE

IF dat_disp = "  /  /  "
   outval = .T.
ELSE
   outval = IF(CTOD(dat_disp) == CTOD("  /  /  "), .F., .T.)
ENDIF
IF outval
   tempdata[x] = CTOD(dat_disp)
ELSE
   SAVE SCREEN
   @ 00,35 SAY SPACE(44)
   @ 00,35 SAY "Invalid date.  (Press SPACE)"
   IF INKEY(0) = 0
   ENDIF
   RESTORE SCREEN
ENDIF
RETURN(outval)

********************

PROCEDURE Editit

SAVE SCREEN
@ 2,62 SAY "  Memo  Edit  "
@ 3,62 SAY "Begin Edit ^Home"
@ 4,62 SAY "Abort Edit ESC"
```

```
    @ 5,62 SAY "Save/Quit  F10"
    SET COLOR TO 0/7
    SET FUNCTION 10 TO CHR(23)
    SET KEY -1 TO
    SET KEY -9 TO
    SET KEY  5 TO
    SET KEY 24 TO
    newtemp = MEMOEDIT(newtemp,6+x,12,6+x,70,.T.)
    RESTORE SCREEN
    SET FUNCTION 10 TO
    SET COLOR TO 7/0
    SET KEY -1 TO Deltit
    SET KEY -9 TO Quitit
    SET KEY  5 TO Upit
    SET KEY 24 TO Dwit

*********************

PROCEDURE Openfile

  IF file = "."
     file = SPACE(14)
     @ ROW(),0 SAY "No database is in USE.  Enter file name: " GET file PIC-
          TURE "@!"
     READ
     file = TRIM(file)
     x = AT(".",file)
     IF X = 0
        file = file + ".DBF"
     ENDIF
  ENDIF
  IF .NOT. FILE("&file")
     ? file + " not found"
     WAIT
     QUIT
  ENDIF
  USE &file
  CLEAR
  SET SCOREBOARD OFF
  GO TOP
  RETURN

*********************

PROCEDURE Drawbord

   *
   * Draw the border of EDIT
   *

   @ 0,1 SAY "Record No. "
   @ 0,60 SAY TRIM(file)
   @ 1,0,6,79 BOX frame
```

```
    FOR aa = 20 to 60 STEP 20
       @ 1,aa SAY CHR(203)
       @ 6,aa SAY CHR(202)
    NEXT
    FOR aa = 2 to 5
       @ aa,20 SAY CHR(186)
       @ aa,40 SAY CHR(186)
       @ aa,60 SAY CHR(186)
    NEXT
    @ 2,2 SAY "CURSOR <--  -->"
    @ 3,2 SAY "Char:   <-     ->"
    @ 4,2 SAY "Field: ^<-    ^->"
    @ 2,22 SAY "       UP   DOWN"
    @ 3,22 SAY "Rec:     " + CHR(24) + "    " + CHR(25)
    @ 4,22 SAY "Page: PgUp  PgDn"
    @ 5,22 SAY "File: Home  End"
    @ 2,42 SAY "        DELETE"
    @ 3,42 SAY "Char:   DEL"
    @ 4,42 SAY "Field:    ^Y"
    @ 5,42 SAY "Record:  F2"
    @ 2,62 SAY "      EDIT"
    @ 3,62 SAY "Begin Edit ^Home"
    @ 4,62 SAY "               "
    @ 5,62 SAY "Save/Quit  F10"
    RETURN

*********************

PROCEDURE Deltit

   PARAMETERS p,l,v

   IF DELETED()
      @ 00,38 SAY "     "
      RECALL
   ELSE
      @ 00,38 SAY "*DEL*"
      DELETE
   ENDIF

*********************

PROCEDURE Upit

   PARAMETERS p,l,v

      good_time = .F.
      REPLACE &intemp WITH tempdata[x]
      CLEAR GETS
      x = x - 1
      IF x < 1
         x = 18
      ENDIF
```

```
*********************

PROCEDURE Dwit

   PARAMETERS p,l,v

   KEYBOARD CHR(13)

*********************

PROCEDURE Quitit

   PARAMETERS p, l, v

   CLEAR
   CLOSE DATABASES
   QUIT

*********************

PROCEDURE Endmemo

   PARAMETERS p, l, v

   * This procedure is called by a SET KEY TO command and simulates
   * a control W key being pushed, thus completing a MEMOEDIT().

   KEYBOARD CHR(23)

*********************

PROCEDURE Dispstat

   * This procedure displays a message if the record in the active
   * and selected database is deleted.

   @ 00,15 SAY LTRIM(STR(RECNO()))
   IF DELETED()
      @ 00,38 SAY "*DEL*"
   ENDIF

*********************

PROCEDURE Adjust

   *  This should be done with most applications.  This simple routine
   *  readjusts the pointer of the currently selected and active database
   *  to the proper position.  Sometimes, when going through a database,if
   *  the EOF() or BOF() markers have been hit and a READ is performed, a
   *  false record or an "image" of a record may show up. The solution is to
   *  check for either a BOF() or EOF() condition and move off the image.
   *  This procedure does just that.
```

```
   IF BOF()
      GO TOP
   ELSE
      IF EOF()
         GO BOTTOM
      ENDIF
   ENDIF

********************

PROCEDURE Loadarry

   FOR x = 1 TO howmany
      temp  = FIELDNAME(x)    && because we can't go directly to the array
      atype[x]  = TYPE(temp)
      names[x] = temp
      DO CASE
      CASE atype[x] = "C"
         length[x] = LEN(temp)
      CASE atype[x] = "D"
         length[x] = 8
      CASE atype[x] = "N"
         length[x] = 10
      ENDCASE
   NEXT

********************

FUNCTION Endfield

   * This function determines the number of the last field in database given
   PARAMETERS File.

   x = 1
   y = 1024
   z = int(y/2)
   DO WHILE X <> Y
      IF LEN(FIELDNAME(z)) = 0
         y = z
      ELSE
         x = z
      ENDIF
      z = x + int((y-x)/2)
      IF LEN(FIELDNAME(z)) > 0 .AND. LEN(FIELDNAME(z+1)) = 0
         y = z
         x = z
      ENDIF
   ENDDO
   RETURN(Y)
```

```
*********************

FUNCTION Bitstrip

   PARAMETERS c

   outstring = ""
   beginning = 1
   DO WHILE .NOT. EMPTY(c)
      IF AT(CHR(141),c) = 0
         outstring = outstring + SUBSTR(c,beginning,LEN(c))
         c = ""
      ELSE
         outstring = outstring + SUBSTR(c,beginning,AT(CHR(141),c)-1)
         beginning = AT(CHR(141),c)+1
         c = SUBSTR(c,beginning,LEN(c) - beginning + 1)
         beginning = 1
      ENDIF
   ENDDO
   RETURN(outstring)

*********************

FUNCTION Big_screen

   PARAMETERS temp_row

   SET KEY 13 TO Endmemo
   data[x] = MEMOEDIT(data[x],temp_row,10,temp_row,80,.T.)
   SET KEY TO
   data[x] = BITSTRIP(data[x])
   RETURN(.T.)
* End of EDIT.prg
```

CENTURY ADJUSTING

```
*********************
* Name          CENTURY.prg
* Date          August 31, 1986
* Notice        Copyright 1988, Stephen J. Straley & Associates
* Compile       Clipper Century
* Release       Autumn '86 only
* Link          PLINK86 fi century lib clipper
* Note          This program shows how you can adjust the internal
*               year mechanisms for Clipper.  This is only necessary
*               if there is a string of a date that is to be converted
*               back into the date format.   If the string contains
*               the century part of the year, it will make no
*               difference to ADJ2000, which is the C subroutine
*               in Clipper that actually makes the adjustment to the
*               date.
*
```

```
*               This section is really necessary for those applications
*               that require string manipulations on dates outside of
*               the currently adjusted century.   Such applications would
*               be those involving mortgages and insurance policies, for
*               example.
*
*               Two other notes:  This routine MUST be activated with a
*               DO and not a CALL.  In order for the DO to work properly,
*               the EXTERNAL command must be added to the routine.
*               Secondly, the variable being passed to the ADJ2000 routine
*               must be passed by VALUE and not by REFERENCE.  To do this,
*               use parentheses when passing it.
*********************

STORE 0 TO year_rng
EXTERNAL _adj2000
atime = DTOC(DATE())            && Turning today's date to character type
DO WHILE .T.
   CLEAR
   TEXT
   Enter in the beginning year of the century to adjust the internal
   mechanisms of Clipper.   For example, if the year is 1986 and the
   beginning year of the century is set to a value less than or equal to
   86, 86 will be considered in the twentieth century.  If, on the other
   hand, the beginning number for the century is greater than the current
   year, the century for the year will be considered as the twenty-first
   century.
   ENDTEXT

   @ 10,10 SAY "Enter beginning year of the century: " GET year_rng PICT "###"
   READ
   newstff = year_rng
   DO _ADJ2000 WITH (newstff)
   btime = CTOD(atime)
   @ 12,10 SAY "The String today is: " + STR(YEAR(btime))
   WAIT
   IF EMPTY(year_rng)
      QUIT
   ENDIF
ENDDO
* End of CENTURY.prg
```

APPENDIX H

Program Generators

There is a set of standard tasks a complete application always does: set up system parameters, create databases, handle prompting functions, and enter, change, scan, and delete data. These tasks become tedious to generate over and over again for even the most enthusiastic developer.

To ease this, there are many programs available, such as Viewgen, HiLite, Quickcode, and Genifer, that either create basic core code for an application or menu code for the front end of an application. However, most of these do not create code specifically for use with Clipper. They, too, have a marketing scheme and must appeal to both the developing market using Clipper and the market using dBASE.

Listed below is source code that generates the front end to an application, to be used strictly with Clipper. It is not intended to compete with other products and should be viewed solely as a demonstration of many of the things we have covered in this book. Pay particular attention to the techniques involved: not only does this program generate Clipper code, it runs under Clipper. Major sections to notice are the creation of the databases and the code for it, a sign-on message routine, and a set of standard procedures and functions.

When this code is combined with MENUGEN, which you will find immediately following GENCODE2, you have a fairly complete application generator. This code is now set for autumn '86 releases of Clipper or later.

A PROGRAM GENERATOR FOR CLIPPER

Create a CLiP file named GEN1.CLP containing the following one line:

```
Gencode1
```

Even though there is only one file in this CLiP file, this is one way to prevent an ASSUMED EXTERNAL message from appearing at the end of the compile when Clipper would try to compile Eleven.prg in with the rest of this code.

```
*********************
* Name          GENCODE1.prg
* Date          April 4, 1988
* Notice        Copyright 1986-8, Stephen J. Straley & Associates
* Compile       Clipper Gencode1 -m
* Release       Autumn '86 or later
* Link          Tlink Gencode1 Gencode2, gencode,,extend + clipper
* Note          The following source is the first half of the code that
*               creates the basic front end of an application.
*               The code generated can then be modified to the
*               needs of the client or user. The second half is in
*               GENCODE2.prg.
```

```
*               The following is a listing of the procedures and their
*               purpose as they relate to the code they generate.
*
*               First:    Writes a standard header to the text or .PRG file.
*               Second:   Asks for the names of the files that must
*                         be present on the disk in order to prevent the
*                         application from regenerating the data files.
*                Third:   Writes the code for the procedure named
*                         SCRINIT.   Eventually sets up
*                         the screen and system parameters for the
*                         application.
*               Fourth:   Accepts input of the name of the application,
*                         any special name for it, the designer's name,
*                         and the code for the initial message for the
*                         application
*                Fifth:   Writes out the function library
*                         that is standard to most applications.
*                Sixth:   Creates the Setup Procedure
*              Seventh:   Creates the Redraw Procedure; this
*                         redraws the top four lines of the application.
*                Eight:   The WHICHWAY function allows a user to choose
*                         which way reports for the application are to
*                         print out.
*                 Nine:   Creates 15 databases, each with 99 fields maximum,
*                         in memory using arrays and macros.
*                         These databases are specific to the application
*                         being developed.
*                  Ten:   Writes the initialization code
*                         for all of the databases created in memory, as
*                         well as writing out memory variables for the
*                         databases.  These variables may be used for a
*                         possible Report Generator.
********************

*
* All this does is display an initial message.
*
STORE SPACE(4000) TO screen
CLEAR
SAVE SCREEN TO screen
SET COLOR TO 7+
STORE "Welcome to the Clipper Code Generator" TO message
over = 5
FOR y = 1 TO 2
   FOR x = 2 TO 18
      @ x,over SAY message
      RESTORE SCREEN FROM screen
      over = over + 3
   NEXT
   FOR x = 18 TO 2 STEP -1
      @ x,over SAY message
      RESTORE SCREEN FROM screen
      over = over + 3
   NEXT
NEXT
```

```
FOR y = COL() TO 20 STEP -1
   @ 2,y SAY message
   RESTORE SCREEN FROM screen
NEXT
FOR y = 2 TO 12
   @ y,20 SAY message
   RESTORE SCREEN FROM screen
NEXT
@ 12,20 SAY message
@ 14,28 SAY "Press Any Key to Begin!"
INKEY(0)

SET CONFIRM ON
SET SCOREBOARD OFF
scrframe = CHR(201) + CHR(205) + CHR(187) + CHR(186) + ;
           CHR(188) + CHR(205) + CHR(200) + CHR(186) + CHR(32)
STORE SPACE(8) TO file
STORE SPACE(30) TO name
CLEAR
@ 0,0,22,79 BOX SUBSTR(scrframe,1,8)
@ 10,10 SAY "What is the name of the Application? " GET file PICT "@!"
@ 12,10 SAY "Enter your Name => " GET name PICT "@X"
READ
pref = SUBSTR(file,1,1) + LOWER(SUBSTR(file,2,1))
file = TRIM(file) + ".PRG"
name = "Copyright - " + SUBSTR(DTOS(DATE()),1,4) + " " + name
SET ALTERNATE TO &file
SET CONSOLE OFF
DO First


*********************

PROCEDURE First

   SET ALTERNATE ON
   ? "*********************"
   ? "* Name      " + file
   ? "* Date      " + DTOC(DATE())
   ? "* Author    " + name
   ? "* Note      This is an application"
   ? "*"
   ? "*********************"
   ?
   ? "CLEAR"
   ? '? "Loading Program..."'
   ? "DO Beginit"
   ? "DO Draw"
   ? "DO " + pref + "menu"
   SET ALTERNATE OFF
   DO Second

*********************
```

```
PROCEDURE Second

   CLEAR
   @ 0,0,22,79 BOX SUBSTR(scrframe,1,8)
   STORE SPACE(12) TO database1, database2, database3
   system1 = pref + SPACE(10)
   @ 4,5 SAY "Enter the Names of the Databases that MUST"
   @ 5,5 SAY "be on the disk in order to prevent the"
   @ 6,5 SAY "application from initializing all of the"
   @ 7,5 SAY "databases.  Give an extension if other than"
   @ 8,5 SAY "a .DBF extension."
   @ 10,20 SAY "->" GET database1 PICT "@!"
   @ 11,20 SAY "  " GET database2 PICT "@!"
   @ 12,20 SAY "  " GET database3 PICT "@!"
   READ
   database1 = TRIM(database1) + IF(AT(".",database1) = 0, ".DBF", "")
   database2 = TRIM(database2) + IF(AT(".",database2) = 0, ".DBF", "")
   database3 = TRIM(database3) + IF(AT(".",database3) = 0, ".DBF", "")
   *
   * Sometimes, an application requires special values to be written to
   * the disk.  Values such as the system date, end-of-year processing
   * date, check numbers, etc.
   *
   @ 15, 5 SAY "Will there be a special system file? "
   IF VERIFY()
      @ 17,10 SAY "Enter full name -> " GET system1 PICT "@!"
      READ
      system1 = TRIM(system1) + IF(AT(".",system1) = 0, ".MEM", "")
      system1 = SUBSTR(system1,1,1) + LOWER(SUBSTR(system1,2))
   ENDIF
   SET CONSOLE OFF
   @ 19,20 SAY "Just a sec...."
   SET ALTERNATE ON
   DO Prochead WITH "Beginit"           && PROCHEAD writes the basic header
   ? '   IF .NOT. FILE("SCREEN.SYS")'    && for a procedure
   ? '      DO Scrinit'
   ? '   ENDIF'
   ? '   RESTORE FROM Screen.sys'
   IF LEN(TRIM(system1)) > 2
      ? '   IF .NOT. FILE(scrdata + "' + UPPER(system1) + '")'
      ? "      DO " + LTRIM(SUBSTR(system1,1,5)) + "int"
      ? "   ENDIF"
   ENDIF
   ? "   IF .NOT. FILE(scrdata + " + CHR(34) + database1 + CHR(34) + ")"
   IF LEN(TRIM(database2)) > 4
      ?? " .OR. .NOT. FILE(scrdata + " + CHR(34) + database2 + CHR(34) + ")"
   ENDIF
   IF LEN(TRIM(database3)) > 4
      ?? " .OR. .NOT. FILE(scrdata + " + CHR(34) + database3 + CHR(34) + ")"
   ENDIF
   ? "      DO " + pref + "init"
   ? "   ENDIF"
```

```
    SET ALTERNATE OFF
    DO Third

********************

PROCEDURE Third

    CLEAR
    @ 0,0,22,79 BOX SUBSTR(scrframe,1,8)
    @ 2,5 SAY "Writing SCRINIT to alternate file"
    SET ALTERNATE ON
    DO Prochead WITH "Scrinit"
    ?
    ? "   SET SCOREBOARD OFF"
    ?
    ? '   scrleft_1    = "Copyright 1988 - SJS & Associates"'
    ? '   scrleft_2    = "All Rights Reserved"'
    ? '   right_1      = "Terminal/System Setup Program"'
    ? '   right_2      = "' + CMONTH(DATE()) + ' - 1986"'
    ? '   temscreen    = SPACE(4000)'
    ?     scrframe     = CHR(201) + CHR(205) + CHR(187) + CHR(186) + ;
    ?                    CHR(188) + CHR(205) + CHR(200) + CHR(186) + CHR(32)
    ? '   CLEAR'
    ? '   center = "Drive Assignment Setup"'
    ? '   @  0,0 SAY scrleft_1'
    ? '   @  1,0 SAY scrleft_2'
    ? '   @  0,80-LEN(right_1) SAY right_1'
    ? '   @  1,80-LEN(right_2) SAY right_2'
    ? '   @  3,40-LEN(center)/2 SAY center'
    ? '   @ 4,0,23,79 BOX scrframe'
    ? '   topspot = "        Move cursor to appropriate option.  Strike RETURN
             key to change        "'
    ? '   @  5, 1 GET topspot'
    ? '   CLEAR GETS'
    ? '   @  6, 0 SAY CHR(204) + REPLICATE(CHR(205),78) + CHR(185)'
    ? '   SCREEN SAVE WITH temscreen'
    ? '   IF .NOT. FILE("SCREEN.SYS")'
    ? '      STORE "C:" TO scrprog, scrdata'
    ? '      STORE .F. TO scrconfirm, scrdelim, scrinten, scrbell, scrtype'
    ? '      STORE .T. TO scrsys, scrshow, scrcolor'
    ? '      STORE "" TO scrframe, scrbar, scrlin'
    ? '      STORE "::" TO scrdelimto'
    ? '      STORE 0 TO scrtimes, scrpass'
    ? '   ELSE'
    ? '      RESTORE FROM Screen.sys ADDITIVE'
    ? '   ENDIF'
    ? '   STORE 4 TO option'
    ?
    ? '   DO WHILE .T. '
    ? '      RESTORE SCREEN FROM temscreen'
    ? '      @  7, 5 PROMPT " 1> System Configured for " + IF(scrsys, "Hard",
             "Floppy") + " Disk "'
    ? '      @  7,45 PROMPT " 2> Program Drive Set to " + scrprog + " "'
```

```
? '        @  8,45 PROMPT " 3> Data Drive Set to " + scrdata + " "'
? '        @ 10, 5 PROMPT " 4> Confirm is " + IF(scrconfirm, "ON ", "OFF") +
        " "'
? '        @ 11, 5 PROMPT " 5> Delimiters are " + IF(scrdelim, "ON", "OFF") +
        " "'
? '        @ 12, 5 PROMPT " 6> Delimiters SET to " + scrdelimto + " "'
? '        @ 13, 5 PROMPT " 7> Screen " + IF(scrcolor, "Bright", "Normal") +
        " "'
? '        @ 14, 5 PROMPT " 8> Field Color is " + IF(scrinten, "ON", "OFF") +
        " "'
? '        @ 15, 5 PROMPT " 9> Bell " + IF(scrbell, "WILL", "WILL NOT") + "
        ring "'
? '        @ 10,40 PROMPT " A> Password " + IF(scrshow, "WILL", "WILL NOT") +
        " echo to screen "'
? '        @ 12,40 PROMPT " B> Change Password "'
? '        @ 14,40 PROMPT " C> " + DLTRIM(STR(scrtimes)) + " tries at the
        Password "'
? '        @ 16,40 PROMPT " D> " + IF(scrtype, "Engage", "Disengage") + "
        Type-Ahead Feature "'
? '        @ 18,33 SAY    "<ESC> to Save Values"'
? '        MENU TO option'
? '        DO CASE'
? '        CASE option = 1'
? '           scrsys = IF(scrsys, .F., .T.)'
? '           IF .NOT. scrsys'
? '              KEYBOARD "2"'
? '           ENDIF'
? '        CASE option = 2'
? '           @ 21,10 SAY "Enter Program Drive: " GET scrprog PICT "!";
                         VALID(SUBSTR(scrprog,1,1) $"ABCDEFGHIJKLMNOP")'
? '           READ'
? '           IF .NOT. scrsys'
? '              IF scrprog = scrdata'
? '                 @ 21,10 SAY SPACE(50)'
? '                 @ 22,10 SAY "Data Drive and Program Drive NOT EQUAL for
        Floppy System"'
? '                 @ 21,10 SAY "Enter Data Drive: " GET scrdata PICT "!";
                               VALID(SUBSTR(scrdata,1,1) $"ABCDEFGHIJKLMNOP"
        .AND. scrprog <> scrdata)'
? '                 READ'
? '              ENDIF'
? '           ENDIF'
? '        CASE option = 3'
? '           @ 21,10 SAY "Enter Data Drive: " GET scrdata PICT "!";
                        VALID(SUBSTR(scrdata,1,1) $"ABCDEFGHIJKLMNOP")'
? '           READ'
? '           IF .NOT. scrsys'
? '              IF scrprog = scrdata'
? '                 @ 21,10 SAY SPACE(50)'
? '                 @ 22,10 SAY "Program Drive and Data Drive NOT EQUAL for
        Floppy System"'
? '                 @ 21,10 SAY "Enter Program Drive: " GET scrprog PICT "!";
                               VALID(SUBSTR(scrprog,1,1) $"ABCDEFGHIJKLMNOP"
        .AND. scrdata <> scrprog)'
```

```
? '             ENDIF'
? '          ENDIF'
? '       CASE option = 4'
? '          scrconfirm = IF(scrconfirm, .F., .T.)'
? '       CASE option = 5'
? '          scrdelim = IF(scrdelim, .F., .T.)'
? '       CASE option = 6'
? '          STORE " " TO choice'
? '          @ 21,10 SAY "Set Left Delimiter:   " GET choice PICT "X"'
? '          READ'
? '          STORE choice TO scrdelimto'
? '          STORE " " TO choice'
? '          @ 21,10 SAY "Set Right Delimiter:  " GET choice PICT "X"'
? '          READ'
? '          STORE scrdelimto + choice TO scrdelimto'
? '       CASE option = 7'
? '          scrcolor = !scrcolor'
? '       CASE option = 8'
? '          scrinten = !scrinten'
? '       CASE option = 9'
? '          scrbell =  !scrbell'
? '       CASE option = 10'
? '          scrshow =  !scrshow'
? '       CASE option = 11'
? '          STORE SPACE(15) TO password'
? '          @ 21,10 SAY "What Password do you want to use? " GET password
       PICT "XXXXXXXXXXXXXXX"'
? '          READ'
? '          scrpass = GENPASS(password)'
? '       CASE option = 12'
? '          @ 21,10 SAY "How may tries for a correct password? " GET
       scrtimes PICT "##" range 0,99'
? '          READ'
? '       CASE option = 13'
? '          scrtype = !scrtype'
? '       OTHERWISE'
? '          EXIT'
? '       ENDCASE'
? '    ENDDO'
?

prmpt_4 = CHR(201) + CHR(205) + CHR(187) + CHR(186) + ;
          CHR(188) + CHR(205) + CHR(200) + CHR(186) + CHR(32)
prmpt_5 = REPLICATE(CHR(177), 8) + " "
prmpt_6 = CHR(218) + CHR(196) + CHR(191) + CHR(179) + ;
          CHR(217) + CHR(196) + CHR(192) + CHR(179) + CHR(32)
prmpt_7 = CHR(222) + CHR(223) + CHR(221) + CHR(221) + ;
          CHR(221) + CHR(220) + CHR(222) + CHR(222) + CHR(32)
prmpt_9 = REPLICATE(CHR(15), 8) + " "

? '    RESTORE SCREEN FROM temscreen'
? '    @ 3,3 SAY SPACE(60)'
? '    @ 3,29 SAY "Installing the Border"'
```

```
? '   SAVE SCREEN TO temscreen'
? '   in_choice = 4'
?
? '   DO WHILE .T.'
? '      RESTORE SCREEN FROM temscreen'
? '      @  8, 5 PROMPT  "1>   *********"'
? '      @  8,32 PROMPT  "2>   ========="'
? '      @  8,59 PROMPT  "3>   ---------"'
? '      @ 10, 5 PROMPT  "4>   &prmpt_4."'
? '      @ 10,32 PROMPT  "5>   &prmpt_5."'
? '      @ 10,59 PROMPT  "6>   &prmpt_6."'
? '      @ 12, 5 PROMPT  "7>   &prmpt_7."'
? '      @ 12,32 PROMPT  "8>    "'
? '      @ 12,59 PROMPT  "9>   &prmpt_9."'
? '      @ 14,20 SAY "Move Cursor to choose preferred boarder"'
? '      MENU TO in_choice'
? '      DO CASE'
? '      CASE in_choice = 1'
? '         scrframe = "******** "'
? '         scrbar   = REPLICATE("*",80)'
? '         scrlin   = "*"'
? '      CASE in_choice = 2'
? '         scrframe = "======== "'
? '         scrbar   = REPLICATE("=",80)'
? '         scrlin   = "="'
? '      CASE in_choice = 3'
? '         scrframe = "-------- "'
? '         scrbar   = REPLICATE("-",80)'
? '         scrlin   = "|"'
? '      CASE in_choice = 4'
? '         scrframe = CHR(201) + CHR(205) + CHR(187) + CHR(186) + CHR(188)
      + ;'
? '                    CHR(205) + CHR(200) + CHR(186) + CHR(32)'
? '         scrbar   = CHR(204) + REPLICATE(CHR(205), 78) + CHR(185)'
? '         scrlin   = CHR(186)'
? '      CASE in_choice = 5'
? '         scrframe = REPLICATE(CHR(177), 8) + " "'
? '         scrbar   = REPLICATE(CHR(177),80)'
? '         scrlin   = CHR(177)'
? '      CASE in_choice = 6'
? '         scrframe = CHR(218) + CHR(196) + CHR(191) + CHR(179) + CHR(217)
      + ;'
? '                    CHR(196) + CHR(192) + CHR(179) + CHR(32)'
? '         scrbar   = CHR(195) + REPLICATE(CHR(196), 78) + CHR(180)'
? '         scrlin   = CHR(179)'
? '      CASE in_choice = 7'
? '         scrframe = CHR(222) + CHR(223) + CHR(221) + CHR(221) + CHR(221)
      + ;'
? '                    CHR(220) + CHR(222) + CHR(222) + CHR(32)'
? '         scrbar   = CHR(222) + REPLICATE(CHR(220),78) + CHR(221)'
? '         scrlin   = CHR(222)'
? '      CASE in_choice = 8'
? '         scrframe = " "'
```

```
   ? '         scrbar   = REPLICATE("",80)'
   ? '         scrlin   = ""'
   ? '      CASE in_choice = 9'
   ? '         scrframe = REPLICATE(CHR(15), 8) + " "'
   ? '         scrbar   = REPLICATE(CHR(15), 80)'
   ? '         scrlin   = CHR(15)'
   ? '      ENDCASE'
   ?
   ? '      CALL _scrrest WITH temscreen'
   ? '      @ 8,10,16,69 BOX SUBSTR(scrframe,1,8)'
   ? '      @ 12,10 SAY SUBSTR(scrbar,1,1) + SUBSTR(scrbar,2,58) + SUB-
          STR(scrbar,80,1)'
   ? '      @ 19,25 SAY "Is this the border you want?  "'
   ? '      IF VERIFY()'
   ? '         EXIT'
   ? '      ENDIF'
   ? '   ENDDO'
   ?
   ? '   writefile = scrprog + "SCREEN.SYS"'
   ? '   @ 22,24 SAY "Now Saving parameters to " + writefile'
   ? '   SAVE ALL LIKE scr* TO &writefile'
   ? '   RESTORE SCREEN FROM temscreen'
   ? '   @ 12,18 SAY  "Finished with Terminal/System Initialization"'
   ? '   IF INKEY(.5) = 32'
   ? '      RETURN'
   ? '   ENDIF'
   SET ALTERNATE OFF
   @ 2,COL() SAY REPLICATE(".",64-COL()) + "FINISHED!"
   DO Fourth

********************

PROCEDURE Fourth

   STORE SPACE(30) TO message1, message2, message3, message4
   @ 15,5 SAY "    Enter Name of Company: " GET message1
   READ
   message1 = TRIM(message1)
   @ 15,5 SAY "Enter Name of Application: " GET message2
   READ
   message2 = TRIM(message2)
   @ 15,5 SAY "     Enter Name of Module: " GET message3
   READ
   message3 = TRIM(message3)
   @ 15,5 SAY "    Enter Designer's Name: " GET message4
   READ
   message4 = TRIM(message4)
   @ 15,5 SAY SPACE(65)
   @ 3,5 SAY "Writing DRAW to alternate file"
   IF LEN(TRIM(system1)) > 2
      endposit = AT(".",system1)-1
      passing = SUBSTR(system1,1,endposit) + "int"
      SET ALTERNATE ON
```

```
    ?
    DO Prochead WITH passing
    temp = pref + "right_"
    ? '    ' + temp + '1 = "' + message2 + '"'
    ? '    ' + temp + '2 = "' + message3 + '"'
    ? '    SAVE ALL LIKE *&pref TO &system1'
    ?
    SET ALTERNATE OFF
ENDIF

SET ALTERNATE ON
DO Prochead WITH "Draw"
?
? '   CLEAR'
? '   RESTORE FROM SCREEN.SYS additive'
? '   IF scrcolor'
? '      SET COLOR TO 7+'
? '   ELSE'
? '      SET COLOR TO 7'
? '   ENDIF'
IF LEN(message1) > 0
   ? '   @ 1,20,7,60 BOX scrframe'
   ? '   @ 3,28 SAY "     GLOBAL SOFTWARE"'
   ? '   @ 4,28 SAY "  in conjunction with"'
   ? '   @ 5,40-LEN("' + message1 + '")/2 SAY ' + '"' +  message1 + '"'
ELSE
   ? '   @ 3,20,7,60 BOX scrframe'
   ? '   @ 5,28 SAY "     GLOBAL SOFTWARE"'
ENDIF
IF LEN(message2) > 0
   ? '       @  9,40-LEN("' + message2 + '")/2 SAY ' + '"' + message2 + '"'
ENDIF
IF LEN(message3) > 0
   ? '       @ 11,40-LEN("' + message3 + '")/2 SAY ' + '"' + message3 + '"'
ENDIF
? '      @ 21,11 SAY "              Designed by Stephen J. Straley
         "'
IF LEN(message4) > 0
   ? '       @ 22,40-LEN("with " + "' + message4 + '")/2 SAY "with " + "' +
         message4 + '"'
ENDIF
?
? '   DO WHILE .T. '
? '      STORE "Today' + CHR(39) + 's Date is " + CDOW(DATE()) + ", " +
         CMON(DATE()) TO prompt'
? '      STORE prompt + " " + STR(DAY(DATE()),2) + ", " +
         STR(YEAR(DATE()),4) TO prompt'
? '      @ 14,40-LEN(prompt)/2 SAY prompt'
? '      @ 18,25 SAY "Is this the Correct Date?  "'
? '      IF .NOT. VERIFY()'
? '         mdate = DATE()'
? '         @ 18, 0 SAY SPACE(80)'
? '         @ 18,28 SAY "Enter in Date:  " GET mdate'
```

```
    ? '          READ'
    ? '          mdate = DTOC(mdate)'
    ? '          RUN DATE &mdate'
    ? '          @ 18,25 SAY SPACE(40)'
    ? '        ELSE'
    ? '          EXIT'
    ? '        ENDIF'
    ?
    ? '     ENDDO'
    SET ALTERNATE OFF
    @ 3,COL() SAY REPLICATE(".",64-COL()) + "FINISHED!"
    DO Fifth

*********************

PROCEDURE Fifth

    SET ALTERNATE ON
    @ 4,5 SAY "Writing FUNCTION FILE to alternate file"
    DO Funchead WITH "Dltrim"
    ?
    ? '    PARAMETER in_string'
    ?
    ? '       RETURN(LTRIM(TRIM(in_string)))'
    ?
    DO Funchead WITH "Endfield"
    ?
    ? '    PARAMETER File'
    ?
    ? '       USE &File'
    ? '       x = 1'
    ? '       y = 1024'
    ? '       z = INT(y/2)'
    ?
    ? '       DO WHILE x <> y'
    ? '          IF LEN(FIELDNAME(z)) = 0'
    ? '             y = z'
    ? '          ELSE'
    ? '             x = z'
    ? '          ENDIF'
    ? '          z = x + int((y-x)/2)'
    ? '          IF LEN(FIELDNAME(z)) > 0 .AND. LEN(FIELDNAME(z+1)) = 0'
    ? '             y = z'
    ? '             x = z'
    ? '          ENDIF'
    ? '       ENDDO'
    ? '       RETURN(y)'
    ?
    DO Funchead WITH "Dayword"
    ?
    ? '    PARAMETER in_date'
    ?
    ? '       in_day = STR(DAY(in_date),2)'
```

```
? '      in_val = VAL(in_day)'
? '      IF in_val > 3 .AND. in_val < 21'
? '         in_day = in_day + "th"'
? '      ELSE'
? '         in_val = VAL(SUBSTR(in_day,2,1))'
? '         in_day = in_day + SUBSTR("thstndrdthththththth", (in_val *
      2)+1,2)'
? '      ENDIF'
? '      RETURN(in_day)'
?
DO Funchead WITH "Expand"
?
? '   PARAMETER in_string'
?
? '      length  = LEN(in_string)'
? '      counter = 1'
? '      out_str = ""'
?
? '      DO WHILE counter <= length'
? '         out_str = out_str + SUBSTR(in_string,counter,1) + " "'
? '         counter = counter + 1'
? '      ENDDO'
? '      RETURN(TRIM(out_str))'
?
DO Funchead WITH "Qwait"
?
? '   SET CONSOLE OFF'
? '   WAIT TO intemp'
? '   SET CONSOLE ON'
? '   IF UPPER(intemp) = "Q"'
? '      RETURN(.T.)'
? '   ENDIF'
? '   RETURN(.F.)'
?
DO Funchead WITH "Chkamt"
?
? '   PARAMETERS figure'
?
? '      final = ""'
? '      IF figure < 0'
? '         final = "Unable to Print"'
? '         RETURN(final)'
? '      ENDIF'
? '      cents = SUBSTR(STR(figure, 15, 2), 14, 2)'
? '      new = INT(figure)'
? '      ********************'
? '      * check for BILLIONS'
? '      ********************'
? '      temp = INT(new/1000000000)'
? '      IF temp > 0'
? '         final = final + GRP_EXPAND(temp) + " Billion "'
? '         new = new - (temp*1000000000)'
? '      ENDIF'
```

```
? '        **********************'
? '        * check for MILLIONS'
? '        **********************'
? '        temp = INT(new/1000000)'
? '        IF temp > 0'
? '           final = final + GRP_EXPAND(temp) + " Million "'
? '           new = new - (temp*1000000)'
? '        ENDIF'
? '        **********************'
? '        * check for THOUSANDS'
? '        **********************'
? '        temp = INT(new/1000)'
? '        IF temp > 0'
? '           final = final + GRP_EXPAND(temp) + " Thousand "'
? '           new = new - (temp*1000)'
? '        ENDIF'
? '        temp = new'
? '        ******************'
? '        * check for UNITS'
? '        ******************'
? '        IF temp > 0'
? '           final = final + GRP_EXPAND(temp)'
? '        ENDIF'
? '        IF SUBSTR(final,1,3) = "One" .AND. LEN(final) = 3'
? '           final = final + " Dollar and " + cents + "/100"'
? '        ELSE'
? '           final = final + " Dollars and " + cents + "/100"'
? '        ENDIF'
? '        RETURN(final)'
?
DO Funchead WITH "Grp_expand"
?
? '    PARAMETER group_val'
?
? '        one_unit  = "One      Two      Three    Four     Five     Six
        Seven    Eight    Nine     Ten      Eleven   Twelve   Thirteen
        Fourteen Fifteen  Sixteen  SeventeenEighteen Nineteen"'
? '        ten_unit  = "Twenty Thirty Forty  Fifty  Sixty  SeventyEighty
        Ninety "'
? '        group_str = ""'
? '        IF group_val > 99'
? '           new1 = INT(group_val/100)'
? '           group_str = group_str + TRIM(SUBSTR(one_unit,(new1*9)-8,9))'
? '           group_val = group_val - (new1 * 100)'
? '           group_str = group_str + " Hundred "'
? '        ENDIF'
? '        IF group_val > 19'
? '           new1 = INT(group_val/10)-1'
? '           group_str = group_str + TRIM(SUBSTR(ten_unit,(new1*7)-6,7))'
? '           new1 = INT(group_val/10)*10'
? '           group_val = group_val - new1'
? '           IF group_val > 0'
? '              group_str = group_str + "-"'
```

```
? '          ENDIF'
? '       ENDIF'
? '       IF group_val > 0'
? '          group_str = group_str + TRIM(SUBSTR(one_unit,(group_val*9)-
       8,9))'
? '       ENDIF'
? '       RETURN(group_str)'
?
DO Funchead WITH "Chktest"
?
? '    in_check = "Y"'
? '    @ 12,10 SAY "Would you like to print a test check? "'
? '    IF VERIFY()'
? '       RETURN(.T.)'
? '    ENDIF'
? '    RETURN(.F.)'
?
DO Funchead WITH "Verify"
?
? '    SET CONSOLE OFF'
? '    STORE "" TO inertemp'
? '    DO WHILE .NOT. inertemp$"YyNn"'
? '       WAIT TO inertemp'
? '    ENDDO'
? '    SET CONSOLE ON'
? '    IF UPPER(inertemp) = "Y"'
? '       ?? "Yes"'
? '       te = INKEY(.25)'
? '       RETURN(.T.)'
? '    ENDIF'
? '    ?? "No "'
? '    te = INKEY(.25)'
? '    RETURN(.F.)'
?
DO Funchead WITH "Prntpage"
?
? '    PARAMETERS normal'
?
? '       IF normal'
? '          @ 63,35 SAY "Page"'
? '          @ PROW(),PCOL()+2 SAY page PICT "@B"'
? '          @ 64,0 SAY ""'
? '       ELSE'
? '          @ 63,65 SAY "Page"'
? '          @ PROW(),PCOL()+2 SAY page PICT "@B"'
? '          @ 64,0 SAY ""'
? '       ENDIF'
? '       RETURN(page)'
?
DO Funchead WITH "Signchng"
?
? '    PARAMETERS amount'
?
```

```
? '      IF amount >= 0'
? '         RETURN (STR(amount))'
? '      ENDIF'
? '      amount = amount * -1'
? '      newfig = "(" + TRIM(LTRIM(STR(amount,15,2))) + ")"'
? '      newfig = SPACE(16 - LEN(newfig)) + newfig'
? '      RETURN(newfig)'
?
DO Funchead WITH "Checking"
?
? '   IF EOF() .OR. BOF()'
? '      @ 22,8 SAY "Cannot continue past end.  Press any key to return to
      the menu."'
? '      te = INKEY(0)'
? '      RETURN(.T.)'
? '   ENDIF'
? '   RETURN(.F.)'
?
DO Funchead WITH "Genpass"
?
? '   PARAMETERS in_string'
?
? '      count = LEN(TRIM(in_string))'
? '      final = 0'
? '      FOR beginning = 1 to (count + 1)'
? '         final = final + ASC(SUBSTR(in_string,beginning,1)) * beginning'
? '      NEXT'
? '      RETURN(final)'
?
DO Funchead WITH "Chkpass"
?
? '   PARAMETERS row, col'
?
? '      IF scrtimes = 0'
? '         RETURN(.T.)'
? '      ENDIF'
? '      IF scrshow'
? '         SET COLOR TO 7/0, 0/7'
? '      ELSE'
? '         SET COLOR TO 7+/0, 0+/0'
? '      ENDIF'
? '      FOR x = 1 to scrtimes'
? '         in_pass = SPACE(15)'
? '         @ row-3,col-5,row+3,col+34 BOX scrframe'
? '         @ row,col SAY "Password --> " GET in_pass PICT "@X"'
? '         READ'
? '         IF LEN(TRIM(in_pass)) <> 0'
? '            temp_count = GENPASS(in_pass)'
? '            IF temp_count = scrpass'
? '               x = 1000'
? '            ENDIF'
? '         ENDIF'
? '      NEXT'
```

```
? '      IF scrcolor'
? '         SET COLOR TO 7+/0, 0/7'
? '      ELSE'
? '         SET COLOR TO 7/0, 0/7'
? '      ENDIF'
? '      IF scrinten'
? '         SET INTEN ON'
? '      ELSE'
? '         SET INTEN OFF'
? '      ENDIF'
? '      RETURN(x > 101)'
?
DO Funchead WITH "Roundit"
?
? '   PARAMETERS in_amount'
?
? '      in_amount = INT(in_amount * 100 + .5) / 100.00'
? '      RETURN(in_amount)'
?
DO Funchead WITH "Printdate"
?
? '   PARAMETERS in_date, whichone'
?
? '   DO CASE'
? '   CASE whichone = 1'
? '      out_str = CMONTH(in_date) + " " + DAYWORD(in_date) + ", " +
      DLTRIM(STR(YEAR(in_date)))'
? '   CASE whichone = 2'
? '      out_str = CDOW(in_date) + ", the " + DAYWORD(in_date) + " of ";
                + CMONTH(in_date) + ", " + dltrim(STR(YEAR(in_date)))'
? '   CASE whichone = 3'
? '      out_str = CDOW(in_date) + ", the " + DAYWORD(in_date) + " of " +
      CMONTH(in_date)'
? '   CASE whichone = 4'
? '      out_str = "The " + DAYWORD(in_date) + " of " + CMONTH(in_date) +
      ", " + DLTRIM(STR(YEAR(in_date)))'
? '   CASE whichone = 5'
? '      out_str = CDOW(in_date) + ", " + CMON(in_date) + " "'
? '      out_str = out_str + STR(DAY(in_date),2) + ", " +
      STR(YEAR(in_date),4)'
? '   OTHERWISE'
? '      out_str = DTOC(in_date)'
? '   ENDCASE'
? '   RETURN(out_str)'
?
DO Prochead WITH "Typeahead"
?
? '   IF !scrtype'
? '      KEYBOARD ""'
? '   ENDIF'
?
DO Prochead WITH "Blink"
?
? '   PARAMETERS temp_row, temp_col'
?
? '      IF scrcolor'
? '         SET COLOR TO W*+'
```

```
   ? '      ELSE'
   ? '         SET COLOR TO W*'
   ? '      ENDIF'
   ? '      @ temp_row, temp_col SAY "Deleted Record"'
   ? '      IF scrcolor'
   ? '         SET COLOR TO W+'
   ? '      ELSE'
   ? '         SET COLOR TO W'
   ? '      ENDIF'
   ?
   @ 4,COL() SAY REPLICATE(".",64-COL()) + "FINISHED!"
   SET ALTERNATE OFF
   DO Sixth

*********************

PROCEDURE Sixth

   SET ALTERNATE ON
   @ 5,5 SAY "Writing SETUP to alternate file"
   ?
   DO Prochead WITH "Setup"
   ?
   ? '    SET FUNCTION  2 TO CHR(22)'
   ? '    SET FUNCTION  3 TO CHR(1)'
   ? '    SET FUNCTION  4 TO CHR(6)'
   ? '    SET FUNCTION  5 TO CHR(3)'
   ? '    SET FUNCTION  6 TO CHR(5)'
   ? '    SET FUNCTION  8 TO CHR(23)'
   ? '    SET FUNCTION  7 TO CHR(20)'
   ? '    SET FUNCTION  9 TO CHR(25)'
   ? '    SET FUNCTION 10 TO CHR(21)'
   ? '    IF scrinten'
   ? '       SET INTENS on'
   ? '    ELSE'
   ? '       SET INTENS off'
   ? '    ENDIF'
   ? '    IF scrdelim'
   ? '       SET DELIM TO "&scrdelimto"'
   ? '       SET DELIM on'
   ? '    ELSE'
   ? '       SET DELIM off'
   ? '    ENDIF'
   ? '    IF scrconfirm'
   ? '       SET CONFIRM on'
   ? '    ELSE'
   ? '       SET CONFIRM off'
   ? '    ENDIF'
   ? '    IF scrbell'
   ? '       SET BELL on'
   ? '    ELSE'
   ? '       SET BELL off'
   ? '    ENDIF'
```

```
   ? '   IF scrcolor'
   ? '      SET COLOR TO 7+'
   ? '   ELSE'
   ? '      SET COLOR TO 7'
   ? '   ENDIF'
   SET ALTERNATE OFF
   @ 5,COL() SAY REPLICATE(".",64-COL()) + "FINISHED!"
   DO Seventh

********************

PROCEDURE Seventh

   @ 6,5 SAY "Writing REDRAW to alternate file"
   SET ALTERNATE ON
   ?
   DO Prochead WITH "Redraw"
   ?
   ? '   PARAMETERS center'
   ?
   ? '      @ 1,0 say scrleft_1'
   ? '      @ 2,0 say scrleft_2'
   IF LEN(TRIM(system1)) > 2
      ? '      RESTORE FROM &system1. ADDITIVE'
      ? '      @ 1,80-LEN(' + pref + 'right_1) SAY ' + pref + 'right_1'
      ? '      @ 2,80-LEN(' + pref + 'right_2) SAY ' + pref + 'right_2'
   ELSE
      ? '      @ 1,80-LEN("Generic Application") SAY "Generic Application"'
      ? '      @ 2,80-LEN("Version 1.00") SAY "Version 1.00"'
      ? '      @ 4,40-LEN(center)/2 SAY center'
   ENDIF
   SET ALTERNATE OFF
   @ 6,COL() SAY REPLICATE(".",64-COL()) + "FINISHED!"
   DO Eight

********************

PROCEDURE Eight

   @ 7,5 SAY "Writing WHICHWAY to alternate file"
   SET ALTERNATE ON
   ?
   DO Prochead WITH "Whichway"
   ?
   ? '   PARAMETERS file, way, d, c'
   ?
   ? '      way = 1'
   ? '      @ d,c,d + 5, c + 40 BOX scrframe'
   ? '      @ d + 1, c + 10 PROMPT " 1> Print to Screen "'
   ? '      @ d + 2, c + 10 PROMPT " 2> Print to Printer "'
   ? '      @ d + 3, c + 10 PROMPT " 3> Print to File "'
   ? '      @ d + 4, c + 10 SAY    "    ESC to RETURN"'
   ? '      MENU TO way'
```

```
    ? '      IF way = 3'
    ? '         FOR fortemp = d + 1 TO d + 4'
    ? '            @ fortemp, c + 5 SAY SPACE(30)'
    ? '         NEXT'
    ? '         @ d + 1, c + 10 SAY "Enter File Name: "'
    ? '         @ d + 3, c + 10 SAY "-> " GET file PICT "@X"'
    ? '         READ'
    ? '         IF LEN(TRIM(file)) = 0'
    ? '            way = 0'
    ? '         ENDIF'
    ? '         IF AT(".",file) = 0'
    ? '            file = TRIM(SUBSTR(file,1,8)) + ".TXT"'
    ? '         ENDIF'
    ? '      ENDIF'
    @ 7,COL() SAY REPLICATE(".",64-COL()) + "FINISHED!"
    SET ALTERNATE OFF
    DO Nine

*********************

PROCEDURE Nine

    SET SCOREBOARD OFF
    SAVE SCREEN
    CLEAR
    DECLARE database[15]
    FOR x = 1 TO 15
       temp = LTRIM(STR(x))
       DECLARE name&temp[99]
       DECLARE type&temp[99]
       DECLARE len&temp[99]
       DECLARE dec&temp[99]
       DECLARE indx&temp[7]
    NEXT
    @ 0,0,23,79 BOX SUBSTR(scrframe,1,8)
    @ 0,30 SAY " Create Databases "
    FOR x = 1 TO 15
       STORE SPACE(12) TO database[x]
       @ 2,3 SAY "Enter Database Name: " GET database[x] PICT "@!"
       READ
       IF LEN(TRIM(database[x])) <> 0
          temp = LTRIM(STR(x))
          trow = 8
          tcol = 0
          FOR y = 1 TO 99
             STORE SPACE(10) TO name&temp[y]
             STORE SPACE(1) TO type&temp[y]
             STORE 0 TO len&temp[y], dec&temp[y]
             @ 3,3 SAY "   Enter Field Name: " GET name&temp[y] PICT "@!"
             @ 4,3 SAY "                Type: " GET type&temp[y] PICT "!"
             VALID(type&temp[y]$"NCLDM ")
             @ 5,3 SAY "              Length: " GET len&temp[y] PICT "####" RANGE
             0, 3000
```

```
            @ 6,3 SAY "           Decimals: " GET dec&temp[y] PICT "##" RANGE
            0,15
            READ
            IF LEN(TRIM(name&temp[y])) = 0
               y = 100
            ELSE
               DO CASE
               CASE type&temp[y] = "D"
                  len&temp[y] = 8
                  dec&temp[y] = 0
               CASE type&temp[y] = "L"
                  len&temp[y] = 1
                  dec&temp[y] = 0
               CASE type&temp[y] = "M"
                  len&temp[y] = 10
                  dec&temp[y] = 0
               CASE type&temp[y] = "N"
                  IF len&temp[y] > 15
                     len&temp[y] = 15
                  ENDIF
               OTHERWISE
                  dec&temp[y] = 0
               ENDCASE
               IF trow > 22
                  trow = 8
                  FOR steve = 8 TO 22
                     @ steve,3 SAY SPACE(47)
                  NEXT
               ENDIF
               @ trow,5 SAY name&temp[y]
               @ trow,COL() + 2 SAY type&temp[y]
               @ trow,COL() + 2 SAY len&temp[y]
               @ trow,COL() + 2 SAY dec&temp[y]
               trow = trow + 1
            ENDIF
         NEXT
         FOR steve = 1 TO 22
            @ steve, 3 SAY SPACE(47)
         NEXT
         @ x, 52 SAY LTRIM(STR(x)) + "-> "
         @ x, COL() SAY database[x]
      ELSE
         x = 17
      ENDIF
   NEXT
   DO Ten

*********************

PROCEDURE Ten

   RESTORE SCREEN
   @ 8,5 SAY "Writing " + pref + "init to alternate file"
```

```
SET ALTERNATE ON
DO Prochead WITH pref + "init"
?
? '   DO ' + pref + 'inthd'
FOR x = 1 TO 15
   IF LEN(TRIM(database[x])) <> 0
      tempstr = pref + "init" + LTRIM(STR(x))
      ? '   DO ' + tempstr
   ELSE
      x = 16
   ENDIF
NEXT
?
? '   @ 12, 6 SAY "All Files/Indexes have been properly created.   Any Key
      to Continue..."'
? '   IF 0 = INKEY(0)'
? '   ENDIF'
? '   CLOSE DATABASES'
? '   @ 12, 2 SAY SPACE(70)'
SET ALTERNATE OFF
SET COLOR TO W*+
SAVE SCREEN
@ 0,0,20,79 BOX SUBSTR(scrframe,1,8)
@ 19,15 SAY "Now writing memory file for Report Generator..."
FOR x = 1 TO 15
   @ 21,00 CLEAR
   writeout = IF(LEN(LTRIM(STR(x))) = 1, "0" + LTRIM(STR(x)),
        LTRIM(STR(x)))
   name = "DB" + writeout
   &name = database[x]
   temp = LTRIM(STR(x))
   @ 21,24 SAY "Now working on data fie ..... " + temp
   FOR y = 1 TO 99
      newout = IF(LEN(LTRIM(STR(y))) = 1, "0" + LTRIM(STR(y)),
         LTRIM(STR(y)))
      fame = "FD" + newout
      tame = "TY" + newout
      lame = "LE" + newout
      dame = "DE" + newout
      &fame = name&temp[y]
      &tame = type&temp[y]
      &lame = len&temp[y]
      &dame = dec&temp[y]
      @ 22,28 SAY "Now working on files .... " + newout
      IF EMPTY(name&temp[y+1])
         y = 100
      ENDIF
   NEXT
   SAVE ALL LIKE FD?? TO Name&temp
   SAVE ALL LIKE TY?? TO Type&temp
   SAVE ALL LIKE LE?? TO Leng&temp
   SAVE ALL LIKE DE?? TO Deci&temp
   RELEASE ALL LIKE FD??
```

```
        RELEASE ALL LIKE TY??
        RELEASE ALL LIKE LE??
        RELEASE ALL LIKE DE??
        IF EMPTY(database[x+1])
           x = 16
        ENDIF
     NEXT
     SAVE ALL LIKE DB?? TO Datafile
     @ 20,00 CLEAR
     SET COLOR TO 7+
     RESTORE SCREEN
     @ 8,COL() SAY REPLICATE(".",64-COL()) + "FINISHED!"
     DO Eleven
     * End of Gencode1
```

Now create a second CLiP file, GEN2.CLP, which will contain the following one line:

```
Gencode2
```

```
*********************
* Name          GENCODE2.prg
* Date          April 4, 1988
* Notice        Copyright 1988, Stephen J. Straley & Associates
* Compile       Cliper Gencode -m
* Release       Autumn 86 or later
* Link          Tlink Gencode1 Gencode2, Gencode,,Extend+Clipper
* Note          The following source is the other half of the code
*               that creates the basic front end of an application.
*               The code generated can then be modified to the
*               needs of the client or user.
*
*               The following is a listing of the procedures and their
*               purpose as they relate to the code they generate.
*
*               Eleven:    This writes the code for the indexing (if
*                          any) routines and their proper prompts.
*                          It also maintains the indexing or file values
*                          for the code that writes the RESORT procedure.
*               Twelve:    Writes the Initial Message and Header for the
*                          initialization procedure.
*             Thirteen:    Writes the code for user-created on-
*                          line HELP.   This also can be used by the
*                          developer after the application has been
*                          designed to write the HELP that will be provided
*                          with the application.
*             Fourteen:    Writes the REINITIALIZATION procedure.
*              Fifteen:    Writes the code to allow the user
*                          of the application to change the subdirectory
*                          he or she is currently working in.   This option
*                          allows an application to be used for multiple
*                          companies.
*              Sixteen:    Writes the code for a Password initialization
```

```
*                         code.
*             Seventeen:  Writes the procedures that
*                         allow the developer to have an application
*                         change the computer's internal system date.
*              Eighteen:  Writes the procedure that allows a user to UNMARK
*                         the records tagged for deletion.  The file names
*                         used are those previously entered when creating
*                         the system initially.
*              Nineteen:  Similar to the procedure for UNMARK, REMOVE actually
*                         removes those records the user has tagged to be
*                         deleted.  Again, the file names are automatically
*                         used from a previous section.
*                Twenty:  Writes the RESORT procedure that
*                         will rebuild the indexes and prompt the user on
*                         the screen as the process is underway.
*********************

PROCEDURE Eleven

   parc_strng = ""
   @ 9,5 SAY "Writing Initializing Procedures to alternate"
   screencnt = 6
   SET ALTERNATE ON
   DECLARE indexkey[105], indexmes[105], indexfil[105]
   FOR x = 1 TO 15
      temp = LTRIM(STR(x))
      IF !EMPTY(database[x])
         tempstr = pref + "init" + temp
         DO Prochead WITH tempstr
         ?
         ? '   SELECT 9'
         IF screencnt >= 22
            screencnt = 5
            ? '   5,0,23,79 BOX scrframe'
         ENDIF
         ? '   @ ' + LTRIM(STR(screencnt)) + ', 5 SAY "Initializing ' +
            TRIM(database[x]) + ' File' + '"'
         ? '   CREATE Template'
         ? '   USE Template'
         FOR y = 1 TO 99
            IF !EMPTY(name&temp[y])
               ?  '   APPEND BLANK'
               ?  '   REPLACE field_name WITH "' + TRIM(name&temp[y]) + '", '
               ?? ' field_type WITH "' + type&temp[y] + '", '
               ?? ' field_len WITH ' + LTRIM(STR(len&temp[y])) + ', '
               ?? ' field_dec WITH ' + LTRIM(STR(dec&temp[y]))
            ELSE
               y = 100
            ENDIF
         NEXT
         ? '   USE'
         ? '   CREATE ' + CHR(38) + 'scrdata.' + TRIM(database[x]) + ' FROM
            Template'
```

```
      ? '   USE ' + CHR(38) + 'scrdata.' + TRIM(database[x])
      ? '   ERASE Template'
      ? '   @ ' + LTRIM(STR(screencnt)) + ', 5 SAY SPACE(70)'
      FOR z = 1 TO 7
         qaz = LTRIM(STR(x))
         STORE SPACE(20) TO indexmes[MATRIX1(x,z)]
         @ 15,2 SAY "Database: " + TRIM(database[x]) + " / " +
         LTRIM(STR(z)) + " Index-> "
         @ 17,COL()-15 SAY "Enter Prompt Message: " GET index-
         mes[MATRIX(x,z)]
         READ
         IF !EMPTY(indexmes[MATRIX1(x,z)])
            STORE SPACE(45) TO key
            @ 19,5 SAY "Enter Index Expression: " GET key
         VALID(!EMPTY(key))
            READ
            indexkey[MATRIX1(x,z)] = key
            screencnt = screencnt + 1
            ? '   @ ' + LTRIM(STR(screencnt)) + ', 5 SAY "Creating ';
                  + TRIM(indexkey[MATRIX1(x,z)]) + ' Index"'
            IF "."$database[x]
               posit = AT(".",database[x]) - 1
               tempname = IF(posit < 6, SUBSTR(database[x],1,posit), SUB-
         STR(database[x],1,6))
            ELSE
               tempname = TRIM(database[x])
            ENDIF


            DO CASE
            CASE AT(".",database[x]) = 0
               tempextn = ".NTX"
            CASE ".DBF"$database[x]
               tempextn = ".NTX"
            OTHERWISE
               tempextn = ".DAT"
            ENDCASE
            indexfil[MATRIX1(x,z)] = tempname + "_" + LTRIM(STR(z)) +
         tempextn
            ? '   temp = scrdata' + ' + "' + indexfil[MATRIX1(x,z)] + '"'
            ? '   INDEX ON ' + TRIM(key) + ' TO ' + CHR(38) + 'temp'
            ? '   @ ' + LTRIM(STR(screencnt) ) + ', 2 SAY SPACE(70)'
         ELSE
            z = 8
         ENDIF
         @ 15,2 SAY SPACE(75)
         @ 17,2 SAY SPACE(75)
         @ 19,2 SAY SPACE(75)
      NEXT
      screencnt = screencnt + 1
   ELSE
      x = 16
   ENDIF
```

```
    NEXT
    SET ALTERNATE OFF
    @ 9,5 SAY "Writing Indexing Files" + REPLICATE(".",37) + "FINISHED!"
    DO Twelve

********************

PROCEDURE Twelve

    SET ALTERNATE ON
    @ 10,5 SAY "Writing Inthead Procedure to alternate file"
    ?
    DO Prochead WITH pref + "inthd"
    ?
    ? '    RESTORE FROM Screen.sys ADDITIVE'
    ? '    DO Setup'
    ? '    CLEAR'
    ? '    DO Redraw WITH "Initializing Databases"'
    ? '    @ 5,0,23,79 BOX SUBSTR(scrframe,1,8)'
    ?
    SET ALTERNATE OFF
    @ 10,COL() SAY REPLICATE(".",64-COL()) + "FINISHED!"
    DO Thirteen

********************

PROCEDURE Thirteen

    SET ALTERNATE ON
    @ 11,5 SAY "Writing HELP to alternate file"
    DO Prochead WITH "Help"
    ?
    ? '    PARAMETERS p,l,v'
    ?
    ? '    SAVE SCREEN'
    ? '    SET SCOREBOARD OFF'
    ? '    p = p + SPACE(10 - LEN(p))'
    ? '    v = v + SPACE(10 - LEN(v))'
    ? '    IF .NOT. FILE("HELP.DBF")'
    ? '       @ 00,10,03,70 BOX scrframe'
    ? '       @ 01,11 SAY "There is no HELP file available.    Would you like a
           help "'
    ? '       @ 02,27 SAY "file to be generated?"'
    ? '       IF .NOT. VERIFY()'
    ? '          RESTORE SCREEN'
    ? '          SET KEY 28 TO Help'
    ? '          RETURN'
    ? '       ENDIF'
    ? '       goback = SELECT()'
    ? '       DO Dohelp'
    ? '       tempgo = STR(goback)'
    ? '       SELECT &tempgo'
    ? '    ENDIF'
```

```
? '    goback = SELECT()'
? '    SELECT 9'
? '    USE Help INDEX Help'
? '    SET FILTER TO search_p = p .AND. search_v = v'
? '    LOCATE FOR search_l = l'
? '    IF FOUND()'
frame  = CHR(201) + CHR(205) + CHR(187) + CHR(186) + CHR(188) + ;
         CHR(205) + CHR(200) + CHR(186) + CHR(32)
? '       @ top,left,bottom,right BOX "&frame."'
? ' MEMOEDIT(helpscr,top+1,left+1,bottom-1,right-1,.F.)'
? ' * for the Summer 87 Release, change the above line to this '
? ' MEMOEDIT(helpscr,top+1,left+1,bottom-1,right-1,.F.,.F.)'
? '       @ bottom-1,left+1 SAY "Any Key to Continue..."'
? '    ELSE'
? '       @ 00,10,03,70 BOX scrframe'
? '       @ 01,11 SAY "There is no HELP for this section.  Would you like
         to make"'
? '       @ 02,28 SAY "a HELP screen for this? "'
? '       IF .NOT. VERIFY()'
? '          RESTORE SCREEN'
? '          SET KEY 28 TO Help'
? '          RETURN'
? '       ENDIF'
? '       APPEND BLANK'
? '       REPLACE search_p WITH p, search_l WITH l, search_v WITH v'
? '       STORE SPACE(4000) TO in_help'
? '       STORE 0 TO temp_top, temp_left, temp_bot, temp_right'
? '       DO WHILE .T.'
? '          @ 00,10,03,70 BOX scrframe'
? '          @ 01,20 SAY "Position cursor with arrow for TOP, LEFT
         corner."'
? '          cursor = 0'
? '          @ 12,40 SAY ""'
? '          DO WHILE.T.'
? '             cursor = INKEY(0)'
? '             DO CASE'
? '             CASE cursor = 5'
? '                @ ROW() - 1, COL() SAY ""'
? '             CASE cursor = 4'
? '                @ ROW(), COL() + 1 SAY ""'
? '             CASE cursor = 19'
? '                @ ROW(),COL() - 1 SAY ""'
? '             CASE cursor = 24'
? '                @ ROW() + 1,COL() SAY ""'
? '             CASE cursor = 13 .OR. cursor = 27'
? '                EXIT'
? '             ENDCASE'
? '          ENDDO'
? '          STORE ROW() TO temp_top'
? '          STORE COL() - 1 TO temp_left'
? '          @ 00,10,03,70 BOX scrframe'
? '          @ 01,20 SAY "Position cursor with arrow for BOTTOM, RIGHT
         corner."'
```

```
? '           cursor = 0'
? '           @ 12,40 SAY ""'
? '           DO WHILE.T.'
? '              cursor = INKEY(0)'
? '              DO CASE'
? '              CASE cursor = 5'
? '                 @ ROW() - 1, COL() SAY ""'
? '              CASE cursor = 4'
? '                 @ ROW(), COL() + 1 SAY ""'
? '              CASE cursor = 19'
? '                 @ ROW(),COL() - 1 SAY ""'
? '              CASE cursor = 24'
? '                 @ ROW() + 1,COL() SAY ""'
? '              CASE cursor = 13 .OR. cursor = 27'
? '                 EXIT'
? '              ENDCASE'
? '           ENDDO'
? '           STORE ROW() TO temp_bot'
? '           STORE COL() TO temp_right'
? '           SAVE SCREEN TO in_help'
? '           DO Temphelp'
? '           @ 00,10,03,70 BOX scrframe'
? '           @ 02,25 SAY "Is this what you wanted?  "'
? '           IF .NOT. VERIFY()'
? '              RESTORE SCREEN FROM in_help'
? '              LOOP'
? '           ENDIF'
? '           REPLACE top WITH temp_top, bottom WITH temp_bot, left WITH
      temp_left, right WITH temp_right'
? '           EXIT'
? '        ENDDO'
? '        DO WHILE .T.'
? '           @ top,left,bottom,right BOX "&frame."'
? '           REPLACE helpscr WITH MEMOEDIT(helpscr,top+1,left+1,bottom-
      1,right-1,.T.)'
? '           @ top,left,bottom,right BOX "&frame."'
? ' MEMOEDIT(helpscr,top+1,left+1,bottom-1,right-1,.F.)'
? ' * For the Summer 87 release, change the'
? ' * above line to this '
? ' * MEMOEDIT(helpscr,top+1,left+1,bottom-1,right-1,.F.,.F.)'
? '           @ bottom-1,left+1 SAY "IS THIS CORRECT?   "'
? '           IF .NOT. VERIFY()'
? '              LOOP'
? '           ENDIF'
? '           EXIT'
? '        ENDDO'
? '        @ bottom-1,left+1 SAY "Press Any key to Continue...."'
? '     ENDIF'
? '     INKEY(0)'
? '     RESTORE SCREEN'
? '     SET KEY 28 TO Help'
? '     tempgo = STR(goback)'
? '     SELECT &tempgo'
```

```
? '    RETURN'
?
? '*********************'
?
? 'PROCEDURE Dohelp'
?
? '   SELECT 9'
? '   CREATE Temp'
? '   USE Temp'
? '   APPEND BLANK'
? '   REPLACE field_name WITH "SEARCH_P", field_type WITH "C", field_len
        WITH 10'
? '   APPEND BLANK'
? '   REPLACE field_name WITH "SEARCH_V", field_type WITH "C", field_len
        WITH 10'
? '   APPEND BLANK'
? '   REPLACE field_name WITH "SEARCH_L", field_type WITH "N", field_len
        WITH 4'
? '   APPEND BLANK'
? '   REPLACE field_name WITH "TOP", field_type WITH "N", field_len WITH 2'
? '   APPEND BLANK'
? '   REPLACE field_name WITH "LEFT", field_type WITH "N", field_len WITH
        2'
? '   APPEND BLANK'
? '   REPLACE field_name WITH "BOTTOM", field_type WITH "N", field_len WITH
        2'
? '   APPEND BLANK'
? '   REPLACE field_name WITH "RIGHT", field_type WITH "N", field_len WITH
        2'
? '   APPEND BLANK'
? '   REPLACE field_name WITH "HELPSCR", field_type WITH "M", field_len
        WITH 10'
? '   USE'
? '   CREATE Help FROM Temp'
? '   ERASE Temp'
? '   USE Help'
? '   INDEX ON search_p + search_v TO Help'
?
? '*********************'
?
? 'PROCEDURE Temphelp'
?
? '   IF scrcolor'
? '      SET COLOR TO W*+'
? '   ELSE'
? '      SET COLOR TO W+'
? '   ENDIF'
? '   @ temp_top, temp_left, temp_bot, temp_right BOX SUBSTR(scrframe,1,8)'
? '   IF scrcolor'
? '      SET COLOR TO 7+'
? '   ELSE'
? '      SET COLOR TO 7'
? '   ENDIF'
```

```
    SET ALTERNATE OFF
    @ 11,COL() SAY REPLICATE(".",64-COL()) + "FINISHED!"
    DO Fourteen

********************

PROCEDURE Fourteen

    SET ALTERNATE ON
    @ 13,5 SAY "Writing Re-initializing Procedure to alternate file"
    DO Prochead WITH "Reinitx"
    ?
    ? '    @ 19,25,23,65 BOX scrframe'
    ? '    tempscr = SPACE(4000)'
    ? '    SAVE SCREEN TO tempscr'
    ? '    @ 20,29 SAY " Data Files are present.  If you"'
    ? '    @ 21,29 SAY "continue, all data will be lost."'
    ? '    @ 22,29 SAY "Do you want to continue? "'
    ? '    IF .NOT. VERIFY()'
    ? '       RETURN'
    ? '    ENDIF'
    ? '    RESTORE SCREEN FROM tempscr'
    ? '    @ 20,29 SAY "Would you like to re-Create"'
    ? '    @ 21,29 SAY "ALL of the databases?"'
    ? '    IF VERIFY()'
    ? '       DO ' + pref + 'init'
    ? '       RETURN'
    ? '    ENDIF'
    scan = 1
    DO WHILE LEN(TRIM(database[scan])) <> 0
       ? '    RESTORE SCREEN FROM tempscr'
       ? '    @ 20,28 SAY "Do you wish to re-create the"'
       ? '    @ 21,40-LEN("' + TRIM(database[scan]) + '")/2 SAY "' +
              TRIM(database[scan]) + CHR(34)
       ? '    @ 22,28 SAY "Database? (Yes / No)"'
       ? '    IF VERIFY()'
       ? '       DO ' + pref + 'inthd'
       ? '       DO ' + pref + 'init' + LTRIM(STR(scan))
       ? '    ENDIF'
       scan = scan + 1
    ENDDO
    ? '    CLOSE DATABASES'
    SET ALTERNATE OFF
    @ 13,COL() SAY REPLICATE(".",64-COL()) + "FINISHED!"
    DO Fifteen

********************

PROCEDURE Fifteen

    SET ALTERNATE ON
    @ 14,5 SAY "Writing Change Default Procedure to alternate file"
    DO Prochead WITH "Default"
```

```
   ? '   @ 19,25,23,65 BOX scrframe'
   ? '   whichone = 1'
   ? '   @ 20,32 PROMPT " 1>  Change Directory "'
   ? '   @ 21,32 PROMPT " 2>  Change System Defaults "'
   ? '   @ 22,32 SAY    "    ESC to RETURN TO MENU"'
   ? '   MENU TO whichone'
   ? '   DO CASE'
   ? '   CASE whichone = 0'
   ? '      RETURN'
   ? '   CASE whichone = 2'
   ? '      DO Scrinit'
   ? '   OTHERWISE'
   ? '      @ 20,26,22,64 BOX SPACE(9)'
   ? '      indir = SPACE(30)'
   ? '      @ 20,28 SAY "Enter in new PATH..."'
   ? '      @ 21,28 SAY "->" GET indir PICT "XXXXXXXXXXXXXXXXXXXXXXXXXXXXXX"'
   ? '      READ'
   ? '      DO WHILE .NOT. FILE(scrprog + "\COMMAND.COM")'
   ? '         @ 20,26,22,64 BOX SPACE(9)'
   ? '         @ 20,28 SAY "Please insert DOS disk in drive :"  + SUB-
      STR(scrprog,1,1)'
   ? '         @ 21,28 SAY "Any key or Q to Quit ......."'
   ? '         IF QWAIT()'
   ? '            RETURN'
   ? '         ENDIF'
   ? '      ENDDO'
   ? '      indir = "CD " + TRIM(indir)'
   ? '      RUN &indir'
   ? '      DO Beginit'
   ? '      RETURN'
   ? '   ENDCASE'
   SET ALTERNATE OFF
   @ 14,COL() SAY REPLICATE(".",64-COL()) + "FINISHED!"
   DO Sixteen

********************

PROCEDURE Sixteen

   SET ALTERNATE ON
   @ 15,5 SAY "Writing Password Procedure to alternate file"
   DO Prochead WITH "Password"
   ? '   @ 19,25,23,65 BOX scrframe'
   ? '   temp = SPACE(15)'
   ? '   @ 20,28 SAY "Leave Blank to keep old Password"'
   ? '   @ 21,28 SAY "Enter New Password: " GET temp PICT "XXXXXXXXXXXXXXX"'
   ? '   READ'
   ? '   IF LEN(TRIM(tem)) <> 0'
   ? '      scrpass = GENPASS(temp)'
   ? '   ENDIF'
   ? '   @ 20,26,22,64 BOX SPACE(9)'
   ? '   @ 21,27 SAY "Enter Times for Password: " GET scrtimes PICT "##"'
   ? '   READ'
```

```
    ? '   SET DEFAULT TO ' + CHR(38) + 'scrprog'
    ? '   SAVE ALL LIKE scr* TO Screen.sys'
    ? '   SET DEFAULT TO ' + CHR(38) + 'scrdata'
    SET ALTERNATE OFF
    @ 15,COL() SAY REPLICATE(".",64-COL()) + "FINISHED!"
    DO Seventeen

********************

PROCEDURE Seventeen

    SET ALTERNATE ON
    @ 16,5 SAY "Writing Change System Date Procedure to alternate file"
    DO Prochead WITH "Olddate"
    ? '   @ 19,25,23,65 BOX scrframe'
    ? '   @ 20,29 SAY "Changing System Date"'
    ? '   STORE "Today'+ CHR(39) + 's Date is " + CDOW(DATE()) + ", " +
             CMON(DATE()) to prompt'
    ? '   STORE prompt + " " + STR(DAY(DATE()),2) + ", " + STR(YEAR(DATE()),4)
             to prompt'
    ? '   @ 21,40-LEN(prompt)/2 SAY prompt'
    ? '   mdate = DATE()'
    ? '   @ 22,40-LEN("Enter in Date:        ")/2 SAY "Enter in Date:  " GET
             mdate'
    ? '   READ'
    ? '   IF FILE(scrprog + "COMMAND.COM")'
    ? '      mdate = DTOC(mdate)'
    ? '      RUN DATE ' + CHR(38) + 'mdate'
    ? '   ENDIF'
    SET ALTERNATE OFF
    @ 16,COL() SAY REPLICATE(".",64-COL()) + "FINISHED!"
    DO Eighteen

********************

PROCEDURE Eighteen

    SET ALTERNATE ON
    @ 17,5 SAY "Writing Unmark Data Procedure to alternate file"
    DO Prochead WITH "Unmark"
    ? '   @ 19,25,23,65 BOX scrframe'
    ? '   tempscr = SPACE(4000)'
    ? '   SAVE SCREEN TO tempscr'
    ? '   updated = .F.'
    scan = 1
    DO WHILE LEN(TRIM(database[scan])) <> 0
       ? '   RESTORE SCREEN FROM tempscr'
       ? '   @ 20,27 SAY "Do you wish to UNMARK data in the "'
       ? '   @ 21,27 SAY "' + TRIM(database[scan]) + ' file? "'
       ? '   IF VERIFY()'
       ? '      SELECT 1'
       ? '      USE ' + CHR(38) + 'scrdata.' + TRIM(database[scan])
       ? '      RECALL ALL'
```

```
      ? '      updated = .T.'
      ? '    ENDIF'
      scan = scan + 1
   ENDDO
   ? '  RESTORE SCREEN FROM tempscr'
   ? '  IF updated'
   ? '     @ 21,27 SAY "Process Complete.  Any Key to Resort"'
   ? '     INKEY(0)'
   ? '     DO Resort'
   ? '  ELSE'
   ? '     @ 21,27 SAY "Process Complete.  Any Key to Continue"'
   ? '     INKEY(0)'
   ? '  ENDIF'
   SET ALTERNATE OFF
   @ 17,COL() SAY REPLICATE(".",64-COL()) + "FINISHED!"
   DO Nineteen

********************

PROCEDURE Nineteen

   SET ALTERNATE ON
   @ 18,5 SAY "Writing Remove Marked Data Procedure to file"
   DO Prochead WITH "Removeit"
   ? '   @ 19,25,23,65 BOX scrframe'
   ? '   tempscr = SPACE(4000)'
   ? '   SAVE SCREEN TO tempscr'
   ? '   updated = .F.'
   scan = 1
   DO WHILE LEN(TRIM(database[scan])) <> 0
      ? '   RESTORE SCREEN FROM tempscr'
      ? '   @ 20,27 SAY "Do you wish to REMOVE data in the "'
      ? '   @ 21,27 SAY "' + TRIM(database[scan]) + ' file? "'
      ? '   IF VERIFY()'
      ? '      SELECT 1'
      ? '      USE ' + CHR(38) + 'scrdata.' + TRIM(database[scan])
      ? '      PACK'
      ? '      updated = .T.'
      ? '   ENDIF'
      scan = scan + 1
   ENDDO
   ? '  RESTORE SCREEN FROM tempscr'
   ? '  IF updated'
   ? '     @ 21,27 SAY "Process Complete.  Any Key to Resort"'
   ? '     INKEY(0)'
   ? '     DO Resort'
   ? '  ELSE'
   ? '     @ 21,27 SAY "Process Complete.  Any Key to Continue"'
   ? '     INKEY(0)'
   ? '  ENDIF'
   SET ALTERNATE OFF
   @ 18,COL() SAY REPLICATE(".",64-COL()) + "FINISHED!"
   SAVE TO Prefix ALL LIKE pref
```

```
    DO Twenty

 *********************

 PROCEDURE Twenty

    SET ALTERNATE ON
    @ 19, 5 SAY "Writing Resort Procedure to File"
    DO Prochead WITH "Resort"
    ?
    ? 'SAVE SCREEN'
    ? 'DO Redraw WITH "Re-sorting Data Files"'
    ? '@ 5,0,23,79 BOX scrframe'
    ? 'SELECT 1'
    beg_row = 6
    scan = UNPARSE(parc_strng)
    DO WHILE !EMPTY(scan)

       ? 'USE ' + CHR(38) + 'scrdata.' + scan
       scan = UNPARSE(parc_strng)
       ? '@ &beg_row.,5 SAY "' + scan + '"'
       scan = UNPARSE(parc_strng)
       ? 'INDEX ON ' + scan + 'TO ' + CHR(38) + 'scrdata."'
       scan = UNPARSE(parc_strng)
       ?? scan + '"'
       ? '@ &beg_row.,5 SAY SPACE(70)'
       beg_row = beg_row + 1
       scan = UNPARSE(parc_strng)


    ENDDO
    ? '@ &beg_row,8 SAY "All Files have been RE-indexed.  Press Any Key to Con-
            tinue..."'
    ? 'INKEY(0)'
    ? 'RESTORE SCREEN'
    CLOSE ALTERNATE
    @ 19,5 SAY REPLICATE(".",69-COL()) + "FINISHED!"
    @ 23,20 SAY "Procedure All Finished.  Output to &file"
    QUIT

*********************        && This is an internal procedure

PROCEDURE Prochead

    PARAMETERS a

    ?
    ? "**********************"
    ?
    ? "PROCEDURE " + a
    ?

*********************        && This is an internal procedure
```

```
PROCEDURE Funchead

   PARAMETERS a

   ?
   ? "**********************"
   ?
   ? "FUNCTION " + a
   ?

****************************

FUNCTION VERIFY            && This is an internal function

   SET CONSOLE off
   WAIT TO inertemp
   SET CONSOLE on
   IF UPPER(inertemp) = "Y"
      ?? "Yes"
      te = INKEY(.25)
      RETURN(.T.)
   ENDIF
   ?? "No "
   INKEY(.25)
   RETURN(.F.)

*********************

FUNCTION Unparse            && This is an internal function

   PARAMETERS string_in

   stop = AT("~",string_in)
   IF stop = 0
      RETURN("")
   ENDIF
   parc_strng = SUBSTR(parc_strng,stop+1)
   RETURN(SUBSTR(parc_strng,1,stop-1))

*********************

FUNCTION Up_down            && This is an internal function

   PARAMETERS a

   front = UPPER(SUBSTR(a,1,1))
   back  = LOWER(SUBSTR(a,2))

   RETURN(front_back)

*********************
```

```
FUNCTION Matrix1

   PARAMETERS left_one, right_one

   * This is for 15 databases and 7 indexes, so the array will be for
   * 105 elements.   The first seven are for the first database; the second
   * seven are for the second, and so on...

   * 1,1 = 1
   * 2,1 = 8
   * 3,1 = 15
   * 1,2 = 2
   * 2,2 = 9
   * 1,3 = 3
   * 2,3 = 10

   first_stop = (left_one * 7) - 7
   RETURN(first_stop + right_one)
 * End of GENCODE2.prg
```

COMPILING AND LINKING THE GENCODE FILES

The batch file list below compiles and links the two files together. This assumes that the subdirectory that holds CLIPPER.LIB is \dbase\. This was linked with the MicroSoft linker (version 3.05), which is the reason for the extra code after the listing of the subdirectory.

```
CLIPPER @gen1
CLIPPER @gen2
LINK gen1 gen2 ,GENER8,, \dbase\/se:1024,,;
```

This incorporates the correct syntax for linking with the Microsoft linker, which is:

```
=>link <object file> [<object file>], [<EXE filename>], [<MAP filename>,
      <path\clipper library> [<all other libraries>]/se:1024,,;
```

In the above batch file, Gen1 and Gen2 are the object files created by GEN1.CLP and GEN2.CLP; GENER8.EXE will be the name of the executable file; the MAP file will assume a default name; and the CLIPPER.LIB is located in the \dbase\ subdirectory.

APPENDIX I

Menu Generator

This program can be used in a stand-alone mode, but it was designed to be used with GENCODE to provide menus for the application generator. Again, this coded section has been upgraded for the summer and autumn releases of the compiler. Please check the header of the file for proper release versions, compiling syntax, and linking syntax. The structure and program flow can best be seen by studying the following flow chart:

PROGRAM FLOW / MAP

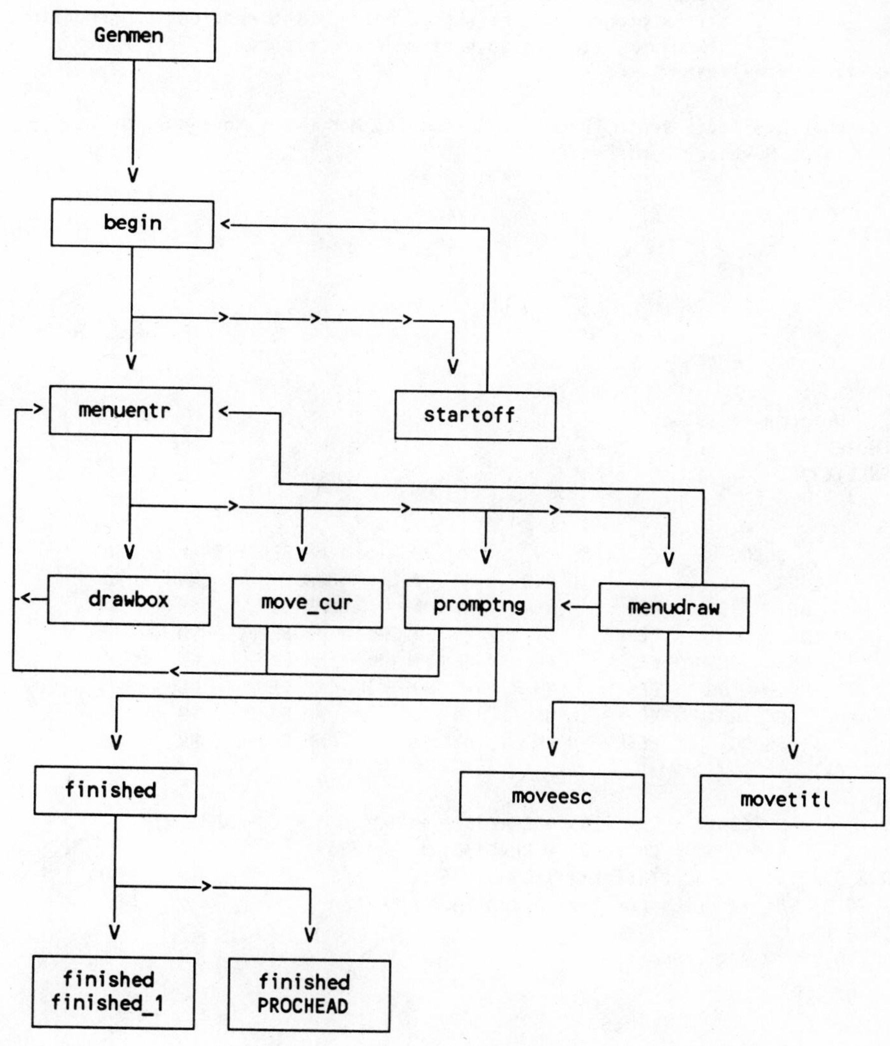

THE PROGRAM FILE

```
*********************
* Name          GENMEN.prg
* Date          April 4, 1988
* Notice        Copyright 1988, Stephen J. Straley & Associates
* Compile       Clipper Genmen
* Release       Autumn '86 or later
* Note          This is a MENU GENerator.  It develops a file of procedures
*               that collectively can generate a menu with prompts and four
*               sublevels.  It writes information to a dBASE III file
*               that may be edited again by this program at a later date.
*               This program is the second half of the application generator;
*               however, it is also a stand-alone program.
*********************

EXTERNAL Startoff, Begin, Promptng, Menuentr, Menudraw, Move_cur, Drawbox,;
Movetitl, Moveesc, Finished


CLEAR

TEXT




    Welcome to ......
ENDTEXT
INKEY(1)
TEXT

         GGGGG      EEEEEEE  NN      NN  MM       MM EEEEEEE NN      NN
        GG   GG     EE       NNN     NN  MMM     MMM EE      NNN     NN
       GG      GG   EE       NNNN    NN  MMMM   MMMM EE      NNNN    NN
       GG           EEEEE    NN NN   NN  MM MM MM MM EEEEE   NN NN   NN
       GG    GGGGG  EE       NN  NN NN  MM  MMM  MM EE      NN  NN NN
       GG      GG   EE       NN   NNNN  MM   M   MM EE      NN   NNNN
        GG   GG     EE       NN    NNN  MM       MM EE      NN    NNN
         GGGGG      EEEEEEE  NN      NN  MM       MM EEEEEEE NN      NN
ENDTEXT
INKEY(1)
frame  = CHR(201) + CHR(205) + CHR(187) + CHR(186) + CHR(188) + ;
         CHR(205) + CHR(200) + CHR(186) + CHR(32)
@ 2,0,22,79 BOX SUBSTR(frame,1,8)
@ 20,23 SAY "< Press Any Key to Continue >"
INKEY(0)
@ 2,0,22,79 BOX frame
```

```
SET FUNCTION 9 TO CHR(25)
SET KEY -1 TO Doitagain
STORE SPACE(4000) TO xscreen
IF .NOT. FILE("Prefix.mem")
   @ 2,0,22,79 BOX frame
   @ 4,5 SAY "The Two Letter Prefix will be attached to the name of all"
   @ 5,5 SAY "procedures so created by this program.  For example,"
   @ 6,5 SAY "the file generated will be xxMENU, and all subsequent"
   @ 7,5 SAy "procedures will have the same root name with varied extensions."
   STORE "  " TO pref
   @ 12,15 SAY "Enter in Two Letter Prefix: " GET pref PICT "!X"
   READ
ELSE
   RESTORE FROM Prefix ADDITIVE
ENDIF
DO Begin

*********************

FUNCTION Center

   PARAMETERS title, width

   midlen = INT(LEN(title) / 2)
   RETURN(width - midlen)

*********************

FUNCTION Short

   PARAMETERS qwert

   RETURN(LTRIM(STR(qwert,2)))

****************************

FUNCTION Verify

   SET CONSOLE OFF
   WAIT TO inertemp
   SET CONSOLE ON
   IF UPPER(inertemp) = "Y"
     ?? "Yes"
     INKEY(.25)
     RETURN(.T.)
   ENDIF
   ?? "No "
   INKEY(.25)
   RETURN(.F.)

*********************

PROCEDURE Prochead

   PARAMETERS a
```

```
   ?
   ? "**********************"
   ?
   ? "PROCEDURE " + a
   ?

********************

PROCEDURE Doitagain

   PARAMETERS p, l, v

   KEYBOARD "0" + CHR(13) + "0" + CHR(13) + CHR(18) + CHR(13)

********************

PROCEDURE Chaina

   PARAMETERS a

   DO &a

********************

PROCEDURE Chainb

   PARAMETERS a, b

   DO &a. WITH &b

* End of GENMEN.prg


********************
* Name          STARTOFF.prg
* Date          April 4, 1988
* Notice        Copyright 1988, Stephen J. Straley & Associates
* Note          This section of the menu generator starts off
*               the program.  The rows, columns, prompts, and messages
*               are stored in two databases.  This section creates those
*               databases if they do not exist.
********************
   @ 18,5 SAY "Creating Files for Menus... One Moment Please...."
   CREATE Template
   USE Template
   APPEND BLANK
   REPLACE field_name WITH "PROC_NAME", field_type WITH "C", field_len WITH 10
   APPEND BLANK
   REPLACE field_name WITH "TOP", field_type WITH "N", field_len WITH 2
   APPEND BLANK
   REPLACE field_name WITH "LEFT", field_type WITH "N", field_len WITH 2
   APPEND BLANK
   REPLACE field_name WITH "BOTTOM", field_type WITH "N", field_len WITH 2
```

```
    APPEND BLANK
    REPLACE field_name WITH "RIGHT", field_type WITH "N", field_len WITH 2
    APPEND BLANK
    REPLACE field_name WITH "ROW_MESS", field_type WITH "N", field_len WITH 2
    APPEND BLANK
    REPLACE field_name WITH "COL_MESS", field_type WITH "N", field_len WITH 2
    APPEND BLANK
    REPLACE field_name WITH "MESSAGE", field_type WITH "C", field_len WITH 30
    APPEND BLANK
    REPLACE field_name WITH "ROW_ESC", field_type WITH "N", field_len WITH 2
    APPEND BLANK
    REPLACE field_name WITH "COL_ESC", field_type WITH "N", field_len WITH 2
    APPEND BLANK
    REPLACE field_name WITH "ESC_MESS", field_type WITH "C", field_len WITH 30
    APPEND BLANK
    REPLACE field_name WITH "SEARCH", field_type WITH "N", field_len WITH 5
    APPEND BLANK
    REPLACE field_name WITH "VARIABLE", field_type WITH "C", field_len WITH 8
    APPEND BLANK
    REPLACE field_name WITH "MENU", field_type WITH "L", field_len WITH 1,
            field_dec WITH 0
    APPEND BLANK
    REPLACE field_name WITH "SET_MESS", field_type WITH "N", field_len WITH 2,
            field_dec WITH 0
    USE
    CREATE Menu1 FROM Template
    CLOSE DATABASES
    CREATE Template
    USE Template
    APPEND BLANK
    REPLACE field_name WITH "SEARCH", field_type WITH "N", field_len WITH 5
    APPEND BLANK
    REPLACE field_name WITH "ROW_PROMPT", field_type WITH "N", field_len WITH 2
    APPEND BLANK
    REPLACE field_name WITH "COL_PROMPT", field_type WITH "N", field_len WITH 2
    APPEND BLANK
    REPLACE field_name WITH "PROMPT", field_type WITH "C", field_len WITH 30
    APPEND BLANK
    REPLACE field_name WITH "PROM_MESS", field_type WITH "C", field_len WITH 50
    USE
    CREATE Menu2 FROM Template
    ERASE Template.dbf
* End of STARTOFF.prg
*********************
* Name          BEGIN.prg
* Date          April 4, 1988
* Notice        Copyright 1988, Stephen J. Straley & Associates
* Note          This section of the menu generator checks to see if the
*               menu databases exist.  If they do, it uses them; otherwise
*               it runs STARTOFF to create them.  It also sets up the
*               screen arrays and chains to the first functional procedure
*               for menu generating, MENUENTR.
*********************
```

```
EXTERNAL Startoff, Promptng, Menuentr, Menudraw, Move_cur, Drawbox, Movetitl,
Moveesc, Finished

   IF .NOT. FILE("MENU?.DBF")
      DO Startoff
      CLOSE DATABASES
      SELECT 2
      USE Menu2
      SELECT 1
      USE Menu1
      APPEND BLANK
   ELSE
      SELECT 2
      USE Menu2
      SELECT 1
      USE Menu1
      GO TOP
   ENDIF
   SET SCORE OFF
   CLEAR
   frame  = CHR(201) + CHR(205) + CHR(187) + CHR(186) + CHR(188) + ;
            CHR(205) + CHR(200) + CHR(186) + CHR(32)
   STORE 1 TO menu, level, asearch
   STORE 0 TO down
   STORE pref + "men" TO name
   STORE SPACE(4000) TO ascreen, bscreen, cscreen, dscreen, tscreen
   STORE .T. TO which
   DECLARE screen[5]
   FOR qaz = 1 TO 5
      STORE SPACE(4000) TO screen[qaz]
   NEXT
   SAVE SCREEN TO ascreen

DO Menuentr
* End of BEGIN.prg


********************
* Name          PROMPTNG.prg
* Date          April 4, 1988
* Notice        Copyright 1988, Stephen J. Straley & Associates
* Note          This section of the menu generator paints the already
*               designed prompts to the screen and waits to see if
*               the drawn menu appears correct.  If it is and a new
*               submenu is chosen, a recursive procedure call is
*               made, and a new menu is entered.  If an Esc key is
*               pressed and the program is at the top level of the program,
*               the option to write the code is displayed.
********************

EXTERNAL Startoff, Begin, Menuentr, Menudraw, Move_cur, Drawbox, Movetitl,
Moveesc, Finished

   PARAMETERS p, l, v
```

```
@ 0,0 CLEAR
IF level = 1 .AND. LEN(TRIM(screen[level])) = 0
   * Just skip over and do nothing right now..
ELSE
   go_down = 1
   DO WHILE !EMPTY(screen[go_down])
      RESTORE SCREEN FROM screen[go_down]
      go_down = go_down + 1
   ENDDO
ENDIF
SELECT 1
IF .NOT. LASTKEY() = 27
   @ top, left, bottom, right BOX frame
   spot  = INT(LEN(TRIM(message))/2)
   point = INT(INT(right-left)/2)
   @ row_mess, col_mess SAY " " + TRIM(message) + " "
ENDIF
IF EMPTY(set_mess)
   SET MESSAGE TO
ELSE
   SET MESSAGE TO set_mess
ENDIF
SELECT 2
SET FILTER TO search = asearch
GO TOP
DO WHILE .NOT. EMPTY(prompt)
   IF !EMPTY(prom_mess)
      temp_mes = AT('("',prom_mess)
      IF temp_mes = 0
         @ row_prompt, col_prompt PROMPT " " + TRIM(prompt) + " " MES-
         SAGE(prom_mess)
      ELSE
         end_mes = AT(")", prom_mess)
         end_mes = end_mes - 2
         @ row_prompt, col_prompt PROMPT " " + TRIM(prompt) +;
                     " " MESSAGE(SUBSTR(prom_mess, temp_mes + 2, end_mes-
         temp_mes+2))
      ENDIF
   ELSE
      @ row_prompt, col_prompt PROMPT " " + TRIM(prompt) + " "
   ENDIF
   SKIP
ENDDO
IF .NOT. LASTKEY() = 27
   @ A->row_esc, A->col_esc SAY TRIM(A->esc_mess)
ENDIF
MENU TO option
IF option = 0
   level = level - 1
   STORE SPACE(4000) TO screen[level+1]
   IF level = 0
      DO Finished
      CLEAR
```

```
         @ 12,30 SAY "Shall I REMOVE all Files?  "
         IF VERIFY()
            ERASE Prefix.mem
            ERASE Menu1.dbf
            ERASE Menu2.dbf
         ENDIF
         @ 12,25 SAY "Thanks for using the Menu Generator!  "
         QUIT
      ENDIF
      asearch = INT(asearch/10)
      DO Promptng
   ELSE
      SAVE SCREEN TO tscreen
      screen[level] = tscreen
      level = level + 1
      asearch = (asearch * 10) + option
      APPEND BLANK
      SELECT 1
      lookfor = name + LTRIM(STR(asearch))
      LOCATE FOR proc_name = lookfor
      IF .NOT. FOUND()
         APPEND BLANK
      ENDIF
      DO Menuentr
   ENDIF
* End of PROMPTNG.prg


*********************
* Name          MENUENTR.prg
* Date          April 4, 1988
* Notice        Copyright 1988, Stephen J. Straley & Associates
* Note          This part of the menu generator enters the
*               menu prompt messages.
*********************
EXTERNAL Startoff, Begin, Promptng, Menudraw, Move_cur, Drawbox, Movetitl,
         Moveesc, Finished

   PARAMETERS p, l, v

   SELECT 1
   IF top + bottom + left + right > 0
      @ 0,0 SAY SPACE(79)
      @ 0,0 SAY "Do you want to edit the menu contents? "
      IF .NOT. VERIFY()
         DO Menudraw
      ENDIF
   ENDIF
   @ 0,0 SAY SPACE(79)
   @ 1,0 SAY SPACE(79)
   @ 1,0 SAY "  Will this be a MENU (No for a data entry screen)? "
   IF VERIFY()
      REPLACE menu WITH .T.
```

```
ELSE
   REPLACE menu WITH .F.
ENDIF
@ 1,0 SAY SPACE(79)
@ 0,0 SAY "Choose the TOP, LEFT coordinates for the menu frame. Do so by
        moving the"
@ 1,0 SAY "the cursor with the arrow keys.    Strike the ESC key for retain
        values."
@ 3,0 SAY "Home"
@ 3,74 SAY "Pg Up"
@ 23,0 SAY "End"
@ 23,74 SAY "Pg Dn"
DO Drawbox WITH .T.
SET COLOR TO 7*/0
@ top, left SAY CHR(201)
SET COLOR TO
@ 0,0 SAY "Choose the BOTTOM, RIGHT coordinates for the menu frame. Do so
        be moving"
@ 1,0 SAY "the cursor with the arrow keys."
DO Drawbox WITH .F.
READ
@ 0,0 CLEAR
IF EMPTY(esc_mess)
   REPLACE esc_mess WITH "ESC to RETURN"
ENDIF
@ 0,0 SAY "Enter Menu Title: " GET message PICT "@X"
@ 1,0 SAY "  Escape Message: " GET esc_mess PICT "@X"
@ 0,50 SAY "Enter Variable: " GET variable
@ 1,50 SAY "Row for Message:" GET set_mess PICT "##" RANGE 0,24
READ
REPLACE search WITH asearch, proc_name WITH name + LTRIM(STR(asearch))
IF LEN(TRIM(variable)) = 0
   SELECT 2
   SET FILTER TO search = asearch
   GO TOP
   DELETE ALL
   PACK
   SELECT 1
   DELETE
   PACK
   DO Begin
ENDIF
SELECT 2
LOCATE FOR search = asearch
IF EOF()
   FOR x = 1 TO 32
      APPEND BLANK
      REPLACE search WITH asearch
   NEXT
ENDIF
SET FILTER TO search = asearch
GO TOP
IF !EMPTY(prompt)
```

```
        @ 3,1 SAY "Do you want to EDIT the prompts? "
        IF .NOT. VERIFY()
           DO Menudraw
        ENDIF
        @ 3,1 SAY SPACE(40)
     ENDIF
     down = 1
     DO WHILE .NOT. EOF()
        @ 3,55 SAY SPACE(24)
        @ 3,1 SAY "   Menu Prompt " + TRANSFORM(down, "99") + "-> ";
              GET prompt PICT "XXXXXXXXXXXXXXXXXXXXXXXXXXXXXX"
        @ 4,1 SAY "Prompt Message " + TRANSFORM(down, "99") + "-> " GET
             prom_mess PICT "@X"
        READ
        IF LASTKEY() = 18
           IF .NOT. BOF()
              down = down - 1
              SKIP - 1
           ENDIF
           LOOP
        ENDIF
        IF LEN(TRIM(prompt)) = 0
           REPLACE col_prompt WITH 0, row_prompt WITH 0
           EXIT
        ENDIF
        IF row_prompt = 0 .AND. col_prompt = 0
           start_look = RECNO()
           SAVE SCREEN
           DO move_cur
           RESTORE SCREEN
        ELSE
           @ 3, 55 SAY "Row: " GET row_prompt
           @ 3, 65 SAY "Col: " GET col_prompt
           READ
        ENDIF
        @ 5,0 SAY SPACE(79)
        IF down > 16
           @ down - 16 + 7,45 SAY prompt
        ELSE
           @ down + 7, 0 SAY prompt
        ENDIF
        @ ROW(), COL()+1 SAY row_prompt
        @ row(), COL()+1 SAY col_prompt
        down = down + 1
        skip
     ENDDO
     DO Menudraw
  * End of MENUENTR.prg
```

```
*********************
* Name          MENUDRAW.prg
* Date          April 4, 1988
* Notice        Copyright 1988, Stephen J. Straley & Associates
* Note          This section of the menu generator actually draws
*               the menu.
*********************

EXTERNAL Startoff, Begin, Promptng, Menuentr, Move_cur, Drawbox, Movetitl,
         Moveesc, Finished

   PARAMETERS p, l, v

   @ 0,0 CLEAR
   RESTORE SCREEN FROM screen[level]
   SELECT 1
   @ top, left, bottom, right BOX frame
   IF row_mess = 0 .AND. col_mess = 0
      REPLACE row_mess WITH top+1
      REPLACE col_mess WITH CCOL(A->right,A->left,LEN(TRIM(message)))
   ENDIF
   @ row_mess, col_mess SAY " " + TRIM(message) + " "
   SELECT 2
   SET FILTER TO search = asearch
   GO TOP
   DO WHILE .NOT. EMPTY(prompt)
      @ row_prompt, col_prompt SAY " " + TRIM(prompt) + " "
      SKIP
   ENDDO
   SELECT 1
   IF row_esc = 0 .AND. col_esc = 0
      REPLACE row_esc WITH bottom-1
      REPLACE col_esc WITH CCOL(A->right,A->left,13)
   ENDIF
   @ row_esc, col_esc SAY TRIM(esc_mess)
   @ 0,0 SAY SPACE(79)
   SELECT 2
   @ 0,10 SAY "Are these the correct values? "
   IF VERIFY()
      @ 0,0 SAY SPACE(79)
      DO Promptng
   ELSE
      @ 0,0 SAY SPACE(79)
      @ 0,0 SAY "Do you want to move the Title Message? "
      IF VERIFY()
         @ 0,0 SAY SPACE(79)
         SAVE SCREEN TO dscreen
         DO Movetitl
      ENDIF
      @ 0,0 SAY SPACE(79)
      @ 0,0 SAY "Do you want to move the ESC message? "
      IF VERIFY()
         @ 0,0 SAY SPACE(79)
```

```
         SAVE SCREEN TO dscreen
         DO Moveesc
      ENDIF
      DO Menuentr
   ENDIF
* End of MENUDRAW.prg


********************
* Name          MOVE_CUR.prg
* Date          April 4, 1988
* Notice        Copyright 1988, Stephen J. Straley & Associates
* Note          This section of the menu generator moves the cursor on the
*               screen, positioning the menu option.
********************

EXTERNAL Startoff, Begin, Promptng, Menuentr, Menudraw, Drawbox, Movetitl,
           Moveesc, Finished

   PARAMETERS p, l, v

   SET KEY -9 TO
   CLEAR
   IF level > 1
      RESTORE SCREEN FROM screen[level-1]
   ENDIF
   @ A->top,A->left,A->bottom,A->right BOX frame
   GO TOP
   DO WHILE .NOT. EMPTY(prompt)
      @ row_prompt, col_prompt SAY " " + TRIM(prompt) + " "
      SKIP
   ENDDO
   GO start_look
   SAVE SCREEN TO dscreen
   cursor = 0
   STORE SPACE(LEN(TRIM(prompt))) TO moving
   @ CROW(A->top,A->bottom),CCOL(A->left,A->right, LEN(moving)) GET moving
   CLEAR GETS
   trow = ROW()
   tcol = COL() - LEN(moving)
   DO WHILE .T.
      cursor = INKEY(0)
      DO CASE
      CASE cursor = 5
         IF trow - 1 > A->top
            trow = trow - 1
         ENDIF
      CASE cursor = 4
         IF tcol + 1 + LEN(moving) < A->right
            tcol = tcol + 1
         ENDIF
      CASE cursor = 19
         IF tcol - 1 > A->left
```

```
            tcol = tcol - 1
         ENDIF
      CASE cursor = 24
         IF trow + 1 < A->bottom
            trow = trow + 1
         ENDIF
      CASE cursor = 13
         EXIT
      ENDCASE
      RESTORE SCREEN FROM dscreen
      @ trow,tcol GET moving
      CLEAR GETS
   ENDDO
   REPLACE row_prompt WITH trow, col_prompt WITH tcol - 1
* End of MOVE_CUR.prg


*********************
* Name          DRAWBOX.prg
* Date          April 4, 1988
* Notice        Copyright 1988, Stephen J. Straley & Associates
* Note          This section of the menu generator draws the box
*               around the menu.
*********************
PARAMETERS whichone

EXTERNAL Startoff, Begin, Promptng, Menuentr, Menudraw, Move_cur, Movetitl,
         Moveesc, Finished

   PARAMETERS whichone

   IF whichone
      newcur = CHR(201)
   ELSE
      newcur = CHR(188)
   ENDIF
   STORE SPACE(4000) TO zscreen
   SAVE SCREEN TO zscreen
   cursor = 0
   trow = 12
   tcol = 40
   @ trow,tcol SAY ""
   DO WHILE .T.
      cursor = INKEY(0)
      RESTORE SCREEN FROM zscreen
      DO CASE
      CASE cursor = 1
         trow = 4
         tcol = 1
      CASE cursor = 18
         trow = 4
         tcol = 79
      CASE cursor = 6
```

```
         trow = 22
         tcol = 1
      CASE cursor = 3
         trow = 22
         tcol = 79
      CASE cursor = 5
         IF trow > 4
            trow = trow - 1
         ENDIF
      CASE cursor = 4
         IF COL() < 78
            tcol = tcol + 1
         ENDIF
      CASE cursor = 19
         IF COL() > 1
            tcol = tcol - 1
         ENDIF
      CASE cursor = 24
         IF ROW() < 22
            trow = trow + 1
         ENDIF
      CASE cursor = 13 .OR. cursor = 27 .OR. cursor = 32
         EXIT
      ENDCASE
      @ trow, tcol SAY newcur
      @ trow, tcol SAY ""
   ENDDO
   IF LASTKEY() <> 27
      IF whichone
         REPLACE top WITH trow, left WITH tcol
      ELSE
         REPLACE bottom WITH trow, right WITH tcol
      ENDIF
   ENDIF
* End of DRAWBOX.prg


********************
* Name          MOVETITL.prg
* Date          April 4. 1988
* Notice        Copyright 1988, Stephen J. Straley & Associates
* Note          Like Menudraw.prg, this section of the menu generator
*               positions the menu title.
********************

EXTERNAL Startoff, Begin, Promptng, Menuentr, Menudraw, Move_cur, Drawbox,
         Moveesc, Finished

   PARAMETERS p, l, v

   SELECT 1
   cursor = 0
   STORE SPACE(LEN(TRIM(message))) TO moving
```

```
    @ row_mess, col_mess SAY ""
    trow = ROW()
    tcol = COL()
    DO WHILE .T.
      cursor = INKEY(0)
      DO CASE
      CASE cursor = 5
         trow = trow - 1
      CASE cursor = 4
         tcol = tcol + 1
      CASE cursor = 19
         tcol = tcol - 1
      CASE cursor = 24
         trow = trow + 1
      CASE cursor = 13
         EXIT
      ENDCASE
      RESTORE SCREEN FROM dscreen
      @ trow, tcol GET moving
      CLEAR GETS
  ENDDO
  @ row_mess, col_mess SAY SPACE(LEN(TRIM(message)))+" "
  REPLACE row_mess WITH trow, col_mess WITH tcol
  @ row_mess, col_mess SAY TRIM(message)
  SELECT 2
* End of MOVETITL.prg

*********************
* Name          MOVEESC.prg
* Date          April 4, 1988
* Notice        Copyright 1988, Stephen J. Straley & Associates
* Note          Similar to MOVETITL.prg, this section of the menu
*               generator moves the Esc message of the menu.
*********************

EXTERNAL Startoff, Begin, Promptng, Menuentr, Menudraw, Move_cur, Drawbox,
            Movetitl, Finished

   PARAMETERS p, l, v

   SELECT 1
   cursor = 0
   STORE SPACE(LEN(TRIM(esc_mess))) TO moving
   @ row_esc, col_esc SAY ""
   trow = ROW()
   tcol = COL()
   DO WHILE .T.
     cursor = INKEY(0)
     DO CASE
     CASE cursor = 5
        trow = trow - 1
     CASE cursor = 4
```

```
         tcol = tcol + 1
      CASE cursor = 19
         tcol = tcol - 1
      CASE cursor = 24
         trow = trow + 1
      CASE cursor = 13
         EXIT
      ENDCASE
      RESTORE SCREEN FROM dscreen
      @ trow, tcol GET moving
      CLEAR GETS
   ENDDO
   @ row_esc, col_esc SAY SPACE(LEN(TRIM(esc_mess)))
   REPLACE row_esc WITH trow, col_esc WITH tcol
   @ row_esc, col_esc SAY TRIM(esc_mess)
   SELECT 2
* End of MOVEESC.prg


********************
* Name          FINISHED.prg
* Date          April 4, 1988
* Notice        Copyright 1988, Stephen J. Straley & Associates
* Note          This section of the menu generator asks the user if
*               all of the menus are entered.  If so, code is generated
*               based on the information in the two databases.  Some
*               of the procedures written in this section refer to
*               procedures generated by GENCODE.EXE.  This section does
*               not write the specific PROMPT commands.
*
*               Inside this .PRG is a procedure called FINISH_1.  This
*               procedure actually writes the PROMPT positions to the
*               alternate file opened by FINISHED.prg.  If a
*               menu option does not have a branch developed,
*               a note will be generated in the code.
********************

EXTERNAL Startoff, Begin, Promptng, Menuentr, Menudraw, Move_cur, Drawbox,
         Movetitl, Moveesc

   PARAMETERS p, l, v

   CLEAR
   @ 12,15 SAY "Do you want to generate the code for the menus? "
   IF .NOT. VERIFY()
      RETURN
   ENDIF
   SELECT 1
   GO TOP
   SET CONSOLE OFF
   STORE name +"u.prg" TO Outfile
   SET ALTERNATE TO &Outfile
   SET ALTERNATE ON
```

```
   ? "CLEAR"
   ? "DO " + name + "1"
   DO WHILE .NOT. EOF()
      IF EMPTY(proc_name)
         SKIP
         LOOP
      ENDIF
      DO Prochead WITH A->proc_name
      tempstr = CHR(LEN(LTRIM(STR(A->search))) + 96) + "screen"
      ? "DO WHILE .T."
      IF RECNO() = 1
         ? "   CLEAR"
         ? "   RESTORE FROM Screen.sys"
         ? "   STORE SPACE(4000) TO ascreen, bscreen, cscreen, dscreen, es-
           creen, fscreen"
         ? "   DO Setup"
         ? "   DO Redraw"
         STORE .T. TO topping
      ELSE
         ? "   IF !EMPTY(" + tempstr + ")"
         ? "      SAVE SCREEN TO " + tempstr
         ? "   ELSE"
         building = SHORT(top) + ", " + SHORT(left) + ", " + SHORT(bottom) +
            ", " +  SHORT(right) +;
                   " BOX scrframe"
         ? '      STORE 0 TO ' + TRIM(variable)
         ? '      @ ' + building
         ? '      SAVE SCREEN TO ' + tempstr
         ? "   ENDIF"
         STORE .F. TO topping
      ENDIF
      ? "   SET MESSAGE TO " + IF(EMPTY(set_mess), "", TRANSFORM(set_mess,
           "99"))
      ? '   @ ' + SHORT(row_mess) + ', ' + SHORT(col_mess) + ' SAY "' +
           TRIM(message) + '"'
      asearch = search
      DO Finished_1
      ? "ENDDO"
      SKIP
   ENDDO
   ? CHR(13) + CHR(12) + CHR(26) + CHR(26)
   SET ALTERNATE OFF
   CLOSE ALTERNATE
   SET CONSOLE ON

********************

PROCEDURE Finished_1

   PARAMETERS p, l, v

   SELECT 2
   SET FILTER TO search = asearch
```

```
GO TOP
DO WHILE !EMPTY(prompt)
   ? '   @ ' + SHORT(row_prompt) + ', ' + SHORT(col_prompt) + ' PROMPT " '
       + TRIM(prompt) + ' "'
   IF !EMPTY(prom_mess)
      temp_mes = AT('("', prom_mess)
      IF temp_mes = 0
         ?? '  MESSAGE ' + '"' +  TRIM(prom_mess) + '"'
      ELSE
         ?? '  MESSAGE ' + TRIM(prom_mess)
      ENDIF
   ENDIF
   SKIP
ENDDO
? '   @ ' + SHORT(A->row_esc) + ', ' + SHORT(A->col_esc) + ' SAY "' +
         TRIM(A->esc_mess) + '"'
? '   MENU TO ' + TRIM(A->variable)
? '   SAVE SCREEN TO ' + tempstr
GO TOP
? '   DO CASE'
counter = 1
DO WHILE !EMPTY(prompt)
   ? '   CASE ' + TRIM(A->variable) + ' = ' + SHORT(counter)
   temp = name + LTRIM(STR(search)) + LTRIM(STR(counter))
   SELECT 1
   back_to = RECNO()
   LOCATE FOR temp == TRIM(proc_name)
   IF .NOT. FOUND()
      ? '      **************************'
      ? '      * Do subprocedure here. *'
      ? '      **************************'
   ELSE
      ? '      DO ' + temp
   ENDIF
   GO back_to
   SELECT 2
   counter = counter + 1
   SKIP
ENDDO
? '   CASE ' + TRIM(A->variable) + ' = 0'
IF topping
   ? '      @ ' + SHORT(A->row_esc + 2) + ', 15 SAY "All Files Closed,
         Returning to Operating System"'
   ? '      QUIT'
ELSE
   ? '      EXIT'
ENDIF
? '   ENDCASE'
?
?
SELECT 1

********************
```

```
PROCEDURE Help

   PARAMETERS p,l,v

   IF p = "HELP"
      RETURN
   ENDIF
   hrow = 23
   hcol = 15
   SAVE SCREEN TO xscreen
   DO CASE
   CASE p = "GENMEN"
      DO CASE
      CASE v = "PREF"
         @ 17,10,24,70 BOX frame
         @ 18,15 SAY "Since the CREATE program has not been executed prior"
         @ 19,15 SAY "to this program, you must enter the 2 letter prefix"
         @ 20,15 SAY "to be attached to all menus built as well as the"
         @ 21,15 SAY "prefix to the output."
      OTHERWISE
         @ 20,10,24,70 BOX frame
         @ 21,15 SAY "No help available...."
      ENDCASE
   CASE p = "PROMPTING"
      DO CASE
      CASE v = "OPTION"
         @ 18,10,24,70 BOX frame
         @ 19,13 SAY "Move the cursor to the menu choice on which to build"
         @ 20,13 SAY "the next menu.  If no menu exists, follow standard"
         @ 21,13 SAY "procedures; otherwise, edit previous menu items."
      OTHERWISE
         @ 20,10,24,70 BOX frame
         @ 21,15 SAY "No help available...."
      ENDCASE
   CASE p = "MENUENTR"
      DO CASE
      CASE v = "MESSAGE"
         @ 17,10,23,70 BOX frame
         @ 18,15 SAY "This will be the title for the menu you are about"
         @ 19,15 SAY "to draw.  For no menu title, please strike F9 to"
         @ 20,15 SAY "leave blank."
         hrow = 22
      CASE v = "VARIABLE"
         @ 18,10,24,70 BOX frame
         @ 19,15 SAY "This will be the name of the variable used for the"
         @ 20,15 SAY "'MENU TO' command.   Leaving blank or striking the F9"
         @ 21,15 SAY "key will delete this menu from the entire system."
      CASE v = "PROMPT"
         @ 17,10,24,70 BOX frame
         @ 18,15 SAY "This will be the character string used for the PROMPT"
         @ 19,15 SAY "command. If no coordinates exist, direct cursor posi-"
         @ 20,15 SAY "tioning is possible by moving cursor within frame. If"
```

```
         @ 21,15 SAY "they do exist, you may modify them directly."
      CASE v = "ROW_PROMPT"
         @ 17,10,24,70 BOX frame
         @ 18,12 SAY "This is the row number for the PROMPT message.  If al-
            ready"
         @ 19,12 SAY "established with cursor keys.  Edit numbers directly or
            "
         @ 20,12 SAY "strike F2 key to allow for re-direct cursor position-
            ing."
         hrow = 22
         hcol = 12
      OTHERWISE
         @ 20,10,24,70 BOX frame
         @ 21,15 SAY "No help available...."
      ENDCASE
   OTHERWISE
    @ 0,0 CLEAR
    @  1,5 SAY "For all questions, either strike Y      F1:  On-line Help"
    @  2,5 SAY "for YES or any other key for NO.        F2:  To clear out row"
    @  3,5 SAY "                                        and column positions"
    @  4,5 SAY "If at any time there is a question      to allow direct cursor"
    @  5,5 SAY "as to what to enter, please strike      positioning for the"
    @  6,5 SAY "the F1 key.   If any help is            entered prompt message"
    @  7,5 SAY "available, instruction will appear."
    @  8,5 SAY "Otherwise, this screen will appear.     F9:   Clear Field"
    @  9,5 SAY "                                       F10:  Flash to Pre-"
    @ 10,5 SAY "                                        vious screen."
    @ 22,10 SAY "  Program name: "
    ?? p
    @ 22,50 SAY "Line number: "
    ?? l
    @ 23,10 SAY "Variable Name: "
    ?? v
    hrow = 24
   ENDCASE
   @ hrow, hcol SAY "Any Key to Continue..."
   INKEY(0)

   RESTORE SCREEN FROM xscreen

********************

FUNCTION Crow

   PARAMETERS in_top, in_bottom

   tempin = in_bottom - in_top
   tempin = tempin / 2
   RETURN(in_top + INT(tempin))
```

```
*********************

FUNCTION Ccol

   PARAMETERS in_left, in_right, width

   tempin = in_right - in_left - width
   tempin = tempin / 2
   RETURN(in_left + INT(tempin))
* End of FINISHED.prg
```

COMPILING AND LINKING THE MENU GENERATOR

Create a batch file named GO.BAT with the commands to compile the menu generator program as follows:

```
GO.BAT:

   CLIPPER GENMEN
   CLIPPER BEGIN
   CLIPPER STARTOFF
   CLIPPER MENUENTR
   CLIPPER DRAWBOX
   CLIPPER MOVE_CUR
   CLIPPER PROMPTNG
   CLIPPER MENUDRAW
   CLIPPER MOVEESC
   CLIPPER MOVETITL
   CLIPPER FINISHED
```

To link the files enter the following command line:

```
C>LINK Genmen Begin Startoff Menuentr Drawbox Move_cur Promptng Menudraw
     Moveesc Movetitl Finished,,,/se:1024,,;
```

INDEX

B

C

D

E

F

G

H

N

O

P

Q

R

S

T

U

V

W

X

Y

Z